MW01503013

China

There is currently widespread and growing interest in the Chinese economy, its rapid growth, and the consequent impact on world business and economic affairs. At the same time, there are concerns about China's political system, the Chinese Communist Party, China's human rights record and the degree to which reform – the development of 'socialism with Chinese characteristics' – represents real liberalization. This book provides full details of economic and political developments in China, focusing in particular on events since 1978. It includes coverage of Hong Kong, Macao, Tibet and Taiwan, together with China's relations, including international trade, with its neighbours and with the international community. It considers the evolution of China's 'open-door' policy in economic affairs, the impact of entry into the WTO and effects of the Asian financial crisis. All the key topics – the growth of the market, the reform of state-owned enterprises, foreign investment, human rights, SARS and bird flu – are comprehensively covered. Overall, this book provides a full account of economic and political developments in China, and will be of importance to all who are interested in this country's affairs, not only scholars but also those within the business and policy-making communities.

Ian Jeffries is Reader in Economics and member of the Centre of Russian and Eastern European Studies at the University of Wales Swansea. He is one of the foremost authorities on the post-communist world and has written extensively on communist and transitional economies. His publications include *A Guide to the Socialist Economies* (Routledge, 1990), *Socialist Economies and the Transition to the Market* (Routledge, 1993) and *The Countries of the Former Soviet Union at the Turn of the Twenty-First Century: The Baltics and European States in Transition* (Routledge, 2004), the last of a five-volume series written by the author.

Guides to economic and political developments in Asia

China

A guide to economic and political developments

Ian Jeffries

Routledge
Taylor & Francis Group

LONDON AND NEW YORK

First published 2006
by Routledge
2 Park Square, Milton Park, Abingdon, Oxon OX14 4RN

Simultaneously published in the USA and Canada
by Routledge
270 Madison Ave, New York, NY 10016

Routledge is an imprint of the Taylor & Francis Group, an informa business

© 2006 Ian Jeffries

Typeset in Times by Wearset Ltd, Boldon, Tyne and Wear
Printed and bound in Great Britain by TJI Digital, Padstow, Cornwall

British Library Cataloguing in Publication Data
A catalogue record for this book is available from the British Library

Library of Congress Cataloging in Publication Data
A catalog record for this book has been requested

ISBN 10: 0–415–38223–8 (hbk)
ISBN 10: 0–203–09966–4 (ebk)

ISBN 13: 978–0–415–38223–6 (hbk)
ISBN 13: 978–0–203–09966–7 (ebk)

Contents

vi *Contents*

Acknowledgements

I am much indebted to the following individuals (in alphabetical order):

At the University of Wales Swansea: David Blackaby; Siân Brown; Dianne Darrell; Michele Davies; Peter Day; Chris Hunt; Frances Jackson; Jaynie Lewis; Nigel O'Leary; Lis Parcell; Mary Perman; Ann Preece; Paul Reynolds; Kathy Sivertsen; Jeff Smith; Syed Hamzah bin Syed Hussin; Clive Towse; Ray Watts; Chris West.

Professors Nick Baigent, George Blazyca, Paul Hare, Lester Hunt and Michael Kaser.

Russell Davies (Kays Newsagency).

At Routledge: Yeliz Ali, Simon Bailey, Amrit Bangard, Tom Bates, Oliver Escrit, Tessa Herbert, Alan Jarvis, Liz Jones, Alex Meloy, Peter Sowden, Alfred Symons, Annabel Watson, Mike Wending, James Whiting, Vanessa Winch and Jayne Young.

At Wearset: Matt Deacon and Claire Dunstan.

Ian Jeffries
Department of Economics and Centre of Russian and East European Studies
University of Wales Swansea

Introduction

Readers will note in the bibliography that I have published extensively on communist and transitional economies, but most books deal with groups of countries. Since the collapse of communism in Eastern Europe and the Soviet Union in and after 1989, the number of countries I have analysed has grown from fourteen to thirty-five! Owing to the large number of languages involved, I have had to rely overwhelmingly on English sources.

I am unable to read Chinese and so cannot undertake frontier research on China. Nevertheless, a vast amount of information is available in English on this increasingly important country. Despite an already vast literature there seems to be a need for a broad-ranging study covering both economic and political developments, with particular emphasis on events since economic reforms began in 1978.

I have tried to write a book which will be of interest to governments, business and academics (from a wide range of disciplines, including economics, politics and international relations). I present a richly endowed 'quarry' of up-to-date economic and political information (presented chronologically where appropriate) to allow the reader to dig out any desired facts and figures. This is not (and is not meant to be) original research but a broad-brush painting of the overall economic and political picture. I make extensive use of quality newspapers such as the *International Herald Tribune* (*IHT*), *Financial Times* (*FT*), *The Times*, the *Guardian*, the *Independent* and the *Daily Telegraph*. Publications such as *The Economist,* the *Far Eastern Economic Review* (*FEER*), *The World Today*, *Asian Survey*, *Transition* and *Finance and Development* have also proven to be invaluable.

A review in *The Times Higher Education Supplement* (29 October 1993) kindly referred to my 'meticulous referencing', even though detailed referencing has the potential to be tiresome to readers. But since this is not original research and I am deeply indebted to many sources, I feel it necessary to make every effort to acknowledge the material used. It is not always feasible to name the correspondents or contributors, but I try, as far as possible, to ensure that credit goes where it is due. For this reason and for accuracy I make extensive use of quotations, although where these include commonly quoted sayings or speeches I leave out specific sources.

China's relations with North Korea are dealt with in a companion volume entitled *North Korea: A Guide to Economic and Political Developments* (2006). This book also deals with the question of how planned economies operate and general issues in the transition from command to market economies.

China: a summary

Population

China is the largest country in the world in terms of population. The population was 1.158 billion at the end of 1991 and 1.259 billion at the end of 1999. A figure of 1.265 billion was announced on 28 March 2001, the result of the fifth national census held on 1 November 2000. In 2001 the figure was 1.272 billion. On 6 January 2005 the figure was 1.3 billion. The world population figure reached 6 billion in October 1999. India is the second largest country in the world by population, reaching 1 billion in August 1999 and 1.033 billion in 2001. (On 1 January 2004 the population of the United States was 292,287,454.) (China is the third largest country in the world in terms of land area after Russia and Canada.)

About 92 per cent of the population is Han.

By official estimates barely half the population can speak the official language [Mandarin] ... A government survey published last year [2004] said only 53 per cent of the population 'can communicate in Putonghua' [Mandarin]. In recognition of this broadcasters commonly include subtitles – the meaning of written Chinese characters is stable even as spoken dialects vary – on television to help people overcome comprehension problems ... China has fifty-five ethnic minorities ... China's Han [is] the ethnic group that makes up more than 90 per cent of the population ... The Han speak as many as 1,500 dialects, with the bulk of them concentrated in the southern half of the country ... Many of the Han dialects are almost entirely mutually incomprehensible.

(www.iht.com, 10 July 2005)

Although the Chinese share a common written language, linguists identify eight major spoken-language groups that are mutually unintelligible. The Communists, like the Nationalists before them, have gone to great lengths to impose a common spoken language, Putonghua, commonly known as Mandarin outside of China, as part of their drive to reinforce national unity. But regional language groups, which include Cantonese and Shanghainese, have been surprisingly resilient ... Cantonese is spoken by about 60 million people in Guangdong province and in Hong Kong and Macao, as well as among ethnic Chinese populations overseas.

(www.iht.com, 15 January 2006; *IHT*, 16 January 2006, p. 9)

China has to support about 22 per cent of the world's population on something like 7 per cent of the world's arable area. 'In 1979 only 11 per cent of the total land area of China was cultivated (50 per cent of India's land is cultivated), with just 0.12 ha *per capita* of the agricultural population (compared with India's 0.42)' (World Bank 1984: 35, cited in Jeffries 1993: 137). 'Only about half of China is habitable . . . [It] has 7 per cent of the world's cultivable land' (*FT*, 27 July 2004, p. 15). 'China is the world's largest agricultural producer, feeding some 22 per cent of the world's population with 10 per cent of its arable land' (*FEER*, 2 May 2002, p. 25). 'China attained food self-sufficiency in the mid-1990s, managing to nourish 20 per cent of the world's population from 7 per cent of its arable farmland' (*The Times*, 8 April 2005, p. 50). Thus it is no coincidence that agricultural reform was first in line after 1978 (see later).

By 1986 life expectancy had risen to 66.9 for men and 70.9 for women (Jeffries 1993: 138). Average life expectancy at birth rose from thirty-five years in 1949 to seventy years in 1989.

> Health experts agree that one of the major achievements of China's health system before 1978 was the provision of basic medical care for all urban and rural Chinese. These services, along with an emphasis on preventative medicine and national campaigns to eradicate endemic disease, contributed to an increase in average Chinese life expectancy from thirty-five years in 1949 to sixty-eight years by 1978. Despite a dramatic increase in prosperity and living standards in China since 1978 average life expectancy has increased by only 3.5 years, about half the gains in longevity in Japan, Singapore, Hong Kong and [South] Korea over the same period . . . Critics note that the government share of national health spending has plummeted from close to 100 per cent during the planned period to about 16 per cent today as the government has steadily withdrawn from providing health services. By comparison, public spending accounts for about 44 per cent of health outlays in the United States and an average of more than 70 per cent in other advanced industrial countries . . . The public's access to health care in China has been steadily declining for more than two decades . . . Critics . . .. [talk of] exorbitant charges for medical services, wasteful over-servicing and widespread over-prescription of drugs . . . A hard-hitting report [was issued] earlier this month by the Development Research Centre, one of the government's top advisory bodies . . . The report was co-sponsored by the World Health Organization . . . [The report] noted 'to our shame' that the World Health Organization ranked the Chinese health system as one of the most unfair in the world. The report said: 'Most of the medical needs of society cannot be met because of economic reasons. Poor people cannot even enjoy the most basic health care' . . . In the absence of widespread medical insurance, many Chinese, particularly the 800 million living in rural areas, cannot afford treatment when they are ill . . . The return [has been witnessed] of deadly diseases including tuberculosis and schistosomiasis [a parasitic disease carried by water snails] that had largely been eradicated before 1978 . . . Health care outlays have now reached 6 per cent of GDP, a relatively high rate for a developing country. During the planned era outlays on health care were about half that proportion.
>
> (www.iht.com, 19 August 2005; *IHT*, 20 August 2005, p. 2)

Policy as regards population growth

Since roughly the mid-1950s the state has tried to control population growth, often in draconian fashion.

The 1953 census revealed a 1952 population of 575 million and shocked the party into a population control programme after 1956. Previously exclusive blame for poverty was based on capitalism and imperialism, Mao opposing birth control as a 'bourgeois Malthusian doctrine' (Fang Lizhi, *Independent*, 18 January 1989, p. 19). It was not until the early 1970s, however, that the programme really took off, with the aim, set in 1980, of restricting population growth to 1.2 billion by the year 2000. A mixture of financial and non-pecuniary incentives and penalties were applied, especially to try to attain the goal of one child per family, formally adopted in 1979. This was relaxed somewhat in 1984–5 and tightened in 1987. After mid-1988 a surprising switch in policy took place, allowing families in rural areas to have a second child if the first was a girl, due to the difficulty of enforcing policy. But the policy was maintained for urban areas and tightened up generally for larger families (Jeffries 1993: 174).

'The population of China will officially reach 1.3 billion [on 6 January 2005] … State media credited the government's population control policies over the past thirty years for delaying the date of arrival at the 1.3 billion figure by four years' (*The Times*, 4 January 2005, p. 32). '[China claims that its population] would today top 1.5 billion … without government intervention' (*The Times*, 7 January 2005, p. 43).

The present policy as population, formally introduced in 1979, is 'one child' per family with exceptions which have grown over time.

> China's one-child policy was first implemented in 1979, but officially proclaimed only in the early 1980s … According to Chinese estimates, only one in five youngsters is an only child. Faced with growing evidence that its population control measures are being ignored [e.g. false claims that children are twins], Beijing is aiming to switch to a two-child policy … [although] there is no official policy change yet … [China says that the one-child policy] has prevented 300 million births during the past decade and brought down China's birth rate from 33 per thousand to fifteen by the end of the 1990s.
>
> (*The Times*, 8 November 2004, p. 35)

> A little-known provision in China's family planning policy allows an only child married to another only child to have two children, providing the kids are spaced four years apart … Now the first generation born under the one-child policy is starting to get married … more and more couples will be eligible for exemption.
>
> (*FEER*, 23 November 2000, p. 98)

> China is starting to move away from its 'one-child' policy and compulsory birth quotas … Targets and quotas have been abandoned in a trial project backed by the UN Population Fund in thirty-two rural counties. Beijing now plans to extend the voluntary approach to a further 800 counties … The one-child rule has already been relaxed in most of rural China, where families are

allowed two children if the first is a girl – and often if it is a boy. City dwellers are still limited to one child, unless both parents are single children themselves ... While birth quotas have been removed in the thirty-two pilot counties, families who exceed two children still have to pay a fine, known as the 'social compensation payment' ... Instead of paying the fine, couples can choose to have an abortion, especially if the pregnancy was unintended. Another important difference under the UN scheme is that families no longer have to apply to have their first child. In the past it might have been refused if the village 'quota' had been filled.

(*Guardian*, 27 July 2002, p. 18)

[On 22 July the USA] withheld $34 million in international family planning funds designated for the United Nations ... [because] any money to the agency ... [the United States claimed] helps the 'Chinese government to implement more effectively its programmes of coercive abortion'.

(*IHT*, 3 August 2002, p. 6)

China's one-child policy ... [was] launched in 1980 after the population topped 1 billion ... But implementation has always been spotty. Today only about 20 per cent of children under fourteen are from single-child families ... The policy has been most effective in cities, where residents face heavy fines and can lose their jobs. But in the countryside, where parents depend on children to help them, especially sons, resistance has been widespread ... By the mid-1980s most rural communities allowed families with one daughter to have a second child after four years – in effect to try for a son ... In 1995 Beijing approved a pilot project in six rural counties where family planning workers would try to limit births by expanding health services for women, providing more information about contraception and allowing couples to make their own decisions. Then, in 1998, the UN population agency encouraged China to take the experiment a step further, providing funding and training to thirty-two rural counties ... that agreed to eliminate the birth permits, targets and quotas and stop promoting abortion as family planning ... [For example] under China's one-child policy, couples in this rural county [the county of Yushi] in Jiangxi province once needed a permit to have a baby. Women as a rule were fitted with IUDs after their first child, sterilized after their second. But times have changed. Yushi abolished the permits several years ago and let women make their own decisions about birth control. It stopped setting birth quotas and sterilization targets for family planning workers, too. The only punishment now for having an extra child is a fine, and even that is only occasionally collected in full ... Four years later ... [it is claimed that] population growth in Yushi has remained steady. In addition, infant mortality and other health indicators have improved ... as have relations between family planning workers and residents. Similar results have been reported in the other thirty-one counties ... [It has also been claimed] that officials across the country had been impressed by the results of the UN project, and that many were also abandoning birth permits and quotas ... [It is said] that cities and counties accounting for nearly a quarter of China's 1.3 billion people had eliminated birth permits and quotas over the last five years ... and about half the population now lives in jurisdictions that allow women to choose which type of contraception to use.

(*IHT*, 21 August 2002, pp. 1, 7)

China's first national family planning law came into effect more than two decades after its one-child-per-family policy was introduced. The legislation is aimed at preventing officials from arbitrarily fining and harshly punishing families which violate the policy. Couples who have more than one child will now pay a weighted form of compensation, while local governments must foot family planning budgets rather than relying on fines levied on parents.

(*FEER*, 12 September 2002, p. 12)

Beijing is considering the value of continuing the one-child policy ... At the time it was adopted in 1979, at the urging of Deng Xiaoping, the one-child policy ... represented a huge change from the historical importance of large families in China and from a Maoist philosophy that encouraged parents to have more children because China would be strengthened by a big population ... Some have said [there have been] cases of forced sterilization, abandonment of unwanted children and infanticide by parents who favoured sons over daughters. According to 2000 census data, China had 117 boys born for every 100 girls ... Fears of instability that could be caused by this imbalance is prompting officials to consider relaxing or scrapping the policy.

(*FEER*, 14 October 2004, p. 28)

China hopes to achieve a normal balance of newborn boys and girls within six years [by 2010] by banning the use of abortions to select an infant's sex and by making welfare payments to couples without sons ... Government figures show that 117 boys are born in China to every 100 girls – a gap blamed largely on a policy limiting most couples to one child. In a society that values sons, many parents abort baby girls, hoping to try again for a boy ... The 'one child' limit allows rural families to have two children if the first is a girl, because Chinese peasants traditionally rely on sons to support them in old age ... Researchers say China has millions fewer girls than it normally should, suggesting that many were aborted or killed after birth ... Another programme gives money to couples who have only one child or two daughters and no sons, or whose children are deceased or disabled ... Couples get 1,200 yuan, or $145, per couple a year after they turn sixty as compensation to families that practise family planning.

(www.iht.com, 15 July 2004)

'Beijing said on 15 July that it would strictly ban selective abortion of female foetuses' (www.feer.com, 29 July 2004).

[In 2003] 117 boys were born for every 100 girls, compared with a global average of 105 to 100 ... Officials said that they would offer welfare incentives to couples with two daughters and tighten the prohibition on sex-selective abortions ... Pilot programmes are already under way in China's poorest provinces. In some areas couples with two daughters and no sons have been promised an annual payment of 600 renminbi once they reach sixty years of age. The money, which is a significant sum in areas where the average income is [low] ... will also be given to families with only one child to discourage couples with a daughter from trying again for a boy ... In parts of Fujian province local governments have given housing grants ... to couples with two girls. The state will expand welfare programmes so poor couples rely less on producing a son to care for them in their old age. It will also push a 'caring for girls' propaganda campaign ... China's demographic distortions have clearly worsened since the introduction of the one-child policy. In 1982 the boy-to-girl ratio was similar to the global average ... Since 1980 family planning officials say the restrictions have prevented 300 million births that would otherwise [have occurred] ... Two laws have been passed banning gynaecologists from telling pregnant women the sex of their foetus once it is confirmed by ultrasound checks.

(*Guardian*, 16 July 2004, p. 19)

Despite some changes, China's one-child family planning programme remains a source of coercion, forced abortions, infanticide and perilously imbalanced boy-girl ratios, [US] State Department officials said [on 14 December 2004] ... Couples who have unsanctioned children have been subject to heavy fines, job losses and forced sterilization ... Testimony [in the United States]... focussed on a Shanghai woman who, since her second pregnancy in the late 1980s, has been assigned to psychiatric wards, coerced into having an abortion and removed from her job.

(www.iht.com, 15 December 2004)

One of the world's least controlled abortion regimes will be tightened ... on 1 January 2005 ... when the city of Guiyang ... the provincial capital of Guizhou province ... introduces a pilot programme aimed at halting the widespread termination of female foetuses. The new policy bans doctors from carrying out abortions on most women who are more than fourteen weeks into pregnancy. In many cases the parents delay making a decision until ultrasound checks can determine the sex of their child ... China's laws do not set time limits for abortions ... In 1982, shortly after the introduction of the one-child policy, the ratio was similar to the global average of 105 boys for every 100 girls ... Because of the stiff financial penalties for second children, many couples have unregistered babies. There may be as many as 100 million of these 'illegal children'.

(*Guardian*, 16 December 2004, p. 14)

'With over 40 million more men than women in the general population, China is seeking to strengthen laws on prohibiting the use of selective abortion of female foetuses' (*IHT*, 8 January 2005, p. 6). The National Population and Family Planning Commission: 'As a new measure, the commission will start drafting revisions to the criminal law in order to effectively ban foetus gender detection and selective abortion other than for legitimate medical purposes' (*IHT*, 8 January 2005, p. 6; *Guardian*, 8 January 2005, p. 18). 'Government figures show that 119 boys are born for every 100 girls, largely because parents abort girls to try again for a boy, under China's one-child policy' (*The Times*, 8 January 2005, p. 44). 'Beijing has set a goal of reversing the imbalance by 2010 . . . But demographers have said that in poor, rural areas girls are often not cared for as well as boys, resulting in higher infant death rates for girls' (*Guardian*, 8 January 2005, p. 18).

> In early January [2005] the government announced that the nationwide ratio had reached 119 boys to every hundred girls . . . China's imbalance has widened since population controls began in the late 1970s . . . [although the] preference [for boys] dates back centuries . . . Selective sex abortions . . . were already banned, but doctors often accepted bribes from parents who wanted to guarantee a boy . . . [Experiments are being conducted to give] rural elderly people annual pensions . . . if they had only one child or if they had daughters . . . [and to give] female students from poor families free tuition as are students from families with two girls.
>
> (*IHT*, 31 January 2005, pp. 1, 7)

(Although great strides have also been made in education, President Jiang Zemin said in August 2001 that there were still 100 million illiterate Chinese: *IHT*, 10 August 2001, p. 3.)

('From the late 1970s . . . Chinese policymakers . . . began allowing Chinese citizens to travel abroad': *FT*, 14 January 2004, p. 17).

Chinese civilization

China is an ancient civilization. The question why China fell behind Europe after being ahead is an interesting one. Factors may include centralization which stifled initiative and enterprise, and a sense of cultural superiority.

China is an ancient and continuous civilization ('The longest continuous civilization in the world': *The Times*, Supplement, 8 October 1999, p. 4). The Shang dynasty was founded in about 1550 BC. But the first centralized Chinese state occurred during the Qin dynasty (221–206 BC). The Han dynasty lasted from 206 BC to AD 220. Disunity followed until China was reunified under the Sui (581–618) and the Tang (618–907). The population of China reached 100 million by the end of the Song dynasty. The Song dynasty was in power from 960 to 1279. The Mongols under Genghis Khan invaded China in the thirteenth century and they established their capital at Beijing (meaning 'northern capital' and formerly called Peking in English). The Mongol Yuan dynasty ruled for nearly a hundred years until the Mongols were expelled by the Ming in 1368. The Ming dynasty lasted until the Qing (Manchu) conquest of China in 1644. That dynasty ended in 1911 and a republic was proclaimed.

> The existence of the shadowy Xia dynasty – and with it Beijing's claims that China's civilization dates back 4,000 or even 5,000 years – has always been the subject of intense debate both in China and abroad. All this is supposed to end later this year [2000] when a government-appointed commission of 170 scholars is due to announce that after four years of research they have blown

away the doubts about China's misty past ... Critics say Beijing's attempts to promote nationalism have driven the project and that as a result the credibility of the findings has been compromised ... Analysts worry that the study could provide new fuel to a growing fire of ethnocentric nationalism in China that could result in a more belligerent foreign policy stance on issues such as Taiwan and China's leadership role in Asia ... Compared with the world's three other ancient civilizations – in present-day Egypt, India and Iraq – the origins of Chinese civilizations have always been controversial. That is because of the long transition period between the various primitive cultures that existed along the Yellow and Yangtze Rivers from roughly 8,000 to 3,000 BC and the beginnings of the country's written record during the Zhou dynasty in 841 BC ... The existence of the Shang dynasty (roughly 1,500 to 1,000 BC) ... as a 'civilization', with an organized state and a class system, is no longer in doubt ... [The Shang dynasty lasted from the sixteenth to the twelfth century BC and the Zhou dynasty lasted from the twelfth to the third century BC] ... The Xia, by contrast has remained the stuff of legend ... Archaeologists working on the project say that the final report ... will conclude that the Xia dynasty – and thus Chinese civilization – began around the year 2150 BC and continued for about 650 years until the Shang dynasty. The report is also likely to conclude that the reign of Emperor Yu, or the Great Yu – a mythical figure – marked the dynasty's founding. It will also trace the origins of the Xia back another 500 years by linking the Xia artefacts to those uncovered ... in north-western Henan. Some scholars believe the site was used by a mythological figure called the Yellow Emperor, the legendary ancestor of all Chinese people.

(Bruce Gilley, FEER, 20 July 2000, pp. 74–7)

In academic circles scepticism abounds over Huangdi ... the Yellow Emperor, regarded as the founder of the Middle Kingdom ... He is credited with the word 'emperor' and the imperial colour yellow, but Chinese legend also claims that he unified three major tribes in the Yellow and Yangtze River areas, invented the cart and the boat, and that his dialogues with the physician Qi Bo were the basis of China's first medical book, the Yellow Emperor's *Canon of Medicine*.

(The Times, 10 April 2002, p. 20)

Zheng He ... explored the Pacific and Indian Oceans with a mighty armada a century before [Christopher] Columbus discovered America ... At its [the armada's] peak [there were] as many as 300 ships and 30,000 sailors ... [compared with Columbus's three ships] ... Zheng He's first mission [was] in 1405 ... [and] his final voyage [was] in 1433 ... By the latter half of the fifteenth century the country had entered a prolonged period of self-imposed isolation that lasted into the twentieth century, leaving European powers to rule the seas.

(www.iht.com, 20 July 2005)

A prominent Chinese lawyer and collector ... Liu Gang ... unveiled an old map on Monday [16 January 2006] that he and some supporters say should topple one of the central tenets of Western civilization: that Europeans were the first to sail around the world and discover America. The Chinese map, which was drawn up in 1763 but claims to be a reproduction of an ancient map dated 1418, presents the world as a globe with all the major continents rendered with an exactitude that European maps did not have for another century and a half, after Columbus, Da Gama, Magellan, Dias and others had completed their renowned explorations. But the map got a cool reception from some scholars ... At issue are the seven voyages of Zheng He, whose ships sailed the Pacific and Indian oceans from 1405 to 1432. Historical records show he explored South-east Asia, India, the Gulf and the east coast of Africa, using navigation techniques and ships that were far ahead of their time ... Gavin Menzies ... a former British Navy submarine commander ... [in] his 2002 book *1421: The Year China Discovered America* ... claims that Zheng He visited America in 1421, seventy-one years before Columbus arrived there ... [The book] laid out extensive but widely disputed evidence that Zheng He sailed to the east coast of today's United States and may have left settlements in South America. Menzies has welcomed Liu's map as evidence that his theory is correct.

(*IHT*, 17 January 2006, p. 4)

The period 1911 to 1949

As already mentioned, the Ming dynasty ended in 1911 and a republic was proclaimed. (China was defeated by Britain in the Opium War of 1841–2 and that was followed by de facto Western domination of China. This humiliating experience has influenced China's foreign policy to the present day.)

The Kuomintang Party (founded in 1924 by Sun Yat-sen) and the Communist Party of China (founded in 1921) co-operated in the drive to break the power of warlords, but in 1927, following the earlier death of Sun Yat-sen and under the new leader Chiang Kai-shek, the former party turned on the latter. The Kuomintang established a new government at Nanking. In 1936 the Communist Party were driven northwards from their rural bases in southern China (the so-called 'Long March'). Japan invaded Manchuria in 1931 and opened full-scale hostilities in 1937. Chiang and the Chinese communists under Mao Tse-Tung then teamed up against the Japanese invaders. But civil war again broke out after Japan's defeat by the Allies in 1945. The communists were the victors.

Taiwan was a Japanese colony between 1895 and 1945. Chiang Kai-shek's forces fled there on 10 December 1949 after losing the civil war. Beijing took over Taiwan's seat in the United Nations in 1971. President Richard Nixon visited China in 1972 and recognized the country and its 'One China' policy. The United States is against Taiwan ever seeking independence but helps Taiwan defend itself and expects any reunification to be achieved peacefully and voluntarily. China says that it will attack Taiwan if the island declares independence. Relations between China and Taiwan have been particularly strained since the election of President Chen Shui-bian in March 2000. The 'anti-secession' law was approved by the National People's Congress on 14 March 2005. This heightened tension, although China stressed that 'non-peaceful' means would be a last resort to prevent secession. The United States has a policy of ambiguity as regards defending Taiwan, but it is generally assumed that it would come to Taiwan's rescue if attacked by China.

Communist China

The People's Republic ('communist' regime) was proclaimed on 1 October 1949 by Mao Tse-Tung (Zedong), who died in September 1976. (The Communist Party was established in 1921.)

The People's Republic of China became a member of the United Nations in 1971.

Although there were pockets of modern industry in the Treaty Ports and a commercial and monetary tradition, at the start of its socialist period China was, in other respects, a classically poor country. In 1949, 89 per cent of its population classified as rural. Average life expectancy was thirty-five years. The literacy rate was 20 per cent. The commodity structure of foreign trade was characterized by mainly primary product exports and manufactured imports. In the period 1931–6 net investment was only about 3 per cent of net domestic product (Riskin 1987: 33). The new communist regime was also confronted with hyperinflation on taking control. In 1952, by which time the economy had largely recovered from decades of foreign and civil war, *per capita* GNP was only $50, while agriculture employed 84 per cent of the work force and contributed 60 per cent to net material product (Riskin 1987: 269)

China is a one-party state, with the Communist Party determined to retain control. It was prepared to shoot protesting students in Tiananmen Square in June 1989. The stress is on 'unity and stability' and the regime is fearful of dissidents linking up with discontented workers and peasants and of mass movements such as Falun Gong.

> The new search for values from China's past is exploited by Falun Gong, a movement ordinarily seen in the West as a sect linked to rather mysterious traditional practices involving physical exercises as a source of well-being . . . Even though it is not a peasant movement, and frames its claims in intellectual terms, Falun Gong resembles popular movements that emerged during the final decades of the decadent Manchu empire . . . Falun Gong reproaches the [Communist] Party for having attacked China's 5,000-year-old traditional culture, attempting to destroy its three ancient religious traditions, Confucian, Buddhist and Taoist. It accuses the Communists of being the only regime in China's history to have attempted to eradicate all three ethical systems, in the past considered the source of legitimate government in China, providing 'the mandate of heaven'. This is a powerful and damaging attack on a Communist Party that presented itself as the vehicle of modernity in China.
>
> (William Pfaff, *IHT*, 25 August 2005, p. 6)

The Communist leaders . . . came to power through mass movements and is likely to lose power only in the same way; it is therefore frightened of any group, even a non-political group like the Falun Gong, that has demonstrated its power to produce mass meetings and demonstrations, or of any publication, like that of *The Tiananmen Papers*, that threatens to embarrass the present Party leaders and undermine their personal position. But the Party is not frightened of purely academic discussions in which only general philosophical opinions and aspirations are mooted ... The government cultivates uncertainty about what it will punish as a policy of deterrence ... Political repression, though often savage and arbitrary, seems pragmatic. It is limited to what the government regards as genuine or potential threats to its position and is intended to discourage open political opposition; it is not an attempt at total mind-control ... [In China reference is made to Russia, whose transition produced] what they [the Chinese] call 'chaos', crime, corruption, inefficiency and vulnerability to separatism and border terrorism.

(Ronald Dworkin, *The New York Review of Books*, 2002, vol. XLIX, no. 14, pp. 66–7)

China is 90 per cent Han. 'The country has fifty-five other groups' (*IHT*, 1 November 2004, p. 1). There has been unrest among ethnic minorities in peripheral areas such as the Uighurs in Xinjiang (which borders Kazakhstan). The United States and China became closer after the 11 September 2001 terrorist attacks on targets in the United States. The United States has named one Uighur group as part of international terrorism, but critics stress the importance in general of not branding genuine independence movements as 'international terrorism' and thus not giving countries like China and Russia (in the case of Chechnya) an excuse for suppressing domestic rebels.

The party is resolved to avoid what it sees as the anarchic conditions prevailing in transitional Russia (and indeed in the Soviet Union just before it disintegrated). Although the party has been somewhat weakened by the devolving of economic decision-making to enterprises and powerful regions, the political situation is stable enough to provide conditions conducive to gradual, partial economic reforms and to the attraction of foreign investment. The remarkable economic progress, however, is in stark contrast to its record on human rights.

China has faced periodic censure votes in the United Nations Human Rights Commission since 1990 (after Tiananmen), although all resolutions have failed to be carried to date. China stresses aspects such as the benefits of rapid economic development when discussing human rights. China does not acknowledge that it has any political prisoners, claiming that over 2,000 people have been jailed for counter-revolutionary offences. The already weak dissident movement has been more or less decimated. Leading dissidents such as Wei Jingshen have ended up in the USA. Attempts to register the China Democratic Party in June 1998 (timed to coincide with the visit of US President Bill Clinton) led to jail sentences of up to thirteen years for allegedly attempting to 'overthrow state power'. There is an extensive labour camp network. (Former camp inmate Harry Wu estimates that there are 10 million inmates, while the Chinese government admits to fewer than 1.5 million: *Guardian*, 19 May 1994, p. 27.)

On 22 July 1999 the Falun Gong movement was formally banned and in October 1999 it was officially described as an 'evil cult'. The regime sees the movement as a threat to the social stability deemed essential for economic reform and as a threat to the authority of the party at a time when ideology is declining and nationalism has not entirely filled the void. On 25 April 1999 more than 10,000 members had staged a peaceful demonstration around the leadership compound in Beijing, complaining about critical comments in the press and demanding legal status. Falun Gong means 'Way of the Law of the Wheel' and is a (slow-motion) exercise and meditation movement. It is influenced by Buddhist and Taoist principles expressed through breathing exercises.

Independent trade unions are not allowed.

Religious freedom has increased but is still severely restricted. For example, Catholics are allowed to practise under the auspices of the Official Chinese Catholic Association. The West estimates that many more practise underground (recognizing the authority of the Pope). China and the Vatican do not have diplomatic relations (although the latter has signalled its desire to establish these – at the expense of those with Taiwan – if agreement can be reached over isues such as the appointment of bishops). Unofficial churches are harshly dealt with.

Tibet remains a sensitive problem for China (which invaded the country in 1950). The Dalai Lama fled to India in 1959 and has still not been allowed to return even though he accepts Chinese sovereignty and acknowledges diplomatic improvements.

China has been criticized over the way it has handled AIDS and SARS in the country.

China has exercised strict control over the internet, seeing its benefits but aware of the threat to party control over information and communication.

It must be said, however, that the present leaders are among the most liberal realistically on offer. Ordinary people have generally benefited substantially in terms of rising living standards and typically enjoy much greater freedom as regards work, movement and information. Many Chinese students now study in Western countries. On 5 October 1998 China signed the International Covenant on Civil and Political Rights, although it has yet to ratify it. Direct elections for village committees, which formally started in 1988, are not to be lightly dismissed despite being essentially under party control. The degree of democracy varies substantially, but they are seen centrally as a way of improving and controlling local government, combating corruption and venting local discontent. The first township election took place on 31 December 1998. In 1999 experiments began with direct elections at the lowest level ('neighbourhood committees') in a number of cities.

Deng Xiaoping

Deng Xiaoping was born on 22 August 1904 and died on 19 February 1997. He was the leading figure in the drive for economic reform, adopting a pragmatic approach (see quotations below). Deng won the struggle within the Communist Party about how to maintain party control. ('In 1976 after Mao's death and the capture of the gang of four, Hua Guofeng, Mao's chosen successor, became top leader. But with little Beijing experience, Hua was no match for Deng, who step by step gained support to become top leader in 1978. At the Third Plenum in December 1978 Deng was anointed and launched his "reform and opening" ... He said he "crossed the river by groping for stones"': *FEER*, 25 November 1999, p. 43.) After he relinquished the titles of political office, Deng Xiaoping's only remaining formal title was 'Most Honorary President of the China Bridge Association'! But he remained the most powerful figure in reality.

Deng's argument (which is still generally accepted) is that concessions to the market and non-state ownership are essential for maintaining party control, while his opponents believed that the party's power is threatened by radical economic reforms (e.g. it leads to demands for political reform). (Deng's ideas on economic reform were influenced by people such as Zhao Ziyang.) Deng was aware of the extraordinary economic progress of the neighbouring 'Asian tigers' (and especially aware of the contrast between China and Taiwan). Deng strongly believed in political stability and considered this a prerequisite of economic progress. He was influenced and personally affected by the anarchy of the Cultural Revolution. He lost positions of power in 1966 and 1976, making political 'comebacks' in 1973 and 1977. He did not become 'paramount leader' until his mid-seventies. He thought that calls for greater democracy and the student demonstrations of 1989 were a threat to stability and was ruthless in stamping them out.

> The goal [of the student protestors of Tiananmen] was to establish a bourgeois republic entirely dependent on the West. Of course we accept people's demands to combat corruption ... However, such slogans were just a front. The real aim was to overthrow the Communist Party and topple the socialist system.
>
> (June 1989)

'We put down a counter-revolutionary rebellion' (June 1989).
The following quotations illustrate, among other things, Deng's pragmatism.

> It does not matter whether a cat is black or white as long as it catches mice.
> (1961, in relation to agricultural reform)

> What do the people want from the Communist Party? First, to be liberated, and second to be made rich.
> (Third Plenum of the Eleventh Central Committee, December 1978)

> If today we still do not set about the task of improving the socialist system, people will ask why it cannot solve problems which its capitalist counterpart can.
> (August 1980)

> We should let some people get rich first, both in the countryside and in the urban areas. To get rich by hard work is glorious.
> (January 1983)

> Socialism must eliminate poverty. Poverty is not socialism.
> (June 1984)

> Development is the core truth.
> Fish grow in muddy waters.
> (1985)

Our experience in the twenty years from 1958 to 1978 teaches us that poverty is not socialism. You cannot eat socialism.

(1985)

If you want to bring the initiative of the peasants into play, you should give them the power to make money.

(October 1985)

A planned economy does not necessarily imply socialism ... a market economy does not necessarily imply capitalism.

(1992)

We in China are faced with the task of transforming our backwardness and catching up promptly with the advanced countries of the world. We want to learn from you.

(1979)

('In early 1979 Deng Xiaoping was barnstorming America to celebrate the historic agreement normalizing relations between the countries. At a stop in suburban Atlanta Deng toured a Ford factory that made more cars in a single month than China produced in a year. Aware of his country's economic inferiority, Deng ... said he hoped to transform China into an industrial power by the distant year of 2000 ... China manufactured 13,000 cars in 1979; last year [2004] the number exceeded 5 million': www.iht.com, 20 November 2005; *IHT*, 21 November 2005, p. 4.)

China after Deng Xiaoping

There was something of a mild power struggle among Deng's successors, but there was essentially continuity of policy.

General secretary Jiang Zemin (12 October 1992):

> We must hold high the great banner of socialism with Chinese characteristics ... If we fail to develop our economy rapidly it will be very difficult for us to consolidate the socialist system and maintain long-term stability ... The goal is to build a socialist democracy suited to Chinese conditions and absolutely not a Western, multi-party, parliamentary system ... [The development of a] social-ist market economy [is the only way forward] ... We are convinced that a market economy established under the socialist system can and should operate better than one under the capitalist system ... [Macroeconomic levers should be the main means of control. The plan should, for example, set] strategic targets [include growth forecasts and deal with investment in the infrastructure. There should be an integrated national market with no regional protectionism].
>
> (Jeffries 1993: 497)

The leading personalities were the following: (1) Jiang Zemin, party leader and president (March 1993); he was described as the 'core' of the collective leadership (note the word 'collective') and he steadily consolidated his position (e.g. he was prominent during the October 1999 celebrations of the fiftieth anniversary of communist China); (2) Li Peng, prime minister until March 1998 when he was elected chairman of the National People's Congress; the least enthusiastic of the three as regards economic reform; (3) Zhu Rongyi, senior vice-premier and the economics supremo until March 1998 when he was elected prime minister (while remaining economics supremo; the foremost economic reformer, he was once governor of the central bank, stepping down on 30 June 1995). Among the economic problems facing them were inflation (though minor compared with that faced by many countries in Eastern Europe and the former Soviet Union in the early years of transition) and, starting in October 1997, deflation (a problem, for example, because large volumes of stocks depressed economic activity; the state has increased its spending to keep growth high enough to keep unemployment under control). (Modest inflation began to be recorded in 2003.) Persistent problems included heavy losses by many state enterprises; worker unrest (caused by factors such as unemployment, the non-payment of wages and benefits and corrupt management); a weak banking system (problems such as high ratios of non-performing loans); farmers' discontent; increasing economic disparities between coastal and inland provinces as well as between town and country; and corruption.

In November 2002 the party charter was revised to include Jiang Zemin's 'three represents'. 'The "three represents" said the party's mission was to represent "advanced production forces" (capitalists and technologists), "advanced cultural forces" (intellectuals) and "the broad masses of the people" (everybody else)' (David Ignatius, *IHT*, 21 September 2002, p. 4).

> The 'three represents': Jiang Zemin's controversial attempt to redefine the party's mission in order to guarantee the party's survival. He holds that the party should represent the needs of 'advanced forces of production' such as hi-tech industries and the private sector, advanced culture and the 'fundamental interests of the overwhelming majority of the Chinese people' – rather than the millions of blue-collar workers laid off by state-owned industries.
>
> (*FEER*, 7 November 2002, p. 29)

'[The term] "advanced productive forces" [is] communist jargon for capitalists' (*The Economist*, 9 November 2002, p. 15). In November 2002 private businessmen (private entrepreneurs) were formally allowed to join the party.

A so-called 'fourth generation' of leaders has appeared since the Sixteenth Communist Party Congress held in November 2002 and the Tenth National People's Congress held in March 2003. The positions mentioned were filled by the following:

1   Hu Jintao: the fifty-nine-year-old vice-president became general secretary of the Communist Party on 15 November 2002, president in March 2003, chairman of the party's Central Military Commission on 19 September 2004 and chairman of the state's Central Military Commission in March 2005. Hu Jintao's mentor was Deng Xiaoping.
2   Wen Jiabao: prime minister. His mentor is Zhu Rongyi.
3   Wu Bangguo: chairman of the National People's Congress. He was previously deputy prime minister dealing with reform of state enterprises and his mentor is Jiang Zemin.

Despite considerable prior speculation about exactly which positions Jiang Zemin would give up, the most orderly and peaceful transfer of power since 1949 has taken place. There was again essentially a continuity of policy, including that of collective leadership and attitudes towards economic reform. There were, however, some differences. For example, Hu seemed to have a more positive attitude towards greater transparency and democracy within the party (such as elections for lower-level party posts). But it is generally thought that his room to manoeuvre was limited. (There was considerable speculation as to who would hold ultimate power, since Jiang Zemin remained chairman of the party's Central Military Commission until 19 September 2004.)

Hu Jintao has not made any startling proposals to date, although he quickly identified himself with those people and areas that have fared less well as a result of the economic reforms. He seemed to be concerned to place greater emphasis of the social costs of growth and less on growth as an end in itself. The term 'a harmonious society' became associated with him. But a communiqué issued on 11 October 2005 at the end of a Central Committee meeting showed that economic growth was not going to be sacrificed in the process. The communiqué stated:

> During the Eleventh Five Year Plan we must maintain fast and stable economic growth and support the building of a harmonious society. The meeting stressed that to push forward economic development and improve the lives of the people is China's major task ... We need to put greater emphasis on social equity, enhance efforts in adjusting income distribution and strive to alleviate the tendency of the widening income gap between regions and parts of society.
> (www.iht.com, 12 October 2005; *FT*, 12 October 2005, p. 11)

(Likewise, although the idea of 'green GDP' implies concern about China's severe pollution problems, it is clear that rapid economic growth is regarded as essential to maintain the rise in living standards and to keep unemployment at socially tolerable levels.) But the widening income inequalities in China (especially between urban and rural areas) are causing increasing concern.

Overall, it seems that Hu Jintao has turned out to be more hard line than expected. There is growing concern that unrest in the countryside (especially over such things as land seizures for urban and industrial development) could threaten social stability.

> Three years after becoming China's top leader, Hu Jintao ... president and Communist Party chief ... has solidified his grip on power and intimidated critics inside and outside the Communist Party with the help of the man once seen as his most potent rival ... Zeng Qinghong, vice president and the man in charge of the party's organizational affairs ... They have clamped down on non-government organizations, tightened media controls and forced all of the 70 million members to submit self-criticisms as an act of ritualistic submission to their authority ... In May Hu and Zeng convened top officials to warn that just as governments in Ukraine, Georgia and Kyrgyzstan had been toppled, the government in China could be, too. They argued that the United States had fostered social unrest in those places and had similar designs on China ... They

have since forced non-government organizations that focus on the environment, legal aid, health and education to find government sponsors or shut down. Many groups are also under pressure to stop accepting money from the United States and other foreign countries. The leadership has also fired editors at publications that defied orders from the party's propaganda department ... They have also tightened rules on foreign investment in China's television industry.

(Joseph Kahn, www.iht.com, 25 September 2005; *IHT*, 26 September 2005, p. 2)

The Communist Party has chosen one of its oldest political tools – a Maoist-style ideological campaign, complete with required study groups. For fourteen months and counting the party's 70 million rank and file members have been assigned readings that include speeches by Mao and Deng Xiaoping, as well as the numbing treatise of 17,000-plus words that is the party constitution. Mandatory meetings include sessions where cadres must offer self-criticisms and also criticize everyone else ... The campaign [is] known as *bao xian* or 'preserving the progressiveness' ... Hu Jintao, who is also general secretary of the party, has insisted that every member complete the programme ... The third and final phase is now under way at village party branches and is to end in June [2006] ... In recent years Hu's predecessor as the country's top leader, Jiang Zemin, ushered in study campaigns. More famously as many as 200 campaigns were introduced under Mao, from the angry purges of the Cultural Revolution era to mass mobilization efforts to exterminate rodents ... In February [2006] the party's Central Discipline Inspection Commission announced that it had disciplined 115,000 party members for corruption in 2005 ... One proposal debated in recent years by Chinese intellectuals calls for intra-party elections. But as yet such reforms have not materialized.

(Jim Yardley, *IHT*, 10 March 2006, pp. 1, 8)

China regained control of Hong Kong from Britain on 1 July 1997 and of Macao from Portugal on 20 December 1999. Hong Kong is much more important than Macao in economic terms, e.g. in terms of foreign trade and foreign capital. But the people of Macao were much more enthusiastic at being under Chinese control than those of Hong Kong, the former hoping to get respite from criminal gangs. Their futures depend crucially on the reform path being maintained in China itself. The Hong Kong takeover was relatively smooth and China was praised by the West during the Asian financial crisis for not devaluing the Chinese yuan or the Hong Kong dollar. Hong Kong is subject to a 'one country, two systems' regime, with a supposedly high degree of autonomy (except for defence and foreign affairs) for fifty years as a Special Administrative Region of China. But this autonomy has been eroded over time, albeit with increasing economic concessions (as regards trade with mainland China and so on). Future democratization in China itself and overall success in Hong Kong and Macao are crucial to any prospects of a peaceful reunification with Taiwan.

China's rapid growth has become a factor of global economic significance (see the section on economic performance). This economic growth has been accompanied by increasing military might and a growing diplomatic stature (e.g. China has, for example, hosted international talks about North Korea's nuclear weapons programme). China's relations with the United States loom large. The war against international terrorism since the 11 September 2001 attacks on the United States has brought the two countries closer together. China has used international terrorism to justify its tough policies on internal unrest among minorities.

China has improved its relations with (much weakened) Russia since the collapse of the Soviet Union, both supporting the idea of a 'multi-polar' world (as opposed to a 'uni-polar' world dominated by the United States). Both China and Russia have sought to use international terrorism to further crack down on internal unrest among minorities and resent what they see as other countries interfering in the internal affairs of others (given the sensitivity of Tibet and Chechnya, respectively). China and Russia have settled their border disputes.

China has also improved its relations with India, although it was disturbed by India and Pakistan conducting nuclear tests in May 1998. China itself announced a moratorium on further tests after it conducted its forty-fifth test on 29 July 1996. (The USA has conducted 1,030 nuclear tests and the former Soviet Union 715: *IHT*, 12 December 1996, p. 7. There have been a total of 2,045 known nuclear tests since 1945: *IHT*, 12 September 1996, p. 17.)

China has gone out of its way to try to allay concern over its growing economic and military power. But many countries in Asia remain worried, not helped by China's territorial claims (over the Spratly Islands, for example).

> President Hu Jintao has a favourite phrase these days: 'harmonious world', in which countries of different outlooks live together in peace. Mr Hu first unveiled this idea ... in a speech at the United Nations on 15 September [2005] ... Before 'harmonious world' came China's 'peaceful rise' – a term that fell by the wayside as officials bickered over whether it sounded a bit too menacing, or perhaps just the opposite as far as Taiwan was concerned.
>
> (*The Economist*, 19 November 2005, pp. 23–5)

President Hu Jintao (20 November 2005): 'China's commitment to a role of peaceful development is a choice that China must make ... China's development is peaceful, open and co-operative in nature' (www.iht.com, 20 November 2005).

Economic reforms

The economic reforms themselves have been variously described by China, e.g. 'planned socialist commodity economy' has given way to 'socialist market economy' (1992: formally enshrined in the new constitution in March 1993) as the reforms have proceeded and ideological concessions have become more and more accepted.

China is the best example of a generally successful policy of gradual and partial economic reform. Success has been achieved on a broad front, in terms of such criteria as output growth, living standards, poverty reduction and inflation. (See Table 1, p. 617.) The discrediting of such extreme and extreme-left policies as the Great Leap Forward (1958–60) and the Cultural Revolution (1966–76) has helped keep the reforms on track. There is no chance of any substantial reversal of the reforms which have been gradually introduced since 1978. China's application for and subsequent entry into the WTO (the successor to Gatt) on 11 December 2001 helped ensure the irreversibility of the economic reform process.

Economic reform has generally moved forward over time, but there have been occasional set-backs (e.g. after Tiananmen Square in 1989 and in prices and privatization).

> In recent years China's leaders have themselves stressed the need to narrow regional imbalances. This was a major theme of the annual ten-day session of the National People's Congress, which ended on 14 March [2006] . . . Yet criticism of these disparities has also become a way for some to air more general grievances about China's embrace of capitalism. The government recently shelved plans to submit a new property law to the congress after a chorus of opposition, led by a Peking University academic, Gong Xiantian.
>
> (*The Economist*, 18 March 2006, p. 62)

> For the first time in perhaps a decade the National People's Congress, the Communist Party-led legislature, now convened in its annual two-week session [5–14 March 2006], is consumed with an ideological debate over socialism and capitalism that many assumed had been buried by China's long streak of fast economic growth. The controversy has forced the government to shelve a draft law to protect property rights . . . It has also highlighted the resurgent influence of a small but vocal group of socialist-leaning scholars and policy advisers. These old-style leftist thinkers have used China's rising income gap [e.g. the gap between the average incomes of urban and rural residents has risen to 3.3 to 1.0, according to the United Nations Development Programme] and increasing social unrest to raise doubts about what they see as the country's headlong pursuit of private wealth and market-driven economic development.
>
> (Joseph Kahn, *IHT*, 13 March 2006, pp. 1, 4)

> A backlash against economic reform has gathered force and the logic of liberalization is being challenged to an extent not seen since the immediate aftermath of the crackdown on pro-democracy protests in Tiananmen Square in 1989 . . . Domestic critics blame market reforms for exacerbating inequality and promoting social unrest.
>
> (*FT*, 16 March 2006, p. 16)

China adopted a policy of gradual and partial price reform. A 'dual' pricing system was used (market prices being allowed for products bought and sold on the market as opposed to state-controlled prices for outputs or inputs forming part of the state plan). Controls have generally been relaxed over time. Nevertheless, temporary retrenchment has occurred, such as the reintroduction of price controls to combat inflation (price ceilings) and (for some time after October 1997) deflation (price floors). Many cases of state interference in price setting can still be found.

In recent years China's rapid growth has been of global significance, e.g. world market prices of commodities such as oil, coal, iron ore, steel and cement have been affected, and China has become a magnet for direct foreign investment. The government is anxious to maintain social stability by keeping GDP growth at at least 7 per cent, the minimum needed to keep unemployment from getting out of hand, i.e. the minimum needed for social stability. Unemployment and labour unrest have both risen. Large-scale, state-determined infrastructure investment programmes (as well as policies such as extended holidays) have been employed by the state to help counter the ill effects of the Asian financial crises (which started in July 1997), and of private consumption depressed by rising unemployment, deflation and reduced social service provision. But in 2004 there was increasing concern about the increasing shortages of goods and services such as energy, raw materials (such as coal and iron ore) and transport. The state set out to try to moderate growth (by restricting sectors such as steel, cement, aluminium, cars and property), but GDP in 2004 was 9.5 per cent (well above the original target of at least 'more than' 7 per cent; the target growth rate for 2005 is 'about 8 per cent'). The inflation rate has on occasion been in double figures, but inflation has never been the sort of problem experienced by many transitional economies in Eastern Europe and the former Soviet Union. For a few years after late 1997, deflation was something of a problem. Modest inflation was recorded for 2003.

As regards agriculture, the Household Responsibility System has taken root and has been improved by lengthening leases (land is not privately owned), in some cases seemingly indefinite in reality if not in law. Private farms are still very small in general, but the state has encouraged the development of larger units in a number of ways: various experiments by the state to lease out larger plots of land; permission given for sub-leasing among farmers; encouragement given to the amalgamation of family plots; and there have even been cases of forcible reassignment of land from less to more efficient farmers (which shows the limitations of leased land in terms of property rights even though there has been legislation to give greater security to leases). The widening gap between urban and rural incomes to the detriment of the latter has caused a mass movement of peasants to the towns (generally put at something like 150 million) and increasing concern to the government. Entry into the WTO has brought real benefits to those farmers willing to switch to products such as those fruits and vegetables in ever greater demand. But there is growing concern about the increasing number of violent protests (sometimes leading to loss of life) in rural areas, caused in particular by the takeover of agricultural land by local officials for redevelopment. Such profitable (and often illegal) redesignation of land can lead to corruption and farmers feeling inadequately compensated for loss of land-use rights. The March 2006 session of the National People's Congress outlined a programme of further aid to rural areas, envisioning a 'new socialist countryside'.

The focus of monetary policy is still on credit control rather than on interest rates. The state-dominated banking system remains a major headache for China, despite various reforms. In market economies the financial system is the means by which saving is transformed into investment. China's financial system is very inefficient because of pervasive state controls. As a result of the 'soft budget constraint' applying to many state enterprises, large amounts of bad ('non-performing') bank loans have been built up. Reforms to try to make state banks more commercially minded have been greatly hindered by, for example, the need to boost spending when deemed necessary by the state. Other reforms include reducing the proportion of non-performing loans held by certain banks via so-called Asset Management Companies and the boosting of the capital resources of certain banks to help prepare them for initial share offerings (IPOs). The central government has begun to refuse to act as an automatic guarantor of debts incurred by regional financial institutions. A start was made in October 1998 when the central bank ordered the closure of the Guangdong International Trust and Investment Corporation after it was unable to repay loans (including foreign ones).

Banking reform has been hindered by the persistence of so many loss-making state enterprises, facing increasing competition from non-state enterprises (able to enter an increasing number of markets). In other words, soft budget constraints still widely apply, especially in the case of larger enterprises. The state is reluctant to see unemployment and enterprise bankruptcies on too large a scale for fear of serious worker unrest. Labour unrest has increased and sometimes takes a violent turn. ('Unity and stability' is a slogan frequently emphasized.) Policies like mergers with healthier state enterprises are preferred to bankruptcy, but many smaller enterprises have been closed down.

In the original system the enterprise was not just a production unit. It was also, as we have already seen, a social unit. The shift to a more Western-type system of social security, health and housing is a difficult, costly and painful one. Such reforms are needed for state enterprises to compete more effectively with private enterprises in a market economy. State enterprises have become increasingly market-orientated.

Large privatization along Eastern European lines has not been adopted in China. Initially China concentrated on deregulation (i.e. gradually opening up certain sectors to private activity). Later on, small enterprises began to be sold off in significant numbers and even some medium-sized and large ones companies have now been sold. Although the state still dominates ownership in medium-sized and large companies, an increasing number of companies have sold a proportion of their shares to private (including foreign) individuals and companies. ('Some 60 per cent of the average listed company remains in state hands': *FEER*, 28 October 2004, p. 32.) The private sector has been given greater encouragement over time and the constitution has been amended to give it greater protection and status. (The private sector still faces problems relating to such things as finance, property rights, corruption and bureaucracy.) 'Public ownership' remains officially the 'mainstay' of the economy, but the term has been interpreted more liberally (e.g. to include mixed-ownership enterprises). China has stuck to its policy of building up conglomerates to compete with the international giants despite the adverse publicity of such organizations as the South Korean chaebols during the Asian financial crisis. Other reforms include separating government administration from enterprise management. China's stock markets are still dominated by largely state-owned companies. For some years prior to mid-2005 (when a revival began) the poor performance of the stock markets was in marked contrast to GDP growth.

By the end of 1998 the People's Liberation Army had carried out the order to divest itself of most of its substantial commercial operations.

'Township–village enterprises' (TVEs) played a very important role in China's overall growth in the earlier reform period. Their star waned as they came under increasing strain as a result of a more individually orientated society, a more mobile population and greater competition from private and the more dynamic of the state enterprises. One response has been the transformation of TVEs into 'shareholding co-operatives', which are becoming increasingly common.

The dramatic increase in the role played by the non-state sector can be seen in the following figures.

According to the International Finance Corporation (the private sector arm of the World Bank), in 1998 the state sector contributed 37 per cent of GDP. Private businesses generated 33 per cent, while the balance came from agricultural companies and businesses (*Transition*, 2000, vol. 11, no. 2, p. 40). 'The non-state sector now accounts for 75 per cent of GDP if collective and agricultural output is included' (*FEER*, 12 July 2001, p. 49).

> The private sector ... now accounts for half of China's GDP and 75 per cent if the essentially privatized activities of agriculture, rural collectives and shareholding companies are included, according to estimates by the World Bank's ... International Finance Corporation. The figure is expected to rise.
>
> (*FEER*, 30 August 2001, p. 19)

(Of course, the 2004 upward revision of GDP, see below, has implications for estimates of the importance of the non-state sector in GDP.)

China has continued to open up its economy to foreign capital, trade and technology (hence the aptly phrased 'open-door' policy). It is a magnet for direct foreign investment because of factors such as cheap and abundant labour and rapidly growing markets. But there are problems, for example as regards remaining state restrictions and with the ensuring of property rights (despite some improvement in this area). '[A] labour shortage in south-east China [especially in Guangdong province]... has persisted for more than nine months' (www.iht.com, 19 April 2005). 'Reports of labour shortages first emerged in late 2004, when the government identified shortages in two critical provinces in south-eastern China, Guangdong and Fujian' (*IHT*, 3 April 2006, p. 1). There have been further reports of regional labour shortages. Investment overseas (even in the United States) by Chinese companies (particularly in energy) is now beginning to attract attention.

China did not succeed in gaining founder membership of Gatt's successor, the World Trade Organization (WTO), when it was established on 1 January 1995. China's entry into the WTO on 11 December 2001 was delayed by such factors as quotas, an extensive licensing system and large subsidies to state industrial enterprises. It has been argued that WTO entry had implications for the overall economic reform process in China. 'Prime minister Zhu Rongyi ... wants to use commitments to the WTO to make it hard for domestic opponents to overturn reforms. Violations of China's commitments to the WTO invite retaliation by China's trade partners' (*New York Times*, editorial: *IHT*, 4 November 1999, p. 8). WTO entry did not eliminate trade friction. There was a surge in imports of Chinese textiles into the United States and the EU (to which both responded) after the lifting (on 1 January 2005) of quotas associated with the Multifibre Agreement. Other trade disputes involve shoe imports into the EU.

Controls on the Chinese economy (such as on capital flows) helped shield China from the worst effects of the Asian financial crisis (which started in July 1997). The crisis had a temporary dampening effect on China's desire to join the WTO.

The yuan (renminbi or 'people's currency') has been gradually made more and more convertible. The first local foreign exchange markets ('swap centres') were set up in 1985 (a valuable boost to direct foreign investment since profits earned by 'foreign-invested enterprises' could be repatriated without having to export). On 1 January 1994 the official and swap rates were unified, with the yuan subjected to a managed float. On 1 December 1996 China formally accepted Article 8 of the IMF's articles of association on current account convertibility (restrictions remaining on capital account transactions). The date of full convertibility of the yuan has been continually put back.

China earned considerable respect in the international community for maintaining the exchange rate of the renminbi (and the Hong Kong dollar) and thus not triggering a further round of competitive devaluations in Asia after the financial crisis started in July 1997. Adverse effects included a decline in exports, but China escaped relatively lightly. Long-imposed controls of the capital account were reinforced by increasingly stringent foreign exchange regulations and indirect ways of boosting exports (e.g. tax rebates for exporters). There was a crackdown on smuggling.

China has integrated into the world economy to an extraordinary degree – the country exports and imports a great deal. China has not typically run large overall balance of trade surpluses, but the surplus surged in 2005 and the increasing bilateral surplus with the United States is a cause of great friction. But many countries fear China's competitive ability in many areas of manufacturing (textiles is but one example). One generally perceived irritant is China's persistence in linking ('pegging') the renminbi to (a generally weakening) US dollar. This generally perceived undervaluation of the Chinese currency further increases China's export competitiveness. (While it is generally thought that the yuan is undervalued, there is considerable disagreement as to the extent to which this is so. See, for example, *The Economist*, 25 June 2005, p. 100.) On 21 July 2005 there was a small revaluation of the yuan against the dollar, with the peg against the dollar scrapped in favour of the yuan moving within a daily trading band of 0.3 per cent either way against a basket of currencies (including the dollar, it later transpired) with unspecified weightings. China tried to discourage speculation that the yuan would gradually appreciate over time.

In December 2005 China announced that it had upwardly revised its official estimate of GDP in 2004 by 16.8 per cent. The main reason given was the considerable underestimation of the private service sector. In January 2006 China presented revised figures for GDP growth rates. From 1993 to 2004 (inclusive) only the figure for 1998 remained unchanged, while all the others were revised upwards.

1   Politics

China and Taiwan

Taiwan was inhabited by non-Chinese peoples who spoke their own language and are ethnically and linguistically closer to modern Indonesians than to Chinese. Chinese fishermen and farmers began to settle along Taiwan's coastal areas, particularly in the sixteenth and seventeenth centuries. Holland seized Taiwan in 1624 (*IHT*, 22 March 2000, p. 2). 'Large-scale settlement from the mainland only began in the seventeenth century and the original Malayo-Polynesian inhabitants remained a majority till the nineteenth century . . . Today 40 per cent of the island's trade is with China' (*IHT*, 27 December 2003, p. 6).

> Except for a tiny aboriginal minority, well over 90 per cent of Taiwanese trace their ancestry to China. But only roughly 15 per cent of the population came to this island since 1949, the start of the communist era. In cultural terms this minority, many of them followers of the nationalist leader Chiang Kai-shek, known here [Taiwan] as 'mainlanders', still identifies closely with the mother-land. To a large degree, today the rest of the population sees itself simply as Taiwanese.
>
> (*IHT*, 27 May 2005, p. 2)

Kinmen is also known as Jinmen or Quemoy (*IHT*, 7 February 2001, p. 7).

China exercised various degrees of control over Taiwan, increasingly settled by Han who drove the non-Han people into the mountains until 1623 (*The Times*, 19 March 1996, p. 11). In 1623 the Dutch demanded a trading post to match Portugal's at Macau and were ceded Taiwan. The Dutch lost control in 1662 when a half-Japanese general fled there from China with the remnants of the Ming dynasty. (The Manchu dynasty conquered China in 1644.) Manchu China gained control of Taiwan in 1683. In 1887 Taiwan's status was upgraded to that of a full province, but eight years later it became Japan's first colony (after the Sino-Japanese War). Japan ruled Taiwan from 1895 to 1945. Chinese sovereignty over Taiwan dates from the 1943 Cairo Declaration, in which the Allies decided what to do with Japan's empire after the war (*The Economist*, 16 March 1996, p. 72). According to Peng Ming-min (leader in Taiwan of the opposition Democratic Progressive Party, which favours independence), the Qing dynasty relinquished sovereignty over Taiwan 'in perpetuity' in the 1895 Treaty of Shimonoseki.

Except for a brief period from 1945 to 1949, when the island was ruled as a part of China by Chiang Kai-shek's Kuomintang regime, Taiwan has had an independent government (*IHT*, 6 March 1996, p. 8). When Chiang Kai-shek's troops took control in 1945 'they treated the island like a captured enemy stronghold, looting it. In 1947 they massacred thousands of indigenous Taiwanese who demonstrated against their "liberators"' (Jonathan Mirsky, *The Times*, 19 March 1996, p. 11). On 28 February 1947 nationalist soldiers launched a month-long massacre, spreading through the island killing thousands of perceived political opponents. After 1949 the nationalists ran a dictatorship. President Chiang Ching-kuo (Chiang Kai-shek's son and successor) took charge in 1975 and it was he who recognized the changes brought about by Taiwan's new affluence. In 1980 an anti-government demonstration was crushed and opposition leaders arrested. But the president then saw that reform was inevitable. 'Chiang recognized that change would come because of Taiwan's ethnic mix – about 88 per cent of the island's population is native to the island' (Keith Richburg, *IHT*, 22 March 1996, p. 12). Mainland-born Taiwanese and their families constitute around 15 per cent of the population. There are about 350,000 aborigines, who, until recently, were known as 'mountain people': 400 years of often violent Chinese immigration had pushed them up into the hills (*The Economist*, 30 March 1996, p. 67). Martial law was lifted in 1987.

'The American Institute in Taiwan administers Washington's unofficial ties with Taipei' (*FEER*, 30 October 2003, p. 22).

[In] the Shanghai Communiqué of 1972 the United States said it 'acknowledges that all Chinese on both sides of the Taiwan Strait maintain there is but one China and that Taiwan is a part of China'. The US government does not challenge that position.

(*FEER*, 23 October 2003, p. 61)

No president of Taiwan was to be allowed a visa to enter the United States after 1979. Thereafter the United States had only 'cultural, commercial and other unofficial relations with the people of Taiwan'. Beijing had taken Taiwan's seat in the United Nations in 1971. According to Steven Erlanger (*IHT*, 13 March 1996, p. 4), the defence treaty the United States had with Taiwan was abrogated after President Nixon visited China in 1972 and recognized China, accepting that it and not Taiwan was the government of a single China. But in return the United States was promised that reunification with Taiwan would take place peacefully. The Taiwan Relations Act of 1979 asserted the United States' right to help Taiwan defend itself, considering 'any effort to determine the future of Taiwan by other than peaceful means, including boycotts or embargoes, a threat to the peace and security of the Western Pacific area and of grave concern to the United States'.

According to *The Economist* (25 May 1996), in 1979 the United States recognized the 'government of the People's Republic of China as the sole legal government of China'. But the United States did not accept that Taiwan was 'part of China'; it merely 'acknowledged' that China thought so (p. 79). The United States abrogated its 1954 defence treaty with Taiwan but in April 1979 Congress passed the Taiwan Relations Act, one of the aims of which was 'to resist any resort to force or other forms of coercion that would jeopardise the security or the social and economic system of Taiwan'. The act also committed the United States to supply 'arms of a defensive character' to Taiwan (p. 80).

> In February 1972 President Richard Nixon ... signed the Shanghai Communiqué: 'The United States acknowledges that all Chinese on either side of the Taiwan Strait maintain there is but one China and that Taiwan is a part of China' ... Taiwan was only ruled in a very desultory manner by the Chinese from 1683 to 1895. For most people in Taiwan this was simply colonialism, no different from what came before – the Spanish (which ruled for seventeen years), the Dutch (thirty-eight years) – and after that, when the Japanese ruled from 1895 to 1946.
>
> (Jonathan Power, *IHT*, 18 March 2004, p. 6)

'In January 1979 China established formal diplomatic relations with the United States' (*IHT*, 17 September 2005, p. 7).

China claims sovereignty (as does Taiwan) over the Diaoyu Islands (known as the Senkaku Islands in Japan). Japan administered the islands from 1895 until its defeat in 1945. The United States handed them over to Japan in 1972.

A chronology of events

7 August 1994. Negotiators from China and Taiwan reach agreement on a number of issues, such as fishing disputes and the possible repatriation of aircraft hi-jackers and illegal immigrants. (The approval of both governments is needed.)

22 May 1995. China vehemently protests about the USA's decision to allow the president of Taiwan a visa for a private visit. (Thereafter China threatened Taiwan on a number of occasions and in various ways, e.g. by holding nearby military exercises for eleven days in August 1995, especially warning against any attempt to declare independence or moves in that direction.)

6 January 1996. The USA issues transit visas to the vice president of Taiwan to enable his plane to refuel on 11 and 16 January 1996.

8–25 March 1996. China conducts missile tests near the coast of Taiwan 8–15 March and holds nearby naval and air exercises 12–25 March. The USA sends extra warships into the area. On 14 March China said that it did not intend to invade Taiwan. On 20 March the USA announced its approval of the sale of new weapons to Taiwan, including surface-to-air missiles.

23 March 1996. The presidential election in Taiwan (the first by direct popular vote) is won by Lee Teng-hui with 54 per cent of the vote (a figure generally considered to have been boosted by China's threats). Peng Ming-min, leader of the pro-independence Democratic Progressive Party, is second with 21.1 per cent. The other two candidates (advocating a more conciliatory stance towards China) receive 14.9 per cent and 10 per cent. There is a 76 per cent turnout. (Lee Teng-hui, leader of the Kuomintang or Nationalist Party, was made president in January 1988. In his inauguration speech given on 20 May 1996 he talked of his readiness to make a 'journey of peace' to China: 'I am ready to meet the top leadership of the Chinese communists for a direct exchange of views'.)

Taiwanese are debunking the myth that Chinese people do not care about politics, that they are more interested in making money than practising noisy, Western-style democracy. More than anything else, that is what is rattling Beijing's communists, who have repeatedly denounced multiparty democracy as unsuited to Chinese culture and Confucian tradition ... In an attempt to disrupt the 23 March election, or at least to influence the outcome, China has staged a series of military exercises and missile tests in the waters close to Taiwan.

(Keith Richburg, *IHT*, 22 March 1996, p. 12)

William Saffire (*IHT*, 26 March 1996, p. 9) asked what explained China's behaviour:

Not fear of a Taiwanese declaration of independence. The Chinese on Taiwan know that would provoke war, on terms that would preclude US military help ... Nor was the blundering in Beijing primarily caused by a need to instil in the regionalized Chinese army a fervent new national spirit supporting the central regime in Beijing as it secretly plans for the succession to Deng Xiaoping ... The key to the communist leadership's willingness to appear bellicose, unstable and, worst of all, unsubtle is this: the spectacle of 21 million Chinese freely choosing their leaders is intolerable to China's established order. Fierce objection must be made lest the billion Chinese under communist political control get democratic ideas.

The former US ambassador to China (1989–91), James Lilley, warns that:

China is now riding the tiger of nationalism, and unless it soon realizes how damaging its actions are to its own interests it may be too late. Communism's appeal is gone, except among opportunists who have something to gain by manipulating the old system. So the Chinese people need a unifying force to counteract the regional decentralization caused by economic growth. Nationalist xenophobia is filling the vacuum ... China is becoming the big man of Asia, and the region will welcome it as a friend. But strident nationalism will set the nation back.

27 November 1996. South Africa announces that it will sever diplomatic relations with Taiwan and establish full diplomatic relations with China by the end of 1997.

14 January 1997. Vice-president and prime minister Lien Chan of Taiwan meets the Pope at the Vatican, the most senior Taiwanese official to do so. The Vatican is one of the thirty remaining states (and the only one in Europe) to maintain diplomatic relations with Taiwan, but not with mainland China.

1 September 1997. China establishes diplomatic relations with St Lucia. This reduces the number of states that recognize Taiwan to thirty (*IHT*, 1 September 1997, p. 6).

9 September 1997. China severs diplomatic relations with Liberia after the latter recognizes Taiwan (having already recognized China).

1 January 1998. South Africa and China establish formal diplomatic relations at the expense of Taiwan. Twenty-nine countries retain diplomatic links with Taiwan (*The Times*, 31 December 1997, p. 13). The number of countries remaining is twenty-nine. The most significant in terms of strategic location is Panama and the largest in terms of population is Guatemala (*FEER*, 30 January 1998, p. 30).

29 January 1998. China resumes diplomatic relations (broken off in 1991) with the Central African Republic. Since the 1970s the number of countries maintaining diplomatic relations with Taiwan has fallen from about a hundred to twenty-eight. 'Most of the holdouts are poor nations in Central America and Africa' (*IHT*, 30 January 1998, p. 5). (In April 1998 Guinea-Bissau reduced the number to twenty-seven: *The Economist*, 2 May 1998, p. 78.)

22–23 April 1998. The first talks between China and Taiwan since 1995 take place (in Beijing). Agreement is reached to hold further talks.

25 June–3 July 1998. President Clinton visits China. Human rights were discussed. (See entry below.)

14–19 October 1998. The head of Taiwan's semi-official Straits Exchange Foundation visits China. He meets his mainland counterpart (the head of China's Association for Relations Across the Taiwan Strait). On 18 October the former met Jiang Zemin. The two heads held their first and only official talks in Singapore in 1993. Their next scheduled meeting was called off in 1995 (*IHT*, 13 October 1998, p. 4).

2 November 1998. China establishes diplomatic relations with Tonga (Taiwan having severed ties on 31 October).

20 November 1998. Taiwan establishes formal ties with the Marshall Islands. (This raised Taiwan's total of countries to twenty-seven. China severed diplomatic relations with the Marshall Islands on 11 December 1998.)

5 December 1998.

> Taiwan's voters have handed a reformed Nationalist Party a crucial victory over the opposition Democratic Progressive Party in mayoral and legislative elections throughout this island of 21 million people. The election Saturday [5 December] marked a major success for the Nationalists' policy of limited engagement with China and a rejection of the Democratic Progressive platform of independence from the mainland communist giant. It also rewarded the Nationalists for economic policies that have generally insulated Taiwan from the Asian financial crisis ... The results will be welcomed in Beijing ... The hard-fought and relatively clean campaign was Taiwan's ninth major election since the Nationalist government ended thirty-seven years of martial law and legalized a multiparty system in 1986 ... Analysts said the Nationalist victory is not a vote for reunification with China. Another opposition group, the New Party, founded three years ago on a platform calling for unification with China, was soundly rejected in the election ... Rather, the election showed the depth of public support for the Nationalists' new policy of firmness with China.

(*IHT*, 7 December 1998, p. 4)

9 February 1999. China severs diplomatic ties with Macedonia owing to the latter's forging of such ties with Taiwan on 27 January 1999.

10 February 1999.

Taiwan said Wednesday [10 February] that China has recently deployed more than 100 ballistic missiles in provinces facing this island of 21 million people ... Western diplomats ... said the deployment more than tripled the number of missiles previously believed to be in that area. The step constituted, they said, China's response to talk in Washington about placing parts of Asia, including Taiwan, under an American missile-defence umbrella.

(*IHT*, 11 February 1999, p. 1)

(The USA subsequently played down the idea that the number of missiles has increased, although China's future plans were of concern. 'Recent reports from Taiwan, which the Pentagon denied, said China has increased missile deployments on its coast opposite the island': *FEER*, 25 February 1999, p. 28.)

5 July 1999. Papua New Guinea establishes diplomatic relations with Taiwan.

10 July 1999. President Lee Teng-hui of Taiwan: 'Since we conducted our constitutional reforms in 1991, we have redefined cross-strait relations as nation-to-nation, or at least as special state-to-state relations' (*IHT*, 15 July 1999, p. 10). (On 20 July he said: 'We are not seeking independence. We will foster dialogue and negotiations with the Chinese Communists on an equal footing ... One China is not now. There is a possibility of one China only after future democratic unification': *IHT*, 21 July 1999, p. 4.)

11 July 1999. 'China Sunday [11 July] poured scorn on a recent statement by President Lee Teng-hui of Taiwan that cross-strait ties were "state-to-state" relations' (*IHT*, 12 July 1999, p. 5).

12 July 1999.

Taiwan's government said Monday [12 July] that its ties with China were 'special relations' between two Chinese states and rejected its earlier position – shared with China – that both sides are 'political entities' within 'one China'. The government in China reacted furiously ... Over the weekend Mr Lee previewed the shift in terminology by asserting that ties with China should be considered 'state-to-state or at least special state-to-state' relations.

(*IHT*, 13 July 1999, pp. 1, 4)

After 1949 China and Taiwan had matching 'One China' policies, both claiming to be the legitimate government of a united China that included Taiwan. In 1991 Taiwan officially abandoned efforts to 'suppress the communist rebellion' and adopted guidelines for eventual reunification until which the two sides were to be referred to as 'equal political entities' (*FT*, 16 July 1999, p. 2).

21 July 1999.

Under intense pressure from the United States and facing military threats from China, Taiwan on Wednesday [21 July] backed away from its announcement that it was dropping its 'one China' policy ... Still, the democratically elected government continued to insist that China treat it as an equal in any subsequent negotiations ... Taiwan's chief government spokesman ... said Taiwan also had no plans to codify the changes in its constitution ... [The spokesman] said

Wednesday that the cabinet had decided to stop using several expressions that in the last few days infuriated Beijing. These include 'two states', 'two Chinas', 'one China, two states' and 'one nation, two countries' ... Finally, the formulation 'special state-to-state relations' was settled on ... With the modification Taiwan's policy becomes essentially a restatement of demands issued by Taiwan's top China negotiator ... to President Jiang Zemin in Beijing in October 1998. They were that Taiwan must be treated as Beijing's equal in any political talks and that China must begin to democratize in order for reunification to occur ... [On 21 July] Taipei suffered a major diplomatic defeat. Papua New Guinea, which had maintained relations with Taiwan for just sixteen days, switched its recognition back to mainland China. Now only twenty-eight recognize Taiwan; more than 160 recognize Beijing.

(*IHT*, 22 July 1999, p. 7)

2 August 1999. Taiwan's mainland affairs council issues a statement: 'The two sides of the straits should return to the consensus on "each having their own interpretation of One China"' (*FT*, 3 July 1999, p. 6).

9 August 1999. China announces that the Pope will not be allowed to make a second visit to Hong Kong (the first was in 1970). The Vatican's diplomatic relations with Taiwan were cited.

30 December 1999. Palau (in the Pacific) and Taiwan establish diplomatic relations. Taiwan now has diplomatic relations with twenty-nine countries.

1 February 2000. The US House of Representatives approves the Taiwan Security Enhancement Act. If it becomes law the Act will establish direct military communications between the USA and Taiwan, expand US training of Taiwan's military officers and force the US administration to make public Taiwan's request for weapons systems. China's response was very critical. 'China's statement was unusual because Beijing does not usually make extensive comment on legislation pending in Congress. In addition, the Clinton administration has said it would veto the bill' (*IHT*, 3 February 2000, p. 5). The bill would lift the long-standing ban on formal US–Taiwan military co-operation, increase Taiwan attendance at US military academies and require an annual Pentagon report on the threats faced by Taiwan. The Clinton administration has threatened a veto. Opposition is growing in the Senate (*IHT*, 4 February 2000, p. 5).

Under the 1979 Taiwan Relations Act the United States is to provide Taiwan only with defensive weapons 'in such quantity as may be necessary to enable Taiwan to maintain a sufficient self-defence capability'. In a 1982 agreement with China President Ronald Reagan also pledged not to increase the quantity or quality of arms sold to Taiwan and said the United States would reduce arms sales if the mainland and Taiwan pursued a peaceful solution to their conflict.

(*IHT*, 2 March 2000, p. 8)

21 February 2000. The State Council (cabinet) issues a statement:

If the Taiwanese authorities refuse indefinitely to peacefully resolve the cross-strait reunification issue through negotiations, the Chinese government can only be forced to take all possible drastic measures, including the use of force ... [But a resort to force] would only be the last choice made under compelled circumstances ... [and only in the event of] a grave turn of events ... Both sides of the Taiwan Strait ... may find ways to solve their political differences and realize peaceful reunification through consultation on an equal footing.

The startling ultimatum, issued in an official white paper from the State Council, the highest organ of China's government, significantly broadened Beijing's threat to invade the island. It had previously said it would storm Taiwan only if the island declared independence from China or if it was occupied by a foreign power ... China's ultimatum was timed to affect the outcome of Taiwan's presidential elections.

(IHT, 22 February 2000, p. 1)

[This represents] a stark toughening of formal policy that comes just weeks before the island holds its second, direct presidential election ... [This represents a] widening of the conditions under which it threatens to use force – previously mainly defined as moves by Taiwan to formalize its autonomy or foreign interference in the island.

(FT, 22 February 2000, p. 12)

One section contained three threats, dubbed the 'Three Ifs': China would attack Taiwan if the island declared independence, if it was occupied by a foreign power or, in a new warning, if Taiwan refused indefinitely to negotiate reunification ... But the added threat in that section of the 11,000-word document was leavened by an olive branch in another: China appeared to agree to one of Taiwan's main conditions for political talks with Beijing – that Taiwan be treated as an equal and not as a 'local government'.

(John Pomfret, IHT, 9 March 2000, p. 6)

'Zigzagging has added to the confusion over what the Chinese government really meant when it issued a policy paper on 21 February (p. 6).

5 March 2000. Prime minister Zhu Rongyi: 'We will not sit idly by and watch any serious separatist activity aimed at undermining China's sovereignty and territorial integrity, such as those advocating the "two-state theory" or "the independence of Taiwan"' (*Guardian*, 6 March 2000, p. 17).

15 March 2000. Prime minister Zhu Rongyi:

Let me advise all these people in Taiwan: do not just act on impulse at this juncture which will decide the future course that China and Taiwan will follow. Otherwise I am afraid you won't get another opportunity to regret ... No matter who comes to power in Taiwan, Taiwan will never be allowed to be independent ... [If the] people who favour independence [win] it may trigger a war between the two sides ... The Chinese people will use all their blood and even sacrifice their lives to defend the unity of our motherland and the dignity of the Chinese nation ... [But] there is nothing new in there [the State Council statement].

Mr Zhu's comments ... were aimed at undermining electoral support for Chen Shui-bian, the independence-minded candidate for the Democratic Progressive Party. Beijing officials are worried over signs that Mr Chen has been gathering support and may now be the favourite to beat Lien Chan, the candidate for the Nationalist party, and James Soong, an independent. Both Mr Soong and Mr Lien are more conciliatory toward the mainland than Mr Chen ... [Although] Mr Chen has done much to moderate his platform ... [He] says that that he would not declare a formal independence.

(*FT*, 16 March 2000, p. 11)

Chen Shui-bian has given 'a promise not to declare independence unless Beijing should attack' (*FT*, 20 March 2000, p. 8). (Chen Shui-bian on 24 March 2000: 'I will not declare independence as long as China does not plot a military invasion of Taiwan': *Guardian*, 25 March 2000, p. 19.)

The contenders [in the 18 March election] are Vice-President Lien Chan (of the governing Nationalist Party), James Soong (a former Nationalist official running as an independent), and Chen Shui-bian of the Democratic Progressive Party, the main opposition party ... Alone among the candidates Mr Chien has long championed a Taiwanese declaration of independence, but he now says a declaration is unnecessary because Taiwan is effectively sovereign.

(*IHT*, 18 March 2000, p. 1)

18 March 2000. Chen Shui-bian of the Democratic Progressive Party wins the presidential election in Taiwan with 39.3 per cent of the vote. James Soong came second with 36.8 per cent of the vote and Lien Chan came third with 23.1 per cent. The turnout was 82 per cent. (The Kuomintang has been in power since 1945. The Nationalist Party, installed by Chiang Kai-shek in 1949, has governed continuously since 1949.)

In a post-election statement, Mr Chen said: 'Most people cannot accept the "one country, two systems" model for reunification, but the determination to seek peace will not be discarded. In order to maintain national security and the benefits of all the people, we would like to immediately negotiate with China on the issue of direct links, direct commerce, investment and military confidence-building measures.'

(*The Times*, 20 March 2000, p. 14)

Late Saturday night [18 March] the Chinese government issued its only reaction to the victory, a brief, moderate statement, which said in part: 'We will listen to the words and observe the actions of Taiwan's new leader, and wait and see in which direction he takes cross-strait relations.'

(*IHT*, 20 March 2000, p. 1)

20 March 2000. Chen Shui-bian:

We can talk about 'one China' as long as it is not a principle. As long as we are treated as equals there is nothing we cannot discuss ... As long as 'one China' is not a precondition or a principle, but a topic for discussion, the two sides of the Taiwan Strait can discuss anything.

Jiang Zemin:

> The 'one China' principle must first be recognized. Under this condition any-
> thing can be discussed ... Dialogue should be on the basis that he [Chen Shui-
> bian] first of all recognize the 'one China' principle. Under this condition
> anything can be discussed.

21 March 2000. The Taiwanese parliament votes to end the ban on direct trade,
transport and postal links between three of its small islands and the Chinese cities
of Xiamen and Mawei facing them across the Taiwan Strait. The government to be
formed by Chen Shui-bian after his 20 May inauguration will have the final say on
whether to implement the scheme (*IHT*, 22 March 2000, pp. 1–2; *FT*, 22 March
2000, p. 38). (Direct postal, trade and transport links are referred to as the 'three
links': *IHT*, 22 May 2000, p. 5.)

11 May 2000.

> A leading economic official in the prospective cabinet of Chen Shui-bian,
> Taiwan's president-elect, has raised the prospect of an easing of the island's
> restrictions on investment in China ... Large companies have clamoured for a
> relaxation of rules that bar them from investing more than 40 per cent of their
> net worth in China or launching projects of more than $50 million without
> special approval ... a policy intended to limit vulnerability to economic pres-
> sure from Beijing.

> *(FT*, 12 May 2000, p. 11)

12 May 2000.

> China and Taiwan for the first time have asked the United States to intervene
> ... On Friday [12 May] ... the top Taiwan official handling China policy said
> in Taipei that Taiwan's new government hoped the United States would play a
> more active role in helping China and Taiwan improve relations. In Beijing a
> Western source said that for the first time Chinese officials in state-to-state
> meetings with their US counterparts had asked Washington to 'play a helpful
> role' in seeking improved relations between the two sides ... A Chinese source
> confirmed that Beijing was seeking this assistance.

> *(IHT*, 13 May 2000, p. 1)

20 May 2000. Chen Shui-bian is inaugurated as president of Taiwan.

> [In his address] Mr Chen side-stepped demands from Beijing that he accept its
> 'One China' principle, but suggested new room for compromise if the prin-
> ciples of 'democracy and parity' were upheld. 'We believe that the leaders on
> both sides possess enough wisdom and creativity to jointly deal with the ques-
> tion of a future One China,' Mr Chen said ... China issued a response that
> while denouncing Mr Chen for 'insincerity' also included a softening of the
> terms of its insistence that he recognize One China before negotiations across
> the Taiwan Strait can resume. The statement said Beijing was ready to autho-
> rize talks if both sides expressed adherence to One China 'in their own way'.

> *(FT*, 22 May 2000, p. 8)

'Mr Chen ... referred to the "question of a possible future One China" ... Beijing ... replied ... that talks might resume if the two sides could "express in their own way orally" their support for the One China principle' (*IHT*, 23 May 2000, p. 6).

> Chen Shui-Bian ... [said] that Taiwan will maintain the status quo and not make explicit its independence unless Beijing militarily challenges its implicit independence ... The new Taiwanese president ... [said] that he won't 'promote a referendum to change the status quo in regards to the question of independence or unification' ... A joint statement from China's Communist Party Central Committee accused Chen of lacking 'sincerity'. His stance on the vital issue of One China was, the statement charged, 'evasive and ambiguous'. But the statement nonetheless struck conciliatory notes. It committed the mainland to working to bring about direct mail, air and shipping links with Taiwan. It also raised the possibility of a return to dialogue on the basis of a 1992 formula that paved the way for historic 1993 talks between the two sides ... In 1992 ... both sides committed to uphold a One China principle. But Taiwan noted in a written statement that 'each side has a different understanding of the meaning of One China', while the mainland agreed in its written statement that the talks would not touch on the 'political meaning' of One China.
>
> (*FEER*, 1 June 2000, pp. 8, 16–18)

20 June 2000. President Chen Shui-Bian:

> If North and South Korea can [referring to the 13–15 June successful summit between North and South Korea], why cannot the two sides of the straits? ... [I invite President Jiang Zemin to] join hands and work to create a moment like the [Korean] handshake ... [A Taiwan–China] summit for peace ... [should be held] in any form or place and not restricted by any preconditions ... Why cannot we continue to work hard to find an interpretation of One China, a real interpretation of One China that both sides can truly accept?

Zhu Bangzao (a Chinese foreign ministry spokesman): 'We demand that Taiwan's leadership recognize the principle that there is one China and Taiwan is part of China. Under this precondition anything can be discussed.'

27 June 2000. President Chen Shui-Bian: 'The new government is willing to accept the consensus of past talks between [Taiwan's] Straits Exchange Foundation and [China's] Association for Relations Across the Taiwan Strait – that of One China, each with their own interpretation.'

> In a surprising concession President Chen Shui-Bian said that he would accept a 1992 formulation that both China and Taiwan could have their own definition of what One China means ... [But] there is disagreement about whether China and Taiwan agreed on anything in 1992, when negotiators for both sides met in Singapore. Chinese officials said both sides agreed that there was One China and that they would not discuss the matter for the time being. Taiwan negotiators said the two sides agreed that there was One China and that each side was allowed its own interpretation ... Mr Chen aid it was 'unacceptable' to view One China as the People's Republic of China.
>
> (*IHT*, 29 June 2000, pp. 1, 7)

Taipei insists that the two sides embraced the One China idea in broad terms but agreed to disagree on how the phrase should actually be interpreted. Beijing insists that the question of how to interpret the principle was left unresolved and the mainland never sanctioned divergent understandings of it.

(*IHT*, 30 June 2000, p. 6)

29 June 2000. Foreign ministry spokesman Zhu Bangzao:

The crux of the issue now is that the Taiwan authorities refuse to accept the One China principle and they have not shown the sincerity for improving cross-strait relations. We have put forward our demands very clearly: that Taiwan's new leader accept the One China principle unequivocally and acknowledge that they are Chinese, clearly, and also promise to seek the goal of national reunification. The Taiwan's side's distortion of that consensus into 'One China, separate interpretations' does not conform to the real situation and is motivated by the intention to insert its separatist stance.

'The Chinese foreign ministry spokesman said it [the 1992 agreement] was an agreement to accept One China period, with no definition of the concept' (*FEER*, 20 July 2000, p. 32).

A document obtained by the *Review* indicates that Taiwan's 'One China, Two Interpretations' approach to the One China issue was indeed part of a 1992 formula that paved the way for talks held the following year. According to the document, which was circulated to Chinese, Japanese and American scholars at a conference in Beijing this May [2000], negotiators for Beijing and Taipei reached a consensus on 16 November 1992, that both sides would orally commit to uphold the One China principle. But the document, authored by Tang Shubei, vice-chairman of the Beijing-based Association for Relations Across the Taiwan Straits, or Arats, says what Taipei's representative actually said was: 'While the two sides are together striving for national unification, although both sides uphold the One China principle, each has a different understanding of the meaning of One China.' That was good enough for Beijing then, but isn't now. 'There has not been a so-called consensus that two sides of the Taiwan Strait would have their own interpretation of the One China principle,' Li Yafei, secretary-general of Arats, told a visiting Taiwan delegation on 17 July. According to the May document, Beijing's statement at the November 1992 meeting was: 'The two sides of the strait both uphold the One China principle and are striving for national unification. But working relations between the two sides of the strait will not touch upon the political meaning of One China.'

(editorial, *FEER*, 27 July 2000, p. 10)

14 August 2000. President Chen Shui-Bian makes a stopover in the USA on the way to the Caribbean and Central America on his first foreign tour. China complains (*IHT*, 15 August 2000, p. 5). '[In August he] left on a thirteen-day tour of Central American and African countries that have diplomatic ties with Taiwan (*IHT*, 1 September 2000, p. 5).

17 August 2000. President Chen Shui-Bian: 'Will reunification be the only and last alternative? I think this is something up for discussion' (*IHT*, 18 August 2000, p. 6).
26–27 August 2000.

> Mainland China has softened its definition of the One China principle ... It has unveiled a new formulation that portrays the two rivals as parts of a greater whole. 'The mainland and China are both parts of One China,' Qian Qichen, Chinese vice-premier, told a delegation from Taiwan's United Daily News media group. Mr Qian's words, reported in the group's flagship daily at the weekend [26–27 August], contrasted with Beijing's standard formula that 'there is one China in the world and Taiwan is part of China' ... There is no sign of Beijing adjusting the much harsher definition of One China that it uses in its international dealings and that forms the basis of official policy on Taiwan. This definition makes clear that Beijing considers its communist People's Republic the sole legal government of all China and that Taiwan's democratic Republic of China is a mere 'local authority'.
>
> (*FT*, 28 August 2000, p. 8)

'Mr Chen [Taiwan's president] yesterday [28 August] waved aside Mr Qian's new formula, saying Beijing continued to insist internationally that it was the sole legal government of all China and that Taiwan's government was a local authority' (*FT*, 29 August 2000, p. 8).
1 September 2000. President Chen Shui-Bian:

> We do not think unification is the only principle. There could be two or three or countless different conclusions. We see Taiwan as a democratic country, with the people in a position to decide ... The KMT [Kuomintang] made unification the only possible conclusion of cross-strait relations. This way of handling it is contrary to public opinion.
>
> (*IHT*, 1 September 2000, p. 5)

'In an interview last week Mr Chen said that a majority of Taiwan's 23 million people did not support unification under the "one country, two systems" formula for autonomy that China has offered' (*IHT*, 6 September 2000, p. 5).
President Chen Shui-Bian: 'Any option is a possibility, but it must respect the free will and the final choice of Taiwan's 23 million people' (*FT*, 6 September 2000, p. 11).
18 September 2000.

> When Taiwan opens limited transportation links with China this year, only residents on two outlying islands will be allowed to sail directly to the mainland, a Taiwanese official said Monday [18 September]. The links will only involve residents on Kinmen and Matsu, which are less than ten kilometres (six miles) from China's southern coast ... When they open, possibly in December, the practice will not extend to residents on Taiwan, who will still have to fly through Hong Kong before travelling on to the mainland ... [The official] said last week that links would gradually open to legalize the trade of fish and vegetables between the outlying islands and China.
>
> (*IHT*, 19 September 2000, p. 4)

13 December 2000.

Taiwan unilaterally announced Wednesday [13 December] that it would ease a ban on Chinese travelling to and trading with two of its heavily fortified islands ... Up to 700 Chinese residents could apply to visit Quemoy, also known as Kinmen, and Matsu at any one time and stay for up to seven days. The rules would also permit residents of the islands to visit Fujian Province on the mainland, but it was not known whether China would go along with the plan. Only Taiwan vessels could be used to ferry passengers and cargo; Chinese ships would still be barred from docking at Quemoy and Matsu. The plan is scheduled to go into effect on 1 January [2001].

(*IHT*, 14 December 2000, p. 5)

[On 28 December 2000 it was announced that] China would not impede Taiwan's plan ... [which] is called the 'small three links'. Effectively it will legitimize the smuggling of goods and people that has gone on for years between the two islands and China's mainland since ties between China and Taiwan began to thaw in the 1980s.

(*IHT*, 29 December 2000, p. 5)

'The "small three links" [refer to] direct trade, postal and transportation links' (*IHT*, 3 January 2001, p. 1).

China's top foreign policy official signalled Thursday [4 January 2001] that China was willing to be more flexible on Taiwan ... Deputy prime minister Qian Qichen said China had adopted a 'pragmatic and more inclusive' version of its longstanding One China policy ... He repeated China's new formula that 'both the mainland and Taiwan belong to one China' adding that it was "pragmatic and more inclusive" than previous formulations.

(*IHT*, 5 January 2001, pp. 1, 4)

31 March–9 April 2001. The Dalai Lama visits Taiwan.
22 April 2001. Lee Teng-hui, the former president of Taiwan, flies to Japan for medical treatment. China objects to the granting of a visa.
24 April 2001. The USA offers to sell a large arms package to Taiwan which includes submarines but excludes destroyers equipped with the state-of-the-art Aegis radar and battle management system. China objects.

Previous administrations refused to sell ... diesel submarines ... on the grounds that they could be used for offensive as well as defensive purposes ... The Bush administration will reconsider the Aegis request in future years. Washington's decisions will then be influenced by whether or not Beijing presses forward with its missile buildup opposite Taiwan.

(*IHT*, 26 April 2001, p. 8)

(China also objects to the granting of a visa to Lee Teng-hui to pass through the USA when he makes his planned visit to Latin America.)

25 April 2001.

When . . . President George W. Bush . . . was asked in an ABC television interview early Wednesday [25 April] if the United States had an obligation to defend Taiwan in event of a Chinese attack, he replied: 'Yes, we do, and the Chinese must understand that.' The interviewer then asked if the president meant with the full force of the US military. 'Whatever it took to help Taiwan defend itself,' Mr Bush replied . . . For decades the United States has regularly assured Taiwan of its support . . . while remaining purposefully vague about the possibility of direct US military involvement should China attack . . . The longtime US balancing act between offering weapons support to Taiwan, to deter any Chinese attack, while leaving the eventual US response vague, to discourage independence-minded Taiwanese politicians, is known as strategic ambiguity.

(*IHT*, 26 April 2001, pp. 1, 4)

13 May 2001.

The US state department said yesterday [13 May] that Chen Shui-bian, Taiwan's president, had been granted a transit visa to stop in New York en route to Latin America . . . Mr Chen would make a three-day stopover in New York on 21–23 May and would spend a further day in Houston on 2–3 June. The decision marks the first time a Taiwanese president has been granted a visa to pass through New York.

(*FT*, 14 May 2001, p. 10)

18 May 2001.

On the eve of a disputed trip to the United States the president of Taiwan, Chen Shui-bian, offered Friday [18 May] to meet his Chinese counterpart, Jiang Zemin, for historic face-to-face talks at a meeting in Shanghai in October. China rejected the talks within hours . . . [Chen Shui-bian's] proposal [is] nearly identical to those he has made before.

(*IHT*, 19 May 2001, p. 8)

18 June 2001. 'Macedonia yesterday [18 June] reestablished diplomatic relations with mainland China, just two years after switching ties to Taiwan . . . leaving the island's government with just twenty-eight diplomatic partners and only one – the Vatican – in Europe' (*IHT*, 19 June 2001, p. 12).

25 June 2001. 'Lee Teng-hui [the former president of Taiwan] . . . has begun . . . a ten-day visit to the USA' (*FT*, 26 June 2001, p. 10).

12 August 2001.

The formation of a new political grouping [has taken place] . . . Its spiritual leader is . . . Lee Teng-hui. His Taiwan Solidarity Union was formed this Sunday [12 August] . . . [It] is widely rumoured [that] it is to join forces with the governing Democratic Progressive Party before or after elections in December for parliament.

(*IHT*, 13 August 2001, p. 8)

Former President Lee Teng-hui threw his support behind a party set up by followers – the Taiwan Solidarity Union – at its inaugural meeting on 12 August. The Taiwan Solidarity Union aims to counter what it says is a shift toward closer ties with mainland China by the former ruling party, the Kuomintang.

(*FEER*, 23 August 2001, p. 10)

26 August 2001.

President Chen Shui-bian on Sunday [26 August] endorsed the proposals of a high-profile economic council to aggressively expand commercial ties with the mainland ... The panel's recommendations include lifting a blanket $50 million cap on single Taiwanese investments in China and allowing Chinese investment in Taiwan's real estate and stock markets. He promised new policies based on the proposals within two weeks ... [Taiwan's] top official for relations with China said the proposals meant an end to the 'no haste, be patient' policy of limiting trade with China.

(*IHT*, 27 August 2001, p. 7)

The existing policy bans single investments worth more than $50 million and any investments in infrastructure and advanced technology ... In the past decade Taiwan has put up about $60 billion into China's economy and many businesses are eager to invest more.

(*IHT*, 28 August 2001, p. 13)

China is expected to gain entry to the WTO by the beginning of next year [2002]. Taiwan is expected to gain admission immediately after China ... The panel recommended that the current $50 million limit on Taiwanese investment in China be abolished in favour of a system by which individual projects would be reviewed case by case.

(*IHT*, 30 August 2001, p. 9)

Among the 120-member [national advisory] committee's proposals was the dropping of the 'no haste, be patient' policy on China investment ... The committee called for a new policy of 'active opening, effective management' that includes replacement of a near-ban on mainland investments of over $50 million with case-by-case reviews and other steps to tighten commercial ties.

(*FT*, 27 August 2001, p. 6)

The panel suggested the government allow Taiwan banks to open branches in China. It suggested the government end a $50 million investment cap on individual investment projects, which would then only be reviewed on a case-by-case basis. The panel also urged the government to let in Chinese tourists.

(*Independent*, 27 August 2001, p. 12)

A panel of leading Taiwanese academics, politicians and businessmen ... stopped short of asking the government to end the ban on direct transport links ... The committee recommended discussions with China about the ban on direct transport under the auspices of the WTO, which both are expected to enter later this year.

(*Guardian*, 27 August 2001, p. 11)

'The previous policy, which places a $50 million cap on individual investments on the mainland ... was a highly ineffective policy. Taiwanese businessmen routinely skirted around the restrictions, pouring at least $40 billion into the mainland in the past decade' (*FEER*, 6 September 2001, p. 28).

('[Prior to this announcement] Taiwan allowed Chinese goods arriving at a southern port to be taken to an airport for trans-shipment off the island in a step toward expanding shipping links with mainland China. Taiwan has allowed limited direct shipping between it and China since 1997. But until this month [August] cargo from China could not leave an offshore centre or be unloaded in Taiwan': *FEER*, 30 August 2001, p. 10.)

7 November 2001.

> Taiwan yesterday [7 November] scrapped most of its controls on direct investment in China ... Taiwan will remove a $50 million cap on spending and simplify application procedures for investments under $20 million. Investments over $20 million will be reviewed by committee. Banks will be allowed to remit money to and from China. The move is part of ... President Chen Shuibian's ... 'aggressive opening, effective management' approach towards China, which replaced former President Lee Teng-hui's more restrictive 'no haste, be patient' doctrine. Despite tight controls and a labyrinth of regulations that forced companies to set up operations in a third country, Taiwanese companies pumped more than $60 billion into China over the past decade ... [But] the new policy keeps old restrictions on investment by certain industries for 'national security' purposes.
>
> (*FT*, 8 November 2001, p. 13)

'Most Taiwanese mainland investment is carried out surreptitiously through overseas subsidiaries, with the investment commission approving only $19 billion of the more than $60 billion that officials estimate have flowed into China over the past decade' (*FT*, 11 January 2002, p. 9).

> Taiwan announced on 7 November that it would scrap a $50 million ceiling on single investment projects in China and simplify the review process for China-bound investments valued below $20 million ... Officials said they hoped ... the moves ... would be implemented in January ... Officials said that direct investment would be allowed and offshore banking units of Taiwan banks would be permitted to remit money to and from the mainland.
>
> (*FEER*, 15 November 2001, p. 30)

> Reversing a five-year-old policy of trying to prevent economic integration with China, Taiwan will lift most remaining restrictions on investments in the mainland on 1 January [2002] ... The changes will include scrapping a $50 million cap on any single investment in China and allowing projects of less than $20 million to be made without approval – up from the current $3 million trigger. Financial institutions will be permitted to invest up to 40 per cent of their paid-up capital or net worth in the mainland, double the present limit. Most of the 1,800 products that currently require approval for investments, such as cars and man-made fibres, will be freed. The number of products where investment is

banned outright – including petrochemicals, infrastructure and computer wafers – will fall to 150 from 200 ... Taiwan government estimates say the island has invested $60 million in China since the late 1980s.

(*FEER*, 22 November 2001, p. 36)

'Taiwan stands to benefit because companies will repatriate more of their profits from China. The new policy requires companies to disclose those profits ... Taiwanese companies have poured an estimated $60 billion into projects in China' (*IHT*, 8 November 2001, p. 9).

23 November 2001.

Taiwan is to ease a half-a-century-old ban on tourism from mainland China early next year [2002] ... The decision to permit Chinese citizens resident abroad to join organized tours marks a concession by Taiwan, which had previously insisted that talks with Beijing were a prerequisite to any opening of its tourist market. Currently mainland citizens are only allowed to visit Taiwan to see relatives or as part of official exchanges. However, the opening is to be conducted on a 'trial basis', visitor numbers are to be limited and Chinese living on the mainland are to remain barred.

(*FT*, 24 November 2001, p. 10)

('Under rules to take effect this month [May] mainland Chinese who are resident in Hong Kong or Macao or part of business delegations or tour groups to a third country will be permitted to visit Taiwan ... [it was] announced yesterday [1 May]': *FT*, 2 May 2002, p. 12.)

1 December 2001.

The strong showing by the Democratic Progressive Party in the Taiwan general elections ... is certain to alarm Beijing ... [President Chen Shui-bian's] Democratic Progressive Party ... won eighty-seven of the 225 seats in the legislature and 37 per cent of the vote. The victory swept aside the Nationalist Party, which supports eventual reunification with China and had governed Taiwan for nearly five decades until Mr Chen came to power last year [2000]. Though Mr Chen failed to win a legislative majority, he was expected to form an alliance with the Taiwan Solidarity Union, a fledgling party founded by former President Lee Teng-hui that has been even more assertive than the Democratic Progressive Party on the issue of independence ... Big gains were also made by the People's First Party, a pro-unification organization that increased its seats to forty-six from twenty and is led by a prominent former Nationalist official, James Soong. The Nationalists, who lost the presidency to Mr Chen last year, won sixty-eight seats in the legislature and 31 per cent of the vote, down from 110 seats. It was a stunning defeat for the party that Chiang Kai-shek led to Taiwan in 1949.

(*IHT*, 3 December 2001, p. 4)

'[The DDP captured] eighty-seven seats ... seventeen more than three years ago ... The Nationalists took only sixty-eight seats compared with 123 in December 1998' (*FT*, 3 December 2001, p. 8).

'Taiwan's Nationalist Party or Kuomintang ... [has] a mere sixty-eight seats, compared with the 123 it captured three years ago ... [and the 114 it held just before the election].' The DDP won eighty-seven seats (up from sixty-six). The People's First Party won forty-six seats (up from seventeen). The new Taiwan Solidarity Union won thirteen seats, while the New Party won one seat (down from nine) (*The Economist*, 8 December 2001, p. 63).

24 January 2002. Qian Qichen (a deputy vice-premier): 'We believe there is a distinction between the vast majority of Democratic Party members and a very small number of stubborn Taiwan independence activists. We invite them to tour and visit in an appropriate status to promote understanding' (*IHT*, 25 January 2002, p. 4).

5 February 2002.

China is pushing to open direct shipping, trade and mail links with Taiwan and is ready to do so without involving the government of either side, a senior Chinese official said Tuesday [5 February] ... The Chinese official ... who spoke on condition of anonymity ... said that mainland Chinese and Taiwanese companies could start negotiations on establishing the links along a pattern similar to that established by Taiwanese firms in talks with counterparts in Hong Kong and Macao.

(*IHT*, 6 February 2002, p. 5)

7 March 2002.

China said Thursday [7 March] that it had protested to Washington over its granting of a [non-transit] US visa to Taiwan's defence minister for the first time since at least 1979 ... The defence minister ... [is to] attend a private, three day [10–12 March] conference in ... Florida, sponsored by US weapons suppliers.

(*IHT*, 8 March 2002, p. 3)

('The USA broke off diplomatic ties with Taipei in 1979': *FT*, 8 March 2002, p. 12.)

US deputy defence minister Paul Wolfowitz met Taiwan's defence minister ... in the highest level documented US–Taiwan defence dialogue in at least twenty-two years ... [They] talked ... at a privately organized conference in Florida about US arms sales to Taiwan.

(*FEER*, 21 March 2002, p. 28)

In a series of recent policy changes ... Taiwan is asserting a separate identity ... It started in January when the government said it would stamp the phrase 'Issued in Taiwan' on Taiwan passports. They now say 'Republic of China', the name Taiwan took when Chiang Kai-shek's forces fled to Taiwan in 1949 after the Chinese civil war. Taiwan is also weighing a plan to rename its overseas liaison offices 'Taiwan Representative Offices'. They are currently called 'Taipei Economic Cultural Affairs Offices' ... Beijing ... has diplomatic ties with many of the countries in which these de facto embassies operate. In another step, in January, Taiwan changed its immigration policy to exclude

Mongolia from the category of territories under China's control. This will allow Mongolians to apply to visit Taiwan as foreigners, rather than as Chinese citizens, which they must now do ... Mongolia declared its independence from China in 1911.

(*IHT*, 8 March 2002, p. 3)

11 July 2002. 'China has allowed its biggest bank ... the Industrial and Commercial Bank of China ... to conduct foreign currency transactions directly with banks in Taiwan' (*IHT*, 12 July 2002, p. 116).

'Beijing this month [July] approved fund transfers between half a dozen mainland banks and more than twenty Taiwanese lenders' (*FT*, 12 July 2002, p. 10).

21 July 2002. 'The tiny Pacific republic of Nauru broke off relations with Taipei in favour of Beijing ... Nauru's switch brought the number of nations that have diplomatic ties with Taiwan to just twenty-seven' (*FT*, 22 July 2002, p. 6).

3 August 2002. President Chen Shui-bian of Taiwan:

I want to sincerely urge and encourage everybody to seriously consider the importance and urgency of passing legislation on a referendum [on formal independence] ... Taiwan is not a part of another country, not a local government or province of another country. In other words, Taiwan and China on the opposite side of the Taiwan Strait is one country on each side. We must be clear about this.

(*IHT*, 5 August 2002, pp. 1, 5)

At his inauguration he [Chen Shui-bian] pledged not to hold a referendum on independence or change Taiwan's constitution unless Beijing moved to take military action against the island. But last week he announced that this promise – along with other concessions – was conditional on Beijing abandoning its threat of the use of force.

(*FT*, Monday 5 August 2002, p. 6)

'At least 500,000 of Taiwan's 23 million people now live on the mainland' (*IHT*, 6 August 2002, p. 3).

6 August 2002.

[Chen Shui-bian said] that he had only meant to put forward a doctrine of equal or parallel sovereignty for Taiwan and China ... The concept of equal sovereignty ... is consistent with the Taiwanese government's position for at least the last two years, although the government has seldom expressed it publicly.

(*IHT*, 7 August 2002, p. 3)

'Mr Chen was quoted] as saying: "My comments were oversimplified and may have caused misunderstanding" ... Mr Chen has now said that "equal sovereignty" was a more appropriate summary of his speech' (*Guardian*, 7 August 2002, p. 12).

7 August 2002. 'On Wednesday [7 August] Taiwan cancelled a routine military exercise scheduled for next week' (*IHT*, 8 August 2002, p. 4).

8 August 2002. The Mainland Affairs Council of Taiwan's cabinet issues a statement:

If Communist China forces Taiwan people to change the status quo in the future, the Taiwan people will have the right to express their opinion through a referendum ... [Taiwan would have] ready but not use [legislation for a referendum unless forced to].

(*IHT*, 9 August 2002, p. 6)

September 2002. 'The [US] House of Representatives votes to designate Taiwan as a "non-Nato ally" for the purpose of United States arms sales to the island' (*FEER*, 24 October 2002, p. 32.)

26 January 2003.

The first authorized flight by a Taiwanese aircraft to mainland China since ... 1949 is due to take place on 26 January [2003] ... the first of sixteen Taiwanese charter services schedule to land in Shanghai during the two weeks of the lunar new year celebrations ... But at Taiwan's insistence the planes will still have to touch down in Hong Kong or Macao on their way from Taiwan to Shanghai ... [and since] Taiwan still bans direct aviation links with the mainland Taiwanese using the charter services will save hardly any time at all. It has all along been possible to fly from Taiwan to the mainland via Hong Kong or Macao without changing planes (only flight numbers), as long as an airline controlled neither by Taiwan nor by the mainland is used ... The two sides have not agreed to repeat this experiment.

(*The Economist* 25 January 2003, p. 62)

'Taiwan this year granted six local airlines permission to fly local businessmen back to the island for the lunar New Year holiday and to return them to China afterwards' (*FT*, 27 January 2003, p. 8).

12 June 2003.

Taiwan decided on Thursday [12 June 2003] to add the word 'Taiwan' in English to the cover of its new passports from September ... Taiwan's foreign ministry originally wanted to add 'Issued in Taiwan' to passports last year [2002], but was forced to shelve that plan after criticism from Beijing ... Passports now say 'Republic of China'.

(*IHT*, 13 June 2003, p. 4)

September 2003.

In September ... Taiwan began describing itself as Taiwan on the covers of its passports ... Previous passports carried the name 'Republic of China' – this was the name that Chiang Kai-Shek's nationalists had used for the whole of China before they fled to Taiwan from the mainland after losing to the communists in the 1940s.

(www.economist.com, 2 October 2003)

November 2003. In November President Chen Shui-bian paid a two-day visit to the United States.

The United States government's rules for visits of Taiwanese leaders have changed. It was the first time a Taiwan president was allowed to make comments on US soil since 1979, when Washington established diplomatic relations with mainland China and severed official ties with Taiwan ... President Chen Shui-bian ... became the first Taiwan president in eight years allowed to make a public speech in the United States and the first since the break in diplomatic relations to make such a speech in a major American city. Chen was also allowed to address a rally in his hotel of hundreds of enthusiastic supporters ... He hosted a lunch for businessmen and a senator, and the media were allowed to cover his opening remarks for the first time ... [In] 2000, when Chen made his first transit through the United States as Taiwan's president ... [he] was confined by the Clinton administration ... to a Los Angeles hotel and allowed to see just fifteen well-wishers. In 2001 the Bush administration allowed him a quota of 150 supporters.

(*FEER*, 13 November 2003, p. 32)

7 November 2003. 'The foreign ministry says that Taiwan had established diplomatic relations with Kiribati. Although only a tiny Pacific island, it brings the number of diplomatic allies back to twenty-seven after Liberia switched recognition to China last month [October]' (*FT*, 8 November 2003, p. 7).

'The mainland called the switch by Kiribati, which hosts one of China's three foreign space-monitoring stations, "an open betrayal"' (*FEER*, 20 November 2003, pp. 28–9).

19 November 2003.

In recent years Beijing has acted with restraint. Yesterday [19 November], however ... [China warned] that efforts by Chen Shui-bian to push for constitutional reform were dragging the cold war revivals to the brink of war ... [The statement said that] any referendum on constitutional reform would be 'an extremely dangerous move ... If the Taiwan authorities collude with all splittist forces to openly engage in pro-independence activities and challenge the mainland and the one-China principle, the use of force may become unavoidable' ... [Chen Shui-bian] has managed to manoeuvre Taiwan's opposition parties into echoing his calls for constitutional reform ... Beijing officials were shocked by the recent endorsement of the need for constitutional reform by Taiwan's pro-reunification opposition.

(*FT*, 20 November 2003, p. 11)

The statement said, 'Taiwan independence means war' (*FEER*, 27 November 2003, p. 28). 'The Kuomintang and People's First Party ... although they remain committed to eventual reunification ... [now] support the idea of referendums' (*IHT*, 25 November 2003, p. 6).

27 November 2003.

Taiwan's legislature ... passed a bill that would allow national referendums on constitutional and sovereignty issues [but] only under very narrow circumstances ... A rival measure, supported by President Chen Shui-bian, would have made it easy for him to call referendums. Most provisions of that bill were defeated ... The final bill bars referendums on changing Taiwan's flag or official name, the Republic of China. The legislation also makes it hard to hold a referendum to amend the constitution and bars referendums to write a new constitution ... A provision ... allows Taiwan's president to call a referendum on 'national security' if the island is faced with a clear foreign threat to national security that could erode Taiwan's territorial integrity. But even this provision stopped short of explicitly allowing a referendum on independence.

(IHT, 28 November 2003, p. 6)

'Taiwan's legislature passed a bill giving the president the power to initiate a referendum on independence in the event of a grave threat or attack from China' *(FT*, 28 November 2003, p. 9).

Chen Shui-bian has suggested that China's missile buildup on the coast facing the island warrants a referendum on unspecified 'national security issues' at the same time as a presidential election next March [2004]. China fears this could be a step towards the island's declaring formal independence from the mainland.

(The Economist, 6 December 2003, p. 60)

5 December 2003.

President Chen Shui-bian said ... that he planned a referendum in March [2004] calling on China to withdraw ballistic missiles aimed at Taiwan and demanding that China renounce the use of force against China ... The question on ballots 'could be for the 23 million people on Taiwan to demand that China immediately withdraw the missiles targeting Taiwan and openly renounce the use of force against Taiwan' [he said] ... Chen said that the planned referendum would not involve independence ... Chen said he planned to hold the referendum on election day, 20 March [2004]. He is seeking reelection.

(IHT, 6 December 2003, p. 3)

7 December 2003.

President Chen Shui-bian announced the island's first referendum yesterday [7 December] ... [a] call for a national vote on missile deployment ... [He] said he would call a referendum on 20 March [2004] – the same day as a presidential election ... Voters will be asked whether they want Beijing to remove the thousands of missiles now aimed across the Taiwan strait.

(Guardian, 8 December 2003, p. 13)

8 December 2003.

The Bush administration's stern warning that Taiwan should avoid provoking China ... effectively blames President Chen Shui-bian for threatening to upset the delicate peace in the region ... The Bush administration's statement on Monday [8 December] made it clear that Washington considered Chen's referendum an election gambit and a possible move toward independence.

(www.iht.com, 9 December 2003)

President George W. Bush, in comments welcomed Tuesday [9 December] by the visiting Chinese prime minister Wen Jiabao, said that the United States strongly opposed a move in Taiwan to stage a referendum ... 'We oppose any unilateral decision by either China or Taiwan to change the status quo,' Bush said, 'and the comments and actions made by the leader of Taiwan indicate that he may be willing to make decisions unilaterally, to change the status quo, which we oppose' ... White House aides had signalled the tougher tone toward Taiwan on Monday [8 December] saying that Taipei should avoid any action that an objective outsider might interpret as a move toward independence. That was coupled with a warning to China not to contemplate any forcible or coercive measures against the island ... Bush said that the United States continued to build on the 'One China' policy that considers Taiwan part of China but rejects political reunification through any but peaceful means.

(*IHT*, 10 December 2003, p. 5)

A senior administration official informed reporters that in Bush's meeting with Wen 'the president did tell the Chinese in no uncertain terms that we, the United States, would have to get involved if China tried to use coercion or force to unilaterally change the status of Taiwan'.

(*FEER*, 18 December 2003, p. 17)

10 December 2003. 'President Chen Shui-bian said Wednesday [10 December] that he would press ahead with plans for a referendum next year [2004] to condemn China's buildup of ballistic missiles aimed at Taiwan' (www.iht.com, 10 December 2003).

5 January 2004.

Taiwan is preparing to offer a compromise on its referendum plans ... The foreign minister said: 'We will not conduct a referendum on 20 March without having reached an understanding with the United States.' Separately, officials preparing for a 'communication mission' to the United States, Japan and Europe, indicated that they would convey the government's willingness to compromise.

(*FT*, 6 January 2004, p. 8)

16 January 2004.

Chen Shui-bian ... will ask voters to decide in a referendum whether it should buy more anti-missile equipment if China continues to pose a military threat. They will also be asked whether the government should resume talks with China on a 'peace and stability' framework. Senior US administration officials signalled their relief at the anodyne nature of the referendum ... Mr Chen released the text of the two questions to be put to voters on 20 March, the same day as the presidential poll in which he is running for reelection ... In the first referendum question voters are asked if Taiwan should buy 'more advanced antimissile weapons' for self-defence in the event that China refuses to withdraw its missiles aimed at Taiwan and to openly renounce the use of force. The Pentagon has long pressed Taiwan to buy its advanced Pac-3 missile defence system.

(*FT*, 17 January 2004, p. 5)

A Taiwan government statement issued on 16 January said that the first of two questions to be put to the electorate will be: 'The people of Taiwan demand that the Taiwan Strait issue be resolved through peaceful means. Should mainland China refuse to withdraw the missiles it has targeted at Taiwan and to openly renounce the use of force against us, would you agree that the government should acquire more advanced anti-missile weapons to strengthen Taiwan's self-defence capabilities?' ... The second question asks voters to endorse a government bid to open talks with the mainland on a framework for 'peace and stability' across the Taiwan Strait ... Chen announced on 2 December [2003] that China had 496 ballistic missiles at bases within 600 kilometres of Taiwan.

(*FEER*, 29 January 2004, p. 24)

26–29 January 2004. President Hu Jintao visits France.
'[On 27 January] President Jacques Chirac proclaimed Taiwan's plans to hold a referendum as "irresponsible"' (*IHT*, 31 January 2004, p. 6).
'Chirac said the referendum ... would be a "grave error"' (*FEER*, 12 February 2004, p. 11).
5 February 2004.

China is putting pressure on the Bush administration to intervene decisively and prevent Taiwan from holding a referendum ... calling the planned vote a 'dangerous provocation' that could lead to war ... Asking the United States to play an intermediary role with Taiwan breaks a longstanding taboo in Beijing, where officials often criticise Washington for meddling in relations across the Taiwan Strait.

(www.iht.com, 5 February 2004)

29 February 2004.

Taiwan held its largest demonstration in its history ... a human chain that stretched the length of the island ... to protest at China's longstanding threat to use military force to take over the territory ... Organizers said [the chain] involved 1.2 million people.

(*Guardian*, 1 March 2004, p. 14)

March 2004. 'China has surpassed the United States and Japan to become Taiwan's leading trade partner' (www.iht.com, 2 March 2004).
19 March 2004.

The president of Taiwan was shot and the vice-president was slightly injured in southern Taiwan on Friday [19 March] on the eve of bitterly contested national elections ... Neither suffered life-threatening injuries ... President Chen Shuibian and vice-president Annette Lu were standing next to each other in the back of an open-roofed red Jeep driving slowly through streets crowded with supporters in Tainan, the president's hometown, when the president was struck in the abdomen by a bullet ... Chen's Democratic Progressive Party and Lien Chan, the presidential candidate of the opposition National Party, each appealed for calm ... While attacks on political figures are almost unheard of in Taiwan, the island does have a long history of serious rioting in response to political developments.

(www.iht.com, 19 March 2004; *IHT*, 20 March 2004, pp. 1, 5)

20 March 2004.

Taiwan President Chen Shui-bian was declared to have won a second term by a razor-thin margin ... but the opposition Nationalist Party called for the election to be annulled and suggested that the president might have staged a eleventh-hour assassination attempt to get votes ... [His opponent was] Lien Chan, the leader of the Nationalist Party ... who says he would like to improve relations with China ... Lien had been narrowly favoured to win until the shooting on Friday [19 March]. One or more bullets grazed President Chen's lower abdomen and vice-president Annette Lu's right knee ... Chen had angered Beijing by holding a referendum on cross-strait issues in tandem with the residential poll ... But the referendum failed to garner the 50 per cent vote participation necessary to be considered valid. While 80.3 per cent of eligible voters cast ballots in the presidential election, only 45 per cent cast ballots on the two referendum questions, both on cross-strait relations, after the Nationalists called for voters to abstain.

(www.iht,com, 21 March 2004)

'[Chen] increased his share of the vote to 50.11 per cent from 39 per cent in 2000' (*IHT*, 22 March 2004, p. 4). '[Chen] increased his share of the vote to 50.11 per cent from 39 per cent in 2000' (*IHT*, 22 March 2004, p. 4).

22 March 2004.

Taiwan's political system remained in turmoil on Monday [22 March], as the opposition Nationalist Party acknowledged it was still searching for evidence that President Chen Shui-bian won reelection because of vote fraud or a staged assassination attempt ... [The incident] appeared to have produced a sympathy vote that decided the election ... Many polls showed a small but potentially decisive lead for Lien in the days before the election ... But after Chen's administration released photos and videos Sunday [21 March] of his medical treatment, the Nationalists switched on Monday to new allegations of widespread vote-rigging, and toned down their earlier assertions that the shooting might have been staged.

(www.iht.com, 23 March 2004)

'Chen defeated Lien by 50.1 per cent to 49.9 per cent' (*IHT*, 23 March 2004, p. 12).

23 March 2004.

Chen Shui-bian agreed on Tuesday [23 March] to a recount of the disputed election last Saturday ... The logistics of a recount, however, remained in dispute between Chen's Democratic Progressive Party and the opposition Nationalist Party. The Nationalists wanted the recount performed immediately ... [But the administration wants it] done on the weekend of 3 April ... Chen and the Nationalists also differed on how to review a mysterious shooting incident ... in which the president received a gash in his abdomen ... Chen said

... that he could accept the participation of outsiders in a review conducted by the government. The Nationalists ... called for an independent task force including foreign experts in ballistics and medicine.

(www.iht.com, 23 March 2004)

26 March 2004.

Hundreds of Taiwan protesters scuffled with the riot police, threw eggs and broke windows Friday [26 March] as they stormed into the Central Election Commission's headquarters, where officials certified the results of last weekend's disputed presidential vote. Opposition lawmakers fired up the anger of about 2,000 with speeches ... China, in its strongest statement on the Taiwan election turmoil, warned on Friday that it would not stand idly by if the situation spiralled out of control. 'The mainland will not sit by watching if the post-election situation spiralled out of control, leading to social turmoil, endangering the lives and property of our Taiwan flesh-and-blood brothers and harming stability across the Taiwan Strait,' the policy-making Taiwan Affairs Office said in a statement ... Certifying the vote is merely a formality required by law within seven days of the election. Those who want to challenge the results can still do so within thirty days of the election. Chen won by a margin of less than 0.2 per cent ... The event [a protest] ... planned for Saturday [27 March] ... is organized by the two main opposition parties, the Nationalists and the People's First Party.

(www.iht.com, 26 March 2004)

27–28 March 2004.

Riot police cleared several hundred Nationalist Party demonstrators from a plaza in front of the presidential party headquarters here [in Taipei] on Sunday [28 March] after hundreds of supporters of the opposition party crowded the city centre in a peaceful protest ... President Chen Shui-bian agreed on Saturday night [27 March] to ... accept an immediate court-supervised recount.

(*IHT*, 29 march 2004, p. 4)

'Half a million people thronged the streets of Taipei' (*FT*, 29 March 2004, p. 9).
29 March 2004.

The political parties reached a rough consensus Monday [29 March] to go ahead with a court-supervised recount of ballots cast on 20 March, although some questions remained about the precise procedures for the recount. Chen won the initial count on election day by 29,000 votes out of 13 million cast.

(www.iht.com, 29 March 2004; *IHT*, 30 March 2004, p. 4)

31 March 2004.

President Chen ... said the 'top priority' of his second term would be to improve relations with China ... [but] 'Taiwan is one country and the other side is another country'. Chen also pledged to keep pushing for a new constitution that he wants voters to approve in a referendum in 2006.

(www.iht.com, 31 March 2004)

'This week ... China announced the establishment of diplomatic ties with ... Dominica. This leaves only twenty-six countries that recognize Taiwan' (*The Economist*, 3 April 2004, p. 61). 'Taiwan's foreign minister accused the mainland of using "dollar diplomacy" to get the Caribbean nation of Dominica to switch its diplomatic relations to Beijing' (*FEER*, 8 April 2004, p. 27). 'China promised $122 million in return for revoking recognition of Taiwan' (*The Economist*, 10 April 2004, p. 47).

'On Wednesday 31 March] the Pentagon announced that Taiwan had been approved to buy a long-range radar system that would detect ballistic or cruise missiles ... [The Pentagon] approved a $1.7 billion military radar' (www.iht.com, 2 April 2004).

'This week the Pentagon announced that it would sell $1.8 billion worth of long-range early-warning radar systems to Taiwan' (*FT*, Friday 2 April 2004, p. 1).

5 April 2004.

> The opposition launched a new challenge to the 20 March presidential vote on Monday [5 April], asking the High Court to nullify the entire election and order another one ... Losing candidate Lien Chan ... last week petitioned the High Court to order a recount, a move the president endorsed. The two sides were scheduled to discuss the process with the High Court on Wednesday [7 April].
>
> (www.iht.com, 5 April 2004)

7 April 2004. 'Taiwan's opposition Nationalist Party had withdrawn a lawsuit that sought to nullify last month's presidential election, saying it would allow a vote recount to take place first' (www.iht.com, 7 April 2004).

> The top US diplomat in the office responsible for relations with Taiwan resigned abruptly after reports that the Chinese government had complained that she was overly sympathetic to the Taiwanese government. The diplomat, Therese Shaheen, is the Washington director of the American Institute in Taiwan, which acts as a de facto US embassy in Taipei ... In her resignation letter ... a [US] State Department said ... Shaheen indicated she 'wanted to spend more time with her daughter'.
>
> (www.ihr.com, 8 April 2004; *IHT*, 9 April 2004, p. 2)

> Therese Shaheen ... told President Chen Shui-bian last year [2003] that President George W. Bush was the 'secret guardian angel' responsible for his trip to the United States, a phrase that lodged in Taiwan's public consciousness as an expression of unconditional US support for Chen. The Taiwan president's push for the right to hold public referendums sounded 'reasonable and logical' she told students in Taiwan last October [2003], just as the US government was trying to signal deep concerns about the initiative ... [In November 2003] she enraged China ... by insisting, incorrectly, to an interviewer that the Bush administration had never said it 'opposed' Taiwan independence ... On 7 April, after a strong push from the State Department, Shaheen submitted her resignation after fifteen months in the post ... Her critics blame Shaheen's

missteps for sending Taiwan's leaders dangerously misleading signals about US positions on sensitive subjects, including Chen's plans for referendums.

(FEER, 22 April 2004, pp. 25–6)

11 April 2004.

A team of American forensic specialists concluded at a press conference Sunday [11 April] that President Chen Shui-bian could not have shot himself in an accident on 19 March that may have helped him with reelection the next day, but said the evidence did not show whether the attack on his motorcade had been staged.

(IHT, 12 April 2004, p. 6)

The protests over Taiwan's disputed presidential election turned violent yesterday [11 April] as an American forensics expert failed to rule out the possibility that the president had staged his own shooting on the eve of the poll. In the fiercest clash since the vote on 20 March more than 100 people were injured outside the presidential palace yesterday when riot police used water cannon on the protesters throwing stones and at least one molotov cocktail. Most of the injured were police. The confrontation came after a rally of up to 300,000 supporters of . . . Lien Chan.

(Guardian, 12 April 2004, p. 13)

14 May 2004. 'Taiwanese police detained three men yesterday [14 May] in connection with the shooting of President Chen Shui-bian the day before his election in March' (*The Times*, 15 May 2004, p. 19).

16 May 2004.

China has offered Taiwan consultations on 'international living space' if Taipei recognizes that it is part of China . . . The inclusion for the first time of an implicit indication that Taiwan should enjoy at least some international recognition is a big concession . . . [The statement said that] once Taiwan recognized that there was only one China, and that Taiwan and the mainland were both part of it, both sides could resume negotiations on the 'formal ending of the state of hostility through equal-footed consultations, establishing a mechanism of mutual trust in the military field, and jointly building a framework for peaceful, stable and growing cross-straits relations' . . . The offer of negotiations appears to be a response to a 'peace and stability framework' proposed by Mr Chen this year. The statement said talks could properly address, through consultations, the issue of international living space of the Taiwan region commensurate with its status 'so as to share the dignity of the Chinese nation' . . . China's statement has been timed to coincide with Taiwan's eighth attempt – today [17 May] – to gain participation in the World Health Organization as an observer.

(FT, 17 May 2004, p. 6)

17 May 2004.

China told President Chen Shui-bian of Taiwan on Monday [17 May] to drop his drive for independence or 'be consumed in his own flames', a sharply worded warning delivered just days before the Taiwanese leader begins his second term of office [on Thursday 20 May] ... But in a statement released Monday morning [17 May] Beijing also offered economic and diplomatic benefits if Chen embraces the 'One China' principle under which China claims sovereignty over Taiwan, and also said it might seek to build a 'mechanism of trust' to reduce military tensions if Chen co-operates ... Beijing said it would resume a political dialogue, offer economic benefits and allow direct transportation links between Taiwan and the mainland. It also dangled the prospect of talks to address 'the international living space of the Taiwan region', suggesting that China might be willing to discuss ways for Taiwan to get more diplomatic recognition under Chinese sovereignty. China has used its clout to block Taiwan's membership in international groups like the World Health Organization.

(www.iht.com, 17 May 2004)

The Chinese statement:

The Taiwan leaders have before them two roads. One is to pull back immediately from their dangerous lurch toward independence, recognizing that both sides of the Taiwan Strait belong to one and the same China. The other is to keep following their separatist agenda to cut Taiwan from the rest of China and, in the end, meet their own destruction by playing with fire ... If Taiwan leaders move recklessly to provoke major incidents of Taiwan independence, the Chinese people will crush their schemes firmly and thoroughly at any cost.

(www.iht.com, 17 May 2004; *The Times*, 18 May 2004, p. 11)

20 May 2004.

President Chen Shui-bian used the occasion of his second inauguration ... to offer China the prospect of renewed dialogue about the island's future ... Chen said he would not use a referendum to change Taiwan's constitution and suggested that any constitutional changes would not broach issues about Taiwan's sovereignty or formal independence ... But China must allow Taiwan to determine its own future ... Chen: 'We would not exclude any possibility, so long as there is the consent of the 23 million people of Taiwan' ... By promising not to hold a referendum on Taiwan's constitution, reversing an election campaign promise, and also implicitly repeating promises he made at his first inauguration four years ago not to formally declare independence or change Taiwan's official name, the Republic of China.

(www.iht.com, 20 May 2004; *IHT*, 21 May 2004, p. 4)

The president said he wanted to see the existing constitution reformed by 2008 without touching on issues related to sovereignty, territory or independence. 'Let me explicitly propose that these particular issues be excluded from the present constitutional reengineering project,' Mr Chen said.

(*FT*, 21 May 2004, p. 7)

'[Chen's] pledge to use existing rules to change the constitution, for example, means super majorities in two representative bodies will be required for revisions' (*FEER*, 3 June 2004, p. 35).

23 August 2004.

Taiwan's parliament voted yesterday [23 August] for sweeping changes, in a move that drastically lowers the risk of a conflict with China ... [The reform was passed] with only one dissenting voice ... Lawmakers agreed that constitutional amendments would have to be confirmed by referendum but denied the people the right to initiate constitutional reform. Changes to the constitution will have to be passed by a three-quarters legislative majority before being enacted by popular vote. The reform virtually excludes the possibility of a future plebiscite on a completely new constitution, which could be interpreted as a declaration of independence by China.

(*FT*, 24 August 2004, p. 7)

25 September 2004.

Taiwan has developed and successfully tested surface-to-surface missiles that could hit coastal or interior Chinese cities ... The development of missiles is a sensitive issue because Taiwan has pledged to buy and make only defensive weapons. But politicians have increasingly proposed making offensive weapons as well, prime minister Yu Shyi-kun said on Saturday [25 September] that the weapons were necessary to maintain the balance of power with China ... The remarks appeared to confirm long-held suspicions that Taiwan has been developing missiles that could reach China's interior.

(www.iht.com, 27 September 2004)

10 October 2004.

President Chen Shui-bian called Sunday [10 October] for the opening of peace talks with mainland China ... He suggested for the first time that Taiwan and mainland China revive a brief flurry of contacts in Hong Kong and Singapore in 1992 ... Taiwan and mainland China agreed then that they both had a 'One China policy', and agreed to disagree on what exactly that policy was.

(*IHT*, 11 October 2004, pp. 1, 4)

In a speech marking Taiwan's National Day President Chen Shui-bian offered peace talks with Beijing, and then invited China to discuss establishing direct charter flights between Taiwan and the mainland. The overtures were dismissed by China's official media as being 'too insincere and vague'.

(*FEER*, 21 October 2004, p. 28)

25 October 2004.

Chinese officials have praised [US] Secretary of State Colin Powell warning Taiwan that it should not seek to become an independent nation. But Taiwan's leaders have sharply criticised him for changing a longstanding policy ... The reactions came after Powell, speaking in two television interviews on Monday [25 October] during a brief visit to Beijing, stressed that Taiwan is not a sovereign nation and that the United States favours its 'peaceful reunification' with China ... Powell: 'There is only one China. Taiwan is not independent. It does not enjoy sovereignty as a nation' ... The comments, which Powell carefully avoided repeating Wednesday [27 October] in Washington, went beyond the ambiguous language American officials have used for several decades ... The United States has recognized China's claim that there is only 'One China', including Taiwan, but has not explicitly backed reunification and has stressed that any change must come only when people on both sides of the Taiwan Strait agree to terms.

(www.iht.com, 28 October 2004)

3 November 2004.

Taiwan ... established formal diplomatic relations with Vanuatu, a small Pacific nation of about 200,000 people that less than two months ago reaffirmed its recognition of Beijing ... Vanuatu becomes the latest of twenty-seven countries – most of them in Latin America and Africa – that recognize Taipei instead of Beijing as the legal government of all China.

(www.iht.com, 3 November 2004)

('Vanuatu has withdrawn a communiqué signed in Taipei to establish ties with Taiwan ... that was signed on 3 November by its prime minister ... Some Taiwan papers said that ... [the prime minister] had not secured the advance approval of Vanuatu's cabinet before he travelled to Taiwan and made the announcement': *IHT*, 12 November 2004, p. 6.)

('Vanuatu is to grant diplomatic recognition to Taiwan despite its ties to China, the office of the prime minister [said on 15 November] ... The prime minister's private secretary said ministers now backed an agreement that ... [the prime minister] signed in Taipei on 3 November to switch formal links to Taipei ... But ... [the] minister for utilities immediately contradicted the prime minister's statement and said Vanuatu's loyalty still lay towards Beijing': www.iht.com, 15 November 2004.)

4 November 2004.

Taiwan's high court upheld yesterday [4 November] the reelection of Chen Shui-bian as president ... The high court said a recount conducted during the trial had not changed the election result enough to invalidate Mr Chen's victory. After the recount Mr Chen's record narrow lead of 29,518 shrank to 25,563 out of more than 13 million votes cast. The court also rejected the opposition's arguments that Mr Chen had distorted the election results by simultaneously holding a referendum and by a mysterious shooting on election eve ... [But the residing judge said]: 'We acknowledge that the holding of a referendum together with the presidential vote was contrary to the referendum law.'

(*FT*, 5 November 2004, p. 12)

15 November 2004. China issues a statement:

If Chen Shui-bian clearly recognizes this [the 1992 agreement] and abandons seeking Taiwan independence [the two sides] could immediately resume dialogue and negotiations, and any topic could be discussed ... If Chen disregards the historical fact of talks in Hong Kong in 1992, refuses to accept the One China principle and sticks to Taiwan independence, it shows that he does not intend to resume cross-straits talks.

(www.iht.com, 15 November 2004)

'Chen has rejected the consensus reached in talks in Hong Kong in 1992, which concluded there was one China and that each side could have its own interpretation of what that China was' (www.iht.com, 15 November 2004).

10 December 2004.

President Chen Shui-bian promised voters a new constitution if his party wins control of parliament in elections on Saturday [11 December] that are seen as a referendum on his policy on relations with China. President Chen Shui-bian: 'Through a referendum by the people in 2006 we will give birth to a new constitution that is timely, fitting and suitable, and implement it in 2008 when I step down as president.'

(*IHT*, 11 December 2004, p. 5)

11 December 2004.

An upset victory [was achieved] by the anti-independence camp ... Nationalist-led opposition parties held on to a slim majority in the legislature. Most polls had predicted that parties close to President Chen Shui-bian would take control ... The Nationalist Party and its allies, the People's First Party and the New Party, preserved their slim majority ... They have vowed to block President Chen Shui-bian's plans to write a new constitution ... Chen's Democratic Progressive Party ... fared much worse than expected, picking up only two seats to claim eighty-nine of the 225 seats in the legislature. The Nationalist Party gained eleven seats, for a total of seventy-nine, while the even more pro-Beijing People's First Party lost twelve seats, retaining only thirty-four, and the New Party kept its only seat. Independents maintained their ten seats.

(*IHT*, 13 December 2004, p. 4)

The most ardently pro-Beijing and anti-Beijing fared worst of all, as voters tended to support more moderate candidates and parties on both sides of the independence issue – those who had taken more pragmatic positions in favour of preserving the status quo with Beijing, and in some cases had taken an interest in the economy instead of solely on ideological differences ... Taiwan now finds itself exporting twice as much to China as to the United States.

(www.iht.com, 13 December 2004)

President Chen Shui-bian submitted his resignation as chairman of the governing Democratic Progressive Party on Tuesday [14 December], taking responsibility for the party's worse-than-expected showing ... Chen had turned the legislative campaign into a debate on the issue of Taiwan's identity versus China. He proposed to de-Sinify the names of state-owned companies and Taiwan's overseas representative offices ... Two-thirds legislative approval ... [is needed] to adopt a new constitution.

(www.iht.com, 14 December 2004)

15 January 2005.

China and Taiwan have agreed to the first direct flights . . . in five decades . . .
The agreement allows forty-eight round-trip charter flights to carry Taiwanese
working in China home for the Lunar New Year holiday . . . Six Chinese and
six Taiwanese airlines will operate the flights from 29 January to 20 February
[2005] . . . Taiwan had banned direct flights since 1949.

(*IHT*, 17 January 2005, p. 18)

'The flights must still pass through Hong Kong airspace, a significant detour, but
they are not required to land' (www.iht.com, 29 January 2005).

20 January 2005.

The Chinese government reacted angrily on Thursday [20 January] to a
planned stopover by President Chen Shui-bian in the US territory of Guam . . .
Chen is planning to visit the Pacific islands of Palau and the Solomon Islands
this month [January] with a transit stop in Guam . . . On the same day China
announced its success in winning the tiny Caribbean nation of Grenada over
from the small group of countries that recognize Taiwan. Grenada had been
one of twenty-seven mainly African and Latin American nations that recognize
Taiwan instead of China . . . The agreement with Grenada . . . followed a
decision in December [2004] by Vanuatu, a Pacific island nation, to scrap an
agreement to form diplomatic ties with Taipei.

(www.iht.com, 20 January 2005)

1 February 2005. 'A private meeting [takes place] in Taipei between delegates
of the semi-official bodies set up by . . . [China and Taiwan] to handle exchanges
. . . [The delegates attended the funeral of a Taiwanese negotiator]' (*FT*, 4 February
2005, p. 10).

19 February 2005.

Japan and the United States will today [19 February] sign a new joint security
agreement . . . Redrafting the 1996 joint declaration on bilateral security, Japan
will for the first time join the United States in identifying Taiwan as a share
security concern . . . [Japan and the United States] are expected to agree
'common strategic objectives' that include security for Taiwan as well as the
Korean Peninsula . . . In December [2004] Japan issued new national security
guidelines that single out China as a threat. This followed the incursion by a
Chinese submarine into Japanese territorial waters last year [2004], which
prompted Tokyo to put its military on alert for only the second time in half a
century. Japan also angered Beijing . . . by issuing a tourist visa last year to Lee
Teng-hui, the former Taiwanese president. In addition, Beijing and Tokyo have
been arguing over energy assets in the East China Sea.

(*FT*, 19 February 2005, p. 6)

'This week [came] news that Washington and Tokyo were openly co-ordinating
their positions over defending Taiwan in case of a Chinese attack on the island'
(*IHT*, 19 February 2005, p. 1).

20 February 2005.

China issued a denunciation Sunday [20 February] of a declaration by Japan and the United States that they had a 'common strategic objective' in the peaceful resolution of Taiwan Strait issues ... The joint statement issued in Washington early Sunday morning, included 'encouraging the peaceful resolution of issues concerning the Taiwan Strait' in a list of 'common strategic objectives' of Japan and the United States ... The statement represented a departure from the previous military agreement between the United States and Japan in 1997, which simply called for the two countries to work together in the 'area surrounding Japan'. The Japanese government has previously called for peace in the Taiwan Strait and offered logistical but not military support to the United States in case of a conflict between Taiwan and mainland China ... The statement does not represent the first time the United States and Japan have co-operated on issues regarding Taiwan. A 1960 security pact between the two countries called for joint co-operation on 'Far East' regional security. Japan publicly interpreted the agreement at the time as covering waters and lands north of the Philippines, including Taiwan. But after Japan and the United States switched their diplomatic recognition from Taipei to Beijing in 1972 and 1979, respectively, subsequent joint security statements tended to omit even vague references to Taiwan.

(*IHT*, 21 February 2005, p. 7)

Taiwan's experience under Japanese colonial rule was much better ... [than that] in most of Asia ... Japan made Taiwan a showcase before World War II, trying to persuade elites in China and south-east Asia to reduce their resistance to Japanese military rule and economic domination ... The Japanese Diet has voted to exempt Taiwanese citizens from visa requirements that still apply to visitors from mainland China.

(www.iht.com, 21 February 2005)

To the east of Taiwan Japanese islands already feel Chinese pressure: Chinese drilling last fall [2004] for gas in an area claimed by Japan; a Chinese submarine caught in November [2004] trying to slip through Japanese territorial waters; and a continuing effort by China to have a Japanese island declared a rock, which would deprive Japan of thousands of square miles of economic rights ... South Korea recently renewed direct flights between Seoul and Taiwan, a link broken more than a decade ago.

(www.iht.com, 22 February 2005)

A conflict with China over rich gas deposits in the East China Sea has escalated since late January [2005] when two Chinese destroyers entered the area, which has been in dispute for decades ... The development of oil and gas in much of the area has been prevented for decades by the boundary dispute. The Japanese government has refused to let companies explore and develop the resources in the area because it says that it could adversely affect relations and negotiations with China on the boundary. But now China is drilling near the boundary claimed by Japan ... In April 2002, after giving proper notification, China resumed its surveys for potential oil and gas in the disputed area.

(www.iht.com, 23 February 2005; *IHT*, 24 February 2005, p. 7)

'Japan recently discovered a Chinese submarine mapping the ocean floor in Japanese territorial waters' (www.iht.com, 13 March 2005),

'Japan demanded (and received) an apology when a Chinese submarine was caught lurking in its waters last November [2004]. Japan has also started to cut back assistance to China' (*The Economist*, 26 February 2005, p. 66).

The United States and Japan agreed a new joint security arrangement, which calls on China to increase its transparency in reporting its military expenditure and expansion ... The United States and Japan tried to mollify China by listing developments of a 'co-operative relationship' with Beijing as another strategic goal.

(*FT*, 21 February 2005, p. 8)

24 February 2005.

President Chen Shui-bian issued a joint statement with a leading opposition politician on Thursday [24 February] ... The declaration included ten points of agreement between Chen ... and James Soong, the chairman of the opposition People's First Party and an advocate of closer relations with China ... [The statement included the following]: 'Any change in the situation across the Taiwan sea must win the agreement of Taiwan's 23 million people, and on the basis of good will between the two sides of the strait we do not rule out any possible model of relations between the two sides ... [The two men promised to] work together to promote mechanism and legal changes related to peaceful developments across the straits ... [Peace with mainland China could be ensured only if Taiwan had] sufficient national defence capabilities' ... [Taiwan announced that former US president] Bill Clinton is to visit Taipei on Sunday [27 February].

(www.iht.com, 24 February 2005; *IHT*, 25 February 2005, p. 2)

'On 24 February Chen concluded a surprise political alliance with the most pro-Beijing party in Taiwan, the People's First Party, a decision that prompted a half dozen of his more pro-independence advisers to quit' (www.iht.com, 27 March 2005).

27 February 2005. 'Bill Clinton arrived in Taiwan on Sunday [27 February] ... despite a warning from Beijing that his visit could violate Washington's "One China" policy' (www.iht.com, 27 February 2005).

8 March 2005. The National People's Congress considers the 'anti-secession' law.

China's leaders on Tuesday [8 March] introduced a law that would effectively preauthorize military action if Taiwan took concrete steps toward formal independence ... The legislation specifies that any changes in the Taiwan constitution seeking to legalize the island's de facto independent status could be a trigger for military action, a direct challenge to President Chen Shui-bian, who made changing the constitution a goal of his second tem in office ... The law ... does not compel China's leaders to initiate military action. It allocates powers to them that they have long been assumed to have and puts the leadership in a position to judge if and when Taiwan has ventured too far toward formal independence ... [The draft] outlines in abstract terms three triggers for the use of 'non-peaceful means'... The law stipulates that the State Council, China's cabinet, and the Central Military Commission, the top military body, 'are authorized to decide on and execute' military action with no more than a notice provided to the legislature ... Much of the law, which has four parts, emphasizes the opportunity for peaceful settlement of the Taiwan issue. It promotes the integration of Taiwan and China and opens the door to new economic, cultural and educational exchanges.

(www.iht.com, 8 March 2005; *IHT*, 9 March 2005, p. 4)

The official summary of the draft law:

So long as there is a glimmer of hope for peaceful reunification we will exert our utmost to make it happen, rather than give it up The draft legislation provides that in the event that the 'Taiwan independence' forces should act under any name or by any means to cause the fact of Taiwan's secession from China, or that major incidents entailing Taiwan's secession should occur, or that possibilities for a peaceful reunification should be completely exhausted, that state shall employ non-peaceful means and other necessary measures to protect China's sovereignty and territorial integrity ... We should be particularly careful of Taiwan authorities trying to use so-called constitutional or legal means through referendum or constitutional reengineering to back up their secessionist attempt with so-called legality.

(www.iht.com, 8 March 2005; *IHT*, 9 March 2005, p. 4)

Copies circulated among cross-strait scholars make clear mainland leaders will retain full freedom of action. While an official English language explanation of the law says authorities 'shall' take military action if any of the three vaguely worded conditions are met, the Chinese word in the context means clearly that they are 'allowed' to do so.

(*FT*, 10 March 2005, p. 12)

Largely overshadowed by Article 8 – the 'non-peaceful means' clause – is Article 7 of the law, which affirms that 'the state stands for the achievement of peaceful reunification through consultations and negotiations on an equal footing between the two sides of the Taiwan Strait' ... [There is also] the acknowledgement that 'these consultations and negotiations may be conducted in steps and phases and with flexible and varied modalities'.

(www.iht.com, 29 March 2005)

14 March 2005. The 'anti-secession' law is approved by the National People's Congress. Prime minister Wen Jiabao: 'This is a law for peaceful reunification' (*IHT*, 15 March 2005, p. 2).

24 March 2005.

President Chen Shui-bian will join a march to protest China's 'anti-secession law' on Saturday [26 March]. He hopes to gather 1 million people to object to the legislation ... Chen will be the first Taiwanese head of state to protest in the streets ... Organizers of the rally ... [which include] members of the ruling Democratic Progressive Party ... called for people to bring their children and their pets ... [Chen] said Thursday [24 March] that the march would be a peaceful expression to protect Taiwan's democracy ... Chen Shui-bian: 'I will bring my family ... I will march with and stand alongside the people of Taiwan. I will neither make a speech nor stand on the front line. But together with every-body I will shout "want democracy, love peace"' ... China has pointed 706 bal-listic missiles at Taiwan. The mainland is increasing its arsenal by 120 a year, according to Chen ... Taiwan's defence ministry said in a report to parliament that the Chinese navy would have sea superiority over Taiwan by 2012. And by 2015 the Chinese navy will be able to form an aircraft carrier battle group, while its submarines will have the ability to retaliate with nuclear weapons.

(www.iht.com, 24 March 2005)

26 March 2005.

President Chen Shui-bian's Democratic Progressive Party organized the march Saturday [26 March], in which he and nearly all of his ministers participated, partly to call public attention to the Chinese [anti-secession] law and partly to discourage the EU from lifting its arms embargo against Beijing. Chanting 'to protect democracy, love peace and safeguard Taiwan', demonstrators denounced the law ... [This was] one of the largest political demonstrations ever on the island ... Organizers said they had met their goal of attracting 1 million protesters, but the police put the crowd at 'over 500,000' ... Even some supporters of Taiwan's opposition Nationalist Party, which backs closer relations with mainland China, ended up joining the march, although the party's leaders did not ... [It is said that] polls were showing that over 90 per cent of the Taiwanese disliked the anti-secession law's mention of using 'non-peaceful means' to regain the island.

(www.iht.com, 27 March 2005)

28 March 2005.

A delegation ... of thirty party officials ... from Taiwan's main opposition party arrived in China on Monday [28 March] on a visit intended to ease cross-strait tensions ... The trip was the first official visit to the mainland by repre-sentatives of the long-governing Kuomintang, or KMT, since the Nationalists' defeat in 1949 by communist forces. Observers said the [five-day] visit was a prelude to a mainland visit by the KMT's leader, Lien Chan ... The party sup-ports eventual unification with a democratic China.

(www.iht.com, 28 March 2005)

The thirty-four-member group, led by Chiang Pin-kung, a vice-chairman of the Kuomintang, or Nationalist Party, was welcomed enthusiastically ... Many

Kuomintang officials have visited the mainland in recent years ... The delegation now touring the mainland appears to be the largest that the party has sent since the end of the civil war in 1949, however ... [On 29 March Chiang] toured the tomb of seventy-two republicans killed trying to overthrow China's last dynasty, the Ching.

(www.iht.com, 29 March 2005)

30 March 2005.

Joseph Wu ... the chairman of Taiwan's Mainland Affairs Council, the cabinet-level agency responsible for relations with China ... [and] a close aide to President Chen Shui-bian ... denounced the visit ... Joseph Wu: 'The Chinese strategy is always to divide and conquer, and the KMT is playing into China's hands' ... President Chen Shui-bian said Tuesday [30 March] that the Nationalists' visit was a backward effort to dominate dealings with mainland China ... Before arriving in Beijing for discussions with central government officials scheduled for Thursday [31 March] the delegation visited sites in southern China that link the Nationalist Party to the mainland, which the Kuomintang ruled before fleeing to Taiwan in 1949 ... The delegation visited the tomb [in Nanjing] of Sun Yat-sen, who is honoured by both Nationalists and Communists as the founder of modern China ... A Nationalist spokesman ... said the delegation's visit would probably be a forerunner to a visit by the party's chairman, Lien Chan, before he retires this year [2005]. Lien's visit would be the first to the mainland by a Nationalist leader since the end of the civil war in 1949.

(www.iht.com, 30 March 2005; *IHT*, 31 March 2005, p. 5)

31 March 2005.

Senior Chinese Communist Party officials formally invite the National Party's chairman, Lien Chan, to visit China ... The Nationalist Party, also known as the Kuomintang ... has been out of power since 2000 for the first time since it established itself in Taiwan in 1949.

(www.iht.com, 31 March 2005)

8 April 2005.

The Vatican is the only [European] state to retain diplomatic ties with Taipei instead of Beijing. That relationship produced an unexpected benefit on Friday [8 April], when President Chen Shui-bian attended the funeral of Pope John Paul II [who died on 2 April aged eighty-four] in the first state visit ever to Europe by a president from Taiwan ... Chen's visit to the Vatican infuriated the Beijing authorities, not least because Italy, which recognizes Beijing but not Taipei, granted landing rights to Chen's jet, as the Vatican lacks an airport ... Top Vatican officials have been negotiating off and on for decades to reach a deal with mainland China, and have redoubled their efforts in the last several years. The Chinese government recognizes the pope as a spiritual leader, but does not recognize the authority of the Vatican. In mainland China Catholics must worship at official government-sanctioned churches, though there is an underground church loyal to the Vatican ... In the days since the pope's death China has reportedly cracked down on Roman Catholic clergy members operating without official approval ... There are 300,000 Roman Catholics in Taiwan. Government figures in mainland China show 4 million Catholics there, Bishop Joseph Zen of Hong Kong said there were at least 10 million. A Communist Party-controlled organization, the Patriotic Association of the Catholic Church, registers and oversees Catholic churches on the mainland and chooses bishops for the country ... The Vatican wants China to provide greater religious freedom for Catholics and to allow the Vatican to choose bishops in China.

(www.iht.com, 11 April 2005)

The Vatican is the only European state to recognize Taiwan, a result of Beijing's decision in 1951 to expel foreign priests from China and bring the Catholic Church under state control ... Chief among ... other issues dividing the two ... is the authority to appoint bishops, a preserve of the Vatican but something Beijing says should be done through its state religious bodies ... The government periodically arrests priests and their followers in the 'underground' churches, but in practice tolerates many of them if they keep a low profile.

(*FT*, 6 April 2005, p. 9)

19 April 2005. German Cardinal Joseph Ratzinger was elected as the new pope. He chose the name Benedict XVI.

20 April 2005. 'China ... warned the new pope, Benedict XVI, that the Vatican and China could establish formal relations only if the Vatican dissolved its diplomatic links with Taiwan and promised not to "interfere in China's internal affairs"' (www.iht.com, 20 April 2005; *IHT*, 21 April 2005, p. 7).

26 April 2005.

Lien Chan, the chairman of the Nationalist Party, or the Kuomintang ... [is] the first KMT chairman to set foot on Chinese soil in fifty-six years [since the Kuomintang left on 10 December 1949] ... [He pays] respect at the tomb of Sun Yat-sen, the revolutionary who founded the KMT 110 years ago and served as China's president from 1923 until his death in 1925.

(www.iht.com, 20 April 2005)

Lien Chan ... became the most senior Taiwanese politician to set foot on the mainland since China and Taiwan were separated ... Nationalists and Chinese officials have choreographed Lien's eight-day visit to China around symbols of the historic links between the Nationalists and the mainland ... Taiwanese attitudes toward Lien's visit were closely divided between support and opposition, reflecting the split between voters who favour Taiwan's outright independence and those who prefer reconciliation with the mainland, several Taiwanese analysts said ... President Chen Shui-bian on Saturday [23 April] reversed his previous opposition to Lien's visit.

(www.iht.com, 26 April 2005; *IHT*, 27 April 2005, pp. 1, 4)

('The president initially condemned [the visit] ... but has since softened his approach since Mr Lien said he was travelling in a private capacity and would not negotiate or sign any agreements with Mr Hu': *The Times*, 27 April 2005, p. 42.)

'Lien has proposed negotiating a fifty-year moratorium on changes in the current status quo that would rule out Taiwanese independence but also oblige the mainland to forswear the use of force against Taiwan' (www.iht.com, 25 April 2005).

'Lien Chan ... supports the idea of an interim agreement lasting thirty to fifty years, whereby Taiwan would agree not to declare formal independence in exchange for a pledge by China not to attack' (*The Economist*, 30 April 2005, p. 61).

'Hu Jintao and Lien Chan ... [greeted each other on 29 April] with a nationally televised handshake ... The Taiwanese government ... [talked of] a blatant attempt to divide Taiwan's political parties and undermine its elected government' (*IHT*, 30 April 2005, p. 1).

> The parties announced that they would establish a platform for regular exchanges allowing discussion of a resumption of cross-strait dialogue, economic co-operation and greater international participation for Taiwan. They said that priority would be given to 'Taiwan's participation in activities of the World Health Organization' – wording that did not suggest Beijing had eased its opposition to full WHO membership for Taipei.
>
> (*FT*, 30 April 2005, p. 6)

'Lien Chan ... agreed with Mr Hu that Taiwan independence should be opposed and proposed discussions on economic co-operation and greater participation for Taiwan on the international stage' (*FT*, 2 May 2005, p. 11).

'During the trip ... Lien and Hu signed a five-point consensus in which they agreed to oppose Taiwan's formal independence' (www.iht.com, 4 May 2005).

'Chinese leaders feted ... Lien Chan ... like a visiting head of state ... [Lien called] for the status quo across the strait and drew attention to China's lack of democracy' (*The Economist*, 7 May 2005, p. 63).

1 May 2005. 'President Chen Shui-bian ... urged Beijing to negotiate with his elected government ... Mr Chen said he has asked James Soong ... to deliver a message to Hu Jintao' (*FT*, 2 May 2005, p. 11).

> A decision [has been made] by President Chen Shui-bian to send a secret message to China's leaders, the most direct contact between the two sides since his election five years ago ... Chen said Sunday [1 May] that he had spoken with James Soong, chairman of the People's First Party ... Soong is scheduled to fly to the mainland Thursday [5 May] for a weeklong trip ... Soong set up the People's First Party, which, even more than the Nationalists, favours eventual reunification of Taiwan with China ... Separate polls published by three Taiwanese newspapers over the weekend [30 April] showed that 51 per cent to 60 per cent of the population supported the trip by Lien.
>
> (*IHT*, 2 May 2005, pp. 1, 6)

2 May 2005.

President Chen Shui-bian ... called on Monday [2 May] for China and Taiwan to set up a procedure for improving communication between their military and security... Chen called for the creation of 'a cross-strait military and security mutual trust mechanism as soon as possible'.

(www.iht.com, 2 May 2005; *IHT*, 3 May 2005, p. 6)

Before Mr Chen took office in 2000 ... [Taiwan accepted] the idea of one China, but explained this in terms of Taiwan's constitution, which suggests the island is part of a Republic of China, just not the communist People's Republic of China.

(*The Economist*, 21 May 2005, p. 69)

3 May 2005.

[On Tuesday [3 May] officials [in China] announced that they would give a pair of giant pandas to Taiwan ... Beijing said it would unilaterally reduce import taxes on Taiwanese fruit ... Officials also said they would ease restrictions on mainland tourists to Taiwan ... Chen Shui-bian invited Hu Jintao to visit Taiwan.

(*IHT*, 4 May 2005, p. 5)

China has previously reserved [pandas] for heads of state on crucial visits ... Chen has said the 'One China' claim can be a 'topic for discussion between the two sides, but not a precondition for those discussions' [a spokesman for the Democratic Progressive Party said].

(www.iht.com, 3 May 2005)

'There have been ten offers of pandas over the years, all rejected' (*The Economist*, 7 May 2005, p. 63).

5 May 2005. James Soong starts his eight-day visit to China.

Until 2000 James Soong was a member of Taiwan's Nationalist Party, but he broke away to form the People's First Party ... The People's First Party is a small presence in Taiwan's legislature and its staunchest advocate of closer relations with China.

(*IHT*, 5 May 2005, p. 4)

[James Soong said on 8 May that] 'Taiwan independence will bring war and disaster. We want factories and markets, not battlefields' ... Soong's People's First Party favours eventual reunification with the mainland ... President Chen Shui-bian has repeatedly said that the constitutional proposals ... such as holding public referendums to approve constitutional amendments ... are aimed at streamlining the political process and are not a step toward declaring independence.

(www.iht.com, 9 May 2005)

11 May 2005. 'In recent days Chen Shui-bian has criticised Soong's and Lien's visits as undermining Taiwan's negotiating position with the Chinese mainland' (www.iht.com, 11 May 2005).

12 May 2005.

President Hu Jintao of China, in a meeting with James Soong ... agreed on a
new, slightly changed linguistic formula to describe relations between the sides
... In a joint communiqué issued by Hu and Soong ... the two men adjusted
the 'One China' phrase from 1992 ... In the 1992 effort at a dialogue both
sides settled on the phrase 'One China' but also agreed to hold different interpretations of what it meant ... Today [12 May] the Hu–Soong communiqué
said that the new wording would be 'two sides of the strait, one China'...
President Chen Shui-bian immediately rejected China's new language.

(*IHT*, 13 May 2005, p. 4)

20 May 2005.

China planned on Friday [20 May] to lift a decades-old ban on mainland
tourists visiting Taiwan, state media said ... A limited number of mainlanders
have been able to travel there on business ... Taiwan has its own tough rules
restricting mainland visitors.

(www.iht.com, 20 May 2005)

27 May 2005.

At Beijing's invitation three cities in Taiwan [including Taipei] have promised
to send delegations to a meeting of Asia-Pacific mayors in China in October
... Officials in all three cities are under the control of the main opposition
Kuomintang, or Nationalist Party ... The trips would need approval from the
government ... China has invited eight Taiwan mayors to the conference.

(www.iht.com, 27 May 2005)

7 June 2005.

A convention adopted sweeping changes to Taiwan's constitution Tuesday [7
June] that favour the top two political parties and require that future amendments go directly before voters – a measure strongly opposed by China. The
300-member National Assembly, chosen by popular ballot last month [May] to
address constitutional change, convened and approved the four amendments
with 249 votes – twenty-four more than the required three-quarters majority.
Both the ruling Democratic Progressive Party and the main opposition Nationalists backed the changes ... Two of the amendments – instituting more of a
winner-takes-all-style system in electoral constituencies and cutting the size of
the 225-seat Legislature in half – are certain to put the DPP and the Nationalists into the dominant position in Taiwanese politics ... Under the existing
electoral system as many as ten lawmakers were elected from Taiwanese constituencies, but the new system would cut the number to one delegate directly
elected by voters, and one chosen proportionally according to party affiliation
... However, Beijing opposed the measure allowing direct popular votes on
amendments, fearing that the ruling DPP might try to use such a poll to push
toward making Taiwan's de facto independence permanent – though the bar
for passing an amendment was set exceptionally high ... Under the changes

constitutional amendments will be difficult to pass because they must be approved by a majority of all Taiwan's eligible voters in a referendum – regardless of how many voters turn out for the poll. A simple majority of the votes cast would suffice only if turnout was 100 per cent. Putting all future constitutional amendments to a public vote signals the death knoll for the National Assembly, a curious remnant of the Nationalists' half century as Taiwan's political rulers. The assembly, originally made up of delegates selected from Chinese provinces, was once charged with voting for Taiwan's president. But that process was scrapped with the institution of direct presidential elections in 1996, and in 2000 a Nationalist presidential candidate was beaten for the first time.

(www.iht.com, 7 June 2005)

The changes are likely to be criticised by Beijing, which opposes the island's efforts to introduce referendums ... In private, however, mainland leaders are likely to welcome the new system which is expected to block radically pro-independence tendencies ... Legislators' terms will be extended from three years to four to bring elections into step with presidential polls. The new rules still require any future constitutional proposal to be passed by a three-quarters majority in parliament before it can be put to a referendum.

(*FT*, 8 June 2005, p. 10)

6 July 2007.

The leader of a small Taiwanese opposition party flew to mainland China on Wednesday [6 July] in a visit [lasting a week] aimed at underscoring his self-governing island's historic ties with the mainland – and promoting eventual unification. Yok Mu-ming [is] chairman of the New Party ... [which] has just one seat in Taiwan's 225-member legislature.

(www.iht.com, 6 July 2005)

14 July 2005.

China should use nuclear weapons against the United States if the American military intervenes in any conflict over Taiwan, a senior Chinese military official ... Major General Zhu Chenghu ... said at an official briefing [on 14 July]. Zhu, considered a hawk, stressed that his comments reflected his personal view and not official policy. Beijing has long insisted that it will not initiate the use of nuclear weapons in any conflict ... China has had atomic bombs since 1964 and has a small arsenal of land- and sea-based nuclear-tipped missiles that can reach the United States, according to most Western intelligence estimates.

(*IHT*, 16 July 2005, p. 6)

('Major General Zhu Chenghu is also a dean at China's National Defence University ... [On 15 July a spokesman for the ministry of foreign affairs in Beijing said]: "What he [Zhu] talked about was just his personal views" ... According to a paper published last month [June] by the *Bulletin of Atomic Scientists*, quoting "the intelligence community", China would increase its strategic nuclear warheads from

"eighteen to seventy-five–100" over the next fifteen years, primarily targeted against the United States': *FT*, 16 July 2005, p. 10.)
  16–17 July 2005.

> The Chinese president, Hu Jintao, on Sunday [17 July] hailed the election of Ma Ying-jeou, the mayor of Taipei, as the chairman of [the Kuomintang] ... Ma defeated the speaker of Taiwan's parliament, Wang Jun-pyng, to succeed Lien Chan ... Ma won 72 per cent of the vote of one million party members Saturday [16 July] ... He is the son of parents who fled China in 1950.
>
> (www.iht.com, 17 July 2005; *IHT*, 18 July 2005, p. 4)

'China's leadership ... has reacted gushingly to the first contested leadership in the 110-year history of the Kuomintang ... Mr Ma was born in Hong Kong to Huanese parents ... Wang Jun-pyng [is] a native Taiwanese' (*The Economist*, 23 July 2005, p. 59).
  20 July 2005.

> A Pentagon report said that efforts to modernize its military could pose a threat to peace in East Asia ... The annual Pentagon report on China's military ... scheduled for release this spring ... said that China is emphasizing efforts 'to fight and win short-duration, high-intensity conflicts' over Taiwan. China's military spending has grown by double digit rates since the mid-1990s and 'appears focused on preventing Taiwan independence or trying to compel Taiwan to negotiate a settlement on Beijing's terms', the report said ... According to the report, China's military modernization has included an estimated 650 to 730 mobile, short-range missiles deployed opposite Taiwan ... China does not yet have the military power to take Taiwan by force, the report said, and Beijing's conventional forces are not capable of threatening US territory, as 'China's ability to project conventional power beyond its periphery remains limited' ... The report called on Taiwan to take a greater role in building up its own defences. New weapons programmes, including equipment sold by American firms, have been languishing in Taiwan's parliament ... The report also says that China's military budget is so opaque, with much of the spending hidden in other accounts, that it 'precludes significant outside analysis'. Although noting that the analysis in imperfect, the report states that 'the defence sector in China could receive up to $90 billion in 2005', the third largest military budget in the world, after the United States, which spends more than four times that figure, and Russia ... The United States is eager for 'a peaceful and prosperous China, one that becomes integrated as a constructive member of the international community', the report stated. 'But we see a China facing a strategic crossroads.' Questions remain about the basic choices China's leaders will make as China's power and influence grow, particularly its military power.
>
> (www.iht.com, 20 July 2005)

The Pentagon estimates that China might be spending up to $90 billion a year on its military, three times the officially acknowledged budget ... [This] signals long-term ambitions to extend its power not only over Taiwan but also deeper into the region, according to the Pentagon ... The Pentagon assessment details advances in China's arsenal of short-range ballistic missiles, with between 650 and 730 deployed opposite Taiwan and notes that Beijing is adding to them at a rate of about 100 missiles a year ... The report said: 'Current trends in China's military modernization could provide China with a force capable of prosecuting a range of military operations in Asia, well beyond Taiwan, potentially posing a credible threat to modern militaries in the area.'

(*The Times*, 21 July 2005, p. 41)

'The report said: "Over the long term, if present trends persist, PLA capabilities could pose a credible threat to other modern militaries in the region"' (*FT*, 21 July 2005, p. 6).

China, says the report, is facing a strategic crossroads. It could choose 'a pathway of peaceful integration and benign competition'. Or ... it could 'emerge to exert dominant influence in an expanding sphere'. It could also become less confident and focus inwards on challenges to national unity and the Communist Party's legitimacy. 'The future of a rising China is not yet set immutably on one course or another' is the cautious conclusion.

(*The Economist*, 23 July 2005, p. 42)

'Total Taiwan military spending is just 2.5 per cent of GDP, compared with roughly double that figure in Singapore' (*IHT*, 4 October 2005, p. 9).

17 August 2005. 'An official investigation into the shooting of President Chen Shui-bian on the eve of the 2004 national election has concluded that a middle-aged, unemployed man, who committed suicide ten days after the incident, was responsible' (*FT*, 18 August 2005, p. 8).

19 August 2005.

Ma Ying-jeou, the popular mayor of Taipei, took over the lead of the National Party [Kuomintang] ... Ma was sworn in ... on Friday [19 August]... [He was] born to parents who emigrated from mainland China ... Ma Ying-jeou: 'We reject Taiwan independence, but we also reject "one country, two systems". We should take our own path' ... Polls show that most of the island's 23 million people support a continuation of the long-standing status quo – maintaining Taiwan's status as a self-governing entity, while not declaring formal independence.

(www.iht.com, 19 August 2005)

25 October 2005. 'Senegal announced it would restore diplomatic relations with China ... China had severed its ties with Senegal in January 1995 after Dakar had recognized Taiwan' (*The Times*, 26 October 2005, p. 47).

16 November 2005. President George W. Bush (speaking in Japan at the start of his Asian tour of Japan, South Korea and China):

As China reforms its economy its leaders are finding that once the door to freedom is opened even a crack, it cannot be closed. As the people of China grow in prosperity, their demands for political freedom will grow as well. Modern Taiwan is free and democratic and prosperous. By embracing freedom at all levels, Taiwan has delivered prosperity to its people and created a free and democratic Chinese society. What I say to the Chinese, as well as to others, is that a free society is in your interest.

(*The Times*, 17 November 2005, p. 47)

18 November 2005. President George W. Bush: 'Our belief that there should be no unilateral attempts to change the status quo by either side' (www.iht.com, 18 November 2005; *IHT*, 19 November 2005, p. 6).

19–20 November 2005. President George W. Bush visits China.

President Hu Jintao (20 November):

I reaffirmed to President Bush that the Chinese government and that the Chinese people are committed to peace and stability in the Taiwan Strait, and we are ready to do our utmost with all sincerity to strive for the prospect of a peaceful reunification of our country. This being said, we will by no means tolerate so-called Taiwan independence. I highly appreciate that President Bush has, on various occasions, stated his commitment to the one China policy, the three Sino-US joint communiqués, and his opposition to so-called Taiwan independence. To oppose and check so-called Taiwan independence and safeguard peace and stability in the Taiwan Strait serves the common interest of China and the United States.

(www.iht.com, 20 November 2005)

3 December 2005. '[In] local elections... the ruling Democratic Progressive Party ... suffered a heavy defeat. The DPP won only six of the twenty-three mayoral and county magistrate posts contested. Parties more sympathetic to China won the rest' (*The Economist*, 10 December 2005, p. 66).

15 December 2005. 'Taiwan said it was building a landing strip on one of the [Spratly] islands' (*The Economist*, 28 January 2006, p. 66).

1 January 2006.

President Chen Shui-bian delivered a highly unexpected New Year's message Sunday [1 January 2006], renewing his pledge to press for a new constitution and a continued arms build-up, and warning citizens of investment risks in China and what he saw as the mainland's military threat ... The president has been widely expected to soften his position toward the mainland after the governing Democratic Progressive Party suffered a stinging setback in closely watched elections last month [December 2005] ... In his New Year's message, however, Chen made clear that he would not respond to domestic political pressure by altering policy ... Chen: '[Taiwan insists upon] sovereignty, democracy, peace and parity no matter how cross-strait relations develop' ... Taiwan's opposition parties have blocked the $10 billion arms purchase package, even though the governing party has scaled it down from $19 billion. The bill ... has yet to win approval by the procedural committee of the opposition-controlled parliament, a necessary step before it can be heard in the full house.

(www.iht.com, 1 January 2006)

In a televised speech ... President Chen Shui-bian said Sunday that Taiwan needed to increase its weapons purchases and warned against greater economic ties with the mainland ... Chen referred as many as seventy times to the island of 'Taiwan' instead of its legal name, 'the Republic of China'. The island's constitution still states that the government in Taipei is the government of 'all China', but Chen has been moving away from that formulation for years ... Chen said that more than two-fifths of all orders placed with Taiwanese companies for manufactured goods were now filled by factories elsewhere; the mainland accounts for 90 per cent of those shipments from factories outside Taiwan, he said ... Chen Shui-bian: 'Although we cannot turn a blind eye to China's markets, we should not view the China market as the only or the last market. Globalization is not tantamount to "China-ization". While Taiwan would never close itself off to the world, we also shall not lock in our economic lifeline and all our bargaining chips in China.'

(*IHT*, 2 January 2006, p. 5)

2 January 2006.

Taiwan's senior official for Chinese affairs, Joseph Wu, sought Monday [2 January] to ease concerns that President Chen Shui-bian's speech on New Year's Day signalled tighter government restrictions on investments in China ... Chen warned of the risks of doing business in China and called on Sunday [1 January] for 'more active management' of growing Taiwanese investments on the mainland ... Wu, chairman of the cabinet-level Mainland Affairs Council, tried to reassure investors Monday by saying Taiwanese investments in China would be allowed to expand as long as it did not harm the island's economy ... Wu: 'We will strengthen our management of these investments. If we can better manage, in fact there will be room for opening [new investments].'

(www.iht.com, 22 January 2006; *IHT*, 3 January 2006, p. 5)

6 January 2006.

China's ... offer of two pandas to Taiwan provoked outrage in the island's government. Officials in Taipei accused Beijing of 'disrespect' and 'pro-unification political warfare' after it announced it would give Taiwan a pair of pandas ... Joseph Wu (chairman of the Mainland Affairs Council): 'They unilaterally announce the pandas will be sent over here in June, without having discussed the matter with Taiwan's government ... That is very disrespectful' ... The pandas support China's claim to sovereignty over Taiwan since Beijing no longer gives the endangered animals to foreign countries ... Opposition parties that support reunification with China have attacked the government as obstinately obstructionist.

(*FT*, 7 January 2006, p. 7)

31 January 2006.

Washington delivered an exceptional rebuke to President Chen Shui-bian [on 31 January] after a speech in which he proposed abolishing a unification

council with China ... Mr Chen proposed ... abolishing the National Unification Council, a non-official advisory body whose responsibility is to co-ordinate unification with China. Mr Chen also called for Taiwan to join the United
Nations under the name 'Taiwan' – instead of the country's official title, the
'Republic of China' – and for the drafting of a new constitution by the end of
the year.

(*FT*, 1 February 2006, p. 11)

The latest fracas in Taiwan over the island's National Unification Council is
especially abstruse. Theoretically charged with reviewing an eventual political
unification of Taiwan with the mainland, the council has not met since April
1999. Its budget has been cut to $31 ... Government officials on other agen-
cies' budgets conduct the council's few administrative tasks ... The National
Unification Council goes beyond dysfunctional to simply being not functional,
but that has not been enough to prevent controversy ... Chen Shui-bian also
suggested that Taiwan might apply this year to the United Nations as Taiwan
instead of ... the Republic of China.

(www.iht.com, 3 1 January 2006)

4–5 February 2006. '[Japanese] foreign minister Taro Aso ... declared over the
weekend [4–5 February] that Taiwan owes its advanced educational level to compulsory education policies imposed on the island during the 1895–1945 period of
Japanese colonization' (*IHT*, 10 February 2006, p. 8).
    27–28 February 2006.

Defying warnings from Beijing and Washington, President Chen Shui-bian
announced Monday [27 February] that he was scrapping the island's council
and guidelines for any political unification with mainland China ... Chen
declared ... that the National Unification Council 'will cease to function' and
that Taiwan's national unification guidelines 'will cease to apply'. Aides said
he would sign the necessary executive order Tuesday [28 February]. The
council has been moribund since Chen took office in 2000, but has considerable symbolic importance. Chen promised in his first inaugural address that as
long as the mainland had no intention of using military force against Taiwan,
he would not undertake any of the five moves toward independence, and
specifically declared that 'there is no question of abolishing the Guidelines for
National Unification and the National Unification Council'. Chen hedged his
remarks Monday by carefully avoiding a repetition of the Chinese term for
abolishing, '*fei chu*', and by saying that he did not want to change existing
relations across the Taiwan Strait ... Chen Shui-bian: 'Taiwan has no intention
of changing the status quo and strongly opposes its alteration by non-peaceful
means' ... The National Unification Council, which has not met since 1999,
has a budget of just $31. This will now be eliminated and the council's staff of
one, a secretary, will be reassigned to other duties in the presidential office.
But Chen is not revoking the executive decision in 1990 that originally created
the council, thereby leaving open the possibility that the council could be
reconstituted someday ... The other four promises were that he would not

declare independence, would not 'promote' a referendum on independence or unification, would not change Taiwan's legal name to something other than the Republic of China and would not rewrite the constitution to define relations with the mainland as 'state-to-state' relations ... The constitution prohibits Chen from seeking a third term in 2008.

(*IHT*, 28 February 2006, p. 7)

Established by the Nationalist Party when it was still in power in 1990, the National Unification Council has not actually met in almost seven years ... The council, and the guidelines it administers, nonetheless hold considerable symbolic importance in Taipei, Beijing and Washington ... Chen first raised the possibility of scrapping the council and guidelines in a speech on 29 January, at the start of the Lunar New Year.

(www.iht.com, 27 February 2006)

Chen Shui-bian ... said the National Unification Council, a body in charge of working towards unification with China, which has been defunct since Mr Chen came into office, would 'cease to function'. Guidelines set by the council that define unification as a national goal would 'cease to apply'.

(*FT*, 28 February 2006, p. 8)

President Chen Shui-bian ... completed the formalities Tuesday [28 February] ... After a concerted diplomatic push by the Bush administration, Chen modified the wording of his order, saying the council would 'cease to function' rather than be abolished, as he had said he would do in late January ... But Beijing ... [said that] 'although he did not use the term "abolish" and changed the term to "cease to function", this is merely a word game' ... An influential lawmaker from Chen's Democratic Progressive Party said Chen had been increasingly worried that China had been trying to gain the upper hand and reshape cross-strait relations.

(www.iht.com, 28 February 2006)

'China does not officially accept this name ... the Republic of China ... for Taiwan, but it much prefers it [to the name being changed to] the Republic of Taiwan' (*The Economist*, 4 March 2006, p. 67). 'James Soong ... says that during his stay Chinese leaders officially accepted "for the first time in history" that Taiwan and the mainland were "equal partners"' (*The Economist*, Survey, 25 March 2006, p. 18).
25 March 2006.

The foreign minister of the Vatican ... Archbishop Giovanni Lajolo ... said the 'time is ripe' for the Holy See and Beijing to establish diplomatic relations, and the Vatican confirmed that it was ready to move its embassy from Taiwan ... Lajolo said it was clear that the spiritual needs of the several million Catholics in China were more urgent than those of Taiwan's 300,000 Catholics ... Lajolo: 'The Holy See has manifested its willingness to transfer the apostolic nunciature from Taipei to Beijing, just as in 1952, on account of the circumstances of the time, it transferred the nunciature from mainland China to Taiwan'.

(www.iht.com, 26 March 2006)

The regaining of sovereignty over Hong Kong on 1 July 1997 and Macao on 20 December 1999

The following are significant dates in Hong Kong's history:

1839–42. The Opium War between China and Britain.

26 January 1841. A British naval contingent raises the British flag on Hong Kong Island. (Hong Kong means 'fragrant harbour'.)

29 August 1842. Hong Kong Island is ceded to Britain in perpetuity in the Treaty of Nanking.

October 1860. The Kowloon peninsula (3 square miles) is ceded to Britain.

9 June 1898. The New Territories (consisting of 235 islands and a mainland area adjoining Kowloon) is leased to Britain for ninety-nine years.

1941–5. Hong Kong is occupied by Japan.

19 December 1984. Britain and China sign the Joint Declaration. China will regain sovereignty over Hong Kong on 1 July 1997. For fifty years Hong Kong will be subject to a 'one country, two systems' regime. The idea is that Hong Kong's laws will remain 'basically unchanged' and that China will grant Hong Kong a high degree of autonomy (except in defence and foreign affairs). Hong Kong will be known as the Hong Kong Special Administrative Region of China.

1989. Britain and China agree that an election for the Legislative Council will be held within a year of the handover on 1 July 1997.

4 April 1990. China promulgates the Basic Law (Hong Kong's future constitution). *1991.* A Bill of Rights is enacted in Hong Kong. China says that anything in the bill that conflicts with the Basic Law will be annulled after the handover.

On 15 September 1991 eighteen members of the sixty-strong Legislative Council were directly elected and twenty-one were indirectly elected by business and professional groups. Eighteen members were appointed and three were ex officio.

30 June 1994. Chris Patten, who became governor in August 1992, has his proposals for enlarging the electorate and for making voting for the council more democratic approved by the Legislative Council. (China did not agree with these proposals.)

September 1995. Democrats and their allies win thirty-one out of sixty seats in the first fully elected Legislative Council. But the twenty directly elected members account for only a third of all legislators, the Democratic Party winning nineteen of the twenty seats.

11 December 1996. Tung Chee-hwa (a Hong Kong shipping tycoon) is chosen as Hong Kong's future chief executive. He will be the head of a sixty-strong provisional legislature. (A 400-strong committee of Hong Kong citizens appointed by China formally made the choices.)

1 July 1997. The provisional legislature passes a series of new laws, including one restricting the right to demonstrate. Protesters need to gain police approval in advance and permission can be refused on grounds of 'national security'.

The population of Hong Kong was some 6.3 million in 1996 (roughly divided into 1.3 million for Hong Kong Island, 2.0 million for Kowloon and 2.8 million for the New Territories). Some 98 per cent of the population are ethnic Chinese. After the 1949 communist victory in China there was a flood of refugees to Hong Kong. After China started to introduce economic reforms in 1978 there was a noticeable movement of manufacturing industry to China, Hong Kong increasingly specializing in banking and financial services.

Hong Kong is China's major source of foreign capital and its largest transshipment centre for foreign trade. By the end of 1996 Hong Kong accounted for 56 per cent of the cumulative totals of both contractual and utilized foreign investment. In 1996 trade accounted for 14 per cent of China's total foreign trade and about a quarter of China's trade is transshipped through Hong Kong. Hong Kong has taken advantage of China's low-cost production base and vast market. This has promoted the economic restructuring of Hong Kong from a manufacturing to a service economy, with significant strengths in financial, transportation and other services (*China Briefing*, September 1997, p. 4).

Other useful information is provided by the *FT* (Survey, 16 June 1997). In 1996 Hong Kong's *per capita* GDP was $25,100 (p. xvii). Some 60 per cent of foreign investment in China comes from Hong Kong (p. xi). Hong Kong is the world's ninth largest exporter and seventh largest importer. Almost half of China's imports and exports pass through Hong Kong and account for about 40 per cent of Hong Kong's international trade (p. xii).

8 July 1997. Tung Chee-hwa announces a new voting system for the Legislative Council. Twenty members will be elected by proportional representation in much larger districts. The remaining forty members will be selected almost entirely by the leaders of Hong Kong's business community and the professions (*IHT*, 9 July 1997, p. 10).

8–12 September 1997. Tung Chee-hwa visits the USA.

26 September 1997. The end of English as the main teaching language in schools is announced.

28 September 1997. The new election system is approved.

> The legislature to be elected next spring will have sixty seats, but only twenty will be directly elected. Thirty will be chosen by 'functional constituencies', such as professional associations and business groups. This is a system devised by the British but in 1995 it was so broadly defined that 2.7 million residents were eligible to vote; the new law reduces the electorate to about 180,000. Thus, where previously garment workers each had a vote, now only garment companies will vote. Another ten seats will be chosen by an 800-member electoral college, itself carefully controlled. Even the system for choosing the twenty elected representatives has been changed to dilute the strength of the most popular, pro-democratic parties.
>
> (editorial, *IHT*, 4 October 1997, p. 6)

24 May 1998. Elections for the Legislative Council take place. There is a record turnout of 53.29 per cent for elections in Hong Kong. Pro-democracy candidates (including Martin Lee of the Democratic Party) win more than 60 per cent of the popular vote but end up with only a third of the sixty seats (fifteen of the twenty directly elected seats and five of the thirty seats determined by 'functional constituencies') (*IHT*, 26 May 1998, pp. 1, 6).

4 June 1998. There is a large candlelit vigil in Hong Kong to commemorate Tiananmen.

30 January 1999. Hong Kong's highest court rules that four mainland-born children will be allowed to remain in the territory. The ruling overturns an April 1998 decision by a lower court. The court ordered their return to mainland China after they surreptitiously joined their parents, who were Hong Kong residents (*IHT*, 30 January 1999, p. 4). The ruling bestows the right to live in Hong Kong on illegitimate children of Hong Kong residents and on children born before either parent became a resident there (*IHT*, 11 February 1999, p. 4).

> The court of final appeal granted residency to children born in mainland China who have at least one parent living in Hong Kong. The court said the right applied to children, regardless of whether the parent was a Hong Kong resident before or after their birth.
>
> (*IHT*, 19 May 1999, p. 4)

'The court of final appeal ruled that all children of Hong Kong residents, including illegitimate children and those born before their parents became permanent residents, were eligible to live in the territory' (*FT*, 19 May 1999, p. 4).

But on 24 June 1999 the Standing Committee of the National People's Congress overturned the ruling after the government of Hong Kong requested a review.

> The government of Hong Kong had expressed fears of a huge influx of immigrants. The decision is expected to reduce the number of mainland Chinese eligible to live in Hong Kong to 200,000 ... The reinterpretation by the NPG stipulates that mainland children of Hong Kong residents can move to the territory only if one parent was a Hong Kong resident at the time of their birth ... Opposition politicians, lawyers and human rights groups warned that the Chinese move threatened the rule of law in Hong Kong.
>
> (*IHT*, 28 June 1999, p. 1)

'The government contended that ... the ruling by the courts in Hong Kong would have opened the gates to more than 1.6 million immigrants from China. Critics said nowhere near that many people would have been eligible for entry' (p. 9).

On 3 December 1999 Hong Kong's Court of Final Appeal said: 'It is clear that the Standing Committee [of China's National People's Congress] has the power to make the interpretation ... The interpretation is binding on the court of HKSAR [Hong Kong Special Administrative Region]' (*FEER*, 16 December 1999, p. 16).

2 November 1999. It is announced that a Disney theme park is to be built, a joint venture with the Hong Kong government.

15 December 1999. Hong Kong's Court of Final Appeal rules that desecration of the Chinese and the regional flag is unconstitutional.

20 December 1999. Macao is reverted to China at midnight on 19 December 1999. Portugal has ruled Macao since 1557.

Jiang Zemin:

> The implementation of the concept of 'one country, two systems' in Hong Kong and Macao has played and will continue to play an important exemplary

role for our eventual settlement of the Taiwan question. The Chinese government and people are confident and capable of an early settlement of the Taiwan question and the complete reunification.

> Portugal negotiated similar guarantees of relative autonomy for Macao that Britain won for Hong Kong ... In this tiny enclave of 430,000 people the main business is gambling and the biggest local concern is curbing the Chinese gangs, whose bloody wars have stained the last days of the Portuguese administration ... The Basic Law, the constitution negotiated between Lisbon and Beijing, allows Macao to keep its own government and laws as a special region of China.
>
> (*IHT*, 20 December 1999, p. 1)

'The Chinese Army streamed into ... [Macao] on Monday [20 December] in a joyful procession that revealed how deeply people here yearn for law and order after the gangsterism that strained the last years of Portuguese colonial rule' (*IHT*, 21 December 1999, p. 1). 'Portugal, which withdrew its soldiers shortly after its revolution in 1974, insisted that Macao was too small to require a military garrison' (p. 8).

1 September 2000.

> Student groups and other critics are demanding that a senior adviser to the chief executive of Hong Kong, Tung Chee-hwa, and two top University of Hong Kong faculty members resign following an investigation that concluded the three men pressured a prominent political scientist to abandon research documenting Mr Tung's steady slide in popularity. Allegations that Mr Tung's allies tried to muzzle the pollster Robert Chung have provoked a furious political debate in this former British colony since details of the case surfaced in July [2000].
>
> (*IHT*, 5 September 2000, p. 5)

> Top officials at Hong Kong University [the vice-chancellor and his deputy] resigned Wednesday [6 September] in the aftermath of an investigation that found they, and an adviser to the territory's chief executive, Tung Chee-hwa, had pressured a prominent pollster not to publish surveys critical of Mr Tung ... The report also implicated Mr Tung's senior special adviser ... Hong Kong University appointed an independent panel, headed by a former high court judge, to investigate the allegations.
>
> (*IHT*, 7 September 2000, p. 4)

10 September 2000. Elections, the second since the return of Hong Kong to China, are held for the Legislative Council.

The turnout was 43.6 per cent, compared with 53.29 per cent in the first election in 1998.

Of the sixty seats twenty-four are chosen by the general electorate in what are known as geographical constituencies. The remainder are elected by tiny groups of professional and business associations, known as the functional constituencies, and by a small, mostly elite group known as the election committee. 'Real power rests with the chief executive, who is hand-picked by Beijing' (*FT*, 11 September 2000, p. 14). The pro-Beijing Democratic Alliance for the Betterment of Hong Kong gained one seat, raising its seats to eleven, while the Democratic Party lost one seat, ending with twelve. The Liberal Party, a conservative business grouping, won eight seats (*FT*, 12 September 2000, p. 10).

> Special interest groups – such as business leaders, lawyers and doctors – picked thirty candidates in a system that gives them a much larger voice than average citizens. Six were selected by a committee under a convoluted system that opponents say ensures control by pro-Beijing figures and business interests.
>
> (*IHT*, 11 September 2000, p. 4)

> Representatives of the business and professional elite . . . get to pick who fills thirty of the legislature's sixty seats. As expected, electors from these 'functional constituencies' cast their votes overwhelmingly in favour of pro-Beijing candidates. The remaining six members on the Legislative Council, chosen by an 800-member committee, whose members are reviewed by Communist Party leaders on the mainland, fell in behind the pro-Beijing slate.
>
> (*IHT*, 12 September 2000, p. 4)

The pro-Beijing Democratic Alliance for the Betterment of Hong Kong's share of popular votes for directly elected seats rose from 25.2 per cent in 1998 to 29.68 per cent. The Democratic Party's share of the vote fell from 42.6 per cent to 34.7 per cent.

> The pro-Beijing Democratic Alliance for the Betterment of Hong Kong . . . unlike other pro-Beijing groups, is all for faster democratization . . . Its success has come from organizing well at the grassroots and concentrating on livelihood issues, areas where the democrats have been notoriously weak.
>
> (*The Economist*, 16 September 2000, p. 98)

> Rather than spend much time on bread-and-butter issues the [Democratic] Party stuck to firmly to its pro-democracy roots, calling for a faster pace of political reform and hammering away at Hong Kong's overseers in Beijing . . . The Democratic Alliance for the Betterment of Hong Kong was forced to spend much of the campaign dealing with a scandal involving vice-chairman Gary Cheng's undeclared stake in a public-relations firm . . . Most analysts agree the party's relative success was due to earlier efforts to appeal to voters' grassroots concerns.
>
> (*FEER*, 21 September 2000, p. 30)

12 January 2001. The head of the Hong Kong civil service, Anson Chan, announces her early retirement. She cites personal reasons (the need to spend more time with her family) but there is speculation of a growing rift with Hong Kong's chief executive, Tung Chee-hwa. Since Anson Chan is a staunch defender of Hong Kong's autonomy, there is also speculation about the prospects of increased mainland influence in the affairs of Hong Kong.

15 February 2001. '[It is announced that] Donald Tsang . . . Hong Kong's financial secretary ... will replace Anson Chan, who stepped down abruptly eighteen months before the end of her term [in June 2002]' (*IHT*, 16 February 2001, p. 5).

11 July 2001.

> [In Hong Kong] ... the legislature passed a bill Wednesday night [1 July] declaring that China's central government could fire Hong Kong's leader ... [But Hong Kong's] constitutional affairs secretary said ... the mainland government would have to follow Hong Kong's constitution before changing the leadership ... The constitution, known as the Basic Law, implies Beijing can oust the Hong Kong leader if he is unable to fulfil his duties and the bill passed Wednesday night does not offer any new powers to the mainland government ... [the secretary] said. It merely spells out Beijing's ability to remove a Hong Kong leader incapable of serving, he said ... Pro-democracy figures tried but failed to stop the measure.
>
> (*IHT*, 12 July 2001, p, 4)

> After a debate in the Legislative Council on 11 July the Chief Executive Election Bill interpreting the powers of the central government to remove the chief executive and laying out procedures for the election in March of Hong Kong's next political leader was passed into law by thirty-six votes to eighteen ... In the debate the secretary for constitutional affairs ... [said] that Beijing already had the power to dismiss the chief executive under the Basic Law, Hong Kong's mini-constitution. He acknowledged this was not explicitly stated but argued that it could be 'reasonably deduced' from provisions in the Basic Law. This meant that nothing changed with the passing of the bill, he said. However, the Law Society contested the official line.
>
> (*FEER*, 26 July 2001, pp. 28–9)

20 July 2001.

> Hong Kong's highest court ruled Friday [20 July] that a three-year-old boy born here to a mainland Chinese mother has the right to residency in the territory. The Court of Final Appeal ruled against the government, which said the decision would open a loophole in Hong Kong's strict immigration laws. But more important it brushed aside the government's request that the court consult the Chinese authorities before handing down the judgement ... [But] the court sided with the government in denying residency to three mainland Chinese children who had been adopted by Hong Kong parents ... The ruling Friday set the stage for a much larger case, involving 5,000 mainland Chinese who refused to leave Hong Kong after the court's landmark ruling on residency was overturned by Beijing in 1999.
>
> (*IHT*, 21 July 2001, p. 4)

'The Court of Final Appeal ... decided that a three-year-old born in Hong Kong while the mother was visiting had the right to reside in the territory' (*FEER*, 2 August 2001, p. 6).

10 January 2002.

> Hong Kong's highest court yesterday [10 January 2002] ruled that a landmark judgement it made in January 1999 could not be broadly applied in assessing the

claims of thousands of mainland immigrants to enter the territory because of a subsequent interpretation of that verdict by Beijing, which effectively overruled it ... In June 1999 China's Standing Committee overruled the Hong Kong court's liberal reading of the territory's immigration laws and limited the right of residence to people who had obtained a one-way exit permit issued by the Chinese government and to those who had at least one parent who was a permanent resident of Hong Kong at the time of their birth ... The Hong Kong Court of Final Appeal in its four-to-one decision yesterday ... ruled that statements by the Hong Kong government that it would abide by the January 1999 judgement before it was handed down, and the 'legitimate expectations' of immigrants arising from those comments, had been superseded by Beijing's ruling. It also said that the January judgement could only be applied to those actually involved in that case. Together the decisions denied the claims of the vast majority of the more than 5,000 immigrants involved in the cases decided yesterday ... The court, however, decided in favour of those immigrants who received letters from the government's legal aid department, saying it was not necessary for them to launch legal proceedings and that their cases would be handled in accordance with the January ruling. It was unclear exactly how many immigrants would be allowed to reside in Hong Kong, with estimates of about 500.

(*FT*, 11 January 2002, p. 9)

28 February 2002. Hong Kong's chief executive, Tung Chee-hwa, won a second term Thursday [28 February] in an election in which nobody dared to challenge him ... [He] was declared the winner after the nomination period expired with no other names put forward' (*IHT*, 1 March 2002, p. 4).

19 *June 2002.*

Hong Kong legislators have voted to approve the most sweeping changes to the territory's government structure since China resumed sovereignty over the former British colony five years ago. Critics fear the changes will undermine the independence of Hong Kong's civil service while also dramatically concentrating power in the hands of the chief executive, Tung Chee-hwa. Under the changes ... billed by supporters as a move toward higher levels of accountability, fourteen civil servants will be replaced by political appointees ... accountable only to him ... The changes mark a major step away from the British civil service traditions built up during Hong Kong's 156 years as a British colony. The danger, critics say, is that without protection of an independent civil service Hong Kong could tarnish the reputation for orderly and relatively corruption-free government on which prosperity is based ... Anson Chan, the territory's senior civil servant, resigned from office last year [2001] in part, some say, because she could not persuade Tung from altering the civil service ... Critics warn that he will name only yes-men to cabinet posts and effectively increase the influence of Beijing over the territory.

(*IHT*, 21 June 2002, p. 10)

'Unlike civil servants who can be dismissed only following a criminal conviction, the new secretaries can be fired by Tung' (*IHT*, 25 June 2002, p. 3).

The new cabinet may not be a step backwards compared with the old British system in which the civil service – accountable only to the Whitehall-appointed governor – implemented policies. But ... Tung has installed a team answerable to himself in place of bureaucrats whose independence was enshrined in Hong Kong's Basic Law.

(*FEER*, 4 July 2002, p. 10)

15 August 2002. 'A Hong Kong court Thursday [15 August] convicted sixteen Falun Gong members of offences related to a public protest [on 14 March] ... All sixteen were found guilty of public obstruction [and fined]' (*IHT*, 16 August 2002, p. 3).

28 January 2003.

It has been a gruelling four months for the Hong Kong government since it unveiled controversial proposals to tighten national security laws ... The Hong Kong government allowed a three-month consultation period after releasing proposals for the new laws on 24 September [2002] ... Chief executive Tung Chee-hwa ... on 28 January [2003] announced the government would water down some of the proposals to outlaw treason, secession, sedition and subversion ... Opposition was a key factor in the government's decision to exempt foreign nationals from prosecution for treason and dump proposals to ban the possession of seditious material. It has also been decided to narrow the offence of obtaining state secrets so that it would only be illegal to obtain classified information by improper means ... The concessions have failed to ease the fears of most critics.

(*FEER*, 6 February 2003, p. 17)

Article 23 of the Basic Law ... requires the enactment of laws against subversion, sedition, secession and treason, as well as the banning of links between local and foreign political bodies, and the theft of 'state secrets' ... The new draft will also make it harder for Hong Kong to ban political organizations that the Beijing government finds disagreeable. Not only would Beijing first have to ban the organization publicly, but Hong Kong's government would then have to prove that the local branch is subordinate to the mainland organization. This seems to protect Falun Gong ... as well as the Roman Catholic Church and most other worried bodies. Best of all, perhaps, the government now proposes that anybody accused under the new laws will have the right to trial by jury. In Hong Kong jurors are selected at random ... [But] the government refuses to publish the exact wording of its proposals.

(*The Economist*, 1 February 2003, p. 58)

29 June 2003.

The governments of Hong Kong and mainland China signed a broad free-trade agreement Sunday [29 June] ... the Mainland and Hong Kong Closer Economic Partnership Arrangement ... providing greater access to the Chinese market for Hong Kong businesses, including the local subsidiaries of multinational corporations. The pact goes beyond the market opening that China pledged when it joined the WTO in November 2001. Hong Kong companies providing services from shipping to management consulting will be allowed to compete in China with fewer or less stringent regulations than the rules for businesses incorporated elsewhere. China will also eliminate most tariffs on 1 January [2004] for goods produced in Hong Kong. By contrast, China has promised the WTO only that it will reduce its average tariff on all imports to 9 per cent by 2007. But Sunday's agreement ... lacked details in a few important areas. And, while China provided unexpectedly broad access to its shipping, logistics and movie industries for companies incorporated in Hong Kong, China gave almost no ground on insurance and securities trading, even for Hong Kong companies, and provided fairly limited concessions on banking ... Hong Kong made few concessions because it already does not collect any tariffs and allows companies of any nationality to set up subsidiaries to offer services. The agreement contains provisions designed to prevent multinationals not already active here from opening shell companies as a way to perform an end run around Chinese trade rules: most of the concessions for service industries require companies to have been doing business here for at least three to five years, depending on the industry.

(IHT, 30 June 2003, p. 9)

Hong Kong retailers, wholesalers, distributors, logistics companies and shipping lines will be allowed to set up wholly owned subsidiaries in China sooner and with fewer restrictions than Beijing had promised when it entered the WTO in November 2001. The Hong Kong subsidiaries of big banks will be able to start offering commercial loans and other services in Chinese currency as well as foreign currencies two years after each branch opens in China instead of three years later. While China has required each branch to become profitable on its own before offering basic services in Chinese yuan, the new rules will allow branches to proceed if all of a bank's branches are profitable ... The minimum assets needed for a bank to enter the Chinese market was reduced to $6 billion from $20 billion ... China allows only twenty foreign movies a year to enter the country ... The agreement exempts from the quota all Chinese-language movies shot anywhere by Hong Kong production companies ... Chinese censors would still vet each movie.

(IHT, 1 July 2003, pp. 1, 4)

[The bilateral agreement] covers trade in goods and services, investment facilitation and also tourism. China will remove tariffs on 273 Hong Kong products from 1 January [2004], accounting for 67 per cent of manufactured goods exported to the mainland. To boost tourism, hit especially hard by SARS, China will issue visas for visits to Hong Kong to people from three cities in neighbouring Guangdong as individuals instead of just as part of tour groups.

(FT, 30 June 2003, p. 7)

From 1 January [2004] China will eliminate tariffs on 273 types of Hong Kong-made goods, accounting for 67 per cent of its exports to the mainland

and including electrical and electronics products, textiles, clothing and jewellery. The zero tariff will apply to most industrial products and the number of goods covered will gradually increase in the next two years. But manufacturing accounts for only 5 per cent of Hong Kong's GDP. Service providers will receive fewer advantages than manufacturers. The deal covers seventeen service sectors, including accounting, advertising, construction and real estate, freight-forwarding, management and consultancy, and logistics and distribution. Hong Kong service providers will have far less onerous capital requirements than those imposed on companies from elsewhere ... The definition of 'Made in Hong Kong', the primary requirement for zero-tariff eligibility, is still being discussed ... [The agreement provides for] the lowering of the asset requirement for Hong Kong banks setting up in China to $6 billion from the $20 billion required of banks from other countries. The minimum experience of operating in China was cut to two years from three for Hong Kong banks seeking a licence to offer services in renminbi.

(*FEER*, 10 July 2003, p. 26)

Hong Kong revealed the fine print of its free-trade pact with China on 29 September, giving international banks, advertising firms, insurers and other multinational companies favoured access to China. The Closer Economic Partnership Agreement signed in June granted Hong Kong companies preferential access to consumers on the mainland for eighteen types of services, including banking, insurance, movies, advertising, construction and shipping. The fine print defined a Hong Kong service company as essentially any business that is incorporated in the city, pays local taxes and has operated for at least three years in Hong Kong, and whose staff is at least 50 per cent local. Tariffs will be eliminated on 273 categories of goods.

(*FEER*, 9 October 2003, p. 36)

1 July 2003. The sixth anniversary of the return of Hong Kong to Chinese sovereignty.

'A large protest is planned ... against the Hong Kong government's decision to bring in tough, new anti-subversion laws' (*FT*, 30 June 2003, p. 7).

An immense crowd marched here [Hong Kong] Tuesday [1 July] to protest government plans to impose stringent internal-security laws ... A police spokesman said that 350,000 people had demonstrated out of a Hong Kong population of 6.8 million. The Civil Human Rights Front, which organized the march, had planned for 100,000 to attend but estimated that more than 500,000 people actually participated.

(*IHT*, 2 July 2003, p. 8)

'[This was] the largest political demonstration in Hong Kong or the mainland since 1989' (*IHT*, 9 July 2003, p. 1).

Hong Kong's chief executive, Tung Chee-hwa ... issued a terse statement on Tuesday night [1 July] saying he would listen to people's concerns ... The rally was mainly against the legislation, although organizers also tapped into public anxiety here about unemployment, falling home prices and the government's slow response to SARS.

(IHT, 5 July 2003, p. 4)

'Protesters were also motivated by Mr Tung's failure to revive Hong Kong's depressed economy, which was recently dealt another severe blow by SARS' (*The Economist,* 5 July 2003, p. 57).

5–6 July 2003. 'Tung Chee-hwa ... agreed [on 6 July] to delay anti-subversion legislation ... withdrawing a demand that the national security bill should be passed on Wednesday [9 July]' (*Telegraph,* 7 July 2003, p. 12).

> Hong Kong's government was last night [6 July] forced to abandon attempts to enact an anti-subversion bill [on 9 July] after a key cabinet minister resigned ... James Tien, chairman of the pro-business Liberal Party and a member of Mr Tung's executive council ... resigned because he believed the government should postpone the reading ... Mr Tien's departure [is] the first such from the cabinet in the six years of its existence ... Tung Chee-hwa tried to defuse the row on Saturday [5 July] by making some concessions.
>
> *(FT,* 7 July 2003, p. 1)

'Beijing said Sunday [6 July] it wanted the bill passed on schedule [on 9 July] ... Tung had sought Saturday [5 July] to push the bill forward by watering down three provisions' (*IHT,* 7 July 2003, p. 1).

> Mr Tung said [on 5 July] he would scrap a provision of the bill that allowed some groups to be banned, add protection for journalists who published classified information and delete a provision that would let police conduct searches without warrants.
>
> *(Independent,* 7 July 2003, p. 12)

> The most contentious clause had required the government to outlaw any group found to be linked to a proscribed mainland organization, such as the Falun Gong sect. This was deleted in the concession announced on Saturday [5 July]. In another concession Mr Tung added a public interest clause for journalists prosecuted for writing about confidential government documents.
>
> *(Guardian,* 8 July 2003, p. 3)

7 July 2003. 'Tung [formally] announced the postponement ... of the vote on Wednesday [9 July] in the Legislative Council on the Article 23 anti-subversion bill ... at 2 a.m. yesterday [7 July]' (*The Times,* 8 July 2003, p. 14).

9 July 2003.

> Tens of thousands of demonstrators gathered here [Hong Kong] Wednesday evening [9 July] before the city's legislature building and called for free elections and the resignation of Hong Kong's leader ... A spokesman for the Human Civil Rights Front, which organized both rallies, said that the peaceful gathering Wednesday night drew the 50,000 people that the group had expected ... The police estimated that at least 30,000 people were present halfway through the two-hour rally and that more may have left earlier or

arrived later ... Speakers called not only for the security legislation to be redone entirely but for Hong Kong's chief executive and all lawmakers to be elected by universal suffrage ... Demonstrators also chanted for the resignation of ... Tung Chee-hwa, although ... [the Front's spokesman] said that this was not the purpose of the rally. Record unemployment of 8.3 per cent, falling home prices and Hong Kong's slow initial response to SARS have sapped Tung's popularity.

(*IHT*, 10 July 2003, p. 1)

Under Hong Kong's current electoral arrangements, only twenty-four members of the sixty-seat Legislative Council are directly elected. Of the remaining seats thirty are elected from professional or occupational constituencies and six by an 800-strong pro-Beijing committee ... Under the Basic Law half of the Legislative Council' will be directly elected at next year's polls [2004], with provisions for further democratic reforms after 2007.

(*FEER*, 17 July 2003, pp. 17–18)

13 July 2003.

Demonstrators ... call for democracy ... The crowd was far smaller than the half million who marched on 1 July ... It was also smaller than the crowd of 30,000 to 50,000 people who showed up [on 9 July] ... The Democracy Development Network, which organized the evening gathering on Sunday [13 July] estimated that more than 15,000 people attended. The police did not have an immediate estimate.

(*IHT*, 14 July 2003, p. 7)

More than 20,000 protestors [took part] ... About 10,000 people had been expected ... The rally was originally scheduled for April, but the onset of SARS meant the date was postponed. The rally's purpose had been to call for democratic elections for the chief executive of Hong Kong by 2007 and for the Legislative Council in 2008.

(*FT*, 14 July 2003, p. 6)

16 July 2003.

Two of Hong Kong's most unpopular senior ministers resigned ... Regina Ip, the secretary for security, resigned citing personal reason ... Many critics believe Ms Ip's fate was sealed when she quipped that if a lot of people attended the massive 1 July protest, it was only because the weather was good and people had nothing better to do ... Anthony Leung, financial secretary, said he too was leaving the government ... His resignation coincided with confirmation yesterday [16 July] that the department of justice was considering whether to charge him with fraud ... [following] a scandal in which the financial secretary ... bought a new Lexus a couple of weeks before he increased vehicle registration fees on luxury cars in his budget.

(*FT*, 17 July 2003, p. 9)

'Officials claim Mrs Ip actually submitted her resignation for unspecified "personal reasons" a week before the 1 July protest' (*The Economist*, 19 July 2003, p. 51).

17 July 2003. Tung Chee-hwa ... announced Thursday [17 July] that he would begin another round of public consultation over [the security bill] ... [but he said that] he was determined not to step down himself' (*IHT*, 18 July 2003, p. 1).

The Civil Human Rights Front, which organized the demonstrations on 1 July and 9 July, is actually a loose coalition of forty-five non-profit groups with different agendas ... The front [was] formed last September [2002] ... The front has refused to ... back calls by many in the streets for Tung to resign. The front has also limited the role of the Democratic Party, which counts as only one group, and vote, among forty-five ... The much smaller Democratic Development Network, a separate coalition, is focussed on achieving universal suffrage as soon as possible. It organized the rally last Sunday [13 July], which drew a crowd estimated at 9,000 by the police and 20,000 by organizers.

(*IHT*, 19 July 2003, p. 2)

August 2003.

This month [August] ... the Chinese authorities [decided] to allow the residents of ... Beijing, Shanghai, Guangzhou and Shenzhen to begin travelling to Hong Kong on their own as tourists, starting 1 September, instead of coming on officially approved business trips or with organized tours.

(*IHT*, 16 August 2003, p. 11)

From 1 September residents of Beijing and Shanghai and several cities near Hong Kong and Macau will be allowed to visit as individuals, dropping a requirement for them to travel in groups ... Since 28 July residents of four cities in Guangdong province that border Hong Kong and Macau may apply for individual travel permits to the two territories.

(*FEER*, 21 August 2003, p. 23)

5 September 2003.

Tung Chee-hwa ... announced Friday [5 September] that he was withdrawing internal security legislation ... [He] said that while he still believed legislation was needed to protect China's national security, he would not introduce a new bill until a clear public consensus supported the legislation. He cancelled the government's plans to issue by the end of this month a 'consultation document' asking the public's views on what provisions should be included in any security legislation. Lawmakers said that the withdrawal of the bill made it unlikely that any security bill could be enacted before next summer's Legislative Council elections.

(*IHT*, 6 September 2003, p. 1)

Tung Chee-hwa said ... Article 23 legislation ... had been withdrawn 'to allow time for the community to study the enactment question'. He reiterated that the government was legally obliged to pass security legislation of some sort by 2007 ... Mr Tung said a special working group would study the enactment question and exhorted people to focus on economic recovery rather than dwell on Article 23.

(*FT*, 6 September 2003, p. 8)

7 October 2003.

Retreating in the face of public opposition for the third time in less than five weeks, the government said Tuesday [7 October] that it would put on hold its plans to fill in part of Victoria harbour to make way for a highway, although it will allow dredging of the harbour in front of the central business district. A judge had ruled Monday [6 October] that the government could not only dredge the harbour's silt but also begin dumping huge quantities of sand and gravel into the water to fill in up to 23 ha, or 57 acres, of the harbour. Two newspaper polls on Tuesday morning showed that two-thirds of the public opposed any landfill, with most of the rest undecided ... Tung Chee-hwa withdrew his security legislation on 5 September and on 26 September the election commission cancelled a plan to reduce voting hours, a measure opposed by democratic activists as a way to suppress turnout.

(www.iht.com, 7 October 2003)

18 November 2003.

The Hong Kong government said Tuesday [18 November] that the city's banks would be allowed to offer credit cards, deposits and other services denominated in yuan ... From January 2004 Hong Kong banks will be able to tap the 65 billion Hong Kong dollars, or $8.38 billion, worth of yuan that is estimated to be in circulation in the city.

(www.iht.com, 18 November 2003)

Banks licensed in the territory will be permitted to accept deposits, arrange remittances, make foreign exchange transactions and issue credit and debit cards in the Chinese currency starting in January 2004. At least initially, however, they will not be allowed to enter the more lucrative market for corporate banking. While there is an estimated 20 billion renminbi to 70 billion renminbi ($2.4 billion to $8.5 billion) circulating in Hong Kong, brought over by visitors from the mainland, the money has so far remained outside the reach of the banking system. As part of China's capital controls, residents can only take a limited amount of money out of the mainland.

(*FT*, 19 November 2003, p. 15)

In a small step toward loosening control over its currency China said it would permit Hong Kong banks to accept deposits in renminbi and convert and remit renminbi for some customers ... Hong Kong banks would be able to take renminbi-based deposits later this year or early next year. It was the first time that China had officially endorsed such services by banks outside the mainland. But Hong Kong banks will probably not profit greatly because they will still not be allowed to lend renminbi. Under the new rules Hong Kong banks can accept renminbi deposits from individual customers and people engaged in tourism-linked businesses. Each customer can exchange as much as 20,000 renminbi ($2,415) per day, or remit as much as 50,000 renminbi a day to bank deposits in mainland China. Chinese visitors will be able to use mainland-issued debit and credit cards in Hong Kong, and Hong Kong banks can offer renminbi-backed credit cards for use on the mainland.

(*FEER*, 27 November 2003, p. 28)

23 November 2003. 'Democracy advocates have won a startlingly broad victory in local elections ... The pro-Beijing Democratic Alliance for the Betterment of Hong Kong fared badly' (*IHT*, 25 November 2003, p. 5).

The chairman of Hong Kong's biggest pro-Beijing party offered to resign after record number turned out and voted against his candidates in favour of pro-democracy parties in local elections ... [There was a] record turnout ... 44 per cent of eligible voters.

(*FT*, 25 November 2003, p. 10)

The Democratic Alliance for the Betterment of Hong Kong won only 38 per cent of the seats they contested ... [Its] chairman felt compelled to resign ... Legislative Council polls [are] scheduled for next September [2004] ... [The] electoral system is heavily tilted in favour of pro-government candidates ... Under the Basic Law, after 2007 it will be theoretically possible for the city's voters to select all their political leaders, including the chief executive, in unrestricted elections. However, changing the system to make this a reality requires the approval of a two-thirds majority of Hong Kong's Legislative Council plus the backing of the chief executive and China's National Congress ... An independent exit poll showed that 80 per cent of voters interviewed wanted a directly elected chief executive and Legislative Council from 2007.

(*FEER*, 4 December 2003, p. 18)

The Democrats have always been the biggest elected party in the legislature, and in elections on 23 November widened their lead as the biggest party in the district councils as well ... [There are] legislative council elections next September [2004] ... The number of directly elected seats in these polls is due to be increased from twenty-four to thirty, half of the total.

(*The Economist*, 29 November 2003, pp. 79–80)

1 January 2004.

Campaigners for democracy are planning on New Year's Day to hold their first big march since a series of rallies last July [2003] forced the government to withdraw a stringent internal security bill. The Civil Human Rights Front, a coalition of groups that brought out 500,000 demonstrators on 1 July [2003], has organized the demonstration for Thursday [1 January] to demand free election of the next chief executive and legislature.

(*IHT*, 31 December 2003, p. 4)

It was the largest demonstration since a big protest on 1 July [2003] forced the government to postpone and later withdraw a proposal for stringent internal security laws ... Activists refrained from further large protests through the autumn after their initial successes in the first two weeks of July ... While the crowd did not match the half-million [of 1 July] ... the spokesman for the coalition of labour unions and non-profit groups that organized the protest said that 100,000 had participated [on 1 January 2004], far more than the 20,000 that the coalition had predicted in obtaining a parade permit from the police ... Demonstrators called for the government to allow the public to elect the next chief executive and the entire legislature ... The demonstrators called for universal suffrage in elections for Tung's successor in 2007 and for the elections for the legislature in 2008 ... Tung Chee-hwa, the current chief executive, was reelected without opposition last year [2002] by an 800-member election committee loyal to Beijing. Various business and professional groups, along with the election committee, also select thirty-six of the sixty members of the legislature, while the public elects the rest ... Pro-democracy candidates mostly routed pro-Beijing candidates on 23 November [2003] for 400 seats on various local councils here. Those results led many here [in Hong Kong] to call for Tung Chee-hwa ... not to exercise his right, granted by Beijing six years ago, to appoint up to 102 more people to the councils. But Tung went ahead on Saturday [27 December 2003] and appointed 102 council members, mostly business executives not active in democratic causes.

(www.iht.com, 1 January 2004; *IHT*, 2 January 2004, p. 5)

7 January 2004.

Objections from Beijing have derailed plans to set a timetable for democratic reforms senior Hong Kong officials said on Wednesday [7 January] as they announced a task force to begin meeting immediately with various mainland Chinese government departments. Hong Kong residents have held numerous rallies in the last six months to demand greater voting rights, with as many as 100,000 taking to the streets on New Year's Day and 500,000 last July [1 July 2003]. But after promising in September [2003] to set a timetable by the end of December for pursuing constitutional changes, senior officials said on Wednesday that they were unable to set any schedule because of Beijing's concerns ... The absence of any timetable for greater voting rights angered democracy advocates, who announced that they would follow up the 1 January [2004] march with a smaller candlelight vigil in central Hong Kong on Thursday evening [8 January] ... Hong Kong's Basic Law, a mini constitution drafted for the territory by China and Britain before Britain's handover of the territory to China in 1997, calls for chief executives after 2007 to be chosen by more democratic means, but it is vague on whether this would include the chief executive selected in 2007 to serve until 2012 ... The Basic Law requires that the chief executive, two-thirds of the legislature and the Standing Committee of the National People's Congress in Beijing approve changes in the method of selection of the chief executive or the members of the Legislative Council.

(*IHT*, 8 January 2004, p. 5)

[A] move to full representative government is technically possible under the Basic Law ... But changing the method of electing the chief executive would require the support of a two-thirds majority in the Legislative Council, the consent of the chief executive and the approval of the Standing Committee of China's National People's Congress. Changing the system of electing the Legislative Council would require a two-thirds majority of that body and the consent of the chief executive. This decision must then be reported to the NPC.

(www.feer.com, 15 January 2004)

9 January 2004.

In a rare victory for a citizens' group in Asia, the highest court here ruled Friday [9 January] that the government had failed to meet legal criteria for filling in part of Hong Kong's famous Victoria Harbour. The ruling blocks the government at least temporarily from further land reclamation ... The Society is a civic group concerned with preserving beautiful views of the harbour and creating more green spaces and restaurants around its shores ... The society's victory marks the first time that the Court of Final Appeal here has ruled against the government in a case brought by a public interest group ... Beijing created the court in 1997 ... Until 1997 appeals of court decisions in Hong Kong went to the Privy Council in London ... The court ruled Friday that the government could proceed only if it showed an 'overriding public need' for the reclamation... The government had already trimmed back its reclamation plans considerably in response to a lower court ruling last year [2003], which imposed a strict standard for land reclamation in the harbour. The Friday verdict by the Court of Final Appeal dismissed the government's appeal of the lower court ruling and replaced the lower court's standard with an even stricter test of when the government can pursue landfills.

(www.iht.com, 9 January 2004)

February 2004. 'The state media began raising questions earlier this month [February] about whether all of Hong Kong's political leaders were patriotic enough, starting a fierce debate among the pro-democracy and pro-China camps in Hong Kong about the qualifications of true patriots' (*IHT*, 26 February 2004, p. 8).

As Beijing expressed increasingly strident opposition to democratic reforms in Hong Kong, a poll ... in late February ... showed the popularity of the Chinese government falling among Hong Kong people ... The results came after weeks of a propaganda campaign by Beijing against growing demands for universal suffrage to be allowed in Hong Kong from 2007. Beijing stepped up verbal attacks on pro-democracy legislators and groups it viewed as 'unpatriotic' and thus unfit to govern. The *China Daily* warned of government collapse if they won a majority in the legislature.

(*FEER*, 11 March 2004, p. 24)

'[A] ban has kept him [Martin Lee] and other democrats away from the mainland for fifteen years' (*FT*, 8 March 2004, p. 18).
9 March 2004.

A Hong Kong court ruled Tuesday [9 March] that a massive reclamation project in Victoria Harbour could go ahead despite charges that it would destroy the waterway. The government says it needs to reclaim the land to build a road and ease traffic congestion ... In January Hong Kong's top court ruled against another reclamation project in the Wanchai district.

(www.iht.com, 9 March 2004)

30 March 2004.

Pro-democracy activists in Hong Kong were dismayed by a 30 March conclusion from a local government task force on future political reform that Beijing
would have the final say on any political change pushed by Hong Kong ...
Earlier, Beijing signalled that the central government would control political
change when it said that a session of the Standing Committee of China's
National People's Congress beginning on 2 April would interpret key sections
of Hong Kong's mini-constitution, the Basic Law.

(*FEER*, 8 April 2004, p. 11)

2–6 April 2004. The Standing Committee of the National People's Congress
considers Hong Kong.

China justified its role in interpreting parts of Hong Kong's mini-constitution
on Monday [5 April] by calling it parliament's 'solemn duty', amid criticism
that Beijing was moving to control the form and pace of democracy there.
Beijing had hosted closed-door deliberations on articles of the law that critics
fear will hand China full control over where and when people in the former
British colony may elect their leaders. China said the leaders of the National
People's Congress, or parliament, had to interpret two clauses that set out how
the territory's chief executive and lawmakers are chosen because of disputes
and confusion in Hong Kong.

(www.iht.com, 6 April 2004)

The Standing Committee of the National People's Congress in Beijing on
Tuesday [6 April] approved new rules interpreting how far Hong Kong can go in
pursuing greater democracy ... The new interpretation requires the government
here [in Hong Kong] to work with the congress in Beijing before making any
changes to how leaders are chosen ... Current law requires only that the congress give its approval after an electoral process change has been approved by
the chief executive and two-thirds of the legislature ... But the new interpretation, which is legally binding under Chinese law, also allows changes to be made
'if necessary' before the next chief executive is chosen in 2007 ... Hong Kong's
mini-constitution, called the Basic Law, had directed that chief executives
elected after 2007 could be chosen by more democratic means. But there had
been considerable debate here over whether that could include elections in 2007.

(www.iht.com, 6 April 2004)

The Chinese authorities declared Tuesday that they would determine if and
when Hong Kong residents could elect their local leaders ... Beijing officials
declared that they intended to 'push forward' Hong Kong's political development, but only when the 'actual situation' permits and only according to a
'gradual and orderly process'.

(*IHT*, 7 April 2004, p. 8)

'The right to amend the law belongs to the National People's Congress,' said
... the deputy secretary-general of the NPC's Standing Committee ... In

practice this means that Beijing will exercise unambiguous control over whether and how quickly the number of directly elected Hong Kong legislators may be increased from a current twenty-four out of a total sixty. The NPC will also decide whether and when to allow the chief executive ... to be directly elected ... [The deputy secretary-general] said it was still Beijing's 'ultimate aim' to allow the selection of chief executive and Legislative Council by universal suffrage but he did not give a timetable.

(*FT*, 7 April 2004, p. 8)

China, without being asked by Hong Kong, suddenly decided less than two weeks ago to 'interpret' parts of ... the Basic Law ... [It was announced that the Standing Committee] had decided the meaning of two crucial annexes about how to elect Hong Kong's chief executive and legislature from 2007; the NPC did not immediately say what its interpretations were ... The Basic Law states these [new, more democratic voting systems] have to be reported by Hong Kong 'only for the record'. It also says only the Hong Kong chief executive and his government ... have the power to initiate changes.

(*FT*, 7 April 2004, p. 16)

The deputy secretary-general: 'Hong Kong can build a bridge to greater democracy, but it must follow China's blueprint' (*Guardian*, 7 April 2004, p. 13).

The Basic Law suggests that changes must be first agreed in Hong Kong then sent to the NPC to be 'approved' (in the case of changes to the chief executive's election), and 'reported for the record' (in the case of Legislative Council elections). Under the new interpretation, the NPC must first agree that there is a need for change ... before discussion can begin. It also gives the NPC the right to refuse to accept any council election reform.

(*Telegraph*, 7 April 2004, p. 16)

China's parliament ruled that Hong Kong is barred from even initiating political reforms for greater democracy without prior permission from Beijing ... The Standing Committee of the NPC ... approved a document requiring Hong Kong's chief executive to seek formal approval from it before changes to the political system could be initiated ... Only the committee has the power to decide whether there is a 'need' for political overhaul in Hong Kong. If it determines there is no need, then chief executive Tung Chee-hwa may not even propose any changes to the system. Polls show that a majority of Hong Kong people want direct elections for the next chief executive in 2007 and for the full legislature in 2008.

(*FEER*, 15 April 2004, p. 24)

Although the NPC has a final power of veto over any change in the system for choosing the chief executive, the procedure for selecting Legco [the Legislative Council] is different. Under the Basic Law it is up to Legco itself to decide on the rules for choosing its members, though these rules must be endorsed by the chief executive. China's NPC is merely to be informed, for the record.

(*The Economist*, 10 April 2004, p. 11)

Only one of the Standing Committee members [173 in all] is from Hong Kong
... a businessman ... Opinion polls suggest strong public support in Hong
Kong for the territory's chief executive and legislature to be returned by universal suffrage ... This is the first time since Hong Kong's handover to China
in 1997 that the NPC has unilaterally taken upon itself to issue an 'interpretation' of the Basic Law.

(*The Economist*, 10 April 2004, p. 54)

11 April 2004.

Thousands of demonstrators ... marched through Hong Kong on Sunday
[11 April] to protest the Chinese government's decision to limit further moves
by the territory to democracy. Organizers estimated that more than 15,000
people participated, while the police declined to provide a figure ... [This was
an] unexpectedly large turnout for an event only scheduled last Tuesday night
and held in the middle of a holiday weekend.

(*IHT*, 12 April 2004, p. 6)

'Lee Cheuk-yan, a legislator and one of the organizers, estimated 20,000 people
had participated, far more than the 5,000 to 10,000 originally expected ... It was
the largest rally since 1 January, when an estimated 100,000 people marched for
democracy' (*FT*, 12 April 2004, p. 8).

'[There were an] estimated 10,000 protesters' (*Guardian*, 12 April 2004, p. 13).

'Up to 20,000 people marched to protest Beijing's requirement that the city
obtain its approval before initiating any political reforms to elect its leader and lawmakers by universal suffrage' (*FEER*, 22 April 2004, p. 22).

21 April 2004.

China is doubling to 150 million the number of citizens who can visit Hong
King without restrictions ... Starting in the next three months, residents from
seven more cities in the nearby province of Guangdong and nine cities in three
other wealthy provinces will be allowed to visit Hong Kong without joining a
tour group.

(www.iht.com, 21 April 2004)

26 April 2004.

Beijing forbade on Monday [26 April] the introduction of universal suffrage in
elections for the chief executive in 2007 and the legislature ... Hong Kong
voters will elect half the legislature in the September elections ... rising to
thirty out of sixty from twenty-four out of sixty in the current session ... and
many here [in Hong Kong] had expected Beijing to increase this proportion in
2008 as a small, conciliatory gesture ... But the Standing Committee of the
National People's Congress ordered Monday that this ratio remain unchanged.
If more democratically elected seats are added, then more seats must also be
added for so-called functional constituencies, which are elected by representatives of specific industries or professions, like banking and accounting, that
tend to follow Beijing's wishes closely. The Standing Committee also ruled on
Monday that no changes would be allowed to a provision that Beijing inserted

into drafts of the Basic Law after the Tiananmen Square killings in 1989. The provision says that while bills backed by the Beijing-appointed chief executive need only a simple majority to pass the legislature, bills and amendments introduced by members of the legislature must clear a higher hurdle. These bills and amendments must win the support of a majority of the democratically elected members plus a majority of the members representing functional constituencies.

(www.iht.com, 26 April 2004; *IHT*, 27 April 2004, pp. 1, 8)

'The Standing Committee of ... the National People's Congress rejected any significant democratic reform in Hong Kong until at least 2012' (*FEER*, 6 May 2004, p. 11).

The decision rules out any meaningful political changes in Hong Kong, at least for another eight years ... China has tried in recent days to reach out to Hong Kong's pro-democracy camp by holding its first official meetings with some of its leaders since [Tiananmen].

(*The Economist*, 1 May 2004, p. 65)

30 April 2004. 'Eight Chinese warships cruised into Hong Kong harbour' (*Guardian*, 1 May 2004, p. 11).
    30 May 2004.

Demonstrators marched Sunday [30 May] to mark the upcoming fifteenth anniversary of the Tiananmen Square killings and growing restrictions on democratic development ... Organizers estimated the crowd at 5,600 people, while the police said that more than 3,000 had participated ... The march coincided with a continuous controversy over why three prominent radio talk shows, all outspoken advocates of democracy, suddenly fled Hong Kong in the past month.

(*IHT*, 31 May 2004, p. 4)

4 June 2004.

Throngs gathered here Friday night [4 June] to mark the fifteenth anniversary of the Tiananmen Square killings in Beijing as the day passed fairly peacefully on the mainland, although at least sixteen people were arrested on the square itself ... As the anniversary neared Chinese authorities reportedly detained activists and the relatives of people killed in 1989 or ordered them to leave Beijing ... An annual candlelight vigil in Hong Kong has become the main remembrance of the military crackdown, drawing tens of thousands of people, including some from the mainland ... Activists for the first time had distributed fliers to tourists from the mainland, urging them to attend the vigil ... Three popular radio talk show hosts in Hong Kong have quit in the last five weeks, complaining of pressure to limit their pro-democracy views. In the past week a succession of mainland officials have stepped forward to insist that the radio hosts had not been intimidated and to suggest that one of them ... had misunderstood a late-night phone call from a former mainland official.

(www.iht.com, 4 June 2004)

'Two of the broadcasters said they had received death threats ... China has denied any role in the resignations' (www.iht.com, 8 June 2004).

'Three popular radio talk show hosts were pressured to resign with threats of violence allegedly backed by the central government in Beijing' (*FEER*, 10 June 2004, p. 12).

'Organizers claimed 82,000 people turned out, but the police said the crowd peaked at 48,000' (*Independent*, 5 June 2004, p. 32).

The vigil ... an annual event in Hong Kong ... usually draws 40,000 to 50,000 people ... The scant police presence at the vigil contrasted with the stringent security measures taken in Tiananmen Square, where sixteen people were reported to have been arrested. Yesterday's tight security followed the disappearance earlier this week of Jiang Yanyong, the military doctor who exposed Beijing's cover-up of SARS and recently wrote to Chinese leaders recommending a reassessment of the 1989 protest.

(*FT*, 5 June 2004, p. 8)

14 June 2004.

The government of China has proposed talks with critics in Hong Kong in a rare conciliatory gesture just days after the city's pro-democracy camp said it would tone down its anti-China rhetoric ... An official in Beijing ... said his proposal was a response to suggestions made by some Hong Kong democracy advocates last week to resolve differences with China ... Both China and the democracy groups have made conciliatory statements in recent weeks in an attempt to defuse tensions before a democracy demonstration set for 1 July and Legislative Council elections in September.

(www.iht.com, Monday 14 June 2004)

30 June 2004.

With one day remaining before what is expected to be a huge pro-democracy march ... Chinese authorities are clamping down to prevent news of the demonstration from spreading to the mainland, while leading democrats here [in Hong Kong] have split over tactics ... Martin Lee, the founding chairman of the Democratic Party here and an acerbic critic of mainland policies for decades, unexpectedly led several other democrats over the weekend in suggesting that marchers avoid the controversial chant 'Return power to the people'. Beijing has taken strong exception to the slogan.

(www.iht.com, 30 June 2004)

1 July 2004.

Hundreds of thousands of residents marched to demand democracy and – to an extent not seen in previous marches – to criticise Beijing ... Demonstrators in earlier rallies ... [demanded] the resignation of Tung Chee-hwa ... But Tung was barely mentioned Thursday [1 July] as protesters boldly denounced mainland China for banning general elections here [in Hong Kong] and for allegedly trying to intimidate democracy advocates ... Demonstrators carried many placards with fairly broad slogans like 'Democracy for Hong Kong'. But also visible were a variety of more controversial signs demanding, for example, 'End one-party rule, establish a democratic China' ... A lawmaker who helped organize the procession said that more than 350,000 people had started the march ... and that more protestors had joined along the route ... But the police estimated the crowd at 200,000 people ... China drastically reduced the number of mainlanders allowed to visit Hong Kong this week and mainlanders were not apparent in the crowd Thursday ... [which was] a public holiday to mark the seventh anniversary of the handover ... The crowd Thursday was only slightly smaller than the estimated 500,000 people who marched on the sixth anniversary.

(www.iht.com, 1 July 2004)

'Organizers estimated that 530,000 joined the demonstration ... Organizers had expected 300,000 for the event ... "Return the power to the people" [was] chanted, a slogan hated by Beijing' (*FT*, 2 July 2004, p. 8). '"Return power to the people" [was] one of the main slogans' (*FT*, 3 July 2004, p. 8).

'Bowing to pressure over a slow and sloppy response to SARS, Hong Kong's health secretary resigned Wednesday [7 July] ... [becoming] a rare political casualty in a territory where critics charge that top aides of ... Tung Chee-hwa often avoid being held accountable for problems' (*IHT*, 8 July 2004, p. 8).

1 August 2004. 'China's military staged its first parade in Hong Kong on Sunday [1 August], with 3,000 soldiers marching crisply in formation as others rode in armoured vehicles and helicopters ... It came two months after a similar naval display' (*IHT*, 2 August 2004, p. 5). 'China's display of military might was a major departure from the military's usually low profile in Hong Kong ... Beijing took the unusual step of inviting Hong Kong's pro-democracy lawmakers' (www.iht.com, 2 August 2004).

China's military garrison in Hong Kong went on public parade to celebrate the seventy-seventh anniversary of the creation of the national army. Some 3,000 People's Liberation Army troops marched through the territory's main military barracks in the rural northern New Territories watched by 17,000 ticket-paying members of the public. The parade also featured tanks, helicopters, weaponry and armoured vehicles.

(*The Times*, 2 August 2004, p. 14)

9 September 2004.

China has used threats and intimidation to skew the [Legislative Council] elections on Sunday [12 September] in favour of pro-Beijing candidates ... [the New York-based] Human Rights Watch ... said on Thursday [9 September] ... The international human rights organization ... [said China] was trying to turn the media, candidates, lawmakers and voters against a pro-democracy movement in Hong Kong ... [The group] said Hong Kong's political community had been plunged into a state of fear unparalleled since sovereignty over the city returned to China from Britain in 1997. Human Rights Watch said the last twelve months had brought some of the most worrying violations of human rights since the handover ... The Human Rights Watch report outlines offences against twenty people. It said the most worrying incidents had been the resignations in quick succession of three outspoken radio talk-show hosts. The talk-show hosts said that they had been threatened over their on-air attacks on the Beijing-backed Hong Kong government. Also cited was the arrest of a politician on 13 August in a hotel room in China on charges of hiring a prostitute. The man, Alex Ho, was sentenced without a trial to six months of 'reeducation through labour'. He remains on the Hong Kong ballot and in mainland detention.

(www.iht.com, 9 September 2004)

12 September 2004. Elections for the Legislative Council are held. 'The 32 million registered voters choose thirty of the Legislative Council's sixty members. That is an increase from the twenty-four elected four years ago' (*IHT*, 13 September 2004, p. 7).

Democratic gains are not as high as once expected.

Despite winning 62 per cent of the vote in a poll where a record 55.6 per cent of the electorate cast ballots, the pro-democracy parties and independents secured only an extra three seats, giving them a total of twenty-five in the sixty-seat chamber ... Of the thirty seats in ... [the] functional constituencies ... the pro-democracy camp gained two extra seats to hold a total of seven.

(*FEER*, 23 September 2004, pp. 26, 28)

Voter turnout hit a record high of 55.6 per cent and the pro-democracy parties garnered 60 per cent of the popular vote, up three points from 2000 ... But this did not translate into the expected increase in seats for the democrats ... They gained three new seats, giving them a total of twenty-five: less than the twenty-seven seats most pundits had predicted ... Half of Legco's seats are returned by generally pro-Beijing business groups and professional associations, via so-called functional constituencies, which represent just 6 per cent of the total votes cast ... These constituencies voted surprisingly heavily for the democrats, giving them seven seats.

(*The Economist*, 18 September 2004, p. 73)

The Democratic Party has become dogged by a series of sex and financial scandals that dominated news ... Before the scandals democracy advocates had hoped for a turnout of 60 per cent or higher ... [compared with the then] record of 53.3 per cent in 1998.

(*IHT*, 13 September 2004, p. 7)

A series of tactical errors and peculiarities in the voting process prevented democracy advocates from winning as many seats as expected ... [For example] a last-minute appeal by the Democratic Party for voters to support its founding chairman, Martin Lee, backfired badly when so many voters in his multi-seat district ... switched their support to him that a key Democratic Party ally lost her seat in the legislature ... Pro-Beijing candidates fared better than expected after a combination of voter incentives and intimidation by mainland officials. Chinese Olympic athletes visited Hong Kong to perform, but democracy supporters were denounced as 'traitors' and one was jailed on the mainland for six months without trial after allegedly soliciting a prostitute ... Candidates from the pro-democracy opposition captured roughly three-fifths of the popular vote; Beijing's allies captured most of the rest. Half of all votes cast by industry leaders and professions, who are allowed to send their own representatives to the sixty-member Legislative Council, also went to democracy supporters ... Yet democracy proponents captured eighteen of thirty members chosen by the general public and only six of thirty members selected by industries and professions [in so-called functional constituencies]. In addition to the twenty-four seats now controlled by democracy advocates, two professions chose candidates for the first with strong democratic credentials, and two industries reelected candidates who sometimes favour greater democracy. That gives the opposition a potential total of twenty-eight votes on some issues, not a majority but enough to give the pro-Beijing local government difficulty, because some lukewarm Beijing backers in the legislature are businessmen who show up infrequently to vote. By contrast democracy advocates have held twenty-one seats in the current legislature, with one independent with strong democratic leanings... and two industry candidates who sometimes favour more democracy.

(*IHT*, 14 September 2004, p. 5)

Pro-democracy politicians won twenty-five of the sixty seats in the legislature, a gain of three. These included two new seats in the so-called functional constituencies which represent professional and community groups and have traditionally been dominated by candidates friendly to Beijing. Although the pro-democracy camp won about 58 per cent of the popular vote, the result was at the lower end of analysts' expectations. Pro-democracy politicians won twelve of the directly elected seats, up from seven last time. The gains by pro-Beijing candidates came despite a record turnout of 55.6 per cent of registered voters ... Candidates are chosen from a list according to the proportion of votes the list gains ... Albert Chen [was elected] ... a former radio talk show host critical of Tung Chee-hwa ... Mr Chen quit his post in May, saying he had been threatened because of his support for democratic reform.

(*FT*, 14 September 2004, p. 10)

Pro-democracy candidates won eighteen directly elected seats, just one more than in the last election, and the pro-Beijing camp took twelve, up from seven in 2000. Results for the other thirty seats, elected by small professional groups, brought the camps' totals to almost the same as in 2000. The Beijing camp took thirty-four, unchanged, the democrats gained three to twenty-five, and independents won one, down from four.

(*Guardian*, 14 September 2004, p. 16)

20 December 2004.

President Hu Jintao publicly urged Hong Kong's leader on Monday [20 December] to improve his management ... a comment widely seen as a rebuke ... In an unscheduled event at the end of a two-day visit ... to celebrate the fifth anniversary of Portugal's return of Macao to Chinese rule ... he delivered his comments directly to Tung Chee-hwa ... Hu started by saying that he believed Hong Kong was 'moving in the right direction' ... but he warned Tung that he should 'sum up experiences, find out the inadequacies, sharpen administrative abilities and continue to raise the quality of governance'.

(IHT, 21 December 2004, pp. 1, 6)

28 February 2005.

Tung Chee-hwa, Hong Kong's chief executive, is preparing to step down early from his post following his appointment yesterday [28 February] to China's leading political advisory body ... [He is] one of ten prominent Hong Kong people appointed to the Chinese People's Political Consultative Conference.

(FT, 1 March 2005, p. 10)

The announcement that Tung Chee-hwa would be travelling to Beijing for elevation to the nation's highest advisory body fuelled speculation Tuesday [1 March] that he would lose his job as Hong Kong's chief executive two years before the end of his term ... The Chinese People's Political Consultative Conference ...made up of retired senior leaders and businessmen ... serves as an advisory role to the central government and is expected to elect Tung to a now-vacant post of vice chairman.

(www.iht.com, 1 March 2005; *IHT*, 2 March 2005, p. 3)

10 March 2005.

Tung Chee-hwa submitted his resignation Thursday [10 March] to China's leaders after eight years as Hong Kong's chief executive, beginning the first transfer of power since Britain returned the territory to Chinese rule in 1997 ... Tung, who is sixty-seven and has a reputation as a workaholic, said that his resignation two years before the completion of his second term on 30 June 2007 was solely the result of declining health and advancing years ... Under the Basic Law ... a chief executive can only step down because of ill health or governal paralysis involving relations with the legislature ... Under the Basic Law Donald Tsang, the chief secretary [a former financial secretary] and second ranking official, will become the acting executive of Hong Kong for up to six months. The 800-member Electoral Committee, composed of prominent businesspeople, professionals and politicians, will meet within 120 days to select a new chief executive. Tsang is widely expected to be chosen then as he has far more experience than any potential rivals. By stepping down this week Tung makes sure that his successor can be elected by current committee members, most of whom are strongly loyal to Beijing. Their five-year terms run until 13 July. A new committee must be elected after that by 160,000 of Hong Kong's 6.9 million people, with mainly business leaders, neighbourhood politicians and professionals allowed to vote ... The consensus of the legal community here [in Hong Kong] is that the Basic Law calls for the next chief executive chosen this summer to serve a full five-year term. But a series of

Beijing officials have said in the past week that Tung's successor should only serve the two-year remainder of his term, following mainland practice. Tung said that mainland officials would decide this point by the time they accept his resignation ... Tung is scheduled to become on Saturday [12 March] a vice chairman of the Chinese People's Consultative Conference.

(www.iht.com, 10 March 2005; *IHT*, 11 March 2005, p. 4)

'Donald Tsang was a loyal civil servant for the British-run government for three decades before the return of Hong Kong to Chinese rule' (www.iht.com, 11 March 2005).

Donald Tsang [became] a civil servant in 1967 ... In 1995 he became the first Chinese to serve as financial secretary. Mr Tsang saw the territory through the 1978 Asian financial crisis, backing Hong Kong's unprecedented intervention in local stock and future markets ... In June 1997, just before Hong Kong's return to Chinese sovereignty, Mr Tsang was knighted by Queen Elizabeth ... In 2001 he became chief secretary for administration, Hong Kong's second-ranking official.

(*FT*, 14 March 2005, p. 10)

12 March 2005.

The Basic Law ... only mentions five-year terms for chief executives. But Elsie Leung, the territory's secretary for justice, announced on Saturday [12 March] that a new chief executive would be chosen this summer [2005] only to complete the two remaining years in the current term of Tung Chee-hwa ... Donald Tsang said that the same 800-member Electoral Committee ... would meet on 10 July to choose a successor. The Hong Kong government plans to amend the local election ordinance to make this possible, Tsang added ... In the Legislature government supporters outnumber democracy advocates by thirty-five to twenty-five ... Leung said that the intent of the drafters of the Basic Law had been to allow for shortened terms for replacement of chief executives. But the secretary for justice also acknowledged that the law itself did not reflect this, and that the Hong Kong government told the Legislature in writing in 2001 and again in 2004 that only five-year terms were possible under the Basic Law ... But she maintained that mainland China's legal system does allow legislative intent to be considered, showing the difference in the way things are done in Hong Kong and in mainland China ... She pointed out that top mainland officials, including the president of China, serve five-year terms, and if the official steps down in the middle of a term the successor only serves the balance of the term ... The terms of current members of the Electoral Committee expire on 13 July. Saturday [12 March] was the last day that Tung could resign and still have his successor chosen by the current committee, which is heavy on Beijing loyalists ... The shorter term could also limit the service of Tsang, the acting chief executive. He is a longtime civil servant not entirely trusted by pro-Beijing politicians because of his three decades of loyal service to the British Crown, for which he was knighted ... Tsang said he would serve as acting chief executive until the Electoral Committee votes on 10 July.

(www.iht.com, 13 March 2005)

Hong Kong lawyers and politicians denounced the government's decision to introduce a two-year term for the territory's next chief executive as evidence of an erosion of the rule of law and autonomy ... Earlier on Saturday [12 March] China's State Council accepted the resignation pf Tung Chee-hwa.

(*FT*, 14 March 2005, p. 10)

14 March 2005. Donald Tsang: 'There is no going back. The next stage will certainly be more democratic than what it is now' (www.iht.com, 14 March 2005).

6 April 2005.

The government here [Hong Kong] asked Beijing to issue a legally binding decision on how long the territory's next chief executive would serve. A ruling on the issue would be the third direct intervention in Hong Kong's legal system ... Donald Tsang, the acting chief executive, said that a binding decision from Beijing was needed to make sure that legal challenges did not prevent elections for the next chief executive from being held as scheduled on 10 July.

(www.iht.com, 6 April 2005)

27 April 2005.

The Standing Committee of the National People's Congress ... issued a legally binding interpretation of Hong Kong's Basic Law ... The interpretation will limit the chief executive to be selected this summer to the two years remaining in the second term of Tung Chee-hwa ... Critics of mainland policies toward the territory described ... the ruling ... as a further erosion of Hong Kong's autonomy ... The interpretation is the third time that the Standing Committee has interpreted the Basic Law.

(www.iht.com, 27 April 2005; *IHT*, 28 April 2005, p. 4)

5 May 2005.

The Court of Final Appeal ... Hong Kong's highest court ... quashed convictions on Thursday [5 May] of eight members of the Falun Gong spiritual group. The eight had been convicted by a lower court of obstructing and assaulting the police during a protest three years ago against China's decision to ban the group on the mainland ... The court ruled that the police officers had not acted properly in arresting people holding a lawful demonstration and so the demonstrators could not be prosecuted for resisting ... Falun Gong is outlawed in mainland China, but not in Hong Kong ... The Court of Final Appeal in Hong Kong based the decision on constitutional rights to demonstrate and to engage in free speech ... The demonstrators had previously been convicted of an additional offence as well, obstruction of a public place. But that decision had been quashed by a lower court, the Court of Appeal, in November 2004.

(www.iht.com, 5 May 2005; *IHT*, 6 May 2005, p. 3)

4 June 2005.

Tens of thousands of people ... [held] a vigil in one of Hong Kong's largest urban parks to commemorate the sixteenth anniversary of the Tiananmen

Square killings ... Organizers put the crowd at 45,000, while the police said it was about half that size. There were visibly fewer people than at the event in the previous two years, when many in Hong Kong were deeply unhappy with economic stagnation and political leadership ... The throngs in Hong Kong were a contrast to the heavy security in Beijing, where large numbers of uniformed and plainclothes officers at the square prevented protests.

(www.iht.com, 2 June 2005)

16 June 2005.

Donald Tsang has secured enough nominations to ensure that he becomes Hong Kong's next chief executive ... [for] the remaining two years of Mr Tung's term ... No other contender secured the necessary 100 nominations from members of the nearly 800-strong election committee ... to qualify as candidates. Mr Tsang said he had 710 nominations and on Thursday [16 June] Hong Kong's returning officer declared him the winner. His appointment still awaits formal ratification by the government in Beijing.

(www.economist.com, 16 June 2005; *The Economist*, 18 June 2005, p. 60)

24 June 2005.

The Chinese government on Friday [24 June] officially appointed Donald Tsang as the chief executive of Hong Kong ... His formal swearing in ceremony in Beijing underscored the mainland's hold over Hong Kong's government ... Beijing appointed him to a truncated term of two years until June 2007, the time left in the term of ... Tung Chee-hwa.

(www.iht.com, 24 June 2005)

1 July 2005.

Pro-democracy and pro-Beijing demonstrations drew tens of thousands of people into the streets. A pro-Beijing parade in the morning drew 30,000 people, according to organizers, while organizers of the pro-democracy march in the afternoon put their event's turnout at 45,000. The police said 20,000 participants attended the pro-Beijing event and 17,000 people arrived at the end of the pro-democracy march. Friday [1 July] was the eighth anniversary of the handover of Hong Kong from Britain to China. Protest marches on the two previous anniversaries had each drawn more than a half million people demanding greater democracy and the resignation of Tung Chee-hwa ... who was widely blamed for the city's years of economic problems ... Tung resigned in March ... and the Hong Kong economy has rebounded to become one of the fastest growing in Asia.

(www.iht.com, 1 July 2005)

21 July 2005. On 21 July there was a small revaluation of the yuan against the US dollar, with the peg against the dollar scrapped in favour of the yuan moving within a daily trading band of 0.3 per cent either way against a basket of unspecified currencies. China tried to discourage speculation that the yuan would gradually appreciate over time.

[Hong Kong's] authorities have made it clear that they intend to maintain its twenty-one-year peg to the American dollar ... The Hong Kong Monetary Authority, the de facto central bank ... had already prepared for a Chinese revaluation. In May it switched from simply maintaining the exchange rate at above HK $7.80 to the American dollar to a trading band of HK $7.75–7.85. For the first time this added a ceiling to the floor by which it had traditionally managed the currency, in a move to discourage investors from using the Hong Kong dollar to speculate against a yuan appreciation. It has worked.

(*The Economist*, 6 August 2005, p. 62)

30 August 2005.

The chief executive of Hong Kong ... Donald Tsang ... invited the territory's entire legislature to come with him next month [25–26 September] in what would be the largest visit of pro-democracy politicians from Hong Kong that the Communist leadership in Beijing has ever allowed ... With very few exceptions China has banned Hong Kong's pro-democracy politicians from crossing the border ever since 4 June 1989, when many of them outspokenly denounced the Chinese Communist Party for the Tiananmen Square killings ... Tsang said the immediate purpose of next month's visit to Guangzhou was to foster greater co-ordination in the Pearl River delta region ... Martin Lee, the founding chairman of the Democratic Party ... said that he would accept the invitation to visit China again for the first time since early 1989 ... Lee Wing-tat, the current chairman of the democratic Party and another lawmaker banned from the mainland since 1989, said that he would accept the invitation ... James To, a senior Democratic Party lawmaker who has been turned back twice in the past five years when he tried to visit the mainland, said that he would also accept Tsang's invitation to go to Guangzhou.

(www.iht.com, 30 August 2005)

12 September 2005.

As Hong Kong Disneyland prepares to open on Monday [12 September] Disney will hold off building a similar park in mainland China until it has been assured that it will be able to air Disney shows on Chinese television ... Disney has a minority stake in the new Hong Kong theme park. The Hong Kong government owns 57 per cent and Disney owns the rest.

(*IHT*, 12 September 2005, p. 10)

25–26 September 2005.

Hong Kong's chief executive ... Donald Tsang ... led all but one member ... who said she could not attend because of a prior commitment ... of the city's executive across the border to mainland China on Sunday [25 September], starting a two-day trip that marks the first time Beijing authorities have let in prominent Hong Kong advocates of democracy since the Tiananmen Square killings of 4 June 1989.

(www.iht.com, 25 September 2005; *IHT*, 26 September 2005, p. 6)

'Beijing invited Hong Kong's entire sixty-member Legislative Council to the southern province of Guangdong. Among them were eleven ardent democracy supporters who had been barred entry for sixteen years after criticizing the government for the Tiananmen Square crackdown of 1989' (www.iht.com, 26 September 2005).

10 October 2005.

The Hong Kong government released on Wednesday [19 October] its plans to pursue somewhat greater democracy, but the plan was assailed by democracy advocates, who called it inadequate and vowed to block it in the legislature ... Constitutional changes require the support of two-thirds of the legislature, or forty of its sixty members. Democracy advocates hold twenty-five seats and vowed to vote as a group against the plan ... The plan calls for doubling the committee of prominent citizens that chooses the chief executive to 1,600 from 800 now. Most of the increase would come from including 529 district councillors who sit on neighbourhood councils. These councils mainly serve an advisory role now, on issues like where to put traffic lights and how to control rainwater run-off. The plan also calls for district councillors to play a greater role in choosing members of the legislature. The general public currently elects thirty members and various business, professional and labour groups choose the rest. Under Wednesday's proposal the legislature would be expanded by ten seats, to seventy, with five of the extra seats to be filled through general elections and the other five to be elected by the district councillors. The government of Donald Tsang, Hong Kong's chief executive, appoints 102 district councillors and the rest are elected by the general public ... [The Democratic Party] had insisted that only the 427 democratically elected councillors should be allowed to vote for the chief executive and members of the legislature and not the 102 appointees. The government proposal calls for the appointees to be allowed to vote in both elections ... Democracy advocates decried the government's decision not to include any timetable for allowing the chief executive and all lawmakers to be elected by the general public ... The government's decision to support greater influence for Tsang's appointees to district councils comes a week after he caused considerable surprise in Hong Kong by saying that he planned to install at least one political appointee near the top of each government department ... The government's proposal Wednesday also said that a chief executive who serves a partial term will only be allowed to serve a single, full five-year term thereafter ... [Thus] the new rule would prevent Tsang from seeking reelection again in 2012.

(www.iht.com, 19 October 2005)

4 December 2005.

Tens of thousands of people marched through Hong Kong streets Sunday [4 December] for the right to choose their political leaders by direct election and as a protest against proposed electoral changes. The intent of the march was to force governments here [Hong Kong] and in Beijing to rethink changes recently proposed by chief executive Donald Tsang.

(www.iht.com, 4 December 2005)

Organizers estimated the peaceful crowd at 250,000 while police officials put it at 63,000. The turnout, much larger than expected by either measure, was especially surprising because Hong Kong's economy is booming ... An abrupt recovery in the economy together with the removal of Donald's Tsang's deeply unpopular predecessor, Tung Chee-hwa, seemed until the last few weeks to have robbed the democracy movement of much of its strength.

(*IHT*, 5 December 2005, pp. 1, 5)

'The turnout was higher than the 50,000 expected by organizers ... [the marchers urging] Beijing to introduce universal suffrage ... [The] protest was prompted by a reform package put forward by Donald Tsang in October' (*FT*, 5 December 2005, p. 9).

'The protesters marched peacefully through central Hong Kong ... In an unprecedented gesture by a top establishment figure, a former head of the civil service, Anson Chan, once Mr Tsang's boss, briefly marched with them' (*The Economist*, 10 December 2005, p. 65).

7 December 2005.

Donald Tsang ... pledged Thursday [8 December] to alter an unpopular package of proposed election pledges ... Tsang said he would not be able to provide a timetable or road map for full democracy ... The changes to come, he said, would be limited ... Tsang: 'We will focus on the study of how to perfect the proposal . . .Everyone understands we do not have a lot of leeway.'

(www.iht.com, 8 December 2005)

'Donald Tsang said ... that he would see what he could do to "perfect" the package, but he had "little scope" to change it' (*The Economist*, 10 December 2005, p. 65).

19 December 2005.

The territory's leaders said Monday [19 December] that they would make small changes to their complex plan for limited democracy and then demand that the Legislature vote on the package on Wednesday. The only change of consequence offered Monday related to the number of local councillors appointed by the chief executive and the number publicly elected. A senior official said Monday the administration would be willing to alter the reform package to increase the proportion of elected councillors.

(www.iht.com, 19 December 2005)

[Tsang proposed] a phasing out of his ability to appoint neighbourhood councillors ... In his legislative proposal this autumn [2005] ... [Tsang called] for five new seats in the Legislature to be filled through general elections and another five members to be chosen by the city's 529 neighbourhood councillors, who count as a functional constituency. While Tsang appoints 102 of the neighbourhood councillors, the rest are elected by the public. Tsang offered on Monday to phase out the appointment of councillors by 2012 or 2016, with the exact schedule to be decided in 2011.

(www.iht.com, 21 December 2005)

21 December 2005.

Democracy advocates defeated a government-backed legislative proposal Wednesday [21 December] to revamp the political system ... Democracy advocates were united in opposing the plan because it did not include a timetable for one-person, one-vote general elections ... The plan was to be voted in two parts, the first involving rules for the election of the chief executive and the second involving rules for legislative elections. The first part was defeated on Wednesday and the second part appeared to be heading for defeat as well in a second vote expected no later than Thursday. Under special rules for constitutional initiatives, Tsang's proposal required a two-thirds majority of the council, or forty votes ... But only the thirty-four pro-government lawmakers voted for the plan, while twenty-four pro-democracy lawmakers opposed it and one lawmaker with democratic leanings ... abstained ... The pro-government president of the council also did not vote ... following a tradition ... It was the first time that the Legislative Council has voted on a constitutional issue requiring a two-thirds majority for approval since Britain returned the territory in 1997.

(www.iht.com, 21 December 2005)

The first part of the package, which gained thirty-four votes, proposed doubling the size of the committee that picks the city's leaders. The second part, which also fell six votes short of approval, called for expanding the legislature. With the rejection of the government plan, the method of selecting Hong Kong's leaders will remain governed by the Basic Law, the mini-constitution used since 1997, and the Chinese parliament's reviews of that law.

(www.iht.com, 22 December 2005)

Tibet

'Tibet's native population is about 2.5 million' (*IHT*, 9 December 2004, p. 2). '[There are] approximately 160,000 Tibetans in exile in India. Tibet's exiled religious leader, the Dalai Lama, maintains headquarters in India' (www.iht.com, 1 April 2005).

A chronology of important events is as follows:

1720. 'China's Manchu Qing dynasty sends its army into Tibet to expel the Dzungar Mongols, bringing the area under Beijing's hegemony. The administration remains in Tibetan hands but the Qing later install their own representatives in Lhasa.'

1912. 'The Qing dynasty is overthrown. Tibet's government expels Chinese representatives.'

1913. 'The Thirteenth Dalai Lama proclaims Tibet independent.'

1918. 'The Tibetan army, led by British-trained officers, defeats the Chinese army. Tibet and China sign a peace treaty but China refuses to ratify it.'

1950. 'The Chinese communist People's Revolutionary Army invades eastern Tibet.'

1951. 'The Lhasa government accepts Chinese sovereignty over Tibet. Beijing promises to maintain the Dalai Lama's power and status and to respect local religious beliefs.'

1959. 'An abortive uprising in Tibet. The Fourteenth Dalai Lama flees into exile in India.'

Late 1970s–early 1980s. 'China softens policy on Tibet and makes contact with the Dalai Lama.'

1989. 'China declares martial law in Tibet after pro-independence riots.'

2002–4. 'The Dalai Lama's envoys hold talks with Beijing . . . The Dalai Lama signals acceptance of China's sovereignty over Tibet but wants genuine autonomy for Tibetan areas.'

The above chronology is taken from *FT* (2 August 2004, p. 15).

May 1995. An Amnesty International report says that political and religious repression in Tibet increased in 1993 and 1994 (*IHT*, 30 May 1995, p. 4).

20 June 1996. The German Bundestag condemns what it calls 'China's continued policy of repression in Tibet'.

23 April 1997. President Clinton meets the Dalai Lama.

10 November 1998. The Dalai Lama meets President Clinton in the USA.

10 March 1999. Today is the fortieth anniversary of the uprising in Tibet (invaded by China in 1950) and the subsequent flight to India by the Dalai Lama.

5 January 2000. The third-ranking Tibetan Lama (the fourteen-year-old seventeenth Karmapa Lama, head of one the four seats of Tibetan Buddhism) arrives in India (in Dharamsala, the seat in exile of the Dalai Lama, who fled Tibet in 1959; China took over Tibet in 1950). He arrived after a long trek from the Tsurphu monastery in Tibet, which he left on 28 December 1999. Both the Dalai Lama and China had recognized the boy's title in 1992. In contrast, the reincarnation of the eleventh Panchen Lama (the second-ranking Tibetan Lama) is in dispute. In May 1995 the Chinese authorities took away the seven-year-old boy recognized by the Dalai Lama and replaced him with another boy appointed by them.

8 February 2001. 'The Chinese government approved a plan to construct a railway from Golmud, in western China, to Lhasa, the capital of Tibet' (*The Economist*, 17 February 2001, p. 78).

23 May 2001. The Dalai Lama meets President George W. Bush at the White House.

'China marked the fiftieth anniversary of its rule over Tibet on Wednesday [23 May] with flag raising, praise for its policies in the region and condemnation of the Dalai Lama's meeting with President Bush in Washington' (*IHT*, 24 May 2001, p. 5).

'Mr Bush's meeting with the Dalai Lama was a step up in protocol from that extended by the previous administration. Bill Clinton used to drop by during a meeting between the Dalai lama and top officials' (*FT*, 24 May 2001, p. 11).

4 April 2002.

Tibet's longest serving dissident . . . the seventy-six-year-old Jigme Zangpo . . . has been released on 'health grounds' after two decades of stubborn refusal to renounce his pro-independence ideals . . . He is the second high-profile Tibetan prisoner to be freed this year. He had not been due for release until 2011.

Earlier this year, in the run-up to the February summit between President George Bush and ... President Jiang Zemin, the authorities ordered the early release of ... Ngawang Choephel.

(*Guardian*, 5 April 2002, p. 17)

('Tanag Jigme Zangpo, seventy-six ... arrived in the United States yesterday [14 July] after winning release on medical grounds ... He was first sentenced ... in 1965 ... [He] is the sixth Tibetan dissident to be freed this year [2002]': *The Times*, 15 July 2002, p. 13. 'He had been released in March and allowed home under a form of house arrest': *FT*, 15 July 2002, p. 6.)

10 September 2002. 'Two envoys from the Dalai Lama began meetings Tuesday with the Chinese government and will later travel to Tibet ... [This] is the first time in more than a decade that Tibetan exile officials have publicly sent an envoy to China' (*IHT*, 11 September 2002, p. 1).

'[They are] the first officials from the exiled government to visit Tibet since 1985' (*Guardian*, 1 October 2002, p. 16).

27 May 2003.

Secret negotiations between China and the Dalai Lama are due to resume after the arrival in Beijing last night [27 May] of two senior envoys of the Tibetan spiritual leader ... Their visit to China last September [2002] was the first formal contact between the Chinese government and the Dalai Lama for ten years.

(*Guardian*, 28 May 2003, p. 11)

(The visit lasted two weeks.)

9 November 2005. 'Last week President George W. Bush welcomed the Dalai Lama ... in the Oval Office, but the White House was careful to give the meeting little publicity' (*The Times*, 17 November 2005, p. 47).

'President George W. Bush ... met the Dalai Lama ... at the White House on 9 November – but without press photographers' (*The Economist*, 19 November 2005, p. 25).

Inner Mongolia

During the 1960s the Chinese–Soviet split kept Mongolia ... apart from Inner Mongolia, a region of China. Today Inner Mongolia is home to 4 million ethnic Mongolians, almost double the 2.5 million in Mongolia. But Chinese migration to Inner Mongolia over the years has left ethnic Mongolians there vastly out-numbered by 18 million Han Chinese ... A Han Chinese-owned company is taking over administration of the Genghis Khan Mausoleum, the region's biggest tourism money-maker. Entrusted to the care of the Darhad Mongolian tribe since 1696, this shrine holds relics of the great conqueror, including his saddle and black bow. The actual burial place of Genghis Khan, who died in 1227, is not known and has been the subject of several archaeological expedi-tions. But construction of a new 'mausoleum' by ... the Chinese company prompted protests by Mongolians who see the move as another power grab.

(*IHT*, 27 November 2004, p. 2)

Uighurs

4–6 February 1997. There were serious riots in Xinjiang (which borders Kaza-khstan). Han Chinese comprise only 38 per cent of the population in Xinjiang, the majority being Uighurs and other Moslem, ethnic Turkic groups (*IHT*, 13 February 1997, p. 4). At least ten people were killed and more than 140 were injured. On 25 February 1997 bombs exploded on three buses in Urumqi, killing nine people and injuring seventy-four. From 1944 to 1949 the Uighurs had their own Republic of East Turkestan in Xinjiang, which is now one of the five autonomous regions of China. Xinjiang covers a sixth of China but its population is only 16.6 million (*IHT*, 26 February 1997, p. 4; 27 February 1997, p. 6; 3 March 1997, p. 6; 6 March 1997, p. 4).

> Fifty years ago the Uighurs were the largest ethnic group in Xinjiang, account-ing for 76 per cent of the population. The Chinese represented only 7 per cent. But after Mao's revolutionaries incorporated the short-lived Uighur republic of East Turkestan into China ... the government encouraged Chinese immigrants to settle in the north-eastern half of Xinjiang ... Now they are a majority.
>
> (*The Economist*, 12 February 2000, p. 78)

On 12 January 1998 it was announced that on 29 December 1997 the govern-ment had executed sixteen people in Xinjiang for murder, robbery and drug ped-dling. In exile in Kazakhstan a spokesman for a Moslem exile group said that China had executed thirteen Uighur separatists. China executed twenty people from April to July 1997 (*IHT*, 13 January 1998, p. 4).

> Xinjiang ... half the size of India in the far northwestern corner of China, is home to 8 million Uighurs, Moslems of Turkish descent. They speak a Turkic language ... and have spawned a sometimes violent autonomy movement. Unlike Tibet, its southern neighbour, Xinjiang has not achieved international prominence over its unrest and longing for self-rule. This is partly because there is no united Uighur diaspora and because it lacks a leader equal to the Dalai Lama ... But Xinjiang's unrest poses as serious a problem to Beijing as does Tibet's. Most of China's continental oil deposits and its main nuclear weapons test sites are in Xinjiang. And unlike the one in Tibet the Xinjiang separatist movement embraces violence. Since the early 1990s there have been scores of uprisings, bombings and killings of Han Chinese officials in this region. Xinjiang separatists have also been blamed for a bombing in Beijing ... Many [Uighurs] live just above the poverty line.
>
> (*IHT*, 23 August 2000, p. 5)

> Xinjiang, with an area of 1.6 million square kilometres, is the largest of China's provinces and autonomous regions ... Islam came to Xinjiang in the tenth century with an Arab invasion, and most minorities in the region are Moslems ... In 1948 75 per cent of Xinjiang's population was Uighurs and 15 per cent Han. Today 40 per cent of Xinjiang's 16 million people are Han ... [It is claimed that] the authorities were alarmed by the 1990 census, which showed Han had declined to 37.5 per cent of the population from 42 per cent in

1978, and they have worked hard to reverse the trend ... Xinjiang is much more ethnically diverse than Tibet, which is inhabited only by Tibetans and Han. Some Xinjiang minorities, such as Kazakhs and Hui – Chinese Moslems – do not necessarily support an independent Xinjiang ... Xinjiang has been volatile for years. As in Tibet unrest increased here in the 1980s after China began to relax policies towards religion ... Some Uighur separatists have received training from Islamic extremist organizations in Pakistan and Iran and have embraced terrorism as a method of dealing with Chinese authorities.

(*IHT*, 18 September 2000, p. 2)

About 40 per cent of Xinjiang's population is now Han Chinese compared to about 15 per cent in 1949. Uighurs ... have declined to about 47 per cent of the population. Other ethnic groups include Kazakhs, Kyrgyz and Tajiks. The population of the region's capital, Urumqi, is now 80 per cent Chinese.

(*IHT*, 6 October 2001, p. 5)

Half the size of India, lying between China's interior and the chaos of Central Asia, and rich in coal, oil and natural gas, Xinjiang is strategically important to China ... [Concerns about Xinjiang] helped inspire an ambitious national campaign, launched by Beijing in March [2000], to develop western parts of China ... Uighurs make up 8 million of Xinjiang's 17 million residents. Uighurs speak a language closely related to Turkish and are traditionally Sunni Moslem. The human rights group Amnesty International in June [2000] identified Xinjiang as one of five global trouble spots where violence is escalating ... From the 1860s until 1949 revolts by Xinjiang's Turkic-speakers against Chinese rule succeeded three times in establishing independent states in parts of the region. The last, the Eastern Turkestan Republic ... existed from 1944 until the communists came to power in 1949 ... In 1949 Han Chinese were 6.3 per cent of Xinjiang's population. Today they are 38 per cent ... religious belief among all under-eighteen-year-olds has been banned in Xinjiang since 1990 ... Foreign Islamic missionaries now target Xinjiang's Moslems and Uighurs are starting to take part in armed Islamic movements from Afghanistan to Uzbekistan and even Chechenia.

(*FEER*, 7 September 2000, pp. 22–4)

(On 8 September 2000 a lorry carrying explosives for disposal exploded in the capital of Xinjiang, Urumqi. At least sixty people died. But the Chinese authorities did not attribute the explosion to terrorism.)

7 March 1997. A bomb explodes on a bus in Beijing. It is thought that the bombing is linked with unrest in Xinjiang. ('After the blast an Istanbul-based group called the Eastern Turkestan Freedom Organization, whose members are exiled Uighurs, took responsibility for the attack: *IHT*, 28 January 2000, p. 4.)

11 September 2001. There are terrorist attacks on New York and Washington.

In recent years there have been occasional acts of violence by Uighur nationalists ... President Jiang Zemin has now used these to assert that Taleban-linked terrorism and Moslem extremism are the problem in Xinjiang ... In fact the only evidence of links is a few Uighurs found to have been serving in the lowest ranks of the Taleban forces. It is not even clear whether or not these were Uighurs from adjacent states with Uighur minorities. The part of Afghanistan bordering China was never in Taleban hands. Militant Islam ... has never been a factor in Uighur nationalism, a phenomenon which long predates the establishment of the People's Republic and is based on language, land and history, of which religion is only a part. China's actual concern is with separatist tendencies in a strategically important region with huge mineral resources, particularly energy ... Oppression of religion has been stepped up. Young people are kept away from mosques and fasting during Ramadan has been banned.

(Philip Bowring, *IHT*, 30 November 2001, p. 8)

A foreign ministry spokesman said Beijing had proof that Uighur militants took part in 'terrorist activities' and had links with 'international terrorist groups or elements' ... Police in the Xinjiang capital, Urumqi, have launched a crackdown. Uighur activists said China was using terrorism as a pretext for attacks on ethnic separatists.

(*FEER*, 25 October 2001, p. 36)

Moslem separatists in western China had been trained and financed by Osama bin Laden as part of a 'holy war' to establish a religious state in the region, according to a long paper released yesterday [21 January 2002] by the Beijing government. The paper outlines in detail China's case for 'separatists' in the vast Xinjiang region to be classified as terrorists by the West ... President George W. Bush has said that China should not use the US-led war on terror as a pretext to suppress religious minorities. The USA has also said it has captured a number of Uighurs ... in Afghanistan recently, but has declined to say if they would be returned to China to face trial. China says in the paper it has arrested more than '100 terrorists' trained in Afghanistan to undertake a violent campaign to establish a state of 'East Turkestan' in Xinjiang ... The paper ... [says] that in the past decade 'East Turkestan' supporters have been responsible for more than 200 terrorist incidents and the deaths of 162 people.

(*FT*, 22 January 2002, p. 6)

26 August 2002. '[It was announced that] the United States had added the East Turkestan Islamic Movement to its list ... of terrorist organizations ... [China] has long campaigned to have Uighur separatists in its north-west frontier region branded as terrorists' (*FT*, 27 August 2002, p. 9).

'The US announcement came a day after China announced new rules to control the export of missile-related technologies' (*IHT*, 27 August 2002, p. 1). '[The Turkestan Islamic Movement is] a small separatist organization in western China' (*IHT*, 4 September 2002, p. 6).

The East Turkestan Islamic Movement [is] one of several, small militant groups seeking independence ... [The United States said it] had acted to freeze any financial assets ... because it [the Movement] had engaged in indiscriminate killing of civilians. In the last week the United States joined China in persuading the United Nations to add the group to its global watch list.

(*IHT*, 14 September 2002, p. 3)

'China hailed the UN placing a Uighur separatist group ... on a list of groups suspected of having links with the al-Qaeda terrorist organization' (*FEER*, 26 September 2002, p. 28).

'The Chinese ... succeeded in persuading the Bush administration to list an obscure Uighur Moslem separatist group in Xinjiang province as a terrorist organization with ties to al-Qaeda' (Zbigniew Brzezinski, *IHT*, 4 September 2002, p. 6).

15 December 2003.

China has issued its first list of terrorist groups, blaming them for a series of bombings and assassinations and calling for international assistance to eliminate them. The groups are accused of trying to create an independent Islamic state called East Turkestan in the Xinjiang region of north-west China, which is populated by the Turkish-speaking Uighur Moslems ... The groups identified were the Eastern Turkestan Islamic Movement, the Eastern Liberation Organization, the World Uighur Youth Congress and the East Turkestan Information Centre. China said the first two groups had received funding from Osama bin Laden to spread religious extremism and carry out terrorist activities. Some of the groups have established bases outside of China to train terrorists and plot sabotage, frequently sending agents into China to guide terrorists acts, according to a ministry statement.

(www.iht.com, 15 December 2003)

China issued its first formal list of terrorists on Monday [15 December], accusing four Moslem separatist groups and eleven individuals of committing violence and acts of terror ... [China is emulating] the list that the United States introduced after the 11 September attacks and has since updated. Critics have argued that China is using the pretence of war on terror to legitimize its harsh treatment of Moslem Uighur minorities that are seeking a separate state in China's western province of Xinjiang.

(*IHT*, 16 December 2003, p. 4)

(Xinjiang means 'New Territory'.)

('China's most wanted terrorist suspect has been ... "recently" [2 October] ... killed in a joint US and Pakistani military operation [near the Afghan border], according to the Chinese state media ... [He is] Hasan Mahsum, a leader of the East Turkestan Islamic Movement (Etim) from China's mainly Moslem north-western region of Xinjiang ... Earlier this month China put Mr Mahsum's name at the head of its list of eleven alleged terrorists ... In 2002 the United States designated Etim as a terrorist group after strong lobbying from Beijing': *FT*, 24 December 2003, p. 5.)

Erkin Alptekin ... [who is] the sixty-five-year-old leader of a new exile group dedicated to self-determination ... [expresses] strong support for non-violence. His group claims to represent the worldwide community of Uighurs, the Turkic-speaking, predominantly Moslem people of north-west China's Xinjiang province. Some 8.4 million Uighurs live in China; another estimated 600,000 live abroad, the greatest number of them in Central Asia, Saudi Arabia and Turkey. This year [2004] US officials disclosed that twenty-two Uighurs are among the nearly 600 prisoners held on suspicion of terrorism at the US detention centre at Guantanamo Bay, Cuba.

(*FEER*, 15 July 2004, pp. 30–1)

March 2004. 'China executed two Uighurs for the murder of a Bishkek-based Chinese diplomat. The two had been handed over by Kyrgyz authorities in July 2002, shortly after the incident' (*FEER*, 4 November 2004, p. 36).

September 2004.

A group of mostly ethnic Uighur exiles has announced the formation of a government-in-exile for north-west China's Xinjiang autonomous region. The announcement came at a September press conference ... in Washington ... The mainstream Uighur exile community has distanced itself from the effort and groups such as the Washington-based Uighur American Association and the Germany-based World Uighur Congress did not attend. The self-proclaimed prime minister of the new East Turkistan government-in-exile is Anwar Yusuf Turani, president of the East Turkestan National Freedom Centre, which describes itself as seeking 'to tell the world about East Turkestan and raise the cause of freedom and independence'. Uighur exiles refer to Xinjiang as East Turkestan. Turani is also the new government's foreign minister.

(*FEER*, 23 September 2004, p. 8)

17 March 2005.

China released its most prominent Moslem political prisoner on Thursday [17 March 2005] as an apparent goodwill gesture that comes days before the US secretary of state, Condoleezza Rice, is to arrive in Beijing on a state visit. The release of Rebiya Kadeer also came as the United States announced that it would not seek to censure Beijing at the current session of the United Nations Commission on Human Rights in Geneva, noting that China has made 'some improvements'. The gestures come as the two countries have still not officially resumed a dialogue on human rights that broke off last year [2004] ... Kadeer was released on a medical parole and was scheduled to arrive in the United States on Thursday ... She was sentenced to eight years in prison in March 2000 for 'illegally providing state intelligence abroad' ... Her crime was sending newspaper clippings about the treatment of Uighurs to her husband in the United States ... [She] is an advocate for women's rights and a business-woman who served on the top advisory board to China's parliament ... Chinese security officials targeted her because of the political activism of her husband, who lives in the United Sates and advocates greater freedoms for Uighurs.

(*IHT*, 18 March 2005, p. 5)

China, which suspended its human rights dialogue with the United States in protest at a resolution sponsored last year [2004], has successfully blocked dis-cussion of all eleven US-sponsored resolutions tabled in the past twelve years. No resolution was put forward in 2003.

(*FT*, 18 March 2005, p. 14)

12 April 2005.

China has stepped up a campaign of religious persecution against its minority Uighur population in the western region of Xinjiang even though the government has already eliminated any organized resistance to Beijing's rule there, two leading human rights groups said in a joint report that was being released Tuesday [12 April]. The US-based groups, Human Rights Watch and Human Rights in China, quoted secret Communist Party and government documents as detailing a range of new policies that tighten controls on religious worship, assembly and artistic expression among Xinjiang's 8 million Turkic speaking Moslems, including strict rules on teaching religion to minors ... The groups said China had used isolated terrorist acts to justify a wholesale crackdown on its Uighur Moslem population ... The Beijing government has promoted rapid economic development in both areas [Xinjiang and Tibet], while encouraging migration of Han Chinese ... to offset the influence of Tibetans and Uighurs in their home communities.

(www.iht.com, 12 April 2005)

The report's key words are these: 'systematic repression of religion continues in Xinjiang as a matter of considered state policy'. Beijing comprehensively denies this. But the reality is exposed by the publication here, for the first time, of secret state documents ... One such regulation, for example, stipulates that 'parents and legal guardians may not allow minors to participate in religious activities'. This ban, the report states, occurs nowhere else in China. Like numerous other regulations in Xinjiang it violates the International Covenant on Economic, Social and Cultural Rights, ratified by China in 2002, as well as the Convention on the Rights of the Child, ratified in 1991, both of which emphasize the rights of children to 'freedom of thought, conscience and religion'.

(Jonathan Mirsky, review of *Devastating Blows in China: Religious Repression of Uighurs in Xinjiang* by Human Rights in China and Human Rights Watch, *FEER*, May 2005, p. 64)

September 2005. 'Moslem separatists in Xinjiang have killed 160 people in a decade, state media admitted' (*Guardian*, 7 September 2005, p. 1).
December 2005.

China has a bottomless thirst for oil and gas, and Xinjiang these days is producing both in ever greater quantities. Moreover, because of its proximity to Central Asia the region has become the favourite route for pipelines bringing energy from Kazakhstan and beyond.

(*IHT*, 21 December 2005, p. 2)

Human rights

The leading dissident is Wei Jingshen, who first came to prominence in the prodemocracy or 'Democracy Wall' movement of 1978–9. He was arrested on 31 March 1979 and sentenced to fifteen years in prison for 'counter-revolutionary activity'. On his release on 14 September 1993 (part of the bid to host the next Olympic Games) he had about six months left to serve of his sentence. He was rearrested on 1 April 1994 (for meeting a US diplomat in February). He was supposed to have been paroled on 4 October 1994, but he disappeared after April 1994; officially he was under 'administrative detention' or 'residential surveillance'. On 21 November 1995 he was formally arrested. He was said to have 'conducted activities in an attempt to overthrow the government after his release on parole'. On 13 December 1995 he was sentenced to fourteen years in jail plus an additional three years' denial of political rights. On 24 October 1996 the European parliament awarded him the Andrei Sakharov human rights prize. After release from labour camp 'on parole for medical treatment' he flew to the USA on 16 November 1997. This occurred after the 26 October–3 November 1997 visit to the USA by Jiang Zemin. (Wei said that the authorities had told him that the only way he would be released on medical parole would be to seek treatment in the USA: *IHT*, 22 November 1997, p. 5.).

Two other well-known dissidents are Xu Wenli, who was released in May 1993 after serving twelve years of a fifteen-year prison sentence (police harassment continued), and Wang Juntao, who was released on 23 April 1994 and allowed to go the USA for medical treatment; he was sentenced to thirteen years in prison in 1991 for his role in Tiananmen.

The regime continually stresses the need for 'social stability' and is especially fearful of the dissident movement linking up with discontented workers and peasants at a time of post-Deng anticipation. China has a huge labour camp network (*laogai*: 'reform through labour'). Former camp inmate Harry Wu estimates 10 million prisoners, while the Chinese government admits to fewer than 1.5 million (*Guardian*, 19 May 1994, p. 27). Harry Wu (then Wu Hongda) was arrested in 1957 for criticizing the 1956 Soviet invasion of Hungary and was a labour camp inmate for nineteen years from 1960 to 1979. He later became famous for undercover reports of life in the camps and for his allegation that China, apart from exporting goods made by prisoners, runs a highly profitable trade in the organs of executed prisoners. After emigrating to the USA in 1985 he became a naturalized American. Harry Wu was detained on 19 June 1995 when crossing into China from Kazakhstan. He was later arrested and charged with spying. On 24 August 1995 he was expelled from China immediately after receiving a fifteen-year jail sentence. There are at least 3,000 political prisoners (*IHT*, 20 May 1994, p. 3). There are 1,700 people in jail for their political or religious beliefs (*IHT*, 4 May 1995, p. 7).

Even tougher regulations against those who threaten the 'social order' were issued on 12 May 1994. Eighteen new rules banned certain activities by unregistered social or religious groups, persons under official surveillance or persons deprived of their political rights.

On 13 July 1994 new laws dealing with internal dissent and espionage were published. Foreign institutions, organizations and foreigners in China were considered hostile if they financed, colluded with or engaged in subversive activities endangering state security. Subversive activities were defined as the organization of terrorist activities, the fabrication or distortion of facts or the spreading of views that endanger state security, and the use of religion to incite ethnic strife.

On 1 October 1994 three dissidents were sentenced to three-year terms of 're-education through labour'. They were Yang Zhou (released in July 1995 on health grounds), Bao Ge and Yang Qinheng. On 18 October Li Guotao received the same sentence.

On 6 November 1994 four dissidents (sentenced after Tiananmen) and four Tibetan dissidents were released from prison.

Nine dissidents were sentenced to prison terms ranging from three to twenty years on 16 December 1994.

On 22 December 1994 Dai Xuechong was jailed for three years, allegedly for tax evasion but in reality for being a member of the Association of Human Rights based in Shanghai. (He was the fourth member to be sentenced in the previous three months.)

A compensation law came into effect on 1 January 1995. Citizens who have been the victims of torture and other physical or mental violence are able to sue government officials.

On 5 January 1995 it was disclosed in the West that China had been operating a blacklist since May 1994. On the list were forty-nine dissidents living abroad, who were to be either banned from entering China or arrested on arrival at the border.

A Justice Ministry official has said that China does not classify its 2,679 'counter-revolutionaries' as political prisoners (*FEER*, 9 February 1995, p. 13).

On 31 March 1997 China said that none of the 2,026 prisoners convicted of counter-revolutionary offences were political prisoners. They had been convicted on the grounds that '[they have] endangered and sabotaged national security, they have conducted activities to overthrow the political power of China'.

By the government's own count about 2,000 people remain imprisoned for the crime of 'counter-revolution', a category eliminated in legal changes in 1997. While records are not public, human rights advocates believe that thousands more political, labour or religious dissidents are serving terms of up to three years without trial in 'education through labour' camps or have been sentenced to jail on trumped-up non-political charges such as 'hooliganism' or economic 'crimes' (*IHT*, 20 April 1998, p. 11). Official figures for the end of 1996 say that 2,026 were in prison for counter-revolutionary crimes (*IHT*, 29 April 1998, p. 1). Amnesty International estimates that there are around 2,000 in prison for political crimes. Around 230,000 people are believed to be held in labour camps (*IHT*, 29 June 1998, p. 4). Of the 2,000, 250 participated in the 1989 Tiananmen protests. Torture routinely occurs even though in 1987 China signed the international convention against torture and other cruel, inhuman or degrading treatment or punishment (*IHT*, 5 November 1998, p. 4).

> Nine years after it crushed the Tiananmen Square democracy movement, China's leadership seems ever so slightly to be loosening its stranglehold on political dissent ... Increased latitude [is being] tentatively allowed for people to campaign in China for limited democratic reforms. Since January [1998] a number of newspapers and journals have printed lively exchanges on subjects like expanding individual rights, extending village elections and shrinking the reach of the government and the Communist Party.
>
> (*New York Times*, editorial in *IHT*, 22 April 1998, p. 8)

A number of petitions were presented to the National People's Congress (which began on 5 March 1995), calling for greater democracy, an independent judiciary and an end to corruption. The petitions were not accepted.

On 8 March 1995 China survived by just one vote a UN Human Rights Commission's resolution (it was defeated by twenty-one to twenty, with twelve abstentions). Since Tiananmen (1989) attempts have been made by Western countries to pass a resolution condemning China's record on human rights, but until 1995 China had successfully ensured that a vote was not even held. (This time Russia supported the holding of the vote, but then voted against the resolution.) The draft resolution 'expressed concern at continuing reports of violations of human rights and fundamental freedoms in China . . . severe restrictions on the right of citizens to freedom of assembly, association, expression and religion, as well as to due legal process and a fair trial'. The resolution cited reports of torture and other accusations of violations, but it also praised China for improving the economic situation of many of its people and changing its legal system.

Forty-five eminent scientists and intellectuals issued a signed petition on 16 May 1995 pleading for the release of those imprisoned after Tiananmen and in general for those incarcerated for their beliefs.

In the run-up to the 4 June anniversary of Tiananmen, further petitions were submitted and more dissidents were detained (e.g. Wang Xizhe on 20 May 1995 and Wang Dan the following day).

An Amnesty International report said that political and religious repression in Tibet increased in 1993 and 1994 (*IHT*, 30 May 1995, p. 4).

> Economic development has generated enormous opportunities, everybody wants to do business there. It is also governed by a brutally repressive regime that violates basic human rights with contempt . . . Despite its phenomenal economic advance in recent years, the People's Republic of China remains a thoroughly repressive society . . . It is also the world's largest killer state: in 1994 China executed three times as many people as the rest of the world put together . . . Perhaps the most extraordinary thing is that amid China's vastness and diversity . . . no-one is safe. Repressive policies combine with the arbitrary and often illegal actions of local officials to produce continuing massive human rights violations . . . You don't even have to do anything. Just for knowing someone – friend or family – who wants political change or religious freedom, you can find yourself, without charge or trial, doing up to four years of 're-education through labour'. At any one time over 100,000 people are held in 're-education through labour' camps. Conditions are often harsh, with long hours of hard labour, poor food and ill-treatment for those who 'resist reform' . . . This is the reality of China today: human rights abuses are still a daily reality and it really can happen to anyone.
>
> (*Amnesty*, Spring 1996, issue 78, p. 4)

> Locked inside more than 300 prisons in this . . . vast penal system . . . are an estimated 300,000 prostitutes, drug users, petty criminals and political prisoners who have been stripped on their legal rights . . . [without] having a lawyer or a trial – rights granted under China's criminal law . . . This system is known

as reform through labour reeducation ... [which means that police can sweep up] people without the complications of court trials ... Sentences can now reach a maximum of four years ... China's labour reeducation camps opened in 1957 ... Specialists say political prisoners constitute 5 per cent to 10 per cent of the total labour reeducation inmate population, while as many as 40 per cent of inmates are drug offenders.

(Jim Yardley, www.iht.com, 9 May 2005; *IHT*, 10 May 2005, p. 2)

'[The] labour reeducation camps allow for imprisonment without trial' (www.iht.com, 11 May 2005).

'China signed the UN Convention on Civil and Political Rights in 1998 but has so far failed to ratify it' (www.iht.com, 21 April 2005).

'Courts can impose the death penalty for almost seventy offences, many of them non-violent' (*IHT*, 15 August 2005, p. 4).

China executes more people each year than all countries combined, according to international human rights groups. They estimate that as many as 15,000 people annually are put to death. China says the number is smaller, but has said it is considering reducing the number of capital offences.

(www.iht.com, 29 August 2005)

A chronology of later developments in human rights

October 1993. China cracked down on satellite television dishes and other forms of telecommunications such as portable telephones (which needed to be registered). But there seems to be significant flouting of the regulations.

13 July 1994. New laws dealing with internal dissent and espionage are published. Foreign institutions, organizations and foreigners in China are considered hostile if they finance, collude with or engage in subversive activities endangering state security. Subversive activities are defined as the organization of terrorist activities, the fabrication or distortion of facts or the spreading of views that endanger state security, and the use of religion to incite ethnic strife.

4–15 September 1995. The Fourth World Conference on Women takes place in Beijing. The Non-governmental Organizations Forum started on 30 August and finished on 8 September. It took place in Huairou, some 50 km from Beijing. (The holding of the world conference in China was controversial and there were protests about restrictions imposed by China on participation and about harassment and excessive surveillance by security officials.)

29 November 1995. The government approves an alternative Panchen Lama to the one approved by the Dalai Lama.

16 January 1996. The State Council orders foreign economic news agencies (e.g. Reuters) to submit to control by the official Chinese press agency (Xinhua or New China) in order 'to safeguard the nation's sovereignty, protect the legal rights and interests of domestic users of economic information and promote the healthy development of our country's economic information industry.' 'Approved foreign economic information providers will be punished ... if their information to Chinese users contains anything forbidden by Chinese laws and regulations, or slanders or jeopardizes the national interests of China.' Economic information agencies owned by foreigners have to register within three months with Xinhua (which will charge a fee and set subscription rates) and will not be allowed to provide information directly to Chinese customers (*IHT*, 17 January 1996, p. 1; *FT*, 17 January 1996, p. 3).

1 March 1996. President Jiang Zemin signs a law making it easier to impose martial law in the event of serious threats to national unity, social chaos or riots. (While the Standing Committee was authorized to impose martial law in provinces or regions, the State Council and premier can do so on their own in 'subregions', precisely as in Beijing in 1989: Matt Forney, *FEER*, 14 March 1996, p. 15.)

17 March 1996. A major reform of the criminal justice system is approved. Defendants are to be assumed innocent until proven guilty (previously courts were usually seen as merely confirming guilt rather than reviewing the evidence). Suspects are to be able to consult a lawyer after being interrogated by the police and are to be held for a maximum thirty days before the police apply for an arrest warrant. But the right of administrative departments to jail suspects without trial is confirmed and the police can continue to keep the detention of a suspect secret from family and to restrict suspects' right to remain silent (*IHT*, 18 March 1996, p. 4).

27 April 1996. Liu Gang flees China. (He arrived in the USA on 30 April. He had been jailed for six years for his role in Tiananmen and was constantly under surveillance and subject to harassment even after his release.)

14 May 1996. It is reported that Fu Shenqui has been released (*IHT*, 15 May 1996, p. 4).

9 June 1996. Ren Wanding is released. (He was first detained in 1979 and imprisoned for four years. He was arrested on 9 June 1989 and imprisoned for seven years.)

2 August 1996. Chen Longde (arrested on 27 May) is sentenced to three years in a labour camp for petitioning the National People's Congress to release all political prisoners. (He spent three years in prison for his role in Tiananmen.)

8 October 1996. Liu Xiaobo is detained and ordered (by 'administrative' procedures, i.e. without trial) to serve three years in a labour camp ('reeducation through labour').

13 October 1996. It is revealed that Wang Xizhe has escaped to Hong Kong. (He arrived in the USA on 15 October.)

30 October 1996. Wang Dan is sentenced to eleven years in prison for 'conspiring to subvert China's government'.

6 November 1996. Chen Ziming is released from prison on medical parole. He has cancer.

29 January 1997. The *IHT* (29 January 1997, p. 1) summarizes the US government's annual report on human rights. By the end of 1996 there were no active dissidents left in China who had not been imprisoned or exiled. 'No dissidents were known to be active at year's end.'

15 April 1997. The fifty-three member UN Human Rights Commission approves a China-sponsored 'no-action motion' on its human rights record by twenty-seven votes to seventeen with nine abstentions. (This was preceded by a split in the EU's attitude to a motion condemning China.)

30 May 1997. For the first time a court reduces the sentences of (four) dissidents on the grounds that it had not been proven that they had tried to overthrow the government during the Tiananmen demonstrations of 1989 (*IHT*, 31 May 1997, pp. 1, 6).

4 June 1997. Bao Ge is released from a labour camp. (He was sentenced in September 1994. He left for the USA on 5 November 1997.)

21 October 1997. It is announced that for the first time UN human rights experts have had private interviews with prisoners, including political ones (*IHT*, 22 October 1997, p. 4).

8 December 1997. Wei Jingsheng meets President Clinton.

26–27 January 1998. Four poets are detained. They are accused of planning to publish an independent literary journal and of plotting to overthrow the government.

30 January 1998. The US State Department, in its annual report, concludes that China took a 'somewhat more tolerant' attitude towards dissent in 1997 but that serious human rights problems remain. 'The government exhibited some limited tolerance of public expressions of opposition to government policies and calls for political reform.' The previous report asserted that by the end of 1996 'all public dissent against the party and the government was effectively silenced' (*IHT*, 31 January 1998, p. 5).

6 February 1998. Wang Bingzhang, now resident in the USA, is captured after entering China illegally in order to set up a new party. He was sent back to the USA on 9 February.

7 February 1998. Gao Feng (a Christian activist) is released.

8–26 February 1998. Three religious leaders from the USA visit China (including Tibet).

15 March 1998. The USA announces that it will not sponsor the annual (since 1990) resolution before the UN Human Rights Commission condemning China's record. (The EU has already decided not to do so in order to avoid open splits between EU members.)

18 April 1998. Wang Dan, the last of the internationally well-known dissidents, is released from prison on 'medical parole' and flown to the USA the following day. (On 30 October 1996 Wang Dan was sentenced to eleven years in prison for 'conspiring to subvert China's government'.)

> A steady flow of arrests did not make the front pages around America or even mention in most newspapers ... There is a danger, as China bargains with its dissidents one by one, of losing sight of the thousands who remain in jail or labour camps, and of those added to the prison population week after week.
>
> (*Washington Post*, editorial in *IHT*, 22 April 1998, p. 8)

25 June 1998. Three political dissidents openly apply to register an opposition party (*IHT*, 26 June 1998, p. 4). (On 10 July nine dissidents who tried to register the Chinese Democratic Party were detained: *IHT*, 13 July 1998, p. 4. Three were released. On 16 July 1998 seventy-nine dissidents signed an open letter calling for the release of the five detainees: *IHT*, 16 July 1998, p. 1.)

6–14 September 1998. The visit of Mary Robinson, UN High Commissioner for

Human Rights. This is the first visit by a UN high commissioner for human rights to communist China.

5 October 1998. China signs the International Covenant on Civil and Political Rights. The treaty was adopted by the United Nations General Assembly in 1966 and went into force a decade later. Since then 140 countries have ratified or acceded to it. The treaty states that all people have the right of self-determination. It prohibits torture, cruel or degrading punishment and provides for freedom of movement, thought, religion and expression, among other things. States that have signed on to the treaty are required to submit an initial report within one year of ratification and periodic reports every five years thereafter. China has now to ratify the treaty. China has already signed the International Covenant on Economic, Social and Cultural Rights but has still not ratified it (*IHT*, 6 October 1998, p. 6).

20–21 October 1998. The first international conference on human rights is held in China (*IHT*, 21 October 1998, p. 4).

10 November 1998. The Dalai Lama meets President Clinton in the USA.

30 November 1998. Five members of the China Democratic Party are arrested, including Xu Wenli and Qin Yongmin. Attempts formally to register the party seem to lie behind the arrests (*IHT*, 2 December 1998, pp. 1, 4).

20 December 1998. Liu Nianchun is released on medical parole (six months before the end of his sentence) and sent to the USA.

21 December 1998.

> Chinese courts on Monday [21 December] sentenced two leading dissidents to lengthy prison terms for attempting to start the country's first opposition party. In meting out sentences of thirteen years to Xu Wenli and eleven years to Wang Youcai for attempting to 'overthrow state power', the communist government issued a sharp reminder to China's 1.3 billion people that it would not tolerate organized dissent. Last week President Jiang Zemin vowed to 'nip' such subversion 'in the bud'. A third dissident [Qin Yongmin] was expected to be sentenced Tuesday [22 December] ... The verdict ... marked the climax of the most widespread crackdown on dissent in China since 1996 ... Next year China will commemorate three important anniversaries – the tenth anniversary of the crackdown around Tiananmen Square, the fiftieth anniversary of communist China's founding and the eightieth anniversary of the 4 May Movement, which established the tradition of Chinese student activism. Chinese set great stock in anniversary celebrations and the Communist Party is known to be afraid that activists will use the anniversaries as an excuse to start protests ... Starting in June the three activists teamed up with dozens of others to push the idea of founding an opposition party – the China Democracy Party. Activists attempted to register the party in fourteen provinces and cities. Mr Wang was the first to attempt to register the party, doing so in Hangzhou on the day that President Bill Clinton arrived in China in June for a summit with Mr Jiang.
>
> (John Pomfret, *IHT*, 22 December 1998, pp. 1, 4)

The official Xinhua news agency quoted court verdicts as saying that Xu and Wang had accepted money from 'foreign hostile organizations'. The Beijing verdict on Xu Wenli said:

Attempting to overthrow the state, Xu in November secretly planned the formation of the Beijing and Tianjin cells of the so-called Chinese Democratic Party. To organize, plan and implement the overthrow of state power. Xu also accepted financial assistance from foreign hostile organizations.

(*The Times*, 22 December 1998, p. 12)

22 December 1998. Qin Yongmin is sentenced to twelve years in prison.

Experience suggests that activists will soon find new ways to challenge the system. As recently as January 1997, after long prison sentences had been given to the prominent dissidents Wei Jingsheng and Wang Dan, the US state department said in a report that no active dissidents remained in the country. For most of 1997 it seemed that way, but towards the end of the year ... activists sensed a slight easing of controls and began to speak out again. People like Mr Xu, fifty-five, and Mr Qin, forty-four – both of whom had previously served long prison terms – began faxing statements to colleagues and the foreign press. Then this year, as President Bill Clinton visited China in June, Wang Youcai founded the Democracy Party. Almost overnight hundreds of people appeared who seemed willing to risk everything for the cause.

(Erik Eckholm, *IHT*, 24 December 1998, p. 4)

On 25 June [1998] ... Mr Clinton arrived in China. On that day Wang Youcai, thirty-two, a student leader during the Tiananmen Square protests, tried to register the China Democracy Party in the eastern city of Hangzhou ... The success of the China Democracy Party surprised everyone ... Within a few months preparatory committees had been established in twenty-three of China's thirty-one provinces and major cities. Applications to register the party were made in fourteen provinces and big cities. Hundreds of people were involved in the effort.

(John Pomfret, *IHT*, 4 January 1998, p. 7)

The dissidents ignored warnings from the authorities.

23 December 1998.

China appeared to move another step closer to full-scale political restrictions Wednesday [23 December] when its state-run press published tough new rules threatening film directors, singers and computer software developers with life in prison if they attempted to 'overthrow state power' or 'endanger national security'. President Jiang Zemin, meanwhile, in his second hardline speech in six days, told a gathering of security officials that their task next year was to ensure China's stability. Mr Jiang's speech ... was a clear signal that the sentencing of three dissidents to lengthy prison sentences was part of a broader pattern to suppress organized dissent and bolster the Communist Party's dictatorship in the coming year. Under the guidelines artists, film directors, singers, producers and computer software programmers could face stiff jail sentences if they 'endangered social order' – in other words did anything to challenge Communist Party rule. They could also be jailed if they encouraged independence movements in Tibet, the north-western province of Xinjiang or on the island of Taiwan.

(John Pomfret, *IHT*, 24 December 1998, p. 1)

A big unknown for the dissident movement is the extent to which younger people may become involved. Virtually all those who became declared members of the Democracy Party were veterans of either the Democracy Wall movement of the late 1970s or the student-led demonstrations in 1989 ... This could change in the event of prolonged economic hardship or other social traumas, which helps explain why President Jiang Zemin in a speech last week, said China must 'fight against factors disrupting social stability and nip them in the bud'. Chinese scholars say the government is especially sensitive about dissident political activities now because of growing unemployment and frequent protests by unpaid workers. The party's ultimate nightmare is a joining of democracy and labour movements against it. Any threat to the supremacy of the Communist Party is, by definition, a threat to national security. This gave officials a neat way to explain why the latest trials did not violate the International Covenant on Civil and Political Rights, which China has signed but not ratified.

(p. 4)

27 December 1998. Labour activist Zhang Shanguang is sentenced to ten years in prison for 'illegally providing intelligence to overseas enemy organizations and people'. He was interviewed by Radio Free Asia (which is funded by the US Congress) about protests by farmers.

11–12 January 1999. 'China and the United States resumed dialogue on human rights Monday [11 January] after a hiatus of more than four years ... Diplomats agreed to the resumption of human rights talks when President Bill Clinton visited China in June [1998]' (*IHT*, 12 January 1999, p. 8). 'US and Chinese officials held their first meeting exclusively devoted to human rights since 1995' (*IHT*, 13 January 1999, p. 4). The two sides agreed to meet again.

20 January 1999. Lin Hai, a computer engineer who owns a software company in Shanghai, is sentenced to two years in prison in China's first internet case. He was accused of supplying VIP Reference (an electronic publication based in the USA) with 30,000 e-mail addresses. Prosecutors argued that the e-mail addresses were used by VIP Reference to distribute in China 'articles aimed at inciting subversion of state power and the socialist system' (*IHT*, 21 January 1999, p. 1).

15 February 1999. The journalist Guo Yu is released early (1 October 1999 being the original date). She was arrested in 1993 and sentenced to six years in jail the following year for 'revealing state secrets'.

23 April 1999. Members of the United Nations Human Rights Commission votes twenty-two to seventeen (with fourteen abstentions) in favour of a Chinese proposal to take no action on the US motion expressing concern at 'continuing reports of violations of human rights and fundamental freedoms in China ... [and] increased restrictions on the exercise of cultural, religious and other freedoms of Tibetans' (*IHT*, 24 April 1999, p. 1). The US resolution was backed by Poland. China has defeated every resolution against it in the commission since 1990, the session that followed Tiananmen. In 1998 the US and the EU decided not to sponsor a resolution (*FT*, 24 April 1999, p. 4).

25 April 1999.

More than 10,000 Chinese followers of a cult-like figure who lives in the USA massed Sunday [25 April] on the streets surrounding the headquarters of the Communist Party in the largest and strangest protest since the student-led demonstrations rocked Beijing in 1989 ... The protesters were demanding action by the Chinese government against a Chinese magazine that last week published an article critical of the cult called Falun Gong [whose Chinese leader moved to the USA in 1998] ... They also said they wanted the government to recognize the sect officially, granting it legal status ... The protest in Beijing was ... a continuation of demonstrations that began last week in the coastal metropolis of Tianjin.

(*IHT*, 26 April, 1999, pp. 1, 6)

'The [sit-down] protesters ... maintained an eerie vigil around the leadership compound in Beijing' (*IHT*, 3 May 1999, p. 3). 'The protest [was] sparked by the arrest of sect leaders' (*IHT*, 7 June 1999, p. 3).

'Falun Gong ... was set up in 1992 by Li Hongzhi ... who [now] lives in New York' (*Independent*, 27 July 1999, p. 16).

That the Communist Party is losing touch with the masses is an open worry to leaders here. The latest shock to the system came last week with the sudden demonstration by the spiritual cult called Buddhist Law, a movement claiming tens of millions of Chinese members. So what is the party chief, Jiang Zemin, doing to create a more relevant Communist Party for the twenty-first century? ... Mr Jiang's top aides have been busy mounting an old-fashioned 'rectification' campaign to promote ideological conformity among the millions of cadres who purportedly run the country, to invigorate the party ... The 'three stresses' campaign, as it is known, is being waged in party offices, government agencies and the army. The senior ranks at universities, research centres and publishing houses are next. Under the command to 'stress study, stress politics and stress rectitude', officials are required to read specially prepared textbooks, including works by Mao Zedong, Deng Xiaoping and, of course, Mr Jiang.

(Erik Eckholm, *IHT*, 3 May 1999, p. 1)

'Falun Gong is a movement that practises a combination of bits of Buddhist and Daoist [Taoist] principles expressed through breathing exercises' (*FEER*, 19 August 1999, p. 34). 'Falun Gong is an exercise and meditation movement' (p. 17).

Falun means the Wheel of Law, which the sect says revolves constantly within practitioners, drawing in good powers and expelling evil forces (*Telegraph*, 29 December 1999, p. 19). Falun Gong means Way of the Law of the Wheel.

2 May 1999. 'Chinese police have detained at least twenty political activists to stop them from planning commemorations of the tenth anniversary of the Tiananmen Square demonstrations, a rights group said Sunday [2 May]' (*FT*, 3 May 1999, p. 3).

4 June 1999. The tenth anniversary of Tiananmen goes off without major incident, although the event is commemorated in Hong Kong. Dissidents were detained in the run-up to the anniversary and months ago Tiananmen Square was walled off for renovations.

In the USA recently declassified documents estimate that 2,600 people died and 7,000 were injured during Tiananmen (*FEER*, 17 June 1999, p. 16).
19 July 1999.

> Police detained at least seventy leaders of Falun Gong, or Buddhist law, in Beijing, Tianjin, Dalian and other cities on Monday night [19 July] ... [In the April demonstration in Beijing] the group was demanding official recognition, which has not been granted ... [Falun Gong has] as many as 70 million adherents.
>
> (*IHT*, 21 July 1999, p. 4)

20 July 1999.

> On Tuesday [20 July] policemen in fourteen cities rounded up more than 100 leaders of ... Falun Gong ... Protests erupted in Beijing and other Chinese cities on Wednesday [21 July] as thousands of followers of the spiritual movement vented their anger ... Falun Gong claims to have 100 million members.
>
> (*IHT*, 22 July 1999, p. 1)

22 July 1999. Falun Gong is formally banned.

> Announcing the ban the ministry of civil affairs said the group had been 'engaging in illegal activities, advocating superstition and spreading fallacies, hoodwinking people ... and jeopardizing social stability' ... A Chinese official said there were about 2 million Falun Gong followers in China, but the group claims it has tens of millions of practitioners.
>
> (*FT*, 23 July 1999, p. 4)

'Falun claims 100 million followers worldwide and says it has 70 million in China' (*FT*, 26 July 1999, p. 14).

'The ministry of civil affairs accused Falun Gong of "inciting and creating disturbances and jeopardizing social stability" ... The government ... estimates [that the group] has 2 million members – far fewer than the 100 million the group claims' (*IHT*, 23 July 1999, pp. 1, 3).

23 July 1999.

> Police rounded up about 200 members of the Falun Gong religious movement yesterday [23 July] after they gathered in Tiananmen Square ... to protest peacefully against the banning of their group ... Falun Gong claims more than 100 million followers worldwide, mostly in China. Beijing says there are 2 million within China.
>
> (*FT*, 24 July 1999, p. 2)

> Security forces detained more than 200 defiant followers of the sect as they staged a sit-in protest on Tiananmen Square ... Thousands of practitioners have been detained in the past two days all over China ... The massive [anti Falun Gong] campaign started by the Chinese Communist Party has involved showing a documentary to each of China's 2.5 million soldiers, special classes for all 60 million Communist Party members and struggle sessions in fifteen major government bodies, involving millions of people.
>
> (*IHT*, 24 July 1999, p. 1)

29 July 1999. An arrest warrant is issued for Li Hongzhi, the New York-based leader of Falun Gong.

30 July 1999.

> Chinese authorities revealed Friday that a retired senior army officer, the highest-ranking leader of the spiritual movement that was banned last week, had confessed his 'mistakes' and renounced his allegiance to the movement ... The general ... has been identified as Falun Gong's top officer in Beijing and the article he wrote two months ago, which was circulated among senior military officers, was a critical item in Beijing's decision to mount such a wide-ranging political campaign against the movement. The Communist Party has mobilized its vast apparatus to demand that government offices and workplaces all over the nation purge Falun Gong members.
>
> (*IHT*, 31 July 1999, p. 1)

> What was apparently most shocking to China's leaders was the discovery that some senior officers in the People's Liberation Army and minister-level government officials not only believed in the mystical healing and all-seeing powers of Falun Gong, but also were openly urging their colleagues to take it up ... In addition to arresting more than 5,000 people, the authorities detained more than 1,200 government officials who are members of Falun Gong for reeducation sessions.
>
> (*IHT*, 30 July 1999, p. 4)

(Falun Gong members have been found in the Communist Party as well as the army. 'Falun Gong, the exercise and meditation movement that staged a daring 25 April sit-in of more than 10,000 people – a surprising number of them party members – outside the compound in Beijing where the Communist Party leaders live and work ... In a relentless propaganda campaign the party has been using that incident, and subsequent revelations about party members' extensive participation in a nationwide Falun Gong network, to drive home the need to instil discipline': *FEER*, 19 August 1999, p. 17.)

2 August 1999.

> China sentenced two leaders of its first opposition party to lengthy prison terms Monday [2 August] ... [A court] sentenced Zha Jianguo to nine years in prison and Gao Hongmin to eight years in prison on charges of subverting state power... Dissidents founded the China Democracy Party in June of last year [1998].
>
> (*IHT*, 3 August 1999, p. 5)

7 August 1999. Liu Xianbin, a grassroots organizer of the banned China Democracy Party, is sentenced to thirteen years in prison for 'subverting state power'. His sentencing followed that of three other party organizers this week (*IHT*, Saturday 7 August 1999, p. 6).

25–30 October 1999. Falun Gong members quietly demonstrating are removed from Tiananmen Square. (Members of Falun Gong held a secretive press conference with foreign journalists on 28 October.)

On 25 October, while on a visit to France, Jiang Zemin called Falun Gong 'an evil cult threatening the Chinese people and society' (*Guardian*, 30 October 1999, p. 23).

'In the official press this week Falun Gong was labelled a cult ... Cults are illegal' (*IHT*, Friday 29 October 1999, p. 4). 'Last Thursday [28 October] ... the party's newspaper, *People's Daily* ... argued that Falun Gong was an "evil cult"' (*IHT*, 5 November 1999, p. 4).

'For the first time China has branded Falun Gong a cult' (*Independent*, 29 October 1999, p. 17).

30 October 1999.

> A new law, passed by the National People's Congress (parliament) on Saturday [30 October] called for the authorities to be 'on full alert for cult activities and smash them rigorously in accordance with the law'. It said that cult organizers, if found guilty, could be sentenced to jail terms of three to seven years. Serious offences, including recruiting, would receive a minimum of seven years.
>
> (*FT*, 1 November 1999, p. 12)

The new law includes the following: 'Heretic cults, operating under the guise of religion, qigong and other illicit forms, which disturbs social order and jeopardize people's life and property, must be banned according to law and punished resolutely' (*Guardian*, 20 January 2000, p. 21). (Qui means life force: *FEER*, 27 January 2000, p. 28.)

(The authorities have charged four principal members of the Falun Gong spiritual sect with violating secrecy laws and 'organizing a cult to undermine implementation of laws'. The four could face the death sentence under the new anti-cult law: *FEER*, 11 November 1999, p. 16.)

31 October 1999.

> China on Sunday [31 October] announced for the first time that it had charged four 'principal key members' of the Falun Gong sect ... The four ... were charged with 'organizing a cult to undermine the implementation of laws' ... [Three] were also charged with violating China's vague state secrets law, a measure also used against political dissidents ... [Two] were charged with running illegal businesses ... The indictments Sunday came as Falun Gong practitioners ... took a day off from protesting the government's ban and the impending legislation ... On Sunday the government-run media cranked up the campaign against the sect again, arguing in a broadcast by the Beijing television station that 'if Falun Gong had been allowed to continue, all economic reforms would have been stopped'.
>
> (*IHT*, 1 November 1999, p. 6)

> [There is the argument] that Falun Gong represents a deep-seated opposition among many of China's dispossessed, who over the last few years have not benefited from economic reforms ... [There is also the argument that Falun Gong] has provided a convenient way to express opposition to the direction the party is taking – towards patronage, corruption and sleaze.
>
> (*IHT*, 30 October 1999, p. 7)

9 November 1999. Four founders of the China Democracy Party are found guilty of 'subverting state power' and given prison sentences of up to eleven years.

12 November 1999. Four Falun Gong members are given prison sentences ranging from two to twelve years.

26 December 1999. Four leading members of the Falun Gong movement (three men and one woman) are sentenced to long terms in prison.

> [Two men] were sentenced to eighteen years [a deputy director in the computer bureau of the national police ministry] and sixteen years [an engineer in the railways ministry], among the harshest sentences China has given to political or religious dissenters this decade ... Chinese leaders ... ordered the legislature to revise a law against cults to allow for harsher penalties against organizers.
>
> (*IHT*, 27 December 1999, pp. 1, 4)

The other two were sentenced to twelve and seven years in prison. All four were party members and held good jobs in government and state business. They were found guilty of organizing a cult to undermine the implementation of laws, organizing protests (including the one on 25 April 1999), illegally obtaining and disseminating state secrets, and of causing deaths. It was alleged that the deaths were caused by advice given to members to forego medical treatment and to rely instead on spiritual techniques to heal themselves. It was alleged that this advice had led to the deaths of more than 1,400 people.

The trial was followed by brief and peaceful demonstrations by Falun Gong members who were arrested or moved on.

3 January 2000. It is reported that two leading figures in the China Democracy Party have been sentenced to prison terms of ten and six years for allegedly attempting to subvert state authority. On 30 December 1999 a member of the Falun Gong movement was sentenced to four years in prison (*IHT*, 4 January 2000, p. 5).

6 January 2000. Two Falun Gong members are sentenced to eight and six years in prison respectively.

11 January 2000. The USA, citing a stepped-up crackdown on political dissent and religious freedoms in China, says it will seek a resolution in the UN Human Rights Commission criticizing China's human rights record (*IHT*, 12 January 2000, p. 6).

14 January 2000. It is reported that a retired air force general has been imprisoned for seventeen years for links with Falun Gong.

16 January 2000. China announces that a two-year-old boy has been chosen as Tibet's seventh Reting Lama.

31 January 2000. 'China has secretly ordered the suppression of a second popular qigong mystic healing group ... Zhong Gong, which was founded in 1988 and claims more than 10 million members ... The founder of the group is in hiding' (*Telegraph*, 1 February 2000, p. 22).

1 February 2000. Amnesty International, citing official Chinese press reports, says that 1,769 people were executed in 1998, more than the rest of the world combined. But Amnesty International says that the real figure was higher because many executions went unrecorded. Many of the executions were carried out during nationwide 'strike hard' crackdowns on crime begun in 1996. China executes people for non-violent crimes, such as tax fraud and embezzlement (*IHT*, 2 February 2000, p. 5). In 1996 the figures was 4,367 (*Independent*, 3 February 2000, p.14).

25 February 2000. The US State Department releases its annual report on human rights. The section on China includes the following:

> The government's poor human rights record deteriorated markedly throughout the year, as the government intensified efforts to suppress dissent, particularly organized dissent ... The government continued to commit widespread and well-documented human rights abuses in violation of internationally accepted norms. These abuses stem from the authorities extremely limited tolerance of public dissent aimed at the government, fear of unrest, and the limited scope or inadequate implementation of laws protecting basic freedoms.
>
> (*IHT*, 26 February 2000, p. 1)

2 March 2000. Mary Robinson (UN high commissioner for human rights): 'I am concerned about three areas that I have expressed my worries about: the areas of freedom of expression, freedom of religion and freedom of association. My major concern is that there does seem to have been a deterioration' (*IHT*, 3 March 2000, p. 1).

18 April 2000. The fifty-three-member United Nations Human Rights Commission accepts by twenty-two votes to eighteen (with twelve abstentions) a 'no-action' motion put forward by China in response to USA resolution to censure China for its record on human rights.

> China once again evaded any international censure of its human rights record on Tuesday [18 April] when it won a procedural manoeuvre to block debate ... China ... has used a procedural manoeuvre to avoid full-fledged examination of its human rights practices. This has worked all but one year since resolutions began to be lodged at the commission following the 1989 killings of protestors near Tiananmen Square. If a no-action motion passes, there is no further discussion of a country's record. In 1995 the effort passed the first hurdle, but the commission members then voted against rebuking the country.
>
> (*IHT*, 19 April 2000, p. 4)

20 April 2000.

> On Thursday [20 April] the official Xinhua press agency made the stunning admission that the protests have been nearly continuous and sometimes very large. 'Since 22 July 1999 Falun Gong members have been causing trouble on and around Tiananmen Square in central Beijing nearly every day,' Xinhua quoted a high-level official as saying.
>
> (*IHT*, 21 April 2000, p. 1)

25 April 2000.

> The Chinese police detained more than 100 members of the banned Falun Gong movement Tuesday [25 April] in Tiananmen Square. The defiant devotees of the movement had come to commemorate the first anniversary of

the huge [1999] demonstration ... Such Falun Gong protests have become nearly daily events at Tiananmen ... But on Tuesday there were more than the usual number of protesters – and law enforcement officials – because of the anniversary ... Although the scattered actions Tuesday on Tiananmen were meagre in comparison to last year's protest, they vividly underline the government's difficulty in controlling Falun Gong.

(*IHT*, 26 April 2000, p. 5)

10 June 2000.

A follower of the banned Falun Gong spiritual movement died ... less than two weeks after his release from detention ... by police in a mental hospital. According to his father, he had been forcibly injected with medication. Twenty-two Falun Gong supporters have died in custody, a Hong Kong-based human rights group reported.

(*FEER*, 29 June 2000, p. 12)

'Some twenty-two Falun Gong believers have lost their lives, according to the Hong Kong-based Information Centre for Human Rights and Democracy' (*IHT*, 24 June 2000, p. 8).

'Two Falun Gong members died in custody this month [July 2000}, bringing to twenty-four the number of such deaths since China banned the sect last year [1999]' (*The Times*, 20 July 2000, p. 15).

7 July 2000. China withdraws its application for a $40 million loan from the World Bank to help finance a controversial plan to resettle nearly 57,000 farmers in what is now China's Qinghai province, land traditionally occupied by ethnic Tibetans. The World Bank approved the loan in 1999 but criticism led to an internal report which was itself critical of the World Bank for violating some of its own guidelines. The president of the World Bank, James Wolfensohn, proposed delaying the project for at least a year to allow for a deeper environmental review. But China says it will finance the entire project itself (*FT*, 8 July 2000, p. 1). (There were also serious ecological concerns about the project, such as the effects of a rapid increase in population and the need for irrigation schemes. Ethnic Mongolians also traditionally inhabited the area.)

Because China's *per capita* income has risen so rapidly, the Qinghai project was the last anti-poverty effort in China eligible for the World Bank's most subsidized loans (*IHT*, 8 July 2000, p. 3).

22 July 2000. The first anniversary of the banning of Falun Gong.

The Chinese police arrested more suspected members of the outlawed Falun Gong spiritual movement Friday [21 July] as they tried to protest in a packed Tiananmen Square ahead of the first anniversary of Beijing's ban on the group ... Defiant members of the Falun Group have staged almost daily protests in Tiananmen Square ... Human rights groups have documented the deaths of twenty-four Falun Gong members in police custody in the last year.

(*IHT*, 22 July 2000, p. 5)

'Chinese police detained about 200 practitioners of Falun Gong who began a series of small protests in Tiananmen Square on Saturday [22 July] to mark the first anniversary of the government decree outlawing the group' (*IHT*, 24 July 2000, p. 5).

> In several parts of China practitioners of Falun Gong's breathing and spiritual exercises say their campaign of civil disobedience, unprecedented in the history of communist China, is yielding results. In Weifang, a medium-sized city in central Shandong province, adherents say they can now practice their faith at home. The public practice of Falun Gong still means jail time and an almost guaranteed beating. Other Chinese regions continue to enforce the ban with apparent brutality ... At least twenty-six practitioners are believed to have died in police custody and an estimated 3,000 people have been sent to labour camps. Chinese law allows the police to dispatch people for three years of 'thought reform through labour' without using the courts. And the courts, controlled by the Communist Party, have sentenced dozens more to jail terms of ten years or more. But Falun Gong practitioners continue to protest in Tiananmen Square, in the centre of Beijing, and they continue to arrive with petitions at the offices of the State Council, China's cabinet, just a few blocks away.
>
> (*IHT*, 24 August 2000, p. 4)

9 August 2000. Liu Wensheng, a student leader during the 1989 democracy protests, is released twenty months before completing a ten-year sentence handed down in 1992 for setting up the underground Social Democratic Party (*IHT*, 16 August 2000, p. 5).

5 September 2000.

> The US government accused China on Tuesday [5 September] of trying to stem a surge in religious activity by harassing, detaining and physically abusing believers. The criticism of Beijing's treatment of Tibetan Buddhists, Falun Gong spiritual practitioners and members of unregistered groups came in the second annual report on religious freedom written by the state department by order of Congress ... The report cited a crackdown on Falun Gong – including thousands of detentions and what it called credible estimates that at least twenty-four practitioners had died in custody.
>
> (*IHT*, 6 September 2000, p. 5)

1 October 2000. What were typically estimated as 'hundreds' of Falun Gong protestors succeeded in disrupting the National Day celebrations and even forced the temporary closure of most of Tiananmen Square. There were violent clashes with the police and mass arrests.

10 October 2000.

> A commentary printed in most of the main media [said of Falun Gong members] ... 'They have completely transformed themselves into an out and out reactionary political force. Its aim is to overturn the People's Republic of China and to subvert the socialist system.'
>
> (*FT*, 11 October 2000, p. 10)

> A commentary on the front page of ... the *People's Daily* ... added that the Falun Gong ... was in league with anti-China forces ranging from separatists

in Tibet and . . . Xinjiang to pro-democracy campaigners and supporters of Taiwanese independence. Enemies of China in the United States were also trying to use the sect to Westernise and weaken the nation.

(*Telegraph*, 11 October 2000, p. 18)

12 October 2000. A former Chinese dissident, Gao Xingjian, wins the Nobel Prize for Literature. He is the first Chinese writer to win the prize. He left China in 1987 and later became a French citizen (*IHT*, 13 October 2000, pp. 1, 14; *FT*, 13 October 2000, p. 12).

20 November 2000.

Mary Robinson, the UN high commissioner for human rights . . . signed an agreement here [in Beijing] for co-operation and training on individual rights and the rule of law. Under the agreement the United Nations will provide advice to China's erratic police, prisons and courts on sound legal procedures. It will also offer detailed scrutiny of legal changes required if China is to comply with two treaties on economic and political rights that it has signed but not ratified.

(*IHT*, 21 November 2000, p. 5)

China has signed an agreement . . . accepting programmes for human rights education, and police and judicial training, after two years of negotiations . . . The technical agreement on training and education . . . will be launched next February [2001], with a workshop on the punishment of minor crimes . . . Mrs Robinson said she had hoped the pact was a precursor to China ratifying two UN covenants, on Economic, Social and Cultural Rights and on Civil and Political Rights.

(*FT*, 21 November 2000, p. 16)

China promised to . . . make all its 300,000 prison guards sit professional examinations every five years. Guards will be required to name prisoners' rights and cite the laws under which China's 12 million prisoners are being held. Any guard who fails the examination twice will be forced to quit the job . . . Prison guards in Xinjiang and Tibet . . . will apparently undergo a separate set of tests.

(*The Times*, 21 November 2000, p. 17)

13–14 January 2001.

More than 1,000 members of . . . Falun Gong . . . [held] a two-day [international] meeting . . . [in Hong Kong] . . . Falun Gong obtained a permit to rent space and gather at City Hall in Hong Kong . . . The meeting was the second gathering of Falun Gong in Hong Kong since Beijing outlawed the group in July 1999, but the first time the group had been permitted to use a government venue . . . On Saturday [13 January] . . . more than 800 members marched in protest to the government's main liaison office in Hong Kong . . . [and] carried wreaths and photographs of 120 people the group contends have been tortured and killed as part of Beijing's suppression.

(*IHT*, 15 January 2001, p. 6)

[Some] 1,000 Falun Gong practitioners from around the world rallied ... in Hong Kong. The Hong Kong-based Information Centre for Human Rights and Democracy contends that as many as 10,000 practitioners are being held in more than 300 labour camps and that ninety-eight sect members have died while in police custody ... [But the Chinese] State Council information office said ... 242 organizers of the sect had been jailed and an unreleased number of 'stubborn elements' who had broken laws against illegal demonstrations had been sent to labour reeducation camps.

(*IHT*, 16 January 2001, p. 4)

23 January 2001. Five people (four female and one male) doused their clothes in petrol and set fire to themselves on Tiananmen Square. One woman died. She was the mother of a twelve-year-old girl who was severely burned. China said the five were members of Falun Gong and used the incident to step up criticism of it. But membership was questioned by Falun Gong representatives in Hong Kong and New York. The 23 January was New Year's Eve in the Chinese lunar calendar, the following day being the start of the new millennium in the Chinese view (*FT*, 24 January 2001, p. 1; *IHT*, 24 January 2001, p. 1).

In New York spokesmen ... denied the protestors were Falun Gong members and said the act was part of a Chinese government smear campaign. The statement said more than 120 practitioners have died in custody but noted that China has only acknowledged a few deaths and attributed them to natural causes or suicide.

(*IHT*, 25 January 2001, p. 4)

(On 16 February the government claimed that another Falun Gong member had burned himself to death, this time in a suburb of Beijing.)

28 February 2001.

The Standing Committee of the National People's Congress ... ratified ... the International Convention on Economic, Social and Cultural Rights one day after a visit to China by the UN's top human rights official, Mary Robinson ... [But] the lawmaking body issued a statement announcing that the Chinese government would assume the obligations prescribed in Item 1(a) of Article 8 of the convention ... which proclaims the right to form and join free labour unions ... in line with relevant provisions of China's constitution, trade union law and labour law ... Chinese law recognizes only one labour union, the state-sanctioned All China Federation of Trade Unions, and prohibits the formation of independent groups. Its constitution prohibits strikes ... The convention allows member countries to enter so-called reservations on clauses of the treaty indicating that such portions will not be followed.

(*IHT*, 1 March 2001, p. 10)

'The partial ratification ... came nearly four years after China signed the treaty' (*Telegraph*, 1 March 2001, p. 20).

18 April 2001.

China blocked debate Wednesday [18 April] at the UN Human Rights Commission on how well it safeguards the basic rights of its citizens. Beijing rounded up enough votes to defeat discussion of the resolution, introduced by the United States, by twenty-three to seventeen, with twelve countries abstaining and one absent . . . China has successfully blocked debate every year since the resolution were first offered, after . . . Tiananmen Square in 1989.

(*IHT*, 19 April 2001, p. 8)

25 April 2001.

Members of the banned Falun Gong spiritual group staged small scattered protests Wednesday [25 April] on Tiananmen Square in an attempt to commemorate the second anniversary of a massive silent sit-in held outside the Chinese leadership compound in 1999, seeking government recognition . . . Since [the January self-immolations] . . . protests have been more sporadic . . . Up to 10,000 followers are in labour camps, according to human rights groups, and more than 100 have died in custody.

(*IHT*, 25 April 2001, p. 6)

4 July 2001.

The Falun Gong said yesterday [4 July] that at least fifteen of its followers were tortured to death in a prison camp in north-eastern China last month, but the claim was denied by local officials. Officials in Harbin. . . said that three Falun Gong practitioners in the prison labour camp had tried to commit suicide but all had failed . . . The incident . . . took place on 20 June . . . Miscreants can be sent [to labour camps] without a trial . . . The almost daily protests in Tiananmen Square . . . have ceased and the incident in Harbin is the first significant report of Falun Gong action for several weeks. A Hong Kong human rights group said that sixteen Falun Gong adherents tried to hang themselves at the Harbin camp after their sentences were extended for launching a hunger strike. The group, the Information Centre for Human Rights and Democracy, said ten people may have died. The Falun Dafa Information Centre, which acts for the sect, gave no evidence to support its claim that fifteen people at the camp had died as a result of police torture. The group also claims that 200 adherents have died in police custody since Beijing banned the movement in July 1999. China says the group is an 'evil cult', responsible for the deaths of 1,660 people by suicide or refusing medical treatment.

(*FT*, 5 July 2001, p. 8)

At least fourteen Falun Gong adherents died . . . The Chinese government said the women had committed suicide as a group, but the Falun Gong web site . . . said they had been tortured to death . . . On Wednesday [4 July] a Heilongjiang provincial official released a statement saying that fourteen women had died. The official said they were among twenty-five followers who attempted suicide on 20 June by hanging themselves . . . Eleven others attempted suicide but were stopped by guards . . . The report came a day after the Hong Kong-based Information Centre for Human Rights and Democracy said that ten followers . . . killed themselves on 20 June to protest their treatment at the labour camp. But Falun Gong's web site in the United States was quick to denounce the reports of mass suicide, saying that fifteen women at the camp had been tortured to death ... Falun Gong's web site says 236 followers have died as a result of confrontations with the police or prison guards.

(*IHT*, 5 July 2001, p. 1)

August 2001.

Expanding its use of torture and high-pressure indoctrination, China's Communist Party has gained the upper hand in its protracted battle against the banned Falun Gong spiritual movement, according to government sources and Falun Gong practitioners ... The government for the first time this year sanctioned the systematic use of violence against the group ... The crackdown had benefited from a turn in public opinion against Falun Gong since five purported members had set themselves on fire in Tiananmen Square, leading many Chinese to conclude the group is a dangerous cult ... Policy changed after the 23 January self-immolations and a Communist Party work conference in early February ... At the start of the crackdown government officials estimated that between 3 million and 6 million people were serious followers of Falun Gong. About 10 per cent, up to 600,000, were considered willing to fight the government crackdown, Chinese officials said. Estimates outside the government have put members much higher – in the tens of millions. Exact figures are not available.

(John Pomfret and Philip Pan, *IHT*, 6 August 2001, pp. 1, 4)

17 August 2001.

A Beijing court convicted four people of murder Friday [17 August] for organizing the self-immolation of followers of the outlawed Falun Gong spiritual movement. One man was sentenced to life in prison and the others received terms ranging from seven to fifteen ... The [23 January] incident has been widely seen as a turning point in the government's campaign to crush the group, which once attracted millions of followers and now appears to have been reduced on the mainland to isolated and desperate remnants ... Over the last year the crackdown has grown harsher, with thousands of members reportedly sent to labour camps, psychiatric institutions or reeducation centres.

(Erik Eckholm, *IHT*, 18 August 2001, p. 2)

19 August 2001.

[It was reported that] Chinese courts sentenced forty-five alleged 'die-hard' members of the banned Falun Gong spiritual movement to prison over the past few days ... The heaviest sentence ... imposed ... [was] a thirteen-year prison term ... Two other men were jailed for ten years.

(*IHT*, 20 August 2001, p. 5)

13 December 2001. 'Six Chinese university students have been imprisoned for downloading and disseminating material from the web site of the Falun Gong spiritual movement ... The students ... [were sentenced] to prison terms of three to twelve years' (*IHT*, 24 December 2001, p. 7).

4 March 2002. 'The [US] state department's annual human rights report contains strong criticism of China ... China is accused of using the world-wide campaign against terrorism as a pretext for cracking down on Moslems in the Xinjiang region' (*IHT*, 5 March 2002, p. 3).

5 March 2002.

> The Chinese state-run news media reported Friday [8 March] that the Falun Gong spiritual movement staged a brief takeover of state television Tuesday [5 March] in the Chinese city where the founder [Li Hongzhi] was born ... Falun Gong members cut into the cable network in the north-eastern city of Changchun at two locations Tuesday evening and used portable video equipment to broadcast their message into homes across the city ... twice during the evening.
>
> (*IHT*, 9 March 2002, p. 4)

('For the second time since March, Falun Gong activists broke into a cable-television system of a Chinese city and broadcast a videotape criticizing the government crackdown on the group. The broadcast broke into regular programming in Harbin on 21 April': *FEER*, 23 May 2002, p. 24.)

23–30 June 2002.

> China has confirmed reports from human rights groups that Falun Gong hacked into signals transmitted by the Sinosat satellite, which is linked from Shanghai, nearly twenty times during the last week in June. In place of the broadcasts, which included the World Cup football final, Falun Gong was briefly able to substitute its own messages.
>
> (*FT*, 10 July 2002, p. 12)

24 July 2002. 'Li Dawei ... a former policeman ... has been sentenced to eleven years in prison on charges of using the internet to subvert the Chinese government' (*IHT*, 6 August 2002, p. 3).

> [This is] the first conviction for downloading 'reactionary' material from the internet ... Private citizens were granted access to the internet only in late 1995 ... According to the best government surveys ... the number of people making at least occasional use of the internet ... reached 37 million by last January. By now the number may have surpassed 50 million.
>
> (p. 2)

26 August 2002. 'The World Psychiatric Association ... voted Monday [26 August] to send a delegation of experts to China to look into charges that Chinese psychiatric hospitals are being used to silence political and religious dissidents' (*IHT*, 27 August 2002, p. 3).

25 September 2002.

> China demanded Wednesday [25 September] that Taiwan stop Falun Gong members from hijacking mainland television from the island nation ... [from] hijacking satellite transmissions and beaming anti-government messages all over mainland China ... but stopped short of blaming the government for the illegal satellite broadcasts.
>
> (*IHT*, 26 September 2002, p. 9)

24 December 2002.

A leading Chinese pro-democracy activist, Xu Wenli, was released from prison Tuesday [24 December] and left aboard a flight to the United States . . . Xu was released early while serving a thirteen-year sentence on subversion charges . . . Xu was arrested in 1998 after trying to set up the opposition China Democracy Party with other activists. The government quickly crushed the party and sent dozens of members to prison . . . Xu, who suffers from hepatitis B, was granted medical parole . . . Xu is the first person convicted of endangering state security – the charge used against leading Chinese dissidents – to be released from prison . . . Xu's co-founders of the China Democracy Party – Wang Youcai and Qin Yongmin – are still in prison on similar charges, serving terms of eleven and twelve years, respectively . . . Xu was first arrested for advocating greater political freedoms during the 1979 Democracy Wall movement. He was imprisoned from 1982 to 1993 on charges of counter-revolution.

(*IHT*, 26 December 2002, p. 5)

10 February 2003.

In one of the toughest punishments meted out to a dissident in years, a Guangdong court convicted United Sates-based dissident Wang Bingzhang on spying and terrorism charges and sentenced him to life imprisonment. Wang was convicted by a court in the southern city of Shenzhen of spying for Taiwan and organizing and leading a terrorist group . . . Wang was the first political dissident to be charged under the country's new anti-terrorism laws.

(*FEER*, 20 February 2003, p. 25)

15 August 2003. 'The Falun Gong spiritual movement disrupted television signals three times this week, a foreign ministry spokesman said Friday [15 August]. The movement . . . hijacked satellite signals Tuesday and Wednesday' (*IHT*, 16 August 2003, p. 4).

4 March 2004.

A Chinese activist who helped organize the 1989 Tiananmen Square protest and later co-founded a democracy party was released from prison Thursday [4 March 2004] and left for the United States . . . Wang Youcai [was released on] medical parole . . . Wang had been sentenced in 1998 to eleven years for activities related to his founding of the China Democracy Party. He was also one of more than a dozen student leaders of the 1989 demonstrations . . . He served a year in prison in 1990 on charges related to those activities . . . Wang is not the first leader of the party he founded to be released. Its co-founder, Xu Wenli, was freed in December 2002 and also left for exile in the United States. Wang has been ill for years . . . He entered prison in 1999 on the latest charges . . . On Wednesday [3 March] China cut one year from the eight-year prison term of Rebiya Kadeer, a prominent Moslem businessman convicted of violating national security after she sent Chinese newspapers to her husband. And last week China released Phutsog Nyidron, a Tibetan nun who was arrested in 1989 on charges of 'counterrevolutionary propaganda and incitement' and sentenced to eight years in prison. She was the last of the fourteen 'singing nuns' who, in 1993, used a tape recorder smuggled into the prison to record songs about their love for their families and their homeland. Their sentences were extended after the tape was smuggled out of prison.

(www.iht.com, 4 March 2004)

One of China's most prominent political prisoners, democracy activist Wang Youcai, was released and sent to the United States. It was the third time in little over a week that Beijing was lenient to a prisoner on a list presented by the Bush administration, which has indicated that it will hit out at China's rights record at an annual United Nations meeting this month.

(*FEER*, 18 March 2004, p. 30)

23 March 2004.

China broke off discussions on human rights with the United States on Tuesday [23 March], a day after Washington said it would seek to criticise Beijing's rights record at the United Nations Human Rights Conference in Geneva ... a fifty-three-member body that began its six-week annual session on 15 March ... [China] has held talks on the issue with the United States, the EU and other governments since the mid-1990s ... In its announcement the US government accused Beijing of not living up to its international commitments to protect the rights of its citizens. The United States has voiced concern over China's arrests of democracy activists and alleged extrajudicial killings, use of torture and mistreatment. It has also highlighted the repression of the Falun Gong spiritual group. The [US] State Department's spokesman ... said Washington had sought the backing of the United Nations Commission on Human Rights ... The United States broke with tradition by not sponsoring the resolution last year [2003] ... But the United States has resumed attacks on Beijing's rights record in recent months ... [The US] State Department's annual rights assessment last month [February] highlighted the arrest of democracy activists and the suppression of religious groups in China.

(www.iht.com, 23 March 2004)

[On 15 April 2004] a United States-backed attempt to censure Beijing before the annual meeting of the United Nations Human Rights Commission in Geneva failed when other developing countries joined China in voting to block any discussion. It was the eleventh time such a resolution was averted.

(*FEER*, 29 April 2004, p. 29)

Beijing's representatives pushed a 'no-action motion' – essentially a decision not to have a vote. That succeeded with the help of twenty-seven countries on the Commission of Human Rights including Cuba, Zimbabwe, Saudi Arabia and Sudan ... The first [attempt to censure Beijing] was in 1990, in a motion resulting from the Tiananmen massacre in June 1989.

(p. 11)

The United States criticised China for 'backsliding' on key human rights issues in 2003. In its annual global rights survey the State Department cited Beijing's arrest of political activists, a crackdown on internet dissent, and the arbitrary arrest, torture and execution of Tibetans.

(*FEER*, 11 March 2004, p. 24)

March 2004. '[On 14 March] the National People's Congress [NPC] voted to adopt significant changes to the national constitution ... [One amendment] enshrined the respect of "human rights" in the constitution for the first time' (*FT*, 15 March 2004, p. 14)

'China's parliament formally approved constitutional amendments Sunday [14 March] to protect private property and human rights ... The 2,900-member legislature approved a series of thirteen changes to the constitution. "The state respects and preserves human rights," one reads' (*IHT*, 15 March 2004, p. 1).

'Also added [was] the first mention of human rights to the constitution ... "The state respects and preserves human rights," the amendment said' (*The Times*, 15 March 2004, p. 16).

> On the last day of the ten-day session the NPC amended the constitution to include formal guarantees of human rights and private property ... 'The state respects and protects human rights' ... But the changes were more symbolic than practical because courts in China do not usually consider whether laws are constitutional. The human rights amendment, for instance, was not at odds with restrictions on public protest because the constitution is subordinate to the Chinese Communist Party.
>
> (*FEER*, 25 March 2004, p. 24)

('[The Communist Party is] proposing to add to the constitution this sentence: "The state respects and safeguards human rights". Once adopted it will be the first time that the term human rights has been used in the document, which, at present, only provides for "rights"': *IHT*, 5 March 2004, p. 8.)

September 2004. 'Falun Gong claims that more than 800 of its members have died in custody since the movement was banned in 1999' (*Guardian*, 13 September 2004, p. 14).

'Falun Gong espouses an idiosyncratic mix of traditional Chinese qigong, or self-healing, exercises and meditation' (www.iht.com, 25 November 2004).

5 April 2005.

> China accounted for the majority of executions reported worldwide last year [2004], but the true frequency of the death penalty is impossible to count because many death sentences are carried out secretly, Amnesty International said Tuesday [5 April 2005]. In 2004 more than 3,797 people were executed in twenty-five countries, including at least 3,400 in China, the rights group said. More than 7,000 people were sentenced to death in sixty-four countries, it said.
>
> (*IHT*, 6 April 2005, p. 7)

23 August 2005.

> China has agreed to allow the UN Human Rights Commission's special investigator on torture to visit the country in an official capacity for the first time. Manfred Nowak will visit China from 21 November to 2 December to meet

government officials and tour Chinese detention centres ... While China outlawed torture in 1996, activists say that it is still widely practised.

(www.iht.com, 24 August 2005)

29 August 2005.

Louise Arbour, the UN High Commissioner for Human Rights, arrived in
Beijing [on 29 August] ... [for a] five-day stay in China ... China executes
more people each year than all countries combined, according to international
human rights groups. They estimate that as many as 15,000 people annually
are put to death. China says the number is smaller, but has said it is considering
reducing the number of capital offences.

(www.iht.com, 29 August 2005)

'The UN delegation's discussions with Chinese officials and judges focused on
strengthening the judiciary, limiting the death penalty and abolishing detention
without trial' (www.iht.com, 2 September 2005).

2 December 2005.

Manfred Nowak, a special investigator for the UN Commission on Human
Rights who focuses on torture ... condemned what he found to be 'widespread' use of torture in the judicial system of China and said Beijing must
overhaul its criminal laws, grant more power to judges and abolish labour
camps before it can end such abuses ... [He] noted some progress by Chinese
officials in reducing violence against prisoners since the country signed an
international covenant banning torture in 1988. But Nowak said that 'obtaining
confessions' and fighting 'deviant behaviour' continue to be central goals of
the Chinese criminal justice system ... Nowak: 'The use of torture, though on
the decline, particularly in urban areas, nevertheless remains widespread in
China' ... Nowak's two-week investigation of Chinese prisons and detention
facilities was the first of its kind for the UN anti-torture unit and took a decade
of diplomacy to arrange. He had rare access to about thirty prisoners in several
elite facilities in Beijing as well as in the remote regions of Tibet and Xinjiang,
where persecutions of religious and ethnic minorities are considered common.
While he expressed appreciation to the Chinese government for allowing his
visit and allowing private interviews with prisoners, torture victims and their
relatives, he said he experienced numerous attempts to 'obstruct or restrict' his
investigation. The police and other security forces put him under constant surveillance that prevented some people from meeting him, he said. He also complained that his prison visits could take place only during daylight 'working
hours' of prison guards ... Nowak: 'There was a palpable sense of fear and
self-censorship' ... The Chinese ban on torture covers only a specific type of
torture ... that meets a narrow definition of violent punishment that leaves a
lasting impact, such as scars or disability, Nowak said ... The initial summary
of his findings noted that the government has taken steps to reduce torture in
recent years, including issuing new regulations in 2004 that prohibit torture
and threats to gain confessions. But he said he found ample evidence that the
courts still relied too heavily on forced confessions in assessing guilt. Nowak

said torture also remained common in Chinese labour camps, which are operated by the police with no oversight from the courts ... The government, he said, should eliminate political crimes, such as 'endangering national security' and 'disrupting social order', which he said leave far too much discretion in the hands of security forces.

(www.iht.com, 2 December 2005; *IHT*, 3 December 2005, pp. 1, 6)

'Manfred Nowak ... said he had been obstructed by security officials, who intimidated some victims and their relatives or prevented them from seeing him' (*Guardian*, 3 December 2005, p. 18).

China broke its silence yesterday [2 December] to admit for the first time that executed prisoners' organs were sold to foreigners for transplant ... and promised to tighten the rules ... The only existing regulation covering the removal of organs from the bodies of executed prisoners is a 1984 draft document that stipulates that such operations can take place only with the consent of the family or if the body goes unclaimed ... Executions have long been carried out with a single bullet to the head or the heart. That practice changed in the late 1990s when the use of lethal injection was introduced to make the organs usable. No official figures are available for the number of executions each year ... However, Amnesty International says more people are executed in China than the rest of the world combined, and estimates the total at about 3,400 each year – and possibly as many as 6,000.

(*The Times*, 3 December 2005, p. 48)

China ... has long designated its number of executions as a state secret. A hint at the number came last year [2004] when a high-level delegate to the National People's Congress publicly estimated that it was 'nearly 10,000'. In 2004 Amnesty International documented at least 3,400 executions – out of 3,797 worldwide that year – but cautioned that China's true number was probably far higher.

(*IHT*, 31 December 2005, p. 2)

Thousands of Chinese who petition the authorities for redress of grievances are attacked, intimidated and detained, Human Rights Watch, a New York-based group, said in a report released Thursday [8 December 2005] ... The group said the report was the first detailed investigation into how China was handling the growing number of petitioners seeking justice over alleged abuses, including police brutality, illegal land seizures and corruption. China's petition system is often seen as last resort because local governments and courts routinely ignore complaints, leaving people no choice but to travel to the capital hoping petition offices there will investigate ... About 10 million petitions were filed in 2004 but success was rare, the group's report said. A recent study found only three of 2,000 petitioners surveyed had their problems resolved, it said.

(www.iht.com, 8 December 2005)

For centuries Chinese who have a grievance against the government have used an elaborate petition system in hopes ... of imperial redress. But that ancient recourse has been so abused by authorities in China that petitioners seem as likely to be harassed, kidnapped, incarcerated and tortured as they are to have their complaint adjudicated by a higher authority ... About 10 million people filed petitions at the provincial and national level in 2004. But only three in 2,000 ... received a result they considered satisfactory. Instead, many who complain are apprehended at petition sites and forcibly sent home to keep them from embarrassing local officials. Repeat offenders have been jailed or sentenced to extra-judicial labour camps. The most ardent activists are tortured until they agree to stop filing complaints.

(*IHT*, 9 December 2005, p. 4)

21 January 2006.

A California businessman has returned to the United States after three years of imprisonment in China for his participation in Falun Gong ... Charles Lee was put on trial based on accusations that he tried to sabotage the government by disrupting broadcasts with videotapes showing government persecution of Falun Gong members.

(*IHT*, 25 January 2006, p. 5)

24 January 2006.

China's propaganda department on Tuesday [24 January] ordered the closing of *Bing Dian* [*Freezing Point*], an influential weekly newspaper that often tackled touchy political and social subjects ...*Bing Dian* [was] published as a supplement to the influential newspaper *China Youth Daily* ... [*Bing Dian*'s] long-time editor, Li Datong ... said ... the authorities cited the publication of a lengthy study of Chinese middle-school textbooks as a reason for the order ... The 11 January [2006] article discussed what the author, Yuan Weishi, a Zhongshan University professor, referred to as official distortions of history to emphasize the humiliations China suffered at the hands of imperial powers. He criticised the textbooks' treatment of events like the Boxer rebellion and the burning of the Summer Palace by British and French troops in 1960, which he said were partly the result of mistakes by then flailing Qing Dynasty leaders ...Li said the article, though provocative, was just an excuse for closing the paper. In August [2005] a letter by Li led to a revolt at the China Youth Daily group after the paper's new party-appointed editor ... sought to impose a review system that graded the staff on factors including the reaction their work elicited from party leaders. The letter, which was posted on the web, and the backlash resulted in modification of the review system.

(www.iht.com, 25 January 2006)

Li Datong, a veteran of the 1989 Tiananmen Square protests, issued an open letter last summer [2005] that forced his masters to abandon the journalist reward scheme. The final straw was an essay published on 11 January that questioned the unbalanced history taught in Chinese schools ... [The essay] said students should be aware that the Boxers – who attempted to expel

foreigners from China in 1900 – could as easily be described as violent xeno-
phobes as magnificent patriots.

(Guardian, 26 January 2006, p. 19)

The closure of ... *Bing Dian* ... was merely the latest in a series of such
moves against publications that have pushed the ever-present limits on expression in China ... The past year saw a steady stream of cases in which editors
and reporters were disciplined, dismissed or even jailed ... In its 2005 Press
Freedom Index, a Paris-based rights group, Reporters Without Borders, put
China near the bottom – in 159th place out of 167 countries ranked. The group
has identified thirty-two imprisoned journalists ... *Bing Dian* had previously
attracted attention and official criticism with articles about corruption, Taiwan
and ... heavy-handed political interference in the work of the media ... The
paper is a weekly supplement in the *China Youth Daily* newspaper, which is
affiliated to the Communist Party Youth League. The Youth League, in turn, is
the institutional power base of China's president and Communist Party chief,
Hu Jintao, so Mr Hu was likely to have been directly involved in the decision
to shut *Bing Dian* down ... Li Datong, the founder and editor of *Bing Dian* ...
[said] that the closure was part of a long-nurtured scheme to silence the paper's
'pursuit of democracy, rule of law, deliberation, liberty and rights'.

(The Economist, 4 January 2006, p. 59)

A dozen former Chinese Communist Party officials and senior scholars, including a one-time secretary to Mao Zedong ... Li Rui ... and the retired bosses of
the country's most powerful media outlets, have denounced the recent closing
of ... *Freezing Point* ... A public letter, issued by party elders, dated 2 February but circulated to journalists in Beijing on Tuesday [14 February], appeared
to add momentum to a campaign by a few outspoken editors ... Among the
others [who have signed the letter] are Hu Jinwei, a former editor of the
People's Daily, the party's leading official newspaper... Zhu Houze, who once
ran the party's propaganda office ... and Li Pu, a former deputy head of the
official Xinhua press agency ... Since late last year [2005] officials responsible
for managing the media have shut down one publication ... *Freezing Point* ...
and replaced editors of three others that had developed reputations for breaking
news or exploring sensitive political and social issues ... Propaganda officials
are facing rare public challenges to their legal authority ... including a short
strike and a string of resignations at one newspaper and defiant open letters
from two editors singled out for censure ... The letter by the former officials,
party leaders and scholars criticised the Propaganda Department's 24 January
order to shut down *Freezing Point* as an example of 'malignant management'
and an 'abuse of power' that violated China's constitutional guarantee of free
speech. They predicted the country would have difficulty countering the recent
surge of social unrest in the countryside unless it allowed the media more
leeway to expose problems that lead to violent protests. 'At the turning point in
our history from a totalitarian to a constitutional system, depriving the public
freedom of speech will bring disaster for our social and political transition and

give rise to group confrontation and social unrest,' the letter said. 'Experience has proved that allowing a free flow of ideas can improve stability and alleviate social problems.'

(*IHT*, 15 February 2006, pp. 1, 8)

'Li Datong enlisted senior party members to resist the decision' (*The Times*, 17 February 2006, p. 23).

Bing Dian ... a four-page weekly supplement of the *China Youth Daily* ... will resume publishing ... on 1 March ... more than a month after being shut down, but its two top editors were fired, one of the editors said Thursday [16 February] ...The editor-in-chief, Li Datong ... said that he and the deputy editor, Lu Yuegang, had been removed from their posts and transferred to another department of the *China Youth Daily* ... As part of the deal to reopen, *Bing Dian* will also have to run an article criticizing a previously published essay by Yuan Weishi, who complained of a political bias in the way that Chinese textbooks present nineteenth century history.

(*IHT*, 17 February 2006, p. 4)

'Li Datong ... said that he and Lu Yuegang, the deputy editor and a well known investigative reporter, had been told that the magazine would restart without them on 1 March. The two journalists were transferred to a research branch of the newspaper, Li said. He also predicted that a new, more compliant tone would be evident in the 1 March issue ... Chinese journalists are increasingly willing to criticise party censors. Li has filed a formal complaint against the Propaganda Department and has described it as an 'illegal organization'. Earlier this year editors and reporters at the party-run *Beijing News* held a short strike to protest the firing of an editor.

(www.iht.com, 17 February 2006)

The editors of the parent newspaper, *China Youth Daily*, will scrutinize each edition ... In recent months ... editors of the popular and often muckraking *Beijing News* were dismissed, prompting a brief strike by journalists, and the editor of *Public Interest* was also dismissed.

(*The Times*, 17 February 2006, p. 50)

Li Datong and Lu Yuegang ... have issued a public letter lashing out at propaganda officials and calling for free speech. Meanwhile, a group or prominent scholars and lawyers who had contributed articles to the journal wrote an open letter to President Hu Jintao, denouncing the crackdown against *Freezing Point* as a violation of the constitution and of the promise made by top leaders for a consistent rule of law.

(www.iht.com, 19 February 2006)

Religion

9 May 1998. It is confirmed that Bishop Zeng Jingmu has been released six months early, officially on humanitarian grounds. He was arrested in November 1995 and sentenced, without trial, to three years of 'reeducation through labour' for holding unauthorized religious services. He had already spent twenty-three years in jail since the 1950s for openly proclaiming allegiance to the Vatican. At least 4 million Catholics practise under the auspices of the official Chinese Patriotic Catholic Association, which rejects the authority of the Pope over the selection of bishops and other church matters. China does not have diplomatic relations with the Vatican (*IHT*, 11 May 1998, p. 4).

'Beijing oversees a 3-million-strong "patriotic church" that rejects the supremacy of the Vatican. But 3 million to 10 million mainland Chinese are said to belong to an underground Roman Catholic Church that does recognize papal authority' (*IHT*, 15 January 1997, p. 6). An internal Communist Party document estimated that in February 1996 there were perhaps 70 million religious believers in China. In 1949 there were only a million Protestants, compared with an estimated 20 million today (although the publicly acknowledged figure is only 6.5 million). Government statistics indicate 4 million Catholics, but church organizations and Western academics say that 8 million to 10 million is a more reliable estimate (*IHT*, 28 January 1997, p. 2).

> China and the Vatican broke ties in 1951 ... The official [Chinese] church says it has ... 4 million followers. Vatican officials have estimated that 8 million Chinese ... remain loyal to the Pope in a parallel, illegal church that faces police harassment.
>
> (*IHT*, 27 September 2000, p. 5)

'Beijing claims some 4 million Chinese belong to the Catholic Patriotic Association, while the Vatican asserts that there are as many as 8 million underground Catholics loyal to Rome' (*Independent*, 25 August 2000, p. 13). 'China set up the Chinese Catholic Patriotic Association in 1957, six years after Beijing cut off diplomatic ties with the Vatican' (*Independent*, 21 November 2005, p. 25).

> In 1951 the government expelled the Roman Catholic Church and many clergy members and believers reconciled themselves to the 'patriotic' church. However, other Chinese Catholics joined underground dioceses that retained allegiance to Rome ... The Vatican is the last European state to continue recognizing Taiwan, not China ... The number of Chinese Catholics has grown steadily since the 1980s, though not as fast as Protestant denominations that rely more on small 'house churches' ... China now has about 12 million Catholics – about half of whom are attached to state-controlled churches – compared with about 3 million in 1949 ... The official churches are strongest ... in the big cities.
>
> (www.iht.com, 4 April 2005)

> The Vatican is the only European state to recognize Taiwan, a result of Beijing's decision in 1951 to expel foreign priests from China and bring the Catholic Church under state control ... Chief among ... other issues dividing the two ... is the authority to appoint bishops, a preserve of the Vatican but something Beijing says should be done through its state religious bodies ... The government periodically arrests priests and their followers in the 'underground' churches, but in practice tolerates many of them if they keep a low profile.
>
> (*FT*, 6 April 2005, p. 9)

6 January 2000. In Beijing the Patriotic Catholic Association (controlled by the state) names five new bishops. China and the Vatican do not have diplomatic relations.

1 October 2000.

Pope John Paul II on Sunday [1 October] canonized 120 Roman Catholics who were killed in China, defying the Chinese government, which condemned the ceremony as an insulting reminder of colonial imperialism ... China had no saints before Sunday ... [The Pope canonized] as martyrs eighty-seven Chinese believers and thirty-three European missionaries killed from 1648 to 1930... The Chinese government denounced the 120 Roman Catholics as 'agents of imperialism'. Most of them died in the anti-Western Boxer rebellion in the nineteenth century ... Chinese leaders fiercely denounced the Sunday ceremony for coinciding with the anniversary of the founding of the People's Republic in 1949 ... The Vatican estimates that 8 million Chinese Catholics are loyal to the Pope.

(*IHT*, 2 October 2000, p. 9)

October 2002.

There are about 12 million practising Catholics in China today ... a number which by all accounts is growing rapidly. Exact numbers are hard to come by because an estimated 50 per cent of these attend underground churches ... In 1980 ... China's government decreed that confiscated land and buildings should be returned to religious organizations. But churches had generally suffered heavy damage and local governments for many years refused to return property they had come to regard as their own.

(*IHT*, 8 October 2002, p. 2)

May 2004.

The country's estimated 20 million Moslems are often said to constitute the second largest religious community after Buddhists, who may number as many as 100 million. Christians of various denominations are also believed to number well over 10 million, and adherents of all these faiths are widely believed to be growing.

(*IHT*, 7 May 2004, p. 5)

September 2004. 'The US based Cardinal Kung Foundation estimates there are 12 million "underground" Catholics, compared with the 4 million who follow the state-authorized church' (*Guardian*, 13 September 2004, p. 14).

19 December 2004.

China ... has announced new rules enshrining religious belief as a basic human right ... The Religious Affairs Provisions formally take effect on 1 March [2005] ... *People's Daily*: 'As China has more than 100 million people believing religion, so the protection of religious freedom is important in safeguarding people's interests and respecting and protecting human rights ... [The set of comprehensive administrative rules] specify that the legitimate rights of religious groups, religious sites and the religious people are protected.'

(www.iht.com, 20 December 2004)

8 April 2005.

The Vatican is the only [European] state to retain diplomatic ties with Taipei instead of Beijing. That relationship produced an unexpected benefit on Friday [8 April 2005], when President Chen Shui-bian attended the funeral of Pope John Paul II [who died on 2 April aged eighty-four] in the first state visit ever to Europe by a president from Taiwan ... Chen's visit to the Vatican infuriated the Beijing authorities, not least because Italy, which recognizes Beijing but not Taipei, granted landing rights to Chen's jet, as the Vatican lacks an airport ... Top Vatican officials have been negotiating off and on for decades to reach a deal with mainland China, and have redoubled their efforts in the last several years. The Chinese government recognizes the pope as a spiritual leader, but does not recognize the authority of the Vatican. In mainland China Catholics must worship at official government-sanctioned churches, though there is an underground church loyal to the Vatican ... In the days since the pope's death China has reportedly cracked down on Roman Catholic clergy members operating without official approval ... There are 300,000 Roman Catholics in Taiwan. Government figures in mainland China show 4 million Catholics there. Bishop Joseph Zen of Hong Kong said there were at least 10 million. A Communist Party-controlled organization, the Patriotic Association of the Catholic Church, registers and oversees Catholic churches on the mainland and chooses bishops for the country ... The Vatican wants China to provide greater religious freedom for Catholics and to allow the Vatican to choose bishops in China.

(www.iht.com, 11 April 2005)

19 April 2005. German Cardinal Joseph Ratzinger was elected as the new pope. He chose the name Benedict XVI.
20 April 2005.

China ... warned the new pope, Benedict XVI, that the Vatican and China could establish formal relations only if the Vatican dissolved its diplomatic links with Taiwan and promised not to 'interfere in China's internal affairs' ... China has 12 million Catholics ... In the past decade more bishops in the official church have also sought authorization from Rome before taking up appointments, and many Chinese Catholics now expect their clergy to carry at least the informal blessing of the Vatican.

(www.iht.com, 20 April 2005; *IHT*, 21 April 2005, p. 7)

It is Protestantism that in recent years has spread most rapidly in China, even among the usually sceptical urban elite ... Officially there are 5 million baptised Catholics and 15 million Protestants. Vatican officials believe there are more than 10 million Catholics. In its report last year [2004] on religious freedom, the American State Department quoted estimates for the Protestant community ranging from 30 million to 90 million ... The most rapid spread occurred in the 1980s after the lifting of China's Maoist-era ban on religious activity and the reopening of thousands of Christian churches. Believers were typically elderly, little-educated and poor. But since then the average age of believers has fallen and worship in places not sanctioned by the government has become more common than in officially approved churches ... Most striking in recent years has been the spread of Christianity among urban intellectuals and businesspeople ... Christianity has flourished on university campuses ... China's leaders last year [2004] ... launched a campaign to promote atheism in schools.

(The Economist, 23 April 2005, p. 68)

The authorities in Beijing have sharply rejected a Vatican invitation to four Chinese Catholic bishops to attend a church conference in Rome [it was reported on 10 September] ... [Two of the bishops] were appointed by China's official church, but senior church officials say they have both subsequently been recognized by the Vatican ... [The third] is a longstanding member of the underground Catholic church loyal to Rome but also has been approved by the official church ... [The fourth] is an active member of the underground church and was most recently arrested last year [2004] ... [In August] the Pope gave twenty-eight priests from China's official church a special greeting at one of his general audiences ... In some Catholic strongholds where bishops appointed by the government have also been tacitly recognized by Rome, congregations of the two churches have effectively merged. Some Catholic officials estimate that more than 80 per cent of China's officially appointed bishops have now reached accommodation with Rome through unofficial channels ... The state-sanctioned church now claims 5 million members ... An underground Catholic church loyal to Rome ... according to Vatican estimates ... has up to 10 million members.

(IHT, 12 September 2005, p. 5)

The contention over naming bishops is largely resolved: most new bishops in China seek and receive Papal approval prior to their consecration, and most bishops ordained without Papal approval have since been legitimized by Rome. The accommodation goes both ways – some 'underground' bishops have also received recognition from the government. An estimated 90 per cent of the bishops in the mainland are accepted by both the Vatican and the Chinese government.

(FEER, September 2005, p. 42)

'Even by conservative estimates there are 100 million regular practitioners of various religious faiths in China, along with at least 100 million others who are more casual in their devotion' (www.iht.com, 15 September 2005).

February 2006.

With almost 21 million followers of Islam, China has roughly as many Moslems as Europe or even Iraq ... With 1.2 billion people, China is so huge and Moslems constitute such a tiny minority that most Moslems intuitively learn to keep quiet ... Islam began arriving in China along trading routes ... [in] the seventh century.

(www.iht.com, 19 February 2006)

Pope Bendict XVI named fifteen new cardinals on Wednesday [22 February 2006], including Bishop Joseph Zen of Hong Kong, an often outspoken critic of China's rulers who has nonetheless played a leading role in efforts to open diplomatic relations between Beijing and the Vatican ... Government figures in mainland China show 4 million Catholics there, but Zen estimated in an interview last year [2005] that there were at least 10 million. Taiwan has just 300,000 Catholics ... The great China region has not had an active cardinal since the resignation in December [2005] of Shan Kuo-his, who turns eighty-three this year [2006], a the bishop of Kaohsiung, an industrial port in southern Taiwan.

(*IHT*, 23 February 2006, p. 3)

The use of the internet and mobile phones

'The first full internet connection in China was recorded on 17 May 1994' (*The Times*, 10 February 2006, p. 40).

4 February 1996. New rules are announced to regulate links to the internet.

30 December 1997. New controls are imposed on the use of the internet (excluding Hong Kong), strengthening those introduced in February 1996 and May 1997. For example, the internet must not be used to 'split the country' or 'defame government agencies' (*IHT*, 31 December 1997, p. 15; *FT*, 31 December 1997, p. 4).

26 January 2000. China imposes further controls on the internet. 'All organizations and individuals are forbidden from releasing, discussing or transferring state secrets on bulletin boards, chat rooms or in internet news groups.' The rules are retroactive to 1 January 2000. Internet companies must be responsible for their own content. Internet content providers must be vetted by authorities to check their 'secrecy preservation systems' are secure before they can obtain 'security certification'. The number of internet users in China quadrupled in 1999 to 8.9 million (*FT*, 27 January 2000, p. 12; *IHT*, 27 January 2000, pp. 1, 9).

'By the end of this year [2000] there may be 20 million internet users, nearly ten times the 2.1 million at the start of 1999' (*FT*, Survey on the World Economy, 22 September 2000, p. xi). 'In the past year the number of internet addresses in China has more than quadrupled to 9 million. This year [2000] the number is expected to grow to more than 20 million' (President Clinton, *IHT*, 25 September 2000, p. 10). 'The number of internet users has increased from fewer than 50,000 in 1995 to the current 16 million' (*IHT*, Survey, 29 September 2000, p. ii).

2 October 2000. New regulations governing the use of the internet are published.

By holding companies responsible for blocking vast quantities of illegal content on their web sites and chat rooms, the rules illustrate Beijing's determination to contain the spread of ideas deemed dangerous to Communist Party rule. The regulations ban any content that is 'subversive', that supports cults, that 'harms the reputation' of China or that hurts reunification efforts with Taiwan, among other things. Internet content and service providers must keep records of all the content that appears on their web sites and all the users who dial on to their services for sixty days, and hand the records to the police on demand, the rules state. Existing commercial internet sites have until the end of November to provide detailed information on their businesses to the ministry of information technology and telecommunications industries in order to obtain licences. Companies without licences and those exceeding their state business scope will be fined or shut down, the rules state ... The rules require internet content providers to win the approval of the ministry before they can receive foreign capital, co-operate with foreign businesses or list domestic or overseas stock. 'The proportion of foreign investment must conform with relevant laws and administrative regulations,' the rules say.

(*IHT*, 3 October 2000, p. 19)

As part of the new rules dotcoms have sixty days from 1 October to provide information to the MII to secure licences ... Dotcoms are to be held responsible for keeping their sites free of content that subverts state power, harms the 'reputation' of China, damages chances of reunification with rival Taiwan or support cults, such as the banned Falun Gong. In addition, internet content and service providers must keep records of all the content that appears on their websites and all the users who dial on to their servers for sixty days, and hand over the records to the police on demand.

(*FT*, 3 October 2000, p. 12)

China's new laws broadly involve restating what content is unsuitable – treachery, subversion, pornography and cult material ... They also demand that internet service providers be state owned and that commercial internet content providers have a licence and keep a sixty-day log of who has visited their sites, and which pages were viewed.

(*FEER*, 19 October 2000, p. 48)

7 November 2000. Regulations aimed at controlling news and chat rooms on the internet are published. Web sites are required to seek approval from a department under the State Council (the cabinet) before they can publish news. Web sites must rely on state press groups, cite the sources of the news and seek permission before publishing foreign news. A document defining 'news' may be published soon (*IHT*, 8 November 2000, p. 20; *FT*, 8 November 2000, p. 16). (On 28 December 2000 a law was passed against 'on-line subversion'. The law bans the 'use of the internet for subverting the government' and makes it illegal to produce or transmit computer viruses or break into military computer networks: *IHT*, 29 December 2000, p. 5. China has made it a crime to use the internet to promote Taiwan's independence, organize "cults" and spread rumours to manipulate stock prices ... [The law] also lists slander of individuals and corporations over the internet ... [and] tampering with personal email accounts as crimes': *FT*, 30 December 2000, p. 6.)

There are now about 20 million internet users on the mainland, compared with 2 million in 1999 (*FT*, Survey, 13 November 2000, p. viii).

'More than 20 per cent of China's 22.5 million internet users were gaining access to the internet via . . . [internet] cafés at the end of 2000' (*IHT*, 15 June 2001, p. 5).

'As of early 2002 official estimates indicate that there were some 22.5 million Chinese with online access' (*Asian Studies*, 2001, vol. XLI, no. 3, p. 377).

'An estimated 16 million . . . are on the net' (*FEER*, 21 June 2001, p. 38). ('[In February 2001] China put the organizer of a web site on trial for publishing articles about democracy, the banned Falun Gong sect and other material deemed subversive. Huang Qi is the first Chinese webmaster known to have been prosecuted for publishing political material': *FEER*, 22 February 2001, p. 15.)

'Beijing estimates there were more than 26 million Chinese internet users in July [2001], compared with only 9 million at the end of 1999' (*IHT*, 31 August 2001, p. 13).

'There are 30 million internet users in China, three times as many as two years ago' (*Guardian*, 1 September 2001, p. 15).

16 June 2002.

Beijing ordered the city's internet cafés to close after an early morning blaze yesterday [16 June] at an illegal web café killed twenty-four people . . . All but 200 of Beijing's 2,400 internet cafés were illegal . . . China keeps strict control over access to the internet and many of the cafés operate in secret with doors locked and windows barred, turning them into death traps.

(*FT*, 17 June 2002, p. 10)

'The mobile phone has outperformed the internet, with 167 million mobile phone users in China compared with about 30 million regular internet users' (*FEER*, 27 June 2002, p. 13). 'A new report said that China was the number three user of internet in the world, with more than 45 million people logging on regularly . . . Only the United States and Japan have more "netizens"' (*FEER*, 1 August 2002, p. 22). 'The number of mobile phone users in China almost quadrupled to 329 million last year [2004] from 85 million in 2000, according to the International Telecommunications Union' (www.iht.com, 29 March 2005).

Internet users number 46 million, according to an official estimate (*The Economist*, 21 September 2002, p. 66).

There are 46 million internet users (*FEER*, 7 November 2002, p. 24).

Internet users number 39.8 million, mobile phones number 176.2 million and fixed-line phones number 198.9 million. 'A decade ago there were only 10 million phones' (*IHT*, 19 August 2002, p. 11).

The number of internet users rose by 48.5 per cent from a year ago to 68 million at the end of June [2003] . . . [China] lags only the United States, which has 178 million users . . . [There are now] 234.5 million mobile phone users, more than any other market.

(*IHT*, 23 July 2003, p. 14)

There were 78 million internet users at the end of 2003 (www.iht.com, 14 January 2004).

There are 80 million internet users (*IHT*, 8 March 2004, p. 13).

'By the end of the year [2004] China will have 111 million internet users (making it the largest online community in the world after the United States)' (*Guardian*, G2, 12 November 2004, p. 4).

'Internet users, who numbered fewer than 17 million in 2000, are now estimated to be somewhere near 90 million' (*IHT*, 6 December 2004, p. 12).

'[There are] 94 million [internet] users' (www.iht.com, 4 March 2005).

'China has more than 100 million internet users, second only to the number of users in the United States' (www.iht.com, 7 July 2005).

'Less than 10 per cent of the nation has internet access ... China has 100 million web users, half the number of users in the United States' (www.iht.com, 15 August 2005).

'China ... has 103 million internet users, second only to the United States, and yet has an internet penetration rate of just 8 per cent' (*FT*, 13 August 2005, p. 8).

Reporters Without Borders, the Paris-based press freedom watchdog, yesterday [7 September 2005] accused Yahoo, the US internet portal, of helping Chinese authorities catch and prosecute a journalist convicted of leaking state secrets ... a vaguely defined charge often used against government critics. Shi Tao was sentenced to ten years in prison in April ... Overseas Chinese websites have said that, in Mr Shi's case, the state secret was a copy of an order from the Communist Party's propaganda department for tighter controls about the anniversary of the 4 June 1989 crackdown on demonstrators in Tiananmen Square ... The internet market is booming but the communist government maintains strict controls on online activity ... The accusation comes less than a month after Yahoo announced it would invest more than $1 billion in Alibaba, the Chinese e-commerce website ... Yahoo rivals Google and MSN, the online arm of Microsoft, have also been accused of being overly willing to assist efforts by the Chinese government to control the internet. The *Financial Times* revealed in June that MSN had banned the words 'freedom' and 'democracy' from parts of its new Chinese website, saying they were 'forbidden speech'. Google has been criticised for tailoring the results of its Chinese search service to exclude websites that are blocked by the government.

(*FT*, 8 September 2005, p. 14)

'In June it emerged that Microsoft's joint venture Chinese internet portal had banned words such as "democracy" and "freedom" from being used to label personal websites' (p. 20).

Yahoo's role in the persecution of Shi was revealed in July by Boxun, a website run by overseas Chinese, and was repeated on Tuesday [6 September] by Reporters Without Borders, a media watchdog group ... The internet giant Yahoo provided information that helped Chinese state security officials convict a Chinese journalist for leaking state secrets to a foreign website, court documents show ... Shi Tao was sentenced to ten years in prison in June for sending an anonymous posting to a New York-based, Chinese language website that the authorities said contained state secrets. His posting summarized a communication from Communist Party authorities to media outlets around the country ... The information involved routine instructions on how officials were to safeguard social stability during the fifteenth anniversary of the 4 June 1989 democracy movement.

(*IHT*, 8 September 2005, p. 4)

A statement by Yahoo (8 September): 'Just like any other global company, Yahoo must ensure that its local country sites must operate within the laws, regulations and customs of the country in which they are based' (www.iht.com, 8 September 2005).

According to the company's co-founder, Jerry Yang ... Yahoo had to comply with a demand by Chinese authorities to provide information about a personal email of a journalist who was later convicted under state secrecy law ... According to Reporters Without Borders, court papers show that Yahoo Holdings (Hong Kong) gave Chinese investigators information that helped them trace a personal email to Shi's computer. It says Shi was convicted for sending notes on a government circular spelling out restrictions on the media ... Yahoo and two of its biggest rivals, Google and MSN, owned by Microsoft, have previously come under attack for censoring online news sites and weblogs, or blogs, featuring content that China's government wants to suppress.

(www.iht.com, 11 September 2005)

Jerry Yang, Yahoo co-founder, has admitted the US portal assisted Chinese authorities' action against a local journalist for leaking state secrets, but said it had had no choice. On Saturday [10 September] Mr Yang acknowledged Yahoo had provided information on Shi Tao as part of a 'legal process' and that the company had had no choice but to obey the law in any country in which it operated ... Reporters Without Borders said information on Mr Shi was provided by Yahoo's business in Hong Kong, which has an independent judiciary and separate legal process.

(*FT*, 12 September 2005, p. 26)

'Yahoo's subsidiary that turned in Shi is in Hong Kong' (*IHT*, 19 September 2005, p. 8). 'According to reports, the identity was established through Yahoo's Hong Kong operation. Hong Kong ... operates under different laws and does not yet have all-embracing "state secrecy" laws' (*IHT*, 21 September 2005, p. 8).

China issued instructions Sunday [25 September] designed to limit information available to internet users and sharply restricting the scope of news and opinion that can be posted on websites ... Under the new regulations major search engines and portals must stop posting commentary articles and instead make available only opinion pieces generated by government-controlled newspapers and news agencies. Also private individuals or groups must register as 'news organizations' under Chinese law before they can run email distribution lists that spread news or views ... The regulations say: 'The foremost responsibility of news sites on the internet is to serve socialism, guide public opinion in the right direction and uphold the interests of the country and the public good.'

(*IHT*, 26 September 2005, p. 12)

China set new regulations on internet news content yesterday [25 September], widening a campaign of controls it has imposed on other websites, such as discussion groups. 'The state bans the spreading of any news with content that is against national security and public unrest,' the official Xinhua news agency said, adding that internet sites must be directed towards serving the people and socialism.

(FT, 26 September 2005, p. 15)

[The] government said Tuesday [6 December] that it had stepped up the monitoring of short-text messages sent by the nation's 383 million cellphone users to prevent fraud, pornography and other 'unhealthy elements' from exploiting the technology . . . The crackdown on short-message services mirrors a tightening of rules on internet content announced in September.

(www.iht.com, 6 December 2005)

Microsoft's decision to shut down the site of a well known Chinese blogger was the latest in a series of measures in which some of the biggest technology companies have co-operated with Beijing to curb dissent or free speech online. Microsoft drew criticism last summer [2005] when it was discovered that its blog tool in China was designed to filter words like 'democracy' and 'human rights' from blog titles. The company said this week that it must 'comply with global and local laws' . . . The site pulled down this past week was a popular one created by Zhao Jing, a well known blogger with an online pen name [An Ti] . . . [who] also works as a research assistant in the Beijing bureau of the *New York Times* . . . Zhao worked as a journalist for a Chinese newspaper and as a research assistant for the *Washington Post* before joining the *Times* in 2003 . . . The blog was removed last week from a Microsoft service called MSN [MSN Spaces sites being maintained on computer servers in the United States] after the blog discussed the firing of the independent-minded editor of the *Beijing News*, which prompted about 100 journalists at the paper to go on strike on 29 December [2005]. It was an unusual show of solidarity for a Chinese news organization in an industry that has long complied with tight restrictions on what can be published . . . Zhao said he had kept a personal blog for more than a year . . . Zhao said that Microsoft chose to delete his blog on 30 December with no warning . . . Zhao's site was taken down after the Chinese authorities made a request . . . A spokeswoman for Microsoft said the company had blocked 'many sites' in China . . . Another American online service operating in China, Yahoo, was widely criticized in the autumn [of 2005] after it was revealed that the company had provided Chinese authorities with information that led to the imprisonment of a Chinese journalist who kept a personal email account with Yahoo. Yahoo also defended its action by saying it was forced to comply with local law.

(IHT, 7 January 2006, p. 17; www.iht.com, 6 January 2006)

'Some of the world's most famous internet companies have lined up to show how to cripple the web. A partial list includes Google, Microsoft, Yahoo, Cisco, Sun Microsystems and Skype' (Jonathan Mirsky, *IHT*, 16 January 2006, p. 6).

It was not so long ago that the internet was seen as a trap for China. The country desperately needed to foster economic growth, and in the early 1990s much of the globe was plugging itself in. Sooner or later, the thinking went, China would have to plug into the web, too, and however efficiently its leaders might have controlled information in the old days, they would be no match for this democratic beast, decentralized and crackling with opinion and information from the four corners of the earth. Things did not exactly turn out that way ... China's leaders were savvy about their internet strategy almost from the moment they began permitting global connections in 1994. Rather than trying to tame the web through sheer technological derring-do, they instead created a multilayered regime of filtering and surveillance, vague legal regulations and stringent enforcement that, taken together, effectively neutralized the internet in China. In September [2005] Beijing issued additional overarching rules forbidding bloggers to post information that is 'bounded by law and administrative rules' or that 'creates social uncertainty' ... Microsoft was only the latest technology company to be criticized for co-operating with the Chinese government. Yahoo, Cisco ... [which] provided much of the hardware forming the backbone of China's internet ... and Google have all been accused of helping to maintain what the United States–China Economic and Security Review Commission, a Congressional investigatory body, has called 'the most sophisticated internet control system in the world' ... *Reporters with Borders*, which tracks censorship around the world ... lists sixty-two 'cyber dissidents' imprisoned around the world for their activities online: fifty-four are in China ... The American internet population is reaching saturation levels, with roughly 203 million users ... China has the second largest online population in sheer numbers, about 103 million users, by the country's official statistics, but that represents less than 8 per cent of 1.3 billion people. In the first six months of 2005 China added almost 10 million new web users.

(Tom Zeller, www.iht.com, 15 January 2006)

[The government uses] sophisticated filtering software to block websites that carry references to such 'prohibited' words as Tibet, Tiananmen or Falun Gong. Cisco Systems has been sharply criticized for selling the filtering equipment to China, and Yahoo, Google, Sun Microsystems and other American companies are complicit in various ways in government censorship abroad.

(editorial in the *Boston Globe*, *IHT*, 17 January 2006, p. 6)

The company motto may be 'Don't be evil' but Google, like other Western internet companies, will adopt self-censorship to build its business in China ... A growing number of visitors from China to the uncensored web address www.google.com will now be redirected to the self-censored www.google.cn, Google executives said Tuesday [24 January] ... Google issued a statement: 'While removing search results is inconsistent with Google's mission, providing no information (or a heavily degraded use experience that amounts to no information) is more inconsistent with our mission' ... The .cn address will offer a stripped-down version of Google's offerings, including a self-censored

version of the Google search engine ... The company said it would not offer
email service, discussion groups, video searches or blogging services ...
Yahoo offers a full range of services, often from China-based servers ...
Google said it had dealt with self-censorship before, notably in Germany over
Nazi memorabilia and in France over racism-related issues ... The company
will notify users in China that their search has been censored ... Google users
in China are now directed to servers in the United States for a Chinese-
language version of all the company's services. Passing the search through the
internet fire wall operated by the Chinese authorities slows response at best and
often blocks results entirely, they [Google executives] said. The full Chinese-
language version of Google with all services will remain available to users in
China who manage to get through the government-operated fire wall.

(*IHT*, 25 January 2006, pp. 1, 8)

Google [is] famous for its 'Do no evil' philosophy ... [and is] dedicated to
making information 'universally accessible' ... [Google is] promising to
inform Chinese users when search results are censored, something other China-
based search services do not do ... Google's overseas-based services have
long suffered from the attentions of Chinese internet censors, who have disrupted access to its news service and disable its 'cache' function for viewing
defunct websites. Users who search on sensitive topics are often blocked from
using the site. China in 2002 briefly denied access to Google ... Google says it
will not offer email and blogging services in China until it is 'comfortable' that
it can protect users' interests.

(*FT*, 25 January 2006, p. 13)

[China has] 110 million online users ... Of the sixty-four internet dissidents in
prison worldwide, fifty-four are from China ... In the United States it [Google]
assists the authorities' crackdown on copyright infringements ... In an attempt
to be more transparent than its rivals, Google said it would inform users that
certain web pages had been removed from the lists of results on the orders of
the government.

(*Guardian*, 25 January 2006, p. 3)

The Chinese authorities used information obtained from the American internet
company Yahoo in 2003 to convict a Chinese citizen of 'inciting subversion'
... Reporters Without Borders ... has said ... The assertion ... came on
Wednesday [8 February] ... a week before [the US] Congress is to hold hearings on human rights policies of American internet companies doing business
in China ... Reporters Without Borders said Li Zhi ... a former civil servant
... had used online discussion groups to criticize corruption among local
government officials. Li was arrested in August 2003 and convicted in December of the same year. He was sentenced to eight years in prison ... According
to the appeal [of Li's attorney], Li was convicted partly on the basis of his
internet communications, which were obtained from Yahoo's Chinese operation in Hong Kong ... [However, Yahoo's] spokeswoman ... said Yahoo
Hong Kong would not have access to Li's Chinese account and that it had not

released information to the Chinese government ... [She] said the company was investigating whether Yahoo China – operated by a partner company – had released the information.

(www.iht.com, 9 February 2006)

'More than 111 million Chinese use the internet, second only to the United States. [About] 16.9 per cent of urban Chinese use the internet. There are an estimated 13.3 million blogs in China. Three years ago there were none' (*The Times*, 10 February 2006, p. 40).

'Microsoft unveiled new guidelines this month [February] after it pulled the plug on a popular blogger on its MSN network at the Chinese government's request. In future, Microsoft said, it would only do so if handed a legally binding request' (*Guardian*, 14 February 2006, p. 19). 'The number of internet users in China has surged from 620,000 in 1997 to 110 million. It is estimated that there are between 5 million and 10 million blogs ... [There are] an estimated 30,000 internet police' (p. 25).

'The official ... [who] supervises internet affairs for ... the State Council ... said there are now 111 million Chinese web users' (www.iht.com, 14 February 2006).

Shi Tao, Li Zhi and Jiang Lijun [are] three Chinese cyberdissidents whom Yahoo helped send to prison for terms of ten years, eight years and four years, respectively ... There are 110 million internet users and 13 million bloggers, hugely outnumbering the 30,000-odd censors.

(*IHT*, 20 February 2006, p. 7)

'Reporters Without Frontiers, based in Paris, ranks China 159th on a list of 167 countries in its global press freedom index. It also labels China one of fifteen that are "enemies of the internet", along with Myanmar, Iran and Syria' (www.iht.com, 27 February 2006).

China [is] the world's biggest mobile phone market ... The number of users on the mainland rose in January [2006] by 5.4 million to 398 million. The country set up its first network in 1987 and ten years later had 10 million customers.

(*The Times*, 24 February 2006, p. 43)

Billed as the next generation of the internet, a new technical standard enthusiastically embraced by China will allow greater traceability of internet users, potentially endangering those expressing views counter to the government's. The standard [is] known as IPv6 ... Adopted in the 1980s, the current system has only 4.3 billion possible addresses and those could be used up within five years. China's online population has grown to more than 110 million, far outstripping the country's allocation of 70 million addresses ... The ability to more closely identify users comes with the IPv6 standard, which expands the number of potential addresses into the trillions. Implementation of the detailed addressing system in China began in 2004.

(*IHT*, 20 March 2006, pp. 1, 8)

Study abroad

'Of the 380,000 Chinese who have left the mainland to study overseas since ... 1978, only 130,000 have returned, according to government figures' (*FT*, 14 March 2002, p. 12).

'According to official figures, 458,000 Chinese have gone abroad to study since the country opened up two decades ago, and only 135,000 have returned' (*Telegraph*, 12 July 2003, p. 19).

SARS

SARS (Severe Acute Respiratory Syndrome) is a highly infectious strain of pneumonia. It first appeared in Guangdong province in November 2002.

'The first case was officially reported in February [2003] ... The earliest cases of SARS appeared in Guangdong in November [2002], but the WTO first heard about the disease in February – and even then through unofficial channels' (*The Economist*, 5 April 2003, p. 13).

'SARS first began to shake public confidence in early January [2003]' (*FEER*, 10 April 2003, p. 13).

'A Chinese medical professor who had been treating infected patients brought the disease from Guangdong province to Hong Kong ... in late February. Travellers from Hong Kong then carried the disease to Beijing, Taiwan, Singapore, Vietnam and Canada' (*IHT*, 24 May 2003, p. 4).

'Beijing has been criticized for not providing adequate information to international health authorities about the spread of the illness in Guangdong' (*FT*, 2 April 2003, p. 10). '[China] kept the outbreak secret for months and even now may not have disclosed its full extent' (*The Times*, 2 April 2003, p. 13). 'China ... [has] continued refusing to give information long promised to medical investigators from the World Health Organization' (*IHT*, 2 April 2003, p. 7).

'The WHO hailed Beijing's decision to provide fuller data and finally [on 2 April] to permit a team of international health experts to travel to Guangdong to investigate the outbreak' (*FT*, 3 April 2003, p. 11).

> SARS ... was not revealed by the Chinese government until February, when Beijing began reporting cases to the WHO ... On 9 February the WHO received its first report about the disease from China ... On 15 March the WHO took a highly unusual step in issuing a global health alert ... Until the past two weeks health officials in China not only were unwilling to share their data, but also denied that the four-month-long pneumonia outbreak affecting Guangdong has anything to do with SARS.
>
> (*IHT*, 8 April 2003, pp. 1, 8)

'The WHO issued an unprecedented warning against travel to Hong Kong and the neighbouring Chinese province of Guangdong' (*IHT*, 10 April 2003, p. 7).

'A senior Chinese military surgeon said the government has understated the spread of the disease in Beijing' (*FT*, 10 April 2003, p. 6). 'China's doctors and nurses are risking prosecution under state secret laws by accusing the government of lying about the spread of SARS ... Passing on information about infectious diseases is covered by state secrecy legislation' (*Telegraph*, 10 April 2003, p. 18).

China's top leaders ... have issued their strongest warning yet [which appeared in the newspapers on 18 April] about SARS and have explicitly cautioned officials not to cover up its spread ... An urgent meeting on SARS [was] held Thursday [17 April] by the country's supreme ruling body, the nine-member Standing Committee of the Politburo.

(*IHT*, 19 April 2003, p. 7)

The United States said yesterday [11 April] it would not offer a United Nations resolution condemning China for human rights abuses, the first time since the Tiananmen Square massacre that Washington has not tried to censure the Beijing government. The decision ... is the latest sign of improving relations between the United States and China as a result of the war on terrorism and China's muted opposition to the war in Iraq.

(*FT*, 12 April 2003, p. 13)

[On 20 April] China announced a ten-fold increase in the number of people infected with the disease in [the capital] Beijing ... China dismissed its health minister [Zhang Wenkang] and the mayor of Beijing [Meng Xuenong] ... The Chinese authorities also cancelled a week-long national [May Day] holiday that runs from 1 May.

(*FT*, 21 April 2003, p. 1)

'Officials said the [Golden Week] vacation would be limited to one day and encouraged people to stay close to home' (*IHT*, 21 April 2003, p. 1).

(The holiday was later reduced from seven to five days but other measures were taken, such as monitoring of passengers.)

Gao Qiang ... the deputy [health] minister ... stressed that from now on 'underreporting, late reporting or failure to report' SARS cases would not be allowed ... Mr Gao also promised aid for China's poor, especially in rural areas, who might avoid hospitals for fear of medical expenses.

(*Guardian*, 21 April 2003, p. 1)

Liu Qi, the communist official in charge of Beijing ... acknowledged [on 21 April] that he provided late, inaccurate data on the SARS epidemic and failed to contain its spread ... [He said] 'There have been obvious deficiencies in our work. I take the responsibility of leadership and make a sincere self-criticism.'

(*FT*, 22 April 2003, p. 1)

On 23 April further measures were taken to combat the disease in Beijing, e.g. primary and middle schools were to be closed for at least two weeks and people and buildings that had been infected were to be quarantined. Beijing and Shangxi province were added to the WHO's list of places where non-essential travel was to be avoided (i.e. in addition to Guangdong province and Hong Kong). University students were told not to travel to their homes outside Beijing.

Fear of SARS has gripped the Chinese capital, sending many workers fleeing to their home towns, prompting companies to order impromptu holidays and emptying hotels, shopping centres and restaurants. Beijing authorities have ordered at least 4,000 people who have had close contact with SARS victims to quarantine themselves at home.

(*FT*, 26 April 2003, p. 10)

Estimates have begun to be made of how much of an impact SARS would make on economic growth (p. 10).

At least 4,000 Beijing residents with exposure to [SARS] ... are being kept in isolation, often in their own homes, the health authorities said Friday [25 April] and a second major hospital was put under total quarantine, with virtually no one allowed to enter or leave. City officials also revealed that 300 college students ... had been sequestered in a military training camp for two weeks' observation ... Friday morning Beijing officials held the first of what they promised would be frequent press briefings on an epidemic that has suddenly become a consuming threat and popular obsession.

(*IHT*, 26 April 2003, p. 1)

'In Beijing the authorities shut theatres, discos and other entertainment venues as ... the Chinese capital appeared set to become the world's worst-hit area, eclipsing ... Guangdong' (*FT*, 28 April 2003, p. 8).

The outbreak of SARS has inflicted the greatest blow to the Chinese economy since the massacre around Tiananmen Square in 1989 ... The initial impact has fallen on businesses that provide services, which ... make up a third of the Chinese economy ... But there are signs that ... the manufacturing sector, which accounts for half of economic output, could also begin to feel the effects ... Service businesses represent close to two-thirds of the economies of developed countries like the United States, and five-sixths of the economy of Hong Kong, which exists as a trading centre and has been especially hurt by its SARS epidemic ... The municipal government in Beijing has ordered the closing of all cinemas, playhouses, internet cafés and other entertainment venues.

(*IHT*, 28 April 2003, pp. 1, 4)

[Manufacturing accounts for] 54 per cent of GDP ... [There is] little disruption so far ... Services are 28 per cent of GDP and there the impact from aviation to retail is large. Agriculture, 14 per cent of the economy, is likely to be largely insulated from a SARS shock, because the vast majority of agricultural production is sold near the place it is grown. There is no real nationwide network to disrupt. Construction makes up the remaining 5 per cent ... There is little sign of it [a real estate slump] now ... Add it all up and you have an economy that is being hit – but not that hard ... This is a slowdown amid a gigantic boom.

(*FEER*, 8 May 2003, p. 30)

'[Beijing's] 12 million residents have either fled the city or chosen to sit out the epidemic at home ... Wu Yi ... known as "China's Iron Lady" ... [has been appointed as] health minister' (*The Times*, 28 April 2003, p. 12). (Wu Yi took a tough stance in enforcing the 'one child' population control programme. She was also an international trade negotiator.)

'The Chinese government on Monday [28 April] ... announced the closure of the stock exchanges in Shanghai and Shenzhen, at least from Thursday [1 May] through 9 May and perhaps longer' (*IHT*, 29 April 2003, p. 5).

Prime minister Wen Jiabao (speaking on 29 April at an international meeting on SARS in Bangkok):

> Our countermeasures are not adequate by far. We have already learned our lesson. The citizens and government of China are in action and action itself represents hope. The SARS situation in China is still grave. Some places are experiencing more and more cases. Those people who violate these principles [about disclosing information on SARS] should be dealt with according to the law.
>
> (*IHT*, 30 April 2003, p. 6; *FT*, 30 April 2003, p. 10)

28 April 2003.

> The World Health Organization on Monday [28 April 2003] declared Vietnam the first SARS infected country cleared of the virus ... Outbreaks of the disease had peaked in Canada, Singapore and Hong Kong, but not in China ... [Vietnam] was one of four countries in which local transmission of the disease took place ... Although sixty-three people became infected with the disease in Vietnam, including five medical workers who died, there have been no new cases since 8 April.
>
> (*IHT*, 29 April 2003, p. 5)

> The disease has killed at least 332 people [worldwide], has infected 4,800 people, mostly in China and Hong Kong ... Hong Kong's death toll has reached 138 ... China has reported 3,106 infections ... The reported number of cases [infections]: China (mainland), 3,106; Hong Kong, 1,557; worldwide, more than 4,800. Reported number of deaths: China (mainland), 139; Hong Kong: 138; worldwide, 332.
>
> (*IHT*, 29 April 2003, p. 5)

Wang Qishan is acting mayor of Beijing. Wang Qishan (30 April):

> As the panic of the public has not yet been alleviated, a great deal of work is needed to ensure social stability. Due to a shortage of beds at designated hospitals not all suspected SARS patients can be hospitalized in a timely manner.

'A surge in the number of cases of SARS in the Chinese capital has sparked fear and panic buying of medicines and staple foods. People are staying at home' (*Independent*, 1 May 2003, p. 16).

'By 30 April the city [Beijing] had reported 1,440 confirmed SARS cases, 1,408 suspected cases and seventy-five deaths from the disease, the worst outbreak in the country' (*The Economist*, 3 May 2003, p. 65). 'The total number of cases [infections] on the mainland [rose] to 3,460' (p. 87).

The May Day (1 May) celebrations were cancelled.

> All seventy sailors aboard a Chinese conventionally powered submarine died after it suffered 'mechanical problems' during a military exercise, the official media said yesterday [2 May] in a rare admission of a serious military mishap ... China has rarely acknowledged military accidents in the past. In the mid-1980s a destroyer exploded ... killing as many as 100. This time, though, diplomats said, the government might have been spurred into greater transparency by the stinging criticism it drew for covering up its SARS pneumonia epidemic in April.
>
> (*FT*, 3 May 2003, p. 13)

'The Chinese submarine accident ... occurred on 16 April' (*IHT*, 5 May 2003, p. 5). 'The cause of death was not given, but toxic fumes have been suggested' (*IHT*, 6 May 2003, p. 10). '[The] submarine accident was the worst acknowledged military accident since the communist takeover in 1949' (*FEER*, 26 June 2003, p. 25). ('China's navy chief ... Admiral Shi Yunsheng ... was sacked this week, taking the blame for the April submarine disaster ... Nine other senior naval officers were dismissed or demoted ... including Mr Shi's deputy and political commissar, Yang Huaiqing': *FT*, 14 June 2003, p. 9.)

> China, with a total of 3,799 cases reported Friday [2 May], including 181 deaths, has more SARS patients than the rest of the world put together ... More than 5,900 probable cases of SARS have been reported worldwide, causing 413 deaths.
>
> (*IHT*, 3 May 2003, p. 2)

> China will not allow foreign tourists to go to Tibet or other western regions of the country ... [it was] reported yesterday [3 May]. Travel agencies have been told to delay all tourism to the region until the end of May ... [China] had banned travel agents from taking Chinese citizens outside their home provinces ... The state tourism administration banned travel to Tibet on 25 April ... The report did not say when travel to other parts of China's west was banned ... No cases [of SARS] have been reported in Tibet.
>
> (*Guardian*, 3 May 2003, p. 22)

'So far ninety-one people in the city [Beijing] have died ... The global death toll now stands at 416' (*The Times*, 3 May 2003, p. 22).

> Beijing announced Saturday [3 May] that it would allow epidemiologists from the World Health Organization to go to Taiwan to help fight the disease there. Beijing replaced Taipei in 1972 in representing China at the WHO and had resisted until this weekend any contact between Taipei and the health organization except by way of Beijing ... On Sunday [4 May] the Beijing authorities ordered that all [elementary and middle] city schools remain closed for an additional two weeks.
>
> (*IHT*, 5 May 2003, p. 7)

'[Beijing's] total number of cases is 1,803 ... and the city's total number of fatalities stands at 100' (*Independent*, 5 May 2003, p. 3).

The reported number of cases is as follows: China (mainland), 4,125; Hong Kong, 1,689; worldwide, 6,242. The reported number of deaths is as follows: China (mainland), 197; Hong Kong, 184; worldwide, 449 (*IHT*, 5 May 2003, p. 7).

Beijing's total of deaths now stands at 103 (*FT*, 6 May 2003, p. 13).

> SARS has left huge swaths of China virtually unaffected ... The illness is almost under control in Guangdong, the wealthy southern province where it first erupted. Shanghai, which with Guangdong contributes 16.7 per cent of the country's GDP, has been almost unaffected ... Many economists are predicting that, overall, SARS could wipe out one or two percentage points from Chinese GDP growth this year [2003]. The World Bank is slightly more optimistic, lowering its forecast from 8 per cent to 7.5 per cent.
>
> (*FT*, 6 May 2003, p. 19)

There is great concern about the spread of SARS to rural areas because of the poor health facilities there.

> China's economic reforms have brought the country's rural health care system to the brink of collapse ... The reforms have undermined many positive gains of the Maoist policy in social welfare. Particularly hard hit have been small rural health clinics ... Hundreds of millions of peasants no longer have even rudimentary health facilities ... Where health care is available it is as a 'pay-as-you-go' system that is unaffordable to most people ... China's leadership is responding [to SARS] by promising to repay hospitals for admitting peasants.
>
> (Joshua Muldavin, *IHT*, 8 May 2003, p. 6)

> The government had begun rethinking rural health even before SARS arrived ... At a national conference in October [2002] officials unveiled an ambitious plan to create a new rural collective medical system into which farmers and the central and provincial government would each pay renminbi 10 billion a year. Trials have already begun in some areas of the system, under which the funds are used to provide insurance against large medical costs.
>
> (*FT*, 8 May 2003, p. 12)

'The WHO announced Thursday [8 May] that it was extending its warning against non-essential travel to the city of Tianjin and Inner Mongolia in China, and to Taipei' (*IHT*, 9 May 2003, p. 5).

> China announced Thursday [8 May] that it would attend the summit meeting of the Group of Eight major industrial nations next month [1–3 June] in France, a significant shift in diplomatic perspective ... [In the past China] derided ... the G8 ... as a rich man's club ... The impetus behind China's reversal Thursday may be an urge to enhance the government's stature following the SARS crisis.
>
> (*IHT*, 9 May 2003, p. 5)

> The Sars epidemic has begun to hit China's export juggernaut ... Most of China's export industries have until this week reported little impact from SARS, but as the disease spreads further into the hinterland, and authorities in Beijing fail to contain it, evidence of trade dislocation is growing. Textiles are

particularly badly hit because face-to-face contact is required to finalize most garment orders ... Many textile products must be seen by eyes and felt by hands ... Textile exports ... [constitute] China's biggest single export item ... There is evidence that SARS is hitting other export sectors, too. Food and agricultural produce appears to be badly affected, partly because of a belief that the virus could survive in a shipment ... There is concern among ... overseas importers ... that the supply chain within China could be affected by the disease, or because their quality inspectors cannot make the trip to a SARS-infected area.

(FT, 10 May 2003, p. 7)

'China has announced a package of tax relief measures for business sectors hit by the outbreak of SARS' *(FT,* 13 May 2003, p. 14).

The legal announcement of 15 May:

Intentional spreading of disease pathogens in sudden epidemics, endangering public security, causing serious injuries or death, or serious loss to private or public properties, will attract a sentence of imprisonment for a minimum of ten years, or life imprisonment, or death sentence.

(Telegraph, 16 May 2003, p. 19)

'The edict, a judicial interpretation of existing disease laws, was announced only days after the government issued new rules holding officials legally accountable for any delays in reporting health emergencies and requiring rapid public disclosure about health threats' *(IHT,* 16 May 2003, p. 5). 'Officials found guilty of negligently allowing the disease to spread face three years in jail' (www.bbc.co.uk, 15 May 2003).

The current estimate of SARS cases in Asia is around 5,000. But that figure is cumulative. It is not the number who have the disease (which is about half that figure), but the total number of those who have it and those who have had it.

(FEER, 22 May 2003, p. 21)

China said on 20 May that SARS had peaked in the capital and other big cities with no sign of it spreading in large numbers to the countryside. 'From mid-April to May it peaked in Beijing ... Cases have mainly occurred in urban areas, with few in rural areas and no cluster cases in the countryside' [the statement said].

(FEER, 29 May 2003, p. 22)

The anxiety about the disease has begun to ease. Beijing high schools opened Thursday [22 May] for the first time since 22 April ... Elementary schools are expected to remain closed until mid-June ... Officials are increasingly confident the worst is over.

(IHT, 23 May 2003, p. 5)

'Taiwan reported a daily rise in cases ... But in mainland China, Hong Kong and Singapore the epidemic appeared to be waning' *(The Economist,* 24 May 2003, p. 6).

The WHO yesterday [23 May] lifted its SARS travel alert on Hong Kong and China's Guangdong province ... SARS has begun to affect southern China's vast manufacturing hinterland in Guangdong ... China reported only twenty new infections, bringing its total to 5,285 cases and 303 deaths. Worldwide there have been 8,113 infections and 688 deaths.

(*FT*, 24 May 2003, p. 7)

The reported number of cases is as follows: China (mainland), 5,316 Hong Kong, 1,726; Taiwan, 585; worldwide, more than 8,100. The reported number of deaths is as follows: China (mainland), 317; Hong Kong, 267; Taiwan, 72; worldwide, 724 (*IHT*, 20 May 2003, p. 9).

On 8 June 2003, China: cases, 5,328; deaths, 339; worldwide: more than 8,300, and 781.

'China on Sunday [1 June] reported no new SARS fatalities and two new cases on its mainland, the lowest figures for a single day since authorities began keeping a daily count in April' (*IHT*, 2 June 2003, p. 5).

'China on 1 June reported no new deaths from SARS – and on 2 June no new cases of SARS – for the first time since it began releasing such figures on 20 April' (*FEER*, 12 June 2003, p. 26).

China on Monday [2 June] reported two new SARS deaths on the mainland and no new cases – the first time since it began reporting figure in April that no new cases were reported. That raised the death toll to 334, while the number of people sickened remained 5,328 ... Chinese health officials are still not co-operating adequately in the fight against SARS, a senior official in the WHO said Monday.

(*IHT*, 3 June 2003, p. 7)

'The WHO declared Thursday [5 June] that the global crisis was receding ... China reported no new cases of the disease for the second day in a row and the eleventh consecutive day of fewer than ten new cases' (*IHT*, 6 June 2003, p. 10).

'On 17 June Hong Kong and mainland China reported no new SARS cases for the sixth straight day' (*FEER*, 26 June 2003, p. 12).

Signalling that the worst of the SARS crisis seems to have passed, the WHO on Tuesday [17 June] lifted its warning against non-essential travel to Taiwan. Only the UN agency's recommendation against travel to Beijing remains in place, but health officials warned that Canada's experience showed how quickly a new outbreak of the disease can erupt ... The number of SARS cases has declined around the world ... The global outbreak has infected more than 8,400 people and killed 801.

(*IHT*, 18 June 2003, p. 5)

The WHO on Monday [23 June] removed Hong Kong from the list of SARS-infected areas, marking the end of a four-month crisis during which the deadly respiratory disease spread around the world ... Since the disease first arose in southern China last November [2002] it has spread to more than two dozen countries, where it infected more than 8,400 people and killed at least 800.

(*IHT*, 24 June 2003, p. 2)

The WHO scrapped its last SARS-related warning Tuesday [24 June], declaring Beijing safe to visit. Beijing was the city most infected by SARS, with more than 2,500 cases and 191 deaths ... The WHO lifted a similar warning from four other areas in China this month [June], removed a warning from Taiwan a week ago and scratched Hong Kong from its list of SARS-infected areas Monday [23 June] ... [The] disease first arose in the southern province of Guangzhou, six months before China began regular reporting of the outbreak.

(*IHT*, 25 June 2003, p. 3)

'Beijing has reported more than 2,500 cases – out of 5,300 in China and 8,450 worldwide – but no new victims have been found in the capital since 29 May' (*FT*, 25 June 2003, p. 11). 'A day after the WTO scrapped its last SARS-related warning ... China on Wednesday [25 June] reported a new case ... in Guangdong province and a death in Beijing' (*IHT*, 26 June 2003, p. 6).

The economic impact [of SARS], though severe in the travel, leisure and catering industries, appears unlikely to result in a big slowdown. Most analysts expect China to achieve at least 7 per cent growth this year [2003] ... That would only be a percentage point or two below what the country would probably have achieved without SARS.

(*The Economist*, 28 June 2003, p. 77)

'With cases of SARS fast on the decline, economists have started revising upward their 2003 economic growth forecasts that were cut because of SARS' (*FEER*, 3 July 2003, p. 22).

'Beijing has been the worst affected city in the world, with 2,521 reported cases and 191 deaths caused by the virus ... [In Hong Kong] 296 people have died from the disease out of 1,734 reported cases' (*FEER*, 3 July 2003, p. 10).

The WHO removed Toronto from its list of SARS-infected areas last Wednesday [2 July], saying Canada's largest city had contained the virus ... All eighteen people receiving treatment for SARS are in the Toronto area in hospital isolation wards ... Deaths remained unchanged at thirty-nine.

(*IHT*, 9 July 2003, p. 4)

The global epidemic of SARS has been contained and is no longer spreading, the WTO declared [on 5 July] ... Taiwan has been declared free of infectious cases by the WTO and was on Saturday [5 July] taken off its list of areas with recent local transmission of SARS ... The SARS virus ... has infected a total of 674 people in Taiwan and led to eighty-four deaths. This makes Taiwan the third most affected country, after China and Hong Kong. Worldwide 8,439 people have been infected and 812 have died from SARS.

(*FT*, 7 July 2003, p. 8)

'Investment banks and analysts, most of whom lowered GDP growth predictions this year during the SARS outbreak, have returned to earlier predictions or, in some cases, raised them ... Recovery from the virus was swifter than many had expected' (*FEER*, 17 July 2003, p. 48).

'China's last two SARS patients have recovered and left the [Beijing] hospital [on 16 August 2003] . . . [SARS] killed 349 people in the country' (*IHT*, 18 August 2003, p. 3). 'They were the last of 4,959 patients in China cured and discharged from hospital, out of a total of 5,327 SARS cases reported on the mainland. China's death toll from the disease stood at 349' (*FEER*, 28 August 2003, p. 24).

'WHO figures show that of the 8,422 people known to have caught it [SARS], 916 died' (*FT*, 10 September 2003, p. 20).

'[In] Hong Kong 1,755 cases and 299 deaths were recorded' (*IHT*, 14 October 2003, p. 2).

'A man has tested positive for SARS in Singapore . . . the first new case for five months' (*Guardian*, 9 September 2003, p. 14).

The Singapore health ministry confirmed Tuesday [9 September] that a . . . researcher who worked in two of the city's medical laboratories was the first case of SARS since the WHO said in July that . . . [it] had been contained worldwide . . . [The ministry] stressed that it had decided to confirm the man's illness even though it did not meet the WHO's definition of the disease.

(*IHT*, 10 September 2003, p. 4)

The Chinese government increased health screenings of travellers and hospital patients on Saturday [27 December] after acknowledging that doctors in this coastal city [of Guangzhou] were treating the first suspected SARS case [a free-lance television journalist who was admitted to hospital on 20 December] since the disease was declared contained by the World Health Organization in July . . . [On 17 December] a SARS case was confirmed in Taiwan. Another case was reported this summer in Singapore. Both those patients were health workers apparently exposed to the disease in hospital settings. In neither case was the virus believed to have spread. If SARS is confirmed as the cause of the illness in Guangzhou, it would raise the possibility of SARS reentering the general population . . . Speculation has abounded for months that SARS could return this winter . . . According to the World Health Organization, SARS has infected 8,099 people and killed 774 of them since its emergence in November [2002].

(www.iht.com, 28 December 2003)

Officials in Guangdong province on Monday [5 January 2004] ordered the immediate killing of every civet cat in captivity in the province after researchers found that a Guangdong man had fallen ill with a new strain of SARS virus that is genetically very similar to the strain found in civet cats . . . All civet cats – relatives of the mongoose widely eaten in winter as a delicacy – will be killed 'in a few days' . . . A Guangdong provincial official said that about 10,000 civet cats would be killed . . . [China's top expert on SARS] said that there would be an effort to trap and kill civet cats in the wild, but the Guangdong provincial official said that at least initially the government would only try to kill civet cats at restaurants, on farms and in wild animal markets . . . The Chinese health ministry and the World Health Organization confirmed Monday that the case in Guangdong province was now regarded as a full-blown case of SARS . . . Meanwhile, the Philippines has isolated a woman there after she was suspected of contracting SARS while working in Hong Kong, but a health official said Monday that it was too early to confirm whether she had the deadly virus.

(www.iht.com, 5 January 2004; *IHT*, 6 January 2004, p. 3)

[A health official from Guangdong said that] 'A decision has been made from today [5 January 2004] to close down all wild animal markets in Guangdong' ... Guangdong also launched a 'patriotic health campaign' to exterminate rats and cockroaches before the Chinese new year holiday, which starts on 22 January, when tens of millions of Chinese travel the country.

(*The Times*, 6 January 2004, p. 8)

'Markets that sold civets were to be closed as part of a campaign also exhorting the extermination of rats and cockroaches' (*FT*, 6 January 2004, p. 8). 'The director of the Guangzhou Institute of Respiratory Diseases said species relating to civet cats will also be killed, including raccoon dogs, Chinese ferret badgers, hog badgers and Eurasian badgers' (*Telegraph*, 6 January 2004, p. 12). 'The Guangdong government lifted controls on sales of civet cats and other species soon after the all-clear on SARS in humans was given last July [2003]. WHO officials criticized the move as "premature"' (*Guardian*, 6 January 2004, p. 16). '[The Chinese man with SARS] was pronounced "fully recovered" ... WHO investigators say no definitive connection has been established and expressed concern that a mass slaughter might spread the germ or eradicate crucial evidence of SARS' origins' (*IHT*, 7 January 2004, p. 2). 'The World Health Organization said the evidence was not strong enough to warrant the mass slaughter and worried that it might eliminate valuable clues and risk spreading SARS further' (www.feer.com, 15 January 2004).

A waitress in Guangzhou, the capital of Guangdong province ... was declared a suspected SARS case on Thursday [8 January], while in Hong Kong two members of a television crew tested negative for the deadly virus ... A television producer confirmed this week as China's first SARS case since last year [2003], and identified only as Luo, has recovered. He left the hospital on Thursday. Three television workers from Hong Kong ... had visited an animal market and a hospital where Luo had been treated before they returned to Hong Kong on 30 December [2003] with fevers ... Test results on the third [were] pending ... The first outbreak of SARS ... killed 349 people in China.

(*IHT*, 9 January 2004, p. 3)

The authorities set a Saturday [10 January] deadline to kill the civets and their order was later expanded to include badgers and other wildlife eaten in Guangzhou ... Three television reporters who showed SARS-like symptoms after visiting Guangdong province have all tested negative for the virus.

(www.iht.com, 9 January 2004)

'A thirty-five-year-old man in Guangdong is suspected of having SARS' (*Guardian*, 12 January 2004, p. 14).

Investigators from the World Health Organization have found strong evidence that animals play a role in SARS. The team revealed yesterday [16 January] that it uncovered traces of the virus in a restaurant in Guangzhou where a waitress believed to be infected with SARS worked and civet cats were served.

(*Independent*, 17 January 2004, p. 14)

The three cases of SARS that have been identified here [Guangzhou] appear to represent a milder strain of the disease, and the public health system appears well prepared to prevent a larger outbreak, a senior World Health organization investigator said Friday [16 January 2004].

(www.iht.com, 16 January 2004)

Three cases of the disease were confirmed [on 18 January] ... All three cases were in Guangdong ... One was a waitress who worked in a restaurant that served civet ... Two have recovered and a third is in a stable condition.

(*FT*, 19 January 2004, p. 6)

'[On 31 January China said] a forty-year-old man became the fourth SARS case since [July 2003]' (*IHT*, 2 February 2004, p. 2).

'China belatedly confirmed its fourth case of SARS this season, but said the patient ... a doctor in Guangzhou ... had left the hospital after a "total recovery"' (*FEER*, 12 February 2004, p. 24).

SARS has failed to stage a significant resurgence this year [2004]. This winter just four people were diagnosed with SARS, all in Guangdong province ... Since the official campaign against the wild-game industry began in January no new SARS infections are known to have occurred ... Whether there are other reasons the disease did not return this winter is still a matter of guesswork ... But the virus is a virtual no-show as of early April.

(*FEER*, 8 April 2004, p. 35)

Analysts indicate that SARS crossed from its original animal hosts to humans in mid-November 2002. But only in early 2003 did it develop an efficient mechanism of spreading between people. That done, it spread around the world within weeks. Airborne influenza viruses are much more easily spread than SARS, partly because still-healthy carriers shed large amounts of virus. This is why the basic containment measures – isolation and quarantine – that worked so well for SARS would not work for a combined avian–human influenza.

(*IHT*, 12 April 2004, p. 8)

The Chinese government announced Thursday [22 April 2004] that a nurse in Beijing had been hospitalized with a suspected case of SARS and that five other people had been isolated with fevers. The authorities in Hong Kong said a second suspected SARS patient had been discovered in eastern China [in Anhui province] ... China has had no reported cases of SARS since January [2004].

(*IHT*, 23 April 2004, p. 7)

China reported two confirmed SARS cases on Friday [23 April] and said one of two other people suspected of having the disease had died. The two confirmed cases – one in Beijing and the other in the province of Anhui – are the first reported in those areas since last summer [2003]. Both are laboratories for China's centres for disease control and were probably infected there ... Besides the two confirmed SARS cases, Beijing and Anhui each have one suspected case ... One of the suspected cases ... has died.

(www.iht.com, 23 April 2004)

The Chinese government said on Friday [23 April] that it had sealed off its main SARS laboratory after an apparent safety breach there led to four confirmed and suspected cases, including a death ... This is the third outbreak from a laboratory accident, the others were in Singapore and Taiwan ... The cases involve two graduate students who worked at the institute ... The other two cases involve ... [one of the graduate's] mother, who died ... and a nurse ... who cared for [the graduate] ... Questions immediately arose about the apparent breach in the laboratory and why doctors and health officials had not been more alert to the possibility that ... [the graduate] had SARS.

(*IHT*, 24 April 2004, p. 1)

'[The graduate] had travelled from Beijing to her home in Anhui by train three times with a fever' (www.iht.com, 27 April 2004).

China announced Sunday [25 April] it was investigating four fresh suspected SARS cases in Beijing and ordered an affected province to gird for the coming May Day holiday when millions of Chinese will be travelling ... The latest four cases brought the total in China for the past week to two confirmed and six suspected. The new suspected cases are the father, mother, aunt and roommate of a ... confirmed SARS patient in Beijing.

(*IHT*, 26 April 2004, p. 4)

Nearly 500 people were in quarantine in China's capital and a southern province on Monday [26 April] as authorities raced to contain a small eruption of SARS before a national holiday puts millions of travellers on the road. Two confirmed cases of SARS and six suspected ones have been announced over the past week, all of them linked to people who worked in a SARS lab in Beijing ... All of the suspected cases announced over the weekend have been traced to a single patient, the government said, suggesting the problem was still tightly confined and not a general outbreak.

(www.iht.com, 26 April 2004)

'[China] announced no new suspected or confirmed cases of the virus Monday [27 April] ... "There appear to have been serious errors along the way" ... [said] a spokesman for the WHO office in Beijing' (*IHT*, 27 April 2004, p. 5).

[On 28 April] a new suspected case [was] reported and the number of people isolated in Beijing during the crisis passed 700. The new case ... shared a Beijing hospital room with one of the two people confirmed to have [SARS] ... It brings to seven the number of suspected SARS patients in Beijing and Anhui province.

(www.iht.com, 28 April 2004)

Two patients in Beijing who had been suspected of having SARS were confirmed Thursday [29 April] as having the disease, one of them in critical condition. The mother and aunt of an infected nurse were the latest cases ... The announcement brought the number of confirmed cases on the mainland to four, with an additional five suspected cases.

(www.iht.com, 29 April 2004)

'Doctors are concerned that an infected nurse may have inadvertently spread the disease during a trip to Anhui province' (*Guardian*, 30 April 2004, p. 20).

The ministry of health said Saturday [1 May] that one of the institute's lab workers ... was confirmed to have SARS ... The announcement raised China's confirmed cases to six. One of those six has died. Another three patients are hospitalized as suspected SARS cases ... The WHO says the cases are not a public health threat because they are limited to a small group with a clear chain of transmission. The agency blames lab security for the outbreak.

(*IHT*, 3 May 2004, p. 6)

Three suspected cases of SARS in Beijing have been confirmed, pushing the number of victims of the latest outbreak to nine, China's health ministry said Tuesday [4 May]. All three newly confirmed cases ... were linked to one viral disease laboratory in Beijing ... The WHO ... wants to find out what went wrong with lab safety ... The experts visited the lab on Tuesday for a second time.

(www.iht.com, 4 May 2004)

Not a single case of SARS has been reported [in any country] this year [2005] or in late 2004. It is the first winter without a case since the initial outbreak in late 2002 ... The epidemic strain of SARS that caused at least 774 deaths worldwide by June 2003 has not been seen outside a laboratory since then. SARS is not even the nastiest bug in its neighbourhood, as health officials warn that avian influenza in South-east Asia poses a far greater threat ... Health officials have categorized SARS into three known outbreaks: the worldwide epidemic of more than 8,000 cases that began in November 2002 and ended in June 2003; the second outbreak from December 2003 through January 2004 that involved a milder strain of the virus; and the nine cases traced to laboratory accidents in China, Taiwan and Singapore between March and May of last year [2004].

(www.iht.com, 15 May 2005)

China has ordered emergency measures to prevent an outbreak of avian flu after investigators said migratory birds found dead in the country's west this month were killed by the virus. Nature reserves were closed to the public and local authorities were ordered to watch wild birds for signs of disease and impose quarantines if necessary ... Migratory birds found dead on 4 May in the western province of Qinghai were killed by the deadly H5N1 strain of the virus ... China's most recent known case of bird flu occurred last July [2004] in the eastern province of Anhui ... Since the SARS outbreak China has set up a nationwide disease-warning network and created emergency plans for possible outbreaks ... The regional death toll in the latest bird flu outbreak rose to fifty-three this week when another fatality was reported in Vietnam.

(www.iht.com, 22 May 2005)

'The outbreak of SARS in 2003 ... killed fewer than 1,000 people but cost Asia $40 billion in economic losses' (*IHT*, 15 July 2005, p. 6).

A worldwide scientific effort identified the cause of SARS in March 2003, four months after the disease had broken out in southern China ... SARS had the biggest impact on China, where the disease originated and caused the largest number of deaths – 349 ... SARS prompted Beijing to launch a $1 billion programme to improve the country's readiness for future epidemics. The programme includes a better reporting system and the founding of a centre for disease control ... Analysts found it hard to estimate the full economic cost of SARS, through travel disruption and lost output, but most authorities put the figure at more than $30 billion ... Although there were a few isolated cases of SARS last year [2004], some caused by escaping viruses from research laboratories, the epidemic strain in effect disappeared in the summer of 2003. Many experts assume that the virus is still lurking in the animals from which it emerged as a human disease ... [One theory is that] SARS started with rats, which infected civet cats, which in turn passed the virus to people.

(*FT*, 30 July 2005, p. 7)

Probable SARS cases and deaths, respectively, in the period November 2002 to July 2003 were as follows: China: 5,327 and 349; Hong Kong: 1,755 and 299; Taiwan: 346 and 37; Canada: 251 and 43; Singapore: 238 and 33; Vietnam: 63 and 5; Philippines: 14 and 2; Thailand: 9 and 2; Malaysia: 5 and 2 (*FT*, 30 July 2005, p. 7).

The SARS virus, which killed 774 people and cause severe economic losses, particularly in Asia, as it spread to Canada and other countries, has long been known to come from an animal. Now two scientific teams independently say that the Chinese horseshoe bat is that animal and is the reservoir of the virus in nature. The reservoir is the hiding place for the virus, where it can survive without causing illness in its host ... SARS first appeared in China in 2002. Then it spread widely in early 2003 to infect at least 8,098 people in twenty-six countries, according to the WHO. The disease died out and no cases have been reported since then ... During the SARS outbreak attention focussed on the role of the Himalayan palm civets in transmitting the disease after scientists identified the virus in this species and in a raccoon dog sold in markets in Guangdong ... But officials of the WHO and scientists elsewhere cautioned that ... civets ... most likely were only intermediaries in the chain of transmission to humans, largely because no widespread infection could be found in wild or farmed civets.

(*IHT*, 30 September 2005, p. 8)

'Later studies found no widespread infection in either wild or farmed civets' (*IHT*, 6 October 2005, p. 8).

The outbreak of SARS in Asia in 2003 only infected around 8,000 people and killed about a tenth of these. According to the most pessimistic estimates, it caused almost $60 billion of lost output, with tourism-related businesses being especially hard hit.

(www.economist.com, 20 October 2005)

'The latest data from the WHO show that a total of 8,097 people contracted SARS and 775 people died from it' (www.iht.com, 21 October 2005).

'[The] SARS outbreak led to estimated losses of between $30 billion and $50 billion' (www.iht.com, 25 October 2005; *IHT*, 26 October 2005, p. 3).

'SARS, which killed 800 people, caused an economic loss of around 2 per cent of East Asian regional GDP in the second quarter of 2003, according to a report from the [World] Bank on 8 November' (*The Economist*, 19 November 2005, p. 95).

'SARS cost east Asia an estimated 2 per cent of GDP in the second quarter of 2004' (*FT*, Survey on the World in 2006, 25 January 2006, p. 6).

Bird flu

On 13 January [2004] the World Health Organization announced that two Vietnamese children and one adult had died of ... bird flu ... Vietnam, South Korea and Japan are scrambling to control a fresh epidemic ... So far, Vietnam appears to be the only country where the dreaded H5N1 avian influenza is affecting humans ... The big question is whether human-to-human transmission will be detected ... The epidemic has triggered a mass poultry slaughter in all three countries.

(*FEER*, 22 January 2004, p. 11)

'The bird flu ... could become a bigger problem for the region than SARS ... The same strain of bird flu killed six people in Hong Kong in 1997' (*IHT*, 15 January 2004, p. 3).

'No confirmed or suspected deaths have been reported in South Korea, Japan and Taiwan, which are all coping with their own bird flu outbreaks' (www.iht.com, 19 January 2004).

An outbreak of the virulent H5N1 strain of bird flu in Hong Kong in 1997 infected eighteen people, killing six. It was the first time an avian virus had been observed crossing directly to humans. Hong Kong authorities slaughtered the territory's 1.5 million chickens. Hong Kong was hit by a second bird flu scare in 2001. Another mass slaughter was ordered ... In February 2003 ... in Hong Kong two cases of H5N1 were confirmed in a nine-year-old boy and his father, who died ... In July 2003 a flu outbreak in Vietnam led to the cull of 20,000 chickens.

(*FEER*, 29 January 2004, pp. 12–13)

Indonesia reported Sunday [25 January 2004] that millions of poultry had fallen ill with avian influenza ... South Korea, Japan, Vietnam, Cambodia, Thailand and Hong Kong have previously confirmed the disease in birds, while Taiwan has reported a less dangerous strain of bird flu in some chickens there.

(*IHT*, 26 January 2004, p. 20)

'The virus has infected millions of chickens in Thailand, Vietnam, Cambodia, South Korea, Japan and Taiwan' (www.iht.com, 26 January 2004).

> China said Tuesday [27 January] that avian flu had been found in fowl in three regions, as three international agencies issued a global appeal for donor nations to help bankroll Asia's fight to forestall a lethal flu epidemic in humans ... Ten Asian governments have reported outbreaks among poultry, with Laos joining the list Tuesday.
>
> (www.iht.com, 27 January 2004; *IHT*, 28 January 2004, p. 4)

> China denied a British publication's report blaming it for the beginning of the epidemic ... The *New Scientist* said it appeared that the bird flu cases began a year ago, most likely in China. It alleged the Chinese authorities hid the emergence of the disease.
>
> (*IHT*, 30 January 2004, p. 5)

> The WHO has said that the current outbreak of H5N1 in birds started in South Korea in December [2003]. However, *New Scientist*, a British magazine, said experts had told it that the outbreak probably began a few months earlier in China.
>
> (*The Economist*, 31 January 2004, p. 56)

> The WHO ... said Sunday [1 February] that China ... must improve its detection and handling of diseases ... [China] must quickly improve its surveillance network of animal diseases or face increased risks that the strain of the bird flu could jump to humans there ... China announced new suspected infections of bird flu in two more provinces on Saturday [31 January] ... The WHO has said that China's chances of halting bird flu are dwindling.
>
> (*IHT*, 2 February 2004, p. 2)

> A teenage boy in Vietnam and a woman in Thailand on Monday [2 February] became the latest deaths from bird flu ... [which] has now killed twelve people ... The two countries are the only ones where humans have died from this strain of avian influenza ... Infections in people have only been reported only in Thailand and Vietnam ... Bird flu spread between humans in a 1997 outbreak in Hong Kong that killed six people.
>
> (www.iht.com, 2 February 2004)

'China reported more confirmed and suspected outbreaks of the virus in its poultry stocks' (www.iht.com, 3 February 2004).

> The death toll from Asia's bird flu outbreak rose to fifteen on Wednesday [4 February] as the virus ravaged poultry flocks in ten countries and spread in China. Vietnamese authorities said tests confirmed a six-year-old boy who died earlier in the week had been infected with the H5N1 virus ... Twelve of China's thirty-one provinces have confirmed or suspected outbreaks of the disease. The UN agency said bird flu had been confirmed in fifty-three of Vietnam's sixty-four provinces ... The death of a seventeen-year-old girl from avian flu in Vietnam was the country's tenth death from the virus. All fourteen

deaths in the region so far are believed to have resulted from direct contact with infected poultry.

(www.iht.com, 4 February 2004)

Asia's human death toll from bird flu rose to fifteen on Wednesday [4 February], while China addressed its broadening zone of infected poultry by creating a bird flu headquarters ... New deaths were announced Wednesday in Vietnam, where a sixteen-year-old girl became the country's tenth bird flu fatality, and Thailand, where a six-year-old boy died, bringing that country's total to five. Human cases of bird flu have not been reported in any other countries. China said Wednesday that it had no human infections, but that officials were investigating cases in poultry in twelve of its thirty-one regions.

(*IHT*, 5 February 2004, p. 2)

'The death toll from the bird flu epidemic sweeping through Asia rose to sixteen on Thursday [5 February] ... as Vietnam announced that a sixteen-year-old girl had become its eleventh flu victim' (www.iht.com, 5 February 2004).

The WHO said on Thursday [12 February] that it could find no evidence that human-to-human transmission of bird flu was responsible for the deaths of two Vietnamese sisters last month [January]. Although the new test results could not prove the sisters did not catch the illness from their brother, they were nonetheless reassuring, officials from the UN health agency said.

(www.iht.com, 12 February 2004)

'Ten governments in the region have dealt with strains of bird flu since South Korean officials reported an outbreak there in early December [2003]' (www.iht.com, 13 February 2004).

Bird flu claimed its twentieth fatality in Asia [on 14 February] ... with the death of a thirteen-year-old boy in Thailand ... It is confirmed to have killed six people in Thailand and fourteen in Vietnam ... WHO officials have expressed concerns that China may also be suffering human cases, given the broad range of poultry infections there.

(*IHT*, 16 February 2004, p. 2)

'[In March] in Vietnam a twelve-year-old boy died, taking Asia's death toll from the virus to twenty-four' (*FEER*, 1 April 2004, p. 13).

According to the available data, all infected people contracted the virus from birds. There is no confirmed evidence of human-to-human transmission yet ... Airborne influenza viruses are much more easily spread than SARS, partly because still-healthy carriers shed large amounts of virus. This is why the basic containment measures – isolation and quarantine – that worked so well for SARS would not work for a recombined avian-human influenza.

(*IHT*, 12 April 2004, p. 8)

'China reported a new outbreak of bird flu Tuesday [6 July 2004] and Thailand said it had a suspected case' (*IHT*, 7 July 2004, p. 8). 'In China official said they had found a single infected bird ... in Anhui province' (www.iht.com, 7 July 2004).

Scientists voiced growing alarm on Wednesday [7 July] that avian flu may have become impossible to eradicate in Asia and could eventually spread easily among humans. The warning came as China, Thailand and Vietnam, which all found chickens dying of the disease again in the past week, began culling thousands of birds in the hope of preventing a human outbreak. Earlier this year [2004] ten countries reported cases in poultry and more than 100 million chickens were killed ... [A journal article] concludes that the disease is firmly rooted in domesticated ducks in southern China.

(www.iht.com, 7 July 2004; *IHT*, 8 July 2004, p. 8)

A senior Chinese health official disclosed on Friday [20 August] her country had found a lethal strain of avian influenza among pigs at several farms, a discovery that could move the virus one step closer to becoming a global problem for humans ... The A(H5N1) strain of avian influenza, or bird flu, infected chickens in at least eight countries this year [2004] and killed twenty-three of the thirty-four people in Thailand and Vietnam who caught the disease directly from poultry ... The discovery of the bird flu strain in pigs is alarming ...because scientists have long regarded pigs as an important conduit for new influenza strains in humans. Most kinds of influenza viruses live only in birds, not people. But pigs can be infected with both bird strains and human strains of influenza. When these viruses mix and reassort genes inside a pig, the result can be a new virus for which humans have little immunity.

(*IHT*, 21 August 2004, p. 5)

'The avian influenza virus ... has crossed another species barrier to infect cats, and can be spread among them as well, Dutch scientists have found' (www.iht.com, 3 September 2004).
'An outbreak of A(H5N1) in Hong Kong in 1997 included several probable cases of human-to-human transmission' (*IHT*, 29 September 2004, p. 5). '[A Thai lady] is the first person believed to have contracted the disease from another human, rather than poultry ... The country's tenth confirmed fatality ... [Her] daughter was cremated and there is no proof she died of A(H5N1) avian influenza' (www.iht.com, 29 September 2004). 'Thai and international health officials confirmed on Tuesday that the first probable human-to-human transmission had been recorded in Thailand' (*IHT*, 30 September 2004, p. 6).

Vietnam confirmed a new bird flu death to bring Asia's human toll to thirty on Wednesday [29 September] ... A baby in Hanoi became Vietnam's twentieth victim ... The recent deaths in Vietnam and Thailand are part of a second wave of outbreaks since ... the start of this year [2004].

(www.iht.com, 29 September 2004)

The strain, A(H5N1) has killed thirty of the forty-two south-east Asians it infected in the past year ... A handful of cases of human-to-human transmission may have occurred during bird flu outbreaks in Hong Kong in 1997 and in Europe a year ago, but neither resulted in a pandemic.

(www.iht.com, 1 October 2004)

The human toll from bird flu reached thirty-one on Monday [4 October] when Thailand confirmed that a nine-year-old girl had died from the disease ... The girl's death brought to eleven the number of human deaths in Thailand ... In Vietnam, the only other country to suffer human cases of the virus, twenty people have died.

(www.iht.com, 4 October 2004)

'As more human bird flu cases occur, the chances become greater for the deadly virus to acquire more ability to be transmitted from person to person. That could spark the next global pandemic – possibly killing millions' (www.iht.com, 21 January 2005).

A conference expected to attract international scientists and representatives from countries battling bird flu will open Wednesday [23 February 2005] in Ho Chi Minh City ... organized by the World Organization for Animal health and the Food and Agricultural Organization ... ... Vietnam is the only country to have suffered bird flu-related human deaths this year [2005]. It has been the worst hit by the disease, with thirty-three human deaths from two outbreaks of the A(H5N1) strain of the bird flu virus since late 2003 ... The bird flu epidemic, which has hit several Asian countries and has killed forty-five people since 2003 ... Bird flu has already affected Cambodia, Thailand and Vietnam in 2005, after being discovered in eight countries in 2004, including China, Indonesia, Japan, Laos and South Korea. Twelve have died in Thailand.

(www.iht.com, 21 February 2005)

Shigeru Omi (regional director of the World Health Organization):

[The virus appeared to be] evolving in ways that increasingly favour the start of a [human] pandemic ... We at the WHO believe the world is now in the gravest possible danger of a pandemic. We must all work together to make sure what is happening in the animal world does not spill over and cause health emergencies for humans ... There are many terrible diseases in Asia, but this one is the most urgent because global health is now at risk ... We are now confident in our judgement that this virus has become endemic in Asia. We have been through three waves of human cases of the virus in Vietnam over the last year.

(*FT*, 24 February 2005, p. 11; www.iht.com, 24 February 2005)

Since 2003 avian flu has killed forty-six people – about 80 per cent of those identified as infected ... Two may have caught it from other humans. International health officials fear the virus may mutate – or recombine with a human flu virus – into a form easily transmitted from person to person.

(*FT*, 24 February 2005, p. 11)

'A sixty-nine-year old man has died of bird flu in Vietnam, the fourteenth fatality from the disease in the country this year' (*IHT*, 28 February 2005, p. 6).
'[This is] the forty-sixth fatality in South-East Asia this year' (*Independent*, 28 February 2005, p. 27).

A twenty-six-year-old male nurse who tended a patient with bird flu has caught the virus that has killed forty-seven people in Asia, a health official said Monday [7 March]. It was not yet clear whether the nurse had caught the virus, known as H5N1 from the patient or through other means ... Experts fear that if the versatile and resilient virus mutates into a form that could easily jump between humans it would kill millions in a global pandemic. Almost all of the Asian victims – thirty-four Vietnamese, twelve Thais and a Cambodian – have caught it from infected poultry. Bird flu kills more than 70 per cent of those known to have been infected, but doctors say victims can be saved if they are diagnosed early.

(www.iht.com, 7 March 2005)

For the first time North Korea confirmed an outbreak of bird flu and said Sunday [27 March] that hundreds of thousands of chickens had been culled ... North Korea had previously declared itself free of the disease, which has swept much of East and South-East Asia, killing forty-eight people and millions of birds since late 2004 ... Since late 2004 the WHO has registered more than sixty-nine cases of humans infected with the H5N1 strain of avian flu. It has killed thirty-four Vietnamese, twelve Thais and two Cambodians.

(www.iht.com, 27 March 2005)

North Korea admitted bird flu had broken out in Pyongyang ... although it remained unclear if the virus spotted was the H5N1 strain, which has been known to spread to humans from birds ... South Korea confirmed nineteen cases of the H5N1 strain at poultry farms between December 2003 and March 2004.

(*FT*, 28 March 2005, p. 6)

'South Korea was the first Asian country to report a bird flu outbreak in December 2003 ... the country reported one case of low-pathogenic bird flu last year [2004]' (*FT*, 29 March 2005, p. 6).

The human toll from bird flu reached fifty yesterday [6 April] that a ten-year-old girl had died ... on 27 March ... She had the H5N1 virus ... Over the last sixteen months bird flu has killed thirty-six people in Vietnam (fifteen of those in the past four months), twelve people in Thailand and two in Cambodia.

(*Guardian*, 7 April 2005, p. 16)

Prior to the latest outbreaks bird flu was thought to be rare in poultry and unlikely to spread between countries. Today, however, it has affected eleven countries all the way from Japan to Indonesia and caused the death of over 120 million Asian birds. This outbreak is without precedent.

(*The Economist*, 16 April 2005, p. 53)

Indonesian health officials confirmed the first human case of bird flu in the country on Thursday [16 June 2005] ... Indonesia is the fourth country to report a case of the bird flu virus in humans ... The virus has infected more than 100 people and killed fifty-four people in Vietnam, Thailand and Cambodia since late 2003.

(www.iht.com, 16 June 2005)

'The World Health Organization has confirmed 107 cases of human infection in South-east Asia, fifty-four of them fatal. China has reported no cases of human infection' (www.iht.com, 22 June 2005).

In response to the possibility of a worldwide avian influenza pandemic, UN experts convening here [Kuala Lumpur] unveiled on Tuesday [5 July] the most comprehensive global strategy to date to address the current crisis in Asia and to prepare other regions for similar outbreaks ... There is no evidence that the highly pathogenic bird flu virus is easily transmissible between humans, but health experts are concerned that the volatile virus, which has surfaced across Asia in various strains, could mutate and trigger a global pandemic. Such a pandemic could kill millions of people, WHO officials said.

(www.iht.com, 5 July 2005)

'[Bird flu has] infected 108 people, killing fifty-four' (*FT*, 7 July 2005, p. 11).

Indonesia confirmed its first human deaths from [the H5N1 strain of] bird flu Wednesday [20 July], a man and his two daughters ... who died earlier this month [July] ... bringing Asia's toll from the disease to fifty-seven people ... Though there is no evidence yet that the three had contact with infected poultry ... [the Indonesian health minister] said human-to-human transmission of the disease appeared unlikely at this stage ... Bird flu has killed thirty-eight people in Vietnam, twelve in Thailand, four in Cambodia and – with latest deaths – three in Indonesia. Experts say most of the deaths so far have resulted from an animal passing the virus to a human.

(www.iht.com, 20 July 2005)

Virologists have long been concerned about bird flu, worrying that the virus which causes it might mutate in a way that allowed it to be transmitted easily from person to person. This, they fear, might result in a catastrophic epidemic among humans, similar to the one just after the First World War that killed 20 million to 40 million people.

(*The Economist*, 23 July 2005, p. 79)

Global health officials fear ... the H5N1 flu virus ... could mutate into a lethal strain that could rival the 1918 Spanish flu pandemic that killed between 20 million and 40 million people. Bird flu was first seen to jump the species gap to people in 1997 in Hong Kong, when it infected eighteen people and killed six ... The spread of H5N1 avian flu has so far been confined to South-east Asia ... However, even though the cost to human health has so far been relatively small, the virus has devastated the poultry trade in many Asian countries. Investment bank CLSA said the crisis had already cost the region between $8 billion and $12 billion. The EU has prolonged its ban on poultry meat and live bird imports from eight Asian nations until September [2005] and this may be extended still further.

(Alan Bullion, *The World Today*, 2005, vol. 61, nos 8–9, pp. 30–1)

Russian authorities confirmed yesterday [Monday 25 July] an outbreak of highly infectious avian flu in Siberia that has already resulted in the death of about

1,200 birds The virus recently detected was different from earlier registered virus strings ... The first cases were registered in the Novosibirsk region last week. Domestic poultry are believed to have been infected by migrating migratory birds. This is the first outbreak of the disease in Siberia or central Asia.

(*FT*, 26 July 2005, p. 12)

'Investigators have determined that a strain of bird flu infecting fowl in Russia is the type that can infect humans ... The agriculture ministry identified the virus as avian flu type A(H5N1)' (*IHT*, 30 July 2005, p. 3).

'Russia will today [2 August] begin a mass cull of poultry in eighteen Siberian villages' (*FT*, 2 August 2005, p. 7).

'In the Kazakh province of Pavlodar officials said they had slaughtered 2,350 geese and 250 ducks after 600 poultry died from bird flu' (*The Times*, 2 August 2005, p. 24).

[Russia] said Tuesday [2 August] that the deadly bird flu virus had been found in a third Siberian province, as officials began a mass culling to contain its spread ... The virus was found in the west Siberian province of Tyumen, following an announcement of outbreaks in the provinces of Novosibirsk and Altai ... The A(H5N1) subtype has killed at least sixty people in parts of South-east Asia since 2003.

(*IHT*, 3 August 2005, p. 5)

'The outbreak began in the Novosibirsk region [of Russia] early last month [July] and has killed thousands of domestic fowl' (*The Times*, 3 August 2005, p. 34).

US government scientists say they have successfully tested in people a vaccine that they believe can protect against the strain of avian influenza that is spreading throughout Asia and Russia. Officials have been racing to develop a vaccine because they worry that if that strain mutated and combined with a human influenza virus to create a new virus it could spread rapidly. Tens of millions of birds have died from infection with the virus and from culling to prevent the spread of the virus. About 100 people have been infected and about fifty have died from this strain of the avian flu virus, called A(H5N1). So far there has been no sustained human-to-human transmission, but that is what health officials fear, because it could cause a pandemic ... An earlier vaccine against A(H5N1) avian influenza virus was prepared after the virus first appeared in the world, in Hong Kong in 1997. That vaccine was never fully developed or used, and the strain has mutated since then ... The only medicine known to work against bird flu [is called] Tamiflu ... Only a few human cases of A(H5N1) influenza have been found. Although a few cases may have been transmitted from person to person in Asia, the A(H5N1) strain has not gathered enough strength to spread widely among humans anywhere. As of Friday night [5 August], according to the WHO, the avian strain has killed fifty-seven of the 112 people it has been known to infect in four countries. The countries are Cambodia (with four cases), Indonesia (with one case), Thailand (with seventeen cases) and Vietnam (with ninety cases).

(www.iht.com, 7 August 2005; *IHT*, 8 August 2005, p. 4)

'A bird flu outbreak in Russian Siberia worsened yesterday [10 August] as neighbouring Kazakhstan confirmed cases of the deadly H5N1 strain of the virus and Mongolia reported its first cases' (*FT*, 11 August 2005, p. 7).

An outbreak of the bird flu virus that health officials are battling in Asia has spread westward in Russia from Siberia to a Ural Mountains region, the agriculture ministry said on Monday [15 August] . . . [The ministry] said in a statement that the A(H5N1) strain had been detected in a settlement in the Chelyabinsk region. . . No cases of human infection have been found. The authorities say they believe the virus was brought to the country by migratory birds.

(*IHT*, 16 August 2005, p. 8)

'An outbreak of avian flu among wild and domestic birds in Russia is spreading west and starting to approach Europe' (*The Times*, 16 August 2005, p. 27).

'The outbreaks in Russia and neighbouring Kazakhstan prompted the EU to declare a Europe-wide ban on imported birds from both to contain the spread of the disease, although neither country exports poultry to the EU' (*FT*, 17 August 2005, p. 10).

Amid further reports of bird deaths in Russia, just over the mountains that separate Asia from Europe, European countries were preparing Tuesday [23 August] for the possibility that migratory birds might carry the dread avian influenza virus to Europe in coming months . . . Until recently scientists believed that the major route of spread was through the transport of infected chickens and meat. But in the last few months outbreaks in which the virus appeared to have hopped from western China, to Mongolia, Russia and Kazakhstan – places that have little poultry trade between them – have highlighted the likelihood that wild birds have also disseminated the virus . . . Although scientists have long known that the disease could be spread by either domestic or infected animals, the shipment of infected animals between farms and market was previously thought to be the major route . . .Because officials had long assumed that domestic poultry was the primary culprit in disease transmission, the EU had previously sought to protect itself from outbreaks by banning all imports of meat from China and south-east Asia. That ban was extended to Russia and Kazakhstan on 12 August, when the disease was discovered in these countries . . . [The Netherlands] declared that as of this week all commercial chickens and turkeys would have to be housed indoors or in outdoor pens that would prevent contact with wild birds . . . An outbreak of a less virulent strain of bird flu decimated the country's poultry industry just two years ago . . . They lost 50 per cent of their poultry population in 2003 . . . Dutch officials had long suspected that their 2003 outbreak may have been caused by migratory birds, since no other origin was ever discovered.

(*IHT*, 24 August 2005, pp. 1, 4)

'Finnish authorities said they found a suspected case of bird flu in the north of the country . . . The case involved a gull. Final results of the tests are not expected for three weeks' (*Independent*, 27 August 2005, p. 24).

Indonesia yesterday [19 September] declared a national 'extraordinary event' after four children were taken to hospital with suspected bird flu and the Jakarta zoo was closed for three weeks after nineteen birds tested positive. None of the patients ... are thought to have caught the H5N1 strain of the illness ... at the zoo. But experts have yet to discover how they became sick, just as they cannot yet pinpoint where the woman who died of bird flu in south Jakarta ten days ago caught the virus. She was the fourth Indonesian to die of bird flu, all of them in unexplained circumstances. At least sixty other people have died of the virus since November 2003 in Vietnam, Thailand and Cambodia ... Indonesia [said it] could not start the culling procedures recommended by the United Nations because it could not afford to compensate poultry owners.

(*Guardian*, 20 September 2005, p. 20)

Indonesia has officially confirmed four human deaths since July from bird flu, all of them in Jakarta ... H5N1 was first found in Indonesian chickens in August 2004 ... The first deaths were confirmed in July. But officials continue to resist calls for a cull, declaring it too costly and impractical ... preferring to vaccinate selectively instead ... Doctors ... were yesterday [20 September] monitoring at least seven suspected human cases ... Indonesia's health minister on Monday [19 September] officially declared an 'extraordinary' outbreak, giving officials legal powers to force treatment on anyone showing symptoms.

(*FT*, 21 September 2005, p. 7)

'Since the deadly H5N1 strain of bird flu was detected in chickens in the archipelago in 2003, Indonesia has conducted only selective culls of poultry' (*FT*, 22 September 2005, p. 10).

[Results of tests relating to] a woman's death of avian flu in Jakarta ... [showed] that the virus had not yet mutated in ways likely to make it more of a threat to people ... The WHO's representative ... [said that it] 'seems like a virus that has gone directly from birds' ... The government of Indonesia had declared Monday that the disease was an 'extraordinary event', a step allowing additional spending beyond usual budget restraints and allowing the government to force suspected victims to be hospitalized and isolated ... The Indonesian government has also begun an extensive slaughter of chickens in or near flocks where birds have been infected with the disease. The culling marks a shift in policy, as Indonesia had resisted large-scale culling last year [2004] when the disease spread through Thailand and Vietnam; Indonesia tried then to vaccinate chickens instead ... The WHO added another bird flu death ... to its count for Vietnam. That brought the total there since the beginning of last year to sixty-four cases, twenty-one of them fatal. There were also seventeen confirmed cases of bird flu in Thailand last year, twelve of them fatal.

(www.iht.com, 21 September 2005)

A five-year-old girl died [in Jakarta] yesterday [21 September] after suffering from bird flu symptoms. Initial tests gave proved negative for the virus, but ... [it was announced that] more tests would be done ... Four Indonesians are confirmed to have died since July from the H5N1 strain of bird flu ... Bird flu has killed sixty-four people in four Asian countries since late 2003.

(Independent, 22 September 2005, p. 29)

'[In] Indonesia a fifth victim died on Monday [26 September]' (www.iht.com, 30 September 2005).

Worried scientists have finally managed to catch the attention of politicians. Last week at the United Nations General Assembly President George W. Bush announced a new international partnership to discuss flu and pandemic influenza. World health ministers will meet in Canada next month [October] to discuss how to pool resources, boost surveillance and improve the capacity to contain and respond to an outbreak. The WHO wants more governments to draw up preparedness plans (only forty have these so far) and agree on how they will co-ordinate their responses ... In the global pandemic of 1918 25 million to 50 million people died. Many scientists now believe that another influenza pandemic is inevitable some time soon.

(The Economist, Saturday 24 September 2005, p. 113)

South-east Asian nations approved the creation of a regional fund to fight bird flu and other animal diseases, officials said Friday [30 September] ... Details of the fund and other measures to curb bird flu were expected to be announced later on Friday at the end of the meeting by the Asian ministers and their counterparts from China, Japan and South Korea ... Asean [comprising Brunei, Cambodia, Indonesia, Laos, Malaysia, Myanmar, Philippines, Singapore, Thailand and Vietnam] will also endorse a global plan to contain avian influenza, which has killed sixty-six people in four Asian countries since late 2003 ... Millions of birds have been destroyed, causing estimated losses of $10 billion to $15 billion to the poultry industry [according to the Food and Agriculture Organization] ... Asean would also endorse the global bird flu plan proposed by the world animal health body OIE [World Organization for Animal Health], the Food and Agriculture Organization (FAO) and the World Health Organization (WHO). The three agencies plan to hold a bird flu conference in December to try to raise the $102 million they say is needed over the next three years to contain the virus ... The WHO, the UN health agency, said on Thursday that if the bird flu virus spreads among humans the quality of the global response would determine whether it ends up killing 5 million people or 150 million.

(www.iht.com, 30 September 2005)

South-east Asia's agriculture ministers endorsed a United Nations plan Friday to combat bird flu – a move they hope will win enough international aid to halt the disease before it becomes a catastrophic epidemic with the potential to kill millions of people globally. The ministers from the ten-member Association of South-east Asian Nations said in a statement that fighting avian flu ... requires 'an all-out co-ordinated regional effort' ... David Nabarro of the WHO has been appointed as the UN co-ordinator to lead a global drive to counter a human flu pandemic, which could strike if the bird virus mutates into a strain that is deadly to humans and can easily spread among people ... Nabarro: '[It would be] extremely wrong [to ignore the serious possibility of a global outbreak] ... The avian flu epidemic has to be controlled if we are to prevent a human influenza pandemic. We expect the next influenza epidemic to come at any time now, and it is likely to be caused by a mutant of the virus that is currently causing bird flu in Asia. Between 5 million and 150 million people could die in a pandemic – the higher figure being likely if governments fail to act now' ... The meeting ended with the endorsement of a regional plan for control and eradication of bird flu and directed a task force to formulate 'a detailed action plan for implementation and proceed to identify potential sources of funding', according to a joint statement. The plan covers 'eight strategic areas over a period of three years from 2006 to 2008 to prevent, control and eradicate the disease', the ministers said. The plan was drafted in May by the UN Food and Agriculture Organization and the World Organization for Animal Health and will be presented to donors in December for implementation early next year [2006].

(www.iht.com, 30 September 2005)

The WHO ... said Friday [30 September] that it was impossible to estimate how many people might die from a new influenza pandemic, though it added that it had warned countries to prepare for a death toll as high as 7.4 million ... Dick Thompson (a spokesman for the WHO): 'We think this is the most reasoned position ... [Even though several estimates could be plausible the agency] cannot be dragged into further scaremongering' ... Scientists' estimates of how many people could die in a flu pandemic have ranged from fewer than 2 million to more than 100 million, depending on how contagious and lethal the virus is. Neither factor can be known until a pandemic strain emerges.

(*IHT*, 1 October 2005, p. 6)

'The WHO said yesterday [30 September] 2 million to 7.4 million deaths was a reasonable forecast for a global pandemic – distancing itself from ... [David Nabarro's] figure of up to 150 million' (*FT*, 1 October 2005, p. 6).

Scientists have made all sorts of predictions, ranging from fewer than 2 million to 360 million. Others have quoted 100 million. Last year [2004] WHO's chief for the Asia-Pacific region predicted 100 million, but until now that was the highest figure publicly mentioned by a WHO official.

(*Independent*, 1 October 2005, p. 29)

Two teams of federal and university scientists [in the United States] announced Wednesday [5 October] that they have resurrected the 1918 influenza virus, the cause of one of history's most deadly epidemics, and have established that, unlike the viruses that caused more recent flu pandemics of 1957 and 1968, it was actually a bird flu that jumped directly to humans ... The new studies find that today's bird flu viruses share some of the crucial genetic changes that occurred in the 1918 flu. [The 1918] virus killed 50 million people.

(*IHT*, 6 October 2005, pp. 1, 7)

'Flu viruses that caused the pandemics of 1957 and 1968 ... were not bird viruses but were human viruses that picked up a few genetic elements of bird flu' (www.iht.com, 6 October 2005).

> The virus responsible for the 1918 Spanish flu pandemic which killed an estimated 50 million people worldwide originated from a bird flu virus, preliminary studies have shown ... The research ... will help scientists find new treatments for the most dangerous types of flu ... In 1957 and 1968 an existing human virus underwent genetic mixing with a bird flu to produce a new 'reassorted' strain in one step. In 1918, however, an entirely avian virus gradually adapted to function in humans through a sequence of mutations.
>
> (*FT*, 6 October 2005, p. 10)

'Scientists have recreated the Spanish flu virus that killed up to 50 million people in 1918–19' (*The Times*, 6 October 2005, p. 31).

'The Spanish flu pandemic killed an estimated 40 million people' (*FT*, 8 October 2005, p. 11).

'The Spanish flu outbreaks of 1918 ... killed between 20 million and 40 million' (*Independent*, 10 October 2005, p. 20).

> More than sixty-five countries and international organizations are participating [in a meeting in Washington] ... The meeting comes a day after two teams of scientists announced that they had reproduced the 1918 Spanish flu virus, the cause of one of history's most deadly pandemics, and found it to be bird flu ... Since 1997 bird flocks in eleven countries have been decimated by flu outbreaks. But so far nearly all the people infected [with bird flu] – more than 100, including more than sixty who died – contracted the sickness directly from birds. However, there has been little transmission between people ... Indonesia lowered its official total of bird flu deaths from six to three in line with WHO's records, the health minister said Thursday [6 October] ... Investigations have produced no evidence that the virus is spreading from person to person.
>
> (www.iht.com, 6 October 2005)

'So far sixty-two people have died from bird flu in the region' (*The Times*, 7 October 2005, p. 43).

> Three cases of suspected bird flu have been reported in Romania, which if confirmed would be the first in Europe. Officials detected the cases in domestic birds in the Danube delta ... [Romania] would not say whether the flu was believed to be the virulent H5N1 strain ... In August Finland reported a suspected case of bird flu in a gull ... Tests are believed to have proved negative ... The H5N1 strain has killed at least sixty-two people, all in southeast Asia and led to the slaughter of about 140 million birds in more than ten countries. No human-to-human transmission has been proved but there has been one case in Thailand where a woman is thought to have caught it from her daughter.
>
> (*Guardian*, 8 October 2005, p. 16)

The birds that tested positive for the disease were domestic ducks, meaning they probably contracted the disease from other birds that had migrated to the area. The WHO has confirmed 116 human cases of bird flu, all in Asia, and sixty-three deaths since the latest outbreak began in December 2003.

(*FT*, 8 October 2005, p. 11)

'The Turkish authorities began slaughtering poultry Sunday [9 October], one day after the agriculture minister confirmed the country's first bird flu case at a turkey farm' (www.iht.com, 9 October 2005).

The Asian flu seemed to continue its westward march as two outbreaks of avian influenza were reported in Europe over the weekend. Romania reported its first cases on Saturday [8 October] and Turkey on Sunday [9 October], both presumed to be carried there by birds that migrate from Asia in the autumn. There was no confirmation that the birds had succumbed to the deadly Asian H5N1 strain ... If the birds are infected with A(H5N1) it would be the first time that the virus has been seen in Europe ... In Romania outbreaks were reported in the region of the Danube Delta, with both wild and domestic birds affected ... The authorities took hundreds of birds from the farms and killed them and then declared a quarantine on the villages and six counties in the area ... [Turkey] confirmed that an outbreak of bird flu had occurred on a farm in the western part of the country ... The village was put under quarantine and all birds and street dogs killed as a precaution.

(*IHT*, 10 October 2005, p. 3)

[In Vietnam] the WHO has recorded ninety-one cases of avian flu, including forty-one that have resulted in death ... The health organization has warned that a possible pandemic of avian influenza could kill as many as 7.4 million people ... 'At present there is no convincing evidence of sustained human-to-human transmission of the H5N1 virus,' the organization said in a statement. 'However, there have been incidents, in Thailand, Vietnam and Cambodia, where limited transmission between humans was suspected.'

(www.iht.com, 10 October 2005)

'The Asian virus does not appear to spread among humans' (*IHT*, 12 October 2005, p. 5).

Bird flu has not been detected in Romania, EU veterinary experts said on Wednesday [12 October] ... Officials stressed, however, that more tests were still being taken of birds in Romania ... The authorities in Bucharest continued with plans to cull thousands of domestic birds in the Danube Delta.

(*IHT*, 13 October 2005, p. 4)

Experts have confirmed that a bird flu virus found in samples taken from dead birds in Romania's Danube Delta is the H5 type, authorities said Thursday [13 October]. The samples are being sent to Britain to identify the specific strain of the virus. So far there are no indications it is the H5N1 strain.

(www.iht.com, 13 October 2005)

'The EU on Thursday said the bird flu virus found in Turkish poultry was the H5N1 strain that scientists fear might mutate into a human virus and spark a pandemic' (www.iht.com, 13 October 2005).

> Thousands of birds that died in Turkey over the past week succumbed to ... the H5N1 virus ... medical test ... confirmed Thursday [13 October] ... It is the first time that the disease has been reported in a European country ... The United Nations Food and Agriculture Organization ... predicted that tests completed in the next few days would probably show that recent bird deaths in Romania were also caused by the virus ... The deadliest strain of all bird flu viruses, H5N1, has also infected 120 humans, generally people in close contact with sick birds. About half of them died.
>
> (*IHT*, 14 October 2005, p. 1)

> Researchers have identified a mutated form of H5N1 bird flu that is resistant to Tamiflu, the drug being stockpiled around the world to counter a feared influenza epidemic ... The strain was found in a case in Vietnam, a fourteen-year-old girl who may have caught the flu from her brother rather than directly from infected birds ... However, tests on lab animals showed that the resistant virus is sensitive to another drug.
>
> (*IHT*, 15 October 2005, p. 3)

'[On 15 October] the European Commission said ... that the virus detected in Romania was identical to the lethal strain that had hit Turkey and Asia' (*FT*, 17 October 2005, p. 9).

> The first known case of the A(H5N1) strain of avian influenza was found in 1996 in a goose in China. While the Beijing authorities insist that no poultry in the country has the disease now, Hong Kong University scientists who have studied the genetic evolution of the virus wrote in *Nature* in July that infected migratory birds in western China appeared to have contracted the disease in southern China; the virus has since spread from western China to East Asia, Russia, Kazakhstan, Turkey and Romania ... Beijing officials criticized the researchers last summer for writing that the disease was still present in poultry in southern China ... Though no human cases of the disease have been reported in China, the size of China's human and poultry populations makes it possible that the spark will happen there ... A lingering concern is whether local and provincial authorities, fearing censure, are hiding cases from the central government. This occurred in the SARS outbreak in late 2002 and again during a flare-up last summer of a pig disease in central China ... While China shared samples of the bird flu virus last year [2004] with international health agencies, it has not done so with migratory bird virus samples this year [2005], preferring to analyse them in Chinese laboratories and showing the results to officials ... [like one from] the UN agriculture organization.
>
> (*IHT*, 17 October 2005, p. 2)

> Greece became the first member of the EU to report a case of bird flu yesterday [17 October], when the H5 virus was identified in a turkey from the Aegean

island of Oinousa ... [Greece said that tests] would determine whether the
virus was from the deadly H5N1 strain.

(*FT*, 18 October 2005, p. 10)

'Bird culls to control probable new outbreaks of bird flu started on farms in
Russia and Macedonia ... The Chinese authorities reported another outbreak of
H5N1 in the province of Outer Mongolia' (*IHT*, 20 October 2005, pp. 1, 8).

'Thailand announced its thirteenth fatal case of the disease ... [The] man who
died Wednesday [19 October] was the first in more than a year to die from the
disease' (*IHT*, 21 October 2005, p. 3).

Taiwan reported its first case of avian flu Thursday [20 October], discovered in
a smuggled cargo of exotic cage birds ... Taiwan said it had encountered the
H5N1 strain of bird flu in birds shipped in a container smuggled from China.

(*IHT*, 21 October 2005, p. 3)

[The H5N1] strain of bird flu ... began circulating in South Korea in 2003 ...
Millions of birds have caught the disease and 150 million poultry have been
culled. Despite this action the virus is now endemic in many parts of Indonesia
and Vietnam, some parts of Cambodia, China and Thailand, and possibly Laos.
Yet only 117 people have caught the virus ... In the unlikely event it is caught
it is lethal. More than half those infected, sixty people, have died. Those most
at risk are poultry workers in these countries, their families and those working
with wild birds ... China's handling of bird flu has been characteristically
secretive ... Outbreaks of H5N1 in Japan, North Korea and Malaysia were
quickly brought under control and are now believed to have been eradicated
... The virus can infect and kill a range of other animals ... The less severe
pandemics in the second half of the last century, in 1957 and 1968, were
caused by a human flu virus that had swapped genes with a bird flu virus. The
more serious 1918 pandemic was caused when a bird flu virus adapted on its
own to become transmissible between humans. The mortality rate was about
2.5 per cent and 40 million to 50 million died.

(*The Economist*, 22 October 2005, pp. 91–3)

The H5N1 strain of bird flu ... has killed sixty-seven people ... Bird flu, a
common ailment among fowl, is difficult for people to contract and most
human cases have been linked to direct contact with sick birds ... There was
confirmation from Moscow on Wednesday [19 October] of an outbreak of the
H5N1 virus in the Tula region, south of the Russian capital.

(www.iht.com, 21 October 2005)

On 23 October it was confirmed that an imported parrot in quarantine in the
United Kingdom had died of the H5N1 strain of bird flu.

'[The] parrot imported from Suriname and under quarantine in Britain ... [is]
thought to have been infected by a consignment of birds from Taiwan' (*IHT*, 25
October 2005, p. 3).

[On 25 October]] Indonesia confirmed its fourth fatality from avian influenza
[a man who died in September] ... H5N1 infections have killed sixty-two

people in Asia since 2003 – more than half in Vietnam ... [China] reported an outbreak of the deadly H5N1 avian flu in the eastern province of Anhui ... In contrast with the widespread criticism of China's initial tardiness in tackling the 2003 SARS outbreak and sharing information with its neighbours, international public health experts have praised Beijing's recent efforts to fight avian influenza ... There is clear evidence that China is promptly sharing information about avian influenza with the international community ... A bird flu pandemic ... would have a devastating impact on Asian countries, the Asian Development Bank warned Tuesday [25 October] ... The economic impact would dwarf the downturn following the 2003 SARS outbreak that led to estimated losses of between \$30 billion and \$50 billion.

(www.iht.com, 25 October 2005; *IHT*, 26 October 2005, p. 3)

[On 26 October] China reported another outbreak in poultry ... In China's latest case of H5N1 infection, the third since last week, hundreds of chickens and ducks died in a village in central Hunan province. China had notified the United Nations of the latest outbreak on [25 October] ... In Europe Croatian officials said tests had confirmed that wild swans found dead in eastern Croatia last week were infected with the lethal H5N1 bird flu strain ... The WHO says 121 people have been infected in four South-east Asian nations and sixty-two have died.

(www.iht.com, 26 October 2005)

On the French island of Reunion in the Indian Ocean preliminary tests on a man who had returned to the island after a trip to Thailand showed he might have the H5N1 strain, the authorities said Wednesday [26 October] ... [It was announced that] the number of suspected bird flu cases in Reunion had risen to three ... The EU Commission announced Wednesday that the H5N1 virus strain, which has killed sixty-two people in Asia, had been found in dead swans in Croatia. It was detected earlier in birds in Romania, Russia and Turkey.

(*IHT*, 27 October 2005, p. 3)

The WHO on Friday [28 October] asked China to conduct further tests to determine whether a twelve-year-old girl died of avian influenza and cautioned that provincial health officials may have acted prematurely in declaring that her death was not linked to the fatal disease ... The death of the girl quickly attracted attention because she lived in a village in Hunan province where the latest outbreaks had occurred. Reports in the Hong Kong and mainland media suggested that the girl and her brother had fallen ill after eating a sick chicken.

(www.iht.com, 28 October 2005)

Romania announced Friday [28 October] that the virulent H5N1 strain of bird flu has spread to the country's north-east from the Danube Delta region, after test on a dead heron proved positive for the virus. The heron was found a week ago ... near Romania's border with Moldova. The announcement marks the first time the H5N1 virus has been reported outside the Danube Delta region.

(*IHT*, 29 October 2005, p. 5)

Vietnam said Monday [31 October] that it needed tens of millions of dollars to fight the spread of bird flu as disaster co-ordinators from Pacific Rim countries met in Australia ... [Vietnam said it] needed $50 million and help building up its stockpile of bird flu drugs ... Vietnam has been hardest hit by bird flu, which has killed more than forty people in the country and prompted the authorities to destroy tens of millions of birds. Vietnam ... [a] country of 82 million ... has enough viral drugs to treat 60,000 people ... Officials said last week that they wanted enough to treat 30 per cent of the population.

(www.iht.com, 31 October 2005)

[On 4 November] China reported its fourth bid flu outbreak in three weeks ... Vietnam also confirmed bird flu outbreaks in three northern villages ... The Japanese authorities have detected signs of bird flu at a northern farm and plan to kill 180,000 chickens after they discovered antibodies in some for the H5 family of bird flu. The deadly H5N1 strain of bird flu, which is the only one that has spread to humans, has not yet been detected in Japan, but the less virulent H5N2 strain hit the country last year [2004].

(*IHT*, 5 November 2005, p. 3)

China and Vietnam each confirmed new bird flu outbreaks [on 4 November] and warned of more infections to come, amid predictions that a flu pandemic could kill up to 3 million people in Asia ... cost the region billions ... and plunge the world into recession. The latest Chinese outbreak [is] the fourth in the past three weeks ... In Vietnam more than 3,000 poultry died or were culled this week in three villages ... Vietnam began vaccinating its 150 million poultry flock in early August, but a shortage of vaccine imported from China may delay the programme's completion by two weeks.

(www.iht.com, 4 November 2005)

China and Vietnam have reported major bird flu outbreaks in poultry ... [In China's case this is] the fourth outbreak in a month ... In Vietnam, where forty-one people have died of avian influenza, a ... woman with a fever and respiratory problems is the latest suspected case after Indonesia said three children were being tested for bird flu ... In Asia it has killed sixty-two people and infected 122 since late 2003. It is difficult for people to catch and is spread almost exclusively through human contact with birds.

(*Independent*, 5 November 2005, p. 31)

In a report released Thursday [4 November] the Asian Development Bank outlined a number of scenarios – some catastrophic – that could face Asian Nations in the event of a global flu outbreak. In a worst-case scenario in which the psychological impact of a pandemic could last a year, the bank said Asia could lose almost $282.7 billion – or 6.5 per cent of its GDP – in consumption, trade and investment and another $14.2 billion due to workers' incapacity and death. The report said 'growth in Asia would virtually stop' and the economic impact would likely force the world into recession. That scenario assumes about 20 per cent of Asia's population would fall ill and 0.5 per cent would die. In a less pessimistic forecast, the bank said that if the psychological impact of an outbreak lasted six months the cost to Asia in lost consumption, trade and investment would be about $99 billion. China, Hong Kong, Singapore, Malaysia and Thailand would likely be hardest hit by the pandemic, the ban predicted. A separate report by the World Bank said a human pandemic triggered by bird flu could cost the world economy as much as $800 billion.

(www.iht.com, 4 November 2005)

'The deadly H5N1 strain of bird flu has killed at least sixty-two people – including forty-one in Vietnam – and resulted in the deaths of more than 100 million birds since 2004' (www.iht.com, 4 November 2005).

In the 1918 Spanish flu epidemic between 20 million and 40 million people worldwide died. There was about a 2 per cent mortality rate. In subsequent pandemics in 1957 and 1968, which killed far fewer people, it was about 0.45 per cent.

(*IHT*, 5 November 2005, p. 3)

The Chinese government said Sunday [6 November] it had asked for help from the WHO in determining whether the H5N1 bird flu virus killed a twelve-year-old last month [13 October] and sickened two others [who recovered]. If any of the cases are confirmed it would be China's first reported case of bird flu in humans ... Meanwhile Indonesian health officials said Saturday [5 November] that a nineteen-year-old woman had died of bird flu ... Her death brings the number of people killed by the disease in Indonesia to five.

(www.iht.com, 6 November 2005)

'As yet the only human cases reported around the world have gotten the disease by direct contact with an infected bird' (*IHT*, 7 November 2005, p. 7).

The [H5N1] virus might infect someone already sick with a strain of human flu, and the two viruses could have sex, thus creating a new virus that contains some genes from each, Such viral hanky-panky is thought to have led to the flu pandemics of 1957 and 1968. Or the virus could mutate in such a way that it becomes able to travel between people. Mutations to an avian flu virus are thought to lie behind the 1918 pandemic.

(p. 8)

The World Bank announced the creation Monday [7 November] of a $500 million loan programme aimed at quickly getting money to poor South-east Asian countries that are struggling to combat an outbreak of avian flu among birds. It also warned that a global human pandemic, should it occur, could cause $800 billion in global economic losses ... or 2 per cent of annual global output ... So far sixty-three people have died from avian flu and 124 people have been infected, all residents of agricultural areas of South-east Asia that came into contact with infected birds.

(*IHT*, 8 November 2005, p. 3)

Vietnam confirmed on Tuesday [8 November] its forty-second death from bird flu, its first in more than three months ... The H5N1 strain of bird flu in Asia, as of Tuesday, is known to have killed at least sixty-three people out of 125 known cases ... Despite ... the fact that those viruses have been circulating in China for more than a dozen years, almost no human-to-human spread has occurred.

(www.iht.com, 8 November 2005)

The World Bank said Wednesday [9 November] that up to $1 billion would be needed over the next three years to fund a global strategy to tackle the spread of the H5N1 bird flu. On the final day of a three-day meeting of the WHO, World Bank officials said it was crucial to stamp out the disease in poultry as well as prepare countries for a potential human flu pandemic ... World Bank officials said the budget estimate did not cover funding for measures in the event of widespread human-to-human transmission leading to a global human pandemic ... The Asian Development Bank said it was making an extra $300 million available to help fight bird flu in countries such as Vietnam, Laos and Cambodia ... The bank has already announced $170 million in grants and loans. The extra $300 million will be focussed on worst-hit countries such as Vietnam, Laos and Cambodia ... Many poor Asian countries lack adequate surveillance and reporting mechanisms and cannot compensate farmers for poultry culls. Africa, which many experts said is likely to be the next front line in the fight against bird flu, faces similar problems ... The Chinese prime minister, Wen Jiabao, warned Wednesday that China faced a serious threat from bird flu, since the disease is still not under control despite massive nation-wide efforts to stop its spread.

(www.iht.com, 9 November 2005)

China on Thursday [10 November] reported two new incidents of avian flu among chickens in its north-eastern province of Liaoning, bringing the total number of reported cases in the past month to six ... Vietnam, the country worst by bird flu so far, said on Thursday that it would send soldiers and the police to help contain the spread of the virus as more outbreaks erupt and the sudden deaths of ducks in two provinces hint at the emergence of a more virulent strain. Bird flu has been spreading fast in Vietnam, but provincial authorities are not showing enough urgency, the agriculture minister said.

(www.iht.com, 10 November 2005)

'China reported two new bird flu outbreaks in poultry Thursday [10 November] and quarantined 116 people, while Kuwait confirmed the first known cases in the Gulf – in an imported peacock and a wild flamingo' (*IHT*, 11 November 2005, p. 4).

The first case of bird flu in the Gulf Arab region was reported in Kuwait yesterday [11 November]. A migrating flamingo ... was carrying the lethal strain of the H5N1 virus ... An earlier case found in a shipment of birds from Asia was found to be the less virulent H5N2 strain.

(*Independent*, 12 November 2005, p. 35)

On Saturday [12 November] China tested an ill poultry worker for bird flu and Vietnam reported two new outbreaks of the virus ... The Indonesian authorities are investigating whether a twenty-year-old woman . . . died from bird flu . . . [She died] late Saturday . . . The H5N1 strain has devastated poultry flocks across Asia since 2003 and jumped to humans, killing at least sixty-four people.

(www.iht.com, 13 November 2005)

'Of the sixty-four people who have so far died of bird flu, forty-two were infected in Vietnam' (www.economist.com, 11 November 2005).

Scientists in Vietnam believe the H5N1 bird flu strain has mutated, allowing it to breed more effectively in mammals, though not necessarily in humans . . . Scientists found significant variations in twenty-four samples from humans and poultry. The findings corroborate the belief that H5N1 would not have to mix with a human flu strain to become a form causing a human pandemic.

(*Guardian*, 14 November 2005, p. 18)

[China] said Tuesday [15 November] that the government plans to vaccinate all the country's 14 billion poultry against bird flu as two new outbreaks of the disease in the far west were announced . . . China has more than 14 billion farm poultry, accounting for almost 21 per cent of the world's total . . . Also Tuesday the government confirmed the tenth and eleventh outbreaks in the past month . . . A total of 320,000 poultry have been slaughtered . . . Infections have been reported in almost every part of the country since 19 October . . . On Tuesday China said it would ship 45 tonnes of bird flu vaccine worth $780,000 to Vietnam, the country hardest hit by the disease . . . Bird flu has killed at least sixty-four people in Asia since 2003, mostly those who have come in contact with infected birds.

(www.iht.com, 15 November 2005)

[China said] said that it would try to vaccinate all of the nation's chickens and other poultry against bird flu . . . China has stocks of 4.2 billion chickens and a billion ducks, geese and turkeys last year [2004] . . . Three-fifths of the poultry in China are kept by families, who let the birds and other domesticated animals wander around the neighbourhood, the yard and the house . . . Experts at the UN Food and Agriculture Organization . . . said that more information was needed to assess the wisdom of China's decision to vaccinate all poultry . . . [China] said it was 'highly probable' that a boy and a girl who suffered high fevers last month [October] – the girl died – had been China's first human cases of bird flu . . . There had been no sign of human-to-human transmission of bird flu . . . China reported fifty outbreaks of bird flu in sixteen provinces last year, and reported eleven more to international health agencies this autumn, including two more small outbreaks Tuesday . . . [China] reported last week that a fake flu vaccine, possibly including active virus, may have actually spread the disease instead of preventing it . . . China has developed its own version of Tamiflu.

(*IHT*, 16 November 2005, p. 7)

[Experts] now believe that the disease was brought to Britain in a consignment of 1001 mesias, or finches, from Taiwan. It was previously thought that the first source of the virus was in a ... parrot from Surinam ... It is not certain how many [of the finches] died of the bird flu ... Experts admitted that they could not be definite about the source of the virus because tissue from the parrot and a sick mesia were mixed for testing. However, 'on the balance of probabilities', they blamed the mesia ... No evidence of the H5N1 strain was found in any of the other birds [in quarantine] ... Crucially, there was no infection in four British chickens used as a 'sentinel' in the quarantine premises.

(*The Times*, 16 November 2005, p. 8)

China confirmed its first three bird flu cases Wednesday [16 November], including two fatalities ... A twelve-year-old girl in central Hunan province and a twenty-four-year-old female poultry worker in Anhui province in the east died of the virus ... The third confirmed infection was the Hunan girl's nine-year-old brother who has since recovered ... Chinese and WHO experts had been reviewing the children's cases ... The two children and a teacher who also fell ill in their village had tested negative for bird flu ... Also Wednesday Vietnamese authorities reported bird flu outbreaks in three more provinces ... bringing to twelve the number of cities and provinces affected in the latest wave, which began about a month ago.

(www.iht.com, 16 November 2005)

The Chinese government announced Wednesday that it had confirmed the country's first three cases of bird flu ... [China said] that bird flu had been confirmed in a nine-year-old boy and his twelve-year-old sister in central China's Hunan province and a thirty-six-year-old woman in Anhui province in east-central China. The boy has recovered and was released from hospital last weekend while the girl and woman died. In confirming all three cases as infections with the H5N1 bird flu virus, the Chinese authorities went even further than the WHO was willing to go. The WHO agreed late Wednesday that the boy and the teacher had been infected with bird flu. But the sister's body had been cremated before her case became the subject of medical attention, and the WHO concluded that samples drawn before she died were not adequate for concluding whether she had bird flu. Determining whether the boy and the girl both had the disease is important because scientists are watching to see if the disease develops the capacity to more easily from person to person, which could lead to a global epidemic in people. The WHO has concluded that most human infections so far have come directly from birds, but has acknowledged that it is very difficult to determine the sources of infection when multiple family members fall ill. The family members are likely to have been exposed to the same birds as well as to each other ... The earliest cases of H5N1 virus were found in birds in south-eastern China in 1996 and researchers have been finding the virus practically every year since then. The widespread presence of the disease in Chinese poultry has prompted suspicions that human cases were also occurring in China but were not being reported to national authorities by local and provincial authorities leery of censure for failing to protect public health ... China becomes the fifth country to confirm human cases of bird flu since the beginning of last year [2004], following Cambodia, Indonesia,

Thailand and Vietnam, and bringing the total to 128 cases, of which sixty-five were fatal. Vietnam has had ninety-two cases of which forty-two were fatal, Thailand has had twenty-one cases and thirteen deaths, Indonesia has had nine cases and five deaths, and Cambodia has had four cases, all dead.

(*IHT*, 17 November 2005, p. 4)

The Food and Agriculture Organization estimates the economic impact [of bird flu] has been more than $10 billion ... [The] director of its animal-production and health division says that a single large outbreak in 2004 cut GDP across South-east Asia by up to 1.5 per cent ... The next influenza pandemic – an event that occurs about three times a century – it could last for up to a year ... [The World Bank] suggests it might cost at least $800 billion.

(*The Economist*, 19 November 2005, p. 95)

Indonesian officials said yesterday [17 November] they had confirmed two more human fatalities from H5N1 ... [bringing Indonesia's confirmed fatalities to seven, with four other people having survived]. Western health experts believe at least two other fatalities can be attributed to the virus and many more cases are probably not being detected.

(*FT*, 18 November 2005, p. 11)

Indonesia's toll [rose] to seven out of eleven infections and the number of global fatalities [rose] to at least sixty-seven ... In China the WHO ruled out human-to-human transmission in the case reported on Wednesday as two new outbreaks in poultry were reported.

(*Guardian*, 18 November 2005, p. 18)

China's plan to vaccinate billions of chickens against avian flu could backfire and end up spreading the disease, according to poultry and vaccine experts. Vaccination teams could easily carry the virus from farm to farm on their shoes, clothes and equipment unless they changed or sterilized them each time ... Also, experts said, the task is likely to be overwhelming because the Chinese eat about 14 billion chickens a year so mass vaccinations would have to be repeated again and again.

(*IHT*, 21 November 2005, p. 10)

'Beijing yesterday [21 November] issued new rules to combat bird flu, threatening to punish local authorities that delay or misreport findings' (*FT*, 22 November 2005, p. 11). '[The] new rules require local Chinese officials to set up disease-warning networks and to stockpile disinfectant and other emergency supplies. Officials who fail to pinpoint and report outbreaks quickly face firing or jail' (www.iht.com, 22 November 2005).

On Monday [21 November] two new outbreaks among poultry, the sixteenth and seventeenth, were reported in China ... A suspected human death from the virus was reported in Jakarta Tuesday [22 November], which, if confirmed, would bring Indonesia's toll to eight ... If confirmed it would be the sixty-eighth avian flu death worldwide.

(www.iht.com, 22 November 2005)

A study published this month [November] by scientists in a global network organized by the WHO pointed out that there was no evidence that the H5N1 virus had acquired human or any other avian influenza genes in the eight years since it had begun infecting humans.

(*FT*, 24 November 2005, p. 21)

'China is preparing to test a bird flu vaccine on people, state media said Thursday [24 November 2005] after officials confirmed the nation's second human death from the virus ... The vaccine trial will involve 100 people' (www.iht.com, 24 November 2005).

With China reporting its first two human deaths from bird flu, international health experts are warning that current tallies may greatly underestimate the problem, both in China and elsewhere. Scientists have long been mystified by the low number of cases in humans reported in China ... The WHO ... [believes] that systems to diagnose a virus like bird flu are often poorly developed and underfinanced in the rural areas that have suffered most ... While Vietnam, Indonesia and Thailand have provided international experts with samples of the virus from each bird outbreak, China has been unwilling to share such material. It has provided only one sample ... Vietnam has reported ninety-one cases of bird flu in humans, with forty-one people dead ... [according to] new data [presented on 23 November].

(*IHT*, 25 November 2005, p. 5)

Roche, the Swiss pharmaceutical company that controls the patent for Tamiflu ... the antiviral drug used to treat bird flu ... gave Indonesia permission Friday [25 November] to start producing it for the domestic market. The company said it did not have a patent there, so Indonesia does not have to obtain a licence ... So far Indonesia and Vietnam are the only countries to have secured permission from Roche to produce Tamiflu on their own. Other countries are in talks with the company ... Jakarta health officials confirmed an eighth ... human death from the H5N1 virus ... but are waiting for definitive tests to come back from Hong Kong.

(www.iht.com, 27 November 2005)

China reported two new outbreaks of bird flu in poultry on Tuesday [29 November] The outbreaks were China's twenty-third and twenty-fourth since 19 October ... China has sent 3 million doses of bird flu vaccine to Indonesia, where H5N1 was found in twenty-three of thirty provinces. Unlike other countries, Indonesia does not routinely cull birds, citing a lack of funds. Indonesia has reported twelve human cases, seven of which have been fatal. China has also exported 43 tonnes of bird flu vaccine to Vietnam., the country hardest hit by the disease ... At least sixty-eight people have died from the H5N1 bird flu virus since it emerged in Asia in 2003 ... So far most human cases have been traced to contact with infected birds.

(www.iht.com, 29 November 2005)

China claims a domestic population of about 14.2 billion birds. The mass vaccinations illustrate ... the immense challenges involved, including the possibility that the rural health workers themselves might spread the virus ... China is estimated to have 640,000 to 1 million villages where birds are raised in close proximity with humans ... International experts say Beijing's official figure of only two human deaths from bird flu is suspicious. Some speculate that dozens or even hundreds may have died already.

(*IHT*, 1 December 2005, p. 7)

'China reported its twenty-fifth outbreak of H5N1 in poultry' (*The Times*, 2 December 2005, p. 54).

Ukraine yesterday [4 December] began combating what appeared to be the biggest outbreak yet in Europe of the deadly strain of bird flu, after more than 2,000 domestic birds died in a remote region of the Crimea. A state of emergency [was declared] in five villages on Saturday [3 December] after the agriculture ministry said it had identified the H5 subtype of bird flu virus ... Confirmation that the outbreak was caused by the H5N1 strain that can kill humans was awaiting the results of tests in Britain and Italy. But officials left little doubt that they were dealing with the same deadly strain that has shown up in Romania and other parts of south-east Europe ... The [Ukrainian] agriculture minister told a press conference he was alerted on Friday [2 December] after the villagers saw up to 20 per cent of their birds die overnight ... Villagers told television reporters they were mystified by the disease that had been killing birds for more than a month ... Romania said at the weekend it was dealing with what appeared to be a new H5N1 outbreak in the country's south-east, its first outside the Danube delta.

(*FT*, 5 December 2005, p. 6)

'A state of emergency [was declared] Saturday after ... Ukraine ... recorded its first case of type H5N1 bird flu' (*IHT*, 7 December 2005, p. 3).

'President Viktor Yushchenko, angry over delays in reporting a virulent strain of bird flu, ordered the dismissal on Monday [5 December] of Ukraine's top veterinarian officer' (*IHT*, 6 December 2005, p. 10).

'A five-year-old boy became Thailand's second bird flu fatality ... since October ... China [reported] its fifth human case' (www.iht.com, 9 December 2005).

A five-year-old Thai boy became the seventieth person to die of bird flu, it was reported yesterday [9 December] ... The boy's death took Thailand's bird flu death toll to fourteen out of twenty-two known cases ... China has reported a new case of H5N1 ... [but] the Chinese victim has since recovered.

(*Independent*, 10 December 2005, p. 31)

'The death of the five-year-old boy from Thailand took the country's bird flu cases to fourteen out of twenty-two known cases since the virus broke out in Asia in late 2003' (*Guardian*, 10 December 2005, p. 18).

Roche, the Swiss drug maker, said Monday [12 December] that it had reached a sub-licensing agreement with China's state-owned Shanghai Pharmaceutical Group to manufacture the influenza drug Tamiflu and is in talks with twelve other companies [in other countries]... The agreement with Shanghai Pharmaceutical is the first full sub-licence that Roche has awarded for Tamiflu ... the anti-viral drug [that] has shown in clinical trials to work against the symptoms of the H5N1 strain of bird flu ... The agreement with Shanghai Pharmaceutical comes after some Asian countries, including China's, said they would allow local companies to produce a generic version of the drug – without Roche's permission, if necessary ... Tamiflu is not protected by patent in Thailand, the Philippines and Indonesia, meaning local companies there are free to produce the drug ... In Vietnam Roche has agreed to allow local companies to put the finished ingredients of Tamiflu into capsules ... So far seventy people in five Asian countries have died of the disease.

(IHT, 13 December 2005, p. 16)

Ukraine on Wednesday [14 December] announced that tests had confirmed that a potentially deadly strain of avian flu ... H5N1 ... had established itself in the Crimean Peninsula, and said that thousands of birds were being culled ... [The] H5N1 [strain] has been responsible for the deaths of at least sixty-nine people in Asia since 2003.

(IHT, 17 December 2005, p. 3)

A thirty-five-year-old man in eastern China became infected with the ... H5N1 virus ... making him the country's sixth human bird flu case, the state news media said Friday [16 December] ... [He] fell ill on 4 December ... [but is] recovering in hospital ... The H5N1 strain of bird flu has killed at least seventy-one people since 2003 ... On Friday Indonesia said a ... man had died from the H5N1 strain.

(www.iht.com, 16 December 2005)

The first scientific study of humans with bird flu who have received the anti-viral drug Tamiflu has found that the bird flu virus can rapidly become vulnerable to the medicine ... In the new study ... colleagues at Vietnam's Hospital for Tropical Diseases in Ho Chi Minh City treated eight patients with Tamiflu. Vietnam has had more human bird flu cases than any other country ... In half of the patients Tamiflu worked brilliantly ... In two patients the bird flu virus rapidly developed strong resistance to the drug. The patients died ... The remaining two patients died despite treatment, although the drug may have been started too late in their illness to help them. From a public health perspective the development of resistance in even a quarter of cases is worrisome, since it means that such patients, before they die, can pass on a resistant form of virus that is even harder to treat.

(IHT, 22 December 2005, pp. 1, 8)

'The reports increase suggested levels of resistance to nearly 10 per cent, or three out of the thirty-one known human cases of H5N1 treated with Tamiflu ... The virus has so far infected 139 people and killed seventy-one' *(FT*, 22 December 2005, p. 12).

Roche, the Swiss pharmaceutical group, has signed a pioneering deal authorizing an Indian drugs company to manufacture and sell its anti-viral flu medicine

Tamiflu under licence in a number of developing countries. Hetero ... becomes the second drug company after Shanghai Pharmaceutical Group to receive a sub-licence that will allow it to sell large volumes of Tamiflu at a price it chooses ... The Indian deal is important because for the first time it authorizes a partner company to produce and sell Tamiflu not only in its home market – as is the case with Shanghai – but also in other less developed and developing countries ... The deal, which initially lasts for two years, would allow Hetero to sell Tamiflu at whatever price it chooses in India and countries where there is no or poor intellectual property protection for the drug.

(*IHT*, 24 December 2005, p. 5)

China confirmed a new outbreak of bird flu in the south-western province of Sichuan on Wednesday [4 January 2006], but the agriculture ministry said the situation there was under control. More than 1,800 birds were found dead on 22 December [2005] at a farm ... On Tuesday [3 January] samples tested at a laboratory confirmed the birds had died form the H5N1 virus.

(www.iht.com, 4 January 2006)

'Turkey has confirmed two cases of bird flu, including a fourteen-year-old farm boy who died ... His sister, who is in a serious condition in hospital, also tested positive. A third sibling is also suspected of having bird flu' (*Independent*, 5 January 2006, p. 21).

Two siblings who lived on a farm in rural Turkey have died of avian influenza, health officials there said Thursday [5 January], making them the first human victims of the disease outside of China and South-east Asia. Both children had close contact with sick poultry ... It has not yet been confirmed that they suc-cumbed to the virulent H5N1 strain virus, although everything points to that conclusion ... [The girl was] fifteen and her [brother was] fourteen ... Their eleven-year-old sister ... and some neighbours have been hospitalized ... All the children were involved in caring for poultry, although there are no offi-cially reported outbreaks in the village where they live.

(www.iht.com, 5 January 2006; *IHT*, 6 January 2006, pp. 1, 4)

Two children [died] in a suspected outbreak of H5N1 ... The brother and sister, who lived close to poultry at their farm in a village near the border with Armenia, were the first human victims of the disease in Europe. Seventy-four people have died of bird flu in Asia in the past three years ... [The fifteen-year-old girl] died early yesterday [5 January]. Her brother [aged fourteen] ... died on Sunday [1 January] ... Their eleven-year-old sister is among the eighteen other patients who were in hospital last yesterday with bird flu-like symptoms ... Samples of the dead birds were due to arrive in ... the UK and would be tested to show whether the birds died of the H5N1 strain.

(*FT*, 6 January 2006, p. 7)

An eleven-year-old girl died Friday [6 January] of suspected bird flu in eastern Turkey, days after her brother and sister succumbed to the disease ... Their doctor said the youngsters most likely contracted the virus while playing with

the heads of dead chickens infected with the disease ... The Turkish agriculture minister ... said the problem of containing bird flu in eastern Turkey was
aggravated by the fact that almost every house has poultry and people keep the
birds inside their homes at night when temperatures drop. Most of those who
have died from the virus have been farm workers in Vietnam, Thailand and
Indonesia, who came into close contact with poultry, said the WHO.

(www.iht.com, 6 January 2006)

Health officials in Europe said they were on 'high alert' Friday [6 January] as a
third child in eastern Turkey was confirmed to have bird flu and more than two
dozen people suspected of having the disease were in a local hospital ... An
international reference lab in England confirmed for the first time Friday that at
least three children in the Turkish cluster had the H5N1 virus and further
testing was under way ... The full extent of the cluster is unclear, as test for
H5N1, which are difficult to perform, are still under way [in England] ... On
Friday the lab confirmed that ... the two siblings who died ... were infected
with H5N1. So was another unrelated boy, who is severely ill in the same hospital in the city of Van ... Even though their chickens were dying, there were
no reports of H5N1 in the remote village when the children fell ill.

(*IHT*, 7 January 2006, p. 3)

A third child from the same family in Turkey died yesterday [6 January] after
tests confirmed that two of the victims had been infected with the H5N1 virus
... The children had all eaten infected chicken that had live partly in their
home.

(*FT*, 7 January 2005, p. 6)

Two young children were being treated for deadly bird flu at an eastern
Turkish hospital Sunday [8 January], the day after health officials confirmed
that at least two of the three siblings who died last week had been infected with
the virus. A British laboratory has confirmed the virus in a five-year-old hospitalized in the Turkish town of Van, near the Iranian border, while tests in
Turkey and Britain also found the strain in a eight-year-old girl ... The British
lab also confirmed that a fourteen-year-old boy and his fifteen-year-old sister,
who died Friday [6 January] ...[had the disease] ... In all thirty-eight people
were hospitalized with symptoms like those of bird flu ... Dozens of people
with flu-like symptoms, who had recently been in close contact with fowl,
were hospitalized across Turkey ... So far the lethal H5N1 strain of the bird
flu has been capable in rare cases of passing from poultry to humans in close
contact with them, but not from human to human.

(www.iht.com, 8 January 2006)

In the eastern town of Dogubayazit, in Van, three children from the same
family died last week ... A local hospital has been besieged by panicked residents seeking treatment for symptoms ... Two children and an adult have tested
positive for the deadly H5N1 bird flu strain in Turkey's capital Ankara, the
city's governor has said. The results have not been confirmed by WHO labs ...

The three people who tested positive in Ankara come from a town about one hour's drive [sixty miles] from the city.

(www.bbc.co.uk, 8 January 2006)

Four children from villages near Van in remote eastern Turkey have now been officially confirmed to have been infected with the H5N1 strain of the flu by the WHO, and at least thirty people are hospitalized in Van City as possible victims. Like many people in these poor villages, the four children – two of whom have died – had close contact with birds, health officials said, and probably became infected as a result. A sibling of the two victims has also died, although tests for the virus have so far been negative. In addition, Turkish officials announced Sunday [8 January] that tests had confirmed five more cases of H5N1, two in Van and three from around Ankara – two young brothers and an elderly man. The Ankara cases have the most alarming implications since bird flu has never been reported in that part of the country. It is a relatively well off area, where it is not the norm for humans and animals to live under one roof. The boys infected had contact with dead wild ducks ... and the man a dead chicken ... The United Nations Food and Animal Organization ... said the organization now believed the outbreaks had been occurring for some time, staring perhaps as early as October or November [2005] ... In one village near Van, Dogubayazit, four children from the same family have apparently come down with the disease. A third also perished, although the first test was negative ... [The test is] being repeated because the test is complicated and is sometimes falsely negative ... A total of fifty patients are in hospitals in Van and Ankara with possible bird flu ... all of whom had close contact with birds ... The cluster of cases in Turkey is extraordinary and concerning, scientists said. In all of East Asia, where the disease has been rampant in birds for years, only about 140 people have ever become infected and there has never been this kind of grouping. Scientists are exploring various theories to explain the Turkish clusters ... When temperatures drop below zero – as they do frequently around Van in the winter – people may be more likely to bring chickens indoors and that could increase exposure.

(*IHT*, 9 January 2006, pp. 1, 8)

The Turkish health ministry said two children and an adult from near the capital, as well as two people in the eastern city of Van, had tested positive for the H5N1 strain of bird flu ... Samples from them are expected to be sent to the UK for testing ... Seven cases of the H5N1 strain [have been] confirmed in Turkey.

(*FT*, 9 January 2006, p. 1)

Preliminary tests showed that five more people have been infected with the deadly H5N1 strain of the bird flu in Turkey, a health ministry official said Monday [9 January], indicating the disease was spreading. Turkish labs detected H5N1 in the five new cases, discovered in four separate provinces ... The new cases raise the number of suspected and confirmed cases in Turkey to fifteen. Ten people had earlier tested positive for H5N1 in tests in Turkish labs, four of which have been confirmed by the WHO. Those four include two siblings who died last week in the eastern city of Van, the first confirmed fatalities cause by the virus outside eastern Asia, where seventy-four people have been killed by H5N1 since 2003. A third sibling died in Van of bird flu, but a WHO lab has yet to confirm H5N1 ... The cases in Ankara included two young brothers and a sixty-five-year-old man, all of whom tested positive for H5N1 in preliminary tests by Turkish labs ... Vietnam has not detected any bird flu outbreaks among its poultry in more than three weeks, but the country still faces a high risk of future flare-ups, an official said Monday ... The northern provinces of Ha Giang and Cao Bag bordering China were the last two provinces where no outbreaks were reported in twenty-one days ... The virus is considered to have been contained if no new outbreaks have been reported in that period, according to Vietnam's animal health decree. Vietnam has been hit harder by the virus than any other country. Since early October [2005] nearly 4 million birds have died or been slaughtered in twenty-four affected provinces nationwide. All those areas have since gone at least twenty-one days without an outbreak ... A thirty-nine-year-old man who died in Indonesia on 2 January had been infected with the bird flu, a senior health ministry official said Monday ... If the results are confirmed by a WHO-sanctioned laboratory, the country's human toll from the disease would climb to twelve.

(www.iht.com, 9 January 2006)

Five more children in Turkey tested positive in preliminary tests for the deadly H5N1 flu strain. The country now has fifteen suspected or confirmed cases of the strain and three children from the same family have died. The new cases were discovered in four provinces, indicating that the disease is spreading ... The WHO said, however, that the Turkish victims appeared to have contracted the virus directly from infected birds, allaying fears that it might now be passing from person to person.

(*IHT*, 10 January 2006, p. 3)

The WHO says fifteen people have been infected with bird flu in Turkey. Five of those – reported by the Turkish health ministry on Monday [9 January] – are considered 'preliminary positive' because the organization has not yet received enough information about them ... A team that began investigating the cases has initially reported that were caused by 'direct contact with diseased poultry' ... The governor of Istanbul ...announced Monday that birds in three districts of this city of 12 million had been diagnosed with the flu, although it was not yet clear if they carried the most dangerous H5N1 strain ... In addition to the fifteen confirmed cases, the governor said that more than twenty people in Istanbul potentially had bird flu.

(pp. 1, 8)

[On 9 January] the [Turkish] health ministry announced that five more people had been infected with the deadliest strain of the virus, bringing the total to fourteen ... Scores of suspected bird flu cases were reported across western and northern Turkey and a mass cull of poultry continued in the east.

(*FT*, 10 January 2006, p. 8)

The [Turkish] health ministry said fourteen people had tested positive for the virus, including the three dead children … A fourth child from the same family, aged six, was discharged from hospital after being confirmed as free of the disease … Worldwide seventy-six people have died of the H5N1 strain of avian influenza and the total number of confirmed cases has reached 146 in Vietnam, Thailand, Cambodia, China, Indonesia and now Turkey. Vietnam has the highest number, with ninety-three cases and forty-two deaths. China has reported seven cases and three deaths.

(*Independent*, 10 January 2006, p. 18)

New research offers some ground for optimism: it is likely that many people who contact the disease will not become seriously ill and will recover quickly. Although not definitive, a study published Monday [9 January] in *Archives of Internal Medicine* suggests the virus is more widespread than thought. But it also probably will not kill half its victims … Anna Thorson (of Karolinska University Hospital in Stockholm): 'The results suggest that the symptoms most often are relatively mild and that close contact is needed for transmission to humans' … The new study involved 45,476 randomly selected residents of a region [in Vietnam] where bird flu is rampant among poultry – Ha Tay province, west of Hanoi. More than 80 per cent lived in households that kept poultry, and one quarter lived in homes reporting sick or dead fowl. A total of 8,149 reportedly had flu-like symptoms, with a fever and cough. Residents who had direct contact with dead or sick poultry were 73 per cent more likely to have had those symptoms than residents without direct contact. The researchers said between 650 and 750 flu-like cases could be attributed to direct contact with sick or dead birds. While most patients said their symptoms had kept them out of work or school, the illnesses were mostly mild, lasting about three days. In contrast, most of the more than 140 human cases linked to bird flu and reported to the WHO since January 2004 have been severe – killing more than half the patients … The study's authors said that without blood tests to prove the Vietnamese residents had bird flu the results were only suggestive and far from conclusive.

(www.iht.com, 10 January 2006)

'[The study] suggested that the H5N1 virus might cause a wide spectrum of disease, but that doctors in Asia might only detect the severest cases, the ones that went to hospital' (*IHT*, 11 January 2006, p. 8).

Swedish researchers said … there could be up to 750 cases of infection compared with the eighty-seven officially reported … Those infected did not seek hospital treatment and were not counted in official figures … The finding indicates the disease may be milder … but it also suggests it is more widespread in humans, increasing the chances of a mutation that could trigger a pandemic.

(*Independent*, 10 January 2006, p. 18)

Japan said Tuesday [10 January] that seventy-seven poultry workers had tested positive for bird flu in the first ever confirmed infections of humans involving the weaker strain of the virus ... H5N2 ... [But] developing countries hit hardest by bird flu rarely bother trying to confirm cases of the weaker strain ... The farm workers ... were infected at some point but ... none of them showed signs of the disease ... Japan has so far suffered one case of human infection of the more deadly virus, but no deaths ... Most of the human infections in the world have been linked to direct contact with sick poultry ... There is no known cure or vaccination for H5N1 in humans.

(www.iht.com, 10 January 2006)

'China on Tuesday [10 January] recorded its thirty-third outbreak of bird flu since early 2005, with the latest epidemic hitting the southern province of Guizhou' (www.iht.com, 10 January 2006).

The WHO said [on 10 January] that preliminarily it supported analyses from Turkish laboratories of fifteen cases of the H5N1 virus in humans, pending confirmation from a second foreign test abroad, which was in line with normal practice. Three siblings from eastern Turkey have died from the H5N1 strain but authorities said yesterday [10 January] that none of the remaining individuals suspected of infection was in a critical condition ... The [Turkish] health ministry said another human case of the H5N1 strain had been found in a woman in Sivas.

(*FT*, 11 January 2006, p. 11)

The WHO said Wednesday [11 January] that two more people sickened by bird flu in China have died, bringing the total number of humans killed by the disease in that country to five and pushing the death toll worldwide to seventy-eight.

(www.iht.com, 11 January 2006)

Fifteen people [in Turkey] have contracted the deadly strain H5N1 ... and more than 100 people are in hospitals under observation ... Massive bird deaths started in mid-December [2005] ... In Dogubayazit ... all four children in the Kocyigit family came down with the disease after helping their mother slaughter sick birds on 24 December ... The government has announced it will provide compensation, but poultry owners must apply after the birds are killed and are on given money on the spot.

(*IHT*, 12 January 2006, pp. 1, 4)

All the human cases of avian influenza in Turkey – at least eighteen have been confirmed – have occurred after close contact with sick birds ... The largest outbreak in Turkey, which has resulted in three human deaths, is in the border town of Dogubayazit.

(*IHT*, 13 January 2006, p. 3)

Turkish officials announce a rise yesterday [12 January], from fifteen to eighteen, in the number of human bird flu cases ... Tests also showed that an eleven-year-old girl who died last week was suffering from H5N1 ... [Her] brother ... and sister ... also died of the disease last week, bringing the number of confirmed bird flu fatalities in Turkey to three – all of them children.

(*Guardian*, 13 January 2006, p. 28)

A twenty-nine-year-old Indonesian woman has died of bird flu, health officials said Thursday [12 January] ... The woman died Wednesday ... Samples have been sent to a Hong Kong laboratory – accredited by the WHO – to confirm the diagnosis ... Indonesia is awaiting results from tests in Hong Kong on a thirty-nine-year-old man who died last week. Local tests, usually reliable, confirmed he had died of bird flu. If tests confirm the two fatalities were caused by bird flu, Indonesia's death toll from the H5N1 virus would rise to thirteen.

(IHT, 13 January 2005, p. 3)

'Indonesia: the WHO confirmed the country's twelfth human death form the H5N1 strain' *(FT,* 14 January 2006, p. 5).

'The virus has killed a twelfth person in Indonesia, a twenty-nine-year-old woman. It brings the death toll worldwide from the disease since it struck Asia in 2003 to seventy-eight' *(Guardian,* 14 January 2006, p. 18).

The Turkish health ministry ... confirmed three more cases of infection by the deadly H5N1 strain of bird flu in humans, bring the total to eighteen ... A four-year-old girl died in hospital in Turkey yesterday [13 January] ... The EU yesterday [13 January] pledged $97 million towards tackling bird flu, adding to contributions from Japan and the United States as leading countries geared up for an international donors' conference in Beijing next week to help prevent a human pandemic. At the close of a conference in Tokyo yesterday ... The WHO ... said $1.5 billion was needed to tackle the problem ... Japan has pledged $155 million.

(FT, 14 January 2006, p. 5)

Health authorities in Turkey are investigating whether a four-year-old girl who died yesterday [13 January] has become the country's fourth child fatality ... Eighteen people have already been infected ... Patients there [in Turkey] have been said to be responding well ... to Tamiflu.

(Guardian, 14 January 2006, p. 18)

The Turkish authorities were trying to determine whether a twelve-year-old girl who died Sunday [15 January] was the country's latest victim of bird flu after her seven-year-old brother tested positive for the virulent H5N1 virus The girl's brother was in a serious condition, officials said ... [They are] from Dogubayazit ... The health ministry said the latest test results on the sick boy brought to at least nineteen the number of people in Turkey known to have contracted the H5N1 strain ... Health authorities have said all those with confirmed H5N1 infections apparently had touched or played with sick birds and that there was no evidence of person-to-person infection ... The virus is now confirmed in twenty-six of Turkey's eighty-one provinces ... The three fatalities in Turkey last week were the first known deaths from the virus outside East Asia and South-east Asia, where at least seventy-seven people have died from bird flu since the outbreak began, according to the WHO tally.

(IHT, 16 January 2006, p. 3)

'So far seventy-nine humans have died from the virus' (*FT*, 16 January 2006, p. 9).

This week ... health ministers, leaders of UN agencies and top officials from the World Bank and other lending institutions gather in Beijing to raise as much as $1.5 billion to fight bird flu ... For now much of the money being offered to poor countries to fight bird flu involves loans, not grants ... The danger, even some managers of bird flu programmes are starting to say, is that donors focus so intently on a single disease that they unintentionally disrupt many other health programmes ... In Laos ... despite the apparent disappearance of bird flu ... it has consumed the time and attention of Laos's best doctors and veterinarians for the past two years ... Not one human case of bird flu was ever confirmed in Laos ... Laotian government officials reported to the UN agency within hours on a weekend last September [2005] the country's only suspected human case of bird flu so far. A laboratory in Japan determined it was a false alarm ... Unlike the situation in neighbouring Vietnam, Thailand and China, where live poultry is often transported large distances to markets, sometimes on bicycles, in sparsely populated Laos most chickens and ducks are raised in backyards and eaten by their owners. This limits the disease's spread.

(www.iht.com, 15 January 2006)

Initial tests carried out by the Indonesian authorities indicate that a thirteen-year-old girl who died over the weekend was infected with bird flu, an Indonesian health ministry official said Monday [15 January] ... The girl would be the thirteenth Indonesian fatality from the virus, which has killed nearly eighty people in Asia since 2003. Three people have also died in Turkey ... The WHO confirmed Friday [13 January] that a twenty-nine-year-old Indonesian woman was the twelfth Indonesian death from bird flu. Indonesia is also awaiting results from test in Hong Kong on a thirty-nine-year-old man who died earlier this month. Local tests, which are usually reliable, confirmed that he also had bird flu.

(www.iht.com, 16 January 2006)

Twenty people in Turkey, all of whom have had close contact with sick birds, have been confirmed as infected over the past two weeks. The most recent victim was a twelve-year-old girl, who ... died Sunday [15 January] ... It was determined Monday [16 January] that she had the virus ... In South-east Asia, where bird flu first appeared in 1997, there have been about 140 cases over a period of three years ... There are now nineteen confirmed outbreaks of bird flu in Turkey and the government announced Monday that it was culling birds in twenty-nine provinces where flu was 'confirmed or suspected'.

(*IHT*, 17 January 2006, p. 3)

Top officials from around the world said here [Beijing] on Tuesday [17 January] that governments would have to spend heavily for years to prevent bird flu from spreading widely among humans, and cannot just rely on the many stopgap steps taken so far. A two-day conference that began here on

Tuesday morning is expected to produce pledges of $1.2 billion to $1.5 billion in bird flu spending from the conference's sponsors – the EU, the World Bank and China – and from other donors, including the United States. The recent spate of twenty human cases of bird flu on Europe's doorstep in Turkey, including four deaths, has prompted criticism at the conference of Turkish officials for not having spotted the disease in local poultry sooner. This failure has led to calls for a broad international effort to build up many nations' veterinary capacity to spot outbreaks early, when they can still be contained fairly easily through steps like culling or vaccinating chickens ... [It was said that] the EU would announce on Wednesday [18 January] an increase in its previous pledge of $120 million ... The predictions of a long and costly campaign came as Roche announced in Basel, Switzerland, that it would donate another 2 million treatment doses of its anti-viral medicine, Tamiflu, to the WHO ... The director-general of the World Organization for Animal Health said it was crucial to catch an outbreak within the first forty-eight hours and that Turkey had failed to do so.

(*IHT*, 18 January 2006, p. 2)

The Roche donation ... [of] another 2 million treatments of Tamiflu ... would have a market value of about $36.2 million if sold at its usual commercial prices to western governments ... [Tamiflu] is designed to both reduce the death and illness from bird flu and to prevent its spread ... The latest Roche donation follows a previous 3 million treatment stockpile it provided for free.

(*FT*, 18 January 2006, p. 7)

Preliminary tests indicate that another Turkish child is infected with the H5N1 strain of bird flu, increasing the total number of human cases in the country to twenty-one ... The child ... was from Dogubayazit, the home town of all four of the other children who have died of H5N1 infection.

(*IHT*, 18 January 2006, p. 2)

'Bird flu has killed at least seventy-nine people since 2003 and nearly 150 people are known to have been infected in six countries' (*Guardian*, 18 January 2006, p. 16).

The international community yesterday [18 January] promised $1.9 billion to fight avian flu in the worst affected countries, with the largest commitments coming from the United States with $334 million and the EU pledging around $260 million ... [Other promises included Japan's $159 million, Russia's $45 million, Australia's $42 and China's $10 million] ... The funding, promised at an international conference in Beijing, was well in excess of an initial target set by the World Bank to raise at least $1.2 billion ... Of the $1.9 billion, about $900 million would be in the form of loans and the rest in grants ... David Nabarro, the United Nations flu envoy, said the funds were intended to fill a gap in flu-related financing in countries with serious outbreaks ... There are widespread concerns that an unmanageable outbreak or virus mutation in a single country may quickly spread beyond borders.

(*FT*, 19 January 2006, p. 10)

Thirty-three countries and multilateral institutions pledged $1.9 billion Wednesday [18 January] to fight the disease. The pledges, at the conclusion of a two-day conference in Beijing, exceed the $1.2 billion to $1.4 billion that the World Bank said was needed over the next three years. The money will pay for such tasks as strengthening veterinary and medical surveillance for outbreaks, stockpiling of surgical masks and other protective equipment and expanding research ... [The World Bank] said that the oversubscription would make it possible for poor countries to rely more on grants than loans in fighting the disease. The $1.9 billion includes $1 billion in grants and $900 million in loans, including $500 million in World Bank loans ... Migratory birds have carried the virus out of southern China and South-east Asia to infect chickens around the Black Sea and the Caucasus, leading to illness in at least twenty-one people in Turkey. The oversubscription also makes it somewhat less likely that money would have to be taken from existing economic development programmes to pay for fighting bird flu [the World Bank said] ...The United States pledged $334 million in grants, for example, of which $31.3 million is money transferred from funds previously earmarked for helping survivors of the tsunami on 26 December 2004. But $280 million comes from bird flu-related legislation passed by Congress just before Christmas [2005], while another $22.7 million comes mostly from money previously set aside for international health issues ... Japan pledged $159, the EU pledged $120 million and the EU members separately promised $138 million ... China pledged $10 million.

(www.iht.com, 18 January 2005; *IHT*, 19 January 2006, p. 4)

'Tests have confirmed that the H5N1 virus killed a teenage girl in Iraq and a thirty-five-year-old woman in China' (*Independent*, 19 January 2006, p. 31).

The near-total absence of adequate health care in much of the [Chinese] countryside has sown deep resentment among the peasantry while helping to spread infectious diseases like hepatitis and tuberculosis and making the country – and the world – more vulnerable to epidemics like SARS and possibly bird flu.

(Howard French, *IHT*, 16 January 2006, p. 4)

Two children from the same family died from bird flu, the WHO has confirmed, bringing Indonesia's toll from the virus to fourteen, the government said Sunday [22 January] ... The four-year-old boy and his thirteen-year-old sister died last week, but confirmation that bird flu was responsible was not known until Saturday ... Like most of the other cases, the victims lived on Java, a densely populated island that is home to more than half of the country's 220 million people ... Doctors suspect a French woman who recently returned from Turkey could have contracted bird flu and are examining her, the health ministry reported Sunday.

(www.iht.com, 22 January 2006)

Initial tests ... [on] a French woman ... were negative ... Hospitalization does not indicate likely infections and it is common when countries are on high alert concerning a disease. Two weeks ago a German who fell ill after being in

Turkey was hospitalized ... Only 150 people worldwide have fallen ill from ... the H5N1 virus.

(IHT, 23 January 2006, p. 3)

On Friday [20 January] the Turkish government accused several of its neighbours of concealing bird flu outbreaks and hampering efforts to prevent the spread of the disease. Turkey did not name the countries it believes are covering up the infections. Turkey has reported possible H5N1 outbreaks of poultry in twenty-six provinces, including areas bordering Azerbaijan, Armenia, Iran, Iraq, Syria and Georgia ... Since 2003 eighty-one people have died from bird flu in Turkey and eastern Asia. All the victims appear to have contracted the disease after close contact with infected poultry and health officials say that so far there is no evidence that the virus can be transmitted from human to human.

(Guardian, 23 January 2006, p. 19)

The costs of the [H5N1] virus cannot be ignored. Already millions of dollars have been lost to economies in Asia where widespread culling has taken place. The World Bank estimates the damage in a country such as Vietnam at up to 0.2 per cent of GDP ... Even SARS ... cost east Asia an estimated 2 per cent of GDP in the second quarter of 2004.

(FT, Survey on the World in 2006, 25 January 2006, p. 6)

The EU authorities have confirmed the presence of the deadly H5N1 strain of avian flu in a sample of poultry taken from northern Cyprus, the European Commission said Sunday [29 January] ... Turkey has reported twenty-one human cases of H5N1, including four deaths, although the WHO has not confirmed the figures.

(www.iht.com, 29 January 2006)

'Bird flu has been detected in northern Cyprus ... Tests on dead birds showed they were carrying the lethal H5N1 strain' (*FT*, 30 January 2006, p. 12).

'Test showed a bird in northern Cyprus ... the Turkish-Cypriot enclave ... was carrying the H5N1 strain' (*Independent*, 30 January 2006, p. 23).

A fifteen-year-old Iraqi girl has died of the H5N1 virus, Iraqi and international health officials confirmed Monday [30 January], indicating the arrival of the disease in yet another country ... More alarming still, officials said, the finding suggests that the disease may be spreading widely – and undetected – among birds in countries of Central Asia that are poorly equipped to pick up or report infections. Bird flu has never been reported in animals in Iraq. As in Turkey earlier this month [January] the spread of bird flu to a new part of the world was heralded by a human death. The girl ... died earlier this month [17 January] in Sulaimaniya, in the Kurdish region of northern Iraq, three days after touching dead birds ... Her uncle, who died last week, is also presumed to have succumbed to the disease, although test are pending ... Two other people in distant parts of Iraq have also been tested for bird flu ... A serious bird flu outbreak has killed four people and hundreds of thousands of birds in the Kurdish part of neighbouring Turkey over the past six weeks ... A large ethnic Kurdish area includes portions of several different countries ... A slow start in Turkey allowed the disease to spread throughout the country and the government is now struggling to contain fifty-five outbreaks in fifteen provinces.

(*IHT*, 31 January 2006, pp. 1, 8)

'The WHO is carrying out tests to confirm the first human case of bird flu in Iraq, following the death of a fourteen-year-old girl ... Preliminary results ... showed the deadly H5N1 bird flu virus, but it [the WHO] was seeking further tests' (*FT*, 31 January 2006, p. 8).

Bird flu has spread from South-east Asia to the borders of Europe, killing at least eighty-five people in six countries. A girl in Iraq also apparently died from the virus, though the WHO has not confirmed the cause of that death and included it in its tally ... [Roche's] Tamiflu and GlaxoSmithKline's Relenza are the only two drugs currently being sold that studies say may help people infected with bird flu.

(www.iht.com, 1 February 2006)

Bird flu appears to be taking root in Hong Kong now that it has surfaced in local wild birds and chickens ... York Chow (Hong Kong's health secretary): 'Since different kinds of wild birds and chickens have this virus we can be quite sure that this virus is endemic in our birds ... [The virus] will exist in neighbouring areas, southern China as well as Hong Kong' ... Later a health bureau spokesman said Chow meant that bird flu is endemic in Asia, not Hong Kong specifically. The UN Food and Agriculture Organization says an area is considered endemic after tests determine a cycle of disease recurrence within a given area, and that the virus has not simply been imported from another place.

(*IHT*, 4 February 2006, p. 5)

[The Hong Kong health secretary] said that positive tests for H5N1 in a bird brought to Hong Kong from China indicated that the virus was endemic ... The chicken was one of four birds that have died from the virus in Hong Kong this year [2006] ... [His comment] raises concerns about detection within the Guangdong region of China, which has not reported any cases of bird flu ... The H5N1 strain was first detected in 1997, in Hong Kong. It has infected 161 people and killed eighty-six since 2003 ... Indonesian officials confirmed yesterday [3 February] that a fifteen-year-old boy had died of the disease.

(*The Times*, 4 February 2006, p. 47)

The bird flu virus continued its alarming global march, confirmed Wednesday [8 February] for the first time in birds in Africa, a continent that is ill-prepared to contain its spread, international health authorities said. The Nigerian health authorities reported the continent's first outbreak to the World Organization for Animal Health in Paris ... In an outbreak that began on 10 January, more than 40,000 chickens have died at a commercial laying farm in Kaduna state in northern Nigeria ... A UN laboratory in Italy confirmed late Tuesday that the culprit was H5N1 ... UN veterinary officials said Wednesday that they were investigating similar rumours of bird deaths in a number of other African countries ... In Nigeria ... home to about 140 million poultry ... the outbreak began with bird deaths on 10 January but was not reported until Wednesday ... Nigerian samples were only sent to the UN reference laboratory in Italy last week ... The food and agriculture agency has been tracking rumours of bird deaths in Nigeria for several weeks ... and is investigating similar rumours in a handful of other African nations, including Mali, Egypt, Malawi and Libya ... Worldwide about 160 people have become infected with bird flu, almost all of whom have had extremely close contact with sick birds. About half of them have died.

(www.iht.com, 9 February 2006)

The World Organization for Animal Health confirmed yesterday that the first recorded case of H5N1 bird flu in Africa had been found in the northern state of Kaduna [in Nigeria], on a farm of 46,000 chickens, geese and ostriches ... The Italian health ministry confirmed that the 'highly pathological strain' of H5N1 found in Nigeria was similar to those discovered in Siberia and Mongolia.

(*Independent*, 9 February 2006, p. 25)

Many people [in Africa] live in close proximity to poultry, just as in South-east Asia ... [There are] fears that bird flu is now spreading through Iraq ... Worldwide eighty-eight of the 165 people confirmed as having been infected with the avian virus have died ... Samples from wild waterfowl in Malawi, Sudan and Kenya will soon be tested ... in South Africa.

(*Guardian*, 9 February 2006, p. 17)

'The H5N1 strain of bird flu has been detected in two more northern states [in Nigeria]' (*Independent*, 10 February 2006, p. 38).

Nigeria struggled Friday [10 February] to contain the first known outbreak in Africa of bird flu, as officials warned it is spreading rapidly through flocks in the north of the country. Overnight the police and agricultural workers moved into a farm at the centre of the outbreak of avian influenza. They shot ostriches and bulldozed the charred remains of 45,000 chickens into the ground ... Azerbaijani officials said Friday that a British laboratory had confirmed the presence of bird flu in dead birds found along the Caspian Sea coast ... Azerbaijan shares a short border with eastern Turkey, where four children died after becoming infected with bird flu.

(www.iht.com, 10 February 2006)

Azerbaijan on Friday became the latest country to report the discovery of the H5N1 strain of avian flu, when migratory birds were found dead on its Caspian Sea coasts. The health ministry said Friday that a British laboratory had confirmed the presence of the H5N1 strain in wild ducks and swans on the Absheron Peninsula, which includes the capital, Baku, and surrounding villages.

(*IHT*, 11 February 2006, p. 6)

The Chinese government said Wednesday [8 February] that a twenty-six-year-old woman in an area with no reported outbreaks in poultry of the virulent flu strain was the latest person to become infected with bird flu in China ... Researchers looking into why many of the eleven people infected with bird flu in China came from areas without outbreaks in birds suspect it might be a result of contamination spread by dead poultry, the Chinese health ministry said Friday [10 February] ... China has reported twenty-nine bird flu outbreaks in poultry since October [2005] in areas throughout the country. The government has destroyed millions of chickens, ducks and other poultry to contain the virus. Seven of the people infected have died.

(www.iht.com, 10 February 2006)

'China announced Friday the death of a twenty-year-old woman, bringing the death toll from the virus to eight' (*IHT*, 11 February 2006, p. 6).

Italian veterinary and health officials gathered Sunday [12 January] to plan a response to the country's first confirmed cases of the deadly H5N1 bird flu virus, which was discovered in wild swans in southern Italy. The cases in Italy and others confirmed in northern Greece on Saturday [11 February] marked the first time the highly infectious strain of the H5N1 virus had been detected within the EU. The virus was detected in five swans in the three southern Italian states of Puglia, Calabria and Sicily ... The swans had arrived from the Balkans, likely pushed south by cold weather ... Bird flu has killed at least eighty-eight people in Asia and Turkey since 2003, according to the WHO in a 9 February update. On Sunday a WHO-sanctioned laboratory confirmed another two deaths in Indonesia. It has been ravaging poultry stocks across Asia since 2003, killing or forcing the slaughter of more than 140 million birds.

(www.iht.com, 12 February 2006)

Indonesia said that two women died last week from bird flu, pushing the death toll from the disease there to eighteen ... European officials announced Saturday that bird flu had been detected in wild birds in Italy, Greece and Bulgaria, the first time its presence had been detected in the EU ... The Italian health minister ... announced that seventeen swans had been found dead in three southern regions.

(www.iht.com, 12 February 2006)

The H5N1 bird flu virus has been detected in wild birds in Italy and Greece ... It was also detected in Bulgaria ... [Italy] confirmed H5N1 in five of the dead swans and tests on others were continuing ... In Greece health officials announced that three swans in the northern part of the country had tested positive for the virus. Hours later EU officials said that some swans in Bulgaria, near the Danube Delta, had as well ... The variant strain of H5N1 found in Turkey and confirmed in Africa last week is identical to one found in a nature reserve in northern China and later in Siberia. It is different from strains circulating among poultry in South-east Asia and Indonesia.

(*IHT*, 13 February 2006, p. 4)

Slovenia imposed controls yesterday [12 February] after a suspect case ... a dead swan ... was discovered near the Austrian border ... Samples have been sent to ... the UK ... to test if it is the strain that can infect humans ... The H5N1 variant of bird flu has killed at least ninety people in seven countries since 2003, according to the WHO.

(*FT*, 13 February 2006, p. 10)

Concerns grew over the weekend after bird flu appeared for the first time in the EU, in swans in Greece and Italy, while Nigeria waited for test results on two children suspected of being the first Africans to be infected ... The virus has killed at least ninety people in Asia and the Middle East ... since late 2003.

(www.iht.com, 13 February 2006)

Iraqi doctors are investigating six suspected cases of bird flu in southern Iraq, including one in which a twenty-five-year-old fisherman died after contact with birds he was keeping in his yard, Iraqi and US health officials said Sunday [12 February] ... Test are being performed to determine whether the fisherman, who died in hospital ... was infected with the H5N1 strain of the virus.

(www.iht.com, 13 February 2006)

Scores of government workers searched rural areas of Hong Kong for poultry on Monday [13 February] to enforce a ban on backyard fowl ... Hong Kong [is] already on edge following eight deaths from bird flu in mainland China, after six wild birds and two chickens in the city were killed by the H5N1 strain of avian influenza in the past three weeks ... Hong Kong has not had any bird flu infections in people since the outbreak began in Asia in late 2003 ... The government wants to wipe out bird flu from the city where the virus made its first known jump to humans in 1997, killing six people.

(www.iht.com, 13 February 2006)

Twelve people died from bird flu in Thailand in 2004 but only two died last year [2005]. In Vietnam, by contrast, fatalities have continued apace, with twenty deaths in 2004 and nineteen last year ... Thailand has mobilized about 750,000 volunteers, one for every fifteen rural households ... The disease first struck Thailand in late 2003 ... [A] six-year-old [boy] ... was Thailand's first confirmed human case of avian influenza ... In Vietnam the government has urged the media to uncover cases and encouraged the general public to report sick or dead poultry, but there is no network of volunteers, according to ... the WHO ... In China surveillance efforts are haphazard [according to the WHO].

(www.iht.com, 13 February 2006; *IHT*, 14 February 2006, p. 8)

'A fourth bird sample ... a wild goose ... has tested positive for the deadly H5N1 strain in Greece' (*Independent*, 14 February 2006, p. 18).

[On 14 February] H5N1 was identified in two dead swans in Germany and at least two swans in Austria ... The swans [in Germany] found on the Baltic Sea island of Rügen registered positive in an initial test for the virus ... Iran also indicated for the first time yesterday [14 February] that it had identified the virus in wild swans ... Morocco was also conducting tests ... To date ninety-one people [in Asia and Turkey] have been confirmed dead as a result of the virus, from 169 identified as infected ... according to the WHO.

(*FT*, 15 February 2006, p. 8)

'Slovenia confirmed six new cases of bird flu near the Austrian border yesterday [15 February' (*Independent*, 15 February 2006, p. 18].

'The Italian press reported Wednesday [15 February] that two swans that died in southern Italy had tested positive for the virus, bringing to eight the number of birds to have died from H5N1 in Italy' (www.iht.com, 15 February 2006).

H5N1 was confirmed in a type of migratory swan in Greece, Bulgaria and Italy on Saturday [11 February] and in Germany on Wednesday [15 February]. Probable cases were detected in the same species in Slovenia and Croatia on Sunday, in Austria on Monday and in Denmark on Tuesday.

(*IHT*, 16 February 2006, p. 1)

'Germany and Austria became the latest countries to confirm cases of avian influenza ... German officials said yesterday [15 February] that the two swans found on a beach on the Baltic island of Rügen had died from H5N1' (*Guardian*, 16 February 2006, p. 24).

'The bird flu that reached western Europe this week seems to have been carried by swans fleeing a Balkan cold snap' (*The Economist*, 18 February 2006, p. 41).

France yesterday [17 February] confirmed that it had found a dead wild duck carrying the H5 virus, joining Italy, Greece, Slovenia, Germany, Hungary and Austria on the list of EU countries that have found cases of bird flu ... The Dutch government ... announced last night that two dead swans had tested negative.

(*FT*, 18 February 2006, p. 9)

On the German island of Rügen tests on Friday [17 February] confirmed that ten wild birds had the H5N1 flu strain. France said a dead duck in the south-east tested positive for an H5 subtype and that more testing was being conducted. In Egypt official confirmed that country's first cases ... in and around Cairo.

(*IHT*, 18 February 2006, p. 3)

[France said] a duck found dead in the east had tested positive for the virus and that it was likely to be the H5N1 strain ... The bird was found dead on Monday [13 February] near Lyon ... The disease has infected chickens in Egypt for the first time and there were cases reported in Azerbaijan and Slovenia.

(*Guardian*, 18 February 2006, p. 16)

France ... confirmed over the weekend that a duck had died from the virus ... France was the seventh European country discovered to have been infected by the H5N1 strain over the past week ... India began the slaughter of ... chickens Sunday [19 February] as health ministry officials investigated the death of a poultry farm owner from the country's first suspected case of bird flu ......

The first reports from New Delhi of suspected infections came on Friday [17 February] ... India is a major poultry producer, with an estimated 500 million birds.

(www.iht.com, 19 February 2006)

First reports of bird flu cropped up this weekend in widely separated countries – India, Egypt and France – highlighting the disease's accelerating spread to new territories ... The recent acceleration has perplexed many experts, who had watched the H5N1 virus stick to its native ground in Asia for nearly five years ... In Egypt the authorities on Sunday [19 February] closed the Cairo zoo and seven other state-run zoos around the country after eighty-three birds died there, some from the H5N1 strain of flu ... Since Friday [17 February], when the first announcement was made about bird flu outbreaks, the Egyptian authorities have reported cases of bird flu among poultry in at least eight provinces.

(*IHT*, 20 February 2006, pp. 1, 4)

Bird flu was detected for the first time on the German mainland yesterday [19 February] ... Bird flu has killed a twenty-three-year-old worker in Indonesia, a government official said on Saturday [18 February] ... The country's nineteen victim of the H5N1 virus died on 10 February.

(*FT*, 20 February 2006, p. 6)

Vietnam, the worst affected country in the world with ninety-three human cases and forty-two deaths, has become the first to successfully contain the disease ... according to the WHO. No new cases of avian flu have been reported in humans since last November [2005] and in birds since last December, Hans Troedsson, director of the WHO in Hanoi said. Vietnam's breakthrough in containing the disease comes as the worldwide outbreak was confirmed in India, France and Iran ... Under WHO guidelines a country is designated disease-free when no new cases have been reported for twenty-one days. Thailand has also recorded no new cases since last November but has been less severely affected than Vietnam with twenty-two human cases and fourteen deaths ... The success curbing the disease in Vietnam and Thailand ... [is] especially encouraging ... [because] it has been achieved in a part of the world where there are tens of thousands of peasant farmers keeping small flocks of chickens. Dr Troedsson said that a combination of vaccination, culling and public communication had proved the disease could be halted, even in a less developed country such as Vietnam. Almost 200 million birds have been vaccinated and up to 5 million culled ... [Places] like Hong Kong, Vietnam and Thailand have been able to contain [the disease] ... But Dr Troedsson warned that the H5N1 virus was almost certainly still in Vietnam and vigilance was essential.

(*Independent*, 20 February 2006, pp. 1–2)

There have been a total of 169 cases of avian flu in humans and ninety-two deaths. The respective figures for countries are as follows: Cambodia, four and four; China, twelve and eight; Indonesia, twenty-five and nineteen; Iraq, one and one; Thailand, twenty-two and fourteen; Turkey, twelve and four; Vietnam, ninety-three and forty-two (*Independent*, 20 February 2006, p. 2).

> Hungary has reported five cases of suspected H5N1 and sent samples to an EU laboratory for testing ... Two dead swans found in central Bosnia have tested positive for an H5 strain of bird flu and samples were sent to the laboratory in Britain to determine the exact strain.
>
> (www.iht.com, 20 February 2006)

> Nigeria confirmed Monday [20 February] that Africa's first bird flu epidemic had spread to three new states and the capital, Abuja, but underlined there had been no human infections ... To date [there are in total] six states ... where bird flu has been confirmed.
>
> (*IHT*, 21 February 2006, p. 4)

> Niger has become the second sub-Saharan country with confirmed cases of the deadly H5N1 bird flu strain ... The tests were confirmed Monday [27 February] ... H5N1 had earlier been confirmed in Nigeria, Niger's southern neighbour, and officials had said in mid-February they were investigating whether it had surfaced in Niger. It has also been confirmed in Egypt ... Bosnia, meanwhile, confirmed its first case [of H5N1] ... The two migrating [wild] swans had died in mid-February ... [The WHO] on Monday raised its tally of officially confirmed human cases of bird flu by three to 173. It said ninety-three of those were fatal, raising the number by one. The new cases of the WHO's list are two people in China reported in critical condition and a twenty-seven-year-old woman from Indonesia who died last week. WHO figures usually lag behind reports in individual countries, because it considers a person to have bird flu only after samples have been sent abroad and confirmed in a foreign laboratory. Almost all human deaths from bird flu have been linked to contact with infected birds.
>
> (*IHT*, 28 February 2006, p. 4)

'Georgia found the H5N1 strain in wild swans' (*Independent*, 28 February 2006, p. 24).

> Health workers in western India were wrapping up a massive slaughter of chickens Tuesday [21 February] to contain the H5N1 bird flu virus, while Malaysia began killing birds after reporting its first case of the disease in more than a year ... The Hong Kong government said a dead magpie ... was infected with bird flu ... On Tuesday bird flu was confirmed [in three dead wild swans] in Hungary, the seventh country in the EU to be affected by the disease.
>
> (www.iht.com, 21 February 2006)

> The spread of the H5N1 strain of bird flu into Hungary and Croatia was confirmed Tuesday [21 February] ... At least fifteen nations have reported outbreaks in birds this month [February], an indication that the virus ... is spreading faster. Migratory birds are thought to be at least one transporter of

the disease. More than thirty countries have reported cases since 2003. Seven have recorded human infections. Hungary said Tuesday that tests had showed the virus in three dead swans found last week. Croatia confirmed that H5N1 had been found in a dead swan on an island in the Adriatic Sea.

(*IHT*, 22 February 2006, p. 3)

'Avian flu can be controlled. In the past three years bird flu broke out in Malaysia, Korea and Japan and all three countries have eradicated it' (*IHT*, 22 February 2006, p. 8).

China and Vietnam have used widespread vaccination of poultry with great success. Vietnam, which has vaccinated 120 million birds since last year [2005], had the highest human death toll from bird flu in 2004. It has had neither a new outbreak nor a human case in more than four months.

(*IHT*, 23 February 2006, p. 8)

Indonesia said Wednesday [22 February] that a twenty-seven-year-old woman had died of bird flu [on 20 February] ... in the capital, Jakarta, after coming into contact with sick chickens ... Indonesia has now recorded nineteen human bird flu fatalities ... The announcement came as international health experts expressed concern over the unprecedented spread of bird flu from Asia to Europe and Africa ... The virus has been detected in birds in fourteen countries since early February ... [and has] killed at least ninety-two people.

(www.iht.com, 22 February 2006)

About 170 people have become infected with bird flu ... For the first time on Wednesday [22 February] the deadly H5N1 bird flu virus was detected in poultry in the twenty-five-country EU. Two chickens in Graz, Austria, were contaminated in an animal compound ... where an injured swan had been housed.

(*IHT*, 23 February 2006, p. 8)

The WHO has confirmed twenty-six cases of human bird flu in Indonesia, nineteen of them fatal. Eight of those deaths have occurred in 2006, more than in any other country this year [2006] ... The more than 12 million residents of Jakarta, where the majority of Indonesia's bird flu deaths have occurred, live in close proximity to chickens and ducks, often with birds running freely on their property. Local tests this week revealed another possible fatality in a twenty-seven-year-old woman from Jakarta, but the WHO-sanctioned Hong Kong lab has yet to confirm the results.

(www.iht.com, 23 February 2006)

France suspects that an outbreak of the H5N1 bird flu virus has hit a turkey farm in the east of the country, the agriculture ministry said Thursday [23 February]. If confirmed it would be the first case of the virus spreading to domestic birds in the EU ... The farm is in the Ain region, where two wild ducks had already been found to have the virus ... The H5N1 version of avian influenza was also reported for the first time in Slovakia ... in a duck and a falcon ... bringing to eight on Thursday the number of EU countries in which the virus has been found ... More than 100 wild birds in Germany have been infected ... The H5N1 virus has killed ninety-two people since 2003, mostly in Southeast Asia, China and Turkey. The victims were all in close contact with birds infected with the virus.

(*IHT*, 24 February 2006, p. 3)

[The] case of bird flu detected at a turkey farm ... raises concerns for the poultry industry because the French turkeys were infected despite being kept indoors ... The French government last week ordered all poultry farmers to move birds indoors.

(*IHT*, 25 February 2006, p. 3)

'The owner of the turkey farm [in France] where the flu was confirmed ... [said] he thought the virus was carried on bales of straw that he had put into his indoors pens' (*IHT*, 27 February 2006, p. 3).

It is increasingly apparent that the real and most immediate issue is to what extent wild birds, or humans themselves, are responsible for the inspection's spread in poultry. A research paper in *Proceedings of the National Academy of Sciences*, published online on 10 February, shows that the H5N1 virus has persisted in its birthplace, southern Russia, for almost ten years and has been introduced into Vietnam on at least three occasions, and to Indonesia. The authors suggest that such transmissions are perpetuated mainly by the movement of poultry and poultry products, rather than by migrating birds ... In Nigeria there is the suggestion that it was trade, and not migratory birds, that caused the outbreak ... In Nigeria, Egypt and India the virus has been discovered to be widely distributed across the poultry flocks.

(*The Economist*, 25 February 2006, p. 89)

A definitive report in the 28 January issue of the medical journal *The Lancet* concludes: 'We could find no credible data on the effects [of Tamiflu] on avian influenza ... Over-reliance on a pharmaceutical solution to the ravages of influenza may impede the development and implementation of broader intervention strategies based on public health measures' ... Influenza is naturally an aquatic migratory bird virus that is carried by ducks, geese and a small list of other waterfowl. Influenza infection is usually harmless to these world travellers, but can kill other types of birds, such as chickens, domestic ducks and swans ... For at least a decade H5N1 has circulated among a small pool of migrating birds, mostly inside China, and occasionally broken out in other animals and people. Last May [2005], however, more than 6,000 avian carcasses piled up along the shores of Lake Qinghai in central China, one of the world's most important bird breeding sites. Most of the dead included species that had not previously evidenced influenza infection. The Lake Qinghai moment was the tipping point in the bird flu pandemic. The virus mutated, evidently becoming more contagious and deadly to a broader range of bird species, some of which continued their northern migration to central Siberia. By June [2005] Russia's tundra was, for the first time, teeming with H5N1-infected birds, intermingling with southern European species that became infected before flying home, via the Black Sea. Not surprisingly, by October countries from Ukraine to Greece were rumoured to have H5N1, but only the Romanian government responded with swift transparency, culling tens of thousands of chickens and ducks. Most of the governments in the region did not confirm their H5N1 contaminations until Turkey, after at least three months of denial, was forced on 6 January [2006] to admit that the virus had infected birds in a third of the country's provinces, and had caused several human infections and deaths. Since then we have learned of confirmed bird and/or human H5N1 cases in Iraq, Azerbaijan, Iran, Greece, Spain, Italy, Croatia, Austria, Hungary, Slovenia, France, Germany, Denmark, Bulgaria and, most disturbingly, Nigeria, Egypt and India. Not a single one of these countries' outbreaks ought to have been surprises. Each of them is located along either the Black Sea/Mediterranean migratory bird flyway, which starts in Siberia and, at its southernmost point, ends in Nigeria and Cameroon, or the European flyway, which overlaps the former, and stretches from northernmost Siberia to Nigeria ... Several countries along the flyway between Saudi Arabia (which has confirmed H5N1 infections in falcons) and Nigeria have not reported H5N1 cases, but much of the region is North Africa's sparsely populated Sahara Desert. Egypt reported widespread bird infection last week, and it is likely that infected birds have landed along the few waterways in the area, such as the Nile, Lake Chad and the Red Sea.

(Laurie Garrett, *IHT*, 27 February 2006, p. 8)

Experts are realizing that they do not fully understand how migrating birds disseminate the H5N1 virus, leaving the continents vulnerable to unexpected outbreaks. Just after new scientific research clarified the role of wild birds in spreading H5N1 out of its original territory in southern China, the virus promptly moved into dozens of locations in Europe and Africa, following no apparent pattern and underlining how little scientists actually know ... While they [scientists] are convinced that the virus can be carried on trucks, shoes and fertilizer, they are not sure how important that route is ... In February new research provided crucial clues about how the H5N1 virus broke out of its original stalking grounds in South-east Asia, moving to western China and on to the edges of Europe late last year [2005]. Bird flu was discovered in Hong Kong in 1997. The critical viral transfer took place in China's southern Guangdong province, new genetic analysis suggests, when wild ducks or geese acquired the virus from domestic poultry in rice paddies where they co-existed ... From there ... China's remote west and Mongolia ... H5N1 predictably moved to Russia, Ukraine, Turkey, Romania and the Balkans. But the recent pattern of spread, into European and African nations, has been far more confusing ... While ornithologists are convinced that most of Europe's cases are tied to migration, they are also quick to note that wild birds are sometimes unfairly blamed. Officials in Turkey and Nigeria said that migrating birds were responsible for H5N1 outbreaks, though scientists said the distribution made that unlikely ... In Croatia ... the Food and Agriculture Organization in Rome ... fertilizer made of manure from infected poultry probably spread H5N1.

Manure from farms is commonly used to fertilize fish ponds, which are frequent stopovers points for migrating birds that probably contracted the virus there ... Nigeria's problem was probably caused by the transport of sick birds or bird products infected with H5N1 from another country or even Asia.

(Elisabeth Rosenthal, *IHT*, 1 March 2006, pp. 1, 8)

There are many indications that migratory birds are not the only – or even the primary – reason the virus has moved beyond Asia. Experts have noticed that the pattern of infections marching westward follows railway lines more closely than the birds' predominantly north-west flyways. Exported chicken manure, used in everything from fishponds to poultry feed to fertilizer spread on fields, may have contributed to the spread. But the French outbreak provides the strongest suggestion yet that migration is part of the problem and that wild birds carried the virus to this poultry-breeding region ... The turkeys ... [had] the same strain of the virus as the wild ducks ... [according to] the World Organization for Animal Health ... Investigators have descended on ... [the French turkey] farm to check everything from fertilizer to feed, trying to determine how the virus got into the sheds. One theory is that the bales of hay he [the farmer] used were contaminated with the virus, possibly from pigeon droppings. Another theory is that journalists who came to interview ... [the farmer] after the dead duck was found carried the virus with them from the edge of the pond ... Poultry have been infected with the virus in Nigeria and Niger, though illegally imported chicks are suspected of being to blame.

(Craig Smith, *IHT*, 2 March 2006, p. 2)

[On 25 February] the Chinese agriculture minister warned of a possible 'massive bird flu outbreak' as China announced two new human cases of the H5N1 flu strain, raising to fourteen the number of human cases reported in China since October [2005]. China has reported eight deaths among its fourteen human cases ... Outbreaks in poultry occurred last year [2005] in thirty-two areas throughout China, killing 163,100 chickens, ducks and other fowl, and the authorities destroyed 22.6 million more birds to keep the virus from spreading ... Outbreaks in China have continued despite a mass inoculation effort. The government says it has vaccinated all of the country's vast flocks of chickens, ducks and other birds. Chinese farmers raised about 15 billion poultry – 21 per cent of the world's total – in 2005 ... China has about 5.2 billion poultry at any one time ... Health officials say the virus is being spread by migratory wild birds ... [In total] the H5N1 virus has devastated poultry stocks and killed at least ninety-two people since 2003, mostly in Asia. Fresh outbreaks have been reported in fourteen countries since early February [2006] ... Most human infections have been linked to direct contact with sick poultry.

(www.iht.com, 26 February 2006; *IHT*, 27 February 2006, p. 8)

'Recent avian influenza outbreaks in Europe, the Middle East and Africa have caused dramatic swings in poultry consumption, increased trade bans and sharp price declines,' the United Nations Food and Agriculture Organization said Tuesday [28 February] in a report ... Bird flu has a devastating effect on the poultry industry because in addition to the birds it kills outright many more must be slaughtered preventively in the surrounding area. More than 200 million birds have been killed or culled as a result of bird flu outbreaks with the variant strain H5N1 in the past seven years. Even as the experts convened in Paris ... [for] a two-day [27–28 February] conference ... there were new reports of bird flu from Russia, Germany, Sweden, Hungary, Greece and Ethiopia on Tuesday. In addition, the German health authorities confirmed the first report of a death in a mammal, a cat on Rügen Island, where dozens of wild birds have perished from the disease. A number of species – including humans and cats – can in rare cases acquire the bird flu from close contact with sick birds, and it is often deadly. There have been previous reports of cats sickened from H5N1 in Asia.

(*IHT*, 1 March 2006, p. 8)

'Mammals can contract the disease from eating the raw carcasses of infected birds and studies have shown that cats can transmit the virus to other cats' (*IHT*, 2 March 2006, p. 2).

'Avian flu was yesterday [28 February] discovered in two wild ducks found dead in southern Sweden ... Initial tests suggested the virus could be H5N1' (*FT*, 1 March 2006, p. 8).

In Geneva the United Nations health agency said Thursday [2 March] that the death of a second person in Iraq has raised to 174 the number of officially confirmed human cases of bird flu and to ninety-four the number of people who have died worldwide from the disease since 2003 ... The man's fifteen-year-old niece, who died earlier, is the only other confirmed human case of H5N1 in Iraq ... The World Organization for Animal Health lists thirty-eight countries and territories from East Asia to Europe and Africa as having confirmed cases of bird flu infections – almost all of the H5N1 – in birds since the strain reemerged in Hong Kong three years ago.

(*IHT*, 3 March 2006, p. 3)

[It was announced on 5 March that] a thirty-two-year-old man in Guangdong province [in China] is confirmed to have died of the H5N1 strain of bird flu ... The man, who lived in Guangzhou, less than a two-hour train ride from Hong Kong ... died Thursday [2 March] ... [He] had repeatedly visited a local market to carry out a survey and spent a long time near where chickens were slaughtered ... [Previously] mainland China had reported fourteen human bird flu infections since October [2005], including eight deaths ... Hong Kong has not reported any human infections since early 2003 ... The H5N1 virus first appeared in Hong Kong in 1997, when it jumped to humans and killed six people, prompting the government to slaughter the entire poultry population of about 1.5 million birds.

(www.iht.com, 5 March 2006)

'The thirty-two-year-old man was the fifteenth bird flu case in [mainland] China ... [and] the ninth death from the H5N1 virus. He died in Guangdong province, which borders Hong Kong' (*IHT*, 6 March 2006, p. 3).

Indonesia said it believed a three-year-old boy who died this week may have succumbed to bird flu. Local tests suggested the presence of the H5N1 strain ... If confirmed the boy would be Indonesia's twenty-first bird flu death ... Last week China said it feared it could suffer a 'massive' outbreak of bird flu this spring [2006], if wild birds returning from their winter migration infect farm poultry.

(www.bbc.co.uk, 5 March 2006)

A lethal strain of bird flu has spread to a region on France's Mediterranean coast, with confirmation Sunday [5 March] that a [wild] swan had died of the H5N1 strain of the virus. Earlier all of France's bird flu cases had been confined to the south-east Ain region.

(*IHT*, 6 March 2006, p. 3)

Two wild swans in Poland have tested positive for the H5N1 strain of bird flu, the first cases to be found in the country, an official said Monday [6 March] ... Samples were being sent to Britain for further tests. The swans were found dead on Thursday [2 March] ... Among the other European countries that have confirmed cases of the deadly H5N1 strain are Poland's western and eastern neighbours, Germany and Ukraine.

(www.iht.com, 6 March 2006)

Three cats from an animal shelter [near Graz] that took in birds infected with bird flu have tested positive for the H5N1 strain of the disease, Austrian state authorities said Monday [6 March], confirming the first case here of the disease's spread to an animal other than birds ... A pattern of disease transmission [has been] seen in wild cats in Asia, where the WHO said several tigers and snow leopards in a zoo, as well as several house cats, had been infected with H5N1 since 2003 ... Serbia's health authorities confirmed on Monday the country's first cases of the H5N1 virus in at least two swans found dead in northern and western parts of the country. The H5N1 virus has been detected in a number of countries neighbouring Serbia, including Croatia and Hungary.

(*IHT*, 7 March 2006, p. 3)

Serbia has confirmed its first case of the deadly H5N1 strain of bird flu, following a UK laboratory test on a swan found dead ... near the Croatian border ... [Serbia] said a second swan was also assumed to be infected with H5N1 ... Albania on Wednesday [8 March] confirmed H5N1 in a domestic chicken.

(*FT*, 10 March 2006, p. 6)

'The H5N1 bird flu virus has been found in a stone marten ... on the Baltic island of Rügen ... a German laboratory said, indicating the disease has spread to another species of mammal' (*Independent*, 10 March 2006, p. 23).

Cameroon has become the fourth African country to be struck by fatal bird flu. The government announced its first confirmed case on Sunday [12 March]. The bird flu strain H5N1 was detected in a duck on a farm ... near the border with Nigeria ... Experts have expressed concern that bird flu is likely to be spreading undetected in Africa, which is ill prepared to deal with the virus and lacks laboratories to detect it.

(IHT, 13 March 2006, p. 5)

Burma has detected the deadly H5N1 strain of bird flu in chickens, pledging to handle the country's first outbreak with vigilance and transparency, while Afghanistan's discovery of the H5 strain of bird flu could prove to be the deadly H5N1 virus, government officials and the UN said yesterday [13 March].

(FT, 14 March 2006, p. 5)

The WHO announced Tuesday [14 March] that it believed test results showing three young women in Azerbaijan had died of bird flu were reliable, but it was awaiting final confirmation from a British laboratory ... Results were pending on two other suspect deaths.

(IHT, 15 March 2006, p. 8)

'The WHO ... on Tuesday [14 March] confirmed that the deaths in Azerbaijan were caused by bird flu' *(IHT*, 18 March 2006, p 3).

'[It was announced on 15 March that] the EU's reference laboratory in Britain has confirmed Sweden's first cases of the deadly H5N1 strain of bird flu in two wild ducks found dead last month [February]' *(IHT*, 16 March 2006, p. 8).

A dog has died of bird flu in Azerbaijan ... where three people have already died from the virus ... The medical investigation is continuing ... Denmark became the latest European country to report a case of bird flu in wildfowl, although it has yet to confirm that it is the feared H5N1 strain.

(Independent, 16 March 2006, p. 22)

'The European Commission on Friday [17 March] banned poultry imports from Israel ... The decision came after the Israeli authorities confirmed that the H5N1 strain had been found in thousands of poultry' *(IHT*, 18 March 2006, p. 3).

The bird flu deaths of five people in Azerbaijan have pushed the world total human deaths from H5N1 past 100, the WHO said Tuesday [22 March]. The UN health agency said that seven of the eleven patients from Azerbaijan had tested positive for the deadly strain of bird flu in samples checked at a major laboratory in Britain. Five of the cases were fatal. The new global total of confirmed deaths from H5N1 is 103. There have been a total of 184 confirmed human cases of H5N1 since 2003.

(IHT, 22 March 2006, p. 4)

AIDS

'[Internationally] the HIV virus [was] first noticed in 1981' *(IHT*, 29 July 2005, p. 6).

For fifteen years or more after China announced its first AIDS related death in 1985, the country's leaders were in denial about HIV. Few cases were reported, and homosexuality and promiscuity, the two agents by which this 'western' affliction was presumed to spread, were said to be limited in China. Then, in November 2002, came the outbreak of SARS in Guangdong province. By the time it had been contained China's leaders had come to realise just how vulnerable the country was to such a plague ... The economic threat posed by such diseases was clear, and suddenly AIDS too looked potent.

(*The Economist*, 30 July 2005, p. 53)

'In 1997 homosexuality was decriminalized, and in 2001 the Chinese Psychiatric Association declassified homosexuality as a pathological condition, thus allowing greater social and legal space for gay groups to increase their HIV-related community activities' (*IHT*, 21 January 2005, p. 6).

23 August 2001.

On 23 August ... the vice-minister of health ... acknowledged that China is 'facing a very serious epidemic' ... [He said that] China had 600,000 people infected with HIV, which can lead to AIDS, at the end of last year [2000] ... A recent report by the United Nations' AIDS office put the number of HIV sufferers in China at over 1 million at the end of 2000.

(*The Economist*, 1 September 2001, pp. 54–5)

('The United Nations on Thursday [27 June 2002] ... warned that the country was "on the verge of a catastrophe" ... [and] criticized the Chinese authorities on numerous fronts, from the lack of education programmes to the absence of treatment for people infected with HIV. "We are witnessing the unfolding of an HIV–AIDS epidemic of proportions beyond belief, an epidemic that calls for an urgent and proper but as yet unanswered, quintessential response," the report said': *IHT*, 28 June 2002, p. 3. 'By the end of last year [2001] 800,000 to 1.5 million Chinese were infected with HIV, the virus that can cause AIDS, up from 500,000 at the end of 1999, according to the United Nations report ... China could have as many as 10 million HIV sufferers by 2010 if no effective countermeasures were taken, the UN said': *FT*, 28 June 2001, p. 10.)

November 2001. 'Last week ... China ... held its first international conference on AIDS' (*FT*, Friday 23 November 2001, p. 1).

('The first reported AIDS victim was in 1985': *IHT*, 14 September 2002, p. 4. 'The [AIDS] epidemic started in the early 1990s among heroin addicts who shared dirty needles, took a huge jump when contaminated blood supplies infected up to a million farmers in central China and is now spreading sexually through prostitutes into the general population': *IHT*, 17 September 2002, p. 4.)

('[In April 2002] China published new statistics on its AIDS epidemic, estimating that 850,000 people were infected with HIV by the end of 2001, up 30 per cent from government estimates issued last summer [2001] ... [Some] 200,000 people might already have progressed to AIDS': *FEER*, 25 April 2002, p. 20.)

('[On 6 September 2002 China raised its] estimate of [HIV/AIDS] sufferers to 1 million and said that China would start manufacturing a full complement of AIDS drugs if the Western pharmaceutical manufacturers who hold the patents did not lower prices by the end of the year [2002]. It was a striking reversal for Chinese health officials, who had previously insisted that, as a new member of the WTO,

China had to be hypervigilant about respecting patents and would not permit the use of generic AIDS drugs. Also for the first time, officials publicly asked for international help in dealing with China's AIDS problems – which they had previously insisted they could handle on their own': *IHT*, 7 September 2002, p. 5. 'The government said ... that by the end of the year at least 1 million of its citizens will be HIV-positive, the condition that can lead to AIDS ... Reports that the government had threatened to produce copies of patented HIV medicines were quickly denied by China. But the government says it has started treating patients with a domestically produced version of AZT, for which patents recently expired, and that ten Chinese firms have applied for permission to make versions of other HIV drugs with expired patents': *The Economist*, 14 September 2002, p. 64).

1 December 2002. 'China will send 1 million students to the countryside ... The mass mobilization – to tell peasants of the AIDS threat – reverses years of public neglect ... It was announced to mark World AIDS Day' (*Telegraph*, 2 December 2002, p. 16).

November 2003. 'Gao Qiang, the executive deputy health minister ... [said] that 5,000 people should get free treatment by the end of the year [2003]. He said 80,000 of the 840,000 HIV-positive people in China have AIDS' (*FEER*, 20 November 2003, p. 28).

1 December 2003.

Wen Jiabao shook hands and chatted with three AIDS patients in a Beijing hospital, becoming the first senior leader to address China's AIDS epidemic. Wen's visit to Ditan Hospital on 1 December, World AIDS Day, was shown on state television and seemed to signal a new commitment by the government to fight a disease that most officials have long ignored. Wen urged all levels of government to provide 'free anti-AIDS treatment, free anonymous tests and free education for AIDS patients' orphans'.

(*FEER*, 11 December 2003, p. 32)

9 May 2004.

The Chinese government has warned that AIDS is continuing to spread rapidly ... and announced new 'urgent measures' to improve prevention and education efforts that include holding local officials responsible for curbing the disease ... The announcement was the latest effort by the government to confront a disease whose spread officials once actively sought to conceal. In the past year China has introduced a limited programme providing some free drugs to AIDS patients and begun a public relations campaign to reduce the stigma associated with the disease and encourage testing ... The government estimates that 840,000 people are HIV carriers, while 80,000 have tested positive for AIDS. More than 100,000 people are believed to have died of the disease ... Experts have predicted that China could have as many as 10 million AIDS patients by 2010 if the government fails to adequately fight the disease.

(www.iht.com, 10 May 2004)

'China says 840,000 people are HIV-positive and 80,000 have full-blown AIDS [2003 figures]' (*FEER*, 29 April 2004, p. 29). 'More than 200,000 people have died of AIDS in China' (*FEER*, 15 July 2004, p. 44). '[The United Nations warns that] unchecked, infections could reach 10 million by 2010' (p. 37). ('[The United Nations] warns that 10 million people may be infected by 2010 unless effective action is taken': www.iht.com, 6 July 2004.)

'China says it has an estimated 840,000 HIV/AIDS patients, of whom some 20 per cent are believed to have been infected through unsanitary and often illegal blood-buying deals. International specialists say the real figure is probably much higher' (www.iht.com, 15 October 2004).

> The country is trying to reverse its once abysmal record on AIDS. In the past eighteen months China's top leaders have made AIDS a national priority ... [although] the police in some cities still arrest and harass AIDS activists or try to conceal the presence of the disease ... Peter Piot, executive director of UNAIDS ...[thinks that] the turning point came in 2003, when the rapid and unexpected spread of SARS showed the government that communicable diseases could pose not just a health threat but also a political one ... Piot: 'Nothing did as much as the fear that SARS instilled in terms of the potential for destabilizing society' ... The shift in attitude was signalled in December 2004 when prime minister Wen Jiabao met with AIDS patients, a step later repeated by President Hu Jintao. These symbolic steps have been accompanied by a doubling of the government's budget for AIDS and several new policies, like needle exchanges and condom promotion. Until 2002 condom advertising was banned ... The Chinese government estimated in 2003 that 840,000 people are HIV-positive, while another 80,000 have AIDS. Roughly 150,000 more people with AIDS are believed to have died.
>
> (www.iht.com, 16 June 2005; *IHT*, 17 June 2005, p. 2)

'China has an estimated 840,000 people infected with HIV, including 80,000 with full blown AIDS, according to official figures. International groups believe the real figure is much higher' (www.iht.com, 14 June 2005).

> China's rulers said this week said they would take the threat of AIDS more seriously, for example by doing more to stop HIV-contaminated blood being used by doctors ... Estimates ... about how many Chinese carry the virus ... range wildly from 430,000 to 1.5 million.
>
> (www.economist.com, 1 December 2005)

'Drug abuse now accounts for half of China's AIDS cases' (*IHT*, 2 December 2005, p. 8).

> China on Wednesday [25 January 2006] countered the long-held suspicion that it has undercounted the number of people with HIV and AIDS by releasing a new, more extensive survey that found the opposite to be true – that the country has actually overestimated how many people are stricken. The new survey, conducted with the World Health Organization and Unaids, lowered the country's estimated number of HIV and AIDS cases to 650,000 from the official 840,000 figure released in 2003. Many experts and AIDS activists have long believed that China has at least 1.5 million cases, possibly far more ...

Chinese and international health officials endorsed the new findings but also warned that China still has a serious AIDS problem that could rapidly worsen if testing, education and treatment programmes are not expanded. Indeed, the survey found that while the overall number of cases is less than previously believed, the rate of infection is rising, with 70,000 new cases in 2005. Drug users and prostitutes transmitted the virus in most of these cases, but the report also found that the disease is now spreading from such high-risk groups into the general population, raising the risk of a broader level of infections ... The study found that 25,000 people died of AIDS last year [2005]. Of that figure 10,000 were former blood and plasma donors, the study found. Overall, Chinese officials estimate that fewer than 100,000 people have died of AIDS in the country ... The new study found that ... drug users living with HIV or AIDS accounted for 288,000 people. Or 44.2 per cent of the estimated total ... Prostitutes and their clients accounted for 127,000 cases, or 19.6 per cent ... China has mounted an aggressive nationwide campaign and introduced pilot programmes that provide condoms, methadone and even anti-retroviral drugs for free ... Some grassroots AIDS activists in China expressed doubts about the lowered estimate ... of people with HIV and AIDS [given in the new study] ... India is estimated to have more than 5 million people living with HIV, the virus that causes AIDS.

(www.iht.com, 25 January 2006; *IHT*, 26 January 2006, pp. 1, 7)

Pig disease

The illness, which was discovered in June [2005], has spread to 155 villages in seven cities in Sichuan province, including the provincial capital of Chengdu ... Victims contracted the bacteria by slaughtering or processing infected pigs or by handling infected pork ... The World Health Organization [WHO] has said that it was baffled by the illness because if the epidemic was caused by the bacteria it would be the first time it had struck so many people at one time. Normally only one or two cases of the rare disease are seen in any instance ... As of Saturday [30 July] the number of people killed by the illness, which is usually spread among pigs, hit thirty-four, while the number of cases increased to 174 ... The first batch of [pig] vaccine for treating the mysterious pig-borne disease ... was flown Sunday to the south-western province of Sichuan.

(www.iht.com, 31 July 2005)

The WHO has urged China to conduct more tests to clarify perplexing aspects of the largest outbreak in humans of a bacterial pig disease, including why the death rate among patients has been unusually high. China has reported that the disease ... infected 206 people in Sichuan province from 24 June through 21 July – or nearly one in five – died, and eighteen are critically ill. Most cases have occurred among adult male farmers who have had close contact with diseased pigs or have eaten uncooked pig products ... Sichuan has one of the largest pig populations in China ... There is no evidence that the illness has been transmitted from one person to another in the outbreak ... There was no immediate evidence that China, which came under fire for covering up the outbreak of SARS ... in 2002 and 2003, was hiding information about the *Streptococcus suis* outbreak ... *Streptococcus suis* infections usually occur sporadically or in small outbreaks ... Health officials say more laboratory tests are needed to determine why the Sichuan outbreak is so large and the death rate so high. Among the questions infectious disease specialists have raised is whether *Streptococcus* has mutated to become more virulent.

(www.iht.com, 5 August 2005)

Direct elections at the local level

Direct elections of village leaders began in certain provinces in 1988 (*World Development*, May 1996, p. 924).

The law relating to villager committees was passed in November 1987 and rural elections began to be organized from 1988 onwards. In many provinces local laws approved by the provincial People's Congress stipulate that peasants can jointly nominate candidates or even nominate themselves as candidates for village committees (Wang 1997: 1437).

> Despite the impressive achievements of economic reforms, the Chinese state faced serious challenges to its ability to govern the countryside by the late 1980s. The decay of the grassroots-level state apparatus and the loss of control over local officials and cadres weakened the capacity of the state to govern the rural areas. The corruption of local cadres, tension in cadre–peasant relations, and resurgence of traditional authorities in the countryside had eroded its legitimacy.
>
> (p. 1436)

> The democratic practice of self-governing villager committees in rural China is a political development with many goals. In a sense, it is the only mechanism available to the state to cope with the crisis of both legitimacy and governability in the countryside incurred by the decay of the party-state apparatus in the grassroots, the loss of control of the state over its local agencies, and tension in cadre–peasant relations.
>
> (p. 1440)

The village democracy programme involves the election of members of village committees. The elected local leaders replaced the appointed chiefs of the dismantled farm collectives. The tasks of village committees include family planning and collection of grain levies. It is officially claimed that 90 per cent of the countryside is affected. There are differences between provinces and even between counties. For example, in a village in Zhejiang province citizens chose from four candidates (all members of the Communist Party) for three open positions on the committee, while Jilin province allows an unlimited number of candidates for all committee positions, including that of chairman (Rone Tempest, *IHT*, 21 May 1996, p. 4).

> The dissolution of the communes left no local governments and led to village elections. By the early 1990s 90 per cent of village committees had been

elected. Progress has been ragged. Local cadres resist losing privileges and non-party members often experience discrimination. Some assemblies require party membership for candidacy. There is some probable ballot fraud and officials decide if voters can choose more than one candidate. Nevertheless, the principle of competitive elections is established. Those who oppose party members are no longer 'enemies of the people'. The concept of rule by law is accepted, with peasants learning about legal procedures and how to protect their rights.

(Henry Rowen, *IHT*, 11 October 1996, p. 6)

The advent of village democracy in China certainly sounds impressive. There are around 900,000 villages in China, housing perhaps three-quarters of the country's 1.3 billion people. Since 1988 over 80 per cent of these villages have elected, through universal suffrage and secret ballots, their own chiefs and village committees, who serve for terms of three years. By next year 95 per cent of villages will have held elections – some will be staging their third election in a row. Although many of the village heads who are elected are communist party members, the majority are not. For China as a whole it marks the party's most sweeping abdication of power since the People's Republic was founded in 1949 ... village democratization has flowed from the economic reforms ... launched in 1978 ... The irrelevance of the old structures seems to have led to the spontaneous emergence of new village committees in southern China in the early 1980s. In 1987 a law was passed by the central government formally allowing villages to elect their own headmen and committees.

(*The Economist*, 2 November 1996, p. 81)

'For ten years the party has allowed direct elections for village committees and for legislatures in small towns ... Almost all of those elected are party members, and in many cases those who are not are quickly recruited' (*IHT*, 18 January 1997, p. 4).

In the last few years villagers throughout China have been taking part in an unprecedented experiment in local self-government through village elections. While there have been many reports of electoral malpractice and manipulation, there have also been many cases of genuinely free and fair elections.

(Tony Saich, *IHT*, 1 February 1997, p. 6)

It is impossible to generalize. But it is fair to say that with each new round of elections, procedures have become more democratic, mainly as a result of education by China's ministry of civil affairs. Peasant power is increased because voters can 'write in' any name if they do not like the candidates. About half the most recent round of village elections have used secret voting booths, and one-third of village leaders standing for reelection have lost their positions.

(Teresa Poole, *Independent*, 21 April 1997, p. 11)

According to official figures, elections (introduced in 1987) have taken place in 60 per cent of China's one million villages (*FEER*, 5 February 1998, p. 5).

In 1987 ... China's leaders began an experiment of holding elections at the village level ... But the village elections are no herald of real democracy. They are held, without exception, under the control of the local communist party organization. Even in the cases where voters have a genuine choice between two candidates, both have arrived on the ballot only after being deemed acceptable to the higher authorities ... Village elections ... [represent an attempt] by the country's leaders to improve their outdated political system without sacrificing central control ... Practices vary from region to region, depending on the imagination of the officials in charge, but all essentially hew to the party's principle of keeping any real threat to its ultimate authority far at bay. The true intention of the authorities in conducting elections is to improve government at the lowest level. Villages are more adept at determining corruption in their immediate leaders than supervising officials are in their subordinates.

(Seth Faison, *IHT*, 30 March 1998, pp. 1–4)

Genuine elections have become commonplace in half of China's 928,000 villages ... The experiment has been confined to communities averaging about 1,000 residents and political parties other than communists are not allowed. In many places vote-buying and ballot-rigging are problems. Still, any resident may be a candidate for the freely elected village council, which has the power to levy taxes and manages local services and schools.

(Steven Mufson, *IHT*, 15 June 1998, pp. 1, 8)

Elections have been held in many of China's 930,000 villages, but, with only seventeen ministry officials monitoring them, abuses are thought to be widespread. Ballot boxes are sometimes used, sometimes not. Candidates are not allowed to oppose the ruling Communist Party or its policies.

(James Kynge, *FT*, 10 December 1998, p. 4)

Apparently without formal approval from Beijing, a remote farming region in central China has held the country's first direct elections for leader of a township. And the leaders in Beijing have signalled that they want this to be the last such election, at least for now. Townships, which are units of about 10,000 or more people, are one administrative step up from the villages, where elections have been promoted for years. Townships have more power over taxation, land use and other matters ... The election [was held] on 31 December [1998] in Buyun ... in central Sichuan province ... China's leaders have promoted village elections as a way to vent discontent and root out corrupt officials. In international forums they often point to the elections as proof that a Chinese democracy is evolving and they have vaguely suggested that elections will gradually be extended to higher offices. None of the elections would meet Western standards of democracy, because no candidates who question the primacy of the Communist Party are allowed, information is controlled and unelected party officials usually continue to set policies. Still, some villages have had lively contests.

(Erik Eckholm, *IHT*, 27 January 1999, p. 1)

'Suining is the city that organized China's first direct township election last December [1998]. The vote in Buyun township, which is administered by Suining, was considered a breakthrough in efforts to democratize China's countryside' (*IHT*, 7 August 1999, p. 6).

> Village elections ... began a decade ago and by now have spread to more than half the country's 1 million villages ... The village elections are revolutionary in that they introduce villagers to the concept of democracy, and to the supervision of leaders by the electorate, including how money is spent ... Last December [1998] Buyun, in Sichuan province, held the country's first elections at the township level. Local Communist Party officials helped organize the elections without informing Beijing – apparently for fear that the central authorities would not approve. Strictly speaking, that election was against Chinese law. However, it was widely publicized by the official Chinese media, with China Central Television praising the initiative of local leaders ... So far Buyun is the only one of the country's 45,000 townships to have held a free election ... [Above them are] 2,000 counties ... thirty provinces and, finally, the central government.
>
> (Frank Ching, *FEER*, 26 August 1999, p. 32)

On 9 September 1999 the Guangdong Provincial People's Congress held a legislative hearing at which members of the public were able to voice their views on a proposed piece of legislation. Guangdong has taken several unique steps towards granting more popular participation in the political process. The provincial congress, for instance, has changed the rules for picking top officials: thirty or more deputies may now jointly nominate officials, including the governor, vice-governor, members of the Standing Committee, the most senior judge and the procurator-general. The 9 September hearing was preceded by another ground-breaking decision to publish drafts of important regulations to solicit public views, in this case on changes to laws governing tendering for building projects. In 1993 Guangdong was the first province to introduce laws on tendering (*FEER*, 30 September 1999, p. 22).

> A law passed in November 1998 by the national legislature is making village elections significantly more free ... China's National People's Congress changed the rules. China's Communist Party had embraced direct elections at the village level a decade earlier to improve the quality of local leaders and ensure popular support for them. The nomination process was compromising those goals, the congress concluded ... [Villages in Hebei province] now hold a primary election at which every voter writes in the name of his or her favoured candidate. Top votergetters from the primary become candidates on the final election ballot ... The Communist Party has allowed a handful of experiments with direct elections at the next higher level up – the township.
>
> (Susan Lawrence, *FEER*, 27 January 2000, pp. 16–17)

Chinese cities [such as Shenyang] are starting to experiment with local elections ... Started last year in twelve cities, the elections are highly restricted, dominated by the Communist Party and generally limited to a few participants

... Still, the voting marks the first time that residents of Chinese cities have had any say about the composition of the neighbourhood committees, which have dominated urban life since the communist revolution in 1949 ... The idea is to reform the neighbourhood committees, the lowest level of political control in China. These organizations, dominated by elderly women appointed by local communist party committees, have been incapable of meeting the new needs of China's cities. In a dozen cities these neighbourhood committees are being amalgamated into 'community governments' and the cities are experimenting with ways to 'elect' these officials.

(John Pomfret, *IHT*, 21 February 2000, p. 6)

The old 'neighbourhood committees' watched over every household ... Over the past twenty years ... the committees waned but never quite disappeared ... Now, with experiments in Shenyang and nineteen other cities the government is trying to reinvent this venerable institution ... Cities are replacing [them] ... with more professional, somewhat younger staffs that can link citizens up with vital social services like finding help for isolated elderly people ... In Shenyang ... officials are ... using local elections to select 'community administrative committee' leaders on the theory that this will energize citizens and improve services like job training, garbage collection and care for the elderly ... The new elections are also firmly intended to promote party loyalists ... Shenyang officials say that with their new neighbourhood elections they are creating the equivalent of the village elections now held in rural China.

(Erik Eckholm, *IHT*, 13 April 2000, p. 7)

On 24 May 2000 the city of Beijing authorized 'open and fair' elections for all neighbourhood committee posts. There had been test elections in 200 of the capital's 5,000 committees. Twenty other cities have begun similar experiments with what are now called 'community service committees'. Among the functions of the new committees are helping old people, finding jobs and obtaining permits for new arrivals (*Independent*, 27 May 2000, p. 18).

The party's main motive in allowing ... village ... elections was to strengthen its control over the countryside ... If villagers could take control of bread-and-butter issues, they might support the party in other areas ... Cheng Tongshun, a political scientist at Nankai University in Tianjin, said in a book published last year [2000] that most villages were still led by party secretaries who took on most, if not all, of the duties which the elected chiefs are supposed to carry out ... Mr Cheng writes that vote-buying and selling, stuffing ballot boxes and violence have had a 'considerable impact' on rural elections. The Chinese media also speak of frequent, sometimes successful, attempts by wealthy businessmen to buy official positions or seats in local legislatures ... In December this year [2001], when fresh elections are due to be held, it is expected that Buyun [the township that conducted an election in 1998 without central approval] will end the experiment. This time it will allow voters to choose the candidates, but the winner will be picked by the (party-dominated) township people's congress.

(The Economist, 30 June 2001, p. 26)

According to ... the International Republican Institute [IRI].... 'A decade of concentration on the development of village elections has resulted in many positive accomplishments ... In many villages governance has substantially improved, finances have become more transparent and villager participation in decision-making has increased' ... Village elections were previously held on an experimental basis, but since 1998 they have been mandated by law, even though no one knows how many of the 900,000 villages are actually holding democratic elections ... IRI reports that about twenty cities have recently begun electoral experiments in urban residential areas. There are also signs that elections may soon be allowed at the township level as well. An unauthorized township election was held in Buyun, Sichuan province, a couple of years ago. Although the central government did not overturn the results, the election was declared unconstitutional because the constitution says heads of townships are not chosen directly but by the local people's congress. However, steps are now being taken to get around this constitutional hurdle. Instead of conducting elections for township magistrates, some provinces are conducting 'voter-survey recommendations'. The first to do this was Wuzai county in Shanxi province which, five months after the Buyun election, held a 'voter survey' on who should become township magistrate ... This type of election has since been tried in other provinces as well ... Last June [2000] the official Xinhua news agency announced the 'first ever' township elections, held in Xincai county in Henan province. According to Xinhua, local residents aged eighteen and above nominated three primary candidates ... The villager then voted for their township magistrate ... The township people's congress was evidently relegated to rubber-stamping the outcome so as to comply with the constitution ... Even more significant is another innovation, known as the 'two-ballot system', which gives villagers a voice not only in choosing village leaders but members of the local party committee as well. This was first pioneered by Hequ county in Shanxi province as early as 1992. The county decided that party members hoping to join the village party branch should first subject themselves to an opinion poll by all eligible voters in the village. If the approval rating for any party member fell below 50 per cent, his candidacy would fail. The two-ballot system for electing local party committee officials has since been introduced into several other provinces. This means that the party, at least at the grassroots level, is allowing non-party people to decide who its leaders should be.

(Frank Ching, FEER, 8 March 2001, p. 26)

China's 1 million villages have mostly set up directly elected governments. But their ability to recall leaders or influence policy remains weak. Township governments, meanwhile, are virtually all appointed by upper-level party officials, despite notable experiments in provinces like Sichuan with direct elections.

(Bruce Gilley, FEER, 5 April 2001, p. 29)

The introduction of direct elections in China's 800,000 villages since the late 1980s has done little to show off the merits of democracy. The problems of

Daling's 3,800 villages illustrate how, in many places, the elections have exacerbated tensions between various tiers of rural administration. The polls are often rigged and the committees elected simply pawns of higher-level government. Some Chinese academics think the peasants are losing interest in the elections ... To the residents of Daling, a village in Hebei province, elections have brought nothing but misery. For opposing the officially approved candidates in the village councils polls held seven years ago, dozens have endured beatings and threats by police and thugs ... Daling's Communist Party committee decided whose names should appear on the ballot ... Despite an unusual intervention by the Politburo ... [which] ordered the Hebei provincial authorities to investigate ... [complaining villagers] remain angry ... In a book published in China last year [2000] Cheng Tongshun of Nankei University estimated that over 60 per cent of elected village committees did little more than carry out the orders of higher-level (unelected) governments ... A glaring deficiency is that the powers of the elected committees relative to those of local party committees or higher level rural governments are too vaguely defined ... The result is administrative paralysis and mounting frustration among peasants ... Township governments, which are responsible for several villages, believe that whoever is in charge should be subordinate to them ... Directly electing township chiefs ... has been tried in [only] one or two places.

(*The Economist*, 29 September 2001, p. 77)

Much publicity about direct elections in most Chinese villages does not deserve as much fanfare as it has been getting. Village chiefs do have a say in how a village invests any collective funds, but they are not government officials and are subordinate to village Communist Party secretaries ... But in Bunyan [in Sichuan province] ... in 1998, without formal permission from the central leadership, the township conducted direct elections to the post of township chief, a person who holds government rank (but remains subordinate to the party secretary at the corresponding level, as is every government leader in China). Party leaders were anxious, but allowed Bunyan to keep its newly elected chief, who happened in any case to be the party's nominee ... Fearing that other townships would follow Bunyan's example, a year ago the party issued 'document number 12' which ordered that the usual indirect method of election be adhered to. But there were loopholes in the document that Bunyang seized upon ... Seeing that the orders allowed reforms in the way that candidates (but not the final winner) were selected, Bunyan conducted competitive direct elections for a single candidate, who was then submitted to the township people's congress for approval ... Nearly one-third of Sichuan's 5,065 townships took advantage of the leeway offered by the document. They allowed the public to nominate candidates freely and then submitted the names to a vote of township officials, people's congress members and village representatives. This method still left plenty of scope for party interference, but it was a small step forward ... Experiments [have taken place] in rural areas of Sichuan and to a more limited extent elsewhere ... Since 1999 the central government has approved cautious experiments with direct elections in a few urban areas, albeit only at the level of the neighbourhood committee. These committees, like their counterparts in the villages, are not a formal branch of government.

(*The Economist*, Survey, 15 June 2002, pp. 7–8)

Thousands of villages have elected their own Communist Party secretaries in the past two years ... Communist Party secretaries are the real power-holders in the villages, unlike the nominal village heads who have been elected for years. They embody the final link in a top-down chain of command that ensures one-party rule nationwide ... Rural communities [were] awakened politically by the elections for those relatively powerless village heads, which began in the 1980s with the end of collectivisation and the return to household farming ... In 1999 local party officials, desperate to reimpose order on Qingdui [a village in Hubei province], allowed angry farmers to elect their communist leader – a move so unorthodox that the officials who arranged it kept it secret from Beijing ... Qingdui's election, when it finally came in 1999 – after being tested in another fractious village – contained safeguards to guarantee party control ... In the past two years, however, similar elections have spread to tens of thousands of villages in more than twenty provinces, by one party researcher's estimate. And they have gained a grudging acceptance from national leaders who see them as a way to calm a discontented countryside and rebuild the party's crumbling political capital ... Beijing officials say they see the elections as a way to enhance party control by cashiering obstructionist officials and promoting popular ones ... But this is not what Westerners call democracy. Candidates must be party members. Party officials supervise the elections, weeding out objectionable candidates. And while the party leadership in Beijing recently lent approval, it has also shown deep ambivalence. It has stifled most reporting on the elections by mainstream national media. The elections for now are termed 'experiments', a sign that the party could try to reverse the process if its control is threatened.

(Charles Hutzler, *FEER*, 5 September 2002, pp. 29–31)

Zeng Qinghong, one of the most powerful figures in the Politburo anointed last November [2002], has ordered that officials cannot assume the post of village party secretary (which outranks that of the elected village boss) unless they have first been elected village chief. This order, quietly written into a law published 1 August [2002], marked the first time since the revolution that communist officials have been required to secure the approval of the ballot.

(*FT*, 13 January 2003, p. 17)

After several years of direct elections of village chiefs, urban areas are now introducing the idea of one person, one vote, secret ballots and independent candidates. But it is a cautious process. This is not about hustings for mayors. The urban equivalents of village chiefs are lowly neighbourhood committee leaders. The committees help the government maintain order and provide services such as medical advice and recreation facilities. Four years ago a few provinces introduced direct elections for some neighbourhood leaders. Now the practice is more widespread. In the first half of this year [2003] some 10 per cent of the capital's 2,400 or more neighbourhoods are holding direct elections for the first time (other prefer China's time-honoured practice of shooing in Communist Party favourites) ... The eastern city of Ningbo [is] the first big town to conduct direct elections in every neighbourhood in an entire district (urban Ningbo has six districts with a total population of 2 million). These elections began last month [March 2003] and are due to finish in June ... Openly attacking the Communists, let alone forming a rival party, is still out of the question, though. And just like the directly elected village chiefs, committee leaders still have to obey the orders of neighbourhood Communist Party secretaries – though they are often one and the same person ... Last August [2002] ... [a] neighbourhood became the first in the capital to conduct direct elections.

(*The Economist*, 5 April 2003, p. 64)

[On 13 October 2003] state media unveiled the nation's latest experiment in enfranchisement – a directly elected community council for a Beijing neighbourhood ... the first in the capital to be under the control of voters ... [But] it would have little direct control over the lives of the 60,000 voters it represents ... The council ... would spend much of its time supervising voluntary activities and arranging such services as helping residents hire domestic staff, said [the] council chairman. He said the council would also keep an eye on local government departments.

(*FT*, 14 October 2003, p. 12)

China's ministry of civil affairs is considering holding direct elections for departmental heads after successfully sponsoring unprecedented elections for lower-level officials earlier this year [2003]. The ministry, which oversees such domestic issues as flood relief and poverty, held the polls in August to fill senior working-level posts for director-generals and deputy director-generals ... More than 100 candidates ran in the unpublicized poll, which was aimed at bringing more accountability to the bureaucracy ... While China formally allows only direct elections of village chiefs, some town and government agencies have been experimenting with their own democratic polls in recent years. The Communist Party is also trying to bring more accountability into the system, most recently requiring top party leaders to give a report of their achievements to the ... Central Committee at a meeting in October.

(*FEER,* 27 November 2003, p. 10)

For the first time in more than two decades some independent candidates stood in district elections in Beijing after nominating themselves. But most independents, who included students and property owners, were stopped from standing by election commissions controlled by the ruling Communist Party.

(*FEER*, 18 December 2003, p. 42)

At least sixty-five candidates who are not members of the Communist Party tried to get their names on the ballot. Half a dozen succeeded but others were rejected by officials overseeing the experiment ... the independents face more than 4,000 official candidates ... Elections take place every five years.

(*The Times*, 11 December 2003, p. 20)

'[There were] more than 4,400 officially sponsored winners' (*The Economist*, 13 December 2003, p. 62). 'While President Hu Jintao ... has not presented himself as a democrat, he has tried to craft a friendlier public image than his predecessors, visiting workers in impoverished areas and tolerating the election of a few independents to neighbourhood people's congresses' (www.iht.com, 7 January 2004).

'Observers are concerned about official interference in village-level elections begun under the Zhao administration in 1987 ... [For example] several provinces require county and township party committees to approve the candidates that villagers nominate for the post of village chief' (*FEER*, 3 June 2004, p. 32).

'In the past two or three years ... China's current leaders ... have sought to re-establish control over village affairs by party secretaries rather than democratically elected village chiefs' (*The Economist*, 5 June 2004, p. 54).

[There have been] moves to have one person act as both village head and party chief ... [The] system of having separate elected and party-appointed leaders has caused widespread power struggles in villages ...[In 2004] the Shandong party leadership ordered that next time the province held village elections ways should be found to ensure that the posts of party chief and village head be held by the same person in more than 80 per cent of villages. Achieving this has involved allowing villagers for the first time to vote for the top party posts as well. The village party committee would still have the final say, but would generally pick the party member 'recommended' by the most villagers as party chief. This person would also be appointed village leader.

(*The Economist*, 9 April 2005, p. 50)

Zeguo ... [is a] township of 110,000 people in Zhejiang province ... [It] recently embarked on a novel experiment in governance, allowing citizens' preferences to determine, after detailed consultations over the pros and cons, which major projects would go ahead and how much money would be spent ... Zeguo's political experiment involved the polling of 257 randomly chosen people, and was conducted in large part on the advice of a Stanford University political scientist, James Fishkin, After lengthy briefings on a long list of potential projects, the electors showed a decided preference for environmental works, including sewage treatment plants and public parks. If unique in form, Zeguo's experiment takes place against a backdrop of a broad effervescence of democratic ideas bubbling up into local politics all over China. By one estimate there will be 300,000 village committee elections in China's eighteen provinces this year alone. In many areas officials are making efforts to involve ordinary citizens in local decision-making.

(*IHT*, 20 June 2005, pp. 1, 7)

In Sichuan ... about 40 per cent of its townships now choose their leaders through semi-competitive elections ... The vast majority of the elections are [however] ... restricted to the party's nomenclature, with an electoral college of 150 to 300 making the decisions; plus the candidates have to be party cadres, so that ordinary citizens could neither stand nor nominate candidates

... One township ... was special. Bunyan township had a direct election. The citizens were allowed to select the candidates for township leader by direct votes, and the nominees were later submitted to the township people's congress for final voting.

(*FT*, Magazine, 9 July 2005, p. 20)

Political developments, congresses and Central Committee sessions since March 1993

The Communist Party hierarchy is as follows: Politburo Standing Committee; Politburo (twenty-two members); Central Committee (193 members). The Central Military Commission has eleven members (*FEER*, 8 August 2002, p. 31).

Communist Party membership has reached 70 million (*IHT*, 21 August 2004, p. 4).

The armed forces number 2.3 million (*The Economist*, 7 August 2004, p. 52).

The Eighth National People's Congress, 15–31 March 1993

There were a number of significant personnel changes. Jiang Zemin, now described as the 'core' of the (collective) leadership, added the title president. (He was already party secretary and chairman of the party's Central Military Commission; this was a sign of the abandonment of the earlier policy of separating party and state.) (He replaced Yang Shangkun as president. Yang's half-brother Yang Baibing, the former chief political commissar of the People's Liberation Army, had been demoted at the Fourteenth Party Congress in October 1992. Yang Shangkun and his half-brother Yang Baibing were thought to be building up a power base in the army and this explains the decline in their influence after October 1992. Note, however, that Yang Shangkun was generally seen as a reformer.) Prime minister Li Peng was re-elected for a second five-year term of office, while Zhu Rongyi was promoted to (sole) senior vice-premier. Rong Yiren, the chairman of CITIC (China International Trust and Investment Corporation), became vice-president. (The new chairman of CITIC is Wei Mingyi.) The phrase 'socialist market economy' was formally enshrined in the new constitution.

In his speech on the opening day of the congress Li Peng reaffirmed that 'our great socialist motherland will stand as firm as a rock in the east for ever'. But the Dengist line on economic policy was strongly proclaimed. He did warn that 'the amount of bank credit and currency put into circulation has risen too fast and there is a constant threat of inflation' and he called for a 'basic balance between supply and demand'. But Li Peng formally raised the target for the average annual rate of growth of national income for the remaining three years of the five-year plan to 8 to 9 per cent (originally it was only 6 per cent). The 1993 target was set at 8 per cent, but the prime minister acknowledged that 'unforeseen circumstances' could cause it to be exceeded. He also mentioned regional variations: 'where conditions permit, a higher rate can and should be achieved'. Should the growth targets be met, the goal of quadrupling the 1980 value of national income could be achieved within five years. Particular attention should be paid over the next five years to infrastructure, services and agriculture.

The prime minister said that 'reforming the administration and structure of the government is essential to the establishment of a socialist market economy and accelerating economic development'. Specifically, he announced that the number of civil servants serving the central government was to be reduced by 25 per cent over the next three years, with the number of ministries and other bodies directly under the State Council falling from eighty-six to fifty-nine. (Note that this was a reflection of the growing decentralization of the economy. Mass unemployment was not envisaged, e.g. some people would be transferred to commercial organizations and some functions were to be transferred to the State Economic and Trade Commission.) Li Peng mentioned the growing importance of labour contracts and added that workers should no longer be seen as 'belonging permanently to one sector or another of the economy'. 'Small' state enterprises could be sold or leased 'by public bidding'. He called for the decontrol of grain prices and the conversion of state agricultural subsidies into a 'relief fund for natural disasters'. In other markets, too, the state should opt for a 'price regulation fund' or 'commodity reserves' as opposed to direct state intervention.

Finance minister Liu Zhongli spoke on 16 March. He warned of 'great financial difficulties'. Another budget deficit was forecast, albeit slightly lower than 1992. Although the losses of state enterprises fell by 4.2 per cent in 1992, Liu warned that the government would 'resolutely stop subsidizing those enterprises that have no prospect of making a profit'. Spending on defence would again increase (by 12.4 per cent in 1993), the fourth annual increase in a row.

Political developments after the March 1993 congress

27–29 April 1993. Representatives of so-called 'semi-official' organizations from China and Taiwan meet in Singapore. This is the first high-level direct contact since 1949. Mostly technical matters are discussed, but regular future talks are to take place.

14 June 1993. Li Peng appears in public for the first time since 26 April after a mystery illness (heart trouble was later suggested). This led to speculation about his political future.

25 August 1993. On the final day of a six-day session of the party's Central Commission for Discipline Inspection a new code of conduct bars party and government officials from the following: engaging in business on their own account or helping relatives and friends to profit from their activities; trading in securities; accepting gifts (of money or securities) or credit cards; using public funds to acquire membership of clubs or to take part in expensive recreational activities; engaging in paid media activities. (A survey of companies in Hong Kong that do business in China suggested that about 5 per cent of their operating costs were taken up in bribes: *EIU Country Report*, 1993, Third Quarter, p. 13.) Over the space of three days, namely 23–25 October 1993, three anti-corruption edicts were issued: (1) various government and party departments were ordered to close down or sell off, because of conflicts of interest, any businesses they operated; (2) there was to be an end to fees being charged for what should be public services (e.g. crime investigation by the police); (3) government-financed trips abroad must have a clear official purpose that cannot include sightseeing (*IHT*, 26 October 1993, p. 7).

7 September 1993. China and India sign a provisional border pact, including a reduction of troops: 'Pending a boundary settlement [to be decided through 'friendly negotiation'], India and China have agreed to respect and observe the line of actual control.' (The border has been a contentious issue, especially after the October 1962 war, which India lost.)

23 September 1993. Beijing fails in its bid to stage the Olympic Games in the year 2000, after a heated debate in international political circles and in the international media on China's human rights record. In the final round of voting Sydney (Australia) wins by forty-five votes to forty-three.

5 October 1993. China conducts an underground nuclear test.

31 October 1993. 'High-level' military contacts with the USA resume (the first since Tiananmen). (This was another sign of warmer relations in general between the two countries, e.g. visits of US officials to discuss agriculture, trade and human rights. Relations reached a low point by mid-September and the Clinton administration determined to improve matters.)

11 November 1993. China and Russia sign a defence co-operation pact and agree to hold regular military exchanges.

15 November 1993. Chancellor Kohl of Germany begins a visit to China.

19 November 1993. President Clinton meets President Jiang Zemin in Seattle during the Asia-Pacific Economic Co-operation (Apec) forum. They clash over the issue of human rights. (Two days earlier China had been informed that a supercomputer would be removed from the sanctions list and that other exceptions were being considered.)

26 December 1993. The 100th anniversary of the birth of Mao Tse-Tung (who died in September 1976).

The third plenary session of the fourteenth Central Committee, 11–14 November 1993

Prior to the session Deng Xiaoping had reportedly called for economic reform and development to be 'as fast as possible'; 'development at a slow pace is not socialism'. His ideas in general were endorsed in the communiqué issued on 14 November 1993 (the document was entitled 'Decision on issues concerning the establishment of a socialist market economic structure'). The aim was to 'speed up the process of establishing a socialist market economic system and bring about sustained, swift and sound development of the national economy ... economic construction should be taken as the central task ... a programme of action to restructure the economy in the 1990s'. The socialist market economy (defined as 'making the market the fundamental factor in the disposition of resources under state macro-control') was to be completed by the end of the century. In the meantime the establishment of 'a sound microeconomic control system would continue' and 'greater efforts should be made in comprehensive improvement of social order. Political stability and unity should be consolidated and developed.' The main points were as follows:

1   Public ownership was to remain the 'mainstay' of the economy (see 'Economy').
2   A new taxation system was to be phased in from the start of January 1994.
3   Strengthening the powers of the central bank along Western lines in order to exercise more effective monetary control. (See 'Economy'.)
4   The income distribution system should be based on work and individual responsibility.
5   The 'open door' policy would be enhanced.

The need for a new social security system stems from such factors as rising unemployment. Such concern led to the following announcement by the ministry of labour on 29 April 1994: enterprises would need government permission to lay workers off; enterprises would have to pay for workers' job searches; state aid should go to unprofitable enterprises with potential, while those that go bankrupt would have to set aside funds from their remaining assets to aid laid-off workers; the central government would send emergency funds to areas where the unemployment rate ran out of control (*IHT*, 30 April 1994, p. 94).

The details of the new taxation system were announced on 1 December 1993:

1   A unified system for sharing tax revenues raised in the localities between the central government and the thirty provinces and municipalities, increasing the proportion received by the central government to 60 per cent (see below).
2   A uniform 33 per cent corporate tax on all enterprises (see below).
3   A simplified and extended VAT (from July 1994 onwards). The rate is 17 per cent for most products and 13 per cent for staple commodities. There will be additional excise taxes on goods such as cigarettes, alcohol, petrol, cars and jewellery. The central government will receive 75 per cent of VAT revenue.
4   A uniform personal income tax system for Chinese and foreign citizens alike (the nine tax rates range from 5 per cent to 45 per cent). But foreigners' personal earnings would be protected by changes in deductions (*IHT*, 6 December 1993, p. 13).
5   A sales tax of 3 per cent to 5 per cent on the turnover of enterprises in the service sector (such as those in entertainment, food, insurance, finance and transport).
6   Special taxes on the extractive industries.
7   Other taxes include those on property, stock exchange dealings and inheritance. (The overall tax burden on enterprises operating in China is supposed to remain unchanged, despite the introduction of new taxes: *IHT*, 27 December 1993, p. 7.)

The unified system for sharing tax revenues (point 1) would increase the proportion received by central government to 60 per cent.

In the late 1980s a new system for sharing tax revenues was introduced whereby each province negotiated a three-to-four-year tax-sharing contract with the central government, but enforcement was difficult. The central government's present share is just under 40 per cent (DIW, *Economic Bulletin*, 1994, vol. 31, no. 9, p. 22). (Note that the fall in central tax revenues has helped undermine fiscal policy as a policy instrument.)

The ratio of budgetary revenue to GNP went down from 31.6 per cent in 1978 to 14.1 per cent in 1993 (Tsang Shu-ki and Cheng Yuk-shing, *Asian Survey*, 1994, vol. XXXIV, no. 9, p. 774). The central government's revenue share in the total budget fell from around 60 per cent to about 40 per cent during the reform period. Up to 1993 central–local revenue arrangements were dominated by the fiscal contract system. There were two sorts: (1) a fixed or adjusted quota arrangement applied to provinces such as Guangdong and Fujian, under which the local government remitted to or received from the central government a fixed amount of revenue or subsidy which could be adjusted upwards and (2) a proportional sharing scheme in which the two levels of government shared revenue according to a pre-agreed ratio. By the mid-1980s most local authorities had adopted the proportional sharing scheme. But a few of them, including Shanghai, shifted to the fixed or adjusted quota arrangement in the late 1980s. In 1994 the government launched a tax assignment system under which taxes were divided into three categories, namely central, local and shared. The goal was to move from the central–local tax revenue ratio of about 40:60 in 1993 to one of 60:40, although no specific date was fixed (pp. 776–8).

The first time that the central government collected taxes direct was in 1994; previously it had had to rely on the provinces to collect taxes. The level of compliance in forwarding revenue to the central government varied greatly. The central bank estimated that on average provinces turned over about half the tax receipts. It has been estimated that the central government's share of total tax revenue rose from about 40 per cent to 65 per cent in 1994 (*IHT*, 7 March 1995, p. 4). In 1994 the central government's actual tax share was 65 per cent (Lincoln Kaye, *FEER*, 16 March 1995, p. 15).

The official budget deficit is probably half the real figure (*The Economist*, 7 March 1995, p. 4). Consolidated budget deficits have averaged 4 to 5 per cent of GDP in recent years, financed primarily from the central bank's printing presses (*The Economist*, Survey, 18 March 1995, p. 10).

The uniform 33 per cent corporate tax (point 2) would be imposed on all enterprises (medium-sized and large state enterprises currently pay 55 per cent, while the standard rate on foreign-invested enterprises is 24 per cent: *IHT*, 6 December 1993, p. 13). The preferential tax treatment of foreign-invested enterprises would be preserved by such devices as tax rebates. Tax refunds would be available for a period of five years or until an enterprise's contract expired, whichever came first (although such refunds would not be available to foreign-invested enterprises set up after 1 January 1994). China has no plans to abolish preferential income tax rates for foreign investors in the special economic and development zones (*IHT*, 13 January 1994, p. 15).

'The unification of the income tax rates at 33 per cent may be regarded as a move to achieve breakthrough as the management contract system implemented since 1987 has been abolished as well' (Tsang Shu-ki and Cheng Yuk-shing, *Asian Survey*, 1994, vol. XXXIV, no. 9, p. 787). 'Management contracts that obliged state enterprises to pay lump-sum income taxes have been cancelled, as have income adjustment taxes. The preferential rate of 15 per cent for foreign-invested enterprises in the SEZs has not been changed' (p. 783).

It was later revealed that a new unified managed floating exchange rate regime would be aimed for in 1994 (with restricted current account convertibility) and full convertibility by about the turn of the century. The new regime was actually introduced on 1 January 1994, somewhat earlier than expected. All import subsidies would be withdrawn in 1994, tariffs were to be reduced over the next few years and all but a few commodities would be freed from licences and quotas over the next four years (*IHT*, 13 December 1993, p. 9). (For actual developments, see below in the section on foreign trade.)

The company law

The first company law came into effect on 1 July 1994, the result of work which began in 1983. Limited liability companies and joint stock companies were covered, regardless of ownership. Companies registered before 1 July 1994 were to be given time to comply. Arbitrary government intervention in company operations was to be reduced and stress laid on the independent economic and legal status of companies. Note that the law relating to foreign-invested companies was to take precedence (*China Briefing*, October 1994, pp. 1–4).

The Ninth National People's Congress, 10–22 March 1994

Prime minister Li Peng delivered the opening speech to the 2,978 delegates. 'In a turbulent and volatile international environment, and amid a worldwide recession, our great socialist motherland stood firm as a rock in the East, enjoying economic growth, political stability, unity among the ethnic groups and social progress.' But there were still 'some major contradictions and problems in the midst of progress', e.g. inflation, excessive growth in fixed investment, loss-making state enterprises, crime and corruption ('the fight against inflation is a matter of life and death for our nation').

> Economic development is the centre of all our work ... Social stability, in turn, is an indispensable prerequisite for economic development and smooth progress in reform ... Government at all levels should try to raise farmers' incomes ... It will be an outstanding achievement if we can keep the GDP growing at 8 or 9 per cent for a few more years.

The target rate of growth of industrial output was to be 10.7 per cent and for inflation 10 per cent. Anti-inflation policies were to include the following:

1   The mayors of big cities were to be held 'responsible' for a 'market basket' system to guarantee the stability of the prices of key goods.
2   The entire budget deficit was to be financed by new (high interest) bonds rather than relying heavily on bank borrowings. (Note that the budget would henceforth be calculated more in line with standard international practice, e.g. an end to the peculiar Chinese practice of counting borrowed funds as revenue.) Defence spending was to increase by 22.4 per cent. The CIA puts the annual defence budget at $16 to $17 billion, more than twice the publicly stated

amount; using the World Bank's purchasing power parity method of calcula-
tion, the figure comes out at around $21 billion, but this is still only about half
the amount spent by Japan and a fraction of the spending of the major nuclear
powers (*IHT*, 21 May 1994, p. 6). The International Institute for Strategic
Studies estimated the 1994 defence budget in the range $28.5 billion to $45
billion (*FEER*, 4 August 1994, p. 16). Independent estimates of China's annual
military expenditure vary from $10 billion to $50 billion. Official figures
reveal a 200 per cent increase since 1988. China has a 2.9 million-strong army
(Nayan Chanda, *FEER*, 13 April 1995, pp. 24–5). The *IHT* (Survey, 24 April
1995, p. 18) cites one US estimate of $20 billion to $30 billion a year. The
International Institute of Strategic Studies estimated that Chinese military
expenditure exceeded $28 billion in 1994, nearly four times the official figure
(*IHT*, 11 October 1995, p. 4). China estimates that the proportion of GDP spent
on defence declined from 2.2 per cent in 1985 to 1.2 per cent in 1995. China's
estimate of $7.5 billion in 1995 compares with defence spending of $260
billion in the USA, $50 billion in Japan and roughly $30 billion each in the
UK, France and Germany (*FT*, 11 October 1995, p. 21). The army was reduced
from 4,238,000 in 1987 to 3,199,000 in 1990. There have been rumours of
plans to reduce it by 500,000 to 2,500,000 (*IHT*, 17 January 1996, p. 4). In
March 1997 it was announced that in 1997 China's defence expenditure would
rise by 12.7 per cent to $9.7 billion. This compares with $32 billion estimated
by the International Institute of Strategic Studies and $36 billion estimated by
David Shambaugh. In 1996 the USA's expenditure on defence was $256.6
billion and Japan's was $50 billion (*IHT*, 6 March 1997, p. 4).

3   Enterprise and banking reforms would continue. Enterprises in 'dire straits'
     would receive some assistance but in the end 'must rely on their own efforts to
     extricate themselves from their predicament'.
4   New capital spending would be restricted to construction projects already
     under way, with special emphasis on infrastructure.

On 23 March President Jiang Zemin repeated the main theme of the congress,
stressing the need to 'protect reforms while preserving stability'.

US secretary of state Warren Christopher visited China on 11–14 March 1994.
Before, during and after his visit China harassed and arrested leading dissidents.
Since a major topic was the link between trade and human rights, this greatly
soured the atmosphere. A similar thing happened during the 7–10 April 1994 visit
of French prime minister Edouard Balladur.

Political developments after the March 1994 congress

18–28 April 1994. Li Peng visits Uzbekistan, Turkmenistan, Kyrgyzstan, Kazakhstan and Mongolia.

26 May 1994. President Clinton announces that 'most favoured nation' status for
China's exports would be renewed (see 'Foreign trade' below).

10 June 1994. China undertakes its fortieth nuclear bomb test since 16 October
1964 (including one on 5 October 1993, two in 1992 and two in 1990).

5–9 July 1994. Li Peng visits Germany. Many economic agreements are signed, but human rights demonstrations upset the Chinese prime minister.

22 August 1994. Deng's ninetieth birthday.

29 August 1994. During the visit of a US trade mission led by the commerce secretary (Ron Brown) the two countries agree on a framework to expand commercial ties and sign a number of contracts. (Ron Brown said that 'private representations' would be made about human rights. China pledged to discuss the topic at the UN in September.)

28 September 1994. At the end of a four-day meeting of the Central Committee a document entitled 'The resolution on strengthening grass-roots party organizations' is published: 'it is necessary to safeguard central authority and forcefully implement the party's line, principles and policies'. The mayor of Shanghai, Huang Ju, is promoted to full membership of the politburo. He is a protégé of President Jiang Zemin, who is described as 'core leader'.

7 October 1994. China conducts an underground nuclear test. (This was China's forty-first nuclear test since 1964, compared with forty-four by Britain, 210 by France and more than 1,000 by the USA: *IHT*, 8 October 1994, p. 8.)

16–19 October 1994. US defence secretary William Perry visits China (the first visit by a defence secretary since 1989). A Joint Defence Conversion Commission is agreed to. The USA will help in the conversion from military to civilian production, e.g. to free air traffic control from the (90 per cent) dominance of the military and to produce 'environmentally safe' vehicles.

The Tenth National People's Congress, 5–18 March 1995

Qiao Shi, who became chairman of the National People's Congress (NPC) in October 1992, has attracted considerable attention, given the imminent demise of Deng Xiaoping. He was made a member of the politburo in 1985 and of the Standing Committee of the politburo in 1987. Qiao Shi abstained in the vote to declare martial law in 1989 (Lincoln Kaye, *FEER*, 11 May 1995, p. 15), but he is thought to be broadly a supporter of Deng's policies.

5 March 1995. In prime minister Li Peng's opening address to the 2,811 delegates familiar concerns came up:

1   Inflation needs to be reduced. The aim was to keep overall output growth in 1995 down to 8–9 per cent (the target for industrial growth was 13 per cent) and inflation down to 15 per cent. The government should tighten 'control and supervision over prices, especially those for daily necessities'. There would be no major price adjustments in 1995.
2   Loss-making enterprises should be merged or declared bankrupt: 'Enterprises which have been operating at a loss for a long time without an end in sight and have failed to repay debts should be allowed to declare bankruptcy.' Those enterprises which produce outdated goods should be allowed to 'change hands'.
3   State enterprises should separate productive activities from social ones, with the latter gradually transferred to the state.

4   The aim of all the measures should be 'to invigorate the state sector as a whole so as to give fuller scope to its dominant role'.

5   Agricultural performance should be improved through measures such as increased investment and action to control the loss of land to agriculture. Provincial governors were to be responsible for grain output (their 'rice bag') and municipal leaders were to be responsible for non-staple food output (their 'vegetable basket'). This has been termed the 'leadership responsibility system' for agricultural output (*China Briefing*, July 1995, p. 8). (Provincial governors are allowed to import from and export to other provinces, but they may not engage in international trade: *FT*, Survey, 20 November 1995, p. ii.)

6   Not only should crime and corruption be combated but 'we should oppose money-worship, ultra-individualism and decadent life styles, advocate healthy and civilized life styles and create a society with high ethical standards'. 'It is necessary to adhere over a long period of time to the principle of plain living and hard struggle, and of building up the country with industry and thrift.'

6 March 1995. The defence budget was increased by 21 per cent (the sixth nominal increase in a row).

17 March 1995. Two members of the politburo, who had the backing of President Jiang Zemin, met resistance from the NPC when it came to voting (by secret ballot) for their elevation to deputy prime minister (thus making six vice-premiers in total). Jiang Chunyun (party secretary of Shandong province) received only 63 per cent support for his agriculture portfolio (1,746 for, 605 against, 391 abstained and ten did not vote). The party secretary of Shanghai, Wu Bangguo (responsibility for the reform of state enterprises), did better, with 86 per cent support (2,366 for, 210 against, 161 abstained and fifteen did not vote).

18 March 1995. The Central Bank Law had only 66 per cent support (1,781 for, 509 against, 360 abstained and twenty-eight did not vote). (See 'Economy'.)

The Education Law had 74 per cent support.

Political developments after the March 1995 congress

22 March 1995. A US warship visits a Chinese port for the first time since 1989 (and only the third time ever; the first visit was in 1986 and the second in May 1989).

9 April 1995. One of Beijing's two vice-mayors (and the chairman of the municipal planning commission), Wang Baosen, commits suicide (apparently) after being accused of corruption. (On 4 July it was announced that he had committed 'serious economic crimes'.)

10 April 1995. Chen Yun dies, aged ninety.

12 April 1995. Li Peng says that 'The core of political leadership has already been transferred from Deng Xiaoping, the second generation leader, to President Jiang Zemin, who represents the third generation of Chinese leadership' (*IHT*, 13 April 1995, p. 1).

27 April 1995. Chen Xitong is forced to resign as party chief (secretary of the Central Committee) of the capital, Beijing (although he remains a member of the national politburo). An old comrade of Deng Xiaoping, Chen Xitong was placed under house arrest and his son was arrested. (On 4 July it was announced that Chen Xitong was to be investigated for corruption. On 28 September 1995 he was dismissed from the national politburo and Central Committee on the grounds that he had 'led a dissolute, extravagant life, abused his power to seek illegal interests for his relatives and accepted valuable gifts for his own use'. The following day he was dismissed from the Beijing municipal and national parliaments. He was expelled from the Communist Party on 9 September 1997. On 16 July 1998 he was charged with 'corruption and dereliction of duty' and on 31 July 1998 sentenced to sixteen years in prison.) This was generally seen not only as part of the anti-corruption drive (reaching high places for a change), but also as part of the process of establishing Jiang Zemin (from Shanghai) as the 'core' of the leadership. In February Zhou Guanwu had suddenly retired as chairman of the Shougang Company (the country's largest steel producer and a company having Deng Xiaoping's personal support) after his son, Zhou Beifang, had been arrested on charges of 'serious economic crimes' in connection with the Hong Kong operations of Shougang's real estate and investment company (headed by Deng Xiaoping's son Deng Zhifang). On 4 May 1995 it was announced that two executives of Shougang subsidiaries had been given suspended death sentences for accepting bribes. In November 1996 Zhou Beifang (the former head of Shougang Concord Enterprise International, a Hong Kong-based subsidiary of Capital Iron and Steel) was sentenced to death for bribery and corruption on a large scale. But he was given a two-year reprieve, meaning that the sentence can be commuted to life in prison for good behaviour (*IHT*, 15 November 1996, p. 4).

3–7 May 1995. The prime minister of Japan visits China.

10 May 1995. The start of a week-long visit by the prime minister of South Korea.

11 May 1995. The Nuclear Non-proliferation Treaty is extended indefinitely.

15 May 1995. China conducts an underground nuclear test (its forty-second).

22 May 1995. Japan announces that, as a protest against the test, it will reduce its grant aid to China (a largely symbolic move, since grants constitute only a small part of the total aid programme).

29 May 1995. State enterprise officials are banned from setting up private businesses, using their influence to help relatives or diverting enterprise assets for themselves. This move followed one the previous week ordering state and party officials to declare their incomes and a string of earlier edicts banning government workers from accepting meals, gifts and other favours from the public (*IHT*, 30 May 1995, p. 4).

30 June 1995. Zhu Rongyi steps down as governor of the central bank and is replaced by Dai Xianglong.

1 August 1995. US secretary of state Warren Christopher meets foreign minister Qian Qichen in Brunei.

17 August 1995. China conducts an underground nuclear test (its forty-third). (Japan announced that it would cut off most grant aid.)

22 August 1995. Deng's ninety-first birthday.

22 September 1995. China approves the USA's nominee for ambassador (James Sasser).

25–28 September 1995. At the Central Committee plenum it is announced that the target of quadrupling 1980 national output will be achieved in 1995 rather than 2000. The new target is a doubling of national output between 2001 and 2010. The target average annual rate of growth of GDP was fixed at 9.3 per cent for the period 1996–2000 and 8 per cent for the period 2001–10.

28 September 1995. The Central Military Commission is expanded, a move generally seen as strengthening the position of President Jiang Zemin.

24 October 1995. President Jiang Zemin and President Clinton meet in New York on the occasion of the fiftieth anniversary of the United Nations (on 22 October).

14 November 1995. Chancellor Kohl of Germany inspects a division of the People's Liberation Army.

1 December 1995. Border questions with Russia are resolved, with Russia ceding about 1,100 ha in the Far East. As many as 500,000 Chinese live illegally in Russia, despite Russia's efforts to organize the border with passport and customs controls (Steven Erlanger, *IHT*, 30 December 1995, p. 5).

The Eleventh National People's Congress, 5–17 March 1996

The new five-year plan statement commented that 'The Communist Party Central Committee, with Comrade Jiang Zemin at its core and the solidarity of the party and the people, is an important guarantee that we will walk from victory to victory'.

Prime minister Li Peng told the 2,793 delegates that 'The maintenance of political and social stability is the basic prerequisite for the promotion of reform and development, and stability in turn is realized through the deepening of reform'. Governments at all levels in China should 'attach equal importance to economic development and the development of socialist culture and ideology'. Li Peng listed the 'conspicuous' problems facing China:

1   'We should consider curbing inflation as the most important task for macro-control and take effective measures to control rising prices.' 'Appropriately tight financial and monetary policies' will continue to be implemented. (The finance minister stated that the aim was to eliminate the budget deficit by the year 2000. Defence spending was to increase by 11.3 per cent. According to Matt Forney, although the official defence appropriation was to increase by 10.2 per cent, off-budget expenditures made for a figure perhaps five times larger: *FEER*, 14 March 1996, p. 15.)

2   Loss-making state enterprises. The state would focus on 1,000 'backbone' and 'pillar' enterprises and a fund would be set up to restructure debt-burdened state enterprises. Enterprise mergers would be encouraged and funding provided for this purpose. (The five-year plan stated that 'State enterprises should declare bankruptcy if their liabilities outstrip assets, if they make long-term losses and if they lose out in market competition.') According to official figures, reforms of loss-making state enterprises, including the shedding of surplus labour, would cost some 500 billion yuan during the next five years. The reforms would mean shedding 8 million jobs at a cost of 160 billion yuan

(representing about 10 per cent of state-employed industrial workers.) About 280 billion yuan would be earmarked to strengthen the balance sheets of loss-making enterprises. These funds would go to 1,000 key enterprises singled out for special assistance, the help taking such forms as debt forgiveness, low-interest loans and technical assistance. Other enterprises would fend for themselves. China had indicated that it would encourage mergers, acquisitions, privatization or bankruptcy for enterprises that cannot make their way. Some 35 billion yuan would be set aside to offset bad debts of state enterprises declared bankrupt (*FT*, 11 March 1996, p. 4). On 14 March 1996 it was revealed that experiments to improve state industries were moving ahead in eighteen cities, in which 366 enterprises had been merged, 103 enterprises in light industry had gone bankrupt and 1.4 million workers had been 'retired from active duties' (*IHT*, 15 March 1996, p. 15).

3   Crime and corruption.
4   'Huge' regional disparities' in wealth. 'Disparate development of different regions is a basic condition in China.' Seven trans-provincial economic regions were to be set up to co-ordinate development and erode the differences among regions. The aim was to direct more than 60 per cent of soft loans to central and western regions.
5   Agricultural development was the most difficult task over the next fifteen years. The shrinkage in agricultural land was a serious problem.

The ninth five-year plan (1996–2000) was outlined. The targets included the following: 8 per cent average annual GDP growth (8 per cent for 1996) (Li Peng claimed that the target of quadrupling the 1980 GDP by the year 2000 had been achieved in 1995); grain production 490–500 million tonnes by the year 2000; an inflation rate of around 10 per cent for 1996.

Political developments after the Eleventh National People's Congress of March 1996

24–26 April 1996. President Boris Yeltsin of Russia visits China.

28 April 1996. Operation 'Strike Hard' against crime is launched.

10 May 1996. The USA announces that it will not impose sanctions on China for alleged sales of nuclear-related technology to Pakistan. The Chinese government says that it was unaware of the sales and promises not to make such sales in the future.

16 May 1996. There is no official commemoration of the thirtieth anniversary of the start of the Cultural Revolution.

15 May 1996. The National People's Congress ratifies the UN-sponsored Law of the Sea, which allows nations to claim waters within 200 nautical miles of their coasts as their economic zones. But China claims that its territorial waters now encompass 2.8 million square kilometres, up from 370,000 square kilometres (*FEER*, 30 May 1996, p. 13).

27 May 1996. Bao Tong is released from prison, but is not allowed to return home until after the Tiananmen anniversary. (He was the top aide to Zhao Ziyang who was opposed to the use of the army to crush the 1989 protests. Bao Tong was political secretary to the Standing Committee of the politburo and a member of the Central Committee when he was arrested on 28 May 1989: *IHT*, 28 May 1996, p. 4.)

8 June 1996. China conducts an underground nuclear test (its forty-fourth). (China said that it would conduct one more test before putting a moratorium into effect in September 1996. China has favoured testing for 'peaceful' purposes – 'peaceful nuclear explosions' – and asked that there should be a review of the issue after ten years.)

1 July 1996. The seventy-fifth anniversary of the foundation of the Communist Party in Shanghai.

29 July 1996. China conducts an underground nuclear test, earlier than expected. This is China's forty-fifth nuclear test and is followed by the announcement of a moratorium on testing. (The USA has conducted 1,030 nuclear tests and the former Soviet Union 715: *IHT*, 12 December 1996, p. 7. There have been a total of 2,045 known nuclear tests since 1945: *IHT*, 12 September 1996, p. 17.)

5 October 1996. Yao Wenyuan, the sole surviving member of the Gang of Four, is released from prison. He was arrested on 6 October 1976.

7–10 October 1996. A plenary session of the Central Committee is held. Support for economic reform is tempered by the endorsement of Jiang Zemin's call to 'build spiritual civilization'.

> The problem of neglect, or being comparatively casual in promoting ideological, education and ethical and cultural progress, while being strong in promoting material progress, has not yet been solved. Ethical and cultural progress should be given a higher status. At no time can we sacrifice spiritual values in the name of momentary economic development.

24 November 1996. Presidents Bill Clinton and Jiang Zemin meet in Manila on the eve of the Asia-Pacific Economic Co-operation (Apec) forum and agree to exchange visits over the next two years.

28–30 November 1996. Jiang Zemin visits India, the first visit by a president of China. A confidence-building agreement calls for a reduction in troops and weapons along the border between the two countries: 'Neither side shall use its military capacity against the other side.'

27 December 1996. China and Russia announce that there will be an (unspecified) reduction in military forces along their common border. (A formal agreement was to be signed in April 1997, when the two countries will be joined by Kazakhstan, Kyrgyzstan and Tajikistan.)

Early 1997. Chongqing municipality is awarded the status equivalent to a province. (Beijing, Chongqing, Shanghai and Tianjin enjoy a status equivalent to that of a province, enabling them to act autonomously on a range of financial and administrative matters and to approve foreign-invested projects valued up to $30 million: *Tianjin in Focus*, Hongkong Bank, September 1998, p. 1.)

19 February 1997. Deng Xiaoping dies. According to the official announcement, he 'suffered the advanced stage of Parkinson's disease, complicated by lung infections'. (He was born on 22 August 1904.)

21 February 1997. Jiang Zemin: 'Hold high the great banner of Deng's theory to build socialism with Chinese characteristics.' Deng's reforms will be pursued 'unswervingly and confidently'.

24 February 1997. Deng is cremated. (Deng requested a simple funeral. The authorities ensured that no opportunities were presented for public demonstrations.)

US secretary of state Madeleine Albright visits China for one day only.

25 February 1997. Jiang Zemin at the memorial ceremony: 'The current world is an open one and the reforms are here to stay ... All our work must be subordinated to and serve this centre [economic construction]. Development is the most essential criterion.'

1 March 1997. Deng's ashes are scattered at sea.

The National People's Congress, 1–14 March 1997

Prime minister Li Peng gave the opening speech at the congress. He stated that Deng's ideas should be followed 'under the leadership of the party Central Committee with Comrade Jiang Zemin at its core'. 'We should speed up reforms.' State enterprises are 'the backbone of the national economy', although the problem of loss-making ones exists. The problem of crime and corruption was once again highlighted.

The economic aims for 1997 included a reduction in inflation, GDP growth of 8 per cent and an increase of 12.7 per cent in defence spending.

There was major revision of the criminal law, the last significant one being in 1979. New offences included forced labour, money laundering, insider trading, breaking into information networks and creating computer viruses. The fifteen 'counter-revolutionary' crimes were replaced by eleven offences of 'endangering state security'.

A clause in the new defence law formally states that 'The armed forces of the People's Republic of China shall be subject to the leadership of the Communist Party of China' (*IHT*, 13 March 1997, p. 4). (The constitution holds that the armed forces 'belong to the people' and report to the State Military Commission, which in turn subordinates itself to the National People's Congress: *FEER*, 13 March 1997, p. 15.)

Defence spending was to increase by 12.7 per cent in 1997, compared with 11.3 per cent in 1996. Some estimates put actual defence spending at at least 2.5 times that stated in the budget (*Transition*, 1997, vol. 8, no. 2, p. 4).

Political developments after the March 1997 National People's Congress

22–27 March 1997. China objects to the (private) visit of the Dalai Lama to Taiwan. (On 27 March he met South Korea's president.)

23 March 1997. The Chinese navy makes its first port visit to mainland USA (San Diego Bay) (*IHT*, 24 March 1997, p. 4).

24–27 March 1997. US vice-president Al Gore visits China. He witnesses the signing of two commercial deals, for the purchase of US aircraft and for a joint car venture.

28 March 1997. Japan resumes its grant aid to China (suspended on 17 August 1995 because of the testing of nuclear weapons).

22–26 April 1997. Jiang Zemin visits Russia.

25 April 1997. China announces that it has ratified the Chemical Weapons Convention.

26 April 1997. Peng Zhen dies.

13 May 1997. A bomb explodes in Beijing. The official explanation is that it was a suicide.

15–18 May 1997. President Chirac of France visits China.

20 August 1997. Chen Xiaotong (son of disgraced Beijing party chief Chen Xitong) is sentenced to twelve years in prison for corruption.

The successful launch of a communications satellite takes place.

4–7 September 1997. The Japanese prime minister visits China.

11 September 1997. China announces new rules to tighten controls over the export of nuclear weapons and technology.

12 September 1997. An unsigned, typewritten letter, purportedly written by Zhao Ziyang, is addressed to the Communist Party's congress presidium and concerns the 4 June 1989 Tiananmen events:

> No matter how radical, wrong and blameworthy the students' movement was, to call it a 'counter-revolutionary rebellion' was groundless. And if it was not a counter-revolutionary rebellion it should not have been solved by means of military suppression. Everyone knows that the majority of the students' demands at that time were to punish corruption and promote political reform and not to overthrow the Communist Party or subvert the republic. Sooner or later the problem of reassessing the 4 June incident must be resolved.

(Zhao Ziyang was last seen in public when he visited Tiananmen Square on 19 May 1989. In his 12 September 1997 speech Jiang Zemin referred to Tiananmen as a 'political upheaval': *FEER*, 25 September 1997, p. 15.)

The Fifteenth Communist Party Congress, 12–18 September 1997

There are 54 million members of the Communist Party. About 1.7 million new members have been added in each of the last two years (*IHT*, 11 October 1994, p. 7). The number of party members has gone up from 48 million in 1989 to 58 million (*IHT*, 2 February 1998, p. 4).

Jiang Zemin put economic reform at the centre of his opening address on 12 September. The most important points were as follows:

1 'The theme of the congress is to hold high the great banner of Deng Xiaoping theory for an all-round advancement of the cause of building socialism with Chinese characteristics to the twenty-first century.'

2 'International competition is becoming increasingly acute ... The quality and efficiency of the national economy as a whole remain fairly low, the irrational economic structure still poses a rather outstanding problem, and especially part of the state-owned enterprises lack vitality ... With the deepening of enterprise

reforms, technological progress and readjustment of the economic structure, it would be hard to avoid the flow of personnel and lay-offs. It will cause some temporary difficulties to some of the workers. Fundamentally speaking it is conducive to economic development, thus conforming to the long-term interests of the working class ... [It is necessary to] increase efficiency by downsizing staff.'

3   The state must retain 'a dominant position in major industries and key areas that concern the life-blood of the national economy' but 'diverse forms of ownership' should be encouraged. China should 'quicken the pace' of state enterprise reform, including 'reorganization, association, merger, leasing, contract operation, joint stock partnership or sell-off'. Ziang did not use the term 'privatization' but stressed an increasing role for 'public ownership'. 'We should strive to seek various forms of materializing public ownership that can greatly promote the growth of productive resources ... Public ownership can and should take diversified forms ... We must have a comprehensive understanding of what is meant by the public sector of the economy. The public sector includes not only the state- and collectively-owned sectors, but also the state- and collectively-owned elements in the sector of mixed ownership ... Even if the state-owned sector accounts for a smaller proportion of the economy, this will not affect the socialist nature of our country ... We cannot say in general terms that the shareholding system is public or private, for the key lies in who holds the controlling share.' (See 'Economy'.)

4   'The fight against corruption is a grave political struggle vital to the very existence of the Communist Party and the state. We should be mentally prepared for a protracted war against corruption.'

5   'In addition to the army reduction by one million men in the 1980s, we shall reduce the armed forces by another 500,000 in the next three years.' (Ziang said that more resources were to be put into higher-grade equipment. The army has fallen from about 5 million to 3.1 million. But the ranks of the People's Armed Police, a paramilitary group designed to guard against domestic unrest or protest demonstrations, has increased by a million: *IHT*, 13 September 1997, p. 7, and 15 September 1997, p. 1.)

6   The aim is to double GNP in the first decade of the millennium (*FT*, Survey, 8 December 1997, p. i).

Personnel changes were seen as strengthening the position of Jiang Zemin:

1   The most surprising move was the departure of Qiao Shi (chairman of the National People's Congress) from the new (192-strong) Central Committee. Other departures included General Liu Huaqing, Yang Baibing, Zou Jianxin, Zhang Zhen, Hu Ping (son-in-law of Deng Xiaoping), Zhou Nan, Lu Ping, Wang Tao, Hu Qili and Wang Hanbin. Among the new members was Dai Xianglong (governor of the central bank)

2   There were two new members of the seven-strong Standing Committee of the Politburo, namely Wei Jiangxing (chairman of the central disciplinary commission) and Li Lanqing (a former foreign trade minister) who replaced Qiao Shi and General Liu Huaqing (leaving no military man among the seven). In order

of rank the members were Jiang Zemin, Li Peng, Zhu Rongyi (who moved from fifth to third place, the ranking formerly held by Qiao Shi), Li Ruihuan, Hu Jintao, Wei Jianxing and Li Lanqing.

3 The politburo was expanded to twenty-two members.
4 On the Central Military Commission, deputy chairmen General Liu Huaqing and General Zhang Zhen were replaced by General Zhang Wannian and defence minister defence minister Chi Haotian.

Political developments after the Fifteenth Communist Party Congress of September 1997

23 September 1997. The USA and Japan formally announce, despite protests from China, details of the revised (1978) defence pact guidelines.

26 October–3 November 1997. Jiang Zemin visits the USA. (Deng Xiaoping visited the USA in 1979 and President Li Xiannian in 1985.)

Jiang Zemin is generally considered to have strengthened his position in China as a result of the visit. There were no dramatic announcements but the following were significant:

1 Agreement to implement the 1985 USA–China Nuclear Co-operation Accord. President Clinton was to certify to the US Congress that China was no longer selling or transferring nuclear technology to other countries for the development of nuclear weapons (especially Iran and Pakistan). (The agreement also covered the sale of missiles such as cruise missiles to countries like Iran.) This would allow the USA civilian nuclear industry to export to China.
2 Agreement to organize regular meetings between the two governments at every level, including annual presidential meetings.
3 A fact-finding visit to China by three US religious leaders.
4 The setting up of a telephone link ('hot line') between the two presidents.

On 31 October the USA named a special co-ordinator for Tibetan issues.

On 1 November, in a comment that many in the West thought referred to Tiananmen, Jiang Zemin stated: 'It goes without saying that, naturally, we may have shortcomings and even make some mistakes in our work.'

10 November 1997. China and Russia sign a declaration on the demarcation of their 2,800-mile (4,300-kilometre) border. ('The short western border, only 50 miles long, is still
under negotiation': *IHT*, 11 November 1997, p. 4.) (There was also an agreement in principle to build a gas pipeline from Siberia to China's Pacific coast.)

19 January 1998. US secretary of defence William Cohen is shown around an air defence command centre in Beijing. China and the USA conclude a formal agreement on preventing accidents at sea. He is assured that China has stopped all transfers of anti-ship cruise missiles to Iran (*IHT*, 20 January 1 1998, p. 1, and 21 January 1998, p. 6).

The National People's Congress, 5–19 March 1998

Nearly 3,000 delegates took part.

The major decisions as regards personnel were as follows:

1   Jiang Zemin was reelected president and chairman of the central military commission, with 98 per cent of the votes in favour. (The vice-president was Hu Jintao.)
2   Li Peng was elected chairman of the National People's Congress, with almost 89 per cent of the votes in favour.
3   Zhu Rongyi was elected prime minister, with 98 per cent of the votes in favour.
4   Xiang Huaicheng (finance minister).
5   Tang Jiaxuan (foreign minister). (Qian Qichen, the former foreign minister, remained responsible for overseeing foreign policy matters. He remained a member of the politburo. He was one of four deputy prime ministers, the others being Li Lanqing, Wu Bangguo and Wen Jiabao.)
6   Sheng Huaren (general manager of the China Petrochemical Corporation) became head of the state economic and trade commission.

Li Peng gave his final speech as prime minister on the opening day of the congress, having completed his second and final term of office. He said that the 1998 target rate of growth of GDP was 8 per cent and that for inflation was under 3 per cent. Growth would be aided by a large-scale, three-year infrastructure investment programme in order to counter the ill effects of the Asian financial crisis that started in July 1997 in Thailand.

The following important issues were discussed at the congress:

1   Bureaucracy. (See 'Economy'.)
2   Businesses and enterprises were to be hived off from government departments and state subsidies to non-administrative units phased out over three years. (See 'Economy'.)
3   The problem of unemployment. There would be an estimated 3.5 million job losses in the state sector in 1998. There were 11.51 million officially counted unemployed at the end of 1997, including 7.87 from the state sector. A deputy minister at the state economic and trade commission: 'Within these [state] enterprises, if a third of the workforce were cut, these enterprises could still operate normally. If half of the workers were to be cut enterprises some enterprises could operate even better. We cannot lay off all the excess workers at once. We have to do it step by step' (*FT*, 9 March 1998, p. 3; *IHT*, 9 March 1998, p. 1). The minister of labour mentioned a current experiment that requires enterprises to contribute 0.621 of wages to an unemployment insurance fund. There was a proposal to increase the percentage to 2 per cent, with employees providing a further 1 per cent of their wages (*IHT*, 9 March 1998, p. 6).
4   The formation of conglomerates was to continue despite the problems experienced in countries like South Korea and Japan. (See 'Economy'.) The deputy minister of the state economic and trade commission: 'While we are going to

learn in real earnest the lessons from the South Korean cases, our overall plan on amalgamating enterprise groups will not be affected. We believe that we will have a smooth process of establishing enterprise groups in China. In some key sectors and fields it is necessary for China to establish very large enterprises or enterprise groups in order to develop economies of scale' (*IHT*, 9 March 1998, p. 6). The deputy director of enterprises at the state commission for restructuring the economy: 'China will not change its strategy of developing large enterprise groups despite the fact that some large enterprises in South Korea have gone bust in the ongoing financial crisis. We are aware of the problems but we will not change our plan' (*IHT*, 10 March 1998, p. 6).

5   The date of full convertibility of the yuan was to be substantially put back because of the Asian financial crisis. The deputy governor of the central bank said that it could take ten years instead of the unofficial target date of 2000 (*IHT*, 6 March 1998, p. 6).

6   The scheme (partially) to recapitalize four state banks afflicted by large amounts of non-performing loans was approved. (See 'Economy'.)

Developments after the 5–19 March 1998 National People's Congress

31 March–7 April 1998. Zhu Rongyi visits the UK and France. The visit included attendance at the Asia–Europe Meeting (Asem) in London.

29–30 April 1998. US secretary of state Madeleine Albright visits China.

5 May 1998. China criticizes India's defence minister for saying (on 3 May) that China was India's 'potential threat number one' (*IHT*, 6 May 1998, p. 4). (On 11 May 1998 India conducted three underground nuclear tests, the first since 1974. Two more tests were carried out on 13 May. On 28 May 1998 Pakistan tested five nuclear devices and another one two days later.)

17 June 1998. Regulations are published, effective immediately, which

aim to strengthen control of dual-use equipment and related technology, halt the proliferation of nuclear technology and promote international co-operation for the peaceful use of nuclear energy ... The nation imposes strict controls of the export of dual-use equipment and related technology and shall strictly carry out all of the international non-proliferation duties it has committed to.

(*IHT*, 18 June 1998, p. 4)

24 June 1998. In the Western press it is reported Zhao Ziyang may have written a letter to the Central Committee of the Communist Party of China, including the following reference to Tiananmen: 'It can be said that China's 4 June problem is one of the biggest human rights problems of this century.'

25 June–3 July 1998. President Clinton visits China (including Hong Kong).

This was the first visit of a US president since George Bush in February 1989. But little was expected and Western critics of President Clinton's visit pointed, among other things, to the following: the official welcoming ceremony (a military one held on 27 June) was to take place before the Great Hall of the People, which is on the edge of Tiananmen Square; the claim that Clinton was stressing commercial links with China at the expense of human rights (it was decided not to allow business executives to be members of the large presidential entourage and not many business deals were actually signed during the visit); in the USA there were ongoing investigations into claims that Chinese money had found its way into Democratic Party campaign funds and into claims that technology of use to the Chinese military had leaked via the launching of US satellites on Chinese rockets.

But the visit turned out to be much more significant than expected, if only symbolically. For example, the issue of human rights was raised in unexpected fashion, as can be seen in the following comments by President Clinton:

1   'Respect for the worth, the dignity, the potential and the freedom of every citizen is a vital source of America's strength and success ... A commitment to providing all human beings the opportunity to develop their full potential is vital to the strengths and success of new China as well' (25 June).

2   On reports that dissidents had been detained just before his visit: 'If true, then this represents China not at its best, not China looking forward but looking backwards.'

3   On 27 June there took place a forthright but good-natured debate on human rights between Clinton and Jiang Zemin, which was (as a result of a last-minute decision by China) broadcast live on television and radio. (Television penetration has increased more than five-fold in the past twelve years and now covers about 90 per cent of households in China: *IHT*, 29 June 1998, p. 4.) Topics included Tiananmen, which brought forth the following statements: Clinton: 'I believe, and the American people believe, that the use of force and tragic loss of life was wrong'; Jiang Zemin: 'With regard to the political disturbances in 1989 ... Had the Chinese government not taken the resolute measures then, we could not have enjoyed the stability that we are enjoying today.' Clinton urged talks with the Dalai Lama over Tibet. Clinton also raised the problem of the relationship between human rights and stability: 'If you limit people's freedom too much then you pay, I believe, an even greater price in a world where the whole economy is based on ideas and information and exchange and debate. I believe stability in the twenty-first century will require high levels of freedom.'

4   On 29 June Clinton addressed audience of students in Beijing and this was followed by a question and answer session. The whole thing was broadcast live. Clinton: 'We are convinced that certain rights are universal'; 'Freedom has reached Asia's shores, powering a surge of growth and productivity'; 'Freedom strengthens stability ... Greater respect for divergent political and religious convictions will actually breed stability'; 'In the world we live in, this global information age, constant improvement and change is necessary to economic opportunity and national strength. Therefore, the freest possible flow of information, ideas and opinions, and a greater respect for divergent political and religious convictions will actually breed strength and stability.'

China and the USA agreed to 'detarget' nuclear weapons aimed at each other.

Clinton's speech in Hong Kong on the final day of his visit: 'Thanks to the leadership of President Jiang Zemin and prime minister Zhu Rongyi, China has followed a disciplined, wise policy of resisting competitive devaluations that could threaten the economy of China, the region and the world.'

14 July 1998. China's science and technology minister attends a conference in Taiwan, albeit in her capacity as a university professor.

26 August 1998. The official loss of life through summer flooding is put at 3,004.

The flooding along the Yangtze has been the heaviest since 1954, when (according to official figures) more than 30,000 people died (*IHT*, 7 August 1998, p. 2).

> The government has made the unusual admission that its land-use mistakes are partly to blame ... Officials have clearly been shocked by the vast scale of damage in southern and north-western China, where severe flooding persists. While the rains this year have been torrential, heavier rainfall in some other years has caused less flooding and damage. In the last few weeks the official press has carried increasingly sharp articles and editorials on the harmful effects of clear-cutting timber along the upper reaches of the Yangtze River and the human invasion of vital wetlands along the river's course. In private some experts are making more pointed charges that, despite repeated warnings, the upkeep of important dikes along China's flood-prone rivers has been badly neglected ... On Tuesday [25 August] the government [announced that it] had decided to shut down logging activities in the upper catchments of the Yangtze River. The deforestation has led to more rapid runoff of rain waters and increased silting of rivers and lakes ... All cleared areas would be replanted ... Large areas of lakes and wetlands in the Yangtze flood plain, which have been drained to make farmland, would be restored to their natural condition. These areas formerly absorbed huge volumes of water during flood periods.
>
> (Erik Eckholm, *IHT*, 27 August 1998, p. 1)

The summer floods killed 3,656 people (*IHT*, 23 November 1998, p. 7).

(The People's Liberation Army played a significant role during the crisis and party propaganda made the most of the situation to improve the image of an army tarnished by factors such as Tiananmen and corruption.)

14 September 1998. Former president (1988–93) Yang Shangkun dies.

23 September 1998. A regulation 'on family planning administration of the transient population' is announced under which migrant workers in urban areas must, from 1 January 1999 onwards, carry a new certificate stating their 'marriage and reproductive status', while employers and landlords of transient workers will be expected to help enforce birth control measures. The local government where the migrant worker is temporarily living must take responsibility for implementing birth control restrictions. Couples found to have fabricated, sold or bought bogus birth-control certificates will be fined up to 1,000 yuan. There are some 100 million migrant rural workers. In most rural areas regulations limit couples to two, well-spaced children. The family planning minister has said that uncontrolled births among the floating population have created 'great pressure' on the government's birth-control efforts (Teresa Poole, *Independent*, 24 September 1998, p. 15).

6 October 1998. British prime minister Tony Blair begins a five-day visit to China.

11 November 1998. More than 200 people demonstrate in Beijing in protest at the collapse (in August 1998) of a futures company in which they had invested.

'Such protests, though still rare, are becoming more common as the economic slowdown scuppers financial institutions' (*FT*, 12 November 1998, p. 1).

22–24 November 1998. Jiang Zemin visits Russia.

25–30 November 1998. Jiang Zemin visits Japan.

Jiang Zemin is the first Chinese head of state ever to visit Japan and the trip had been intended as a milestone in the process of healing the suspicions between the two countries. Instead, the meeting of the two leaders [Jiang Zemin and Japanese prime minister Keizo Obuchi] on Thursday [26 November] seemed to inflame the antagonisms ... A joint declaration by the two leaders was delayed for more than five hours and in an unusual move it was released without being signed by anyone. Mr Jiang had wanted ... a clear-cut written apology to the Chinese people for World War II behaviour by Japan, similar to the apology Japan gave South Korea last month [October] ... Japan rebuffed Mr Jiang ... offering an oral apology to China ... 'The Japanese government expresses again its remorse and apology to China on this occasion,' Mr Obuchi added ... 'Japan feels acute responsibility for the grave misfortune and harm to the Chinese people during a certain period of aggression toward China and we express deep remorse about this,' the declaration said. However, the declaration did not use the word 'apology', which many Japanese feel is more serious than the word for remorse.

(Nicholas Kristof, *IHT*, 27 November 1998, pp. 1, 4)

The joint declaration between South Korea and Japan signed on 8 October 1998:

Prime minister Obuchi regarded in a spirit of humility the fact of history that Japan caused, during a certain period in the past, tremendous damage and suffering to the people of the Republic of Korea through its colonial rule, and expressed his deep remorse and heartfelt apology for this fact.

Prime minister Obuchi speaking to President Jiang Zemin: 'The Japanese government expresses anew its feeling of deep remorse and heartfelt apology for Japan's colonial rule and aggression.'

The unsigned declaration: 'The Japanese side is keenly conscious of the responsibility for the serious distress and damage that Japan caused to the Chinese people through its aggression against China during a certain period in the past and expressed remorse for this.' (*FEER*, 10 December 1998, p. 21.)

29 November 1998. 'China has ordered its vast bureaucracy to cut ties with all its businesses next year [1999] in a bid to stamp out corruption ... Organs of the Communist Party and the government were told to give up enterprises under their control' (*IHT*, 30 November 1998, p. 17). (See 'Economy'.)

China's top leaders vowed Wednesday [9 December] to maintain a stable yuan and to press ahead with market-opening measures next year [1999], official media reported. Maintaining the stability of the yuan will be one of the three major tasks for 1999 ... The others are to stabilize and strengthen the agricultural sector and to deepen the restructuring of state-owned companies. The decisions were made at a three-day conference attended by President Jiang

Zemin, prime minister Zhu Rongyi and other top party and government leaders. China will 'implement an appropriate monetary policy as necessary to maintain support for economic growth', Xinhua [the official news agency] said ... There has been concern that China was backtracking on its restructuring programme to shield itself from the impact of the Asian financial crisis ... Participants at the conference ... called for 'vigilance' because of a decrease in exports, slowdown of income growth for urban and rural residents and increasing economic pressure from unprofitable state companies ... On the reform of state companies, the report said measures would be taken to separate the administration from the management of enterprises, prevent duplication of projects and set up a social security system. Financial reform efforts, especially at state-owned commercial banks, will be accelerated, state radio said.

(*IHT*, 10 December 1998, p. 18)

14 December 1998. Government media report that the government's intention is to make at least a third of loss-making state enterprises profitable in 1999 by stepping up the pace of reforms. At a senior-level conference held on 12–13 December deputy prime minister Wu Bangguo urged further streamlining of state enterprises in 1999 in order to reduce losses. He called for tough measures to stop duplicate investments and for closing inefficient small mines, oil refineries and steel mills, oil refineries and steel mills that waste energy and cause heavy pollution (*IHT*, 15 December 1998, p. 17).

18 December 1998.

Jiang Zemin made ... a speech marking twenty years of economic reforms that have changed the face of the country. He stressed that the economy would continue to be dominated by the state-run sector. But he added that private enterprise also played an important role in China's development. Mr Jiang's speech underscored the party's current preoccupation with stability – a word he repeated throughout his seventy-five-minute speech ... 'From beginning to end we must be vigilant against infiltration, subversive activities and separatist activities of international and domestic hostile forces,' Mr Jiang said ... 'The systems must not be shaken, weakened or discarded at any time,' he continued. 'The Western mode of political systems must never be copied.'

(John Pomfret, *IHT*, 19 December 1998, p. 8)

30 December 1998. Deng Liqun (eighty-four) is a 'hardline Marxist ... once China's propaganda chief and still regarded as the country's leading leftist figure' (*IHT*, 31 December 1998, p. 15). In a speech delivered in December he said:

In their hearts [reformers in the party] it is no longer 'only socialism can save China' but 'only capitalism can save China' ... The rights of an overwhelming majority of people would be guaranteed if state-owned enterprises were in the hands of Marxists and Leninists ... Public ownership should be the mainstay and non-public ownership supplementary. The sale of state enterprises to capitalists has transformed workers from the masters of enterprises to the hired hands of bosses.

After a six-month investigation a bipartisan committee of the US House of Representatives concludes that US technology transfers to China over the last twenty years have harmed US national security. The transfers covered militarily significant technology, including satellite missile technology. The committee was created after abortive launchings in 1996 of US communications satellites atop Chinese rockets. Both mishaps brought charges that two US companies had allowed militarily sensitive technology to fall into Chinese hands (*IHT*, 31 December 1998, pp. 1, 8). The committee accused China of a persistent campaign over twenty years to acquire technology that could be used to bolster its military strength. Methods included knowledge-sharing between Chinese and US aerospace companies and covert means such as espionage (*IHT*, 2 January 1999, p. 3). The enquiry began in June 1998 after it was reported that two US companies may have improperly helped China to fix problems in rocket design (p. 8). (On 23 February 1999 it was announced that the USA would not allow the sale of a commercial satellite to a consortium with close ties to the Chinese government: *IHT*, 24 February 1999, p. 1.)

8 January 1999. 'China has targeted economic growth this year [1999] at about 7 per cent' (*IHT*, 9 January 1999, p. 13).

11–12 January 1999. 'China and the United States resumed dialogue on human rights Monday [11 January] after a hiatus of more than four years ... Diplomats agreed to the resumption of human rights talks when President Bill Clinton visited China in June [1998]' (*IHT*, 12 January 1999, p. 8). 'US and Chinese officials held their first meeting exclusively devoted to human rights since 1995' (*IHT*, 13 January 1999, p. 4). The two sides agreed to meet again.

28 February–1 March 1999. US secretary of state Madeleine Albright visits China.

5–15 March 1999. The Ninth National People's Congress is held.

Prime minister Zhu Rongyi (opening speech):

[There exists a] grim environment at home and abroad ... Financial discipline is lax and economic disorder is somewhat in disarray. Demand in the market is feeble ... The leaders of enterprises operating at a serious loss because of poor management will be shown a yellow warning card in one year and will be dismissed from their post in two years ... The deterioration of the ecological environment remains a glaring problem ... With the exception of a number of projects designed to raise the technological level of production, upgrade products and manufacture marketable products, government at all levels should stop examining and approving industrial development projects and banks should stop granting loans to them ... If projects are launched in a rush, resulting in serious duplication and shoddy engineering, they will become a heavy burden on public finance and sooner or later lead to serious inflation.

Infrastructure investment is again set to increase, however, in order to help achieve the official growth target of 'around 7 per cent' for 1999. (But Zhu Rongyi mentioned many cases of poor quality infrastructure work.) The inflation target is 4 per cent.

The budget deficit will rise by 57 per cent in 1999. There is to be a 12.7 per cent increase in the military budget (partly to compensate for the loss of businesses run by the military).

Article 11 of the constitution is altered. It will now state that the 'non-public sectors' constitute 'an important component of China's socialist market economy' rather than merely 'a complement to the socialist public economy'. (State banks are to be encouraged to make more loans to non-state enterprises by allowing the former to charge higher interest rates, i.e. by allowing them greater latitude in the pricing of risk: *IHT*, 12 March 1999, p. 13; *FT*, 12 March 1999, p. 6.)

The congress votes to add 'Deng Xiaoping theory' to the constitution's 'Marxist–Leninist–Mao Zedong thought' (*The Economist*, 13 March 1999, p. 94).

Measures to combat crime and corruption are again given great attention.

The central bank governor announced that foreign banks would be allowed to set up branches in all major cities. Previously they had been restricted to twenty-three cities and Hainan Island (*FEER*, 25 March 1999, p. 22).

6–21 April 1999. Prime minister Zhu Rongyi begins a visit to the USA. The talks concentrated on trade issues and considerable progress was made in negotiations relating to China's admission to the WTO. China offered concessions in sectors such as agriculture, telecommunications, internal distribution and financial services (including insurance and banking).

'Zhu Rongyi offered Mr Clinton market-opening measures, especially in telecoms and financial services – concessions the Chinese must have found hard to make. Mr Clinton said they were not enough. This, his advisers admit, was a mistake' (*The Economist*, 14 August 1999, p. 53). (The US president judged that the concessions made by China would not be enough to convince Congress, while the Chinese prime minister was criticized in some quarters in China for the concessions he did make. China was annoyed by US publicizing of China's concessions.)

7 May 1999. Nato bombs the Chinese embassy in Belgrade, the capital of Serbia. Nato described the bombing as a 'terrible accident'. It was the result of 'faulty information' as regards targeting, mistaking the building for the federal directorate of supply and procurement (a military office). (It was later revealed that an outdated map had been used.) Three Chinese journalists were killed. Angry demonstrations followed in China, including three days of mob attacks on US and UK embassies. On 10 May China suspended co-operation with the USA on stopping proliferation of weapons of mass destruction, discussions on human rights and high-level military contacts. A US delegation, led by undersecretary of state Thomas Pickering, arrived in Beijing on 16 June 1999 to explain the bombing of the Chinese embassy in Belgrade. The following day China announced that it had rejected the US explanation. On 24 June China banned US military aircraft from landing in Hong Kong; the ban was lifted on 29 July 1999. A US ship did not dock in Hong Kong until 7 September 1999. On 30 July 1999 the USA agreed to pay $4.5 million to the families of those killed and wounded when the Chinese embassy in Belgrade was bombed on 7 May. The money was to be given to the Chinese government, which would decide how to divide the funds among the three people killed and twenty-seven injured. No mention was made of compensation for the embassy building. (The Chinese foreign minister and the US secretary of state met on 24 July and senior trade negotiators from China and the USA resumed bilateral talks on 26 July: *IHT*, 31 July 1999, p. 4.) (On 16 December 1999 it was announced that the USA had agreed to pay $28 million by way of compensation for the embassy building, while China agreed to pay $2.87 million for damage caused to US diplomatic buildings in China during demonstrations: *IHT*, 17 December 1999, p. 4. 'The CIA has fired one intelligence officer and reprimanded six managers, including a senior official, for errors that led to the US bombing of the Chinese embassy in Belgrade ... The Yugoslav arms agency ... was the only target chosen by the CIA ... According to the CIA, an intelligence officer ... obtained the correct address of the Yugoslav Federal Directorate of Supply and Procurement ... But the detailed two-year-old map used for targeting did not show the numbers of the buildings on that street, so the officer used the numbering of buildings on parallel streets ... A cross-check of various databases listing sensitive sites, such as schools, hospitals and embassies, failed to catch the error because the data had not been updated after the Chinese embassy moved there from another part of Belgrade in 1996': *IHT*, 10 April 2000, pp. 1, 5. A spokesman for the Chinese foreign ministry on 10 April 2000: 'The Chinese embassy in Yugoslavia has unmistakeable markings and is also clearly indicated on US maps. The US claim that it did not know its exact location does not hold water. It is hard for people to believe that the bombing was the fault of several officials whose mistake was not corrected in a review process. The Chinese government strongly demands a comprehensive and thorough investigation into its bombing of the Chinese embassy in Yugoslavia, bring the perpetrators to justice and give the Chinese government and people a satisfactory explanation': *FT*, 11 April 2000, p. 12; *IHT*, 11 April 2000, p. 5.)

> The embassy strike occurred at a time of mounting quarrels between Washington and Beijing over the alleged theft by China of nuclear secrets at US weapons laboratories over the past twenty years, the administration's enthusiasm for a missile-defence system over the Pacific that could involve Taiwan, and human rights issues ... A House of Representatives report on an inquiry into Chinese espionage ... tells of 'pervasive' penetration by Beijing agents into a wide range of military activity, from computers, electronics, jet engines, telecommunications, machine tools and missiles to the latest in nuclear warheads.
>
> (*IHT*, 17 May 1999, p. 4)

> On 26 June [1999] Beijing overruled a Hong Kong court on a landmark immigration case ... A few days earlier the US Senate passed a bill stipulating that Hong Kong be treated the same as the rest of China for purposes of exporting technology with military applications.
>
> (*IHT*, 1 July 1999, p. 1)

24 May 1999.

> Chinese strategists view the new US–Japan defence guidelines, which passed in Japan's parliament on 24 May [1999], as a plot to contain China because the rules contain language authorizing Japan's self-defence forces to support US forces in areas 'surrounding Japan'. That vague language has led Chinese strategists to conclude that Japan, with the United States, might be willing to come to Taiwan's aid if China attacks the island ... Strategists see the decision

by the Philippine Senate on 28 May to reopen its territory for joint exercises with US forces as another link in an American chain of military agreements blocking the expansion of China's influence. To the west Nato expansion has alarmed Chinese strategists. Over the past three years US forces have also held exercises or seminars with the armies of Tajikistan, Kazakhstan and Kyrgyzstan, which border China. In a peacekeeping seminar ... in Florida in mid-May [1999] officers from neighbouring Mongolia came to observe.

(John Pomfret, *IHT*, 12 June 1999, p. 4)

25 May 1999. A previously publicized US congressional report is finally published.

In a far-reaching breach of US security, China has stolen [in a two-decade long campaign] classified information on every deployed warhead in the US ballistic missile arsenal, as well as on the neutron bomb, the chairman of a congressional investigating committee said Tuesday [25 May].

(*IHT*, 26 May 1999, p. 1)

(There were many critics of the report even within the USA. On 21 September 1999 it was announced that a three-year FBI investigation of an alleged Chinese spy at the Los Alamos National Laboratory had been so mismanaged that the bureau planned to restart the enquiry by examining more than 500 potential suspects at scores of sites across the USA: *IHT*, 24 September 1999, p. 12.)

15 July 1999.

China has designed a neutron bomb, the [government] report said, as well as miniaturized nuclear weapons ... Scientists have known for years that China had neutron weapon capability ... but Thursday [15 July] was the first time that China had publicly asserted owning such technology.

(*IHT*, 16 July 1999, p. 1)

2 August 1999. 'China test-launched a new type of long-range missile Monday [2 August] and ... excoriated the United States for selling military equipment to Taiwan ... The new missile ... is capable of reaching the United States' (*IHT*, 3 August 1999, p. 1).

25–26 August 1999. The presidents of Russia, China, Kazakhstan Kyrgyzstan and Tajikistan meet in Bishkek (the capital of Kyrgyzstan). The five countries are called the 'Shanghai Five', named after the Chinese city where a treaty on easing border tension was signed in 1996. A declaration is signed:

The importance of fighting international terrorism, the illegal drugs trade, arms trafficking, illegal migration and other forms of transborder crime, separatism and religious extremism [is stressed] ... The signatories also consider that creating a multi-polar world is the common path for development and will ensure long-term stability.

(*IHT*, 26 August 1999, p. i)

'Under pressure from Jiang Zemin, the following clause was inserted in the final Bishek document: "Human rights should not be used as a pretext for interfering in a state's internal affairs"' (*CDSP*, 1999, vol. 51, no. 34, p. 15).

2 September 1999. China and the USA announced that negotiations about China's bid to join the WTO are soon to resume. (They resumed on 12 September.)

11 September 1999. Presidents Jiang Zemin and Bill Clinton meet in New Zealand at the annual Apec summit.

19–22 September 1999. A Communist Party plenum is held.

Hu Jintao, fifty-six, already a politburo Standing Committee member and state vice-president, was named vice-chairman of the Central Military Commission, strengthening civilian leadership over the military – as well as speculation that Hu is firmly in line to succeed Communist Party general secretary Jiang Zemin.

(*FEER*, 7 October 1999, p. 14)

1 October 1999. The fiftieth anniversary of the establishment of the People's Republic of China is celebrated with a massive military and civilian parade.

'Among the ninety floats were separate portraits of Mao, Mr Deng and Mr Jiang, the first time the current leader has been placed on a par with his predecessors in such a public way' (Seth Faison, *IHT*, 2 October 1999, p. 4).

2–6 October 1999.

China and Russia held their first joint naval exercises. A guided-missile escort vessel from the Russian Pacific fleet took part in the 2–6 October manoeuvres, held 50 kilometres off Shanghai ... On 2 October China began ... unprecedented joint naval exercises with Russia.

(*FEER*, 14 October 1999, pp. 16, 27)

18–28 October 1999. Jiang Zemin visits the UK, France and Portugal. (He then visited Morocco, Algeria and Saudi Arabia.)

21 November 1999. China announces a successful launching (the previous day) and recovery of an unmanned spacecraft. The spacecraft is called *Shenzhou* ('magic vessel').

6 December 1999.

The World Bank is reviewing the policies that govern its lending to China ... in the light of the country's changed economic circumstances and the cessation of lending from the bank's soft-loan counter ... China 'graduated' in June this year [1999] from lending under the World Bank's International Development Association (IDA), which dispenses soft loans with long maturities to countries with a *per capita* income of less than $800 per year.

(*FT*, 7 December 1999, p. 14)

9 December 1999. President Yeltsin of Russia visits China and signs two border agreements with China. Provision is made for demarcation in the western region and along the eastern river frontiers. Economic co-operation across the border also featured (*Guardian*, 10 December 1999, p. 15; *IHT*, 10 December 1999, p. 5).

23–25 January 2000. A senior Chinese general visits the USA, the first military contact since the bombing of the Chinese embassy in Belgrade.

February 2000.

Preparations for the Sixteenth Party Congress in 2002 provided the impetus for the party to begin exploring ways to remake itself and adapt to the challenges

the twenty-first century ... The project was the brainchild of Jiang Zemin ...
In a late February [2000] speech in Guangdong province Jiang kicked off the
project by claiming that if the party could represent 'the development needs of
advanced forces of production', 'the forward direction of advanced culture'
and 'the fundamental interests of the broad masses' it would be 'forever unde-
featable'. The short version of that formulation was the 'Three Represents'.

(*FEER*, *Asia 2001 Yearbook*, December 2000, p. 107)

5–15 March 2000. The Third Session of the Ninth National People's Congress is
held.

Prime minister Zhu Rongyi gave the opening speech on 5 March. He stressed
the need for economic reform and to combat corruption:

[Industry and government should] lose no time [in preparing for membership
of the WTO... Fighting corruption is still a tough task ... Corruption and
undesirable practices have not been brought under control ... Unremitting
efforts [will be made to combat corruption] ... All major cases, no matter
which department or who is involved, must be thoroughly investigated and
corrupt officials must be severely punished ... [He attacked] travelling, enter-
taining and dining in luxurious style at public expense ... We still fall far short
of what the central authorities require of us and what the people expect of us
... We must resolutely put an end to the extravagance, waste and squandering
seen in some areas, departments and institutions. Such practices must be
stopped ... Bureaucracy, formalism, falsification and exaggeration are rampant
... In particular, leading cadres should stay clean and honest and self-
disciplined and be sure that their relatives and office staff do the same.

(*IHT*, 6 March 2000, p. 6, and 9 March 2000, p. 1; *FT*, 6 March 2000, p. 13;
Guardian, 6 March 2000, p. 17; *FEER*, 16 March 2000, p. 30)

'For the first time in China's communist era the government at this year's NPC
declined to set a precise target for economic growth' (*The Economist*, 11 March
2000, p. 84).

Budgetary defence spending is to increase by 12.7 per cent in 2000.

'Though much military spending is not revealed, the official figure for 2000 will
rise by 12.7 per cent to $14.6 billion' (*The Economist*, 11 March 2000, p. 84).

'China's military spending is still only about a tenth of what the United States
spends, or less than 2 per cent of the country's GDP' (Craig Smith, *IHT*, 20 March
2000, p. 3).

'China has deployed a minimal [nuclear] force, which consists primarily of
eighteen single warhead land-based CSS-4 missiles ... It also has twelve missiles
on a submarine that rarely strays far from its port' (*IHT*, 29 May 2000, p. 3).

8 March 2000. The former deputy governor of Jiangxi province, Hu Changqing,
is executed for corruption.

'China executed the highest official ever put to death for corruption in its fifty-
year history on Wednesday [8 March] ... for taking bribes worth more than
$600,000' (*IHT*, 9 March 2000, p. 1). 'He was executed after being found guilty of
taking about $660,000 in bribes and receiving property worth $200,000 in return

for issuing exit permits for people wanting to move to Hong Kong, as well as business licences' (*FEER*, 23 March 2000, p. 14).

The Communist Party announced on Thursday [20 April] that it had expelled a senior official in one of its biggest corruption cases. Cheng Kejie ... a deputy chairman of the national legislature ... is one of highest-ranking officials to fall foul of a nationwide campaign against wrongdoing.

(*IHT*, 21 April 2000, p. 4)

'The Communist Party expelled one of the most senior officials ever targeted for corruption. Cheng Kejie, a vice-chairman of the National People's Congress, will be prosecuted for allegedly taking $4.8 million in bribes' (*FEER*, 4 May 2000, p. 14).

In recent weeks Chinese authorities have executed two high-ranking officials on corruption charges; they have removed one of the top legislators from his post because he is being investigated for malfeasance. But they have also refused to release information about one of the nation's biggest smuggling scandals – a $10 billion ring based in the southern city of Xiamen – because the case has implicated a close political ally of President Jiang Zemin.

(*IHT*, 13 May 2000, p. 11)

('Major Case 4–20, so named because the party formed a task force on 20 April last year [1999] ... is being called the biggest smuggling scandal since the revolution in 1949 ... Among the suspects are Lin Youfang, the wife of Jia Qinglin, the Communist Party secretary of Beijing [who has been a Jiang ally since the mid-1960s] ... and relatives of a former member of the Politburo and Central Military Commission ... Many inquiries are stopped halfway for fear of roiling the upper echelons of the party and the military': *IHT*, 24 January 2000, p. 8. 'For the past week rumours have circulated in Beijing that the wife of the city's Communist Party chief had been detained as part of an investigation in the southern province of Fujian. Communist Party sources said the party chief, Jia Qinglin, had been forced to divorce Lin Youfang, his wife of thirty years ... But now the government and Ms Lin have strongly denied all the allegations ... A principal government press office [said] ... "Mme Lin Youfang has no links whatsoever to the Xiamen smuggling case and is not at all involved"': *IHT*, 27 January 2000, p. 5.)

14 May 2000. President Jiang Zemin orders the Communist Party to set up cells in the private sector (*IHT*, 16 May 2000, p. 8).

'Mr Jiang said that private companies needed party help "to guarantee the healthy development of the sector" and that cells "should work hard to unite and educate entrepreneurs to advocate various policies of the party"' (*FEER*, 1 June 2000, p. 8).

7 July 2000. China and the USA resume arms control talks frozen since the bombing of the Chinese embassy in Belgrade. Military contracts were resumed in January 2000 with the visit of a senior Chinese general to the USA (*FT*, 8 July 2000, p. 7).

11–13 July 2000. US secretary of defence William Cohen visits China.

18 July 2000. President Putin of Russia and President Jiang Zemin sign a joint statement during the former's 17–19 July visit to China:

The [US] plan to develop a national missile defence system (NMD) seeks unilateral military and security advantages that will pose the most grave, adverse consequences not only to the national security of Russia and China and other countries but to the security and international strategic stability of the US itself ... [It] will trigger a new arms race ... [Incorporating Taiwan] in any foreign missile defence system is unacceptable.

China is opposed to the US proposal to set up a national missile defence (NMD) system, a missile shield to defend the whole of US territory against a small number of strategic (intercontinental) nuclear missiles from what are now called 'states of concern' (formerly 'rogue states) such as North Korea, Iran and Iraq. China is concerned that its own, relatively limited number of nuclear missiles will become less effective. China is also concerned about a possible US theatre missile defence (TMD) system in Asia which it feels could be extended to cover Taiwan.

(On 1 September 2000 Bill Clinton announced that a decision regarding deployment of the NMD would be left to his successor as US president. Factors included technical failures during tests.)

31 July 2000.

China sentenced a former central government official to death Monday [31 July] for taking almost $5 million in bribes, the highest profile case yet in the country's marathon anti-corruption drive. The former official, Cheng Kejie, who until April was one of nineteen deputy chairmen of the National People's Congress ... would be the most senior Chinese official executed for corruption since the communists first took power in 1949. Mr Cheng was found guilty of taking bribes while he ran the Guangxi Zhuang Autonomous Region, a poor, mountainous province bordering Vietnam and populated largely by ethnic minorities, including the Zhuang people. Mr Cheng is a Zhuang, the largest ethnic group in China after the Han ... There has been almost no media coverage of the country's biggest ongoing corruption case, which centres on the smuggling of hundreds of millions of firearms, cars and crude oil through a south-eastern port. The case has reportedly implicated 200 people, including Xiamen police officers, bankers and customs agents, and the former wife of a Communist Party Politburo member. She has denied any wrongdoing. According to widespread rumours, the case also implicates Ji Shengde, the former head of the army's intelligence department and son of one of China's most vaunted revolutionary leaders ... Many of the largest corruption cases involve border areas with rampant corruption that depends on the collusion of local officials.

(*IHT*, 1 August 2000, pp. 1, 5)

Cheng ... was convicted for 'soliciting and accepting bribery' from 1992 to 1998 during his tenure as chairman of the Guangxi provincial government ... Bar an unlikely stay of execution, Cheng Kejie will become the highest-ranking official to be executed for corruption since the Communist Party took power in 1949.

(*Independent*, 1 August 2000, p. 13)

Cheng Kejie was executed on 14 September 2000.

2 August 2000. A US navy cruiser begins a visit to a naval port in China, 'the first visit to China by a US warship in two years' (*IHT*, 3 August 2000, p. 7).

1 November 2000. A new national census begins. This is the fifth, the others being in 1953, 1964, 1982 and 1990. Smaller samples have been taken in between the national ones.

9 November 2000. Eighty-four people are convicted of corruption and embezzlement. Fourteen death sentences are handed out, although three people are granted a two-year reprieve (which usually means death sentences being commuted to life sentences in prison). The remaining eleven include the former deputy major of Xiamen, the former deputy head of the public security bureau for Fujian province, the former head of Xiamen customs and the head of the Industrial and Commercial Bank of China in Xiamen. Also handed down were twelve life sentences and fifty-eight fixed-term prison sentences. But the businessman who is said to have masterminded the scheme has fled the country (*FT*, 9 November 2000, p. 20; *IHT*, 9 November 2000, p. 8; *Independent*, 9 November 2000, p. 15; *FEER*, 30 November 2000, p. 15).

The Xiamen case ... [is] the biggest corruption case exposed since ... 1949 ... in which up to $10 billion in cars, oil and several other goods were brought into China over several years ... Nevertheless, official sources said the relatives of top Communist Party and military figures have been spared investigation, indicating that high-level political connections can still be a shield against the law ... Those sentenced to death ... were middle-ranking officials.

(*FT*, 9 November 2000, p. 20)

'[These represent] the first punishments meted out in connection with an embarrassing multi-billion-dollar smuggling scandal in the port city of Xiamen in Fujian province' (*IHT*, 9 November 2000, p. 8).

'If deputy party secretaries and vice-mayors were bribed ... most observers conclude that more senior officials must have known something ... So far, though, the party has drawn the line at pursuing them' (*FEER*, 30 November 2000, p. 16).

China's justice minister has been removed from his post and is under investigation for 'economic irregularities', making him one of the most senior officials to fall victim to a widening crackdown on official excesses. Gao Changli left the ministry on Monday [27 November] ... The manner of his detention and investigation suggested he might be under suspicion for some form of corruption ... [Some say] Mr Gao's problems stemmed from poor relations with senior members of the Communist Party.

(*FT*, 2 December 2000, p. 10)

The Chinese minister of justice ... has been relieved of his duties ... A Hong Kong newspaper reported Thursday [30 November] that Mr Gao was under investigation for 'economic and political problems' ... If Mr Gao falls from power he would become one of the most senior government figures to be ensnared in the current campaign to stamp out official corruption ... But it remains unclear how high up the political hierarchy Chinese investigators will be allowed to go. Many analysts maintain that the crackdown will never touch close associates of President Jiang Zemin or other top leaders and that the fight against corruption is sometimes simply a proxy for political infighting. When a senior official is arrested, they say, it means he has fallen out of favour with the leadership and lost his protection from prosecution . . . [Gao Changli is] best known for a widely publicised campaign to improve the country's weak legal system . . . He has also spoken out against corrupt judicial officials.

(*IHT*, 2 December 2000, p. 4)

21 November 2000.

President Bill Clinton's administration has announced a waiver of penalties against China for supplying missile parts to Iran and Pakistan after Chinese officials formally pledged to end the practice . . . The imposition of sanctions would have barred US–Chinese co-operation on commercial space ventures, such as launches of US satellites on Chinese rockets, which are a major source of hard currency for China . . . The announcement of the waiver was timed to coincide with a declaration Tuesday [21 November] by the Chinese foreign ministry. 'China has no intention to assist, in any way, any country in the development of ballistic missiles that can be used to deliver nuclear weapons,' the ministry said in Beijing. China pledged to put into effect a formal system of export controls, including restrictions on 'dual use' technology, those with military and civilian applications.

(*IHT*, 23 November 2000, p. 5)

9 January 2001.

A trove of newly released documents reveals the secret conversations of top Chinese leaders as they battled one another over the decision to crush the student-led protests around Tiananmen Square . . . during the spring of 1989 . . . The compilation is being published as a book entitled 'The Tiananmen Papers' . . . The documents . . . shed light on the decisive role played by . . . Deng Xiaoping and a group of eight retired and semi-retired 'elders' who wielded ultimate power in the Chinese Communist Party . . . The documents were spirited out of China by a Chinese official who wants to promote political reform. He wants to remain anonymous. The documents were translated by two leading American scholars, Andrew Nathan of Columbia University and Perry Link of Princeton University . . . The documents confirm that Li Peng, who was prime minister at the time, led the internal campaign to crack down on the students . . . Li Peng spurred the elders' support for a crackdown . . . They show that the party's standing committee was indeed split over whether to continue dialogue with the students, with only two of the five committee members voting for martial law and one abstaining. And they show Mr Deng as having little sympathy for the demonstrators . . . The documents confirm that Zhao Ziyang, who was the Communist Party's general-secretary at the time, consistently opposed martial law . . . Mr Deng convened the elders and they voted to install . . . Jiang Zemin, then Shanghai party chief . . . as general-secretary, a decision that theoretically should have been made by the standing committee. The leaders also reshuffled the rest of the committee, ousting Hu Qili, an ally of Mr Zhao's, and adding others to bring the committee membership up to seven. Mr Zhao remains under loose house arrest ... Qiao Shi, the intelligence chief who had previously abstained in the martial law vote, endorsed an immediate army crackdown ... [The documents] do not offer new information about how many people died in the massacre; the Chinese government number of 218 civilians is widely considered too low.

(*IHT*, 8 January 2001, pp. 1, 9)

The documents [are] carried in the American journal *Foreign Affairs* ... Mr Li comes across as a manipulator intent on crushing the demonstrators by violent means. It is Mr Li who brings his colleagues a report of the casualties in the operation: 200 civilians and twenty-three soldiers killed, figures much lower than the estimates of most independent observers.

(*Independent*, 8 January 2001, p. 13)

'[On 9 January] the Chinese government ... [described the claim as a] "fabrication" ... Casualty estimates run from 200 to 2000 dead and wounded' (*Independent*, 10 January 2001, p. 14; *Foreign Affairs*, 2001, vol. 80, no. 1).

Extracts will be published tomorrow [9 January 2001] ... Deng, although he had officially retired from office ... had the final say ... Deng and the elders ... [were] entitled to intervene in the event of a committee stalemate ... The documents put the death toll in the region of 200 – fewer than most estimates though independent scholars no longer believe claims that thousands died.

(*Guardian*, 8 January 2001, p. 15)

'The government on Tuesday [8 January] ... suggested that the papers are fake ... It was the first official reaction to the papers, which were said to have been smuggled out of China by a disgruntled civil servant' (*IHT*, 9 January 2001, p. 1).

The book, *The Tiananmen Papers*, is compiled by Zhang Liang (a pseudonym), edited by Andrew. J. Nathan and Perry Link and published by Public Affairs. Jonathan Mirsky provides a detailed review of the book and examines the question of the authenticity of the papers in *The New York Review of Books* (2001, vol. XLVIII, no. 2, pp. 25–8).

The Standing Committee were not unanimous on what to do ... Three of them wanted to reassure the students that there would be a great campaign against corruption. They included prime minister Zhao Ziyang, Hu Qili, the party official in charge of ideology and propaganda, and the security chief Qiao Shi.

(p. 28)

During those turbulent days in the spring of 1989 China was under the control not of its usual high party officials, led by the five-member Standing Committee of the Politburo, but of eight 'elders' ... When it became clear that at least two if not three Standing Committee members were unwilling to take a harsh line with the students, the eighty-five-year-old Deng summoned six elders from retirement. (Deng and President Yang Shangkun still held official positions.).

(p. 25)

According to official figures, '218 civilians had been killed, including thirty-six students, and 7,000 people wounded (5,000 of whom were soldiers)' (p. 28).

10 January 2001.

> China launched a spacecraft carrying animals and microbes into orbit around the Earth on Wednesday [10 January], taking a significant step forward in its quest to join the United States and Russia as the only nations to send humans into space ... The long-awaited launching begins China's second test of a ship designed to carry humans into space ... The first test [was] in late 1999.
>
> (*IHT*, 11 January 2001, p. 5)

> The highly secretive Chinese space programme has never before publicly claimed to have sent live animals into space, but a Chinese aeronautical expert said last March that the country had sent into space and recovered a rat, a rabbit and a dog in a series of test flights since 1997.
>
> (*Telegraph*, 11 January 2001, p. 17)

March 2001.

> The Chinese Communist Party is debating whether to drop its ban on private enterprise owners being allowed to join its ranks ... Rules formulated in 1989 specifically bar private enterprise bosses from joining the party ... 'Between private enterprise owners and workers there in fact exists the relationship between an exploiter and the exploited. Private enterprise owners cannot be absorbed into the party,' says Communist Party Central Committee Document No. 9, issued on 28 August 1989 ... For those already in the party there are strict demands, including 'voluntary acceptance of supervision from party organizations' and agreeing to put the 'vast majority' of after-tax profits into a fund for further developing the business and for public welfare. Violators are not allowed to stay in the party ... The party does not make public how many private enterprise heads are also party members. Many ... joined before entering the private sector. Others were recruited in the 1990s ... The party wants private businesses to have party organizations ... The party's lingering suspicion towards the private economy still keeps private businesses out of lucrative sectors that the party deems strategically sensitive ... As part of its WTO agreement with the United States China agreed to allow foreign companies to invest in its telecom companies, while it still prohibits Chinese private businesses from doing the same.
>
> (Susan Lawrence, *FEER*, 8 March 2001, pp. 14–17)

5–15 March 2001. The annual session of the National People's Congress takes place.

Prime minister Zhu Rongyi (5 March): '[The government] must hold a controlling stake in strategic enterprises that concern the national economy, but not necessarily in others' (*IHT*, 6 March 2001, p. 5). His speech emphasized the problems facing China and the need for continued reforms.

The official defence budget was to rise by 17.7 per cent in 2001, compared with 12.7 per cent in 2000. The GDP growth target for 2001 was set at 7 per cent.

(*IHT*, 7 March 2001, pp. 1, 5; *FT*, 7 March 2001, p. 12; *The Times*, 7 March 2001, p. 19; *Guardian*, 7 March 2001, p. 19.)

6 March 2001.

> An explosion ripped through a rural elementary school in south-eastern China [in the province of Jiangxi] where third graders were forced to make firecrackers for teachers seeking extra cash ... The blast killed at least thirty-seven children and four teachers ... The explosion ... underscores both the widespread practice of child labour in China and a crisis in primary education ... China used to provide nine years of free education for its children. That practice ended in the early 1990s ... While Chinese officials still claim that primary education is free in China, the reality is otherwise ... Since the 1980s the central government has encouraged schools to go into business to supplement dwindling resources.
>
> (*IHT*, 8 March 2001, pp. 1, 5)

(The final toll was forty-two. 'The government's initial finding was that a suicidal madman caused the explosion.' But the government was to make further inquiries: *IHT*, 16 March 2001, p. 6.)

'As the central government does not put any funds into primary education, it is up to local authorities to raise the cash for the nine-year compulsory education' (*The Times*, 8 March 2001, p. 15).

'Rural schools have been badly hit by economic reforms which have shifted education budgets on to local governments, which are often unable to pay teachers their full salary or buy equipment' (*Guardian*, 8 March 2001, p. 9).

'Many rural families struggle to pay [school] fees ... Third-grade pupils [are] aged between eight and nine' (*Telegraph*, 8 March 2001, p. 13).

16 March 2001. Four explosions rip through accommodation blocks owned by cotton enterprises, killing 108 people. The blasts occurred in Shijiazhuang, the provincial capital of Hebei province. Rumours attached blame to various sources, including disgruntled workers dismissed by the enterprises, crime and corruption. One person was arrested later on and was said to have confessed. The official explanation was that his motive was revenge on relatives who lived in the buildings. (In April he was sentenced to death. Three others were also sentenced to death for allegedly supplying explosives and detonators.)

28 March 2001. Results from the fifth national population census held on 1 November 2000 are announced.

> China yesterday [28 March] hailed the preliminary results of its latest census, which recorded a population on the mainland of 1.265 billion, as well within the government's planned ceiling of 1.3 billion by the year 2000 ... The figures followed preliminary results from India's 2001 census this week that ... [shows a population of] 1.027 billion ...China is now willing to acknowledge the problem of its millions of 'missing baby girls' ... but they do not accept that widespread infanticide is the product of the one-child policy instituted two decades ago.
>
> (*FT*, 29 March 2001, p. 13)

'About 36 per cent of the population now lives in cities and towns, an increase of nearly 10 percentage points since 1990 ... The fertility rate, which was four births for each mother in 1970, fell to 1.8 last year [2000]' (*FT*, 31 March 2001, p. 13).

> The world's largest population grew by 132.2 million after 1990 ... said ... the director of the national bureau of statistics. Annual growth was 1.07 per cent – down 0.4 per cent from the rate in the 1980s ... The census shows that China's population is becoming more educated and more urbanized, even though most Chinese – 64 per cent – still live in the countryside ... A 1999 survey found there were 117 male births for every 100 girls – up from a ration of 111 boys to 100 girls in the 1990 census ... He said women may be using ultrasound to detect and abort female babies and that families may not be reporting female babies to the authorities ... Hong Kong ... [has] a population of 6.8 million ... Macau ... 440,000 ... and Taiwan 22.3 million.
>
> (*IHT*, 29 March 2001, p. ii)

'The director of the ... National Bureau of Statistics ... said this showed China's compulsory birth control policies were effective in holding down population growth' (*FEER*, 12 April 2001, p. 12).

1 April 2001. A US surveillance plane and a Chinese fighter plane collide in international airspace over the South China Sea south-east of Hainan Island. The Chinese plane crashes and the US plane is forced to make an emergency landing in Hainan Island. China claims the area as its air space. A diplomatic row ensued and there was disagreement about the cause of the accident. The crew flew home to the USA on 12 April. The diplomacy was handled by Hu Jintao while President Jiang Zemin was abroad. (He left for a twelve-day visit to Latin America, including Cuba, on 4 April.) The relatively satisfactory outcome to the negotiations after early friction was generally seen as a plus for Hu Jintao, generally considered to be Jiang Zemin's favourite to succeed him. (On 24 May China said it was prepared to let the USA dismantle the plane and take it home in pieces. The pieces were returned to the USA on 5 July.)

The incident was complicated by the recent arrest by China of several academics with US citizenship or residency status (e.g. on 11 February and 25 February) and the defection of a Chinese military officer to the USA (seemingly in December 2000). There was speculation that China was searching for academics connected with the publication of *The Tiananmen Papers*. (See the entry for 9 January 2001.)

(The USA resumed surveillance flights off the Chinese coast on 7 May: *IHT*, 8 May 2001, p. 6.)

29 April 2001. 'The Chinese parliament has passed legal provisions prohibiting bigamy and cohabitation outside marriage' (*IHT*, 30 April 2001, p. 9).

> A controversial marriage law passed in China at the weekend takes aim at the rampant concubinage corrupting the morals of the communist elite ... The revised law ... is 'against bigamy, against a married person cohabiting with somebody else [and] against behaviour that is not conducive to monogamy'. But while bigamy is punishable by imprisonment under criminal law, the risks associated with keeping a concubine appear rather mild. The worst outcome,

the new law indicates, is that a concubine's patron may be forced to pay compensation to his wife if she decides to divorce him ... Many [concubines]
double as secretaries and housemaids ... Commentators said the government's motivation in moving against concubinage was to cleanse the morals
of China's mandarinate. In many recent cases philandering officials have been
lured into embezzling state funds by the high maintenance costs of keeping
mistresses ... A recent study by the country's disciplinary commission found
that 95 per cent of officials convicted of corruption in southern China supported mistresses ... There is no specific punishment for marital rape
although compensation can be claimed for 'spouse abuse' – but only upon
divorce.

(*FT*, 30 April 2001, p. 10)

May 2001.

At the end of last year [2000] China's Academy of Social Sciences conducted
a survey of mid-ranking officials attending the Central Party School, the training centre for China's ruling elite. It found that political reform had displaced
reform of state enterprises as their foremost concern ... The academy's report
said the interest shown in this subject reflected 'new contradictions and problems' in Chinese society – the euphemism for corruption, unemployment and
unrest. 'If there are no channels for letting off steam, the repressed discontent
of individuals could well up into large-scale social instability,' concluded a
report published in May by the party's Organizational Department. What is the
party doing about this? So far, very little. President Jiang Zemin ... early last
year [2000] ... rolled out a new theory called the 'Three Represents'. According to this, the party stands for 'advanced productive forces, advanced Chinese
culture and the fundamental interests of the majority' ... Mr Jiang appeared to
be redefining the party as everybody's best friend, not just the proletariat's ...
The party still cannot decide whether to let private businessmen join the ranks
of its 65 million members ... In fact, nearly a fifth of the more than 1.5 million
owners of private companies are party members anyway ... In 1991 China had
about 107,000 private businesses (defined as those with more than eight
workers), employing 1.8 million people. Today more than 24 million people
work in such enterprises, and perhaps another 30 million run smaller, or individual, concerns. Yet private businessmen are still officially barred from
joining the party.

(*The Economist*, 30 June 2001, pp. 25–6)

The depth of China's internal problems was confirmed in a remarkably candid
report published last month [June] by a group under the Communist Party's
Central Committee. It details mounting and increasingly confrontational
'collective protests and group incidents' on a greater scale than had otherwise
been reported. It cites corruption as 'the main fuse exacerbating conflicts
between officials and the masses' and adds that those involved 'are expanding
from farmers and retired workers to include workers still on the job, individual
business owners, decommissioned soldiers and even officials, teachers and

students ... If there are no channels for the letting off of steam, the repressed discontent of individuals could well up into large-scale social instability.'

(*IHT*, 18 July 2001, p. 7)

5 June 2001.

A leaked text of an address given by Zhu Rongyi ... on 5 June [included the statement that] it was necessary to be 'safe and slow down somewhat a few major reforms in light of the current situation'. Mr Zhu indicated that one casualty would be the government's plans to promote badly needed tax reforms in the countryside. The aim of these is to eliminate various fees and levies arbitrarily imposed on farmers by local authorities and rely instead on a single tax based on income from crop production ... As an experiment China made changes to the taxes levied in rural Anhui province in early 2000. These have exacerbated other problems ... [e.g. plummeting] revenues of village-level governments ... The original plan had been to extend the tax experiment to most of the rest of the country this year [2001] ... Other reforms to be slowed down ... are plans to impose a fuel tax in place of the random charges imposed on vehicle owners by local governments, as well as the introduction of a social security system that will remove the burden on employers to provide welfare benefits.

(*The Economist*, 16 June 2001, p. 72)

[There has been] a temporary slowdown in some important reforms ... [including] the 'tax-free conversion programme' designed to reduce illegal levies on farmers, the introduction of a fuel tax and the transition of the urban social security programme towards a near fully funded system.

(Deutsche Bank, *Global Markets Research: Emerging Markets*, July 2001, p. 11)

1 July 2001.

In a significant reversal of policy ... President Jiang Zemin announced Sunday [1 July] that private business could join the party. Mr Jiang made his announcement in a speech to commemorate the party's eightieth anniversary ... Mr Jiang stressed that the party would still be based on 'workers, farmers, intellectuals, servicemen and cadres'. However, he added 'it is also necessary to accept those outstanding elements from other sectors of the society' ... Thousands of entrepreneurs have already entered the ranks – about 113,000, according to a senior party theoretician. Most of these people were party members before they started businesses. Mr Jiang's announcement constitutes part of a reform package for the party, which has more than 64 million members. The package, called the 'Three Represents', argues ... that the Chinese Communist Party should represent the interests of all of Chinese society ... A report issued in May [2001] by a Central Committee research unit spoke of tense relations between the party and the people. The report, '2000–2001: Study of Contradictions within the People under New Conditions' ... spoke about the collapse of state-owned industry, a social security safety net incapable of dealing with millions of unemployed. strained relations with China's ethnic minorities, a restive peasantry increasingly willing to take up arms against the system and an unjust legal system. To quash debate about these issues Mr Jiang has recently ordered an intensive crackdown on China's state-run media.

(John Pomfret, *IHT*, 2 July 2001, pp. 1, 4)

'[Jiang Zemin's] theory, called the "three represents", asserts that the party must represent "advanced productive forces, advanced Chinese culture and the fundamental interests of the majority"' (*IHT*, 17 August 2001, p. 6).

Jiang recently announced that private business people should be welcomed into the party, reversing his veto on the proposal to allow millionaires to join after it was first made in 1988. According to some estimates, one-fifth of the one and a half million owners of private enterprises are party members already.

(Stephen Green, *The World Today*, 2001, vol. 57, no. 10, p. 25)

According to ... Xu Yaotong, chairman of the political teaching department at China's National School of Administration, the country's top training ground for state officials ... official surveys show that the party already has among its members anywhere between 20,000 private-business leaders (according to the party's Organization Department) and 300,000 (according to the semi-official Federation of Industry and Commerce). Most joined when they were working for the state and kept their memberships when they moved into the private sector ... [There are an] estimated 4.5 million private-enterprise leaders ... [The party has] 64 million members.

(*FEER*, 18 October 2001, p. 40)

13 July 2001. It is announced that the 2008 Summer Olympic Games are to be held in Beijing.

In round one Beijing received forty-four votes out of a possible 105 cast by the International Olympic Committee. Toronto came second with twenty votes, Istanbul third with seventeen votes, Paris fourth with fifteen votes and Osaka, with six votes, was eliminated. In round two Beijing received fifty-six votes, Toronto twenty-two, Paris eighteen and Istanbul nine.

In 1993 Beijing was second in the bidding to host the 2000 Summer Olympic Games, two votes behind Sydney. Beijing did not bid for the 2004 Games, which went to Athens.

The modern Olympic Games began in Athens in 1896, but China did not participate until 1932 in Los Angeles, where it sent a single athlete ... After the Communist Party took power in 1949 China stopped competing and did not return until 1984 in Los Angeles. China won fifteen gold medals in those games, which were devalued by a Soviet boycott. Last year [2000] in Sydney the Chinese finished third in the medals table, with twenty-eight gold medals, sixteen silvers and fifteen bronze ... Doping scandals have tarnished the country's reputation ... [but] in the last four years ... Chinese officials have cracked down on the use of performance-enhancing substances ... But the drug issue was not as powerful or emotional an issue in the lead up to Friday's vote as human rights.

(IHT, 14 July 2001, pp. 1, 16)

15 July 2001.

China has convicted an American business professor of spying for Taiwan and ordered him to be expelled. The decision . . . resolved the first of several cases . . . The professor, Li Shaomin, a naturalized American citizen who was born in China and had been teaching in Hong Kong, had been held since 25 February, when he was arrested in southern China . . . [A number of] American citizens and permanent US residents . . . have been arrested in China on spy charges . . . At least four other Chinese-born scholars [other than Li Shaomin] with ties to the United States are awaiting trial on spy charges in China. Among them is Gao Zhan . . . She was picked up on 11 February.

(IHT, 16 July 2001, p. 4)

15–18 July 2001. President Jiang Zemin visits Russia. On 16 July a twenty-year Good Neighbourly Treaty of Friendship and Co-operation was signed, the first being signed by China and the Soviet Union in 1950. The treaty included the following:

[Russia and China] pledge not to use force or the threat of force in their mutual relations, not to use economic or other means of pressure against each other, and to resolve differences solely by peaceful means in accordance with the provisions of the UN Charter and other generally recognized principles and rules of international law . . . In case of the emergence of the threat of aggression, the two sides shall immediately make contact with each other and carry out consultations in order to eliminate the emerging threat . . . [The treaty is] not directed against third countries . . . [The two sides] stand for strict observance of the generally recognized principles and norms of international law against any actions aimed at forced pressure or at interference, under any pretext, into the domestic affairs of sovereign states . . . Russia and China stress the basic importance of the Anti-Ballistic Missile Treaty, which is the cornerstone of strategic stability and the basis for reducing offensive weapons, and speak out for maintaining the treaty in its current form . . . The government of the People's Republic of China is the sole legitimate government representing the whole of China . . . Taiwan is an integral part of China.

The treaty promises closer economic, security and cultural ties . . . The treaty bars Russia and China from concluding other treaties with third countries threatening the 'sovereignty, security or territorial integrity' of the other signatory . . . The countries declare they have no 'territorial claims' on one another. They promise to resolve by negotiation remaining disagreements over two small sections of the common border . . . China is already the largest export market for Russian arms . . . China takes roughly a quarter of Russia's $4 billion annual arms exports. Total official two-way trade between China and

Russia reached $8 billion last year [2000], though unofficial border trade may be worth half as much again.

(*FT*, 17 July 2001, p. 10)

'Aside from a few disputed islands in the Amur River, which marks the border, the 2,500-mile frontier has been recognized by both countries' (*The Times*, 17 July 2001, p. 16).

[Only] 2 per cent of the approximately 4,000-kilometre border remains in dispute. This includes two islands in the Amur river and one in the Argun. Under treaties signed by Tsarist Russia and imperial China the border ran along the Chinese bank, which meant that all of the islands were considered Russian. Under Khrushchev, however, Moscow acknowledged that this was unfair and that the border should run through the main navigating channel. Thus arose the problem of the islands.

(*CDSP*, 2001, vol. 53, no. 29, p. 1)

The treaty ... said two sections of the 4,259 kilometre border had yet to be agreed and would remain the subject of negotiations. The more delicate of these points ... consists of two islands, Bolshoi Ussuri and Tarabarov, lying off Khabarovsk where the Amur and Ussuri rivers meet. Russia took them, along with other strategic islands in the Amur and Ussuri, when it fortified the border in the 1930s, despite claims that they lay on the Chinese side of the river.

(*FT*, 27 August 2001, p. 14)

'China's trade with Russia last year [2000] was $8 billion, while Chinese–US trade came to nearly $120 billion' (*CDSP*, 2001, vol. 53, no. 29, p. 1).

The treaty ... covers politics, economy, trade, science and technology, culture and more ... Despite recent agreements delineating almost the entire China–Russia border, there is still deep suspicion in Russia's Far East of China's territorial ambitions ... Trade [between China and Russia] ... is worth $8 billion annually ... [but] China's trade with the USA is worth over $110 billion and climbing rapidly.

(*FEER*, 26 July 2001, p. 15)

On 16 July 2001 Russian President Vladimir Putin and Chinese President Jiang Zemin signed the Good Neighbourly Treaty of Friendship and Co-operation, replacing the outdated 1950 version that expired in 1980 ... The overall trade turnover between Russia and China was about $8 billion in 2000 and it is expected to have topped $10 billion last year [2001]. In comparison with the US–Chinese annual trade volume of $120 billion the Russian–Chinese trade activity seems puny. However, the statistics do not reflect the real cross-border 'grey economic activities' in the neighbouring regions. And one should not forget that annual US–Russian trade amounted to only $10 billion.

(*Rusi Newsbrief*, 2001, vol. 22, no. 1, pp. 9–10)

[On 17 July] Russian and Chinese officials ... agreed to formulate a plan for a long-discussed oil $1.7 billion pipeline to carry oil from Siberia to north-eastern China ... The 2,400-kilometre (1,500-mile) pipeline could be completed as early as 2005 and ship 20 million tonnes (147 million barrels) a year to China.

(*IHT*, 18 July 2001, p. 5)

24 July 2001.

A US-based sociologist and another scholar with US ties were convicted of espionage ... and both sentenced to ten years in prison ... Gao Zhan, a researcher based at American University, and Qin Guangguang, a pharmaceutical company executive who has taught at Stanford and other US universities, 'collected intelligence for spy agencies in Taiwan, causing a serious threat to China's national security', according to the Xinhua new agency. A third Chinese intellectual and a longtime friend of Mrs Gao, Qu Wei, was sentenced to thirteen years in prison ... Mrs Gao and Mr Qin are Chinese citizens who hold American green cards ... They are among at least six US citizens and permanent residents detained by China ... Mrs Gao ... was detained on 11 February ... Mr Qin has been held since December ... The case against Mrs Gao appeared to turn on academic papers she obtained from Mr Qu and gave to another friend, Li Shaomin ... A Beijing court convicted him of spying for Taiwan on 14 July and ordered him deported, but China has still not released him.

(*IHT*, 25 July, 2001, pp. 1, 5)

25 July 2001. Li Shaomin ... was released on Wednesday [25 July] and flew back to the United States' (*IHT*, 26 July 2001, p. 8). (Li Shaomin returned to Hong Kong on 30 July and on 3 August City University voted to allow him to retain his post teaching marketing.)

26 July 2001.

Gao Zhan ... flew to Detroit [USA] on Thursday [26 July] ... Mrs Gao, a Chinese citizen employed as a researcher at American University in Washington, was granted medical parole by the Chinese government ... Another permanent US resident, Qin Guangguang, was also released. Mr Qin, who has done research for several leading American universities, decided to remain in China ... China released the two scholars just days before [US secretary of state] Colin Powell is scheduled to visit Beijing [arriving on 28 July] ... [The USA has] expressed concern about other cases, too. They include Wu Jianmin, a US citizen detained but not yet charged, Liu Yaping, a US resident held in Inner Mongolia ... and Teng Chunyan, a US resident and Falun Gong follower.

(*IHT*, 27 July 2001, pp. 1, 10)

('Mr Qin ... is expected to leave China for the United States next week. Fearing that he will never be able to see his mother again once he leaves China this time, he has gone to visit her in rural Sichuan province': *IHT*, 28 July 2001, p. 5.)

'China granted her [Mrs Gao] medical parole for what her lawyers said was a heart condition. Medical parole was also granted to Qin Guangguang' (*FT*, 27 July 2001, p. 9).

28 July 2001. US secretary of state Colin Powell visits China.

'China agreed to resume a dialogue with the USA on human rights that was frozen after Nato bombers struck the Chinese embassy in Belgrade in 1999' (*FT*, 2 August 2001, p. 7).

1 August 2001.

A Chinese-born American writer detained in China was formally arrested on charges of endangering China's security, an America diplomat said Wednesday [1 August]. Wu Jianmin, detained in April [8 April], was arrested on 26 May on charges of collecting information that endangered state security ... Qin Guangguang left China on Wednesday.

(*IHT*, 2 August 2001, p. 4)

'[On 2 August] the Chinese foreign ministry confirmed ... that Wu Jianmin ... had been charged with spying for Taiwan' (*IHT*, 3 August 2001, p. 5). 'About 50,000 Chinese students go to American colleges today. That is an increase of 10,000 over the past twelve years' (*IHT*, 2 August 2001, p. 7).

(Wu Jianmin was released on 28 September 2001 and left China. President George W. Bush was scheduled to meet Jiang Zemin at a summit meeting of the Asia-Pacific Economic Co-operation forum in Shanghai on 20 October.)

15 August 2001.

Jiang Zemin's ... decision last month [July] to allow private entrepreneurs to become Communist Party members ... has drawn fierce criticism from the party's old guard, led by Deng Liqun ... An ideological monthly and bastion of the old guard, *The Pursuit of Truth*, was closed this month [August] after publishing a number of articles critical of Mr Jiang and his policies, Chinese academics said yesterday [15 August].

(*FT*, 16 August 2001, p. 6)

The shutdown is the first to come to light since party propaganda chiefs gave warning last month [July] that they would close journals that broke rules called the 'seven nos'. These forbid spreading 'rumours', publishing articles contrary to Marxist theory, endangering state security and harming national ethnic unity.

(*Telegraph*, 16 August 2001, p. 13)

He [Jiang Zemin] shut down the critical leftwing magazine, *Zhenli de Zhuiqiu* (The Search for the Truth) ... The controversial change ... to allow private business leaders to join the Communist Party for the first time since its founding ... is expected to be inscribed in the party constitution later this year.

(*FEER*, 30 August 2001, p. 18)

16 August 2001.

In the late 1950s, at the time of the Great Leap Forward, China established its *hukou*, or household registration system, which required people to live and work only where they were officially permitted to ... According to official estimates, China's migrant labour force now numbers somewhere around

100 million. The government expects another 46 million to come looking for jobs in the city in the next five years as the number of surplus rural workers swells to 150 million ... China announced on 16 August that it plans to revamp the registration system ... The government is working on a plan that will do away with migration restriction over the next five years ... On 27 August the ministry of public security, the main administrator of the *hukou* system, confirmed its support for the reforms.

(*The Economist*, 1 September 2001, p. 54)

From 1 October residents of rural China will be able to apply for 'residence permits' in smaller cities if they can prove a legal home and a stable source of income in their new urban environment. The planned changes represent one of the most significant reforms thus far to ... [the] *hukou* (residence permit) system ... It is believed to have been first formulated during the Han dynasty around 2,000 years ago ... Its pervasiveness has in recent years been eroded by various economic imperatives ... On the black market in Beijing each permit is currently worth around 100,000 renminbi ... The changes planned in October are prompted by economic necessity. The number of excess workers in rural areas already exceeds 150 million, according to conservative official estimates. In addition, farming is expected to become less labour-intensive as the imperative for efficiency grows with China's [prospective] entry into the WTO.

(*FT*, 30 August 2001, p. 9)

China ... says it needs to build thousands of [up to 12,000] new towns to provide ... migrant workers ... with work ... The migrant work force in China's cities is estimated at 100 million – although no one knows for sure ... The migrants must obtain temporary permits without which they may be sent back to the countryside. However, a central planning commission in Beijing said that it was working on a scheme to abolish restrictions within five years ... Beijing introduces a tentative reform today [1 October] to grant permanent residency to a small number of rural entrepreneurs who have made good [in terms of taxes paid and jobs provided] in the city.

(*Guardian*, 1 October 2001, p. 17)

The central government announced its intention to conduct a gradual overhaul of the *hukou* system, which is a holdover from the 1950s ... A handful of smaller cities have [already] begun offering residency rights to outsiders, both to attract skilled workers and to cope with increasing dissatisfaction of rural migrants already there.

(*IHT*, 24 October 2001, p. 4)

('To help the transition to a market economy authorities began dismantling a system that for more than forty years has allowed people to work only where they are registered to live. State media said on 9 October that people could now move to over 20,000 cities and towns. The government says it will end the *hukou* system, which allows people to live only where they are registered, over the next five years': *FEER*, 18 October 2001, p. 34.)

'Beijing ... ordered the effective closure of the Left's two main mouthpieces, *The Pursuit of Truth* and *Indomitable* ... after criticisms by leading leftists of President Jiang Zemin's decision to welcome capitalists into the Communist Party' (*FEER*, 6 September 2001, p. 74).

11 September 2001. There are terrorist attacks in the United States on the World Trade Centre in New York and on the Pentagon in Washington. The USA took the war on international terrorism to Afghanistan. Bombing started on 7 October and on 19 October US special forces began the ground phase of the war in Afghanistan. The USA considers the Taleban regime to be harbouring terrorists, notably the Moslem fundamentalist Osama bin Laden.

Jiang Zemin condemned international terrorism and China supported a US resolution at the United Nations condemning the attacks and upholding the USA's right to self-defence. China has merely requested that military retaliation be justified by evidence, done in accordance with the United Nations Charter and international law, targeted at specific objectives and done so as to avoid civilian casualties. China has co-operated with the USA over intelligence. China has branded Moslem Uighur separatists in Xinjiang as being linked with the international terrorists headed by the Moslem fundamentalist, Osama bin Laden. For example, China claims that Uighur rebels are being trained in Afghanistan. China has also requested international support for its policies in Tibet and Taiwan. ('The government estimates that 1,000 Chinese Moslems have trained in camps run by Osama bin Laden and his Qaeda network in Afghanistan': *IHT*, 12 November 2001, p. 5.)

President Jiang Zemin promised China's support for the struggle against terrorism and offered its co-operation to ... President George W. Bush ... Jiang told Bush by telephone that China opposed all types of terrorism, backed United Nations anti-terror resolutions and supported action against terrorist groups. Jiang noted Bush's assertion that US attacks in Afghanistan were not aimed at ordinary Afghans or Moslems and that civilian casualties should be avoided.

(*FEER*, 18 October 2001, p. 35)

In a telephone conversation with US President George W. Bush, Mr Jiang said that China had taken note of Mr Bush's statement that military action was aimed at 'terrorist activities' and not the Afghan people or Moslems. Earlier [the Chinese newsagency] Xinhua carried a statement saying that any military action should be 'targeted at specific objectives so as to avoid hurting innocent civilians'.

(*FT*, 9 October 2001, p. 3)

[There was a] phone call on Monday [8 October] from President Jiang Zemin to his US counterpart, George W. Bush, offering broad support for the retaliatory strikes on Afghanistan ... [Jiang Zemin] stressing the role of the UN and the importance of sparing innocent civilians by targeting only 'terrorist activities'.

(*FT*, 10 October 2001, p. 2)

Jiang Zemin (during a meeting with President Bush in Shanghai on 19 October): 'We hope anti-terrorism efforts can have clearly defined targets and also should be hit accurately and avoid innocent casualties. What is more the role of the United Nations should be brought fully into play' (*Telegraph*, 20 October 2001, p. 10). 'The Chinese leader said his government was "opposed to terrorism in all its forms". He promised further intelligence support and action against terrorist finances' (*FT*, 20 October 2001, p. 5).

8 October 2001. Prime minister Junichiro Koizumi of Japan (on a one-day visit to China): 'I looked at the various exhibits [in the museum] with a feeling of heartfelt apology and condolences for those Chinese people who were victims of [Japanese] aggression.'

> The friendly tone of the conversations reflected a sudden thawing in bilateral ties that have been badly strained in recent months. China took offence at Mr Koizumi's visit [on 13 August] to a Japanese shrine to its war dead, which includes the name of war criminals, and at his refusal to ban a textbook that downplays Japanese atrocities in World War II. There have also been nasty trade disputes ... The statement [by Mr Koizumi on 8 October] was similar to one made by another Japanese prime minister in 1995.
>
> (*IHT*, 9 October 2001, p. 5)

17–21 October 2001. Shanghai hosts a summit of APEC leaders. APEC, the Asia-Pacific Co-operation forum, was founded in 1989 and then comprised twelve members. There are now twenty-one members, including China and Taiwan.

'China ... refused the representative Taipei nominated to come to APEC, former vice-president Li Yuan-zu, put forward after Beijing rejected entreaties to allow Chen Shui-bian, Taiwan's president, to attend ... Beijing has insisted that Taipei find an 'economic representative' (*FT*, 19 October 2001, p. 15). 'Taiwan said yesterday [19 October] it would boycott ... [the] summit ... Chen Shui-bian, Taiwan's president, said Beijing's refusal to invite his chosen representative, former vice-president Li Yuan-zu, made it impossible for Taiwan to take part in the APEC meeting' (*FT*, 20 October 2001, p. 5).

On 19 October there took place the first meeting between President George W. Bush and President Jiang Zemin.

A statement was issued after the APEC meeting concluded on 21 October:

> Leaders consider the murderous deeds [of 11 September]... as a profound threat to the peace, prosperity and security of all people, of all faiths, of all nations. Terrorism is also a direct challenge to APEC's vision of free, open and prosperous economies.
>
> (*FT*, 22 October 2001, p. 11)

'The statement issued by the APEC leaders promised co-operation to block funds for terrorists, step up security at ports and airports, and limit the economic fallout from the attacks' (*Telegraph*, 22 October 2001, p. 9). 'Leaders ... agreed to step up efforts to cut off funding for terrorists. They also called for efforts to improve aviation, maritime and energy security and to co-operate to bring the perpetrators of the 11 September attacks to justice' (*FT*, 22 September 2001, p. 11). '[The statement] pledged economic and financial measures to prevent "all forms of terrorist acts" in the future' (*Guardian*, 22 October 2001, p. 2).

The statement itself committed the nations to: 'Bring the perpetrators to justice ... [to take] appropriate measures to prevent the flow of funds to terrorists ... [and to develop] a global electronic customs network and electronic movement records' (*IHT*, 22 October 2001, pp. 1–6).

'[At the APEC meeting President Bush said that] "No government should use our war against terrorism as an excuse to persecute minorities within their borders"' (*Guardian*, 22 October 2001, p. 2).

Jiang Zemin: 'We are fighting a battle against international terrorism' (*The Times*, 22 October 2001, p. 1).

'[Albeit reluctantly, China has accepted] new legislation going through the Diet in Tokyo that will allow Japan to offer logistical (though not direct military support) to America' (*The Economist*, 27 October 2001, p. 26).

23 October 2001.

China has quietly ordered a virtual freeze on the bankruptcy of its larger state-owned enterprises in the clearest sign to date that crucial industrial reforms are being slowed as Beijing concentrates on warding off social unrest. People inside government said yesterday [23 October] that the supreme court ... has ordered provincial courts not to proceed with bankruptcy cases of state-owned enterprises with assets in excess of 50 million renminbi ($6 million) unless they have prior supreme court approval ... The order has not been publicly announced ... Beijing announced this week that ... the sale of state-owned shares on domestic stock markets was being suspended after domestic A shares had fallen... The suspension of state share sales may reinforce the government's reluctance to allow bankruptcies.

(*FT*, 24 October 2001, p. 15)

24 October 2001.

Pope John Paul II ... apologized for errors of the colonial past and pleaded for the establishment of diplomatic relations ... China and the Vatican broke formal relations in 1951 ... The Vatican maintains diplomatic relations with Taiwan ... Beijing says normalization of diplomatic ties is possible only if the Holy See severs relations with Taiwan ... The Beijing-backed Patriotic Church says it has 4 million members. The Vatican says 8 million Chinese are loyal to the Pope and worship in secret.

(*IHT*, 25 October 2001, p. 5)

'About 5 million Chinese participate in the official church while as many as 8 million worship in the unapproved church' (*IHT*, 26 October 2001, p. 4). 'The Vatican's representative was expelled from China in 1951 and replaced by a state-backed organization, the Chinese Patriotic Church ... [There are] an estimated 8 million Chinese Catholics ... Those who continue to support the Holy See have gone underground' (*IHT*, 10 November 2001, p. 6).

27 October 2001.

A revised union law maintains the ban on strike action and on independent unions, while at the same time significantly widening the scope and powers of the official All-China Federation of Trade Unions. The revised law, passed by the National People's Congress standing committee on 27 October ... says all enterprises with twenty-five or more workers must set up branches of the ACFTU, whose leaders should be chosen through elections. In the past only state and collective enterprises were obliged to set up the unions, which will now extend to foreign and private firms. The new law also stipulates legal liabilities for violations of the right to join a union and deals in greater detail with the rights of workers in bankrupt enterprises. The right to strike ... had a brief life in China's constitution from 1975 to 1982.

(*FEER*, 8 November 2001, p. 32)

28 October 2001. Hu Jintao starts his visit to five countries (Russia, the United Kingdom, France, Germany and Spain).

13 December 2001. 'President George W. Bush formally announced Thursday [13 December] that the United States was withdrawing from the Anti-Ballistic Missile treaty ... Mr Bush said he had given Russia formal notice of the move on Thursday' (*IHT*, 14 December 2001, p. 1).

President Putin:

This step was not a surprise for us. However, we consider it a mistake ... It is not a threat to the security of the Russian Federation ... We must not allow a legal vacuum in strategic stability ... One should not undermine the regime of non-proliferation of weapons of mass destruction ... I think the current level of bilateral relations between the Russian Federation and the USA should not only be retained, but also used in order to work out the new framework of strategic relationship as soon as possible.

(*IHT*, 14 December 2001, pp. 1, 3; *Guardian*, 14 December 2001, p. 16)

China (13 December): 'We have taken note of the reports and express our concern over them. It is of crucial importance to maintain the international and arms control efforts. China opposes the missile defence system' (*FT*, 14 December 2001, p. 3).

Senator Joseph Biden (chairman of the US Senate Foreign Relations Committee): 'A year ago it was widely reported that our intelligence community had concluded that pulling out of the ABM would prompt the Chinese to increase their nuclear arsenal ten-fold, beyond the modernization they are doing anyway' (*IHT*, 15 December 2001, p. 1). Joseph Biden: 'China will speed up. And I just saw the Indian ambassador, who nodded and said that would pressure India to do the same. And then, of course, the Pakistanis match the Indians. Pretty soon you've started another arms race' (*IHT*, 17 December 2001, p. 3).

'According to US intelligence estimates, China has from twenty to twenty-four long-range nuclear missiles created in the 1950s and 1960s as a minimal deterrent. China is now in the process of replacing those missiles with mobile, solid-fuel intercontinental ballistic missiles' (*IHT*, 7 September 2001, p. 5). 'China has about twenty long-range nuclear missiles that could reach the United States. While it apparently has the ability to place multiple warheads on its missiles, it has not done so' (*IHT*, 8 September 2001, p. 4).

11 January 2002. 'The extent of crooked banking in China was brought into focus with the sacking of China Construction Bank president and former Bank of China president Wang Xuebing' (*FEER*, 31 January 2002, p. 31).

21–22 February 2002. President George. W. Bush visits China. (President Richard Nixon started his visit to China on 21 February 1972.)

5 March 2002. The annual meeting of the National People's Congress begins. There are 2,987 delegates attending the meeting.

Party membership is 64 million, up from 50 million in 1990 (*The Economist*, 1 June 2002, p. 66).

In his opening address prime minister Zhu Rongyi contrasted China's achievements with its problems. Among the latter were corruption, the waste of resources, unemployment, the environment, rural living standards, delays in the payment of the salaries of rural teachers and delays in the payment of pensions.

> Mr Zhu reaffirmed the need to 'deepen' the reform of state-owned enterprises and restructure state companies to form 'as quickly as possible a number of large companies and enterprise groups that are internationally competitive'. Beijing is currently engaged in directing mergers in the airline, telecommunications and power industries.
>
> (*FT*, 6 March 2002, p. 10)

The defence budget was increased by 17.6 per cent.

'In the thirteenth straight year of double-digit increases, spending on the 2.5 million member People's Liberation Army will grow by 17.6 per cent to $20 billion' (*FEER*, 14 March 2002, p. 27).

> Beijing announced in March last year [2001] that its published defence budget was jumping more than 17 per cent to $17.2 billion. Real annual spending, including payments for foreign weapons and technology, is estimated by many analysts at more than $60 billion ... Up to half of Russia's $4 billion in military sales last year [2001] went to China.
>
> (*FEER*, 24 January 2002, p. 30)

'[A] report [released by the US department of defence on 12 July] estimates that China spends $65 billion a year on military modernization' (*FEER*, 25 July 2002, p. 16).

> The defence report from the State Council, or cabinet ... asserts that China's defence spending ... [at] $14.6 billion in 2000, is only 5 per cent of US military spending. Independent experts contend China's public total excludes major sums spent on research and procurement that are concealed in other budgets.
>
> (*IHT*, 17 October 2000, p. 4)

'Real [military] expenditure is estimated at two to two-and-a-half times the size of this year's $20 billion' (*IHT*, 16 July 2002, p. 6).

21 April 2002. 'Jiang Zemin [in Iran] ... said that Beijing opposed the US military presence in Central Asia and the Middle East' (*IHT*, 22 April 2002, p. 7).

27 April–3 May 2002. Hu Jintao visits the United States. 'The two sides agreed to resume military contacts, frozen since last spring when China seized a US spy plane' (*The Times*, 3 May 2002, p. 20).

14 May 2002.

> Companies from Russia and China are the most likely to bribe foreign officials to win contracts ... according to a survey released [on 14 May 2002] ... by Transparency International ... The Bribe Payers Index, based on a Gallup poll of 835 business executives in fifteen emerging economies, showed that companies from Russia and China were paying bribes on an 'exceptional and intolerable scale'. Russia and China scored worst in the survey of twenty-one major trading countries.

> (*IHT*, 15 May 2002, p. 14)

7 June 2002. 'The leaders of Russia, China, Kazakhstan, Kyrgyzstan, Tajikistan and Uzbekistan have signed the security pact that China once envisaged as a counterweight to Nato. However, Western diplomats said that the pact had become irrelevant after 11 September' (*The Times*, 8 June 2002, p. 23).

23 July 2002. 'A US army team arrived in China on the first mission to search for the remains of Americans who went missing in action during the Cold War ... [to] look for the remains of two pilots whose aircraft crashed in north-east China on a spying mission in 1952' (*FEER*, 1 August 2002, p. 23).

'The Bush administration scrapped its $34 million payment for 2002 to the United Nations Population Fund, saying the fund indirectly helped China to force women to have abortions under the one-child policy' (*FEER*, 1 August 2002, p. 22).

27 August 2002.

> A district court [in Tokyo] ruled Tuesday [27 August] that Japan conducted germ warfare in World War II, bluntly contradicting the continued resistance by the government that there was no proof of such crimes. But the court rejected claims for compensation by elderly Chinese ... The court said: 'No international law that enables individuals to sue for war crime damages was established at the time or has been now' ... The court decision follows the pattern by which Japanese courts have, with rare exceptions, rejected claims for compensation. Lawsuits brought on behalf of slave labourers, women forced into prostitution ['comfort women'], torture victims, Koreans forced into military duty and Allied prisoners of war all have been dismissed ... The United States made a secret deal to exclude the biological crimes from the trials held in Tokyo after the war in return for getting the results of the gruesome experiments.

> (*IHT*, 28 August 2002, p. 7)

'Tokyo's refusal to aid victims of wartime atrocities, on the grounds that all claims were settled in bilateral peace treaties signed after the war, is usually backed by the Japanese courts' (*The Times*, 28 August 2002, p. 14).

> The government's official stance is that war reparations were settled by the 1951 San Francisco peace treaty that formally ended the Pacific war ...

However, in April [2002] a court in Fukuoka, western Japan, ordered Mitsui Mining to pay ... compensation to fifteen Chinese people forced to work in coal mines during the War.

(*FT*, 28 August 2002, p. 8)

22–25 October 2002. Jiang Zemin visits the United States.
4 November 2002.

The Chinese government signed agreements Monday [4 November] with the ten countries of South-east Asia to prevent open conflict over long-disputed areas of the South China Sea and to establish the world's largest free-trade zone over the next decade. The two deals [were] approved at a summit meeting in Phnom Penh of the Association of South-East Asian Nations ... [Asean] reached agreement with China on a non-binding political declaration intended to reduce the chances of military confrontation over the Spratly Islands and other disputed areas ... But the accord did not lay down the detailed, binding 'code of conduct' that negotiators had made their goal ... [China's] 1.3 billion people dwarf the scattered markets of its Asean neighbours, which have about 500 million people ... Under the [free-trade] agreement the more developed member countries will cut their tariffs first, to between 0 per cent and 5 per cent on most goods, and the other countries will follow over the next decade.

(*IHT*, 5 November 2002, p. 5)

South-east Asian nations and China yesterday [4 November] signed a framework agreement to establish a comprehensive free-trade area by 2010 ... the world's largest free-trade area of more than 1.7 billion billion ... The agreement provides for special treatment for the weakest Asean members – Vietnam, Cambodia, Laos and Burma – which will have until 2015 to comply with the deal ... Negotiating the details, starting early next year [2003], is likely to be tough and painful ... Although Asean's trade with China has expanded significantly in the last decade – rising to about $41 billion in 2000, up from about $8 billion in 1991, China still absorbs just 3 per cent of the exports of the six biggest Asean economies and provides just 5 per cent of those economies' imports ... Along with agreeing yesterday to refrain from provocative activities in the disputed South China Sea, China and Asean issued an unexpected declaration on joint efforts to combat non-traditional security problems, like the smuggling of arms, drugs and people, money laundering, cyber-crime and terrorism.

(*FT*, 5 November 2002, p. 14)

The two sides issued a joint 'declaration on the conduct of parties in the South China Sea', rather than the code of conduct Asean had originally sought ... China and Asean did pledge to abide by international law, avoid the threat or use of force and refrain from any action that might 'complicate or escalate disputes and affect peace and stability' ... China flatly rejected an Asean effort to include the Paracel Islands, which are claimed by Vietnam but controlled by China ... The Spratly Islands are claimed in whole or in part by six countries ... [There is to be a] prohibition against 'inhabiting ... presently uninhabited' locations'.

(*FEER*, 14 November 2002, p. 26)

8–14 November 2002. A Communist Party Congress is held, the sixteenth since the party was founded in 1921. Congresses are held every five years. The number of delegates attending was 2,114.

Despite considerable speculation about exactly which positions Jiang Zemin would give up, the most orderly, peaceful and voluntary transfer of power since 1949 took place. The so-called 'fourth generation' of leaders took over the formal reins of power. But there was continuity of policy, including that of collective leadership. It was also generally thought that Jiang Zemin would be 'the power behind the throne'. ('In his secret acceptance speech ... Hu Jintao pledged that on important matters he would "seek instruction and listen to the views" of ... Jiang Zemin, according to two party officials who attended briefings on the meeting': *IHT*, 21 November 2002, p. 1.)

'The turnover in leading party councils is enormous, largely thanks to a recent unwritten rule that officials older than seventy should step down. This does not portend, however, equally striking changes in policy' (*IHT*, 16 November 2002, p. 3).

Hu Jintao (fifty-nine) was the only member of the old seven-man Standing Committee of the Politburo to be named as a Central Committee member. The new Central Committee has 356 members (198 full members and 158 alternates). Hu Jintao took over from Jiang Zemin (seventy-six) as General Secretary of the Communist Party on 15 November. (Jiang Zemin is expected to relinquish the title of state president to Hu Jintao in March 2003.) Jiang Zemin retained his position as chairman of the Central Military Commission.

The new Standing Committee comprises nine members. In order of ranking and with their mentors in brackets they are: Hu Jintao (Deng Xiaoping); Wu Bangguo (he was deputy prime minister dealing with reform of state enterprises; Jiang Zemin); Wen Jiabao (Zhu Rongyi); Jia Qinglin (former Beijing party secretary; unexpected choice because of the huge corruption scandal in Fujian; Jiang Zemin); Zeng Qinghong (Jiang Zemin); Huang Ju (former Shanghai party secretary; Jiang Zemin); Wu Guangzheng (Shandong province party secretary; Jiang Zemin); Li Changchu (Jiang Zemin); Luo Gan (Li Peng).

The party charter was revised to include Jiang Zemin's 'three represents'. Thus private businessmen (private entrepreneurs) were formally allowed to join the party.

'The capitalist delegates at the congress are managers-turned-owners of former state-owned enterprises. Often party members, they became capitalists by virtue of privatization. Genuine entrepreneurs who financed and built their own businesses were not invited to the congress' (*The Times*, 12 November 2002, p. 17). 'It was made difficult to calculate how many private-sector tycoons were attending the meeting. Lists of names that journalists put together on their own suggested the number was about ten' (*FEER*, 21 November 2002, p. 32).

> [As regards] private business people ... although pre-congress reports predicted that as many as four chiefs of non-state-owned enterprises might be elevated to the Central Committee, in the end only one made it, and then only as an alternate Central Committee member. He is Zhang Ruimin, president of the

white-goods manufacturer Haier Group, a so-called 'collectively-owned' enterprise [which means that it was formerly fully state-owned but now has some privately owned shares] that enjoys strong financial backing from the Qingdao city government.

(*FEER*, 28 November 2002, p. 62; 26 December 2002, p. 62)

'Private businessmen ... were welcomed to the congress as delegates for the first time since 1921, and one capitalist entrepreneur was elected to the Central Committee' (*FT*, 16 November 2002, p. 7).

The new politburo comprises twenty-four members. The only woman member is Wu Yi, a former foreign trade minister.

Jiang Zemin (8 November):

> We must move forward or we will fall behind ... It is of vital importance we take economic development as the central task ... [Economic] reform and opening up are ways to make China powerful ... We need to respect and protect all work that is good for the people and society and improve the legal system for protecting private property ... [The] dominant role [is played by the state sector] ... Controlling shares in lifeline enterprises must be held by the state ... [The private sector is] an important component part ... We should admit into the party advanced elements of social strata [including private entrepreneurs, employees of foreign funded firms and the self-employed] who accept the party's programme and constitution in order to increase the influence and rallying force of the party' in society at large.

Jiang predicted a quadrupling national output by 2020

> The economy last year [2001] was already triple its size in 1989, according to government statistics ... China needs growth of at least 7 per cent a year to create jobs for an estimated 8 million people, according to the government.

(*IHT*, 11 November 2002, p. 11)

The official growth target for 2002 is 7 per cent but 8 per cent looks likely.

Urban unemployment at the end of 2001 was 3.6 per cent; 4 per cent seems likely at the end of 2002.

> [On 10 November it was officially revealed that] in the past few years state-owned enterprises have laid off 24 million to 25 million workers. Each year 10 million more people enter the work force ... State companies have dismissed more than 26 million workers since 1998.

(*IHT*, 12 November 2002, pp. 8, 11)

'[It was announced on 11 November that] private businesses would be granted equal access to bank credit ... [More] areas closed to private businesses in the past ... would be opened to private capital soon' (*IHT*, 12 November 2002, p. 8).

'[It was said on 11 November that] China had begun an experiment to let farmers amass larger parcels of land' (*IHT*, 12 November 2002, p. 8).

> [In his speech of 8 November 2002 Jiang Zemin] indicated that farmers should be able to sell their land use rights for profit. 'We must respect farmer

households as market players,' he said ... The government also wants to consolidate land holdings to build bigger, more productive farms ... New rules on selling rural properties were quietly passed by a committee of the National People's Congress in August, but will not take effect until March [2003] ... All land is officially owned by the state ... Chinese in both the countryside and the towns enjoy 'land use rights' of anything from thirty to seventy years.

(FT, 13 November 2002, p. 14)

The Rural Land Contracting law was passed on 1 March [2003]. It helps farmers secure existing rights of tenure for thirty years on their holdings and restricts the ability of local officials to change the size of a holding ... It contains provisions that give farmers the right to transfer or lease their land and includes safeguards against local officials pressuring farmers to surrender their holdings to development companies or farming corporations.

(FEER, 10 April 2003, p. 47)

'The "three represents" said the party's mission was to represent "advanced production forces" (capitalists and technologists), "advanced cultural forces" (intellectuals) and "the broad masses of the people" (everybody else)' (David Ignatius, *IHT*, 21 September 2002, p. 4).

The 'three represents': Jiang Zemin's controversial attempt to redefine the party's mission in order to guarantee the party's survival. He holds that the party should represent the needs of 'advanced forces of production' such as hi-tech industries and the private sector, advanced culture and the 'fundamental interests of the overwhelming majority of the Chinese people' – rather than the millions of blue-collar workers laid off by state-owned industries. The congress will write the 'three represents' into the party charter.

(FEER, 7 November 2002, p. 29)

'[The term] "advanced productive forces" [is] communist jargon for capitalists' (*The Economist*, 9 November 2002, p. 15).

In March this year [2002] Beijing announced that it was boosting military outlays by 17.6 per cent to about $20 billion this year ... On 12 July the Pentagon estimated that actual annual spending had reached $65 billion. If so, this would mean that China has the second biggest defence budget in the world – though Beijing is still dwarfed by US outlays this year of $350 billion ... Taiwan's defence budget for this year is about $8 billion.

(FEER, 12 December 2002, p. 34)

(There is a two-year draft for the 2.5 million People's Liberation Army: *FEER*, 15 April 2002, p. 31.)

28 December 2002.

Zhou Xiaochuan, the reformist head of the China Securities and Regulatory Commission, [is appointed] as governor of the People's Bank of China, the central bank. Mr Zhou's replacement at the CSRC is Shang Fulin, president of the Agricultural Bank of China and a former deputy governor at the People's

Bank of China ... [There are] plans to hasten interest rate deregulation. Interest rates are mostly fixed but significant experiments are under way in rural areas to allow banks latitude in setting interest rates within certain bands.

(*FT*, 31 December 2002, p. 6)

Zhou Xiaochuan ... will replace Dai Xianglong as governor of the central bank ... In addition to the securities commission he [Zhou Xiaochuan] has headed the state administration of foreign exchange and China Construction bank ... At the central bank foreign investors will be expecting Zhou to make China's exchange rate policy more flexible ... Zhou is also expected to lead interest rate deregulation ... Shang Fulin, president of Agriculture Bank of China, was appointed Monday [30 December] to be China's top securities regulator ... Shang is a former deputy governor of the central bank who since February 2000 has headed Agriculture Bank, China's number four lender ... The bulk of Agriculture Bank's loans go to rural factories and agricultural projects on government orders. Agriculture Bank transferred about 300 billion yuan to an asset management company in 1999 and 2000 to get non-performing loans off of its books. Even after the transfer it has the highest non-performing loan ratio among the top four lenders.

(www.iht.com)

Dai Xianglong after eight years as People's Bank of China governor, was named both mayor and a vice-mayor of Tianjin, China's fourth largest city ... Authorities allowed Chinese citizens to buy gold bullion for the first time since the Communist Party took power in 1949.

(www.feer.com)

31 December 2002. Shanghai inaugurates the world's first maglev (magnetic levitation) railway, based on German technology.
'China has awarded Germany a potentially lucrative contract to lengthen the world's first commercial magnetic-levitation rail system to cities surrounding Shanghai' (*IHT*, 2 January 2003, p. 7).
7 January 2003.

China announced yesterday [7 January 2003] that it would phase out a job-for-life system for the country's 30 million civil servants ... Over the next five years the government will put into place a system under which civil servants work according to contracts and can be dismissed if they fail to perform in line with a set of transparent goals ... In reality a previous cast-iron guarantee of life-long employment for government officials evaporated some years ago, with about 17,000 civil servants being dismissed over the past six years and 22,000 resigning ... In places such as Shenzhen ... such reforms have already begun, along with a rudimentary feedback system that allows the local administration to consider public opinion on the performance of government departments ... A more common reform, also practised at some central government bureaux in Beijing, has been to recruit through an examination and interview system, rather than purely through appointment by superiors.

(*FT*, 8 January 2003, p. 12)

The announcement formalises changes already under way ... It is part of civil service reforms which also includes open recruitment examinations and an attempt to encourage educated Chinese to return from considerably more lucrative jobs abroad ... The idea of an 'iron rice bowl' to give security to those favoured by China's rulers predates the communist era.

(Telegraph, 8 January 2003, p. 14)

The official Xinhua news agency reported yesterday ... [that] China [is] to end lifelong tenure for public employees ... Within five years judges, policemen, soldiers, teachers and nurses will be forced to sign contracts and ... could be dismissed ... [An] administrator at the foreign trade ministry ... [said that] 'Already my ministry signs contracts with young students, who join the ministry when they graduate from university. Contracts are for five to ten years.' He explained that the aim was to make public sector employment more attractive.

(The Times, 8 January 2003, p. 14)

Civil servants should be recruited 'through a system of open examinations in order to build quality and competence'. State employees include everyone working for a government-funded institution, from artists at fine arts academies to junior clerks in tax offices ... Educational institutions and research centres, while still technically under state management, are increasingly obliged to pay staff with money they have raised themselves.

(Guardian, 8 January 2003, p. 10.)

('China recently returned to the council of the International Labour Organization, the ILO, after it was ejected twelve years ago in the wake of the [1989] Tiananmen crackdown': *IHT*, 8 February 2003, p. 4.)

5 March 2003. The start of the two-week Tenth National People's Congress. (The first congress was in 1954.)

'A total of fifty-five private businesspeople are among 2,985 delegates elected to the National People's Congress this year' *(FEER*, 13 March 2003, p. 33). 'There are 133 bosses of private enterprise in the congress ... nearly three times the number in the last congress' *(IHT*, 13 March 2003, p. 5).

[In 2001 Jiang Zemin launched an initiative] to allow private business people to play an open role in Chinese political life. The idea is for them to invigorate politics and for the party to head off the danger of politically frustrated private business people setting up alternative organizations that might challenge party power ... The constitution still holds China is 'a socialist state under the people's democratic dictatorship led by the working class and based on the alliance of workers and peasants.'

(FEER, 27 March 2003, p.31)

Key political changes were as follows: Hu Jintao, president; Wen Jiabao, prime minister; Zeng Qinghong, vice-president; Wu Bangguo, chairman of the National People's Congress; Li Zhaoxing, foreign minister. Jiang Zemin remained chairman of both the party and state Central Military Commissions. Liu Mingkang was appointed head of the new Banking Regulatory Commission, set up during the session.

'Hu still isn't allowed to call himself the "core" of the leadership, as Jiang did. So the party's membership is instead pledging allegiance to "the party centre with Hun Jintao as general secretary"' (*FEER*, 27 March 2003, p. 31).

'A key experiment in political reform is soon to be launched in . . . Shenzhen . . . The party will be forbidden from interfering in the daily business of government. Its role will be limited to that of long-term policy-making' (*FT*, 4 March 2003, p. 12). 'Du Qinglin, the agriculture minister . . . [said] that a test campaign in twenty provinces and cities to replace local government fees on farmers with regulated taxes has reduced the burden on them by more than 30 per cent' (*FT*, 11 March 2003, p. 12).

> The National People's Congress will preside over the slimming down of the central government from twenty-nine to twenty-one ministries and oversee efforts to separate ministries from the state enterprises they own. The symbiotic relationships between enterprises and their owner/regulators has been blamed for both high levels of official corruption and unfair competition in certain industries . . . The congress is expected to approve the establishment of a new body, the State Asset Management Commission. Over time . . . the transfer process may take at least a year . . . the commission and its local offshoots will assume ownership from ministries and other regional organs of . . . 190,000 state-owned enterprises . . . Central and local authorities will decide which level of government owns which enterprise. This will enable local authorities to sell stakes in the corporations they own without seeking permission from Beijing.
>
> (*FT*, 4 March 2003, p. 12)

> A new ministry of commerce replaced the ministry of foreign trade and economic co-operation and the state economic and trade commission . . . Also new are a ministry-level commission to manage and supervise state assets and a ministry-level commission broken out from the central bank to oversee bank regulation – leaving the central bank to concentrate on monetary policy.
>
> (*FEER*, 20 March 2003, p. 22)

Zhu Rongyi:

> Maintaining the good momentum of economic growth is the basis of success for all fields of work . . . We must do everything possible to increase farmers' income and lighten their burden. Agricultural, village and farmers' problems relate to the overall situation of China's reform, opening and modernization. We cannot neglect them or relax at any time. If we do not change these conditions, they will severely dampen farmers' enthusiasm to produce, undermine the foundations of agriculture and even threaten the overall health of the national economy . . . We must exert a great deal of effort to resolve the problems of back pay for workers and overburdened farmers.
>
> (*IHT*, 6 March 2003, p. 2; *FT*, 6 March 2003, p. 11; *Independent*, 6 March 2003, p. 17; *Guardian*, 6 March 2003, p. 17)

'One measure that should be taken, Mr Zhu said, was the nationwide application of a pilot scheme [in Anhui province] to decrease the imposition of fees and replace them with taxes' (*FT*, 6 March 2003, p. 11).

The defence budget was increased by 9.6 per cent.

20 March 2003. The United States starts its attack on Iraq, aided principally by British troops, without submitting a second resolution to the UN Security Council (thus saving Russia from having to make a formal decision about whether to use its threatened veto). Australia and Poland also sent troops into action. ('Poland has sent fifty-six troops': *IHT*, 3 April 2003, p. 4. 'Poland ... has fifty-four soldiers involved in ground operations in Iraq': *Baltic Times*, 10–16 April, p. 2.) The United States insisted on referring to 'coalition' forces. The Saddam Hussein regime effectively collapsed after three weeks, US troops entering the centre of Baghdad on 9 April, although some fighting continued.

The action of the United States deeply divided world opinion, including Nato itself. France and Germany were leading critics of the United States, suggesting that UN inspectors should have been given more time to complete their task. Russia and China (less vehemently) were broadly in agreement with France and Germany. China issued a statement on 20 March:

> We strongly urge relevant countries to immediately stop military action. They ignored the opposition of most countries and peoples of the world and went around the UN Security Council to begin military action against Iraq ... The norms of international behaviour [have been violated].
>
> (*IHT*, 21 March 2003, p. 3; *The Telegraph*, 21 March 2003, p. 8)

But both countries remained on relatively good overall terms with the United States.

26 May 2003. President Hu Jintao meets President Putin. This is the first foreign tour by the new Chinese president since he took office. (The entire tour of a number of countries lasted ten days.)

1 June 2003. 'China began filling the reservoir of the Three Gorges Dam ... The dam will not be completed until 2009' (*Guardian*, 2 June 2003, p. 5).

22 June 2003. Indian prime minister Atal Behari Vajapyee begins a six-day visit to China.

1 July 2003.

> In his first major speech as head of the Communist Party ... President Hu Jintao ... on Tuesday [1 July] urged the party's 67 million members to toe the political line laid down by Jiang Zemin and made no mention of reform policies ... In a speech marking the eighty-second anniversary of the Chinese Communist Party ... Hu urged citizens to show 'even greater enthusiasm' in studying the so-called Three Represents theory coined by Jiang in 2000.
>
> (*IHT*, 2 July 2003, p. 8)

> The state news agency announced that Mr Hu had given the speech, but did not publish its text ... Analysts speculated that Mr Hu was forced to abandon plans to call for more open discussion, as well as competitive elections for some Communist Party posts because of tension between senior party leaders.
>
> (*The Times*, 2 July 2003, p. 14)

'Defying some predictions, a speech by Hu Jintao ... contained no word of political reform' (*The Economist*, 5 July 2003, p. 8). '[There was] speculation that Hu Jintao ... would outline plans for low-level party democracy in a key speech, [but] he did no such thing' (www.economist.com).

In a speech marking the eighty-second anniversary of the Chinese Communist Party's founding, President Hu Jintao urged bolder policies to tackle economic and social problems, but did not reveal any sweeping plans to reform the political system as some foreign commentators had hoped he would ... He ordered improved welfare programmes for laid-off workers, the poor and other groups ... and demanded change from the bureaucracy that had impeded the response to the SARS outbreak. Hu also said the party should show 'still greater enthusiasm' for the political theories of ... Jiang Zemin.

(*FEER*, 10 July 2003, p. 24)

14 July 2003.

Yang Bin, a former flower magnate once dubbed the nation's second richest man, [is sentenced] to eighteen years in prison on charges ranging from bribery to financial deception and misuse of agricultural land ... Mr Yang [is] a Chinese-born Dutch national with close ties to North Korea ... [He] won Dutch citizenship after claiming political asylum ... after the crushing of China's 1989 pro-democracy movement ... Mr Yang ... [was] appointed by North Korea as head of a proposed free-trade enclave on its border with China.

(*FT*, 15 July 2003, p. 10)

'Yang Bin ... was ranked as China's second richest man by *Forbes* magazine in 2001' (*The Times*, 15 July 2003, p. 14).

'Yang's fortune was estimated by *Forbes* in 2001 at $900 million ... Yang moved to the Netherlands in 1987' (*Independent*, 15 July 2003, p. 12).

His orchid and real estate empire collapsed when he was detained last October [2002] shortly before he was due to take up a post as head of a special economic zone in North Korea. The Chinese leadership was apparently not notified in advance of Pyongyang's plans for Yang.

(*FEER*, 24 July 2003, p. 26)

July 2003. 'The first two 700 megawatt generators [of the Three Gorges Dam] started up last month [July] and two more are to go into operation later this year [2003]' (*FEER*, 28 August 2003, p. 25).

'The Three Gorges Dam recently began generating' (*The Economist*, 13 September 2003, p. 67).

3 August 2003.

China's new leaders launched a campaign to revive industries and create jobs across three provinces in the north-east, the rust belt of shuttered state enterprises, unemployment and simmering labour unrest. Premier Wen Jiabao attended a meeting on 3 August in the industrial centre of Changchun to announce the 'rejuvenate the north-east' campaign, after visiting eleven state-owned factories in the region. 'Use new thought, new systems, new mechanism and new methods to work out new ways to speed up the rejuvenation of the old industrial production,' he said.

(*FEER*, 14 August 2003, p. 25)

For the past half-century ... the Communist leadership has decamped to a resort [Beidaihe] on the Bohai Sea ... [But] Hu Jintao has cancelled the seaside retreat ... The decision to end the secretive meetings marks Hu's most formal break with Communist tradition. It is also the strongest signal that he intends to manage party affairs differently from Jiang Zemin ... Beidaihe provided elders who had given up formal titles with a casual setting [to continue to exercise influence].

(*IHT*, 5 August 2003, p. 1)

1 September 2003.

China is to cut 200,000 troops from the 2.5 million-strong People's Liberation Army by 2005 ... The announcement was made by Jiang Zemin ... The cut follows a 500,000 reduction in PLA numbers in the late 1990s ... However, the latest cuts are less than the initial target of another 500,000 reduction by 2005 ... Jiang Zemin: 'A further reduction in the scale of the army will help us concentrate our limited strategic resources and accelerate the pace of building the information technology capability of our army' ... The PLA's official budget is $22.4 billion, but with many big-ticket items kept off-budget real military spending is estimated to be about $60 billion.

(*FT*, 2 September 2003, p. 12)

'At the height of its strength in the 1950s the People's Liberation Army numbered 5 million. In the late 1990s it was cut from 3 million to its current 2.5 million' (*Telegraph*, 2 September 2003, p. 14).

('An estimated 1.3 million soldiers have been demobilized in the last fifteen years': *IHT*, 17 October 2002, p. 5. 'Beijing has trimmed manpower by more than 1.6 million to a total of 2.3 million over the last fifteen years ... The PLA now has an annual budget of about $30 billion, according to David Shambaugh': *FEER*, 19 June 2003, p. 51. '[The US has] estimated that China has an annual military budget of $45 billion to $65 billion compared with the $20 billion figure announced by Beijing last year [2002]': *IHT*, 31 July 2003, p. 1.)

1 September and 1 October 2003.

In China couples must have permission from their employers before they can legally marry ... or, if they do not work for the state, from their Communist Party organized neighbourhood committees or village committees. That is finally set to change on 1 October ... Under the new rules couples who present themselves at marriage registries will need to bring only national identification cards and household-registration books ... The new marriage rule follows several other popular initiatives. In thirty-four cities concentrated on the east coast can now apply for passports without having to present letters from their state employers or street committees. From 1 September applicants in all those cities may also apply for travel passes to visit Hong Kong and Macau as individual tourists, again without the need for official letters ... [The aim is] to expand those programmes to 100 cities by the end of this year [2003] ... Another change in the marriage-registration rules [is] the scrapping of a requirement for couples to undergo premarital physical [health] check-ups.

(FEER, 11 September 2003, pp. 30–1)

On 1 September Beijing joined the ranks of Chinese cities that allow residents to apply for passports without written permission from a state employer or the police. From 1 October China will no longer require citizens to obtain permission before getting married or divorced. And a new policy announced last week bans employers from blocking owners of state-assigned housing from selling properties ... It was only in 2001 that China took tentative steps to scrap the requirement that *danwei* [the government-controlled work unit] approval – or if a citizen has no state-owned *danwei*, police permission – be given for the issuing of passports. Last year [2002] Shanghai joined the handful of cities to try this out. Officials say that this group, which Beijing has now joined, will grow to 100 cities by the end of this year [2003]. By 2005 every city in China, officially 658 of them, is supposed to be included ... More recently a *danwei* might have vetoed a marriage because of concerns about providing housing (a practice that the *danwei* abandoned only four years ago). Bribery was often the only way of getting permission. From 1 October the *danwei* will no longer be involved and couples will not have to undergo health examinations before getting married ... Housing reforms in the 1990s did not entirely release the *danwei*'s grip. Although employees were no longer given free housing, and instead had to buy or rent it, they often could not resell without their *danwei*'s permission. According to last week's directive, the *danwei* can no longer stop them except for legal or contractual reasons (such as the property being under joint ownership of the *danwei* and the occupier). Beijing has announced that from 1 October 800,000 homes that were once owned by central government organizations may be put on the market, a move that could double the amount of second-hand housing available in the capital.

(The Economist, 6 September 2003, p. 66)

October 2003.

In a speech on the eve of National Day ... President Hu Jintao ... called for a bigger public role in government, more 'socialist democracy' and a fairer legal system. 'We must enrich the forms of democracy, make democratic procedures complete, expand citizens' orderly political participation and ensure that the people can exercise democratic elections, democratic decision-making, democratic administration and democratic scrutiny,' Hu said.

(FEER, 16 October 2003, p. 32)

Relations between India and China ... took a marked turn for the better yesterday [8 October] when it emerged that Beijing has quietly conceded New Delhi's sovereignty over the Himalayan state of Sikkim ... High level envoys meet this month to discuss the remaining differences over their 3,500 kilometre common border.

(*FT*, 9 October 2003, p. 14)

11–14 October 2003.

The 'Third Plenum' meeting of the party's ruling Central Committee ... called for more equal treatment for private business, action to narrow the income gap between rich and poor and greater government emphasis on job creation – goals that largely reflected the socially orientated approach of Mr Hu's administration ... It underlined Mr Hu's desire to shift the government's focus while staying within the policy framework set by ... Jiang Zemin ... The communiqué made clear leaders' commitment to greater legal guarantees for private business ... 'Non-state sector enterprises [should] enjoy equal treatment in such areas as investment, taxation, land use and foreign trade,' it said. It softened the call, however, by offering only a vague promise of protection for property rights rather than explicit guarantees for private ownership, and stressed a continuing commitment to the role of state industry ... 'Increasing employment should be given a more prominent position in economic and social development,' the communiqué said, adding that greater effort should be made to spread wealth more evenly.

(*FT*, 16 October 2003, p. 11)

There was talk of the need to perfect the 'socialist market economy' (*FT*, 22 October 2003, p. 17).

Mr Hu and Mr Wen have made a habit of making high-profile visits to poor herders, rural schools and hard-toiling coalminers, the kinds of people and places that have been left behind by the wealthy coastal cities. Such concerns were clearly reflected in the communiqué ... 'Increasing employment should be given a more prominent in economic and social development,' the communiqué said. 'Emphasis should be put on resolving the excessive widening of the income gap between some parts of society' ... The communiqué committed the government to delivering 'a modern system of property rights' ... At the moment, however, legal protection for business profits, and the right of individuals to get compensation for forcible removal of property are based on administrative discretion rather than any clear or enforceable set of laws ... The final communiqué offered only a vague reference to the need actively to 'promote political system reform and widen socialist democracy'.

(*FT*, 18 October 2003, p. 15)

The new leaders ... have closed a secretive annual planning session [known as a plenum and lasting four days] with a broad pledge to deepen market reforms and to help the poor, but without detailing any new economic or political policies ... A communiqué ... did not reveal details about a plan to amend the constitution that had been widely discussed in state-controlled media ... The statement issued at the close of the party meeting did not depart markedly from past policies. But it emphasized the need to guarantee legal property rights, a key demand of private entrepreneurs. It also promised to allow the use of private capital in traditionally public endeavours, like building hospitals and schools. Officials said they intended to alter the constitution, but they did not say how or when … The party is committed to pursuing a more balanced vision of economic development by addressing sensitive social issues. It pledged to reduce unemployment in declining industrial cities and the country-side, to narrow gaps in income between rural and urban labourers, to set minimum income levels and to pursue other 'mechanisms for sustainable economic and social development'. No details were provided.

(www.iht.com, 16 October 2003)

This was the third plenum since the 16th Party Congress in November 2002 … China's 356 top politicians met amid discreet press coverage … [There are] 198 full members of the Central Committee … [There is also] the nine-member Politburo Standing Committee and twenty-four-member Politburo … At the end of a four-day, low-key meeting, the party's Central Committee plenum backed legal and regulatory changes that it said would 'perfect' the economic system, including fairer treatment for private enterprises and equal 'treatment in investment, financing, taxation, land use and foreign trade'. It said private enter-prises should be encouraged to enter previously closed sectors, such as infra-structure and public utilities. The official Xinhua news agency said the plenum approved a proposal to revise the constitution, but gave no details of what it was … 'We should protect all kinds of property ownership – and private ownership as well' … Hu Jintao [said on television] … Xinhua said the plenum approved a decision on improving the 'socialist market economic system', but gave no specifics. But an overall change of public stress under Hu in tackling the gap between rich and poor is a reaction to a strategy that favoured hard infrastruc-ture projects – roads, bridges and buildings – to keep the economy growing rapidly and producing new jobs. This worked, but at the cost of investment in soft infrastructure such as the health system, social welfare and rural education. Economist Zhang Zhuoyuan … [says] the blow from the outbreak of SARS earlier in the year contributed to a rethink of Beijing's pursuit of GDP growth while paying less attention to social management, public services and the devel-opment of society … His point chimes with the more caring image of Hu and premier Wen Jiabao projected by the party propaganda machine and also in private meetings with both men. Since taking power they have stressed the need for a more broad-based development and being seen to care more about ordin-ary people. 'Economic growth is not our only goal. We aim to balance eco-nomic growth, political developments and social undertakings,' Hu [said recently] … Hu said after the plenum that it was important that jobs should be found for people in the north-east. That focus sets Hu and Wen apart from Jiang's high-profile drive to develop the west and plays to their image of being truly concerned for those who lost out in reforms under Jiang and former premier Zhu Rongyi … The government has stated that it wants to see the establishment of a full market economy in China by 2010.

(*FEER*, 23 October 2003, pp. 34–7)

The Central Committee called for a narrowing of the rural–urban gap, for a better social security system and for private firms to be treated as equals of their state-owned counterparts. It also called for 'greater efforts' to accelerate the growth of cities – essential if the 300 million people in the countryside with little or nothing to do are to get a chance to work.

(*The Economist*, 18 October 2003, p. 69)

15 October 2003.

The Chinese spacecraft *Shenzhou 5* blasted off from the Gobi desert on Wednesday [15 October] carrying a single astronaut ... Yang Liwei ... The *Shenzhou 5*, or Divine Vessel, is expected to orbit Earth fourteen times before returning after a voyage of roughly twenty-one hours ... [The actual flight lasted twenty-one and a half hours] ... First with the Great Leap Forward of the late 1950s, then later the Cultural Revolution in the 1970s, China's domestic turmoil slowed, and at some points stopped, the space programme. In the early 1970s China had started a secret programme to send a man into space ... [but] the project was cancelled ... In 1992 Jiang Zemin ... signalled China's renewed ambitions in space with a new programme to send a man into orbit. Since then China has launched four unmanned spacecraft, beginning with *Shenzhou 1* in November 1991 ... Compared with the United States, where NASA has an annual budget of roughly $15 billion, the Chinese space budget of $2 billion is small ... The Chinese plan to begin exploring the moon, to launch a Hubble-like space telescope and, possibly, to construct a rival space station to the existing International Space Station.

(www.iht.com, 16 October 2003)

'China's first satellite [was] launched in 1970' (*IHT*, 16 October 2003, p. 6).

China is expected to launch its first manned space flight within a few days. It would be only the third country after the United States and Russia to develop an independent capacity to send people into orbit ... Western experts expect it to carry a crew of up to three military pilots into orbit for a few days ... Chinese officials spelled out longer-term plans to prepare for a lunar landing. China is expected to send an unmanned probe to the moon in around 2008.

(*FT*, 6 October 2003, p. 8)

Shenzou [means] Sacred Vessel ... Taikonaut [is derived] from *Taikong*, meaning space ... Between 1985 and 2000 twenty-seven foreign-made satellites were successfully launched ... An early attempt to develop it [manned space flight] in the 1970s was abandoned because of funding shortages ... China has ambitious plans for its manned programme, which may culminate in a mission to Mars ... The manned element ... includes development of a space station, a lunar base and missions to Mars ... [There are] plans for a manned orbiting space station ... A demonstrated capability of this sort might be used as a leverage with which to gain a role in the International Space Station from which China has been excluded.

(Michael Sheehan, *The World Today*, 2003, vol. 59, no. 11, pp. 16–17)

An astronaut is known as a 'taikonaut' in China. '"Taikonaut" [is] derived from the Chinese word for space, *taikong*, meaning too empty' (*The Times*, 16 October 2003, p. 24).

'China is investing more than $200 million in the European Galileo satellite navigation system, the proposed rival of the US Global Positioning System ... China has already fired seventy satellites into orbit' (*FT*, 16 October 2003, p. 20).

'[China] relied heavily on Russian technologies ... [The] spacecraft was based on the Russian *Soyuz* design and upgraded by the Chinese themselves ... Whether they can develop pioneering technologies, not just adapt old Russian designs, is yet to be determined' (*IHT*, 20 October 2003, p. 8).

(The first man in space was Yuri Gagarin of the Soviet Union, who orbited the earth on 12 April 1961. The United States followed soon afterwards.)

30 October 2003. 'Chinese and EU leaders exchanged pledges of closer economic co-operation and signed agreements paving the way for Beijing to join Europe's Galileo satellite navigation system and for more Chinese tourists to visit Europe' (*FT*, 31 October 2003, p. 11).

> [China is] to join the EU's radio navigation system, Galileo, to rival the US-run GPS system ... The two sides initialled an agreement on visas to make it easier for groups to travel to Europe. Approved Chinese travel agencies will be given preferential treatment for visas, provided their holidaymakers all return to China.
>
> (*Independent*, 31 October 2003, p. 13)

5 November 2003.

> China announced plans Wednesday [5 November] to send two more astronauts within the next two years on the country's second manned mission ... On Tuesday [4 November China] said they planned to launch a space station within ten years. They had announced plans for such a station on the day Yang Liwei returned but had no timetable until this week ... [On Tuesday China said it] had no plans in place for a human moon landing and that the nation would work at its own pace ... The military-linked manned space programme had been extremely secretive for years.
>
> (www.iht.com, 5 November 2003)

('Beijing says it will launch its own permanent manned space station within fifteen years ... The nation's chief designer of its space programme ... said China does not plan to send a man to the moon': *FEER*, 7 May 2004, p. 12.)

11 November 2003.

> China yesterday [11 November] announced a bold new drive to reform its state-owned enterprises ... Li Rongrong, chairman of the cabinet's state-owned assets and supervision commission (Sasac) said the 'acceleration and intensification of a process of selling state enterprises to foreign and private companies over the next two years would result in a shrinkage of the state-owned economy' ... At the moment 196 of China's largest and most strategic state enterprises are managed by Sasac, but Mr Li indicated for the first time

that even these companies could be at least partly privatised, especially if they did not perform well over the next two years. The state council (cabinet) has instructed Sasac to oversee the emergence of thirty to fifty internationally competitive enterprises, which would also constitute the leaders in their industry, Mr Li said ... Mr Li added that managers of state enterprises would be chosen from the open market rather than appointed by the Communist Party ... The party has decided ... it must sell parts of its biggest companies to foreign or private companies, officials said. Smaller companies could be released from state ownership ... The Communist Party's meeting last month [October] decided to accelerate the privatization of the economy. In line with that senior officials in Sichuan and Yunnan provinces in south-west China said they planned to put about 1,000 state companies up for acquisition by foreign or private companies next year [2004]. Mr Li said there would be no guidelines or minimum prices for state assets sold. 'The mechanisms of such transfers will be set by market forces,' he said. In the past Sasac has insisted that state assets could not be sold for less than the net asset value of a company, as judged by a local asset valuation firm. This stipulation has been a big hurdle to some foreign investors ... Beijing remains committed to retaining control of many state companies but is open to the idea of its shareholding falling to below 51 per cent, Mr Li said.

(*FT*, 12 November 2003, p. 11)

'China announced a new drive to reform its state-owned enterprises. It will speed up the sale of foreign assets to foreign and private companies over the next two years' (*The Economist*, 15 November 2003, p. 6). 'The government wants to sell to overseas investors and private entrepreneurs 2.6 trillion yuan, or $314 billion, worth of shares it holds in 189 of the country's most important companies' (*IHT*, 20 November 2003, p. 12).

12 November 2003.

An Indian navy flotilla ... has docked in Shanghai in a friendly visit ... The visit by the Indian navy follows on the heels of joint naval exercises off Shanghai between China and Pakistan ... Indian officials said the joint exercises would be focused purely on maritime search and rescue operations and improving safety at sea.

(*FT*, 13 November 2003, p. 15)

China Yangtze Power's initial public offering attracted fifteen strategic and 1,272 institutional investors ... Yangtze Power, the listing vehicle of the Three Gorges Dam project, issued 2.33 billion A shares at 4.3 renminbi (51 US cents) each to raise 10 billion renminbi.

(*FEER*, 20 November 2003, p. 29)

14 November 2003.

China and India began their joint naval exercises off Shanghai's coast on Friday [14 November] ... Three Indian Navy ships are taking part in the maritime safety and search-and-rescue exercises, which also included helicopters and fixed-wing aircraft ... The day of drills follows similar exercises off Shanghai last month [October] involving the Chinese Navy and warships from Pakistan, China's longtime ally and India's nuclear neighbour with whom relations are tense. Those exercises marked the first joint naval exercises between Chinese ships and the navy of another nation since the founding of the People's Republic of China in 1949 ... The exercises [with Pakistan] were nearly identical to the China–India exercises, involving two Pakistani ships and about 700 sailors and men in a simulated joint search-and-rescue and anti-terror operation.

(www.iht.com, 14 November 2003)

19 November 2003. 'The Chinese government gave a temperate response Wednesday [19 November] to the Bush administration's decision to restrict imports of certain Chinese fabrics and apparel, contending that the move [on 18 November] violated free-trade principles' (*IHT*, 20 November 2003, p. 11).

25 November 2003. 'The Chinese government said Tuesday [25 November] that it regretted a US decision to levy duties of up to 46 per cent on colour television imports' (www.iht.com, 25 November 2003).

18 December 2003.

[A US annual report says that] China has made little progress in lowering trade barriers and implementing proposed reforms promised when it joined the WTO ... [The report said that China's] 'uneven and incomplete WTO compliance record can no longer be attributed to start-up problems' ... The report noted major problems in agriculture, services, enforcement of intellectual property rights and transparency of government regulations ... The Bush administration cited China's 'questionable use' of tax policy to favour domestic production. Beijing was also accused of using industrial policies to encourage domestic industries at the expense of imports or foreign businesses operating in China.

(*IHT*, 20 December 2003, p. 11)

[This was] the strongest US criticism yet ... [The report said that] China's efforts to implement its WTO commitments had 'lost a significant amount of momentum' ... The report says that market mechanisms still operate poorly and that government officials intervene too frequently to direct or restrain trade flows. It also said that China had increased its use of industrial policies that encourage domestic companies at the expense of imports or foreign businesses operating in China. The report does praise China for progress in several areas, including better administration of its agricultural quotas, and improvements in financial services and motor vehicle financing.

(*FT*, 20 December 2003, p. 7)

22 December 2003.

China is changing its constitution to protect private property rights for the first time since the 1949 communist revolution ... A constitutional amendment endorsed by the Communist Party was put before legislators on Monday ... The proposed amendment on property says 'private property obtained legally shall not be violated', according to the official Xinhua press agency. The press agency said that would put private property 'on an equal footing with public property'. The amendments were submitted to the Standing Committee of the National People's Congress, a smaller, party-controlled body that handles law-making when the full legislature – which only meets two weeks a year – is out of session ... The party leaders also sent the National People's Congress a proposed amendment to enshrine in the constitution the theories of Jiang Zemin ... who invited capitalists to join the party ... The amendment on Jiang's theories says they shall be considered guiding principles along with the ideology of Mao Zedong and the late leader Deng Xiaoping, who initiated China's economic reforms ... Xinhua did not say whether Jiang would be mentioned by name.

(www.iht.com, 22 December 2003)

China's Communist Party has called for protection of private property to be written into the constitution, along with references to the political theory of Jiang Zemin ... though it is unclear if Mr Jiang's name will be written into the constitution ... Xinhua said Mr Jiang's political ideas – known as the 'Three Represents' ['advanced forces of production, advanced culture and the interests of the majority of the people'] – would be established as 'guiding principles of the nation', alongside Marxism, Leninism, Mao Zedong Thought and Deng Xiaoping Theory ... The constitutional proposals must still win formal approval from the National People's Congress [meeting in March 2004].

(*FT*, 23 December 2003, p. 5)

'A revised Article 5 will read: "Citizens legal private property is not to be violated ... The state protects citizens' property rights and inheritance rights according to the law"' (*FT*, 14 January 2004, p. 19).

23 December 2003.

At least 191 people were killed ... when a natural gas well in south-western China erupted and released a plume of toxic fumes ... The blast did not cause a fire ... The gas well burst on Tuesday [23 December] throwing a high concentration of natural gas and sulphurated hydrogen 30 metres [about 100 feet] into the air at the Chuandongbei field, which is owned by China National Petroleum, parent of the oil giant PetroChina ... The disaster happened in the densely populated Chongqing municipality in the Kaixian region.

(*Independent*, 26 December 2003, p. 20)

An explosion rocked a natural gas field in south-western China and spread poisonous fumes into the area ... The field ... [is] in Kaixian county, near the major municipality of Chongqing ... A plume of toxic chemicals [was created] ... Sulphurated hydrogen is a poisonous chemical that can kill when inhaled ... Local hospitals reported receiving victims of chemical burns ... China has a notoriously poor record for work safety, especially in low-end factories, coal mines and raw material processing industries. Natural gas is a high-priority industry for China. The authorities are eager to replace coal-burning furnaces with cleaner natural gas generators to fight air pollution.

(*IHT*, 26 December 2003, p. 3)

(The final death toll was 242.)

30 December 2003.

China yesterday [30 December] successfully launched a high-altitude research satellite that for the first time carried instruments provided by the European Space Agency (Esa). The first of two launches under the Sino-European 'Double Star' programme to research the Earth's magnetic field underlines China's growing clout in the space industry and its interest in greater international collaboration ... Esa said it had supplied eight of the instruments carried by the satellite ... the first time the agency had put scientific experiments on a Chinese spacecraft. The Europeans also supplied some funding for the mission, which was put together and controlled by the China National Space Administration.

(FT, 31 December 2003, p. 6)

2 January 2004.

South Korea and China yesterday [2 January 2004] lodged protests with Japan about the visit by prime minister Junichiro Koizumi to Yasukuni shrine, which honours the country's war dead ... [The shrine] commemorates the 2.5 million Japanese who have died in war since the 1850s, including fourteen class A war criminals. On New Year's Day Mr Koizumi made his fourth visit to the shrine since becoming prime minister in 2001 ... Taiwan urged Japan to be more sensitive to the painful wartime memories the shrine invokes in its neighbours.

(FT, 3 January 2003)

26–29 January 2004. President Hu Jintao visits France.

The EU could decide this spring to lift its ban on arms sales to China ... Reported defence spending grew 17.6 per cent to $20 billion in 2002, but foreign analysts say the true spending is likely to be four times the official figures.

(IHT, 27 January 2004, p. 3)

'President Jacques Chirac of France ... threw his weight behind moves to end the arms embargo imposed on China by the EU after the 1989 Tiananmen Square massacre' *(FT*, 28 January 2004, p. 13).

12 February 2004. 'The signing in Beijing [is to take place] on 12 February of an agreement – known as "approved destination status", or ADS – that will allow Chinese tour groups much easier access to most EU member states' *(FEER*, 12 February 2004, p. 27).

China granted twelve EU-member countries the status of 'approved destinations', making it easier for tour groups to travel to Europe. Beijing also promised it would facilitate the return of any of its citizens caught using this easier access to illegally migrate to the EU ... The ten new countries acceding to the agreement on 1 May will also be party to the agreement after they join.

(FEER, 26 February 2004, p. 27)

16 February 2004.

John Bolton, US undersecretary of state for arms control ... yesterday [16 February] urged China to help curb the spread of weapons of mass destruction but stopped short of criticizing Beijing over reports that nuclear weapons designs found in Libya came from China via Pakistan ... A *Washington Post* report [said] that the US government had documents showing China was involved in Pakistan's nuclear programme, a charge long suspected by Washington but denied by Beijing. The report said the documents were found in Libya and some included text in Chinese as well as detailed instructions for assembling an implosion-type nuclear bomb.

(*FT*, 17 February 2004, p. 10)

China yesterday [18 February] expressed concern about reports that Chinese nuclear weapon blueprints were found in Libya ... [The foreign ministry] said the Chinese authorities were looking into the issue ... The Chinese origin of the Libyan weapons designs was first reported on Sunday [15 February] by the *Washington Post* ... US intelligence has long contended that China provided Pakistan with a nuclear warhead design in the early 1980s. However, the new disclosures raise questions about what else has been exchanged.

(*FT*, 18 February 2004, p. 10)

24 February 2004.

Army surgeon Jiang Yanyong's letter to state media last year [2003] revealed Beijing's burgeoning epidemic of SARS ... In a letter to party and government leaders dated 24 February Jiang suggested 'rectifying the name of the 4 June 1989, patriotic student movement'. He recounts in grisly detail treating the wounded and dying at his hospital in western Beijing ... Even the late President Yang Shangkun and late vice-premier Chen Yun condemned the Tiananmen Massacre as a grave mistake, Jiang asserts.

(*FEER*, 18 March 2004, p. 15)

Jiang Yanyong refers to the students in the square as innocent patriots 'fighting corruption and bureaucratic racketeering' ... Jiang Yanyong: 'A small number of leaders who supported corruption resorted to means unprecedented in the world and in China. They acted in a frenzied fashion, using tanks, machine guns and other weapons to suppress totally unarmed students and citizens, killing hundreds of innocent students in Beijing, and injuring and crippling thousands of others. Then the authorities mobilized all types of propaganda machinery to fabricate lies and used highhanded measures to silence the people across the country.'

(*IHT*, 12 March 2004, p. 6)

5 March 2004. The annual session of the National People's Congress begins. The session is due to last ten days.

Prime minister Wen Jiabao:

[The economy has reached] a critical juncture ... Deep-seated problems and imbalances in the economy over the years have not been fundamentally resolved, and new problems and imbalances keep cropping up in the process of rapid development. Excessive investment; shortages in energy, transport capacity and important raw materials; a decrease in grain output in recent years; and an obvious trend in rising prices [are challenging the government]. This test is no less severe than the SARS episode we had to deal with last year [2003]. Macro-control [of the economy] is more difficult than ever. If we adjust well we may be able to keep the ship of the Chinese economy steady at a relatively fast clip. If we do not it will be difficult to avoid setbacks ... I am somewhat troubled by the last two aspects [referring to the recapitalized Bank of China and China Construction Bank taking responsibility for cutting bad loans and hiring competent staff], but there is no alternative. This reform for us is a make or break reform, and success is the only acceptable option ... Unity and stability are of overriding importance [referring to the letter about Tiananmen Square sent by Jiang Yanyong on 24 February].

(*FEER*, 25 March 2004, pp. 24–5)

('A 2004 growth rate target of "more than 7 per cent" [was set]': www.iht.com, 2004).

Prime minister Wen Jiabao ... vowed Friday [5 March] to cool China's surging economy and focus more resources on millions of people left behind in the boom ... [He] implicitly criticized his predecessors for stimulating high growth through heavy state investment. He said this had led to rampant waste and had done too little to raise the incomes of peasants ... 'Rural incomes have grown too slowly, and development if different regions of the country is not balanced,' Wen said ... China has a 'serious problem of haphazard development', he said, adding that peasants had suffered 'widespread illegal appropriation of farmland' ... He outlined a broad plan to restructure the rural economy, promising to revamp the state-controlled grain procurement system, eliminate some rural taxes and reduce others, and increase agricultural investment this year [2004] by 20 per cent ... For the urban unemployed, Wen said, the government will nearly double spending on retraining ... He said the government would insist that companies 'strictly obey minimum wage regulations', which are routinely ignored, even by some prominent foreign companies. Wen also pledged that the government would eliminate the widespread problem of unpaid wages for rural workers, especially in the construction industry, within three years. 'We will concentrate on resolving prominent conflicts in economic and social development and promoting all-round balanced and sustainable development,' he said.

(www.ihr.com, 5 March 2004)

Wen Jiabao ... in his first opening address to the National People's Congress ... promised to eliminate agricultural taxes and rein in over-investment as part of a new push by the central government to reduce yawning income and geographical disparities in favour of more balanced economic growth ... to create a sustainable and balanced growth ... [He promised] to cut agricultural taxes by 1 percentage point each year – eliminating them by 2007 ... Wen signalled a renewed determination to quell overheated investment, especially in certain sectors such as steel, cement, property and aluminium. One way in which these projects would be reined in was by enforcing stricter environmental standards and land-use laws. 'Projects that do not meet standards for environmental protection, safety and energy consumption and technology should be blocked and those already under construction should resolve such problems,' the premier said ... 'Macro control should be neither too loose or too tight,' Mr Wen said ... Mr Wen called for faster production of coal, electricity, oil and other raw materials that are in considerable shortage across China. The construction of transport capacity, such as roads, railways and ports had also to be speeded up.

(*FT*, 6 March 2004, p. 5)

('[It has been announced that] authorities would eliminate central government taxes on farmers in three years instead of the five announced by premier Wen Jiabao in March': *FEER*, 22 April 2004, p. 23.)

'Rural incomes have grown too slowly and development in different regions of the country is not balanced ... The income gap is too wide among some members of society,' Mr Wen said ... Mr Wen said he expected growth of 7 per cent in 2004 ... Lawmakers will review measures to stamp out corruption.

(*The Times*, 6 March 2004, p. 22)

('"China is ranked among countries at level fifty-nine on a scale of 102 in Transparency International's 2002 Corruption Perception Index': www.iht.com, 8 September 2003. In the 2004 index Finland remained the least corrupt at number one. China ranked seventy-one out of 145 countries: *The Economist*, 23 October 2004, p. 118.)

'[The prime minister] said agriculture would now be a "top priority" ... Grain production would be directly subsidized by the central government' (*Telegraph*, 6 March 2004, p. 16).

China is widely forecast to become a net grain importer in 2004 or 2005 ... US economist Lester Brown said in a report released during the NPC that China's grain harvest fell in four of the past five years – to 322 million tonnes in 2003 from 392 million tonnes in 1998.

(*FEER*, 25 March 2004, p. 25)

In a bid to relieve pressure from inequalities that threaten social stability, China's leaders unveiled policies at the annual National People's Congress (NPC) to slow economic growth and lift hundreds of millions of farmers out of poverty ... Premier Wen Jiabao announced cuts to state investment in sectors that provided much of the rapid growth in recent years, and forecast 7 per cent growth this year. Also agricultural taxes will be phased out by 2007 and official spending will aim to raise rural incomes by 5 per cent in 2004 ... In the budget announced at the NPC military spending rose 11.6 per cent, from 9.6 per cent growth in 2003 when the public military budget was 185 billion renminbi ($22 billion). Analysts said hidden spending makes the real figure much higher ... Wen Jiabao and economic planners announced a range of measures to end energy shortages endangering economic growth. They told the NPC that the government aims to put its $20 billion west-to-east natural gas pipeline project into full commercial operation this year, months ahead of schedule. And it wants to build 40 gigawatts of power generating capacity.

(FEER, 18 March 2004, p. 30)

[On 14 March] the NPC voted to adopt significant changes to the national constitution, for the first time protecting the legitimacy of 'legally obtained' private property ... Another amendment enshrined the respect of 'human rights' in the constitution, also for the first time.

(FT, 15 March 2004, p. 14)

China's parliament formally approved constitutional amendments Sunday [14 March] to protect private property and human rights, and the new prime minister vowed to rein in the overheated economy ... Wen indicated that the government would maintain a cautious, piecemeal approach to political changes while focussing on the overheating economy and rickety banking system ... The 2,900-member legislature approved a series of thirteen changes to the constitution. 'The state respects and preserves human rights,' one reads. Another change states that 'citizens' lawful private property is inviolable' and it says that the state will protect private property and give compensation when it is confiscated. The legislature also authorized introducing into the constitution some key slogans of ... Jiang Zemin [the 'three represents'].

(IHT, 15 March 2004, p. 1)

The amendment reads: 'Private property obtained legally is inviolable' ... [with] 2,863 voting in favour, ten against and with seventeen abstentions ... The constitutional protection of private property was the first since ... 1949 ... Also added [was] the first mention of human rights to the constitution ... 'The state respects and preserves human rights,' the amendment said.

(The Times, 15 March 2004, p. 16)

On the last day of the ten-day session the NPC amended the constitution to include formal guarantees of human rights and private property. 'Legally obtained private property of the citizens shall not be violated,' said one the most significant of thirteen amendments passed by the NPC. 'The state respects and protects human rights,' said another. But the changes were more symbolic than practical because courts in China do not usually consider whether laws are constitutional. The human rights amendment, for instance, was not at odds with restrictions on public protest because the constitution is subordinate to the Chinese Communist Party. The NPC also enshrined in the constitution former President Jiang Zemin's 'three represents' theories.

(FEER, 25 March 2004, p. 24)

'Even now public ownership retains preferred status. The constitution refers to it as "sacred"' (*The Economist,* Survey, 20 March 2004, p. 16).
16 March 2004.

The navies of China and France begin today [16 March] joint exercises off the north Chinese coast ... The exercises involve search-and-rescue missions, refuelling and tactical helicopter exchanges ... This was the first time two French warships had taken part in exercises, although the two navies had co-operated on twelve occasions.

(*FT*, 16 March 2004, p. 10)

'[This is China's] biggest naval drill with a foreign country' (*IHT*, 17 March 2004, p. 3).

25 March 2004.

Seven Chinese activists have reignited a bitter dispute between China and Japan over who owns a group of rocky, uninhabited islands in the East China Sea. China on Thursday [25 March] denounced Japan's decision to detain the seven activists, who landed on one of the disputed islands on Wednesday [24 March]. It called the arrest of the men a violation of its sovereignty over the islands, which provide access to rich fishing grounds and possible oil deposits in the area ... Japan has formally claimed sovereignty over the islands since 1895 and has said Beijing did not stake its claim until the 1970s, when information emerged about possible oil deposits in the area. China and Taiwan have said their claims go back to ancient times.

(www.iht.com, 25 March 2004)

26 March 2004.

The Japanese authorities said on Friday [26 March] that they would immediately deport without charge seven Chinese activists ... It was the first landing since 1996 and the first time activists had even been detained. Japan declared sovereignty over the islands when it defeated China in an 1895 war. They were temporarily put under US control after World War II and were returned to Japan in 1972, along with Okinawa. In the early 1970s China and Taiwan made claims to the islands after oil deposits were confirmed in the area by a United Nations agency. Both of them say that their claims date back centuries.

(www.iht.com, 26 March 2004)

5 April 2004.

Zhao Ziyang [eighty-four], who became a potent symbol of thwarted political reform after he was purged during the 1989 crackdown on dissent, is in critical health and is being kept alive by a respirator at his home in Beijing, people close to his family said Monday [5 April]. Though he has long been under house arrest and out of public view, Zhao's death could pose a challenge to China's leadership ... Officials have already been trying to squelch demands that they revise their own account of what happened in Beijing on 3 and 4 June 1989 ... They could face the possibility that Zhao, who was stripped of his post after taking a soft line on the protests, could die and provide an additional impetus to those seeking redress for the crackdown, which killed hundreds around Beijing ... China's long tradition of paying homage to the dead makes it unseemly for the police to repress mourners, potentially allowing a window for people to express grievances along with condolences ... Anointed in the 1980s as a successor to Deng Xiaoping ... Zhao favoured a relatively bold pace of political and economic reform. His hold on power weakened, however, when the mainly state-run economy overheated, sparking inflation, and students organized peaceful but huge demonstrations in the heart of the capital. Zhao's last public appearance came on 19 May 1989 when he made an impromptu visit to Tiananmen Square. He pleaded with students to leave the square, apologizing for having arrived too late and warning them that the police planned to remove them by force. Martial law was declared the following day and Zhao was stripped of power. The army moved in on the night of 3 June with tanks and armoured personnel carriers, gunning down hundreds who tried to stop their advances ... Most analysts say they believe the leadership is united in its view that the crackdown was a necessary price to pay for a long period of political stability.

(www.iht.com, 6 April 2004)

'Zhao Ziyang [was] ... named General Secretary of the Communist Party in 1987 ... [After Tiananmen he] was sacked as General Secretary' (*The Times*, 7 April 2004, p. 14).

Zhao Ziyang's last public appearance was on 19 May 1989, when he visited Tiananmen Square and begged students to leave. Martial law was declared the next day and he was fired. Analysts said his death could be a rallying point for reformers and those who lost out from China's economic success.

(*FEER*, 15 April 2004, p. 24)

7 April 2004.

Prime minister Junichiro Koizumi of Japan vowed Wednesday [7 April] to continue his controversial visits to a war shrine despite a court ruling that declared the pilgrimages unconstitutional. The visits have drawn ire from China and South Korea [and North Korea], which were occupied by Japan during World War II ... In the first such ruling against Koizumi's visits ... [the court said] that the prime minister's visit to Yasukuni Shrine on 13 August 2001 had violated the constitutional separation of church and state ... Koizumi went four times to Yasukuni.

(www.iht.com, 7 April 2004)

27 April 2004.

Asian governments have signed a landmark UN-brokered agreement to complete a vast international highway network that officials hope will rival the ancient Silk Road. The accord to set up a highway network was signed by twenty-three nations. The road network will link Tokyo with Singapore, Istanbul and St Petersburg in some 140,000 kilometres [87,500 miles] of routes.

(*FT*, 28 April 2004, p. 11)

Yesterday [27 April] India joined twenty-three countries, including China and Japan, in signing up to the Asian Highway network ... Russia is expected to join the pact today [28 April], followed by seven more countries in the next few months ... The idea of the Asian highway was mooted in 1959 ... The Asian highway will use existing routes improved to international quality.

(*The Times*, 28 April 2004, p. 14)

9 May 2004.

Police have detained forty-seven people accused of selling fake infant formula that led to the deaths of dozens of children in an eastern city, the government announced yesterday [10 May]. The deaths prompted a national crackdown on safety violations in China's food and drugs market, where phoney medicines and other products regularly cause deaths and injuries. State media say fifty to sixty children, mostly from poor farm families, died of malnutrition in the city of Fuyang after being fed the bogus formula.

(*FT*, 11 May 2004, p. 8)

1 June 2004.

Struggling to keep up economically with Shanghai and the rest of the Yangtze River basin, the leaders of nine provinces and the two special administrative regions in south-eastern China announced here [in Hong Kong] on Tuesday [1 June] the creation of a regional forum to co-ordinate economic policy ... the Pan-Pearl River Delta Regional Co-operation and Development Forum ... The new grouping will align Hong Kong and Macau with the provinces of Yunnan, Guizhou, Guangdong, Fujian, Hunan, Jiangxi, Hunan, Guangxi, Hainan and Sichuan against Shanghai and its neighbours ... The grouping [ranges] ... from impoverished and landlocked Yunnan and Guizhou provinces to wealthy Hong Kong ... The national and provincial leaders here called for the elimination of many of the non-tariff barriers that currently discourage trade between provinces, as well as closer co-ordination of provincial government policies.

(www.iht.com, 1 June 2004; *IHT*, 2 June 2004, p. 17)

Leaders from Hong Kong, Macau and nine provinces in southern China agreed on 3 June to construct a regional economic bloc to compete with Shanghai's rapidly growing economy. The leaders agreed to co-operate in energy production, education, transport and environmental protection. This pan-Pearl River Delta region already accounts for roughly 40 per cent of China's GDP.

(*FEER*, 17 June 2004, p. 30)

4 June 2004.

Throngs gathered here [Hong Kong] Friday night [4 June] to mark the fifteenth anniversary of the Tiananmen Square killings in Beijing as the day passed fairly peacefully on the mainland, although at least sixteen people were arrested on the square itself ... As the anniversary neared Chinese authorities reportedly detained activists and the relatives of people killed in 1989 or ordered them to leave Beijing ... An annual candlelight vigil in Hong Kong has become the main remembrance of the military crackdown, drawing tens of thousands of people, including some from the mainland ... Activists for the first time had distributed fliers to tourists from the mainland, urging them to attend the vigil ... Three popular radio talk show hosts in Hong Kong have quit in the last five weeks, complaining of pressure to limit their pro-democracy views. In the past week a succession of mainland officials have stepped forward to insist that the radio hosts had not been intimidated and to suggest that one of them ... had misunderstood a late-night phone call from a former mainland official.

(www.iht.com, 4 June 2004)

'Organizers claimed 82,000 people turned out, but the police said the crowd peaked at 48,000' (*Independent*, 5 June 2004, p. 32).

The vigil ... an annual event in Hong Kong ... usually draws 40,000 to 50,000 people ... The scant police presence at the vigil contrasted with the stringent security measures taken in Tiananmen Square, where sixteen people were reported to have been arrested. Yesterday's tight security followed the disappearance earlier this week of Jiang Yanyong, the military doctor who exposed Beijing's cover-up of SARS and recently wrote to Chinese leaders recommending a reassessment of the 1989 protest.

(*FT*, 5 June 2004, p. 8)

Jiang Yanyong [was] detained before the fifteenth anniversary of the 4 June Tiananmen Square massacre [has] since been held incommunicado ... Jiang was detained along with his wife ... while en route to the US embassy on 1 June to get a visa.

(www.iht.com, 10 June 2004)

'[In Tiananmen] on the night of 3–4 June 1989 ... officially 240 died, but most people think the true number was hundreds more – if not thousands' (*Telegraph*, 4 June 2004, p. 18).

'[There were] 1,500 to 2,000 civilian deaths on 4 June 1989. About 2,000 individuals are still in prison, and thousands more are in exile' (www.iht.com, 22 February 2005).

15 June 2004.

China is sending nuclear technology to Iran in exchange for oil and allowing North Korea to use Chinese air, rail and seaports to ship missiles and other weapons, congressional investigators reported Tuesday [15 June] ... The US China Economic and Security Review Commission [was] established by Congress in 2000 ... 'Continuing intelligence reports indicate that Chinese cooperation with Pakistan and Iran remains an integral element of China's foreign policy,' the commission reported ... Chinese leaders have told the Americans that any nuclear-related trafficking is done without the government's knowledge ... Beijing 'continues to permit North Korea to use its air, rail and seaports to transship ballistic missiles and WMD [weapons of mass destruction]-related materials', the commission said.

(www.iht.com, 15 June 2004)

('Beijing has a long history of missile and missile-related sales overseas, and in the 1980s provided Pakistan with enriched uranium and a working bomb design, which was later sold to Libya and possibly North Korea and Iran': *FT*, 13 April 2004, p. 1.)

20 June 2004. 'Britain and China conducted their first joint naval [search and rescue] exercises off the Chinese coast' (*Guardian*, 21 June 2004, p. 14).

19 July 2004.

The military authorities have released the prominent surgeon who exposed China's SARS cover-up and condemned the 1989 crackdown on democracy protesters ... Jiang Yanyong, seventy-two, was allowed to return home late Monday night [19 July] after about forty-five days in military custody, where he was subjected to political indoctrination sessions and investigated for possible criminal activity, according to one person told about his case ... Jiang [is] a senior member of the Communist Party who holds a rank that corresponds to lieutenant general or major general in the West ... [On] 1 June ... Jiang and Hua Zhingwei [his wife] were intercepted on their way to an appointment and taken into custody. She was released in mid-June.

(*IHT*, 21 July 2004, pp. 1, 10)

'[Jiang Yanyong and his wife] were detained on 1 June while going to the US embassy for visas to visit their California-based daughter' (*Guardian*, 21 July 2004, p. 13).

18 August 2004. Li Peng:

In the spring and summer of 1989 a serious disturbance broke took place in China. With the boldness of vision of a great revolutionary and politician, comrade Deng Xiaoping – along with other party elders – gave the leadership their firm and full support to put down the political disturbance using forceful measures ... Comrade Xiaoping said: 'What I am worried about is that you are not bold enough to carry out your work. You have to learn hard and train yourself in work in order to make yourself more mature.'

(*IHT*, 19 August 2004, p. 8, and 25 August 2004, p. 8)

('A few months ago Jiang Yanyong, a senior doctor in Beijing's Army Hospital 301, daringly described – before he was made to disappear for several weeks – the reasons for the civilian carnage he treated in his hospital in the first week of June 1989: "A small number of leaders who supported corruption resorted to means unprecedented in the world and in China. They acted in a frenzied fashion, using tanks, machine guns and other weapons to suppress the totally unarmed students and citizens, killing hundreds of innocent students in Beijing, and injuring and crippling thousands of others. Then, the authorities mobilized all types of propaganda machinery to fabricate lies and used high-handed measures to silence the people across the country"': *IHT*, 25 August 2004, p. 8. 'Jiang Yanyong, the military doctor who blew the whistle on the SARS cover-up, urged the party to reconsider the acts of the [Tiananmen] demonstrators as "patriotic"': *Guardian*, 19 August 2004, p. 19.)

22 August 2004. The 100th anniversary of the birth of Deng Xiaoping. (There was a week of celebrations.) He died in 1997.

19 September 2004. '[A] closed [four-day] meeting of the 198-member Central Committee of the Communist Party [ends]' (*The Times*, 20 September 2004, p. 14).

President Hu Jintao consolidated power ... as Jiang Zemin, seventy-eight, ... stepped down as chairman of the party's Central Military Commission [CMC] and Mr Hu ... sixty-one ... took his place Mr Jiang failed at the plenum to secure a post for Zeng Qinghong, his protégé, within the CMC. Party sources said Mr Jiang had been insisting that Mr Zeng, who is a Politburo member and vice-president, be appointed to a role as vice-chairman ... Hu Jintao became party chief in 2002 and national president [in 2003].

(*FT*, 20 September 2004, p. 10)

'It completes the most orderly transition of power since the 1949 revolution, adding the military post – the final panel of the Chinese triptych of power – to Mr Hu's leadership of the Communist Party and the state' (p. 18).

President Hun Jintao replaced Jiang Zemin as China's military chief ... completing the first orderly transfer of power in Chinese Communist Party history ... Jiang's resignation, which came as a surprise to many party officials, who expected the tenacious elder leader to cling to power for several more years, came after tensions between Jiang and Hu began to affect policy-making ... some political analysts said ... Hu and Jiang did not publicly spar. But there were signs that their relationship had become strained ... Jiang may be suffering from health problems ... [He] submitted a letter of resignation earlier this month ... The letter was dated 1 September ... [Jiang] failed to arrange for vice-president Zeng Qinghong to be elevated to the Central Military Commission. Party officials had said that they expected Zeng ... to become either a regular member or a vice-chairman of the commission.

(*IHT*, 20 September 2004, pp. 1, 4)

'Deng Xiaoping retained his position as the chairman of the military commission at the Communist Party's Thirteenth Congress in October 1987 and turned over the chairmanship to Jiang Zemin in November 1989' (*IHT*, 21 September 2004, p. 8).

'[Jiang's] term of office as chairman of the Central Military Commission had been scheduled to expire in 2007' (*The Times*, 20 September 2004, p. 14).

'The state's Central Military Commission exists only on paper. Mr Jiang will remain its nominal chief until next March when the legislature next convenes' (*The Economist*, 25 September 2004, p. 80).

China's Communist Party ... has managed for the first time to engineer a leadership transition without the turmoil and bloodshed that accompanied earlier changes at the top ... Hu Jintao (15 September): 'History indicates that indiscriminately copying Western political systems is a blind alley for China' ... The party plenum focussed on 'strengthening the building of the party's ability to govern' ... Membership of the Central Military Commission was broadened from four to seven.

(*FEER*, 30 September 2004, pp. 31–2)

1 October 2004. '[China] attended a working dinner of the Group of Seven industrialized nations on Friday [1 October] ... The dinner was the first time that China ... had attended a G7 meeting' (*FT*, 4 October 2004, p. 7).

14 October 2004.

China and Russia settled the last of their decades-old border disputes during a visit to Beijing by President Vladimir Putin, signing an agreement fixing their

2,700-mile-long border for the first time ... Beijing and Moscow had reached agreements on individual border sections ... but a stretch of river and islands along China's north-eastern border with Russia's Far East had remained in dispute ... At one point the Soviet Union was believed to have as many as 700,000 troops on the border, facing as many as 1 million soldiers from China.

(*IHT*, 15 October 2004, p. 3)

Russia and China had reached a 'final settlement' of their border, which stretches 3,483 kilometres, or 2,164 miles. To resolve a dispute over three river islands controlled by Russia, one was allotted to China [Tarabarov] and one to Russia. The largest one [Bolshoi Ussuriisky Island] was split down the middle.

(*IHT*, 22 January 2005, p. 2)

A supplementary agreement [was signed] on the eastern part of the Russian–Chinese border, an accord that decided the fate of the disputed islands in the Amur and Argun rivers. The agreement capped forty years of efforts to delineate the border ... In December 1999 the leaders of Russia and China signed basic demarcation documents on the western section (54.57 kilometres) and eastern section (4,195.22 kilometres) of the border. The sides divided 2,444 islands and sandbars in the border rivers roughly in half. Damansky Island went to China. That agreement did not include the islands of Bolshoi Ussuriisky and Tarabarov near Khabarovsk, or Bolshoi Island in the Argun river ... The islands [of Tarabarov and Bolshoi Ussuriisky] are to be transferred to China.

(*CDSP*, 2004, vol. 656, no. 42, pp. 2–4)

17 January 2005.

Zhao Ziyang, the former General Secretary of the Communist Party who was stripped of power for supporting students during their 1989 pro-democracy Tiananmen Square protests, died in a Beijing hospital on Monday [17 January 2005] ... He was eighty-five and had been in a coma since Friday [14 January] after suffering a series of strokes. For the past fifteen years Zhao had lived under house arrest ... No charges were brought against him ... During his long confinement he had become a powerful symbol for those Chinese who believe the government must reassess its bloody crackdown at Tiananmen. He blamed top leaders for ordering the military assault, and he refused to embrace the official line that the demonstrations had been a 'counter-revolutionary rebellion'. In what would be his last public appearance, Zhao visited students at Tiananmen on 19 May 1989. He pleaded with them to leave, apologized for having arrived 'too late', and warned that the authorities were planning to remove them. It is now clear that Zhao made the visit directly after being fired by China's Politburo. Martial law was introduced the next day in a prelude to the crackdown on 3–4 June, when soldiers fired on protesters throughout Beijing, killing hundreds, possibly more ... Zhao's role at Tiananmen came to overshadow his other legacy as a principal architect of the sweeping economic changes [including agricultural reforms and special economic zones] that began under Deng Xiaoping, then China's paramount leader.

(www.iht.com, 17 January 2005; *IHT*, 18 January 2005, p. 4)

'The army killed hundreds, perhaps thousands of demonstrators around the capital on 4 June [1989]' (*IHT*, 18 January 2005, p. 1). ('On 4 June [1989] the People's Liberation Army seized Beijing ... killing hundreds ... Thousands of protesters were killed in Beijing and other Chinese cities': *FT*, 18 January 2005, p. 9.)

'The government statement yesterday [17 January] said: "Comrade Zhao died of illness in a Beijing hospital"' (*The Times*, 18 January 2005, p. 27).

Zhao Ziyang (19 May 1989, addressing the demonstrators in Tiananmen Square): 'We have come too late and it is only right that you criticize us' (*The Times*, 18 January 2005, p. 51)

The official Communist Party report on Zhao Ziyang after Tiananmen said:

> Comrade Zhao Ziyang committed the serious mistake of supporting the turmoil and splitting the party. He had the unshirkable responsibility for the shaping up and development of the turmoil ... The nature of his mistakes is very serious ... [He had connived in the spread of] bourgeois liberalization].
>
> (*The Times*, 18 January 2005, p. 52; *Telegraph*, 18 January 2005, p. 23)

'Zhao Ziyang wrote several letters to his successors to call for "reversing the verdict of Tiananmen Square"' (*Guardian*, 18 January 2005, p. 23).

'Market reforms he [Zhao Ziyang] said were necessary in the "primary stage of socialism"' (*The Times*, 19 January 2005, p. 17).

'The "gold coast" policy ... referred to the policy of opening up the entire coastal region to trade and foreign investment' (*The Times*, 18 January 2005, p. 51). 'Zhao was also responsible for helping to father the special economic zones and attracting investments, especially export manufacturing jobs, to the "gold coasts" of Guangdong, Fujian and Zhejiang provinces' (*Independent*, 18 January 2005, p. 34).

'[Zhao Ziyang pushed for] political reforms intended to separate party and state' (*FT*, 18 January 2005, p. 9). '[In 1986 Zhao Ziyang called] for elections offering a choice of candidates from village level to the membership of the Central Committee. The following year, at the Thirteenth Communist Party Congress, he proposed separating government from the Communist Party' (*Telegraph*, 18 January 2005, p. 23). 'The aim of the [political] programme was always rather vague. It included direct voting in the Politburo, elections with more than one candidate, more transparency, more consultation and individual responsibility for mistakes' (*Independent*, 18 January 2005, p. 34).

20 January 2005.

> The Chinese authorities will hold a low-key service for Zhao Ziyang ... and have given permission to bury his body in a cemetery reserved for senior party officials ... The State Council, China's cabinet, issued a statement: '[The government will hold a] farewell service for the body [of Zhao Ziyang] ... We will follow this format for Comrade Zhao Ziyang, who was a veteran member of our party.'
>
> (www.iht.com, 20 January 2005; *IHT*, 21 January 2005, p. 3)

27 January 2005.

> Senior Communist Party officials and the family of Zhao Ziyang ... have agreed to hold a public burial service for Zhao on Saturday [29 January] ... A

public 'farewell ceremony for the body' is to be held at the Babaoshan cemetery, where many ranking party officials are buried ... The government will
issue the traditional official 'life assessment' ... But in a modest compromise
the assessment will be released by Xinhua after the burial service rather than
be presented at the service itself.

(www.iht.com, 27 January 2005)

'[A] "farewell to the body" [is] a far more restrained event than a state funeral –
with only the state news agency Xinhua authorized to report on proceedings' (*FT*,
28 January 2005, p. 12).

'Memorial gatherings after the death of premier Zhou Enlai ... sparked three
days of anti-government protests on Tiananmen Square in 1976. Police broke up
the gatherings, killing some protesters and arresting others' (*Independent*, 29
January 2005, p. 34).

29 January 2005.

Zhao Ziyang was officially memorialized and cremated Saturday [29 January]
... [Some] 2,000 mourners filed past Zhao's body ... [There was] an overwhelming policy presence, as well as careful vetting of the guest list ... [There
were no] open expressions of dissent ... Scores of opposition figures were kept
under guard and barred from attending ... Xinhua issued a traditional ... life
assessment that noted Zhao's contributions to 'the party and the people' to
soften the longstanding condemnation of his 'grave errors', which the life
assessment reiterated.

(www.iht.com, 30 January 2005; *IHT*, 31 January 2005, p. 4)

5–14 March 2005. A session of the National People's Congress is held.
'This year [2005] Chinese parliament leaders are treating the [Taiwan] "anti-
secession law" as their top issue' (www.iht.com, 10 March 2005). (See the section
on Taiwan.)

On Friday [4 March it was announced that] China intended to increase its officially declared spending on its military by 12.6 per cent this year [2005] to
$29.9 billion ... This latest rise comes after increases of 11.6 per cent in 2004,
9.6 per cent in 2003, 17.6 per cent in 2002 and regular double-digit increases in
the decade before that. China's official military budget is dwarfed by the
United States' military budget of $400 billion for 2005 and it is less than half
the size of Japan's military budget. But some Western experts estimate that the
real size of China's military spending is several times the official number,
placing it third behind the United States and Russia in military spending, and
there is no doubt China has embarked on an ambitious effort to develop or buy
advanced aircraft, naval vessels and missiles ... [It was also announced that]
this year's military budget increase will be used to cut troop numbers by
200,000, but it was unclear whether this referred to previously announced cut-
backs of that number or new reductions. Currently China's military has about
2.4 million personnel.

(www.iht.com, 4 March 2005)

'The official military budget rises to $30 billion in 2005. Western analysts say that actual spending may be two or three times higher' (www.iht.com, 13 March 200). 'China has 2.5 million regular troops and around one million paramilitary policemen' (*IHT*, 19 April 2005, p. 9).

'Actual [military] spending is far higher [than the figure in the budget] ... since the official figure does not include much of China's weapons purchases from abroad or spending on research and development' (*The Economist*, 12 March 2005, p. 70).

> The defence budget for 2004 ...did not include the budget for the vast military police, reserve forces, major weapons acquisition and military R&D. In addition, the People's Liberation Army also receives significant revenues from arms sales to foreign countries and its many affiliated business undertakings. It is safe to say that the actual number [for military spending] triples the published figure [for the defence budget].
>
> (Sheng-ren Liu, *RUSI Newsbrief*, 2005, vol. 25, no. 4, p. 48)

('China's military spending far exceeds what is officially acknowledged but is far less than many experts believe – less than a fifth of what the Pentagon spends and on a par with other nuclear powers, a report funded by the US Air Force said Friday [20 May 2005]. The report, by the RAND research group, said that in terms of purchasing power, China's People's Liberation Army – which includes the country's naval and air forces – spends $69 billion to $78 billion a year, estimated in 2001 US dollars. This is well below some estimates by the US government and some outside experts. Actual spending ranges between 2.3 per cent and 2.8 per cent of China's GDP, the study found. The 2.5 million-members Chinese army received double-digit increases to its official budget in most recent years as China has stepped up efforts to improve training and outdated weapons technology. ... "China's defence spending has more than doubled over the past six years, almost catching up with Great Britain and Japan," Keith Crane, a senior economist at RAND and lead author of the study [said] ... The authors of the report said their estimates included, in addition to the official military budget, items such as foreign weapons purchases, spending on paramilitary forces such as the People's Armed Police, nuclear weapons, subsidies to defence industries, defence-related research and revenue channelled to the military from outside the official budget. For example, the official budget in 2003 of 185 billion yuan, or $22.4 billion, was well below the estimate for 2003 of as much as $38 billion. On average actual spending would be 1.4 times to 1.7 times the publicly reported amount ... Outside calculations of China's defence spending usually put it at several times the official figure; rough estimates range as high as thirteen times the official figure, the report noted ... China faces chronic difficulty in producing high quality weapons systems and military aircraft, partly because of its lack of expertise in those areas and also because export controls limit Beijing's access to sensitive technology. But the report said that China was quickly catching up in some areas. It noted major improvements n Chinese-made destroyers and missiles': www.iht.com, 20 May 2005. 'US Defence Secretary Donald Rumsfeld: 'China's defence expenditures are much higher than Chinese officials have publicly admitted. It is estimated that

China's is the third largest military budget in the world and now the largest in Asia': www.iht.com, 5 June 2005.)

> The new slogan of choice for Chinese leaders is the need to build a 'harmonious society' ... Creating a 'harmonious society' was officially declared a top priority in September last year [2004] ... Prime minister Wen Jiabao ... stressed the idea in a speech to the legislature on 5 March.
>
> (*The Economist*, 19 March 2005, p. 72)

'Hu Jintao formally completed his accession to China's top posts with the formal retirement of Jiang Zemin from his position as chairman of the Central Military Commission, Jiang's last major title' (www.iht.com, 8 March 2005; *IHT*, 9 March 2005, p. 4).

'Hu Jintao ... will be "elected" head of the state's military commission – a body that exists only on paper – on 13 March' (*IHT*, 12 March 2005, p. 69). 'The government commission has no real power ... [but the move symbolically completes] a transfer of power to a younger generation of Communist leaders ... Neither Hu Jintao nor Jiang Zemin has military experience' (www.iht.com, 13 March 2005).

> Delivering the main opening address to the National People's Congress on Saturday [5 March] prime minister Wen Jiabao set an economic growth target of 8 per cent [for 2005 from 7 per cent in 2004], down from the 9.5 per cent growth recorded in 2004. He also vowed to eliminate the main tax imposed on China's peasantry for the first time in two millenniums. The government also announced that it would increase spending on China's rapidly modernizing military by 12.6 per cent in 2005 ... Wen emphasized continuing a campaign to cool China's economy and narrow the growing urban–rural wealth gap, which has led to severe social tensions.
>
> (www.iht.com, 6 March 2005)

('[The target rate of GDP growth for 2005 is] "about 8 per cent"': *FT*, 15 March 2005, p. 7.)

> The agriculture minister ... Du Qinglin ... on Thursday [10 March] promised to protect farmers' land rights and spend more on irrigation as China's leaders seek to ease chronic rural poverty, seen as posing their biggest risk of anti-government unrest ... The ministry introduced pilot projects last year [2004] aimed at arbitrating disputes over land contracts ... Average annual incomes for farmers rose 12 per cent last year [2004], but still total just 2,936 yuan, or $355 per person, according to Du. By contrast the government says annual incomes in China's booming cities average more than $1,000 per person ... Premier Wen Jaibao promised [on 5 March] ... to eliminate farm taxes by 2006 – a promise repeated Thursday by the finance ministry ... China said this week that it would start cutting school fees in rural areas this year [2005] in response to growing domestic criticism that the country's education system is corrupt and discriminates against poor, rural students. The new policy will begin with the removal of fees for 14 million students in the country's poorest countries and will continue until 2007.
>
> (www.iht.com, 10 March 2005)

Prime minister Wen Jiabao on Monday [14 March] ... spoke about China's need to balance its economic growth and to spread its wealth to the vast, impoverished countryside. He said that China had passed into a new era of development in which industrial development has to 'replenish' agriculture. This would involve further reducing taxes on farm products, improving irrigation and farming infrastructure, and improving rural schools and health care, he said.

(*IHT*, 15 March 2005, p. 2)

'Per capita disposable income in towns and cities ... rose 7.7 per cent to 9,422 yuan last year [2004], while incomes in rural areas rose 6.8 per cent to 2,936 yuan' (www.iht.com, 14 March 2005).

This year's budget calls for more spending on a new rural health care programme aimed at reversing the near collapse of rural medical services in recent years. It also calls for an increase in central government handouts to rural areas, to make up for their loss of revenue as a result of reforms intended to reduce peasants' tax burdens. The government plans to abolish agricultural tax by 2006, two years earlier than it had originally planned. And it also says it will abolish primary school fees for all children in rural areas by 2007.

(*The Economist*, 19 March 2005, p. 72)

17 March 2005. '[Japan's foreign minister said] that the Japanese government would end its development aid to China by 2008 ... [ending] new yen loans by the start of the Beijing Olympics' (www.iht.com, 17 March 2005). 'Japan has given more than $28 billion in low-interest loans since 1980 in what has been widely seen a substitute for compensation. Japan has said it will end loans to China by the 2008 Olympics – although some technical assistance could continue' (www.iht.com, 5 June 2005).

22 March 2005. 'EU plans to lift its arms embargo against China by June [2005] appeared to be collapsing Tuesday [22 March] after months of intense lobbying by the United States and a negative reaction to China's recent ['anti-secession' law]' (*IHT*, 23 March 2005, p. 1).

The EU ... may not press the issue until next year [2006], US and European officials said ... The Chinese action, they said, jolted France to undercut its efforts to end the embargo before June ... The embargo was imposed after China's crackdown on pro-democracy demonstrators in Tiananmen Square in 1989 ... European officials say that the EU will not back off its commitment, made last December [2004] and pressed by President Jacques Chirac of France, to lift the embargo at some point ... Chirac first proposed lifting the embargo in late 2004.

(www.iht.com, 22 March 2005)

In March the government selected four state-owned space technology companies to oversee research and development as part of China's participation in the Euro 3.2 billion, or $4.15 billion, Galileo network, which is due to enter service in 2008 ... China in September 2003 agreed to invest Euro 200 million in the system. Of the Chinese investment all but Euro 5 million would be spent on research and development that China undertakes ... [Critics] warn that Beijing will score a military victory when Chinese companies begin research on the EU's Galileo satellite navigation system ... Galileo is a network of thirty satellites and ground stations designed to provide a highly accurate navigation and positioning system. The system has both civilian and military applications ... Senior EU officials have rejected suggestions that China could gain a military advantage from Galileo ... A more accurate encoded signal is to be available for EU police and military forces to fight crime and illegal immigration ... [but] would be withheld from China.

(www.iht.com, 18 April 2005; *IHT*, 19 April 2005, pp. 1, 4)

China first tested a nuclear weapon ... in 1964 ... [China today has] a mere twenty-four intercontinental nuclear missiles that are able to reach the United States ... [China has] no aircraft carrier group for projecting its power and very few destroyers. China is constructing no long-range bombers and has no military bases abroad. Its seventy submarines rarely venture outside Chinese territorial waters. Even vis-à-vis Taiwan, against which it has deployed 600 short-range missiles, China does not have the makings of an invasion force that could overwhelm Taiwan's defences.

(Jonathan Power, *IHT*, 8 April 2005, p. 7)

9–10 April 2005.

A second day of angry mass protests against Japan erupted on Sunday [10 April] ... About 3,000 demonstrators gathered near the Japanese consulate in Guangzhou ... In Shenzhen up to 10,000 protesters surrounded the Japanese-owned Jusco supermarket ... The weekend's protests were the largest seen in China since 1999, when demonstrators surrounded the US embassy in Beijing to protest the bombing of the Chinese embassy in Belgrade ... [There was a] large protest in Beijing on Saturday [9 April] ... [An estimated] 10,000 demonstrators joined the march ... [The government] recently denounced the Japanese government for approving history textbooks that China says underemphasize the violence and bloodshed Japan inflicted on China ... An effort in China to rally public opinion against Japan began last month as word spread that the United Nations was prepared to consider proposals to make Japan a permanent member of the council this year.

(*IHT*, 11 April 2005, pp. 1, 4)

Demonstrations against Japan have spread across China since last week, after Tokyo approved a revised edition of a school textbook that critics say whitewashes Japan's brutal wartime collaboration of Asian nations last century ... About 1,000 people threw rocks and broke windows at the Japanese embassy in Beijing on Saturday ... [They were] mostly student demonstrators ... The history books, written by nationalist scholars, were approved by Japan's education ministry for use in schools beginning April 2006 ... Anti-Japanese sentiment runs deep among Chinese, with many resenting what they see as Tokyo's failure to atone for its wartime aggression ... In early April [2005] up to

10,000 Chinese protesters attacked a Japanese department store in Chengdu, the capital of Sichuan province ... Another Japanese store was mobbed in Shenzhen. A week later students massed in central Beijing ... Tensions between Japan and China have been evident for some time now. They erupted violently at a soccer match last year [2004], have been simmering over a territorial dispute in the East China Sea, and most recently surfaced with a petition circulated by a Chinese internet portal aimed at preventing Japan from gaining a seat on the United Nations Security Council ... The Imperial Japanese Army is alleged to have killed ... 35 million Chinese ... in the Pacific War ... [China is also critical about] the absence of a full apology from Tokyo ... [and the fact that Japanese prime minister Junichiro Koizumi has visited] the Yasukuni shrine in Tokyo, dedicated to Japan's 2.5 million war dead [including some war criminals].

(www.iht.com. 11 April 2005)

'The police, who routinely deny permits for protest marches, approved the anti-Japan protest [in Beijing] with little advance notice' (*IHT*, 15 April 2005, p. 4).

'Protests [took place] against recent revisions to a Japanese history textbook and Tokyo's efforts to win a seat on the United Nations Security Council' (*FT*, 11 April 2005, p. 8). '[Japan says that China has] rejected Japan's proposal to take the dispute over the exclusive economic zone to international arbitration' (*FT*, 15 April 2005, p. 11).

At least 5,000 people joined a rally on Saturday ... Most of ... the protesters ... were in their teens ... Japan's attempt to become a permanent member of the UN Security Council ... has been opposed by more than 20 million people in an online petition ... The leaders of [China and Japan] ... have not visited each other since 1998.

(*Guardian*, 11 April 1005, p. 16)

'[China complains that a] new school history book whitewashes the brutal events in the 1930s and 1940s [1931–45] ... There has been no official visit to China by Mr Koizumi since 2001, and none by a Chinese leader to Japan since 1998' (*Guardian*, 13 April 2005, p. 21).

China and South Korea have excoriated Japan over its approval of new school books which they say whitewash the atrocities committed during Japanese occupation ... Japan's prime ministers and its emperors have apologized to China for the brutal conduct of the occupying Japanese army in the 1930s–1940s [1931–45] on seventeen occasions since the two countries restored diplomatic relations in 1972. Seven years ago Japan also made a written apology for its harsh colonial rule of the Korean Peninsula, in 1910–45. But its expressions of regret have never been seen as quite sufficient, especially by China ... The latest such act of perceived impenitence is the Japanese government's approval of a set of school books written by nationalist historians, which reportedly omit or gloss over such wartime atrocities as the rape of thousands of 'comfort women', captured and used as sex slaves by the Japanese military. Furthermore, to South Korea's fury, one of the books asserts

Japan's claim to a group of rocky islets that Korea possesses and calls Dokdo, which the Japanese call Takeshima ... Rows over the wording of Japanese history books have been flaring up for a quarter of a century, most recently in 2001 when a previous version of the books at the centre of the current controversy was submitted for approval. Then the Japanese government demanded over 100 revisions to try to answer the accusations of 'airbrushing history'. The government points out that Japanese schools are not obliged to use the approved texts and, indeed, many do not. But to the Chinese and South Koreans that is beside the point ... Japan and its neighbours did not set up an equivalent of the Franco-German history textbook commission that, soon after 1945, sought agreement on a common account of the two countries' bitter history. Shortly after the 2001 row over history books Junichiro Koizumi, on becoming Japan's prime minister, caused even deeper offence by visiting the Yasukuni shrine in Tokyo, where the souls of all of Japan's 2.5 million war dead since 1853 are symbolically interred, including those of fourteen class-A war criminals who were executed in 1948. Mr Koizumi now visits the shrine annually ... Recently the Japanese government took control of a lighthouse built by its nationalists on another set of disputed islands, which it calls the Senkaku, while China, which also claims them, calls them Diaoyu ... There has been no official visit to China by Mr Koizumi since October 2001 and none by the Chinese president to Japan since 1998, when Jiang Zemin went.

(www.economist.com, 14 April 2005)

'The protests first turned violent in ... Chengdu on 2 April' (*The Economist*, 16 April 2005, p. 54).

'[China highlights what it sees as] the forcing of Chinese into sexual slavery as "comfort women", the 1937 massacre of unarmed civilians in Nanjing [some 300,000 deaths, according to China] and the experiments in biological warfare' (*IHT*, 29 April 2005, p. 8).

11 April 2005.

India and China ... signed an agreement for a 'strategic partnership for peace and prosperity' on Monday [11 April] ... At a meeting in New Delhi prime minister Wen Jiabao and his Indian counterpart, Manmohan Singh signed a series of accords aimed at ending a decades-old border dispute and improving economic ties ... The eleven agreements included a road map aimed at resolving the dispute over the neighbours' 3,500-kilometre, or 2,200-mile, Himalayan border, which has troubled relations for more than four decades, ever since the two countries fought a short war over the boundary in 1962 ... No precise details of how the dispute would be settled were given and the statement merely stressed that both India and China would have to make 'meaningful and mutually acceptable adjustments to their respective positions' ... China was also understood to have promised to back India's bid for permanent membership of an expanded UN Security Council.

(www.iht.com, 11 April 2005; *IHT*, 12 April 2005, pp. 1, 4)

[On 12 April] Wen Jiabao presented his Indian counterpart ... with a freshly printed map of the long-contested area, clearly showing Sikkim as part of India

... This principality [was] annexed by India in 1975 and fiercely contested by China ... The two leaders agreed to boost bilateral trade to $20 billion by 2008, from $13.6 billion last year [2004].

(www.iht.com, 12 April 2005)

What has long seemed the only feasible solution [is] something not far from the status quo. China would drop its claim to the Indian state of Arunachal Pradesh, and India would accept China's rule in part of Ladakh. There would be some adjustments to the borders there and elsewhere ... China is already India's second largest trade partner after America, though India accounts for only 1.2 per cent of China's trade.

(*The Economist*, 16 April 2005, p. 55)

12 April 2005.

Wen Jiabao, the prime minister, said on Tuesday [12 April] that Japan would not be ready for a permanent seat on the United Nations Security Council until it faced up to its history of aggression and won its neighbour's trust. His comments were the most direct Chinese declaration yet on the subject.

(*IHT*, 13 April 2005, p. 4)

13 April 2005.

Japan said Wednesday [13 April] that it would allow drilling for oil and gas in waters claimed by China ... Japan will start reviewing oil company applications for exploration in a long-disputed section of the East China Sea ... Although [Japan] ... described the waters as 'the eastern part of the Japan–China boundary', China does not accept the line to which Japan adheres, essentially a median line between mainland China and Japan's Okinawa prefecture. In recent weeks Japan has accused China of preparing to send gas to Shanghai this summer from undersea reservoirs that stretch across the line into what Japan claims as its exclusive economic zone ... Last year [2004] China supplanted the United States as Japan's most important trading partner and destination for Japanese investment ... The increase last year in Japanese exports to China is credited with keeping Japan from falling into deep recession. China accounted for 16.5 per cent of all Japanese foreign trade in 2004, up from 4 per cent in 1991 ... The $2.7 billion in China accounted for almost 15 per cent of Japan's overseas investment last year, up from 1 per cent five years earlier ... In Okinawa this week Japan flexed its diplomatic muscles against China by pulling together a coalition that successfully blocked China's bid to join the Inter-American Development Bank. Working with the United States, Japan and a group of Central American and Caribbean countries with close ties to Taiwan managed to delay China's entry into the development bank at least until 2008.

(www.iht.com, 13 April 2005; *IHT*, 14 April 2005, p. 16)

[Japan] said the companies would be permitted to analyse energy deposits in the Xihu Trench, an area east of Shanghai that spans a maritime economic zone partially claimed by both China and Japan ... China has already conducted test drilling on its side of the Xihu Trench, but Japan contends any reserves China discovers could come from the Japanese side and has demanded a halt to Chinese exploration.

(*FT*, 14 April 2005, p. 11)

China is planning to ban smoking at all venues for the 2008 Beijing Olympic Games, signalling an official determination to address a mounting public health crisis in a country of 260 million smokers ... The WHO estimates a minimum of 1.3 million people die each year [in China] from tobacco-related illnesses ... The state has a monopoly on tobacco production and distribution ... China is the world's biggest tobacco producer, accounting for about 30 per cent of production. The tobacco industry employs about 60 million people... [In China] 67 per cent of men and 4 per cent of women smoke.

(www.iht,com, 13 April 2005; *IHT*, 14 April 2005, p. 4)

14 April 2005. 'China backed Germany for a new permanent seat on the expanded United Nations Security Council, but ... said Japan was not ready' (*The Times*, 15 April 2005, p. 41).

After weeks of hints Chinese leaders said outright on Wednesday [14 April] that Japan did not have the moral qualifications to become a permanent member of the United Nations Security Council ... The foreign ministry spokesman said: 'Only countries that care about history and are able to win the trust of neighbouring countries can play a large role in international affairs' ... China [said it] would support Germany's bid for a permanent seat on the Security Council, calling Germany a 'country that follows a path of peaceful development'.

(*IHT*, 15 April 2005, pp. 1–2)

15 April 2005. 'Authorities are trying to limit popular anti-Japanese demonstrations planned for this weekend [16–17 April], warning activists that unapproved protests are illegal and disrupting their attempts to use the internet to organize' (*FT*, 16 April 2005, p. 8).

Authorities issued urgent messages Friday [15 April] to local governments, companies and police officials warning that popular protests like those authorized by Beijing a week ago now threatened to get out of control ... Beijing tolerated – some say helped organize – protests against Japan last weekend ... Grass-roots organizing activity could further upset relations with Japan and undermine China's own social stability ... Unrest of any kind could open the door for people to rally against [the] government ... In the mid-1980s a string of protests against Japan's World War II-era atrocities spilled over into anti-government protests ... China is to be host to the Japanese foreign minister ... on Sunday and Monday [17–18 April].

(Joseph Kahn, *IHT*, 16 April 2005, p. 2)

'EU foreign ministers yesterday [15 April] insisted they still wanted to lift the bloc's arms embargo on China, but admitted it could take more than a year to accomplish' (*FT*, 16 April 2005, p. 9).

17 April 2005.

Japan's foreign minister, Nobutaka Machimura. arrived in Beijing [for a two-day visit] on Sunday [17 April] ... as sometimes violent demonstrations against Japan swept across China for a second week ... In many Chinese cities on Sunday crowds marched to denounce Japan's wartime past and its bid for membership of the United Nations Security Council ... About 10,000 people protested outside a Japanese-owned department store that was also the target of demonstrators last week. In Shenyang, in north-east China, 1,000 protesters marched on the Japanese consulate ... In Shanghai on Saturday [16 April] about 20,000 protesters surged through the streets ... Beijing remained outwardly calm Sunday.

(www.iht.com, 17 April 2005)

Japan requested an official apology and compensation from China for damage done to Japanese property ... [But] Chinese foreign minister Li Zhaoxing curtly rejected Tokyo's demand for an apology: 'The Chinese government has never done anything for which it has to apologize to the Japanese people' ... The two sides discussed steps to improve bilateral relations, including a proposal by the Japanese minister to set up a group of experts to study the history of relations between the two countries.

(*FT*, 18 April 2005, p.1)

Demonstrators also vandalized a number of Japanese restaurants and shops. Police at the Japanese consulate building [in Shanghai] ... kept protesters back from the building but rarely intervened to stop the vandalism ... As many as 10,000 people are reported to have protested in the eastern city of Hangzhou and there was also a protest in Tianjin ... The marches also come days after an extraordinary riot in a south-western village in Zheijiang province, where locals protesting against environment damage took control of the village from the police.

(*FT*, 18 April 2005, p. 9)

[Japan also proposed] a fund to promote exchanges of students ... The authorities ... blocked a follow-up march in Beijing ... The [Japanese] foreign ministry spokesman ... quoted him [foreign minister Nobutaka Machimura] as saying: 'Japan as a nation expresses deep remorse, deep regret and sincere apologies to the people of China and other Asian countries.'

(*Guardian*, 18 March 2005, p. 13)

('Nobutaka Machimura was telling the press in Tokyo [on his return] that he had not expressed "deep apologies" during a private meeting with Li Zhaoxing': *Independent*, 20 April 2005, p. 27.)

'In Beijing hundreds of police blanketed Tiananmen Square to block a planned demonstration' (*The Times*, 18 April 2005, p. 33).

'Activists in Beijing obeyed a government directive not to take part in anti-Japanese rallies ... About 4,000 people demonstrated in Hong Kong' (*Independent*, 18 April 2005, p. 23).

'[The reissued book was] produced by a Japanese right-wing group and used in only a tiny minority of schools' (*Telegraph*, 18 April 2005, p. 14).

Damage to Japanese facilities in China has been extensive in two weekends of riots ... The protests in China have triggered reprisals in Japan, including paint smeared on the Chinese ambassador's residence in Tokyo and pellets shot at a Chinese language school.

(www.iht.com, 10 April 2005)

19 April 2005.

[It was announced that] Australia had granted China market economy status, removing it from the list of countries whose exports are assumed to be subsidized by state payments ... [The status] makes it more difficult for foreign companies to apply for protective measures against Chinese exports ... [China wants] the EU and the United States [to grant it market economy status.

(www.iht.com, 19 April 2005; *IHT*, 20 April 2005, p. 16)

Foreign minister ... Li Zhaoxing ... called Tuesday [19 April] for an end to anti-Japanese protests ... Li Zhaoxing: 'Cadres and the masses must believe in the party and the government's ability to properly handle all issues linked to Sino-Japanese relations. Calmly and rationally express your own views,. Do not attend marches that have not been approved. Do not do anything that might upset social stability' ... Li's comments, carried on national television, amounted to the first direct call by a top official to wind down the protests ... [which took place] on three successive weekends ... Urban residents have been sending text and email messages to one another calling for major marches on 1 May, China's traditional Labour Day, and on 4 May ... [4 May] is the anniversary of the first major student-led nationalist uprising in 1919. Popular outrage over the Versailles Treaty, which gave German-controlled territory to Japan after World War I, sparked the protest.

(www.iht.com, 20 April 2005)

22 April 2005. Junichiro Koizumi:

In the past Japan, through its colonial rule and aggression, caused tremendous damage and suffering to the people of many countries, particularly to those of Asian nations. Japan squarely faces these facts of history in a spirit of humility. And with feelings of deep remorse and heartfelt apology always engraved in mind, Japan has resolutely maintained, consistently since the end of World War II, that it will never turn into a military power... [Japan is committed to peace and resolving differences] without recourse to force.

(*IHT*, 23 April 2005, pp. 1, 8; *The Times*, 23 April 2005, p. 48)

'Hu Jintao said: "China will unwaveringly follow the path of peaceful development" ... [China propounds the idea of a] "peaceful rise" – the idea endorsed by leaders that the country can become a global power while avoiding territorial expansion or war' (www.iht.com, 24 April 2005).

Junichiro Koizumi, the Japanese prime minister, made an unusually public apology for his country's World War II aggression at a conference here

[Jakarta] Friday [22 April] ... [He was] speaking to representatives of more than 100 governments at the Asian–African summit ... While Japanese leaders have extended such apologies in the past, it is rare for a prime minister to address the issue in so public a forum ... The Chinese–Japanese matter and Japan overshadowed the opening of the Asian–African summit. The meeting ... marks the fiftieth anniversary of a gathering of twenty-nine countries from the two regions in the Indonesian mountain city of Bandung. That gathering gave birth to the Non-Aligned Movement. At the time of the first Asian–African summit in April 1955 many of the countries present were emerging from long periods of colonial rule and trying to assert their independence in the midst of the Cold War ... Japanese lawmakers made a pilgrimage Friday [22 April] to a shrine that honours World War II dead, including war criminals ... About 168 legislators or their representatives made the early morning visit to the Tasukuni Shrine for the annual spring festival ... [The] minister of internal affairs was the only member of Koizumi's cabinet to go to the war shrine on the day.

(*IHT*, 23 April 2005, pp. 1, 8)

'In 1961 many of the countries that attended the [1955] Bandung summit meeting met in Belgrade to create the Non-Aligned Movement, declaring their neutrality [in the Cold War]' (*IHT*, 25 April 2005, p. 6).

'China made clear on Friday [22 April] that it would no longer tolerate anti-Japanese protests, declaring that any "unauthorized marches" were illegal and warning that the police "would mete out tough blows" to marchers caught vandalizing property' (*IHT*, 23 April 2005, p. 5).

Thousands demonstrated in China against the textbooks, which critics say play down the 1937 Nanking Massacre, when Japanese soldiers killed up to 300,000 Chinese civilians, and ignore mention of 'comfort women', a euphemism for women forced into sex slavery for the Japanese military.

(*FT*, 23 April 2005, p. 8)

Beginning in 1931 Japan occupied and colonized Manchuria in north-eastern China and six years later invaded the rest of the country ... [The most controversial Japanese history textbook] does skate over the details of Japanese wartime atrocities, but only eighteen of Japan's 11,102 junior high schools have adopted it, even though the publishers are giving it away ... [Japan] is the only country whose constitution outlaws force as a means of settling international disputes.

(*The Times*, 23 April 2005, p. 48)

Previous statements of regret by Japan included the following: prime minister Kakuei Tanaka (September 1972): 'The Japanese side is keenly conscious of the responsibility for the serious damage that Japan caused ... and deeply reproaches itself'; prime minister Zenko Suzuki (August 1982): 'I am painfully aware of Japan's responsibility for inflicting serious damages during the past war'; Emperor Hirohito (June 1984): 'It is indeed regrettable that there was an unfortunate past between us [Japan and South Korea] for a period in this century and I believe it should not be repeated again'; Emperor Akihito (May 1990): I cannot but feel the deepest remorse'; prime minister Tomiichi Murayama (August 1995): 'Japan, through its colonial rule and aggression, caused tremendous damage and suffering to the people of many countries, particularly those of Asia. I ... express deep remorse and state my heartfelt apology' (p. 48).

23–24 April 2005.

The leaders of Japan and China [prime minister Junichiro Koizumi and President Hu Juntao had] ...a fifty-five-minute meeting Saturday [23 April] on the sidelines of an Asia–Africa [three-day summit conference in Jakarta that ended on 24 April] ... [They] pledged to improve ties.

(www.iht.com, 24 April 2005)

At the Jakarta meeting, on the sidelines of a three-day Asia–Africa summit ... Mr Hu and Mr Koizumi both stressed the need for good ties and an ongoing dialogue between the two countries ... [although] the Chinese assessment of the meeting was less upbeat ... China has quelled violent protests against Japan for the first time since they began a month ago after a summit meeting eased tensions between [the two countries] ... [There were] three weekends of often violent unrest ... Apart from one small anti-Japanese march ... [on Sunday 24 April] reported in Zhuhai, in southern China, China's major cities were free of large-scale protests.

(*FT*, 25 April 2005, p. 12)

The Japanese government is to conduct a survey of bias and propaganda in Chinese school textbooks. Nobutaka Machimura, the Japanese foreign minister, announced the survey yesterday [Sunday 24 April] ... He said: 'Chinese textbooks appear to teach that everything the Chinese government has done has been correct. There is a tendency toward this in any country, but the Chinese textbooks are extreme in the way they uniformly convey the "our country is correct" point of view' ... There were no significant anti-Japanese demonstrations in China over the weekend.

(*The Times*, 25 April 2005, p. 35)

('The authorities [in China] have detained some people involve in vandalism [during the demonstrations]': *IHT*, 27 April 2005, p. 3.)

4 May 2005.

A sensitive political anniversary passed without incident Wednesday [4 May] despite the government's concern that protesters wanted to renew angry marches against Japan ... The date, which is often abbreviated as 5/4, is the anniversary of a 1919 student uprising against Western colonialism – specifically against the decision by World War I allied powers to give Japan control of German colonial territories in Japan.

(*IHT*, 5 May 2005, p. 4)

7 May 2005.

Foreign minister Li Zhaoxing of China ... and his Japanese counterpart, Nobutaka Machimura, said there was 'some improvement' in rocky relations [according to a Japanese spokesman] ... The two ministers met Saturday [7 May] on the sidelines of a two-day Asia–Europe meeting in Kyoto ... The two have feuded over the ownership of islands, natural gas exploration rights and the division of exclusive economic zones in the East China Sea. Machimura and Li agreed to resume talks this month on those issues, including the possibility of jointly exploring natural gas resources there. They also agreed to set up a joint panel to study history ... Both sides will name members to the panel by the end of the year.

(www.iht.com, 8 May 2005)

10 May 2005.

[It is announced that] Zhang Chunqiao, a member of the Gang of Four, the radical communist leaders who were blamed for the worst turmoil and persecutions during the Cultural Revolution of 1966 to 1976, has died at the age of eighty-eight ... [He] died from cancer on 21 April ... With Zhang's death, the only member of the Gang of Four [which included Mao's Zedong's wife Jiang Qing] believed to be alive is Yao Wenyuan.

(www.iht.com, 10 May 2005)

'Jiang died in 1991, reportedly a suicide. Another Gang member, Wang Hongwen, died in 1992' (*IHT*, 11 May 2005, p. 7).

20 May 2005.

Waving a Japanese rising sun flag, Tokyo's outspoken nationalist governor landed on a pair of Pacific islets at the centre of a dispute with China on Friday [20 May] ... Governor Shintaro Ishihara arrived at one of the cement-covered outcroppings ... China claims rights to oil and other underseas resources around Okinontoroshima, arguing that the outcropping – which Japan has fortified with extensive cement embankments against the encroaching waves – is too small to qualify as an island that Japan can use to delineate its exclusive economic zone. Japan, however, says the islets are full-fledged islands, meaning that Tokyo can lay exclusive claim to the natural resources 200 nautical miles from its shares into the Pacific. Okinontoroshima is legally part of Tokyo.

(www.iht.com, 20 May 2005)

23 May 2005.

[On 25 May] the Chinese media drove home the point that the Japanese leader's defence of his [Yasukuni] shrine visits had prompted the Chinese deputy prime minister, Wu Yi, to abruptly cancel a meeting with him in Tokyo on Monday [23 May] The cancellation Monday caught Japan off guard. The Chinese had requested the meeting with the Japanese prime minister.

(www.iht.com, 25 May 2005)

The Yasukuni shrine [is] a Shinto memorial to Japan's war dead. Fourteen war criminals [are] enshrined in Yasukuni ... The shrine was built in 1869 as part of Japan's drive to create a nationalistic state religion centred around a divine emperor.

(www.iht.com, 22 June 2005)

4 June 2005.

Tens of thousands of people ... [held] a vigil in one of Hong Kong's largest urban parks to commemorate the sixteenth anniversary of the Tiananmen Square killings ... Organizers put the crowd at 45,000, while the police said it was about half that size. There were visibly fewer people than at the event in the previous two years, when many in Hong Kong were deeply unhappy with economic stagnation and political leadership ... The throngs in Hong Kong were a contrast to the heavy security in Beijing, where large numbers of uniformed and plainclothes officers at the square prevented protests ... This year's vigil [in Hong Kong] coincided with a furore over a secret book reportedly written by a retired Communist Party official, Zong Fengmin, based on conversations he had with Zhao Ziyang ... A correspondent for the leading English language newspaper in Singapore, *The Straits Times*, was detained in southern China on 22 April, after what his wife has described as an effort to obtain a copy of the book.

(www.iht.com, 5 June 2005)

The Chinese authorities have pressured the author, Zong Fengming, an old friend of Zhao's, not to publish the book ... Zong Fengming: 'He [Zhao] said China's development must be on the path to democracy and rule of law. If not, China will be a corrupt society. He believed China's economic reforms need democracy, otherwise they will not work. He believed that if there were no political reforms it would bitterly disappoint the people' ... The manuscript also airs Zhao's opinion that the government blundered in cracking down on democracy protest, a move that led to the deaths of hundreds it not thousands of citizens, the author said.

(www.iht.com, 2 June 2005)

11 June 2005.

In the most recent dispute over land use the police arrested twenty-two people over an attack on village residents in Dingzhou city in Hebei province ... On 11 June up to 300 thugs had descended on a village in Dingzhou to force the residents' evacuation after they had refused to make way for a new power plant. Six farmers were killed.

(*IHT*, 20 June 2005, pp. 1, 7)

(The attack gained international attention because it was filmed by one of the farmers.)

('Thousands of farmers in Guangdong province demonstrated against government-backed land requisition policies, with clashes erupting after the police detained some protesters ... The first day of the protests [was 30 June] ... Saturday [2 July saw] the third consecutive day of protests ... The demonstrations centred around the fact that about 7,000 farmers are being evicted from the land that they farm ... [On 30 June] about 600 people from a village in eastern Zhejiang province took control of a battery factory that they said was poisoning their children': www.iht.com, 3 June 2005. 'In a sign that top leaders are growing increasing worried about unrest in the countryside, the government has warned citizens that they must obey the law and that any threats to social stability will not be tolerated ... Many disgruntled farmers have turned to protests. In recent weeks 2,000 farmers in Inner Mongolia protested to block local officials from seizing their land, a common point of contention in the countryside. Other recent riots have seen villagers protesting industrial dumping that poisons streams and farmland. In Zhejiang province tens of thousands of villagers fought off an estimated 3,000 police officers so that they could continue protesting against local chemical plants': *IHT*, 1 August 2005, p. 4. 'In response to unrest the government has introduced new policies. In May it announced rules to restrict petitions and visits to government offices. Last week the People's Liberation Army introduced rules barring soldiers from joining protests and petitions': www.iht.com, Tuesday 23 August 2005.)

30 June 2005. Hu Jintao begins a four-day visit to Russia.

14 July 2005.

Japan on Thursday [14 July] approved a request by Teikoku Oil to drill for natural gas in the East China Sea along a disputed sea border with China ... Tokyo would allow test drilling east of the line that Japan considered its sea boundary with China – a demarcation that Beijing disputes.

(www.iht.com, 14 July 2005)

China should use nuclear weapons against the United States if the American military intervenes in any conflict over Taiwan, a senior Chinese military official ... Major General Zhu Chenghu ... said at an official briefing [on 14 July]. Zhu, considered a hawk, stressed that his comments reflected his personal view and not official policy. Beijing has long insisted that it will not initiate the use of nuclear weapons in any conflict ... China has had atomic bombs since 1964 and has a small arsenal of land- and sea-based nuclear-tipped missiles that can reach the United States, according to most Western intelligence estimates.

(*IHT*, 16 July 2005, p. 6)

('Major General Zhu Chenghu is also a dean at China's National Defence University ... [On 15 July a spokesman for the ministry of foreign affairs in Beijing said]: "What he [Zhu] talked about was just his personal views" ... According to a paper published last month [June] by the *Bulletin of Atomic Scientists*, quoting "the intelligence community", said China would increase its strategic nuclear warheads from "eighteen to seventy-five–100" over the next fifteen years, primarily targeted against the United States': *FT*, 16 July 2005, p. 10.)

20 July 2005.

A Pentagon report said that efforts to modernize its military could pose a threat to peace in East Asia ... The annual Pentagon report on China's military ... scheduled for release this spring ... said that China is emphasizing efforts 'to fight and win short-duration, high-intensity conflicts' over Taiwan. China's military spending has grown by double digit rates since the mid-1990s and 'appears focused on preventing Taiwan independence or trying to compel Taiwan to negotiate a settlement on Beijing's terms', the report said ... According to the report, China's military modernization has included an estimated 650 to 730 mobile, short-range missiles deployed opposite Taiwan ... China does not yet have the military power to take Taiwan by force, the report said, and Beijing's conventional forces are not capable of threatening US territory, as 'China's ability to project conventional power beyond its periphery remains limited' ... The report called on Taiwan to take a greater role in building up its own defences. New weapons programmes, including equipment sold by American firms, have been languishing in Taiwan's parliament ... The report also says that China's military budget is so opaque, with much of the spending hidden in other accounts, that it 'precludes significant outside analysis'. Although noting that the analysis is imperfect, the report states that 'the defence sector in China could receive up to $90 billion in 2005', the third largest military budget in the world, after the United States, which spends more than four times that figure, and Russia ... The United States is eager for 'a peaceful and prosperous China, one that becomes integrated as a constructive member of the international community', the report stated. 'But we see a China facing a strategic crossroads.' Questions remain about the basic choices China's leaders will make as China's power and influence grow, particularly its military power.

(www.iht.com, 20 July 2005)

The Pentagon estimates that China might be spending up to $90 billion a year on its military, three times the officially acknowledged budget ... [This] signals long-term ambitions to extend its power not only over Taiwan but also deeper into the region, according to the Pentagon ... The Pentagon assessment details advances in China's arsenal of short-range ballistic missiles, with between 650 and 730 deployed opposite Taiwan, and notes that Beijing is adding to them at a rate of about 100 missiles a year ... The report said: 'Current trends in China's military modernization could provide China with a force capable of prosecuting a range of military operations in Asia, well beyond Taiwan, potentially posing a credible threat to modern militaries in the area.'

(*The Times*, 21 July 2005, p. 41)

'The report said: "Over the long term, if present trends persist, PLA capabilities could pose a credible threat to other modern militaries in the region"' (*FT*, 21 July 2005, p. 6).

China, says the report, is facing a strategic crossroads. It could choose 'a pathway of peaceful integration and benign competition'. Or ... it could 'emerge to exert dominant influence in an expanding sphere'. It could also become less confident and focus inwards on challenges to national unity and the Communist Party's legitimacy. 'The future of a rising China is not yet set immutably on one course or another' is the cautious conclusion.

(*The Economist*, 23 July 2005, p. 42)

('In an official defence report released this month [August], Japan said China was clearly expanding its military reach ... The report said: "Beijing is shifting from using its air and sea forces for defensive purposes to unifying its defensive and offensive capabilities"': *IHT*, 15 August 2005, p. 7.)

15 August 2005. The sixtieth anniversary of Japan's surrender on 15 August 1945. It is commonly known as VJ Day (Victory over Japan Day), while VE Day (Victory in Europe Day) was celebrated on 8 May.

'Japan invaded China ... [and] erected a puppet state in Manchuria in 1932' (*IHT*, 15 August 2005, p. 1).

'[The] first shots in the Sino-Japanese War were fired on 7 July 1937 ... A [controversial Japanese] revisionist history textbook ... was adopted by the Tokyo Metropolitan Board of Education for use in junior high schools two weeks ago' (*Independent*, 15 August 2005, p. 24).

Junichiro Koizumi:

> Our country has caused great damage and pain to people in many countries, especially our Asian neighbours, through colonization and invasion. Humbly accepting this fact of history, we again express our deep remorse and heartfelt apology and offer our condolences to the victims of the war at home and abroad. We will not forget the terrible lessons of the war and will contribute to world peace and prosperity.
>
> (*Guardian*, 16 August 2005, p. 6)

> Junichiro Koizumi ... also reached out to China and South Korea by saying that the three countries should work together 'in maintaining peace and aiming at development in the region' ... On Monday [15 August] Koizumi chose not to visit the Yasukuni shrine, the Shinto shrine where Japanese war criminals are enshrined along with other Japanese war dead, ending weeks of intense speculation. But members of his cabinet and about fifty other lawmakers prayed at the shrine.
>
> (*IHT*, 16 August 2005, p. 4)

'Instead of visiting Yasukuni, Mr Koizumi laid flowers at the tomb for the unknown war dead at the Chidorigafuchi National Cemetery' (*FT*, 16 August 2005, p. 6).

'Mr Koizumi joined the emperor at a secular service at the Nippon Budokan hall in honour of the Japanese soldiers and civilians who died during the Second World War' (*Guardian*, 16 August 2005, p. 11).

> In a written statement, approved by his cabinet, he repeated an unambiguous expression of 'deep remorse and heartfelt apology' for Japan's 'colonization and aggression' during the war. But the similarly worded speech that he read out aloud at a ceremony attended by Emperor Akihito and members of the government omitted all references to colonialism, aggression or apology. Although Mr Koizumi himself did not make an appearance, two members of his cabinet and forty-seven MPs joined 200,000 Japanese visitors to the controversial Yasukuni shrine in central Tokyo.
>
> (*The Times*, 16 August 2005, p. 28)

'[During the Japanese] war in China from the late 1930s to 1945 ... some estimates of Chinese deaths in those years approach 20 million' (*IHT*, 25 August 2005, p. 6).

18 August 2005.

> China and Russia are due to begin their most ambitious joint military exercise Thursday [18 August], with naval ships, bombers, fighter planes and 10,000 troops massing on China's north-east [Pacific] coast ... China and Russia say the exercise, named 'Peace Mission 2005', is not intended to threaten other countries but to improve their ability to thwart terrorism and separatist uprisings on their borders ... China will contribute 8,000 troops, while Russia will send 1,800, including elite paratrooper and commando forces ... [In 2004] Russia sold more than $2 billion in military equipment to China – a third of its arms exports.
>
> (www.iht.com, 17 August 2005)

'The first-ever joint military exercises China and Russia are ... [being held] over the next eight days on China's north-eastern coast' (www.iht.com, 18 August 2005). 'Thousands of Chinese and Russian troops concluded their historic first joint military exercises Thursday [25 August] with a mock invasion by paratroopers on China's east coast. The eight-day exercises ... [involved] 7,000 Chinese troops and 1,800 Russians' (www.iht.com, 25 August 2005).

> The fictional scenario ... [in the] eight-day exercise ... envisages an imaginary state engulfed in a wave of violence fuelled by 'ethnic and religious differences' ... Moscow and Beijing are keen to stress that they are rehearsing a peacekeeping mission that would be conducted under United Nations auspices.
>
> (*Independent*, 19 August 2005, p. 27)

'The week-long games ... [involve] Vladivostok [in Russia] and the Yellow Sea' (*Guardian*, 19 August 2005, p. 15).

'"Peace Mission 2005" ... [was] launched in ... Vladivostok and involves manoeuvres in and near China's coastal province of Shandong' (*FT*, 19 August 2005, p. 8).

'Chinese and Russian troops concluded their historic first joint military exercises Thursday [25 August] with a mock invasion by paratroopers on China's east coast ... The eight-day exercises [involved] 7,000 Chinese troops and 1,800 Russians' (www.iht.com, 25 August 2005).

5 September 2005.

> Hu Jintao will arrive in Seattle next Monday [5 September] for a twelve-day tour that will take him to Washington, Canada, Mexico and the United Nations General Assembly in New York ... This visit will be Hu's first to the United States since he became China's president.
>
> (www.iht.com, 30 August 2005; *IHT*, 31 August 2005, p. 2)

> President Hu Jintao, because of problems occasioned by Hurricane Katrina [in the United States], has postponed an official visit to the United States this week, but he and President George W. Bush have agreed to meet during a

United Nations assembly in New York this month . . . The meeting in New York will occur when Hu and Bush attend ceremonies beginning 14 September for the sixtieth anniversary of the founding of the United Nations . . . Hu talked by phone and the two agreed to postpone their meeting, planned for Wednesday [7 September] . . . The announcement came after Hu's government on Saturday [3 September] offered $5 million in aid to Katrina survivors and said it would send medical personnel if necessary.

(www.iht.com, 4 September 2005)

12 September 2005.

China will no longer treat the death toll in natural disasters as a state secret . . . officials said Monday [12 September] . . . The declassification of disaster-related death tolls . . . [was] implemented last month [August] . . . The rules will apparently apply mainly to purely natural disasters, like earthquakes, floods and typhoons. They may allow officials and the state media greater leeway to report on such events as they unfold, rather than waiting for the official version to be released . . . An official spokesman: 'Declassification of these figures and materials is conducive to boosting our disaster prevention and relief work' . . . Information about casualties in storms and floods [is] no longer routinely suppressed . . . The new rules are unlikely to lead to the release of data that are not currently available in some form. But the revised regulations may make it more difficult for local officials to cover up accidents on the grounds of protecting state secrets, as they have often done.

(*IHT*, 13 September 2005, p. 4)

7 October 2005.

Japan, concerned that China will receive most of Siberia's . . . annual oil and gas exports, will urge President Vladimir Putin of Russia in November to accelerate plans to build an oil pipeline to Japan. Russia will build a pipeline from East Siberia to China first, and then a smaller line to the Pacific coast near Japan, Putin said on 5 September. Gazprom, Russia's gas exporting monopoly, will make China a priority in Asian sales [the company said on 21 September] . . . China will get two-thirds of the 30 million tonnes of oil that Russia plans to export to Asia within four years, Putin said on 8 July . . . When Putin visits Tokyo in November Japan plans to push for an $11 billion Siberian oil pipeline directed to the Pacific, and not to China . . . [Japan] said on 7 October that Putin would be asked to reconsider Japan's offer to fund the proposed oil pipeline to the Pacific coast and to help develop Siberian oil fields . . . [Japan] in 2003 offered Russia $7 billion of low-interest loans in return for an oil pipeline to the Pacific coast, enabling shipments to Japan . . . Russia now directs most of its . . . oil and gas exports to Europe. Japan last year [2004] received less than 1 per cent of its oil from Russia, which supplied 8.8 per cent of China's imports. Neither Asian nation currently buys gas from Russia, which holds the largest reserves of the fuel . . . Rosneft, Russia's biggest oil supplier to China, said on 12 October that it had granted China Petroleum & Chemical a 25 per cent stake in a project to develop oil and gas fields near

Sakhalin Island. Rosneft and the Chinese company, known as Sinopec, agreed to form a venture for the Sakhalin-3 project on 1 July, the day after President Hu Jintao of China met with Putin. Russia said this month [October] that it might cancel two planned oil pipelines to the Arctic Ocean, which could help supply the United States, to focus on expanding sales to China and the rest of Asia.

(www.iht.com, 17 October 2005)

The [Russian] government has shelved plans to build a pipeline from West Siberia to Murmansk ... Plans to build a pipeline to China or Japan have been discussed for years ... At a recent meeting with foreign analysts and journalists President Vladimir Putin confirmed that Russia would first build a pipeline from Taishet near Lake Baikal to Daqing [in China] and only later to Japan. Oil to Japan would be carried by rail until output from East Siberia justified the second part.

(*FT*, Survey, 11 October 2005, p. 5)

This is a policy reversal. '[On 31 December 2004] Russia approved an ...oil pipeline linking Siberia with the Pacific, effectively ending dreams of a rival project to China ... [Oil will be exported] to Japan and the United States' (*The Times*, 1 January 2005, p. 44). 'Russia will by May [2005] draw up detailed plans for the financing and construction of an estimated $11.5 billion oil pipeline to the Pacific following a decision ... to adopt a Japanese-proposed route over one that would have favoured China' (*FT*, 4 January 2005, p. 7).

8 October 2005. The start of the Fifth Plenum of the Sixteenth Central Committee of the Communist Party.

'The four-day ... closed-door session is taking place at the Jingxi Hotel, a Soviet-era building in Beijing' (www.iht.com, 10 October 2005).

[Hu Jintao's] 'five balances' policy [involves] a call to strike an equilibrium between the 'domestic and international, the inland and the coast, the rural and urban, society and the economy, and nature and man'. In each of the 'balances', say Chinese officials, the central and local governments should favour the first consideration over the second ... The [five year] plan is also expected to enshrine the notion of 'green GDP' in policy-making, a fashionable tag for the need to ensure that growth does not continue to come at the expense of environmental destruction.

(*FT*, 9 October 2005, p. 9)

Leaders of China's Communist Party began drawing an economic road map for the next five years in a major meeting ... The plan will focus on social services to narrow the widening gap between the rich and poor ... A main priority is to enact President Hu Jintao's calls for a 'harmonious society' to improve the lives of poor farmers, migrant workers and others left behind as the economy surged.

(www.iht.com, 10 October 2005)

[A] communiqué was released after a four-day closed meeting of the party's 354-member Central Committee in Beijing, which approved a draft of the latest economic plan spanning five years from 2006 ... China will continue to pursue high-speed economic growth ... but will attempt to temper its impact by improving social security, the health system and the incomes of its poorest citizens ... The communiqué: 'We need to put greater emphasis on social equity, enhance efforts in adjusting income distribution and strive to alleviate the tendency of the widening income gap between regions and parts of society.'

(*FT*, 12 October 2005, p. 11)

'A vague communiqué [was issued] that gave something to everyone – balanced growth and fast growth ... [The Central Committee] did agree on one change ... by scrapping the word "plan" and calling China's Eleventh Five Year Plan a "blue-print"' (*The Times*, 12 October 2005, p. 38).

The Communist Party leadership ... approved a new economic blueprint that it says will address the country's yawning wealth gap and reduce 'outstanding contradictions' that have led to a rash of social unrest ... The work report describing the plan ... was filled with slogans, such as building a 'harmonious society' through 'scientific development' ... The party's statement [was] issued at the conclusion of the four-day meeting: 'During the Eleventh Five Year Plan we must maintain fast and stable economic growth and support the building of a harmonious society. The meeting stressed that to push forward economic development and improve the lives of the people is China's major task' ... The Five Year Plan ... will not be implemented until the spring [of 2006].

(www.iht.com, 12 October 2005)

The Communist Party's annual meeting on economic policy ended on Tuesday [11 October] with word of a strategic shift: from now on there will be more emphasis on redressing the inequality and social disruption that market reforms have left in their wake ... Amid all the talk of addressing the wealth gap, the party's plenum reiterated a commitment to rapid growth by restating a goal of raising China's GDP to double its 2000 level by 2010.

(www.economist.com, 12 October 2005)

[China's] leaders have just approved a five-year 'programme' rather than, as in the past, a plan. The document is intended to mark a shift to a more sustainable growth model ... The five-year programme for 2006 to 2010 ... by no means abandons the pursuit of high growth. But, according to a communiqué ... it is 'essential' for China to 'speed up the transformation of the economic growth pattern'. Details of the programme are still secret (it will not be promulgated until the annual session of parliament next March). But officials say the transformation includes ensuring that growth is more evenly shared across the country, is less investment-driven and less polluting ... Among the very few specifics suggested by the communiqué is a goal of reducing energy consumption per unit of GDP by 20 per cent over the next five years ... More vaguely, it calls for 'big improvements' in education and public health. The social security system ... should be put on a 'relatively firm basis'.

(*The Economist*, 15 October 2005, p. 76)

An elaborate points system that determines the careers of officials is often blamed for many of China's problems. In their drive to meet targets for economic growth local mandarins squander money, ride roughshod over citizens and ravish the environment. So now China is trying to devise and embed into its assessment of officials a way of calculating a 'green GDP' – which allows for environmental costs in national accounts – to help mitigate some of these excesses ... Green GDP would be calculated by subtracting the cost of the natural resources used and the pollution caused from regular GDP ... President Hu Jintao first endorsed the idea in March 2004 ... Last February the government said that ten regions, including Beijing, were carrying out a pilot project in green GDP assessment ... A 'framework' for a green GDP accounting system could be unfolded [it is said] within three to five years. This would make China the pioneer of a statistical approach that no other country has adopted – and which many economists around the world eschew as an attempt to quantify the unquantifiable ... The exercise is riddled with complexity ... China's top leaders themselves may be getting cold feet. A draft of the national economic development plan for the next five years ... stresses the need for 'a resources-saving and environment-friendly society'. But it makes no mention of a green GDP.

(*The Economist*, 22 October 2005, pp. 69–70)

12 October 2005.

A rocket carrying two Chinese astronauts ... Fei Junlong and Nie Haisheng ... blasted off Wednesday [12 October] ... the mission [is] reportedly to last up to five days... The launch ... [of] *Shenzhou 6* ... [was] shown live on state television ... The *Shenzhou* – Divine Vessel – capsule is based on Russia's workhorse *Soyuz*, though with extensive modifications ... China has had a rocketry programme since the 1950s and fired its first satellite into orbit in 1970. It regularly launches satellites for foreign clients aboard its giant *Long March* boosters. Chinese space officials say they hope to land an unmanned probe on the moon by 2010 and want to launch a space station.

(www.iht.com, 12 October 2005)

'China's ultimate goal for the Shenzhou programme is to launch three-pilot missions that can remain aloft for several days ... China's goals in space ... [are] larger orbital missions, piloted lunar missions and the construction of a space station' (www.iht.com, 12 October 2005).

'China sent its first man, Yang Liwei, in space in October 2003 ... China has had a space programme since 1958 and put its first satellite into orbit in April 1970' (*Independent*, 12 October 2005, p. 26).

'The 2003 flight made it the third country after Russia and the United States to send a human into space' (*IHT*, 12 October 2005, p. 6).

17 October 2005.

The *Shenzhou 6* flight ended early Monday [17 October] ... China hopes to conduct a spacewalk in 2007 and might recruit women into its next group of astronaut candidates ... China [said it] had a number of other goals, including launching a lunar probe and setting up a permanent space station ... China said last year [2004] that it would launch a moon-orbiting satellite in 2006 ... The lunar programme – named Chang'e after a legendary Chinese goddess who flew to the moon – aims to place an unmanned vehicle on the moon by 2010. Plans also call for a vehicle to land by 2010 to collect soil samples and conduct other tests, possibly in preparation for a manned moon base.

(www.iht.com, 17 October 2005)

US Secretary of Defence Donald Rumsfeld begins a visit to China, his first in that capacity. (The visit ended on 20 October.)

[Japanese] prime minister Junichiro Koizumi's visit to a nationalist war memorial Monday [17 October] drew immediate and fierce criticism from Asian countries ... [China] cancelled bilateral talks on the North Korean nuclear crisis that had been scheduled for Monday. South Korea also announced that it would cancel or postpone a trip scheduled for December to Japan by President Roh Moo Hyun, citing the visit. The visit also drew protests from Taiwan and Singapore ... The South Korean government [said it] was no longer planning for a summit meeting in December or talks between the two leaders next month [November] at an Asian-Pacific Economic Co-operation forum in South Korea ... Koizumi said he visited the shrine as a private citizen ... The muted tone of the visit appeared to be a concession to growing criticism at home, with most polls showing opposition to continuation of the visits.

(www.iht.com, 17 October 2005; *IHT*, 18 October 2005, p. 7)

'Mr Koizumi has visited the shrine each year since taking office in 2001' (*FT*, 18 October 2005, p. 7).

'Mr Koizumi has visited Yasukuni five times since he took office in April 2001' (www.iht.com, 20 October 2005).

18 October 2005. 'China cancelled a visit ... to Beijing ... by the Japanese foreign minister ... scheduled for [23 October] ... Nearly 200 other Japanese lawmakers and aides followed Koizumi's example by paying follow-up visits to the shrine' (www.iht.com, 18 October 2005).

19 October 2005.

China issued its first white paper on democracy on Wednesday [[19 October] but included no new initiatives for political reform and left little doubt of the Communist Party's determination to maintain its grip on power ... The report, entitled 'The Building of Political Democracy in China', emphasized the paramount importance of economic development and social stability. It also declared that the continued rule of the Communist Party was 'the most important and fundamental principle for developing socialist political democracy in China' ... The white paper: 'The democratic system is not yet perfect. There is still a long way to go in China's building of political democracy ... [The current political system has allowed the Chinese people] to become masters of their own country and society, and enjoy extensive democratic rights.'

(*IHT*, 20 October 2005, p. 4)

The document [is] the first policy white paper on the subject [of democracy] ... The white paper: 'Democratic government is the Chinese Communist Party governing on behalf of the people ... while upholding and perfecting the people's democratic dictatorship ... China's socialist political democracy has vivid Chinese characteristics.'

(*FT*, 20 October 2005, p. 11)

'The document did not even mention a suggestion last month [September] by the prime minister, Wen Jiabao, that elections to the leadership positions ... in townships could be possible within a few years' (*The Economist*, 22 October 2005, p. 70).

('Each year Transparency International draws on surveys of businessmen and country experts to gauge perceptions of corruption in 159 counties around the world. It defines corruption as the abuse of public office for private gain. This year [2005] Chad shared the bottom slot [158] with Bangladesh. Corruption has declined significantly over the past year in a number of countries, including ... Taiwan [ranked number thirty-two]': *The Economist*, 22 October 2005, p. 124. Iceland was ranked the least corrupt country at number one, with Finland and New Zealand joint second. China was ranked at number eighty-two, India at number eighty-eight and Russia at number 126: p. 124.)

26 October 2005.

Rong Yiren, the businessman dubbed a 'red capitalist' before tycoons became commonplace in China, died in Beijing on Wednesday [26 October] at the age of eighty-nine ... In one of the most intriguing personal stories of survival and influence ... Rong chose to remain in mainland China after the Cultural Revolution, when most wealthy industrialists chose to flee to Hong Kong or Taiwan ... Private companies were nationalized in 1956 ... Rong set up China International Trust and Investment Corporation (CITIC) in 1978. It became a sprawling conglomerate and a vehicle for massive foreign investment ... In 1993 he was appointed to the largely ceremonial post of vice president. He retired in 1998 and in 1999 *Forbes* magazine ranked him the richest man in China ... His son, Larry Yung, heads the Hong Kong-listed subsidiary of the company, CITIC Pacific.

(www.iht.com, 27 October 2005; *IHT*, 28 October 2005, p. 8)

Rong Yiren ... ceded many of his family's business holdings after the 1949 revolution and lost the rest during the Cultural Revolution of 1966–76 ... [In] 1956, when he handed over large stakes in his family businesses to the government, he was given 30 million yuan ($12 million) compensation ... In 1979, at the party's behest, he founded CITIC ... as the investment arm of the Chinese state.

(*The Economist*, 5 November 2005, p. 114)

(Larry Yung, chairman of CITIC Pacific and the son of a former vice president of China [Rong Yiren], retained the top spot on the *Forbes* list of the nation's wealthiest, *Forbes* said Thursday [3 November]. Yung's net worth was estimated at $1.64 billion. The property tycoon Zhu Mengyi and his family ranked second with

$1.43 billion, followed by the Netease.com founder William Ding with $1.27 billion': www.iht.com, 3 November 2005.)
  13 November 2005.

A 13 November explosion at a chemical plant killed five people in the city of Jilin in Jilin province. The plant is about 380 kilometres from Harbin [on the Songhua river], capital of the north-eastern province of Heilongjiang ... A toxic slick of polluted water reached ... Harbin [on 24 November] ... a city of 3.8 million people ... [A] decision to shut off water service [was made] on Tuesday [22 November] ... A Harbin environmental protection group recently issued a report documenting widespread chemical pollution along the Songhua river. The report warned that many factories were secretly dumping waste water and chemicals into the river ... The Songhua river is the main source of drinking water for the Russian city of Khabarovsk, home to 600,000 people, just across the border from China ... The Songhua is a tributary of the Amur river marking the border between Russia and China.

(www.iht.com, 24 November 2005)

A pollution spill allowed an 80 kilometre slick of toxic benzene to reach this northern city of almost 4 million people on a river that normally supplies it with running water ... Authorities in Harbin ... said the slick was expected to have passed the city by Saturday [26 November] and that water could be restored by Sunday ... [This is] one of China's worst environmental disasters ... Even before the benzene spill there were serious problems with water quality along the 1,850 kilometre Songhua river, according to the Asian Development Bank.

(*IHT*, 25 November 2005, pp. 1, 4)

'The Chinese government cut off the city's water supply on Wednesday [23 November]' (www.iht.com, 25 November 2005).
  '[Harbin's] residents have had their water cut off for four days ... The Harbin government began by ... announcing that water supplies were cut off for maintenance purposes' (*FT*, 25 November 2005, p. 6).

The government did not publicly confirm that the Songhua had been poisoned with benzenes until Wednesday [23 November], ten days after the explosion [on 13 November], which killed five people ... The Songhua flows into the Heilong river, which flows into Russia, where it is called the Amur.

(*Independent*, 25 November 2005, p. 37)

China on Friday [25 November] sent investigators to probe the handling of a two-week-old chemical spill that forced a major city to shut off the water supply to 3.8 million people as the state media gave uncharacteristically critical coverage to the environmental crisis ... Officials kept news of the spill secret for days and initially said they were shutting off water merely for maintenance.

(www.iht.com, 25 November 2005)

The explosion at the chemical plant occurred on 13 November, but factory officials announced only that the accident posed no threat of air pollution. They denied that chemicals had spilled into the river ... Government officials in Jilin told their downstream neighbours in Heilongjiang province, home of Harbin, that there had been no chemical spill. But Jilin officials finally told their peers in Heilongjiang on 19 November that there was a problem ... Environmental officials in Jilin – instead of telling the public – had tried to dilute the spill with reservoir water. By Monday [21 November] officials in Harbin were preparing to shut down the water supply, but feared news of the chemical spill would start a panic ... Instead, they announced that they had cut off the water to do maintenance work.

(IHT, 26 November 2005, p. 1)

Even when announcing Harbin's water was to be shut off for four days on Tuesday [22 November], the city government first said it was for 'maintenance', only to admit a few hours later that the real reason was the contamination of the river.

(FT, 26 November 2005, p. 6)

China apologized to its neighbour [Russia] for the environmental disaster and any damage it might cause, state media reported Sunday [27 November] ... The contamination is expected to take about two weeks to reach Russia ... The explosion at a PetroChina chemical plant in Jilin province on 13 November, which spilled an estimated 100 tonnes of benzene compounds into the Songhua, has become a major international and domestic embarrassment for the Chinese government. An 80-kilometre, or 50-mile, slick of contamination flowed downriver ... The authorities ... in Harbin ... reconnected the water supply Sunday evening after it had been suspended for the previous five days ... [However, there was a] warning that what was coming out of the tap was still too dirty to drink ... The government said ... it would announce on radio and television when the water was safe enough to bathe in and drink ... Officials in Jilin suppressed news of the spill about 380 kilometres upriver from Harbin for more than ten days. The Chinese government has now ordered a full investigation and threatened punishment for those responsible ... On Saturday [26 November] ... a tour of Harbin [was] made by the prime minister, Wen Jiabao. He urged local officials to keep the public informed about pollution levels in the river downstream from the city ... After initial panic buying of bottled water in Harbin last week, calm was quickly restored when the authorities demonstrated they could arrange ample supplies of bottled drinking water ... Heating systems in Harbin, a major city in China, had enough water to remain in operation and additional supplies of water were drawn from existing and newly dug wells to keep the city going. Over the weekend teams of soldiers and workers delivered more than 1,000 tonnes of active carbon to city water treatment plants. Hydroelectric plants upstream also increased the amount of water released from reservoirs into the river in a bid to dilute the contamination.

(www.iht.com, 27 November 2005; *IHT,* 28 November 2005, pp. 1, 4)

Officials in Harbin initially failed to inform residents of the pollution threat, announcing instead that the water system would be shut down for routine repairs. But that notice set off rising panic and wild rumours, including growing speculation that the local government had detected signs of an earthquake. Harbin officials responded with a new announcement confirming the chemical spill.

(www.iht.com, 28 November 2005)

'Rising water in Harbin was restored Sunday after a five-day shutdown ... Officials have been criticized for their slow response [27 November] and for allowing the construction of a facility handling such dangerous materials near a key water source' (www.iht.com, 28 November 2005).

'Water drawn from the river ... was passed fit to drink Tuesday [29 November], almost a week after pumping was suspended' (www.iht.com, 29 November 2005).

The chief environmental regulator ... the director of the state environmental protection administration ... quit Friday [2 December], taking the blame for the [13 November] chemical spill ... But the environmental director, Xie Zhenhua, is also a member of the Communist Party's Central Committee ... and there was no indication he would lose that post ... Xie's deputy said officials in Beijing were not told of the disaster until 17 November ... [and that] local officials ruined the best chance of containing the spill by failing to report it promptly.

(*IHT*, 3 December 2005, p. 6)

'The general manager of Jilin Petrochemical Company ... blamed for a toxic spill ... has been removed from his post, the company said Monday [5 December ... China National Petroleum Company owns Jilin Petrochemical' (www.iht.com, 5 December 2005).

Li Yizhong (director of the state administration of work safety): 'People who are found to have provided false information to investigators will also be punished severely. Any move to cover up the cause of the accident and any passive attitude toward the probe are deemed deception and a defiance of law' ... Contamination from the spill is still threatening water supplies in remote towns and cities in China's northern Heilongjiang province, and Russian emergency services are on alert as the toxic slick heads for the border city of Khabarovsk. Reports in the Chinese media suggested that Communist Party officials in Jilin had initially attempted to withhold information about the spill from government agencies, authorities in the province of Heilongjiang further downstream and the central government ... [It was reported on 7 December] that the deputy mayor of Jilin, Wang Wei, who earlier told reporters that the explosion had not contaminated the river, had been found dead at his home on Tuesday [6 December] ... The cause of death remained unclear.

(www.iht.com, 7 December 2005)

[On 9 December Russia] said that it no longer expects an emergency ... The authorities said that they were taking adequate measure to head off a water crisis in Khabarovsk, a city of about 580,000 people that sits along the Amur river ... The benzene was expected to dissipate by the time it hit Khabarovsk.

(*IHT*, 10 December 2005, p. 8)

14 November 2005.

President Hu Jintao began the final leg of his European tour on Monday [14 November] ... Spain is the last stop on the visit to Europe that began last week to Britain and Germany ... Hu is scheduled to leave Tuesday [15 November] for South Korea, where he will attend the annual Asia-Pacific Economic Co-operation conference.

(www.iht.com, 14 November 2005)

18 November 2005.

Despite strong internal opposition, China's Communist Party later this week will officially restore the reputation of a liberal-leaning party leader whose death in 1989 helped spark pro-democracy protests. The party has not publicly honoured Hu Yaobang since his death in April 1989 gave rise to student demonstrations in Tiananmen Square ... President Hu Jintao early this year decided to mark the ninetieth anniversary of Hu Yaobang's birth. Party observers said President Hu aimed to soften his hard-line image and strengthen the Communist Youth League, his political base within the Communist Party. The Youth League was considered the support network of Hu Yaobang, who lost his position as Communist Party General Secretary after a power struggle in 1897 ... The Youth League, with 72 million members, is a bit larger than the Communist Party itself and President Hu has often targeted youth league alumni for promotions and favourable treatment as a way of expanding his network ... Jiang Zemin often protected and promoted people associated with the Shanghai party apparatus, his lifelong base ... President Hu has dropped plans to attend the memorial ceremony in person and has rescheduled the event to take place on 18 November instead of 20 November, the actual ninetieth anniversary of Hu Yaobang's birth. President Hu will be in South Korea on 18 November to attend the Asia-Pacific Co-operation forum ... The commemoration service will be held at the Great Hall of the People in Tiananmen Square ... The memorial will amount to a posthumous rehabilitation for Hu Yaobang, who is remembered as favouring a faster pace of political change than party elders and rival officials considered prudent at the time.

(www.iht.com, 14 November 2005)

Amid heavy security and a veil of secrecy China on Friday [18 November] officially rehabilitated ... Hu Yaobang ... whose death in 1989 set off massive student demonstrations ... About 350 people attended what the state media called a 'discussion meeting' at the Great Hall of the People in Tiananmen Square to remember ... [It is said that] four of the nine members of the ruling Politburo Standing Committee raised concerns about holding an event to remember Hu ... President Hu Jintao changed the date of the ceremony to coincide with a trip to South Korea, where he attended the Asia-Pacific Economic Co-operation forum ... Even so prime minister Wen Jiabao, Vice President Zeng Qinghong and Wu Guangzheng, China's anti-corruption chief, attended. Zeng delivered the main address. All three men are members of the Politburo Standing Committee ... Further commemorative events will take place in Hunan province, where Hu Yaobang was born, and Jiangxi province, where he is buried ... Hu Yaobang, who would have been ninety on Sunday [20 November] ... [He] remains popular for his role in guiding China away from Mao's extremist politics ... [He] has languished in obscurity since his death, largely because students marched to Tiananmen Square shortly after he died to protest corruption and call for democracy ... Hu helped guide China's initial market-orientated economic reforms, rehabilitated many people who had been purged or disgraced under Mao, and pursued ideas for deeper political change through much of the 1980s. He left power under pressure in 1987, accused by party conservatives of having 'bourgeois' tendencies that undermined stability.

(www.iht.com, 18 November 2005)

'Hu Yaobang became General Secretary of the Communist Party in 1980 but was sacked in 1987' (*The Times*, 17 November 2005, p. 41).

('Hu Jintao ... has launched an overhaul of the party, a kind of communist-style EMBA dubbed a "re-rejuvenation" campaign which requires all 70 million party members to recommit themselves to the organization and promise to improve their work': *FT*, Survey, 8 November 2005, p. 1. '[The] year-old campaign ... requires all 67 million members to repledge their allegiance': *The Times*, 3 January 2006, p. 34.)

19–20 November 2005. President George W. Bush visits China. (See the entry for Taiwan.)

'The Chinese government not only failed to release dissidents on a list of human rights cases turned over to Hu Jintao in September, China actually detained more dissidents ahead of Bush's arrival' (www.iht.com, 21 November 2005).

21 November 2005.

Japan won a promise Monday [21 November] from President Vladimir Putin of Russia that a planned pipeline would bring Siberian oil to the Pacific ... Putin: 'We plan to build the pipeline to the Pacific coast with eventual supplies to the Asia-Pacific region including Japan' ... The construction calendar was set for the end of next year [2006]. Later he and prime minister Junichiro Koizumi of Japan signed preliminary accords on the pipeline, which could cost $11 billion [and] run 4,100 kilometres, or 2,550 miles ... Japan had lobbied for the pipeline to the Pacific, believing that it could cut the country's reliance on imports from the Middle East by up to 15 per cent. But last summer Putin dashed Japanese hopes for an exclusive pipeline when he announced that the first leg of the pipeline would carry oil to China. Russia's ministry of industry and energy this month [November] said that work on the China phase would start next July and would be completed by the summer of 2008.

(*FT*, 22 November 2005, p. 17)

6 December 2005.

Liu Binyan, the forceful dissident writer who repeatedly exposed official corruption and openly challenged the Communist Party to reform itself before and after he was expelled from China to the United States in the late 1980s, died

Monday [6 December] . . . He was eighty . . . He was expelled from the party in 1987, along with two other leading dissident intellectuals, Fang Lizhi, an astrophysicist, and Wang Ruowang, a poet. A year later he visited the United States to teach and write. He was never allowed to return home.

(www.iht.com, 6 December 2005)

7 December 2005. Taro Aso (foreign minister of Japan):

It is necessary to maintain continuously a spirit of remorse as well as thoughtfulness . . . [The Japanese people] must continue to reflect deeply and with a spirit of humility . . . [because nationalism] brought great suffering to innocent people in the countries of Asia, notably the Republic of Korea and China.

(www.iht.com, 7 December 2005)

9 December 2005.

In the worst act of violence by Chinese security forces since the Tiananmen massacre in 1989, residents of a fishing village near Hong Kong said that police and paramilitary forces had invaded their hamlet and opened fire on crowds to put down a demonstration this week, killing as many as twenty people. Villagers said as many as fifty residents remain unaccounted for since the shooting, which began after dark in the town of Dongzhou on Tuesday evening [6 December] . . . The villagers of Dongzhou said their dispute with the authorities had begun with a conflict over plans by a power company to build a wind turbine in their area . . . [Apart from the issue of compensation for the use of land for the plant, farmers said] plans to reclaim land by filling in a bay as part of the construction were unacceptable because people have made their livelihoods there as fishermen for generations. When a small group of villagers went to complain recently to the authorities about the plant, they were arrested, infuriating other residents and sparking a larger demonstration.

(www.iht.com, 9 December 2005)

Residents of a fishing village near Hong Kong said that as many as twenty people had been killed by the paramilitary police in an unusually violent clash that marked an escalation in the widespread social protests that have roiled the countryside. Villagers said that as many as fifty other residents remain unaccounted for since the shooting that occurred this week as villagers staged a protest over government land appropriations. It is the largest known use of force by security forces against ordinary citizens since the killings around Tiananmen Square in 1989. That death toll remains unknown, but is estimated to be in the hundreds. The violence began after dark in the town of Dongzhou on Tuesday evening [6 December] . . . The use of live ammunition to put down a protest is almost unheard of in China, where the authorities have come to rely on rapid deployment of huge numbers of security forces, tear gas, water cannons and other non-lethal measures. But the Chinese authorities have become increasingly nervous in recent months over the proliferation of demonstrations across the countryside, particularly in heavily industrialized eastern provinces like Guangdong, Zheliang and Jiansu. By the government's tally there were 74,000 riots or other significant public disturbances in 2004, a big jump from previous years. The villagers of Dongzhou said their dispute with the authorities had begun with a conflict over plans by a power company to build a coal-fired generator in their area, which they feared would cause heavy pollution ... [Farmers] said plans to reclaim land by filling in a local bay as part of the power plant project were unacceptable because people have made their livelihoods there as fishermen for generations ... Early reports from the village said the police opened fire only after villagers began throwing home-made bombs and other missiles, but villagers ... denied this, saying that a few farmers had launched ordinary fireworks at the police as part of their protest.

(*IHT*, 10 December 2005, p. 1)

The government is defending fatal police shootings in a southern village, saying officers opened fire after protesters angered by land acquisitions assaulted police. It said three people were killed, while residents put the toll at up to twenty. In its first statement on the violence the government said Saturday [10 December] that hundreds of people attacked a wind power plant Tuesday [6 December] in Dongzhou, a village north-east of Hong Kong, and assaulted police ... [The government said that] the villagers attacked the plant using knives, steel spears, sticks, dynamite, gasoline bombs and explosives used in fishing ... It said the police dispersed the crowd with tear gas and arrested two people accused of inciting the violence.

(www.iht.com, 11 December 2005)

The Chinese news reports said that 170 villagers, led by a few instigators, attacked a local wind power plant as part of their protest against another planned development there, a coal-fired plant, using knives, blasting caps and Molotov cocktails ... [On Sunday 11 December] the authorities announced the arrest of a local commander who was in charge during the incident ... They said he had mishandled the situation under 'extremely urgent circumstances' ... Villagers said they had been told of two arrests ... of officers ... The villagers said they had set off fireworks and exploded blasting caps ... Villagers also repeatedly spoke of injured people being approached by security forces and fatally shot at close range ... Dongzhou residents also said that at least forty villagers are still unaccounted for, and it is not known whether the missing were killed, arrested or remain in hiding ... The effort to manage public information about the incident was also apparent on Saturday [10 December] in Shanwei, where villagers said some of the wounded were taken by the police ... Villagers said they had not been adequately compensated for the use of their land ... and feared pollution from the plant would destroy their livelihood as fishermen. The construction plans called for a bay beside the village to be reclaimed with landfill.

(www.iht.com, 11 December 2005)

In the first widely circulated account of the incident, which occurred in the village of Dongzhou, in southern Guangdong province, the Xinhua press agency website cited the information office of the nearly city of Shanwei, saying a 'chaotic mob' had begun throwing explosives at the police on Tuesday night, forcing the police to 'open fire in alarm'.

(IHT, 12 December 2005, p. 1)

The authorities have arrested a police commander who ordered officers to open fire ... Officials quoted by the state news agency said more than 300 people took part in Tuesday's protest in the village of Dongzhou. At the urging of a few 'instigators' the demonstrators reportedly attacked the police with petrol bombs, knives and dynamite. 'It became dark when the chaotic mob began to throw explosives at the police,' the report said. 'Police were forced to open fire in alarm' ... But villagers say only fireworks, not explosives, were thrown at police ... It is extremely unusual for Chinese police to use live fire to suppress a demonstration ... Witnesses at the time ... [said] the incident happened after hundreds of police tried to disperse up to 1,000 demonstrators near Shanwei.

(www.bbc.co.uk, 11 December 2005)

Police opened fire on protesters in a confrontation over demands for higher compensation for the loss of land to make way for the construction of a power plant ... Xinhua, the state news agency ... said '170 armed villagers' led by a number of ringleaders used 'knives, steel spears, sticks, dynamite powder, bottles filled with petroleum and fishing detonators' to launch an attack on a wind power station ... After the initial demonstration was cleared with tear gas, the protesters regrouped and threatened to blow up the power plant, the official account says ... Xinhua: 'It became dark when the chaotic mob began to throw explosives at the police, who were forced to open fire in alarm. In the chaos three villagers died, eight were injured with three of them fatally injured.'

(FT, 12 December 2005, p. 7)

According to Amnesty International, it is the first time Chinese authorities have fired on protesters since the Tiananmen Square massacre of 4 June 1989. Villagers in Dongzhou, near the coastal city of Shangwei, said hundreds of camouflage-clad members of the People's Armed Police confronted the protesters, before using automatic weapons to fire on them at around 8 p.m. on Tuesday evening ... The incident is the latest in a series of increasingly bloody clashes between people living in rural areas and the authorities. Official government figures say that 3.76 million people took part in at least 74,000 protests in 2004, but many more go unrecorded ... Matters came to a head at the beginning of last week, when about 1,000 protesters blockaded a wind power plant n the neighbouring village of Shigongzhai in an effort to pressure the local government into increasing the compensation on offer for the [loss of land] ... Guangdong has become the epicentre of protests by rural residents. Thousands of factories [are there].

(Independent, 12 December 2005, p. 26)

Guangdong's provincial government issued a statement Sunday [11 December] saying that the 'wrong actions' of the commander ... were to blame for the deaths of civilians in Dongzhou village in coastal Guangdong province near Hong Kong ... The official Xinhua news agency had said that three people were killed ... Villagers have given varying estimates of the death toll, including some who said as many as twenty people were killed ... The agency's account, quoting local authorities, initially laid blame for the violence exclusively on villagers ... But the subsequent statement by the provincial government suggested a different conclusion ... [Since 1989] shootings of unarmed demonstrators have been unusual. China had 74,000 mass incidents of unrest in 2004, according to a police tally. While some of them resulted in deaths and a few led to local declarations of martial law, very few involved the police or paramilitary troops opening fire on civilians.

(www.iht.com, 12 December 2005)

[On] 4 June 1989 army units cleared demonstrators out of Beijing's Tiananmen Square and killed hundreds – at least – in the process ... Officials say that the number of 'mass protests' taking place throughout China each year has risen from around 10,000 in 1994 to 74,000 in 2004 ... In the past these [grievances] were often to do with the levying of unfair taxes, but more recently they have centred, as in Dongzhou, on inadequate compensation for the loss of land.

(*The Economist*, 17 December 2005, p. 63)

The Dongzhou episode is something of a watershed because it was the first time that villagers are known to have used explosives, albeit crude and ineffective ones, against security forces ... During a tense standoff ... fireworks, blasting caps and crude gasoline bombs were thrown by the villagers ... The government is doing everything possible to prevent eyewitness accounts of what happened from emerging. Residents of Dongzhou, a small town now cordoned off by heavy police roadblocks and patrols, said in scores of interviews on the telephone and with visitors that they had endured beatings, bribes and threats at the hands of the security forces since their protest against the construction of a power plant was violently put down. Others said corpses had been withheld, ostensibly because they were so riddled with bullets that they would contradict the government's version of events. And residents have been warned that if they must explain the death of loved ones ... they should simply say their relatives were blown up by their own explosives.

(www.iht.com, 18 December 2005; *IHT*, 19 December 2005, p. 5)

'The spill has flowed into the Amur river where China is building a dam to divert the toxic water before it reaches the Russian city of Khabarovsk, a Chinese foreign ministry spokesman [said on 20 December]' (www.iht.com, 21 December 2005).

The Songhua river toxic spill reached Khabarovsk on Thursday [22 December]. Chinese workers completed a dam to divert the pollution away from the intake pipes for the Khabarovsk water supply ... The spill had diluted to a level that was not hazardous, the authorities in Khabarovsk said.

(www.iht.com, 22 December 2005)

A toxic spill from China flowed Thursday [23 December] into Khabarovsk in far eastern Russia ... [and] was met with confusing official messages ... The regional governor ... appealed for calm, reassuring residents that neither the municipal drinking water nor the city's central heating system will be turned off ... The regional chief of the federal natural resources service said, however, that it was not safe to use tap water at all.

(*IHT*, 23 December 2005, p. 3)

A toxic waste spill from a zinc smelter ... forced one city ... Shaoguan, which has a population of half a million ... to halt supplies from a southern Chinese river for eight hours and threatened other cities downstream, state media said on Wednesday [21 December] ... 'It has been confirmed that the Shaoguan smelter illegally discharged the cadmium waste water during an overhaul of equipment' ... the *Guangzhou Daily* said ... The latest spill dumped the chemical cadmium into the North river, which cuts across the southern Chinese province of Guangdong.

(www.iht.com, 21 December 2005)

In Shaoguan, where the water supply was shut off on Tuesday [20 December], another fourteen small smelters had been shut down. Some villages and factories between Shaoguan and the downstream city of Yingde had also turned off their water supplies.

(www.iht.com, 22 December 2005)

Two recent chemical spills have forced officials in different regions of China to take emergency precautions to protect water supplies for millions of people ... The new spills were reported in the past week along the Yellow river in northern China and on a tributary of the Yangtze in southern China's Hunan province ... Some experts believe the flurry of news coverage is revealing how common such accidents have become ... In Hunan province a spill occurred on 4 January [2006] in the industrial city of Zhuzhou after workers cleaning up a waste-water ditch mistakenly diverted the sewage water into the nearby Xiangjiang river. The water was laced with cadmium ... Last month [December 2005] a different cadmium spill on the Beijiang river in Guangdong province threatened water supplies to millions of people and forced some temporary water supply shutdowns in the densely populated region ... A second major accident occurred on 6 January when a spill in Henan province created a slick of diesel fuel flowing down the Yellow river ... A smaller spill was reported on 6 January [2006] in central China along the Qijing river after a sulphur leak forced communities along the river to go without running water for two days ... This week officials announced plans to spend an additional $3 billion to clean up the Songhua river.

(www.iht.com, 11 January 2006)

15 December 2005.

A Communist Party official ... the former Communist Party secretary of the city of Dingzhou, near Shengyou ... and twenty-six other people ... [went on trial on 15 December] on charges of organizing a bloody attack on protesting villagers that killed six people ... In the conflict in June, in Hebei province, as many as 300 men with knives, clubs and guns attacked villagers protesting the seizure of land for construction of a power plant in the village of Shengyou, 200 kilometres, or 125 miles, south of Beijing ... Villagers were unhappy over what they said was inadequate compensation for the seized land ... A month later state media reported that Hebei officials decided to give the villagers their land back, citing the shortage of land compared to the population in the area ... Confrontations are increasing in intensity and frequency as local authorities confiscate land for construction of factories, power plants, shopping malls and other projects. Farmers often complain they are paid little or nothing and some-times accuse local officials of stealing compensation money.

(www.iht.com, 16 December 2005)

('Farmers need only be compensated for lost farm income, generally far below soaring real estate market values. Government-linked middlemen can make a fortune': *IHT*, 28 December 2005, p. 7.)

14 December 2005.

[There takes place] the first East Asia Summit ... [involving] sixteen nations ... It is the largest association of Asian nations – representing nearly half the world's population – as well as the first to include China and India together. It is the first in the postwar era to exclude the ... United States ... China, Japan and India are represented at the summit talks, along with the ten South-east Asian Nations [the Association of South-east Asian Nations or Asean] plus South Korea, Australia and New Zealand. Russia is attending as an observer ... The sixteen-member group accounts for about 3 billion people and a fifth of global trade ... Washington opposed the idea of the East Asian Summit and formed the Asia-Pacific Economic Co-operation forum in 1989.

(www.iht.com, 12 December 2005)

The one-day meeting [in Kuala Lumpur, the capital of Malaysia] ... lasting just three hours Wednesday morning ... followed a conference of the ten-member Association of South-east Asian nations ... The United States declined to join the Summit because of a reluctance to sign a pledge renounc-ing the use of force and interference in internal affairs in the region ... Presid-ent Vladimir Putin of Russia attended as an invited observer and lobbied hard for full membership when the second Summit is held in Manila [Philippines] next year [2006] ... Russia meets two of the three requirements for member-ship. It has agreed to renounce the use of force in the region and has signed an economic co-operation agreement. But, unlike the United States, Russia has only minimal economic and political involvement in the region .... Because prime minister Junichiro Koizumi of Japan had once again visited a shrine to Japanese who died in World War II, some of them war criminals, prime minis-ter Wen Jiabao of China refused to meet him ... South Korea was also at log-gerheads with Japan over what it sees as Tokyo's failure to acknowledge and adequately address wartime atrocities ... The new group's annual meetings will follow the precedent of the first one, coinciding and led by the host nation of the annual Asean summit talks.

(www.iht.com, 14 December 2005)

'The United States [was] absent from an Asian association for the first time in the postwar era . . . New Zealand [was admitted]' (*IHT*, 15 December 2005, p. 2).

> The sixteen countries said they would talk about 'broad, strategic, political and economic issues of common interest'. But they agreed that Asean would be the 'driving force' behind the new forum and that Asean+3 would continue to play a 'significant role' . . . Asean+3 includes China, Japan and South Korea . . . The focus of China's efforts will remain establishing its own free-trade area with Asean . . . Asean's internal free-trade plans are lagging, and a plan to sign a deal with South Korea at the Summit foundered over rice . . . Normally China, Japan and South Korea would hold a separate summit on the sidelines of the Asean talks. This time . . . they held no meeting, though the prime ministers of China and Japan managed a chilly handshake at the end of the gathering.
>
> (*The Economist*, 17 December 2005, p. 62)

> Rather than play a leading role at the WTO ministerial talks this week [in Hong Kong] the 100-strong delegation from Beijing . . . has carefully avoided taking a strong stand along any of the fault lines on market access that divide developed and developing world. Instead, China has been content to defend its compliance with the undertakings it made almost four years ago when it joined the WTO. Since then it has taken a back seat while other developing nations, including India and Brazil, have the fight against EU and US farm subsidies . . . China has put most of its effort into negotiating bilateral or regional free-trade deals. In November [2005] China concluded its first bilateral free-trade deal with Chile . . . The Chinese government has said that it is now negotiating with a further twenty-seven countries, including Australia, New Zealand and the ten members of the Association of South-east Asian Nations [Asean], in a bid to strike bilateral or regional free-trade agreements . . . A report from the office of the US trade representative on Monday [12 December] praised the progress China had made in meeting WTO obligations, although it attacked Beijing's failure to enforce copyright laws and open some key markets . . . Under the WTO agreements it is required to open its banking and finance market to full competition from 2007 . . . Beijing is seen as reluctant to push for new binding commitments in the Doha Round.
>
> (www.iht.com, 15 December 2005; *IHT*, 16 December 2005, p. 13)

22 December 2005.

> [It is announced that] Major General Zhu Chenghu . . . has been punished for telling reporters . . . in July . . . that China would have no choice but to resort to nuclear weapons in the event of US intervention in a conflict with Taiwan . . . [He] received an 'administrative demerit' recently from the National Defence University, which bars him from promotion for one year . . . An administrative demerit is the second lightest punishment on a scale of one to five, but still potentially damaging to an officer's career . . . Zhu is not the first Chinese general to warn the United States of possible nuclear conflict. Xiong Guangkai warned . . . in 1995 that China could use nuclear weapons in any conflict over Taiwan and that Americans cared more about Los Angeles than Taipei.
>
> (www.iht.com 22 December 2005; *IHT*, 23 December 2005, p. 6)

Taro Aso (the foreign minister of Japan): '[China is] a neighbouring country with one billion people, nuclear arms, military spending that has shown double-digit growth for the last seventeen years, with extremely little transparency. It is becoming a considerable threat' (*IHT*, 23 December 2005, p. 6).

> Aso's comments were the bluntest yet by a Japanese government official ... Both Japanese and foreign critics of Junichiro Koizumi's visits to the Yasukuni shrine have called for the construction of a secular war memorial ... [But on 22 December Japan's] chief cabinet minister ... said that the government had decided against allocating funds in next year's budget to consider the possibility of building a new memorial, saying that the project lacked public support.
>
> (*IHT*, 23 December 2005, p. 6)

27 December 2005.

> Tian Fengshan, a former minister in charge of China's influential land and resources ministry was sentenced Tuesday [27 December] to life in prison on charges of taking $500,000 in bribes ... He was accused of taking bribes while serving as a provincial governor.
>
> (*IHT*, 28 December 2005, p. 7)

> Tian Fengshan was fired as minister of land and resources in 2003 ... [This was] the highest level bribery trial in four years ... Tens of thousands of communist cadres have been sacked, fined, imprisoned or executed for corruption in recent years, but it is rare for such a senior figure to be implicated. Before Tian joined the cabinet he was governor of Heilongjiang province ... From 1995 to 2000 he oversaw a system oiled by bribery ... The top level of the Heilongjian administration ... [was] decimated ... According to the party's anti-corruption watchdog, the central commission for discipline inspection, nearly 50,000 officials have been prosecuted and punished in the past two years. More than 1,000 cadres have committed suicide and 8,000 fled overseas.
>
> (*Guardian*, 28 December 2005, p. 15)

28 December 2005.

> China and Japan are locked in a bitter war of words after the Japanese government accused spies from China of being responsible for the suicide of one of its diplomats. The unnamed official, who was based in Japan's consulate in Shanghai and committed suicide in May last year [2004], left a series of suicide notes claiming he was being blackmailed by a Chinese intelligence agent in a karaoke bar. The allegations [were] first voiced on Wednesday [28 December] by the Japanese foreign ministry.
>
> (*Independent*, 30 December 2005, p. 23)

> A Japanese statement on Wednesday [claimed] that the employee of the Japanese consulate in Shanghai killed himself in May 2004 because of 'an impermissible act by the Chinese security authorities' ... China accused Japan on Thursday [29 December] of 'vile behaviour' after Tokyo blamed the suicide of a Japanese consulate employee ... [who] had handled communications

between the consulate and the foreign ministry in Tokyo ... on the Chinese security authorities.

(www.iht.com, 29 December 2005)

28–30 December 2005.

In a rare protest against an official media crackdown, about 100 journalists from one of China's most aggressive daily newspapers have gone on strike after the paper's editor and two of his deputies were fired, local journalists said Friday [30 December]. The editor of the *Beijing News* ... and deputy editors ... were dismissed Wednesday [28 December] ... The striking journalists, about a third of the staff, stopped work on Thursday [29 December] after editors from the *Beijing News*'s conservative parent paper, the *Guangming Daily*, were appointed to replace the editor and his deputies ... Founded as a joint venture in 2003 between the Communist-Party controlled but financially struggling *Guangming Daily* and the *Southern Daily* newspaper group, the *Beijing News* enjoys a reputation as one of mainland China's boldest newspapers ... The paper made its name for aggressive reporting of official misconduct, including a violent crackdown in June on villagers protesting plans to build a controversial power plant in Hebei province. Local officials reportedly hired thugs to break up the protest and six villagers died from beatings. Two officials were later arrested after other newspapers and the electronic media picked up the story. There has also been speculation that sharply critical editorials on official corruption and poor government decision-making had angered senior government officials. The dismissals on Wednesday were not the first time the newspaper had experienced official steps against its staff. In March 2004 ... [the previous editor of the *Beijing News*] was arrested on charges of embezzlement arising from an earlier period when he was the editor of the Guangzhou *Southern Metropolitan Daily*, the sister paper of the *Beijing News*. After strong protests ... the charges were dropped ... Earlier in December the deputy editor of the *Southern Metropolitan News* was fired over a report that a senior official had been officially punished for a fatal coal mine accident ... Editors of other mainland Chinese newspapers that tackled sensitive subjects have also been purged this year [2005] ... The demands for an increasingly competitive market for circulation, viewers and advertising means that even state-controlled media companies are under pressure to provide the public with news that is likely to anger the authorities ... There were encouraging signs when, soon after taking office, Hu Jintao called on the media to play a more active watchdog role in the battle to combat widespread official corruption and government inefficiency. However, by the end of 2003 critics complained that Hu had begun a campaign to suppress the media.

(www.iht.com, 30 December 2005; *IHT*, 31 December 2005, p. 2)

4 January 2006. Prime minister Junichiro Koizumi of Japan:

I cannot understand why foreign governments would intervene in a spiritual matter and try to turn it into a diplomatic problem ... [I visit the Yasukuni shrine to pray for peace] . . . I have never once closed the door to negotiations with China and South Korea.

(www.iht.com, 4 January 2006)

An imprisoned Chinese journalist . . . Jiang Weiping . . . whose release was sought by the American government has been freed [on Tuesday 3 January] in advance of a trip to the United States by President Hu Jintao, an activist based in the United States announced Wednesday [4 January] . . . Hu is scheduled to visit the United States this year [2006] . . . He was arrested in 2000 after writing articles for a Hong Kong-based monthly magazine . . . reporting on corruption scandals in the north-eastern province of Liaoning . . . Jiang was convicted under China's vague state secrets law, which has been used recently against other journalists.

(www.iht.com, 6 January 2006)

5 January 2006.

A Chinese businessman . . . Feng Bingxian . . . who led a group of investors in protesting the seizure by local authorities of privately owned oil wells was sentenced Thursday [5 January] to three years in prison . . . Two other defendants were convicted on similar charges. The landmark ruling . . . appeared to undermine a government pledge to protect private property . . . The case underscored the uncertainty about control of private property even after the government amended the constitution in 2004 to add the first guarantee of property rights since the 1949 revolution . . . [The] case has drawn international attention since it first came to light . . . Feng Bingxian and the other defendants were convicted of disturbing social order . . . Feng was arrested after leading protests by investors who challenged a local government's seizure in 2003 of hundreds of privately developed oil wells in Jingbian . . . in the central province of Shaanxi . . . The other defendants . . . were convicted of the same charges, but received lighter sentences of two years in prison, suspended for three years.

(www.iht.com, 5 January 2006)

'Feng Bingxian said the compensation [offered] was insufficient' (*Guardian*, 6 January 2006, p. 35).

6 January 2006.

Yao Wenyuan, the final surviving member of the Gang of Four that terrorized China during the violent 1966–76 Cultural Revolution by persecuting thousands of people, has died, the government said Friday [6 January]. He was seventy-four. Yao's death on 23 December [2005] was blamed on diabetes . . . The Gang of Four [was] reported given its name by Mao Zedong . . . The members of the Gang of Four were arrested one month after Mao's death in September 1976 . . . Yao was the group's propagandist, later dubbed the killer with a pen by state media . . . Yao, a Shanghai journalist, was convicted of trying to gain power by persecuting officials and members of the public. He spent twenty years in prison before his release in 1996 . . . Mao's wife, Jiang Qing, died in 1991 in custody, reportedly by suicide. Another member, Wang

Hongwen, died in 1992. The third member, Zhang Chunqiao, died last May
[2005].

(*IHT*, 7 January 2006, p. 5)

12 January 2006.

A government environmental review has recommended reducing the number
of dams included in a hydroelectric proposal on the Nu river in south-western
China to limit environmental damage and decrease the number of people who
would be resettled ... The recommendation calls for four hydro dams instead
of the thirteen in the original Nu proposal ... The source cited ... described
the four dams as 'a pilot proposal'. The source said more research would be
needed to assess the larger project. The original NU river proposal, which
would have generated more electricity than the massive Three Gorges Dam,
has become an international controversy ... A coalition of environmentalists,
lawyers, journalists and non-governmental organizations has called for the
release of the report as well as public hearings on the project. They have cited
a 2003 environmental law that required public participation, including hearings, in deciding such major projects.

(www.iht.com, 12 January 2006)

16 January 2006.

A week of protests by residents of a town in China's southern industrial heartland exploded into violence last weekend with thousands of police officers
brandishing automatic weapons and using electric batons to put down the
protest and seal off the village, residents said Monday [16 January] ... In
Panlong village, about an hour's drive from the capital of Guangdong province
[Guangzhou], residents said that as many as sixty people were hurt and that at
least one person – a thirteen-year-old girl – was killed by security forces. The
police denied any responsibility, saying the girl had died of a heart attack ...
Eventually, they [villagers] said, as many as 10,000 police officers were
deployed, roughly twice the number of protesters at the peak of the demonstrations The clash in Panlong was the second time in a month that large numbers
of security forces, including paramilitary troops, were deployed to put down a
demonstration ... Like thousands of other demonstrations roiling rural China,
it took place over land use and environmental issues.

(*IHT*, 17 January 2006, p. 1)

Villagers say a thirteen-year-old girl was killed, and now say another person
died, as a result of the suppression of a local demonstration by police officers
using electrified truncheons that resemble cattle prods. Local officials say the
demonstration was broken up without the use of tear gas, electrified truncheons
or water canons, and that the girl died the day before the protest in a hospital
... Just as the protests are becoming more and more common, so is the use of
overwhelming force to put them down. A major threshold was crossed early
last month [December 2005] in the village of Dongzhou ... where residents
estimate that as many as thirty people were killed by paramilitary security

forces that opened fire on a crowd of demonstrators ... The strands that come together in the trouble in Panlong, a village in the township of Sanjiao, are so typical of rural protests as to be very nearly generic. People are dispossessed of their land to make way for industries or development projects. There are fruitless efforts to seek help from the government, from city hall to the provincial administration and all the way to Beijing. There is environmental destruction on a huge scale and the loss of long-reliable livelihoods. When a spark ignites the people's discontent, local officials use police-state tactics to suppress the protests and enforce a silence over the details of the matter. Ultimately, there are brass knuckles, jail and, lately, death for those who refuse to take the hint and desist ... Many villagers told stories of having been deceived by corrupt local officials who they say have enriched themselves by selling off rights to the villagers' farmland ... A particular focal point for the protests was the Minsen garment factory, the land for which villagers said had been acquired through corrupt deals with local political figures.

(www.iht.com, 18 January 20006)

'Villagers say two people were killed, but the corpse of a thirteen-year-old girl was rapidly destroyed to protect an official story line that she had succumbed to a heart attack' (www.iht.com, 25 January 2006).

[Villagers said the] police clubbed a teenage protester to death and the authorities then bribed her family to keep quiet about the killing ... [The girl] aged about fourteen was reportedly one of the stone throwers [and] fatally beaten on Saturday night [14 January] ... Villagers in Sanjiao, in one of China's most developed and polluted areas, were enraged by a government programme to buy land for an industrial zone. They were told the land would be used for a road, but later found out it would be turned over to chemical and garment factories ... Many considered [the compensation] inadequate to cover lost earnings ... The number and intensity of such demonstrations is rising sharply. According to official data, 3.8 million people took part in 'incidents involving the masses' in 2004. The 74,000 protests represented a sevenfold rise on the 1994 figure.

(*Guardian*, 18 January 2006, p. 20)

17 January 2006.

Two journalists in eastern China were sentenced to up to ten years in jail for publishing an unauthorized magazine that exposed local land disputes ... The two ... were convicted by ... [a court in Zhejiang province] for publishing the magazine without having the approval of the media authorities ... A third person was sentenced to one year in jail. The person and the charges were not identified.

(www.iht.com 18 January 2006)

20 January 2006.

Land grabs by officials ... are provoking mass unrest in the countryside and amount to a 'historic error' that could threaten national stability, prime minister Wen Jiabao said in comments published [on 20 January but delivered to a Party Central Committee meeting held on 29 December 2005] ... Local officials operate with impunity on the one-party state and have little to fear from a legal system that answers to the Communist Party. Endless harangues by central government leaders to pay more attention to inequality have done little to address the root causes of the wealth gap and surging social unrest, analysts say. China in the past two years has abolished taxes on peasants and staple farm crops, relieving one historic source of grievance in the countryside ... The government said in 2004 that new factories, housing, offices and shopping malls had consumed about 5 per cent of total arable land in the previous seven years.

(*IHT*, 21 January 2006, p. 5)

Wen called for keeping grain prices steady, while curbing 'excessive' increases in the prices of farming inputs. He said the government would focus in coming years on improving living and working conditions in rural areas, increasing spending ... rural public schools, hospitals and cultural facilities must be improved, said Wen ... and doing more to protect migrant workers who face unsafe and unstable working conditions and are often denied fair wages ... The government promised Thursday [19 January] to improve treatment of rural migrants who move to urban areas to work ... In many parts of China these workers' incomes have stagnated or risen only slightly for the past decade ... Without legal recourse, many go unpaid and are vulnerable to abuse ... In the past twenty years about 140 million farmers and their families have moved to find work in towns and cities, according to estimates from the national bureau of statistics.

(www.iht.com 20 January 2006)

'Local officials can make huge profits by getting hold of rural land and having it rezoned for industrial use' (*FT*, 21 January 2006, p. 6).

When land is seized it is often done without adequate compensation. As there is no independent court system, it is usually impossible to seek legal redress ... On Thursday the ministry of public security said there were 87,000 protests, riots and other 'mass incidents' last year [2005], up 6.6 per cent on 2004.

(*Guardian*, 21 January 2006, p. 21)

Wen Jiabao:

We absolutely cannot commit a historic error over land problems ... Some local governments have taken over farmland illegally without giving reasonable compensation and this has sparked mass incidents in rural areas ... This is still a key source of instability in rural areas and even the whole society ... In the final analysis we must protect the democratic rights and provide material benefits to rural citizens. Improving the rural quality of life and ensuring social fairness and justice are extremely important and urgent tasks ... [There are local officials who impose] arbitrary fees [on peasants] ... [The expansion of cities has involved] reckless occupation of farmland ... In the long run the contradiction between population growth and shrinking farmland, as well as a shortage of water resources, will assert itself, and raising food production will become more and more difficult ... In 2006 grain production will encounter adverse circumstances such as unstable grain prices, arable land shrinkage and an unpredictable climate.

(*IHT*, 21 January 2006, p. 5; www.iht.com, 20 January 2006; *FT*, 21 January 2006, p. 6; *Guardian*, 21 January 2006, p. 21)

31 January 2006.

Taro Aso ... Japan's foreign minister ... backtracked Tuesday [31 January] from his call for Emperor Akihito to visit ... The Yasukuni shrine ... [which] honours 2.5 million Japanese war dead from eleven wars, including fourteen World War II war criminals ... In a speech Saturday [28 January] Aso said it would be 'best' if the emperor paid a visit ... Akihito's father, the late Emperor Hirohito, halted visits to the shrine in 1978 after the war criminals were enshrined. Akihito has refrained from going to Yasukuni since becoming emperor in 1989 ... [Taro Aso said on Saturday] that foreign criticism encouraged visits to the shrine.

(www.iht.com 31 January 2006)

1 February 2006.

Japan's government has adopted a statement saying it does not consider China to be a threat ... A [Japanese] foreign ministry spokesman: 'We think that threats become evident when a capability to invade is coupled with an intent to invade' ... Foreign minister Taro Aso caused a diplomatic flap in December [2005] when he said China's military buildup was a threat given its lack of transparency.

(www.iht.com, 1 February 2006)

Toxic wastewater was flushed untreated into a river in southern China, prompting the government to cut water supplies to 28,000 people for at least six days [it was announced on 20 February] ... A power plant on the upper reaches of the Yuexi river in Sichuan province was to blame for the pollution, which prompted environmental officials to suspend water supplies to the town of Guanyin last week ... Under new regulations enacted earlier this month, serious accidents must be reported directly to the national state environmental protection agency or to the State Council, the Chinese cabinet, within an hour ... Since the spill in the Songhua river, the national environmental agency has received forty-five reports of environmental accidents as of 1 February [2006], six of them serious.

(www.iht.com, 20 February 2006)

22 February 2006. '[On 22 February prime minister] Wen Jiabao ... met the Japanese trade minister ... Toshihiro Nikai [in Beijing]' (*FT*, 23 February 2006, p. 5).

A Chinese journalist was released from prison on Wednesday [22 February 2006] after nearly seventeen years for splattering paint on a portrait of Mao Zedong during the 1989 pro-democracy protests in Tiananmen Square ... The journalist, Yu Dongye, and two friends hurled eggs filled with red paint at the famous portrait of Mao, which still stares out on Tiananmen Square from the entrance to the Forbidden City .. Yu's original twenty-year sentence had twice been reduced ... In 2004 Reporters Without Borders ... said Yu had gone insane after being tortured in prison ... President Hu Jintao is to visit the United States in April.

(*IHT*, 23 February 2006, p. 4)

'It did not appear to be meant as a gesture to Washington: Yu served his full sentence, unlike other prisoners who have been released early in connection with diplomatic trips' (*IHT*, 24 February 2006, p. 1).

The Chinese government has formally announced major initiatives to expand health, education and welfare benefits for farmers, but left unresolved the fundamental issue of whether farmers should be allowed to buy or sell land ... The National People's Congress ... is expected to make the rural programme the centrepiece of a new five-year plan during its annual meeting next month [March]. The programme, which emerged in broad form last October [2005], includes free education for many rural residents, increased subsidy payments for farmers, new government funding for medical care and further government investment in rural infrastructure projects ... At a news conference Wednesday [22 February] Chen Xiwen, the top government adviser on rural issues, outlined pieces of the programme and said the government must also help defray the huge debts held by rural governments as China enters 'a new historical period' in which the central government can better balance economic development ... Chen acknowledged that China would eventually need 'to propose steadily reforming the land acquisition system itself'. But he said changes must happen slowly to protect the country's farming output. Instead, Chen said, farmers would now be given more compensation after land is confiscated and suggested that urban social welfare benefits should be extended to peasants who are left landless.

(www.iht.com, 22 February 2006; *IHT*, 23 February 2006, p. 4)

Beijing has launched a 'new deal' for farmers, aimed at raising rural incomes with a combination of crop subsidies, tax cuts and infrastructure spending in inland areas. The plan [is] called the 'new socialist countryside' ... Chen Xiwen ... said yesterday [22 February]. China had the 'strictest' rules in the world to prevent the conversion of farmland for industrial use but their implementation would take time. 'The issue is whether land for construction and development should be monopolized by the state,' he said ... Mr Chen said this issue was 'still being considered' ... About 940 of China's 1.3 billion population are registered as living on farms or in villages but about 200 million of these have left their homes to seek higher paid jobs in towns or cities. Mr Chen said China, even with mass migration to cities, would have to manage

600 million rural residents by the time the population peaked at about 1.5 billion in about 2030. The government is committed to spending about renminbi 100 billion ($12 billion) in the next financial year on transfer payments from the centre to county-level governments and below to make up for the abolition of agriculture tax. Mr Chen offered no other figures for the cost of the new rural policy. He said they would be released with the latest five-year economic plan at next month's National People's Congress ... Mr Chen said many rural governments had 'misunderstood their role in the economy' by borrowing money from local banks to invest in property projects or by acting as guarantors for others. Mr Chen acknowledged the policy was not an instant remedy, saying 'it will take a long time in history for the new socialist countryside to materialize in China'.

(*FT*, 23 February 2006, p 5)

The new policy promises that, by 2007, rural students will no longer have to pay for books and heating in schools. Students from the poorest families will receive free textbooks and boarding subsidies. And the government will also increase subsidies for rural health co-operatives ... Last month [January] the ministry of public security said there were 87,000 protests, riots and other 'mass incidents' last year [2005], up 6.6 per cent on 2004 ... The policy proposes that China should remain 'basically self-sufficient' in grain. It promises increased subsidies for farmers growing grain, as well as continued revenue 'bonuses' for local governments in the grain belt, and says the government will continue setting prices for grain purchases.

(*Guardian*, 22 February 2006, p. 16)

5–14 March 2006. The annual session of the National People's Congress was held. The number of delegates in attendance was 2,927.

China's new 'historic task' is to narrow the politically volatile gap between rich and poor and enliven the economy of the country's vast but still impoverished rural areas, prime minister Wen Jiabao said in a national ... televised address Sunday [5 March] ... Wen said officials must find a way to ensure that the two-thirds of China's 1.3 billion people who live in rural areas share the prosperity that has flowed mostly to coastal and urban areas ... 'We need to see clearly that there are many hardships and problems in economic and social life,' Wen said ... But Wen promised only a modest increase in government spending to address the problems ... Wen focussed a large section of his speech on the recently announced effort to build a 'new socialist countryside', in which the central government has pledged to spend more on agriculture and rural infrastructure, crop subsidies and social services for the country's 800 million farmers and rural residents. He said he had earmarked $42.3 billion in such spending this year [2006], an increase of 14.2 per cent over 2005 ... That rate of growth is not particularly high for a country that recorded 9.9 per cent economic growth last year [2005] and has had ballooning tax revenue ... Central and local government revenue rose 19.8 per cent in 2005 ... He said that China's less wealthy western regions this year would completely eliminate tuition and fees associated with required schooling through lower middle school.

(IHT, 6 March 2006, p. 1)

China says it plans to ... launch a series of initiatives to overcome the 'deep-seated problem' of the gaping rich–poor divide between wealthy cities and rural areas ... Wen Jiabao: 'All of society should energetically support rural development' ... However, the initial figures provided by Mr Wen and a separate report by the finance ministry record relatively modest spending commitments for rural areas, home to about two-thirds of China's 1.3 billion people. Central government spending on farmers and rural areas will total renminbi 339.7 billion ($42 billion) in 2006, an increase of about 14 per cent from last year [2005], equal to the percentage increase in the military budget. The rise in central government spending on rural initiatives is also likely to lag behind the rate of growth in central government tax revenue, which rose by 20 per cent in 2005 year-on-year. The central government tax take has grown rapidly in recent years, reaching 17.3 per cent of GDP in 2005, four points higher than in 2000 and nearly double the rate a decade ago, when China faced a fiscal crisis. Despite the spending restraint thus far in the government's effort to revive the countryside, the political focus of Mr Wen's speech was firmly on the problems of lifting farm incomes and grain production. Conflict between farmers and local governments, mainly over the confiscation of land, has been behind a rapid rise in violent disputes in the countryside in the last two to three years ... China is also concerned that the continued loss of scarce arable land to industry will leave it dependent on grain imports, long a worry of top leaders. 'This poses a threat to the nation's food security,' Mr Wen said ... The Chinese premier also promised to accelerate the introduction of rural co-operative mutual funds, to help farmers afford at least basic health care. Few people in the countryside have insurance and the public health system has all but collapsed.

(FT, 6 March 2006, p. 7)

Prime minister Wen Jiabao: 'Building a "new socialist countryside" is a major historic task' (www.cnn.com, 5 March 2006).
Prime minister Wen Jiabao:

> Some deeply seated conflicts that have accumulated over a long time have yet to be fundamentally resolved, and new problems have arisen that cannot be ignored ... [China must] pay more attention to social equity and social stability so that all the people can enjoy the fruits of reform and development.

(www.bbc.co.uk, 5 March 2006)

Prime minister Wen Jiabao ... promised an extra 42 billion yuan in spending for poor rural areas ... The central government will lift spending on rural areas by 15 per cent this year [2006] to 339.7 billion yuan ... Considering the scale of the problem the sums are relatively small.

(Guardian, 6 March 2006, p. 23)

Wen Jiabao's remedies for the countryside contained little new. They included the scrapping of agricultural tax this year [2006], extending an experimental health care insurance scheme to 40 per cent of counties and the elimination by the end of next year [2007] of tuition and other fees for rural residents receiving compulsory education ... Central government spending on rural areas for everything from health care to subsidies for grain producers is to increase by 14.2 per cent this year to 340 billion yuan ($42 billion). And government spending on infrastructure will be shifted towards rural areas. More will be spent on projects such as rural roads, water and power supplies, schools and hospitals ... How much more will be spent on rural infrastructure is unclear ... Central government spending on the countryside will still amount to only 8.9 per cent of total government expenditure, up from last year's 8.8 per cent but down from 9.2 per cent in 2004. Abolishing the agricultural tax and other fees imposed on peasants will save each rural dweller on average of 156 yuan ($19) a year – about 4.8 per cent of net income. But despite promised transfers of 103 billion yuan annually to fill the resulting hole in local finances, it is not clear that these funds will be sufficient. A quarter of the money is supposed to come from local governments, which may well have other plans for it ... The proposed 14.2 per cent in total central spending on all rural projects is not that remarkable. It is only a little higher than the projected increase of 13.8 per cent in all government spending (central and local) this year. And the increase is smaller than the 14.7 per cent rise, to 281 billion yuan, planned in military spending in 2006 ... Total government revenues ... increased by nearly 20 per cent [in 2005] and are predicted to rise by 12 per cent this year [2006]. The target for the budget deficit is a manageable 1.5 per cent of GDP in 2006, down from 1.6 last year [2005].

(*The Economist*, 11 March 2006, pp. 63–4)

'Even though the amount to be spent [on rural areas] has risen to 340 billion yuan ($42 billion), or 8.9 per cent of the entire budget, China's vastness makes it trivial. Some 800 million people still live in the countryside' (p. 14).

China is ... drawing up plans to reform the rules governing state requisitions of farmers' land. The reform would introduce a 'market mechanism' for compensation payments for farmland seized for commercial use ... [An official spokesman]: 'The basic thinking of the reform is to take a different approach to land requisitions depending on the use to which the land is to be put. If the land is being requisitioned for use for the public good, then there must be a raised standard for compensation. If it is to be used commercially then the market mechanism must be introduced ... There certainly is a phenomenon of farmers' interests being harmed by low-price requisitioning of their land' ... Under current rules requisition compensation is supposed to be calculated only according to the land's agricultural value, allowing local governments and developers to reap huge profits when converting it to commercial use ... [The official spokesman] warned that if both public use and commercial requisition orders continued to be the preserve of local governments, it would remain very difficult for farmers to protect their land.

(*FT*, 9 March 2006, p. 9)

Although it received only passing attention in Wen's report, China also announced over the weekend [4 March] that it would increase military spending this year [2006] at a higher rate than the increase in rural investment. The official military budget will grow 14.7 per cent to $35.3 billion, continuing a long streak of double-digit increases in outlays for its 2.5 million-strong armed forces.

(*IHT*, 6 March 2006, p. 8)

China has said it will increase its military spending by 14.7 per cent this year [2006] to 283.8 billion yuan ($35.3 billion) ... A spokesman said: 'The proportion of the budget given over to defence spending is much the same as in past years' ... China says its military spending is dwarfed by the United States. The US Department of Defence had a base budget of $400 billion in 2005 ... [The United States has said that defence spending by China in 2005] was not the $30 billion stated but closer to $90 billion.

(www.bbc.co.uk, 5 March 2006)

Prime minister Wen Jiabao ... said the government would try to reduce the rate of economic growth to 8 per cent this year [2006]. But he announced the same target a year ago, after which the economy expanded nearly 10 per cent. He said officials must do more to slow the growth of fixed-asset investment.

(*IHT*, 6 March 2006, p. 8)

'The government is aiming to keep inflation under 3 per cent and the urban unemployment rate under 4.6 per cent, Wen Jiabao said' (*FT*, 6 March 2006, p. 7).

Prime minister Wen Jiabao ... highlighted a fresh commitment to environment controls and energy efficiency. He said China must reduce the amount of energy to takes to produce each dollar of output by 4 per cent in 2006 and by 20 per cent in five years ... After five years, he said, China will also reduce the quantity of pollutants released into the air and water by 10 per cent ... He made no mention of ... 'green GDP'.

(www.iht.com, 5 March 2006)

China is revising a draft property law after delaying its passage because of fierce ideological debate among officials and academics over its balancing of state and private rights. The dispute over the long-awaited legislation highlights political sensitivities that continue to surround China's embrace of the market and echoes differences on other issues such as the degree to which the economy should be opened to foreign and private investment ... [There has been] a surge of objections from conservative academics and officials who believe the draft gives too much weight to protection of private property. The most widely cited opposition came from Gong Xiantian, an expert in Marxist jurisprudence at Peking University, who issued an open letter arguing that the draft law would 'undermine the legal foundation of China's socialist economy' ... Professor Gong argued that property protections in the law could shield those who stole state assets or who took bribes ... The law is now scheduled to be voted on at the 2007 NPC plenary session.

(*FT*, 10 March 2006, p. 9)

In recent years China's leaders have themselves stressed the need to narrow regional imbalances. This was a major theme of the annual ten-day session of the National People's Congress, which ended on 14 March ... Yet criticism of these disparities has also become a way for some to air more general grievances about China's embrace of capitalism. The government recently shelved plans to submit a new property law to the congress after a chorus of opposition, led by a Peking University academic, Gong Xiantian. He argued that the draft, which protected property rights, was un-Marxist and unconstitutional.

(*The Economist*, 18 March 2006, p. 62)

For the first time in perhaps a decade the National People's Congress, the Communist Party-led legislature, now convened in its annual two-week session [5–14 March 2006], is consumed with an ideological debate over socialism and capitalism that many assumed had been buried by China's long streak of fast economic growth. The controversy has forced the government to shelve a draft law to protect property rights ... It has also highlighted the resurgent influence of a small but vocal group of socialist-leaning scholars and policy advisers. These old-style leftist thinkers have used China's rising income gap [e.g. the gap between the average incomes of urban and rural residents has risen to 3.3 to 1.0, according to the United Nations Development Programme] and increasing social unrest to raise doubts about what they see as the country's headlong pursuit of private wealth and market-driven economic development. The roots of the current debate can be traced to a biting critique of the property rights law that circulated on the internet last summer [2005]. The critique's author, Gong Xiantian, a professor at Beijing University Law School, accused the legal experts who wrote the draft of 'copying capitalist civil law like slaves' and offering equal protection to 'a rich man's car and a beggar's stick'. Most of all he protested that the proposed law did not state that 'socialist property is inviolable' ... The proposed property law has taken eight years to prepare and is intended to codify a more expansive notion of property rights added to China's constitution in 2003.

(Joseph Kahn, *IHT*, 13 March 2006, pp. 1, 4)

'The news came this past week that ... the National People's Congress ... was seriously debating, for the first time in a decade, whether the country had drifted too far from its socialist roots' (*IHT*, 18 March 2006, p. 13).

A meeting of the National People's Congress ... coincided with unrest in China over the pace of market-based reforms and attacks on the alleged creeping controls of parts of the economy by multilateral companies ... Prime minister Wen Jiabao ... said China would sustain the pace of reform, but added that the state must keep a dominant controlling share in the state-owned commercial banks.

(*FT*, 15 March 2006, p. 11)

A backlash against economic reform has gathered force and the logic of liberalization is being challenged to an extent not seen since the immediate aftermath of the crackdown on pro-democracy protests in Tiananmen Square in

1989 ... Domestic critics blame market reforms for exacerbating inequality and promoting social unrest.

(FT, 16 March 2006, p. 16)

17 March 2006.

The authorities made a surprise legal manoeuvre on Friday [17 March] in the state secrets case against a Chinese researcher for *The New York Times* that left unclear whether he would soon be released or whether the case would be further delayed as President Hu Jintao prepares to visit the United States next month [April]. A court here [in Beijing] issued a decision Friday that granted a request by prosecutors to withdraw at least part of the case against Zhao Yan ... His lawyer said court officials told him Friday that the decision meant that both charges against Zhao were being withdrawn. He said his client could possibly be released within days. But the court made no mention of a release date and gave no definitive statement about his status ... The court decision is written in muddled language that does not rule out the possibility that prosecutors intend to withdraw the lesser charge but leave intact the state secrets charge, which carries a prison sentence of at least ten years.

(IHT, 18 March 2006, p. 22)

The researcher, Zhao Yan, worked in the newspaper's Beijing bureau ... Less than three months [ago] ... Zhao was indicted for disclosing state secrets to *The New York Times* and a lesser charge of fraud. Zhao has denied the allegations ... [Zhao's] arrest was tied to a 7 September 2004 article in *The Times*, which disclosed that the former president, Jiang Zemin, had unexpectedly offered to give up his final leadership position as head of the military. The story later proved accurate when Jiang resigned ... Zhao 'was arrested on 17 September, ten days after the publication of the article in *The Times* ... Zhao had been an investigative journalist for several Chinese publications before joining the Beijing bureau of *The Times* as a researcher in April 2004.

(www.iht.com, 17 March 2006)

21–22 March 2006. President Putin visits China.

Russia yesterday [21 March] promised to build two natural gas pipelines to China and to become one of the country's biggest gas suppliers within the next decade ... The pipelines would cost as much as $10 billion to build and the agreement would see Russia supplying China and the Asia-Pacific region with 60 billion to 80 billion cubic feet of gas, twice China's total consumption in 2004. Russia said the first gas could flow to China as early as 2011.

(FT, 22 March 2006, p. 8)

The first deal announced was plans for two gas pipelines to open within five years ... But there was no word of an agreement to build a separate pipeline sought by Beijing to deliver Siberian oil. A Russian minister said Moscow would finance a feasibility study for the oil pipeline and could not offer a construction timetable until then ... On the gas pipelines ... the western route was likely to be developed first and could start supplying China in five years ... On

Tuesday [21 March] Putin and Hu Jintao discussed a possible spur line off the future [oil] line leading directly to China and agreed to a feasibility study.

(*IHT*, 22 March 2006, p. 13)

President Vladimir Putin said Wednesday [22 March] that there was 'no doubt' that a pipeline carrying Siberian oil to Russia's Pacific coast would extend to China ... China National Petroleum ... will contribute $400 million to help finance the link to China ... President Hu Jintao wants an $11.5 billion oil pipeline from eastern Siberia to the Pacific port of Nakhodka to include a 70 kilometre, or 43 mile, spur to his country ... China National Petroleum on Tuesday [22 March] signed agreements to work with Russia's Transneft, Rosneft and Gazprom ... Russia is set to start building the Pacific oil pipeline this year [2006]. The pipeline's first phase will start operating by the end of 2008 ... China National Petroleum plans to build a branch to the Russian border to link up with the Siberian pipeline once that happens.

(www.iht.com, 22 March 2006)

'Russia says that Chinese–Russian trade grew 37 per cent last year [2005] to $29.1 billion and was expected to pass $60 billion a year by 2010' (www.iht.com, 19 March 2006).

22 March 2006.

The government will increase existing taxes and impose new ones on 1 April [2006] for items from gas-guzzling vehicles to chopsticks so as to improve the country's environmental record, conserve energy and narrow China's wide gap between rich and poor, official media said Wednesday [22 March]. New or higher taxes will fall on vehicles with engines of more than 2 litres, disposable wooden chopsticks, planks for wood floors, luxury watches, golf clubs, golf balls and certain oil products.

(*IHT*, 23 March 2006, p. 12)

23 March 2006.

Japan announced Thursday [23 March] that it was freezing its yen loans to China at least through the end of this month because of worsening relations between the two countries ... Japan [said it] would not release any more of the loans to China in the current financial year, which ends 31 March, but that the government might start releasing the loans again if the situation improves ... [There is] an agreement that Japan would end new loans to China by the start of the Beijing Olympics in 2008. Japan's loans to China began in 1979 and Tokyo has so far provided a total of $25 billion, as of May 2005.

(www.iht.com, 23 March 2006)

Japan has suspended decisions on new yen loans to China, blaming its increasingly strained ties with [China] ... The chief cabinet secretary said yesterday [23 March] that Tokyo would 'put off making a decision on yen loans for this fiscal year to China ... because of various situations surrounding Sino-Japanese relations' ... However ... [he said] the freeze signalled a delay, not a suspension and that yen loans would continue with the aim of securing 'future-orientated Sino-Japanese relations'. Japan announced last year [2005] that it was winding down aid to China from 2008 ... However, this is the first time that a reduction or freeze in loans has been linked with politics.

(*FT*, 24 March 2006, p. 7)

2 April 2006.

Foreign minister Taro Aso [of Japan] ... called China a military threat Sunday [2 April] ... Taro Aso, who has angered China in recent months with a series of critical comments, questioned China's rapid military spending increases and its lack of transparency ... Taro Aso: 'It is not clear what China is using the money for. This creates a sense of threat for surrounding countries' ... President Hu Jintao made a conciliatory gesture last week by offering to hold a summit meeting with prime minister Junichiro Koizumi if he ended his visits to the Yasukuni shrine ... Beijing has refused top-level talks since Koizumi last visited the shrine in October 2005 ... But the chief cabinet spokesman, Shinzo Abe, a front-runner to succeed Junichiro Koizumi when his term [as president] runs out in September, rejected that offer Sunday.

(www.iht.com, 2 April 2006)

3 April 2006.

Beijing is scheduled Monday [3 April] to sign an agreement with Australia ... to buy uranium for use in China's nuclear power plants ... The deal also opens the door for Chinese investment in Australian uranium mines. The agreement ... is the highlight of a three-day trip to Australia by prime minister Wen Jiabao ... [Australia] has stressed that China has agreed not to use Australian uranium in its weapons programme or for other military purposes. The Australians also stress that China, unlike India, which the Bush administration agreed last month to provide with nuclear technology, has signed the Nuclear Non-proliferation Treaty ... Australia holds an estimated 40 per cent of the world's reserves of easily extractable uranium.

(*IHT*, 3 April 2006, p. 10)

Australia and China signed deals Monday clearing the way for Beijing to buy Australian uranium for use in its nuclear power stations ... The two countries' foreign ministers signed agreements intended to ensure that Beijing does not divert Australian nuclear fuel into its atomic weapons programme ... [The ministers] signed two pacts: a nuclear transfer agreement and a nuclear co-operation agreement ... Australia refuses to sell uranium to nations that have not signed the Nuclear Non-proliferation Treaty. The signing came on the third day of a visit to Australia by Wen Jiabao, the first by a Chinese prime minister for eighteen years.

(www.iht.com, 3 April 2006)

'Under the terms of the deal Australia will export 20,000 metric tons of uranium to China each year, beginning in 2010 ... Beijing wants to build forty to fifty reactors over the next twenty years' (www.bbc.co.uk, 3 April 2006).

2 The economy

Introduction

The economic reforms themselves have been variously described by China, e.g. 'planned socialist commodity economy' has given way to 'socialist market economy' (1992: formally enshrined in the new constitution in March 1993) as the reforms have proceeded and ideological concessions have become more and more accepted.

China is the best example of a generally successful policy of *gradual and partial* economic reform owing to factors such as (1) the consequences of making drastic mistakes in a poor country with a history of natural and man-made disasters and (2) disagreements within the ruling elite. As we have already seen, those advocating 'big bang'/'shock therapy' for the countries of Eastern Europe and the former Soviet Union argue that China's model cannot be copied in these cases because circumstances are different. (Woo is an exception in that he argues that 'gradual reform in China was not the optimal reform for China': 1994: 306.) The Great Leap Forward (GLF, 1958–60) and the Cultural Revolution (1966–76; a chaotic and anarchic period and one which was basically a means of reasserting Mao's personal power after his authority had waned in the wake of the disastrous GLF) were the result of extreme-left policies. The discrediting of such extreme and extreme-left policies have had a profound effect, both on the decision to implement economic reforms after the watershed year 1978 and on the basic continuity of the reforms. (The Third Plenum of the Eleventh Central Committee in December 1978 was the crucial political event.)

It is generally recognized that China had no detailed blueprint for economic reform in 1978 and thus groped its way forward in a gradual and partial fashion. In addition, China was generally in a more favourable position in 1978 than the countries of Eastern Europe/the former Soviet Union generally were in 1989/1991. For example, China had a relatively low foreign debt, did not suffer from severe inflationary pressures and had substantially reorientated its trade towards the West. (China had quarrelled with the Soviet Union, e.g. in 1960 the Soviet Union withdrew its aid personnel).

Economic reforms have sometimes been put on hold or even regressed, e.g. after the Tiananmen crisis in 1989. The Asian financial crisis (which started in July 1997) and deflation in China (after October 1997) had an impact. In the second half of 1998 some price controls were introduced while there were slowdowns in housing reform, in small privatization and in the downsizing of bureaucracy.

A leaked text of an address given by Zhu Rongyi ... on 5 June [2001 included the statement that] it was necessary to be 'safe and slow down somewhat a few major reforms in light of the current situation'. Mr Zhu indicated that one casualty would be the government's plans to promote badly needed tax reforms in the countryside. The aim of these is to eliminate various fees and levies arbitrarily imposed on farmers by local authorities and rely instead on a single tax based on income from crop production ... These have exacerbated other problems ... [e.g. plummeting] revenues of village-level governments ... Other reforms to be slowed down ... are plans to impose a fuel tax in place of the random charges imposed on vehicle owners by local governments, as well as the introduction of a social security system that will remove the burden on employers to provide welfare benefits.

(*The Economist*, 16 June 2001, p. 72)

China has suspended the sale of shares in state-owned companies used to fund a national social security fund in a policy reversal which it hopes will steady its weakening stock market ... [The commission's] statement last night backed the continuing sale of state shares but said it was a 'long-term task which needed constant improvement'.

(*FT*, 23 October 2001, p. 17)

China unexpectedly suspended the sale of state-owned shares in listed companies ... The China securities regulatory commission said the government would maintain its long-term policy of reducing the state's holdings in listed companies, but it would implement the plan step-by-step, rather than through dramatic sell-offs.

(*IHT*, 24 October 2001, p. 13)

In recent years China's leaders have themselves stressed the need to narrow regional imbalances. This was a major theme of the annual ten-day session of the National People's Congress, which ended on 14 March ... Yet criticism of these disparities has also become a way for some to air more general grievances about China's embrace of capitalism. The government recently shelved plans to submit a new property law to the congress after a chorus of opposition, led by a Peking University academic, Gong Xiantian. He argued that the draft, which protected property rights, was un-Marxist and unconstitutional.

(*The Economist*, 18 March 2006, p. 62)

For the first time in perhaps a decade the National People's Congress, the Communist Party-led legislature, now convened in its annual two-week session [5–14 March 2006], is consumed with an ideological debate over socialism and capitalism that many assumed had been buried by China's long streak of fast economic growth. The controversy has forced the government to shelve a draft law to protect property rights ... It has also highlighted the resurgent influence of a small but vocal group of socialist-leaning scholars and policy advisers. These old-style leftist thinkers have used China's rising income gap [e.g. the gap between the average incomes of urban and rural residents has risen to 3.3 to 1.0, according to the United Nations Development Programme] and increasing social unrest to raise doubts about what they see as the country's headlong pursuit of private wealth and market-driven economic development. The roots of the current debate can be traced to a biting critique of the property rights law that circulated on the internet last summer [2005]. The critique's author, Gong Xiantian, a professor at Beijing University Law School, accused the legal experts who wrote the draft of 'copying capitalist civil law like slaves' and offering equal protection to 'a rich man's car and a beggar's stick'. Most of all he protested that the proposed law did not state that 'socialist property is inviolable' ... The proposed property law has taken eight years to prepare and is intended to codify a more expansive notion of property rights added to China's constitution in 2003.

(Joseph Kahn, *IHT*, 13 March 2006, pp. 1, 4)

'The news came this past week that ... the National People's Congress ... was seriously debating, for the first time in a decade, whether the country had drifted too far from its socialist roots' (IHT, 18 March 2006, p. 13).

A meeting of the National People's Congress ... coincided with unrest in China over the pace of market-based reforms and attacks on the alleged creeping controls of parts of the economy by multilateral companies ... Prime minister Wen Jiabao ... said China would sustain the pace of reform, but added that the state must keep a dominant controlling share in the state-owned commercial banks.

(*FT*, 15 March 2006, p. 11)

A backlash against economic reform has gathered force and the logic of liberalization is being challenged to an extent not seen since the immediate aftermath of the crackdown on pro-democracy protests in Tiananmen Square in 1989 ... Domestic critics blame market reforms for exacerbating inequality and promoting social unrest.

(*FT*, 16 March 2006, p. 16)

Agriculture

Agriculture has been subject to great policy swings. The land reform of 1950–3 involved a massive redistribution of land and property to poorer peasants. Learning the lessons of Soviet collectivization of the 1930s, China progressed through increasing degrees of co-operation until 'advanced agricultural producer co-operatives' (AAPC) became dominant.

During the Great Leap Forward (1958–60) an attempt was made to accelerate economic development and the transition to communism. For example, 'Chairman Mao Tsetung (Zedong) exhorted his countrymen to make enough steel to "overtake Britain in fifteen years and America in twenty years"' (*FT*, 6 May 2003, p. 19). 'People's communes' were set up, reaching an average size of 4,550 households.

Pronounced moves towards egalitarianism severely dampened work incentives and the removal of peasants from the land (especially at peak periods) to work in local industry ('backyard' steel furnaces, etc.) were factors that contributed to drastic falls in agricultural output and massive loss of life. After the GLF the main unit of production became the AAPC and then the team.

'Roughly 10 million people ... were killed in Mao's post-1949 political campaigns and the other 30 to 40 million ... died as a result of his Great Leap Forward famine of 1958–61' (*FEER*, 13 September 2001, p. 66).

> Chronic soil erosion and extreme poverty [are among] the after-effects of the Great Famine of 1959–61, which flowed from Mao's decision to leave the 1958 harvest unpicked and clear forests to create mega-farms and power 'backyard' steel furnaces ... Rivers [have been] polluted by a recent boom in coal mining; this was inspired by Mao's madcap idea that with sufficient coal China's steel industry could surpass Britain's in a year: the so-called Great Leap Forward.
>
> (*FEER*, 27 September 2001, p. 65)

('The countryside was stripped of trees for fuel to fire backyard [steel] furnaces, causing widespread floods': *IHT*, 12 April 2004, p. 6.) 'The Great leap Forward [left] at least 30 million dead and the Cultural Revolution perhaps 3 million' (*FEER*, 13 March 2003, p. 54). '[Mao's] regime brought about the deaths of perhaps 50 million people during its first calamitous quarter century of rule' (p. 54).

'Jung Chang and Jon Halliday [*Mao: the Untold Story*] ... assert that Mao was responsible for upwards of 70 million peacetime deaths, including at least 37 million in the 1959–61 famine that arose from Mao's harebrained economic policies' (Jonathan Mirsky, *IHT*, 6 July 2005, p. 7).

Penny Kane (1988) puts the number of excess deaths in the three years between 1959 and 1961 at between 14 million and 26 million. Some put the upper figure much higher. For example, Roderick MacFarquhar calls it 'the worst man-made famine in history ... There were 30 million excess deaths between 1958 and 1961', while Liu Binyan puts the figure at 50 million (cited in *The New York Review of Books*, 5 February 1998, pp. 31–2). 'From 1959 to 1961 probably 30 million died of hunger – the party admits 16 million' (Jonathan Mirsky, *IHT*, 9 January 2004, p. 6).

Chang and Wen (1997) analyse the famine of 1958–61. It resulted in about 30 million additional deaths. Causal factors included bad weather, a reduction in the sown acreage, the government's high grain procurement, forced collectivization, the allocation of resources away from agriculture to heavy industry, bad management, the collapse of the incentive system and the elimination of farmers' withdrawal rights from the collectives (pp. 1–2). There was also a lack of democracy. For example, a free press would have reported correct information about the severity of the crisis. In China local officials tried to please central authorities by providing falsely optimistic news (pp. 28–9).

> The key problem remaining unsolved is that the starvation started actually as early as late 1958 when grain availability was adequate in the suffering regions ... While we admit that the magnitude of the catastrophe should be explained

by a combination of multidimensional factors, it is the communal dining system that first started and then greatly aggravated the famine.

(p. 2)

In the autumn of 1958, 70–90 per cent of peasants were driven into the communal dining system. In this system the entire grain output of a commune (after the deduction of seed, feed and the quota delivered to the state) was sent to the communal dining halls (p. 19). Fearing deprivation, those who had private grain stocks hastily consumed them. The communal dining halls encouraged a huge waste of food and 'the free food supply also induced enormous overconsumption' (p. 20). Incentives were severely damaged since members found that everybody ate the same quantity of food whether or not work was done (p. 21). 'Individuals lost their essential consumption rationality required for survival in a poor economy with a limited food supply' (p. 28).

> The avoidance of such economic disasters as famines is made much easier by the existence, and the exercise, of various liberties and political rights, including the liberty of free expression. One of the remarkable facts in the history of famine is that no substantial famine has ever occurred in a country with a democratic form of government and a relatively free press ... It is now estimated that the Chinese famines from 1958 to 1961 killed close to 30 million people ... The so-called Great Leap Forward, initiated in the late 1950s, was a massive failure, but the Chinese government refused to admit it and continued dogmatically to pursue much the same disastrous policies for three more years. It is hard to imagine that this could have happened in a country that goes to the polls regularly and has an independent press. During that terrible calamity the government faced no pressure from newspapers, which were controlled, or from opposition parties, which were not allowed to exist. The lack of a free system of news distribution even misled the government itself. It believed in its own propaganda and the rosy reports of local party officials competing for credit in Beijing. Indeed, there is evidence that just as the famine was moving toward its peak, the Chinese authorities mistakenly believed they had 100 million more metric tons of grain than they actually had. These issues remain relevant in China today. Since the economic reforms of 1979 official Chinese policies have been based on an acknowledgement of the importance of economic incentives without a similar acknowledgement of the importance of political incentives. When things go reasonably well the disciplinary role of democracy might not be greatly missed; but when big policy mistakes are made this lacuna can be quite disastrous.
>
> (Amartya Sen, *IHT*, 16 October 1998, p. 8)

I worked on a farm for half a year in Wu Wei County in 1958 and I know how the county and provincial Party Commission Secretaries disregarded human lives by 'launching satellites' (a nickname for forging astronomically high food production records). This resulted in higher quotas of grain to be handed to the state ... Large numbers ... fled and ... died of starvation.

(Bao Tong, *FEER*, 5 September 2002, www.feer.com)

Some general facts and figures about agriculture

China has to support about 22 per cent of the world's population on something like 7 per cent of the world's arable area. 'Only about half of China is habitable ... [It] has 7 per cent of the world's cultivable land' (*FT*, 27 July 2004, p. 15). 'China is the world's largest agricultural producer, feeding some 22 per cent of the world's population with 10 per cent of its arable land' (*FEER*, 2 May 2002, p. 25). 'China attained food self-sufficiency in the mid-1990s, managing to nourish 20 per cent of the world's population from 7 per cent of its arable farmland' (*The Times*, 8 April 2005, p. 50).

Agricultural workers accounted for 84.2 per cent of the work force in 1952 (*The Economist*, 19 January 2002, p. 57). 'Agriculture accounted for 71 per cent of employment in 1978 and 49 per cent in 2003' (*FEER*, April 2006, pp. 41–2). 'Agriculture accounts for half of the work force but only 15 per cent of GDP' (*IHT*, 20 November 2001, p. 8). 'Agriculture still employs half of China's population, but produces only 14 per cent of its GDP, down from 33 per cent in 1982, according to the World Bank' (*FEER*, 1 April 2004, p. 31). 'Nearly half of the country's labour force remains in agriculture (about 60 per cent in India)' (*IHT*, 3 November 2005, p. 6). 'According to a report by the OECD ... agriculture employed 40 per cent of China's workers, but produced only 15 per cent of economic output' (*FT*, 15 November 2005, p. 10).

'[Some] 600 million people [are] dependent on farming ... [Some] 330 million people [are] engaged in agriculture, or 70 per cent of the rural labour force. They financially support about 70 per cent of the 870 million people in rural China' (*FEER*, 2 August 2001, p. 24). '[There are] 900 million peasants, who represent three-quarters of the population but account for only 15 per cent of GDP' (*FEER*, 27 September 2001, p. 66).

More than 80 per cent of people live in the countryside (*IHT*, 13 November 1999, p. 4).

'Three-quarters of Chinese live in rural areas, far above the world average of a half' (*FEER*, 14 March 2002, p. 24). '[Some] 70 per cent of China's 1.3 billion live ... [in] the countryside' (*FEER*, 13 March 2003, p. 24).

'China ... has an agricultural work force of 300 million' (*FT*, 22 May 2001, p. 14). At the end of 2002 the urbanized population was 502 million, about 39 per cent of the total population. Thus about 61 per cent of the population was classified as rural (*FT*, 28 November 2003, p. 9).

The rural population accounts for 62 per cent of the total population (www.iht.com, 25 December 2003).

'[In China] 800 million people, about 60 per cent of the population, live in the countryside' (*The Economist*, 9 April 2005, p. 49).

'China keeps its rural and urban populations distinct through population controls, classifying most rural residents as peasants even when they migrate to the cities to find work ... [There are] 800 million rural residents' (*IHT*, 3 February 2005, p. 1).

(Note that the huge flows – perhaps 150 million – of temporary migrants from the countryside to the towns provides abundant and cheap labour. This spurs industry and attracts direct foreign investment.)

In 1979, 80 per cent of the population was classified as rural compared with 58 per cent in 2005 (*The Times*, 4 March 2006, p. 54).

Reforms: the Household Responsibility System

Agriculture was the first sector to be reformed. (Agriculture's share of the work force has fallen from 71 per cent in 1978 to less than 50 per cent today.) The Household Responsibility System (HRS) arose from below in the form of local experiments which gained central approval. Once generally accepted the HRS was rapidly introduced countrywide. (By 1983–4 the HRS had become overwhelmingly dominant: Hartford 1987: 212.) Private (family) farms do not own agricultural land (this is owned by the village community), but are allowed to lease land. Originally leases of three to five years were common, but the length has been increased substantially (some argue indefinitely in reality in some cases). Leases are inheritable and peasants have subsequently been allowed to lease land to one another. Family farms are 'responsible' for meeting quotas for specified products (at state-determined prices), tax obligations and payments for collectively provided services (such as irrigation). But then the private farms are free to determine their own output and to whom to sell (at market prices). Farmers now enjoy wide-ranging production freedom. In 1993 only 5 per cent of their production was set by the state plan. Leases are usually fifteen-year ones (Sachs and Woo 1996: 2; Cao *et al.* 1997: 20).

At the Sixteenth Party Congress held in November 2002 it was announced that peasants would be able to sell land-use rights and that encouragement would be given to larger plots.

> China has secretly launched an experiment ... which has won approval from Beijing ... Several cities will be allowed to sell the usage rights for a certain category of land to construction developers without first obtaining the permission of the central government. Currently local authorities must seek permission from Beijing every time they wish to turn country land into a building site, though this regulation is often ignored. Not all rural land is eligible to be sold under the new scheme; the 86 million hectares contracted to some 200 million farming families will remain off limits to developers ... Only portions of an estimated 41 million hectares of 'collectively owned' land in rural areas would be eligible for transfer ... Four cities in central China have so far been chosen to conduct the experiment – Hangzhou and Huzhou in Zhejiang province, Anyang in Henan, and Wuhu in Anhui.
>
> (*FT*, 10 December 2002, p. 13)

> A recently revised Land Management Law stipulates that land-use leases for farmers nationwide should be at least thirty years, up from the fifteen- to twenty-year leases concluded in the early 1980s. In Shanxi [province] contracts are even longer ... [in some cases] fifty years ...[in some cases] effectively ... permanent ownership [so long as the land is worked].
>
> (Susan Lawrence, *FEER*, 22 October 1998, p. 24)

Last month [October 1998] a government statement following a legislative review of farm policy made clear that the sector was a vital part of overall economic policy ... confirming the plan to allow farmers thirty-year leases on their land instead of fifteen-year agreements as before.

(*FT*, Survey, 16 November 1998, p. iv)

About 70 per cent of China's approximately 1.2 billion people are still classified as rural residents ... Many of the fifteen year leases that were drawn up in 1984 are being renewed for thirty more years ... China's three-tier system of collective ownership was inherited from the old commune system in which land was owned through a top-down hierarchical structure that included the commune, the production team and the production group ... Communes disappeared and were replaced by townships, which are not economic units but administrative units representing the lowest level of government administration. Production teams were replaced by administrative villages, which govern a number of villagers' groups. And production groups were replaced by villagers' groups.

(Wang 1999: 13)

Problems include the following:

It has not been clarified which collective units may claim ownership rights. Although ownership rights should generally be assigned to local villagers' groups, bureaucrats of administrative villages often appropriate the rights to contract out land and to collect proceeds from its use. The law defines contractual rights ambiguously ... The vague term 'overall stability with small adjustment' in land policies offers an excuse for many local bureaucrats of administrative villages to make unilateral changes in land use and contracts.

(p. 13)

There are 197 million rural households in China.

The adoption of a revised land management law on 29 August 1998 represented a watershed in the reform process. The new law requires that collectively-owned arable land be contracted to collective members for a term of thirty years and that a written contract be executed detailing the rights and obligations of both parties ... The central government called for full implementation of thirty-year land-use rights by the end of 1999 ... The law also restricts land readjustments. Land readjustments have occurred in about 80 per cent of rural villages in China since the introduction of the Household Responsibility System. Under this practice the collective leadership periodically (in some cases once a year) redistributed village land to reflect changes in household population size since the previous land allocation ... Land readjustments have allowed China to maintain an extremely egalitarian distribution of land within villages, but the uncertainty they have created represents the single greatest obstacle to long-term land tenure security in China.

(Brian Schwarzwalder, *Transition*, 2000, vol. 11, no. 5, pp. 21–2)

'A policy was implemented in 1984 stating clearly that the length of tenure on farmers' contracted plots was good for fifteen years' (Kung 2000: 793).

In rural China collective land ownership allows villagers the right to an equal share of arable land (dubbed the equal entitlement rights). As new members are entitled to partake in this equal sharing of land when they become part of the community (whose membership is acquired either by birth or through marriage), land reallocations are inevitable.

(p. 701)

Drawing upon a unique village survey [however] ... this paper shows, first, that land reallocations occurred rather infrequently during the period covered by the survey [up to 1993: p. 707]. Second, and most important, the majority of such reallocations actually occurred on a partial basis.

(p. 715)

On 1 March 2003 the Rural Land Contracting law came into effect:

1   '[In his speech of 8 November 2002 Jiang Zemin] indicated that farmers should be able to sell their land use rights for profit. "We must respect farmer households as market players", he said ... The government also wants to consolidate land holdings to build bigger, more productive farms ... New rules on selling rural properties were quietly passed by a committee of the National People's Congress in August, but will not take effect until March [2003] ... All land is officially owned by the state ... Chinese in both the countryside and the towns enjoy "land use rights" of anything from thirty to seventy years' (*FT*, 13 November 2002, p. 14).
2   '[The law] details the rights of thirty-year contract farmers, attempts to ban reallocation almost completely, and, most radically, allows the transfer of leases for money' (Stephen Green, *The World Today*, 2003, vol. 59, no. 4, p. 27).
3   'The Rural Land Contracting law was passed on 1 March [2003]. It helps farmers secure existing rights of tenure for thirty years on their holdings and restricts the ability of local officials to change the size of a holding ... It contains provisions that give farmers the right to transfer or lease their land and includes safeguards against local officials pressuring farmers to surrender their holdings to development companies or farming corporations' (*FEER*, 10 April 2003, p. 47). '[The law] gives farmers more secure rights to the tiny plots of land they hold under thirty-year leases ... Millions of peasants are sub-leasing their land to move to the cities, where they can make a better living. The plots vacated are being stitched together into sizeable holdings, so that in many places subsistence farming is being replaced by commercial farming' (*FEER*, 14 October 2004, p. 33).
4   'In 2003 new legislation gave farmers the right to a thirty-year lease on their land, but this law has not yet been fully implemented' (OECD 2005: website Chapter 1).

Changes in procurement and prices

In April [1998] Beijing introduced the first market-style mechanisms for the cotton industry, allowing the price to float by 5 per cent around a level of 650 renminbi per kilo. The government-fixed cotton price had previously been 700 renminbi per kilo ... China plans to abolish purchasing price controls over cotton next year [1999].

(*FT*, 3 August 1998, p. 3)

Traditionally the government has sought to keep retail food prices down and farm income up by buying from farmers a proportion of their crop at guaranteed prices and then making the grain available to consumers in the cities at a lower, subsidized price. But after bumper harvests in the past three years ... this system is no longer working. With silos overflowing farmers found the government buyers unwilling to purchase much grain. As a result it was being dumped in the cities at rock-bottom prices, fuelling the deflation in China's economy. Recently, therefore, a new policy was introduced. Now the government effectively sets a floor price by agreeing to buy all available grain at a predetermined price. Responsibility for selling the grain on has been devolved down to provincial governors who are charged with the task of reselling it at prices that do not involve a loss. The aim is thus to reduce the burden of subsidies and to shift the benefit of government intervention away from city dwellers towards the rural areas.

(*FT*, Survey, 16 November 1998, p. iv)

In May 1998 the state council banned all private enterprises and vendors from buying grain directly from peasants, which had been allowed since 1993 (*FEER*, 30 July 1998, p. 47).

In 1992 grain prices soared ... Private traders bought up large supplies, much of which was stockpiled. The government ... intervened ... by selling its grain reserves to keep prices down ... It made provincial governors individually accountable for ensuring that each province grew as much grain as it consumed. And it raised the prices at which state offices guaranteed to buy grain ... High, guaranteed prices helped produce recent record harvests of nearly 500 million tonnes ... Zhu Rongyi, the prime minister, has decreed that private traders will be forbidden to buy grain from farmers, giving the state the monopoly. The state will buy all the grain that farmers wish to sell: they are to get a 'quota' price for that part of their harvest they are obliged to offer to the state, and a lower, fixed 'protected' price for any of the remainder ... The grain offices ... have been ... forbidden to resell grain at less than the procurement price.

(*The Economist*, 30 January 1999, p. 66)

For decades the government pushed farmers nationwide to produce ever-greater quantities of grain, devoting two-thirds of farmland to rice, corn and wheat ... [to] avoid repeats of devastating famines ... Agriculture hid behind protective barriers. Now the prospect of those barriers falling with WTO entry

... adds urgency to the shift that has been quietly under way in the countryside for the last few years: planting what will sell best in the market. That means planting less grain ... In an effort to boost their spending power the government raised grain procurement prices above international market levels in the mid-1900s, but it has been back-pedalling for the past three years, unable to sustain the financial burden. Since January [2000] the central government has stopped paying artificially high prices for certain low-grade strains of corn, wheat and rice, in what is likely to be the first step toward abolishing all grain support prices.

(*FEER*, 29 June 2000, pp. 44–5)

Record grain harvests have become a burden because the government, which monopolizes grain purchases, is opting not to buy all the grain – while also banning farmers from selling it elsewhere. In some areas the government is forcing farmers to pay for storing their harvests in its warehouses.

(*IHT*, 5 September 2000, p. 5)

'Although most prices have been liberalized for most agricultural products, the state still dominates the purchase, sale, and import and export of staple agricultural products such as foodstuffs, cotton and vegetable oil' (Chi Fulin, *Transition*, 2001, vol. 12, no. 3, p. 12).

Early agricultural successes

The boost to incentives and other factors (such as higher prices) led to a remarkable improvement in farm incomes during the first half of the 1980s. (There is considerable debate about the relative importance of the various factors.) Johnson (1988a: 234) estimates that the real income of farm people doubled during the period 1978–86. The United Nations (*World Economic Survey*, 1993, pp. 187, 197) estimates that rural income increased at an average annual rate of 12.8 per cent 1978–85, the figure for rural *per capita* income in real terms being 7.5 per cent.

Since the mid-1980s things have not been so rosy and in recent years there has been considerable peasant discontent, e.g. complaints about the prices they receive for output and have to pay for inputs and the taxes, and charges imposed upon them by local authorities (in some cases illegally; corruption is one commonly cited factor).

Cao Jinqing ... a Shanghai-based scholar ... pinpoints the state's policy of under-investing in agriculture and taxing farmers the heaviest as the biggest problem. The central government simply does not provide the funding needed for public services in rural China ... The result is local officials resort to an array of special taxes.

(Bruce Gilley, *FEER*, 29 November 2001, p. 38)

China [has launched] a sweeping overhaul of rural taxation designed to solve the problem of excessive and arbitrary taxes in the countryside ... The plan, announced at the March [2001] session of the national parliament, calls for all fees and taxes normally levied by the lowest two levels of rural government – the village and the township – to be abolished. Instead a new single tax would be levied by the next highest level – the county – and divided up among the three. Premier Zhu Rongyi has promised 20 billion to 30 billion renminbi ($2.4 billion to $3.6 billion) to villages and townships to make up for any shortfalls in their budgets, which pay for items like road repairs, infrastructure, education, welfare and health ... State law dictates that farmers should not pay more than 5 per cent of their net income in taxes – excluding the taxes they pay when they sell their produce or on the profits from their rural factories.

(Bruce Gilley, *FEER*, 5 April 2001, pp. 28–9)

('A leaked text of an address given by Zhu Rongyi ... on 5 June [2001 included the statement that] it was necessary to be "safe and slow down somewhat a few major reforms in light of the current situation". Mr Zhu indicated that one casualty would be the government's plans to promote badly needed tax reforms in the countryside. The aim of these is to eliminate various fees and levies arbitrarily imposed on farmers by local authorities and rely instead on a single tax based on income from crop production ... These have exacerbated other problems ... [e.g. plummeting] revenues of village-level governments': *The Economist*, 16 June 2001, p. 72. 'The central government's proposed solution involves ... [the abolition of] the fees paid by farmers to support township governments. Instead, farmers will pay tax to provincial governments, which in turn will finance lower-tier rural administrations. This in theory should prevent the townships from demanding excessive fees from peasants in order to meet their debts. It should also force them to trim their staff ... The "tax-for-fee" reform, as China calls it, has been tried out in the eastern province of Anhui and parts of other provinces in the past two years. The results have been mixed. Many peasants find they are now paying out less to officialdom, which is good news for Chinese leaders worried about a potential explosion of rural discontent caused by growing fees and widespread corruption. But many township governments have ended up even poorer ... The central government has offered $2.4 billion to help make up shortfalls, which is nowhere near enough. China announced this week that a third of its provinces would try out the tax-for-fee system next year [2002], but it was too soon to impose it on the whole country': *The Economist*, 15 December 2001, p. 62.)

China received its final shipment of food aid yesterday [7 April 2005], a historic moment as the most rapidly developing country marked the end of twenty-five years as a recipient of United Nations help ... Dominique Frankefort (deputy director of the UN World Food Programme): 'There are fewer and fewer hungry people in China. There are around 26 million ultra-poor left and the government will take care of them now using a variety of activities, probably cash for work rather than food for work programmes' ... During the twenty-five years that China has been receiving food aid it has lifted 300 million people out of poverty. The WFP reckoned that since 1979 it has distributed nearly 4 million tonnes of wheat to more than 30 million people in China ... [The final WFP shipment is Canadian] wheat intended for distribution to more than 400,000 poor farmers and their families to support food-for-work schemes in four of China's poorest provinces: Gansu, Guangxi, Ningxia and Shanxi ... The WFP will officially end its assistance programme to China at the end of this year ... China attained food self-sufficiency in the mid-1990s ... James Morris (the WFP executive director): 'China is now one of the world's leaders in fighting hunger. We need China's help and resources to apply the crucial lessons learnt here to other countries still struggling with hunger.'

(*The Times*, 8 April 2005, p. 50)

To young Chinese and certainly to the outside world it must seem astonishing that ... [China] has been receiving any free grain ... Over twenty-five years the WFP fed some 30 million Chinese and provided aid worth almost $1 billion ... Since the launch of market reforms China has lifted 300 million out of grinding, humiliating poverty, sucked in massive investment, become the fastest growing major economy and itself provided funds to feed the hungry elsewhere in Asia and Africa.

(p. 23)

'The World Food Programme began shipments in 1979' (*FT*, 12 April 2005, p. 6).

The gap between urban and rural incomes

The gap between rural and urban incomes has widened considerably in recent years to the detriment of farmers.

In 1978 the annual *per capita* income of urban residents was ... two-and-a-half times the ... average income of rural residents ... In the early 1980s the income gap between urban and rural residents narrowed. In 1984 the income ratio dropped to 1.6:1, a historic low that was never repeated thereafter. The gap narrowed because economic reform focused on rural areas and policies were favourable to the agricultural sector ... Beginning in 1985 the focus of China's economic reform shifted to cities and the income gap grew. In 1994 the ratio of urban to rural incomes reached a record 2.9:1. In 1999 the gap narrowed slightly to 2.7:1.

(*Transition*, 2001, vol. 12, no. 1, p. 13)

('By 2000 ... [the ratio] had risen to] 2.8 times and [is] still rising': *IHT*, 20 November 2001, p. 8.)

'While urban *per capita* income climbed 8.7 per cent in the first half of the year [2000], to 3,208 renminbi ($387), rural *per capita* income rose just 1.5 per cent to 1,013 renminbi' (*FEER*, 24 August 2000, p. 57).

Annual *per capita* income in rural areas rose just 2.1 per cent last year [2000] to 2,253 renminbi, according to official figures, compared to a year-on-year rise of 6.4 per cent to 6,280 renminbi for urban residents. That puts the urban-to-rural ratio dangerously close to three to one (compared to two to one in 1985) ... [There are] 800 million farmers.

(*FEER*, 5 April 2001, pp. 28–9)

'In 2000, the fifth straight year of reduced growth, [rural] incomes rose just 2.1 per cent, to an average of $272, compared to $763 in the cities' (*FEER*, 2 May 2002, p. 25).

'*Per capita* net income for rural residents was 2,366 yuan ($285) in 2001, up only 4.2 per cent from 2000 ... That increase compares with a 8.5 per cent rise to 6,860 yuan for disposable income of city dwellers' (*IHT*, 1 March 2002, p. 15).

'Rural households ... [had a] disposable income of 2,620 yuan per person in 2003 ... Urban dwellers ... [had] disposable incomes of 8,500 yuan per person' (*The Economist*, Survey, 20 March 2004, p. 1).

'The 2003 rise [of 4.3 per cent] resulted in an annual *per capita* net income for rural residents of 2,622 renminbi ($316). Urban residents recorded a 9.3 per cent rise in incomes' (*FEER*, 5 February 2004, p. 22).

'Average rural incomes last year [2003] were 2,622 renminbi; up 4.3 per cent. By comparison urban incomes climbed 9.3 per cent to 8,500 renminbi' (*FT*, 10 February 2004, p. 10).

'In a report earlier this year [2004] the Chinese academy of social sciences said that average urban incomes were 3.1 times higher than those in the countryside' (*Guardian*, 20 July 2004, p. 11).

In 2004 there were signs of a significant improvement in rural incomes owing to such factors as rising prices for agricultural products.

'[But in 2004] average urban income was 3.2 times higher than in rural areas' (*IHT*, 3 February 2005, p. 1).

'Per capita disposable income in towns and cities ... rose 7.7 per cent to 9,422 yuan last year [2004], while incomes in rural areas rose 6.8 per cent to 2,936 yuan' (www.iht.com, 14 March 2005).

> The agriculture minister ... Du Qinglin [said on 10 March that] average annual incomes for farmers rose 12 per cent last year [2004], but still total just 2,936 yuan, or $355 per person ... By contrast the government says annual incomes in China's booming cities average more than $1,000 per person.
>
> (www.iht.com, 10 March 2005)

Migration from the countryside

There is now a huge 'floating population' in the towns and cities as people have left the land. Estimates vary.

An early official figure of 20 million was mentioned, but that figure has climbed considerably.

> Since China's economic reforms of the late 1970s, millions of farmers have left the land to seek work in the cities. The combination of the need for cheap labour and the relative relaxation of state controls over the movement of people has meant that the 'floating population' of Chinese living away from their place of *hukou* registration now amounts to about 120 million, according to the latest official figures ... At birth every Chinese person is assigned to a particular location, called the household registration or *hukou*.
>
> (Sophia Woodman, *The New York Review of Books*, 11 May 2000, vol. XLVII, no. 8)

(For changes in the *hukou* system, see below.)

'Significant numbers of Chinese have been leaving their villages only since 1984, when the government eased somewhat its residency system, allowing people to travel for temporary jobs ... [There are now] 100 million migrants' (*IHT*, 26 February 1999, p. 2). '[Some] 120 million internal migrants move around the country each day' (*IHT*, 3 August 2000, p. 2).

'Nobody knows exactly how many economic migrants there are, but the number is huge: estimates range from 80 million to 130 million' (*The Economist*, Survey, 8 April 2000, p. 15).

Temporary migration to cities was made legal in 1983 (*FEER*, 7 October 1999, p. 64). Roughly 100,000 farmers have migrated to the cities (*FEER*, 25 May 2000, p. 78). 'The floating population ... [is] an estimated 100 million' (*FEER*, 12 July 2001, p. 54). 'Today 120 million migrant workers roam the cities in search of jobs' (*FEER*, 14 March 2002, p. 24).

'[There has been] an influx of 150 million farmers into Chinese cities looking for work' (*IHT*, 2 July 2001, p. 4).

'In addition to the 150 million migrant workers, around half ... [of those] currently employed in farming are thought to be surplus to requirements, Chinese academics estimate' (*FT*, 29 October 2002, p. 11). ('[The National Research Institute in Beijing says] there are 300 million to 400 million surplus rural labourers': *FEER*, 1 April 2004, p. 28.)

Official figures claim that migrant labour amounted to 94 million in 2002 and 120 million in 2003 (*FT*, 21 January 2004, p. 11). 'Some 99 million rural residents were in urban employment last year [2003] ... up 5 million from 2002' (*FT*, 10 February 2004, p. 10).

'There are 120 million transients' (www.iht.com, 25 March 2004).

'The government estimates that 144 million migrant workers have already flocked from the country to the city' (*Guardian*, 26 October 2004, p. 19).

> Prime minister Wen Jiabao ... said [on 29 December 2005 that] the government in coming years ... [would do] more to protect migrant workers who face unsafe and unstable working conditions and are often denied fair wages ... The government promised Thursday [19 January] to improve treatment of rural migrants who move to urban areas to work ... In many parts of China these workers' incomes have stagnated or risen only slightly for the past decade ... Without legal recourse, many go unpaid and are vulnerable to abuse ... In the past twenty years about 140 million farmers and their families have moved to find work in towns and cities, according to estimates from the national bureau of statistics.
>
> (www.iht.com 20 January 2006)

Changes in the hukou *system*

> [Communist] China had isolated rural and urban economies for about forty years. Such segregation was mainly implemented through two important institutional restrictions. One of them was a strict Household Registration

System (HRS) [*hukou* system], which required individuals to register with local authorities to gain residency and thereby determined where people lived and worked. Basically people remained in their place of birth. Accompanying and reinforcing the HRS was the food rationing system, which allowed people to buy food only in the area of their household registration ... Essentially households in urban areas were given coupons for food that were distributed through the HRS ... Without coupons no food of any kind could be bought at official prices in the city ... Migration was tightly controlled until the mid-1980s ... Both supply and demand forces pushed the government to relax restrictions on rural–urban migration. In addition, by the mid-1980s the food rationing/distribution system was dismantled and individuals could buy food at a market price. Hence rural migrants could survive in urban areas. As a result the number of rural migrants working in urban areas began to increase dramatically during the late 1980s and in the early 1990s. In 1988 about 25 million migrants were working in urban areas: this figure increased to 64 million in 1994 and to 80 million in 1995 ... By the mid-1990s rural migrants accounted for about 18 per cent of the total rural labour force or 34 per cent of the total urban labour force ... Restrictions on rural–urban migration still exist. For example, almost all urban cities require three certificates and one card from rural migrants.

(Meng and Zhang 2001: 486)

'Mao Zedong instituted the *hukou* system in 1958' (*FEER*, 14 March 2002, p. 24).

In the late 1950s, at the time of the Great Leap Forward, China established its *hukou*, or household registration system, which required people to live and work only where they were officially permitted to ... According to official estimates, China's migrant labour force now numbers somewhere around 100 million. The government expects another 46 million to come looking for jobs in the city in the next five years as the number of surplus rural workers swells to 150 million ... China announced on 16 August [2001] that it plans to revamp the registration system ... The government is working on a plan that will do away with migration restriction over the next five years ... On 27 August the ministry of public security, the main administrator of the *hukou* system, confirmed its support for the reforms.

(*The Economist*, 1 September 2001, p. 54)

From 1 October residents of rural China will be able to apply for 'residence permits' in smaller cities if they can prove a legal home and a stable source of income in their new urban environment. The planned changes represent one of the most significant reforms thus far to ... [the] *hukou* (residence permit) system ... It is believed to have been first formulated during the Han dynasty around 2,000 years ago ... Its pervasiveness has in recent years been eroded by various economic imperatives ... On the black market in Beijing each permit is currently worth around 100,000 renminbi ... The changes planned in October are prompted by economic necessity. The number of excess workers in rural areas already exceeds 150 million, according to conservative official estimates. In addition, farming is expected to become less labour-intensive as the imperative for efficiency grows with China's [prospective] entry into the WTO.

(*FT*, 30 August 2001, p. 9)

China ... says it needs to build thousands of [up to 12,000] new towns to provide ... migrant workers ... with work ... The migrant work force in China's cities is estimated at 100 million – although no one knows for sure ... The migrants must obtain temporary permits without which they may be sent back to the countryside. However, a central planning commission in Beijing said that it was working on a scheme to abolish restrictions within five years ... Beijing introduces a tentative reform today [1 October] to grant permanent residency to a small number of rural entrepreneurs who have made good [in terms of taxes paid and jobs provided] in the city.

(*Guardian*, 1 October 2001, p. 17)

The central government announced its intention to conduct a gradual overhaul of the *hukou* system, which is a holdover from the 1950s ... A handful of smaller cities have [already] begun offering residency rights to outsiders, both to attract skilled workers and to cope with increasing dissatisfaction of rural migrants already there.

(*IHT*, 24 October 2001, p. 4)

'Residence permits that give access to education and social benefits are very hard to acquire. In Shanghai you need a postgraduate degree' (*IHT*, 20 November 2001, p. 8).

To help the transition to a market economy authorities began dismantling a system that for more than forty years has allowed people to work only where they are registered to live. State media said on 9 October that people could now move to over 20,000 cities and towns. The government says it will end the *hukou* system, which allows people to live only where they are registered, over the next five years.

(*FEER*, 18 October 2001, p. 34)

'The government views the rural areas as self-sufficient places to which workers can return if they lose their jobs in the towns ... Concerned about social stability, the government wants an urban income safety net in place before full-scale liberalization' (Philip Bowring, *IHT*, 20 November 2001, p. 8).

The number of rural dwellers in China seeking jobs as workers in big cities grew last year [2002] by 5.2 per cent to more than 92 million. In January [2003] the government began dismantling regulations that institutionalised discrimination against migrant workers by setting aside most urban jobs for city residents and hindering migrants from changing their jobs.

(*FEER*, 30 January 2003, p. 22)

[The *hukou* system] dictates where someone is legally allowed to live and work. It enables wealthy cities like Shanghai and Beijing to block access to jobs, schools and hospitals. Because of the system China's 120 million transients cannot compete for the best jobs created by the booming economy. Occasionally Chinese can escape the system if they find a company willing to sponsor them. Sometimes they convince private companies to hire them illegally ... Families without the city's *hukou* must pay steep tuition fees to sue local schools. So their children attend substandard institutions, established by migrants, which local authorities refuse to recognize or support.

(Seth Kaplan, *IHT*, 26 March 2004, p. 7)

It is difficult for workers and their families to permanently change their place of residence. Even for a temporary move many permits are required and many local services, such as education and health, are either not available to migrants or only available on unfavourable terms. Moreover, if a rural person moves permanently to a city his rural landholdings are forfeited without compensation.

(OECD 2005: website Chapter 1)

China plans to abolish legal distinctions between urban residents and peasants in eleven provinces as the government tries to slow the widening of the country's wealth gap and reduce social unrest, state media said Wednesday [2 November]. Under an experimental programme local governments in the eleven provinces will allow peasants to register as urban residents and enjoy the same rights to housing, education, medical care and social security that city dwellers have. If carried out as advertised the programme would eliminate a cornerstone of the population control policies first put in place by Mao Zedong in the 1950s. The system, known as *hukou*, or residence permits, ties every individual to a locale and at one time made it difficult to travel without permission. In practice the *hukou* system has been fading for more than a decade. An estimated 200 million peasants have already left the country to live, some of them full time, in urban areas. Their access to urban services varies widely, depending on local rules and the kinds of employment they find ... The once comprehensive socialist benefits bestowed on urban residents carry far less weight. Most people rely on their own resources or those of their employers to pay for health care, housing and schooling ... [But some analysts believe] that even if the *hukou* system disappeared local governments would retain administrative control over their populations. They would still set conditions on registration for urban residents and prevent the growth of slums ... Shenzhen emerged from rice fields in the early 1980s to become one of China's most prosperous metropolitan areas and nearly all of its 10 million residents were born somewhere else. Shanghai pioneered the concept of a 'blue card' for qualified migrant workers in the mid-1990s, giving them full access to housing and city services if they met certain criteria. The central government first declared that it intended to do away with the *hukou* system at the Sixteenth Party Congress in 2002 and has been making incremental changes since. The overhaul got a major boost in 2003 after a college-educated migrant in Guangdong province ... was beaten to death in police custody after being detained for vagrancy. His death brought nationwide outrage and led to the abolition of vagrancy laws.

(*IHT*, 3 November 2005, p. 3)

China plans to abolish the legal division between urban and rural residents in eleven provinces to protect the rights of migrants needed for labour in booming cities, though a similar experiment failed four years ago, the official media said Wednesday [2 November] ... China is one of three countries, along with North Korea and Benin, that still have strict residency rules ... The reforms would theoretically end the pattern of unfair treatment, including regular denial of payment to migrant workers ... The moves could also help stem growing unrest over China's widening wealth gap ... Among the provinces considering cancelling residency restrictions is booming Guangdong in the south, where migrants make up more than one-quarter of its population of 110 million. Yet Guangdong needs more workers ... In 2001 Zhenzhou, a city in Henan province in central China, allowed anyone with relatives living in the city to get a free residence permit. Increased pressure on transport, education, health care and a rise in crime forced the city to cancel the measure three years later [it has been reported].

(www.iht.com, 2 November 2005)

('Slavery is on the rise in China as migration flows grow and private business blossoms. Unlike the forced labour of China's state-sponsored prison factories, the illegal forced labour happening in the countryside is little known and even less understood. That is because it exists mostly in remote areas where underground or even semi-legal private businesses – often brick factories, stone quarries and greenhouse farms – are plentiful. But it is also because of Beijing's embarrassment about the revival of a problem that the communist revolution was supposed to have ended ... The earliest reports of slavery in China surfaced in the mid-1990s ... In 1994, for example': Bruce Gilley, *FEER*, 16 August 2001, pp. 50–1.)

Problems in agriculture

Major problems include the following:

THE LOSS OF FARMLAND

'Due to urbanization and desertification its [China's] cultivated land is shrinking by about 2 per cent a year' (www.iht.com, 7 July 2004).

'Last year [2003] alone the amount of farmed land fell by 4.3 per cent due to pressure from development and reforestation, according to the World Bank' (*FEER*, 7 October 2004, p. 27).

China has said it will keep controls on use of farmland after a six-month development ban ended to prevent a rebound in building projects that have eroded harvests and prompted protests among the nation's rural residents. China has lost 5 per cent of its farmland in the past seven years.

(*FT*, 4 November 2004, p. 12)

'[According to the CIA, there has been an] estimated loss of one-fifth of agricultural land since 1949 [due] to soil erosion and economic development' (*The Spectator*, 8 January 2005, p. 13).

'The government said in 2004 that new factories, housing, offices and shopping malls had consumed about 5 per cent of total arable land in the previous seven years' (*IHT*, 21 January 2006, p. 5).

There is growing concern about the increasing number of violent protests (sometimes leading to loss of life) in rural areas caused in particular by the takeover of agricultural land by local officials for redevelopment. Such profitable (and often illegal) redesignation of land can lead to corruption and farmers feeling inadequately compensated for loss of land-use rights.

'Officials say that the number of "mass protests" taking place throughout China each year has risen from around 10,000 in 1994 to 74,000 in 2004' (*The Economist*, 17 December 2005, p. 63). 'According to official data, 3.8 million people took part in "incidents involving the masses" in 2004. The 74,000 protests represented a sevenfold rise on the 1994 figure' (*Guardian*, 18 January 2006, p. 30). 'On Thursday [19 January 2006] the ministry of public security said there were 87,000 protests, riots and other "mass incidents" last year [2005], up 6.6 per cent on 2004' (*Guardian*, 21 January 2006, p. 21).

'In the past these [grievances] were often to do with the levying of unfair taxes, but more recently they have centred ... on inadequate compensation for the loss of land' (*The Economist*, 17 December 2005, p. 63).

'When land is seized it is often done without adequate compensation. As there is no independent court system, it is usually impossible to seek legal redress' (*Guardian*, 21 January 2006, p. 21).

'Local officials can make huge profits by getting hold of rural land and having it rezoned for industrial use' (*FT*, 21 January 2006, p. 6).). 'Conflict between farmers and local governments, mainly over the confiscation of land, has been behind a rapid rise in violent disputes in the countryside in the last two to three years' (*FT*, 6 March 2006, p. 7).

> Land grabs by officials ... are provoking mass unrest in the countryside ... Local officials operate with impunity on the one-party state and have little to fear from a legal system that answers to the Communist Party. Endless harangues by central government leaders to pay more attention to inequality have done little to address the root causes of the wealth gap and surging social unrest, analysts say.
>
> (*IHT*, 21 January 2006, p. 5)

Prime minister Wen Jiabao (29 December 2005):

> We absolutely cannot commit a historic error over land problems ... Some local governments have taken over farmland illegally without giving reasonable compensation and this has sparked mass incidents in rural areas ... This is still a key source of instability in rural areas and even the whole society ... [The expansion of cities has involved] reckless occupation of farmland.
>
> (*IHT*, 21 January 2006, p. 5; www.iht.com, 20 January 2006; *FT*, 21 January 2006, p. 6; *Guardian*, 21 January 2006, p. 21)

> China is ... drawing up plans to reform the rules governing state requisitions of farmers' land. The reform would introduce a 'market mechanism' for

compensation payments for farmland seized for commercial use ... [An official spokesman]: 'The basic thinking of the reform is to take a different approach to land requisitions depending on the use to which the land is to be put. If the land is being requisitioned for use for the public good, then there must be a raised standard for compensation. If it is to be used commercially then the market mechanism must be introduced ... There certainly is a phenomenon of farmers' interests being harmed by low-price requisitioning of their land' ... Under current rules requisition compensation is supposed to be calculated only according to the land's agricultural value, allowing local governments and developers to reap huge profits when converting it to commercial use ... [The official spokesman] warned that if both public use and commercial requisition orders continued to be the preserve of local governments, it would remain very difficult for farmers to protect their land.

(*FT*, 9 March 2006, p. 9)

INADEQUATE INVESTMENT

There is inadequate investment in the (originally collectively provided and extensive) rural infrastructure (such as irrigation and flood control) as private incentives now dominate in the HRS.

China is not only short of water. It has problems on all fronts – pollution, floods, drought, distribution and pricing among them. *Per capita* water reserves are a quarter of the world average and most of the nation's water resources are in the south of the country. In the north deserts and arid land areas are expanding ... [With the HRS] communal duties, including upkeep of the irrigation systems, became more haphazard and competition for water was often fierce ... Small-scale water charges were first introduced to the Chinese countryside in 1983 ... [There have been experiments with water user associations [WUAs] .... [The WUA replaces] the local government as the supplier of water to farmers ... There are about 1,500 WUAs scattered across China ... The associations, whose officials are directly elected by the farmers, are responsible for ensuring the supply of water to all farmers in their areas. That involves organizing the repair and maintenance of irrigation canals and regularly opening locks ... The associations buy water – with funds pooled by their members – from a water supply company ... Supply companies charge WUAs for the volume of water they use. In the past villages were charged for water based on the amount of land they had under cultivation, regardless of the amount of water they used. Under that system there was no incentive to save ... Raising water prices in northern China, where the crisis is most serious, and charging by volume rather than by land area, would further encourage conservation, say experts ... Farm holdings in China are small and fragmented. That makes it difficult to impose individual user charges ... Charging individual farmers rather than villages or water user associations for the water they use would further encourage conservation, experts say.

(*FEER*, 24 January 2002, pp. 36–9)

The Chinese government authorized one of the world's biggest engineering projects yesterday [26 November 2002]: to pump water from the flood-prone south to the drought-stricken north ... Mao Zedong ... is credited with first suggesting the project ... Three man-made rivers [canals] will transfer water from the Yangtze ... to the crowded north ... The first imported water could reach Shandong province by 2005 ... The project was trailed tentatively last year [2001] ... Construction was ready to begin on one segment.

(*Guardian*, 27 November 2002, p. 16)

'The project's construction phase is scheduled to run until 2050 and will comprise three separate canals' (*The Times*, 27 November 2002, p. 17).

The State Council gave the go-ahead to a multi-dollar project to divert water from the south to the dry north despite environmental and costs concerns. The project aims to divert water along three canal systems from the nation's largest rivers in the south to northern cities. It is expected to take fifty years to complete and to cost more than $48 billion.

(*FEER*, 5 December 2002, p. 36)

Nearly seven years ago Wen Jiabao, then a vice prime minister, uttered a stark warning: 'The survival of the Chinese nation is threatened by the country's shortage of water' ... Water industry executives say that up to 40 per cent of the population live on supplies that are less than half of international danger levels; and because of severe pollution supplies are often unsafe ... In March [2005] a senior environmental agency official ... said more than 70 per cent of China's rivers and lakes were polluted. Also in March the water resources minister ... said that more than 300 million rural people lacked access to clean drinking water ... In recent years China has lifted most of the protectionist barriers that kept foreign firms out of the water sector. But significant structural obstacles make it hard for companies to [make a] profit. The most basic issue is China's pricing of water. Up until 1985 water was supplied free of charge ... In order to encourage both conservation of water and investment in new projects, the government in recent years has allowed prices to rise, but gradually ... According to China's own estimates, the country uses four times more water per unit of economic output than the global average. Its rate of industrial water reusage stands at only 55 per cent, far below the rate of 80 per cent in most advanced countries.

(www.iht.com, 16 December 2005; *IHT*, 17 December 2005, p. 20)

Since 1980 China's average *per capita* water consumption actually declined by nearly 5 per cent – and not because the country has become an impressively more efficient consumer of irrigation, industrial or residential water ... One of the most frequently cited figures in the Chinese media refers to the country's low average availability of water resources – as of 2005 ... less than a third of the global average and just a quarter of the US rate ... China's [spatial] disparities are particularly large. South China, with roughly 55 per of the population and 35 per cent of the cropland, has about 80 per cent of the water resources

... The north ... [has] 45 per cent of the population and nearly 60 per cent of all cropland, but less than 15 per cent of the water ... More than half of China's waste water does not receive even the simplest primary treatment ... In November 2005 the first national inland lakes symposium was told that a recent survey found 70 per cent of the country's rivers contaminated with industrial pollutants and 75 per cent excessively enriched with nitrogen leached from fertilisers.

(*FEER*, November 2005, pp. 30–2)

LAND DISTRIBUTION

Land is distributed relatively equally and the average farm is not only tiny (something like 0.5 ha) but is also divided up into something less than ten plots (which makes mechanization difficult).

'The average family farm is 0.55 ha and there are, on average, nine plots per farm' (Feder *et al.* 1992: 6).

'Each Chinese worker farms 0.1 ha on average, compared with 1.4 ha in the USA and 0.5 ha in Europe' (*FT*, 16 November 1999, p. 26). 'Holdings average half a hectare in size' (*FEER*, 18 December 2003, p. 33).

'According to a report by the OECD ... fully 200 million of China's 248 million rural households farm on plots of about 0.65 hectares' (*FT*, 15 November 2005, p. 10).

There have been various experiments by the state to lease out larger plots of land, to encourage the amalgamation of family plots (in forms such as shareholder farms where contributing families share in the output and profit), and even to forcibly reassign land from less to more efficient farmers (which shows the limitations of leased land in terms of property rights). 'As many as 70 million farmers have lost their land in the past decade' (*IHT*, 9 December 2004, p. 2). 'As many as 70 million farmers have been left without land' (*IHT*, 22 January 2005, p. 3).

'Forced appropriations by local governments have already deprived as many as 40 million peasants of some or all of their land since the early 1990s' (*The Economist*, 25 March 2006, p. 9). 'Estimates vary, but most agree that tens of millions have lost some or all of their land since the early 1990s, often without compensation' (*The Economist*, Survey, 25 March 2006, p. 6).

'The *Jingji Ribao* (*Economic Daily*) estimated that there might now be 200 million farmers displaced by the rapid conversion of agricultural land for development' (Gallagher 2005: 23).

Across China ordinary people are losing their land as the country struggles to find space for its expanding cities and attempts to make tiny farm plots more efficient by merging them into large agri-businesses. The scale of the change is staggering ... Given China's record many will have their land confiscated by local officials and will receive scant compensation. Such corruption is only rarely exposed ... Illegal land confiscation – a result of highly ambiguous laws, lack of central monitoring and short-sighted greed – is now 'very pervasive', says Li Ping, China representative for the United States-based Rural

Development Institute. For the government in Beijing it is also very worrying. Confiscation ... has sparked large-scale riots in southern Guangdong and Fujian provinces ... In the early 1980s Beijing gave local governments the right to lease land to the peasants. Increasingly local officials began carving out their own fiefdoms. That trend continues. All land transactions are done through the land bureaus of local governments and the proceeds are then distributed to peasants via their township or village collective. This gives land bureaus every incentive to sell rights to as much land as possible, without regard for the needs of the peasants or China's diminishing stock of arable land, says Chen Jianbo, director of the agriculture bureau in the State Council Development and Research Centre, a cabinet-level think-tank. And, as Li Ping [of the Rural Development Institute] points out, the local collectives are not averse to skimming off as much as possible from the income of the sale. The peasants often end up with little or nothing ... In May 2000 a frank report from the Land Ministry stated that of almost 170,000 land-related violations (which covers mainly illegal land seizures), just over 15 per cent involved local officials. Another report in 2000 by the Rural Development Institute and Beijing's People's University found that only half of China's peasants possessed the actual land-use contract, because local officials wanted to maintain as much power as possible.

(Jiang Xueqin, *FEER*, 7 February 2002, pp. 57–9)

(See 'Agriculture', above, for recent changes in legislation.)

LACK OF A LAND OWNERSHIP SYSTEM

The lack of a land ownership system holds back rural development. People cannot sell the land they till; this prevents consolidation into more efficient units. Meanwhile, fear of loss of land use rights is a deterrent to moving off the land permanently.

(Philip Bowring, *IHT*, 20 November 2001, p. 8)

LAND USE AND STATE PREFERENCES

Land use has not always coincided with state preferences. China has a history of famines and so the state was particularly concerned with the grain harvest.

'Many [farmers] are forced to grow grain crops to feed the Communist Party's paranoia of a Western food embargo' (Bruce Gilley, *FEER*, 29 November 2001, p. 36).

'Chinese peasants are [however] increasingly freed of government orders to grow grain' (*FEER*, 18 December 2003, p. 30).

MALE LABOUR

Male labour in particular has become a more valuable asset on the farm (to carry on the farm and provide for parents in their old age) and this has helped undermine the population control programme.

MEDICAL PROVISION

[Some] 90 per cent of the 900 million people who live in the countryside ... have no medical insurance ... With health insurance coverage shrinking, while medical costs rise faster than incomes, China faces a humanitarian disaster that threatens to undo one of the country's proudest achievements of the last twenty years: the lifting of an estimated 210 million people out of absolute poverty ... From the 1950s to the 1970s ... China's rural health infrastructure ... [there were] set up village health centres, township health centres and county hospitals. At the village level agricultural collectives paid the salaries of so-called 'barefoot doctors' and put money into collective welfare funds for drugs and treatment. Patients paid modest premiums and a nominal fee for consultations and medicines. Local government also contributed ... After 1979, however, Deng Xiaoping dismantled the agricultural collectives ... Because he did not make any new provisions for funding rural health care, the health infrastructure collapsed ... This year [2002] ... building a rural health-insurance system has become one of the [health] ministry's top three priorities.

(*FEER*, 13 June 2002, pp. 30–2)

[In] rural areas the former system of free clinics has disintegrated ... Until the beginning of the reform period in the early 1980s the socialized medicine system, with 'barefoot doctors' at its core, worked wonders. From 1952 to 1982 infant mortality fell from 200 per 1,000 live births to thirty-four, and life expectancy increased from about thirty-five years to sixty-eight, according to a recent study published by *The New England Journal of Medicine* ... In the last several years China has experimented with reforms aimed at improving health care for peasants. The most important is an insurance plan in which participating farmers make an annual payment of a little more than a dollar to gain eligibility for basic medical treatments. Many peasants have complained that even the dollar payment is too big a burden and that in any event the coverage the plan theoretically provides is inadequate ... The government ... recently announced an expansion of this experiment, with increased fees and increased coverage, but it has yet to make an impact on the health crisis. As a result, according to government estimates, in less than a generation, a rural population that once enjoyed universal if rudimentary coverage has become 79 per cent uninsured. More than half urban residents, by comparison, have some kind of coverage, which is supplied by their employers. The near-total absence of adequate health care in much of the countryside has sown deep resentment among the peasantry while helping to spread infectious diseases like hepatitis and tuberculosis and making the country – and the world – more vulnerable to epidemics like SARS and possibly bird flu.

(Howard French, *IHT*, 16 January 2006, p. 4)

The state began cutting hospital subsidies in the early 1980s and by the mid-1990s it covered just 20 per cent of urban state hospitals' costs ... About 130 million people in China have health insurance, leaving almost 90 per cent of the population without coverage ... The majority of the uninsured – most of them rural residents – avoid going to hospitals for treatment because they cannot afford it.

(*IHT*, 30 March 2006, p. 17)

Changes in agricultural policy since 2005

The government is trying to improve rural living standards. For example, 'Chinese officials are promising to slash taxes on peasants and increase farm subsidies' (*IHT*, 3 February 2005, p. 1).

Delivering the main opening address to the National People's Congress on Saturday [5 March 2005] prime minister Wen Jiabao ... vowed to eliminate the main tax imposed on China's peasantry for the first time in two millenniums ... Wen emphasized continuing a campaign to cool China's economy and narrow the growing urban–rural wealth gap, which has led to severe social tensions.

(www.iht.com, 6 March 2005)

Prime minister Wen Jiabao on Monday [14 March] ... spoke about China's need to balance its economic growth and to spread its wealth to the vast, impoverished countryside. He said that China had passed into a new era of development in which industrial development has to 'replenish' agriculture. This would involve further reducing taxes on farm products, improving irrigation and farming infrastructure, and improving rural schools and health care, he said.

(*IHT*, 15 March 2005, p. 2)

'Per capita disposable income in towns and cities ... rose 7.7 per cent to 9,422 yuan last year [2004], while incomes in rural areas rose 6.8 per cent to 2,936 yuan' (www.iht.com, 14 March 2005).

The agriculture minister ... Du Qinglin ... on Thursday [10 March] promised to protect farmers' land rights and spend more on irrigation as China's leaders seek to ease chronic rural poverty, seen as posing their biggest risk of anti-government unrest ... The ministry introduced pilot projects last year [2004] aimed at arbitrating disputes over land contracts ... Average annual incomes for farmers rose 12 per cent last year [2004], but still total just 2,936 yuan, or $355 per person, according to Du. By contrast the government says annual incomes in China's booming cities average more than $1,000 per person ... Premier Wen Jiabao promised [on 5 March] ... to eliminate farm taxes by 2006 – a promise repeated Thursday by the finance ministry ... China said this week that it would start cutting school fees in rural areas this year [2005] in response to growing domestic criticism that the country's education system is corrupt and discriminates against poor, rural students. The new policy will begin with the removal of fees for 14 million students in the country's poorest counties and will continue until 2007.

(www.iht.com, 10 March 2005)

This year's budget calls for more spending on a new rural health care programme aimed at reversing the near collapse of rural medical services in recent years. It also calls for an increase in central government handouts to rural areas, to make up for their loss of revenue as a result of reforms intended to reduce peasants' tax burdens. The government plans to abolish agricultural tax by 2006, two years earlier than it had originally planned. And it also says it will abolish primary school fees for all children in rural areas by 2007.

(*The Economist*, 19 March 2005, p. 72)

Already twenty-seven out of China's thirty-one provinces and municipalities ... have abolished agricultural taxes, with the rest soon to follow. 'The agricultural tax will be exempted throughout the country next year [2006],' announced premier Wen Jiabao at the National People's Congress in March 2005.

(*FEER*, November 2005, p. 27)

China's parliament yesterday [29 December 2005] approved a motion phasing out a decades-old agricultural tax from the start of 2006 ... The tax raised only 1.5 billion renminbi ($186 million) this year [2005] and amounted to just 1 per cent of China's total tax revenue last year [2004]. It was introduced in 1958 but has long been held to be unfair – farmers had to pay it regardless of how little they earned or even whether they planted crops.

(*FT*, 30 December 2005, p. 6)

'Late last year [2005] in Guangdong province, one of China's most affluent regions (and also the scene of some of the most violent peasant protests reported recently), the authorities began allowing villages to trade land that had already been converted to industrial use' (*The Economist*, Survey, 25 March 2006, p. 9).

The March 2006 session of the National People's Congress paid particular attention to increasing economic inequalities in China, especially between urban and rural areas. A programme of further aid to rural areas was outlined, envisioning a 'new socialist countryside'. (See the entries for 22 February and 5–14 March 2006 in the political chronology.)

Agriculture and the World Trade Organization (WTO)

Many [farmers] are forced to grow grain crops to feed the Communist Party's paranoia of a Western food embargo ... With WTO entry China's average tariff on agricultural imports will fall to 15 per cent from 22 per cent in trade-weighted terms. More significant is the end of quotas and the state food distribution monopolies that will make China one of the world's most open countries for food imports ... The pain will be concentrated in a few sectors – wheat, corn, rice and cotton – where Beijing reckons 13 million people will lose their jobs, most of them in the north ... Lower tariffs and a relaxation of state quotas and other controls are expected to bring a surge of food imports that will throw 13 million farmers ... [out of a total of] 328 million farmers ... out of work, according to officials estimates ... At the same time WTO membership will bring significant new opportunities for fruit, vegetable and meat producers with access to foreign markets. Beijing believes that 2 million jobs will be added to produce everything from walnuts to pork ... According to a book ... edited by China's chief trade negotiator Long Yongtu ... on the WTO's impact on agriculture published last year [2000] by the foreign trade ministry ... farmers forced to grow grain for food security should be freed to switch crops and allow China to rely on its foreign exchange reserves to import grains ... 'For many years our state's price, investment and tax policies have created a situation of negative protection of agriculture. That means that after WTO entry we will still have a lot of room to expand support for agriculture' [the book says] ... China's big advantage in introducing a more rational policy now is that it does not have a huge system of agricultural protection to dismantle ... As a poor country it never needed high tariffs because people could not afford imported food. The government saw no need for subsidies because farmers were traditionally at the bottom of the pile ... [In 2000] public investment in infrastructure and production-related subsidies was just $14 billion, far less than the 10 per cent allowed by WTO rules and far below investment support in Western countries ... The agriculture ministry plans to liberalize distribution, phasing out the state trade companies that dominate many sectors like grain, and building the transport, storage and marketing means for market efficiency ... Cao Jinqing ... a Shanghai-based scholar ... pinpoints the state's policy of under-investing in agriculture and taxing farmers the heaviest as the biggest problem. The central government simply does not provide the funding needed for public services in rural China ... The result is local officials resort to an array of special taxes.

(Bruce Gilley, *FEER*, 29 November 2001, pp. 36–8)

'China began importing large amounts of grain as far back as 1961 and its annual imports during the 1980s averaged above 11 million tonnes, more than the 9.3 million tonne import quota it has agreed to under WTO' (*IHT*, 1 February 2002, p. ii.)

'The state runs a costly monopoly to purchase and supply grain' (Jasper Becker, *IHT*, 27 November 2002, p. 6).

Entry to the WTO has brought real benefits to those willing to switch to products such as those fruits and vegetables in ever greater demand.

The market gradually replacing central planning

The nearest China came to emulating the traditional Soviet-type command planning system was during the First Five Year Plan (1953–7). But even from the beginning Chinese planning devolved greater powers to the regions (although the degree fluctuated over time), there was no labour market initially (manpower was allocated to enterprises) and greater use was made of consumer good rationing (partly to control population movements). Prior to the 1978 reforms Communist China's development had been erratic, with alternative periods of centralization and decentralization and periods when politics and economics were alternatively in command. For example, the Great Leap Forward (1958–60) and the Cultural Revolution (1966–9/76) were anarchic periods of extreme administrative decentralization when extreme-left politics took priority over economics. These traumatic episodes helped secure the market-orientated reforms of 1978 and after, by giving extreme leftist policies a bad name. The lack of effective medium-term (five years) and long-term planning during the period 1958–76 was reflected in severe bottlenecks in the provision of infrastructure, especially energy, transport and communications. The situation improved. 'Power supply and transportation bottlenecks ... are now seemingly things of the past' (*China Briefing*, January 1998, no. 59, p. 5). But continued rapid growth led to the reappearance of bottlenecks in the early years of the new millennium.

The increasing importance of the market can be judged by the following:

1   'Whereas in 1978 around 700 kinds of producer goods were allocated by the plan, by 1991 the number was below twenty. Even in the case of state enterprises, according to one estimate, in 1989 around 56 per cent of inputs were purchased outside the plan and almost 40 per cent of output was sold outside the plan. Today the market distributes almost 60 per cent of coal, 55 per cent of steel and 90 per cent of cement' (*The Economist*, Survey, 28 November 1992, p. 7).

2   By 1993 central (mandatory) plans controlled only 7 per cent of industrial output (Jefferson and Rawski 1994: 63). The proportion of planned production of total industrial output value fell from 91 per cent in 1978 to 80 per cent in 1984, 16.2 per cent in 1991, 12 per cent in 1992 and 5 per cent in 1993 (Cao *et al.* 1997: 20).

3   'Moving more quickly than political reform ... is China's "marketization" – the degree to which its economy is responsive to market forces. The results of a study on the topic [in the November 1998 issue of a Chinese journal] indicate that after twenty years of reform, half of China's economy is now "marketized", with some parts lagging far behind ... Market forces in China today influence 70 per cent of labour allocation, 62 per cent of product pricing and distribution, 51 per cent of enterprise management, 23 per cent of land transfers and 17 per cent of capital distribution ... Bringing China up to the level of "countries with relatively developed market economies" would take thirty years' (Susan Lawrence, *FEER*, 17 December 1998, p. 22).

4   '[China's] extraordinary economic performance has been driven by changes in government economic policy that have progressively given greater rein to market forces. The transformation started in the agricultural sector more than two decades ago and was extended progressively to industry and large parts of the service sector' (OECD 2005: website Chapter 1). 'Changes in government policies have created a largely market-orientated economy in which the private sector plays a key role' (ibid.: website Chapter 2).

Prices

China adopted a policy of gradual and partial price reform. A 'dual' pricing system was used (market prices being allowed for products bought and sold on the market as opposed to state-controlled prices for outputs or inputs forming part of the state plan). Controls have generally been relaxed over time. Nevertheless, temporary retrenchment has occurred, such as the reintroduction of price controls to combat inflation (price ceilings) and (for some time after October 1997) deflation (price floors).

> On 1 September 1992 central price control was ended on 593 materials and industrial products, including soda ash, high quality steel, glass and electrical machinery. This reduced the number directly priced by the government to eighty-nine, from 737 at the end of 1991. On 28 November 1992 the government announced the removal of price controls on rice and other basic grain products in Sichuan province (this having been accomplished in the autumn in Anhui and a number of other provinces). The intention was to do the same throughout the country in one to three years. On 1 December 1992 the prices of meat and eggs in Beijing were decontrolled (the only ration coupons remaining being for grain and cooking oil). Income compensation was to be given in all cases.
>
> (*IHT*, 30 November 1992, p. 2)

On 3 January 1993 it was announced that in 1993 around 57 per cent of coal output would be sold at market prices, compared with about 20 per cent in 1992 (*FT*, 4 January 1993, p. 13).

'On 12 September 1998 price controls [were ordered] on cars and a range of machinery to halt deflation' (*FEER*, 1 October 1998, p. 72).

> China is to impose selective price controls ... aimed at shielding companies from cut-throat competition [which] has been exacerbated by eleven consecutive months of deflation ... Yesterday [14 September it was said that] floors were to be set for products such as passenger cars, computerized machine tools, three-wheel farm trucks, loading machines and power generators ... The deflationary trend began in October last year [1997].
>
> (*FT*, 15 September 1998, p. 3)

> In the past fortnight China has ordered several new price controls ... The price controls, ordered on various machines, textiles, construction materials and petrochemicals, were necessary to prevent dumping on the domestic market and to end price wars ... Retail prices fell 3.3 per cent in August [1998], compared with the same month a year ago.
>
> (*FT*, 29 September 1998, p. 8)

> Chinese authorities announced new price controls on a range of industries, including cars, steel, chemicals and sugar ... The authorities appear to be trying to protect Chinese companies that are suddenly competing with low-cost imports from neighbouring countries where currencies have been devalued.
>
> (*IHT*, 30 September 1998, p. 13)

On 5 August 1999 the government set out detailed rules designed to stop enterprises from dumping (selling their goods below manufacturing cost). The state development planning commission said it aimed 'to curb cut-throat dumping in the industrial, commercial and service sectors' (*FT*, 6 August 1999, p. 5).

Government-set limits [i.e. ceilings, have been imposed] on drug prices and manufacturers' profit margins ... as part of efforts to slash state spending on health care ... Drug makers in about half of China's thirty-one provinces have had to report their production costs since last year [1998]. They are then restricted to profit margins of between 8 per cent and 24 per cent.

(*FEER*, 26 August 1999, p. 46)

Chinese officials like to boast that 96 per cent of all prices are officially set by the market. But that is extremely misleading. The government's influence remains widespread and deeply felt. And shortages, not rising prices, are the main release valve when demand is stronger than supply ... [For example] globally oil prices have rocketed, but in China petrol prices have barely budged in weeks ... Capitalism with Chinese characteristics increasingly seems to mean nonsensical pricing. From the cheap $1.2 flag-fall in Shanghai taxis to the artificially low prices for many key commodities like electricity, government regulation, intervention and outright fiat have become critical tools for suppressing prices ... Today price bureaus in Shanghai and all over China enforce caps and other controls on such key products as fertilisers, fuel, medicines and transport services.

(*FEER*, 26 August 2004, p. 19)

China's pricing of power is a source of inefficiency. China is only beginning to experiment with charging more for higher electricity usage, or for power during peak times to encourage a more even distribution of demand. In fact, the business of power generation is an easy one to get squeezed in. Coal prices are increasingly set by the market, but electricity prices are still established by the government ... The government is conducting some experiments to let market mechanisms set prices. In June, following a surge in coal prices, authorities announced higher rates for household electricity in seven cities and provinces, which followed a small increase for commercial and industrial users.

(*FEER*, 16 September 2004, p. 39)

Tight regulations on retail prices for diesel and electricity ... have made increasingly profit-orientated refiners and power companies reluctant to sell either. Global markets set wholesale prices for diesel and for heavy fuel oil used by power stations, but the government still insists on setting retail prices.

(*IHT*, 19 April 2005, p. 13)

'Price regulation was essentially dismantled by 2000' (OECD 2005: website Chapter 1). The OECD survey (ibid.: website Chapter 1) provides information on the share of transactions (per cent of transactions volume) conducted at market prices for the years 1978, 1985, 1991, 1995, 1999 and 2003 for both producer goods and retail sales. For producer goods the respective figures for market prices for the six years are as follows: 0.0 per cent; 13.0 per cent; 46.0 per cent, 78.0 per cent; 86.0 per cent; 87.3 per cent. (The respective figures for state-guided and state-fixed prices for the six years are as follows: 0.0 per cent and 100.0 per cent; 23.0 per cent and 64.0 per cent; 18.0 per cent and 36.0 per cent; 6.0 per cent and 16.0

per cent; 4.0 per cent and 10.0 per cent; 2.7 and 10.0 per cent.). For retail sales the respective figures for market prices for the six years are as follows: 3.0 per cent; 34.0 per cent; 69.0 per cent; 89.0 per cent; 95.0 per cent; 96.1 per cent. (The respective figures for state-guided and state-fixed prices are as follows: 0.0 per cent and 97 per cent; 19.0 per cent and 47.0 per cent; 10.0 per cent and 21.0 per cent; 2.0 per cent and 9.0 per cent; 1.0 per cent and 4.0 per cent; 1.3 per cent and 2.6 per cent.)

Monetary policy

There is now greater emphasis on indirect steering of the economy through such policies as prices (see above), taxes and credit. (The Chinese talked of 'guidance planning' in which targets were suggested rather than mandated. 'China ... had converted the State Planning Commission into the ... National Development and Reform Commission': *The Economist*, 13 November 2004, p. 72.)

In market economies the financial system is the means by which saving is transformed into investment. China's financial system is very inefficient because of pervasive state controls.

> Banks continue to bear the brunt of capital raising in China – about 95 per cent of financing comes through banks – because of the dysfunctional local stock market ... [in turn] because of the poor quality of listed companies and the dominant role still played by the state as a shareholder.
>
> (*FT*, Survey, 7 December 2004, p. 4)

('Some 60 per cent of the average listed company remains in state hands': *FEER*, 28 October 2004, p. 32.)

> The price of capital plays a relatively small role in how it is allocated. China has no corporate bond market to speak of and its stock markets, in Shenzhen and Shanghai, are still thin and patchy. Most capital is thus provided by banks, and the most important banks are still owned by the state ... Perhaps two-thirds of the banks' loans serve to prop up state-owned enterprises.
>
> (www.economist.com, 5 November 2004)

> China's banks are mere conduits for pouring money into local governments and state-owned companies, with little regard for risk or profit ... Because China's capital markets are underdeveloped the domestic economy relies on bank loans: bank assets comprise 77 per cent of all financial assets compared with 26 per cent in America ... By end-2003 outstanding loans had surged to 145 per cent of GDP, the highest such ratio in the world. Bad debts to banks at 40 per cent of GDP are a threat to fiscal stability.
>
> (*The Economist*, 6 November 2004, p. 87)

At present nearly 90 per cent of household savings are held in deposits with state-owned banks, partly because of a lack of alternatives. Most of these deposits are lent to SOEs. By contrast most of the investment in the dynamic, private non-SOE sector that is propelling China's industrial growth is self-financed, or dependent on foreign capital. With few of these non-state growth enterprises being willing – or allowed – to issue shares, trade on domestic stock exchanges is mainly in SOEs, whose non-transparent accounting practices and perceived lack of viability deter households from holding much of their savings in them directly. Hence the thinness and volatility of the domestic stock markers, as even a little news from the opaque SOEs can trigger big price movements.

(Deepak Lal, *FT*, 29 December 2004, p. 11)

Oversized, undermanaged and enfeebled by long histories of funnelling money to favoured projects without regard to future results, these organizations [banks] are fertile ground for corruption. The traditional Chinese practice of *guanxi*, doing business on the basis of personal relationships instead of objective criteria, have turned these money-laden institutions into gold mines for the sleazy and well connected.

(Seth Kaplan, *IHT*, 22 December 2004, p. 6)

Broadening financial markets is a crucial aspect of improving the allocation of capital. At present such markets have a limited role and this generates a concentration of financial risk in the banking sector to a greater extent than in OECD economies.

(OECD 2005: website Chapter 3)

Thus one of the major problems China faces is its state-dominated banking system. For example, as part of the 'soft budget constraint' the state-owned and state-controlled banking system has built up a large amount of 'non-performing' loans, i.e. those bank loans likely never to be paid back. ('Virtually unrecoverable loans': www.iht.com, 7 March 2005.) (Note the role played by banks in those Asian counties especially adversely affected by the Asian financial crisis, e.g. providing loans to 'their' enterprises in the financial–industrial conglomerates rather than putting capital to its most profitable use.)

State ownership is still overwhelmingly dominant.

The Industrial and Commercial Bank of China, the China Construction Bank (formerly the People's Construction Bank of China), the Bank of China and the China Agricultural Bank hold about two-thirds of renminbi deposits and issue a similar share of total loans (mainly to state enterprises). China's second tier of banks includes ten joint stock banks (banks with diverse shareholders) that have permission to operate in more than one city. The shares of most are held by local governments and state corporations. One is mainly owned by private businesses, but was founded and remains largely directed by a state commercial organization.

(*FEER*, 16 September 1999, p. 60)

One of the ways of indirectly steering the economy is through monetary policy. But the emphasis is still on credit restrictions as opposed to using interest rates. 'China's one-year lending rate is 5.31 per cent. It was last raised in July 1995' (www.iht.com, 15 June 2004). '[The state-determined] one-year bank deposit rate is ... 1.98 per cent' (*FT*, 13 December 2003, p. 8). (Note that there is a very high savings ratio in China and very few alternative outlets to domestic banks. Hence the large savings deposits in banks. '[The] deputy governor of the People's Bank of China: "The savings rate in China is more than 40 per cent [of GDP]. In the United States it is less than 2 per cent"': *FT*, 3 November 2004, p. 9. 'The savings rate in China climbed to more than 43 per cent of income in 2004 from about 26 per cent in 1985, according to official figures ... In the United States the savings rate fell to less than 1 per cent in the first quarter of this year [2005], according to the ... [US] Department of Commerce ... In many West European economies savings rates now stand at about 10 per cent or slightly higher, according to the Organization for Economic Co-operation and Development [OSCE]': *IHT*, 14 June 2005, p. 2. 'At more than 40 per cent of GDP, and 25 per cent of household income, it [China's savings rate] is among the world's highest and vastly exceeds existing investment needs: *FT*, 25 July 2005, p. 15.) '[China] has one of the highest rates of savings in any economy – the gross saving rate approaches half of GDP' (OECD 2005: website Chapter 1).

'On 24 January 1994 the central bank began Western-style open market operations, trading the first batch of 1994 Treasury bonds on the Shanghai securities exchange; the move came after decades of limiting money supply by imposing bank lending quotas' (*IHT*, 24 January 1994, p. 11).

Although the liberalization of interest rate setting has been slow, there are some signs of change.

China plans to push forward the deregulation of its interest rates next year [2003] to boost lending to private companies ... The People's Bank of China [PBOC] has applied to the State Council, China's cabinet, to approve a system that would allow banks more latitude in deciding what interest to charge to small and medium-sized enterprises. Many such SMEs are privately owned. Chinese banks are currently allowed to set interest rates of 30 per cent higher than the PBOC fixed rate when lending to SMEs, but only 10 per cent higher that that rate when lending to state-owned enterprises.

(*FT*, 9 December 2002, p. 7)

China's central bank on Wednesday [10 December 2003] sharply raised interest rates that banks are allowed to charge for commercial loans, a step that, paradoxically, is likely to make credit more widely available to private enterprises ... Beginning January [2004] banks will be allowed to charge as much as 9.03 per cent for commercial loans and 10.62 per cent for agricultural loans, considerably more than before. This will allow big Chinese banks to lend money to risky private ventures at appropriately higher rates ... For years China has restricted interest rates to a tight range. For a one-year loan, for example, banks are only allowed to charge a rate of 4.78 per cent to 5.84 per cent for medium-size and large businesses and as much as 6.9 per cent for small businesses ... The current cap on loans by agricultural credit agencies, which go to small businesses in rural areas as well as to farmers, is 7.97 per cent. Loans have not been available in many small villages since the collapse and government takeover of many rural credit co-operatives in the 1990s ... Chinese banks issue most of their loans at the lowest allowed rate and to big borrowers. The People's Bank of China said it would leave that minimum rate, of 4.78 per cent, unchanged ...

The People's Bank slightly reduced the interest that it pays banks that keep more reserves on deposit with the central bank than required by law. The effect of this measure is a slight encouragement to banks to lend more.

(*IHT*, 11 December 2003, pp. 1, 6)

China will allow commercial banks to charge higher lending rates ... Banks and urban credit co-operatives would be allowed to set rates on one-year loans at between 4.78 per cent and 9.03 per cent from 1 January 2004 ... The highest allowed rate will be 1.7 times the central bank's basic, or benchmark, rate, currently 5.31 per cent. At present banks are allowed to charge up to 1.1 times the basic rate when lending to big companies and up to 1.3 times when making loans to smaller companies.

(*FT*, 11 December 2003, p. 16)

[On 29 October 2004] the People's Bank of China lifted its benchmark one-year lending rate from 5.31 per cent to 5.58 per cent ... The deposit rate rose from 1.98 per cent to 2.25 per cent. It was the first rise in the lending rate since July 1995 and in the deposit rate since July 1993 ... The PBOC further loosened controls on loans by lifting the ceiling on the range in which commercial banks can adjust lending rates ... Banks have been given greater flexibility to increase lending rates for riskier customers ... Until yesterday [28 October] the home mortgage rate was 5.04 per cent. Inflation [on an annual basis] was 5.2 per cent in August ... Many depositors ... [have been] taking their business ... to the illegal, informal financial sector ... so-called underground banks.

(*FT*, 30 October 2004, pp. 1, 6)

China's central bank raised interest rates ... in a bid to slow ... economic growth and control inflation ... the first [move] in what many economists predict may be a series of increases ... The People's Bank also ended ... years of regulations that had tightly limited the maximum interest rates that banks could charge on loans. After concluding last spring [2004] that the economy was expanding at an unsustainable pace and fuelling inflation, Chinese leaders initially chose mostly administrative methods to limit growth, like the denial of zoning and environmental approvals ... Prices for consumer goods were 5.2 per cent higher last month [September] than a year earlier despite controls on many products. Price increases are running at nearly twice that pace for goods traded between companies, for which fewer price controls exist ... The average price of goods in transactions between companies soared 9.6 per cent in the year through September ... In recent months [there has been a] slowing growth of deposits at Chinese banks. Affluent urban Chinese families in particular increasingly seem to be forgoing the extremely low interest rates offered for bank deposits and lending money directly to struggling businesses at double-digit interest rates.

(*IHT*, 30 October 2004, pp. 1, 8)

'China had begun tightening economic policy last spring [2004] when it imposed stringent administrative controls on the volume of bank loans and the issuance of zoning and environmental impact approvals' (*IHT*, 30 October 2004, p. 16).

'Market-based initiatives last year [2004] were mostly confined to bond sales, a single small increase last autumn in regulated lending rates and three small increases a year ago in reserves that banks must keep on deposit with the central bank' (www.iht.com, 25 January 2005).

'The People's Bank of China on 17 March [2005] raised the minimum interest rate on home loans of more than five years' duration to 5.51 per cent from 5.31 per cent' (www.iht.com, 14 April 2005).

Developments in monetary policy

The old monobank system has given way to a more complicated structure with a central bank at the apex (the People's Bank of China: PBOC). Private banks were banned after the communist takeover in 1949. The banking system is still over-whelmingly state-owned but things are changing.

> China currently has only one nominally private bank, Minsheng Banking Corp., which was established in [January] 1996 as an 'experiment' and which still has numerous government ties ... Minsheng Bank [is] the first bank in China to have a majority of non-state shareholders ... [However] Minsheng is 12 per cent owned by state enterprises and has not completely avoided loans to state-run companies ... [It] successfully listed its shares on the Shanghai stock exchange on 19 December 2000, becoming one of only four Chinese banks to go public ... China is taking its first tentative steps to allow privately owned banks to operate ... Central bank regulators in Beijing are now considering applications to establish five private banks that would compete against the nation's state-owned behemoths, the biggest four of which, control 59 per cent of China's banking sector ... The private banks would be tiny ... and would operate under government constraints ... Still, the private banks would be the first in China to be 100 per cent backed by private investors ... It may take regulators up to a year to make a decision on whether to even proceed with the programme ... The private banks are part of China's efforts to prepare ... for the onslaught of competition that is expected in 2007, when, under WTO guidelines, the country must open itself up to foreign banks ... There are 180 foreign banks in China today ... But [they have] only a 2 per cent market share.

(FEER, 18 September 2003, pp. 46–9)

'Foreign banks' ... share of total assets in the Chinese banking system fell to 1.1 per cent [in 2002] from 2 per cent [in 2001]' (p. 28).

('China is set to back the establishment of a series of private banks ... The banks will be a new category of institution in China, called Rural Commercial Banks (RCBs), three of which were quietly created last year [2002] in the eastern province of Jiangsu as an experiment in rural financial reform ... Local govern-ments cannot take an ownership stake in the RCBs, the stakeholders of which should be local bank employees and farmers ... This structure, it is hoped, will free the new banks from the local government manipulation seen as a key cause of the high bad loan levels at credit co-operatives ... No single shareholder in a new bank may hold more than 5 per cent of its share capital ... The new banks will lend mainly to rural enterprises and other private business springing up in the suburbs of China's towns and cities': *FT*, 10 January 2003, p. 18.)

In December 1993 details were announced of a major reform of the banking system. The People's Bank of China (though still controlled by the government) was to become more like a Western central bank in that it would not henceforth directly engage in commercial or even policy-related lending and would concentrate on monetary policy. State banks were to be divided into state-owned 'policy' banks (which make loans according to state preferences, e.g. infrastructure) and 'commercial' banks (which make loans according to commercial criteria). 'Policy loans' were to become the prerogative of three new 'policy banks (Long-term Development and Credit Bank, Export-Import Bank and Agricultural Development Bank). The existing four 'specialized banks' (Industrial and Commercial Bank, Agriculture Bank, People's Construction Bank and Bank of China) were to become 'commercial banks' But this has not proven to be very effective because all state banks have come under pressure to make loans (for investment purposes, for example), e.g. to counter deflation after October 1997 and to generally make sure that growth does not fall below the minimum 7 per cent needed to prevent unemployment rising to a level sufficient to cause social instability.

State banks are burdened with 'non-performing loans', a result of the persistence of 'soft budget constraints' for many state enterprises. Official figures show that non-performing loans increased from 20 per cent at the end of 1994 to 25 per cent at the end of 1997 (Lardy 1998: 79). 'Some put the total amount of non-performing loans [in the big four state banks as a whole] at 40 per cent, compared with the official estimate of 25 per cent' (*FT*, 14 May 2001, p. 10).

In January 1999 it was announced that Asset Management Companies (AMCs) would be set up to relieve the larger state-owned banks of some of their non-performing loans. The AMCs issued bonds to the banks in exchange for the non-performing loans. (The face value of the non-performing loans was $169.3 billion.) As part of the policy the AMCs would try to recover as many of the loans as possible, to sell the loans at a discount to those interested (including foreigners: the first time was in November 2001) and to indulge in debt-for-equity swaps (the equity of state enterprises in debt to the banks). Problems include still-growing non-performing loans (as state banks have come under pressure to make loans) and questions about the ability of AMCs to exercise corporate governance even after debt-for-equity swaps (since 'soft budget constraints' still operate for important state enterprises).

Western estimates of the extent of non-performing loans are much higher than official Chinese estimates:

> The Bank of China, the nation's most prestigious state bank, announces a level of bad debt that is much higher than previously acknowledged ... The bank's non-performing loans amount to 28 per cent, compared with previous estimates that have ranged between 11 per cent and 15 per cent ... Some put the total amount of non-performing loans [in the big four state banks as a whole] at 40 per cent, compared with the official estimate of 25 per cent ... Last year [2000] the banks transferred 400 billion renminbi in bad loans to asset

management companies ... The selling of assets through the asset management companies is expected to be an uphill struggle, meaning the finance ministry will eventually have to foot most of the bill.

(*FT*, 14 May 2001, p. 10)

Central bank chief Dai Xianglong said [in November 2001] banks must do more to reduce bad loans, and estimated that non-performing loans at state banks accounted for 26.6 per cent of their total lending at the end of September. Some foreign analysts put non-performing loans at about half the lending of the 'Big Four' state banks – China Construction Bank, Bank of China, Industrial and Commercial Bank of China and Agricultural Bank of China.

(*FEER*, 15 November 2001, pp. 30–1)

Dai Xianglong admitted in public that bad loans at [the four] big state banks were higher than official estimates. He said they could be up to 30 per cent of the banks' total lending if international accounting standards were used. Some Western estimates put the level of bad loans at 50 per cent. Dai said in January [2002] the combined level of the 'big four' state banks stood at 25.37 per cent in 2001, down 3.81 percentage points from 2000.

(*FEER*, 11 April 2002, p. 25)

'The four Asset Management Companies (AMCs) set up in 1999 to help China's biggest banks get rid of bad debt are themselves turning into a substantial financial risk, according to a report by the Bank of International Settlements (BIS)' (*FEER*, 19 September 2002, p. 25).

Four government Asset Management Companies [were] set up in 1999 to help dispose of non-performing loans, which by some estimates amount to more than $450 billion, or just under half of China's annual economic output. The companies took over almost $170 billion in bad loans from four state banks in the past three years.

(*FEER*, 31 October 2002, p.30)

In 1998 $33 billion was injected into [the big four state banks] to improve capital adequacy. A year later ... $169 billion in non-performing loans was stripped from their books and shifted to four government-owned Asset Management Companies, or AMCs. In return the AMCs issued bonds worth $141 billion to the banks, topped up with $28 billion in cash.

(*FEER*, 14 November 2002, p. 32)

New estimates [have been made] by outside analysts of China's bad-debt problem. According to probably imprecise official figures, 25.4 per cent of all loans by Chinese banks are unlikely to be repaid in full. The true figure is more like half, maybe $500 billion to $600 billion say independent experts. Goldman Sachs thinks it would cost between 44 per cent and 68 per cent of China's GDP to clean up the mess.

(*The Economist*, 18 January 2003, p. 69)

'No interest is being paid [on non-performing loans]' (*IHT*, 19 June 2003, p. 17).

China's debt-recovery firms retrieved 22.4 per cent of the face value of bad debts disposed of by the end of 2002 ... well below a government target of 30 per cent ... The four Asset Management Companies (Huarong, Cinda, Orient and Great Wall) ... had recovered 67.5 billion renminbi ($8.16 billion) in cash by year end and had disposed of 301.4 billion renminbi in bad assets.

(*FEER*, 6 February 2003, p. 23)

Unofficial estimates put bad loans at 40 per cent or more of the total ... Nicholas Lardy now puts bad loans in the system at around $500 billion or over 50 per cent of the total ... In 1999 four Asset Management Companies [were set up] ... Over the following couple of years the government transferred, at face value, roughly $170 billion of bad loans from the four big banks to their respective AMCs, equivalent to more than one-fifth of the banks' loan books ... Since then another $40 billion of bad loans appear to have been transferred to the AMCs ... Even after the relief provided by the first batch the banks' bad loan ration still stands at 22 per cent, according to ... the Bank for International Settlements ... In order to buy the $170 billion of banks' bad loans the AMCs needed to be capitalized. At the outset the finance ministry injected capital of $1.2 billion into each new AMC ... accounting for just 3 per cent of assets acquired. The People's Bank of China put in. . . up to $50 billion. But in return for that cash a big chunk of state banks' liabilities to the central bank appears to have been transferred to the AMCs: that is, state banks' debts were forgiven, while new ones owed by the AMCs were created. Lastly, the AMCs themselves issued $140 billion worth of ten-year interest-bearing bonds. These were given to the banks, along with $40 billion-odd in cash, in return for the bad loans ... So far only 25 per cent of loans, by face value, have been sold ... The central bank's claim on the AMCs is larger than its own capital base.

(*The Economist*, Survey, 8 February 2003, p. 12)

'[According to official figures] the "big four" state banks ... had cut non-performing loans to 24.1 per cent at the end of March [2003], down from 26.1 per cent at the end of 2002' (*FT*, 30 May 2003, p. 9).

'In China's financial system, says Nicholas Lardy ... 31.4 per cent of loans – the equivalent of 44.6 per cent of GDP – were non-performing at the end of 2002' (*The Economist*, 30 August 2003, p. 62).

US investment bank Morgan Stanley and state-run China Construction Bank finalized an agreement to set up an asset management joint venture to handle 4.3 billion renminbi ($519.3 billion) of the bank's non-performing loans. The agreement was delayed for months by regulatory barriers because authorities preferred that foreign investors work through AMCs.

(*FEER*, 17 July 2003, p. 26)

The Chinese government announced on Tuesday [6 January 2004] a complex transfer [actually accomplished at the end of 2003] of $45 billion from China's soaring foreign exchange reserves to two of its four big state-owned banks, the third large Chinese banking system bailout in less than six years. The transaction is intended to help shore up the banks, the Bank of China and the China Construction Bank, so that they can sell stock for the first time ... The central bank, the People's Bank of China, admonished the banks to do a better job of controlling fraud and limiting bad loans. 'When dealing with bad assets they have to strictly investigate the responsibility of the related officials,' the central bank said. 'They have to fight fiercely against those who have tried to run away from bank loans through illegal behaviour' ... The big four Chinese banks claim that 20 per cent of their loans are non-performing, but Western analysts say that as many as 45 per cent of borrowers do not repay, although this percentage may be falling. By contrast, big American banks commonly fail to obtain repayment on as few as 1 per cent of their loans ... [The money was being transferred] to a new, specially created management company, the Central Huijin Investment Company, which would then invest in the banks ... The two banks were required to keep the money in dollars, which would make it easier for the central bank to continue preventing traders from bidding up the value of the yuan in currency markets. The central bank has been printing yuan on a huge scale to buy dollars and prevent the yuan's appreciation. While the government has been able to take some of the extra yuan out of the financial system by selling bonds and withdrawing money from circulation that is used to pay for them, enough yuan have been issued to allow banks to lend more money in the first seven months of 2003 than in all of 2002. This has prompted fears that the banks might have engaged in another round of reckless lending ... The government has promised the two banks that they could exchange the dollars for yuan later, if necessary, at a rate of 8 yuan to the dollar. This would provide a hedge against losses if the yuan did appreciate. The arrangement could suggest an acknowledgement by Beijing of an eventual appreciation of the yuan, which currently trades at 8.28 to the dollar ... Accounting rules would let the banks count dollars as capital for purposes of meeting international capital adequacy standards without converting them to yuan ... The banks would be able to write off loans as uncollectable and make corresponding accounting entries against their equity without converting the dollars into yuan.

(www.iht.com, 6 January 2004; *IHT*, 7 January 2004, pp. 1–8)

China recently used $45 billion of its reserves to recapitalize debt-strapped banks. This marks the second time Beijing has stepped in to rescue state-owned banks bogged down by non-performing loans that analysts say could amount to 50 per cent of all lending in the country. In 1998 the government raised a 270 billion renminbi bond to help four of its largest banks ... Beijing aims to cut the average bad loan ratio of the big four banks to 15 per cent by 2005 to help them list shares eventually.

(*FT*, 6 January 2004, p. 10)

Officials said the capital injection, completed on 31 December [2003] but announced yesterday [6 January 2004], was the first step in a strategy to spend more than $100 billion in public funds on strengthening the 'big four' state banks – the weakest link in China's booming economy ... The funds were to remain in US dollars and stay invested in their current instruments, mainly US treasuries. However, the ownership of the funds had been transferred to the two banks [each of which received $22.5 billion], both of which must pay interest to a new state company, Central Huijin Investment Company ... Officials said Central Huijin was eventually set to become a shareholder in the two banks by transferring what is now in effect a loan into equity.

(*FT*, 7 January 2004, p. 8)

Since 1998 China has spent roughly $200 billion in recapitalizing its banks and writing off bad loans, to little effect. Politically directed lending to favoured industries has continued as before, and the old, written-off bad loans were soon replaced by new ones. Today some independent estimates put the level of bad loans at around $400 billion, or nearly 40 per cent of GDP.

(*The Economist*, 10 January 2004, p. 13)

'Previous capital injections and write-offs total 1.67 trillion yuan ($200 billion) ... Even official estimates put the bad loans of the big four at $290 billion. Independent analysts think the true figure is closer to $420 billion' (p. 65). 'The big four hold 67 per cent of the country's deposits and make 61 per cent of its loans' (www.economist.com, 9 January 2004).

In the first step of a new drive to prepare debt-laden state-run banks for stock market listing by cleaning up their books, Beijing injected a total of $45 billion from its swollen foreign exchange reserves into the Bank of China and China Construction Bank. The move will reduce bad debt ratios for the two banks ... In 1998 the state injected $33 billion into the Big Four. A year later regulators carved out $170 billion in bad debts from them and put the debts into four Asset Management Companies in exchange for government bonds. The mechanism this time involved the funds being split evenly and shifted to the banks by a new company, Central Huijin Investment, set up to manage the process, which analysts said apparently amounted to loans that would be exchange for equity later. The $45 billion was a tenth of China's foreign exchange reserves and will stay in dollars, mostly in US treasuries.

(*FEER*, 15 January 2004, p. 26)

It is bailout time again for China's Big Four state-owned banks. For the third time since 1998 the government has stepped in to prop up these technically insolvent behemoths that account for more than 70 per cent of lending and deposits in China. Beijing doled out a total of $45 billion to Bank of China and China Construction Bank in late December. Analysts say that the full bill could reach $120 billion by the time the other two banks are recapitalized as part of the same programme. That is on top of two earlier rescue efforts that cost a total of $202 billion ... The unusual way in which the money was pumped in and its unconventional source – China's foreign exchange reserves – left some analysts believing the injection will merely feed the banks' long-standing addiction to reckless lending. For unless the Big Four can make real progress in curbing the accumulation of new bad loans, this bailout, like its predecessors, will simply amount to another exercise in flushing money down the drain ... There is the stipulation that the money cannot be used for writing off non-performing loans, or NPLs ... Officials described the money as a loan, on which the banks would have to pay interest, and said that the funds were not to be used for writing off bad assets, but for strengthening the banks' capital bases ... The new capital is in dollars, which are fine for capitalizing Chinese banks, but not much good for writing off bad loans denominated in renminbi. There is little chance that the banks will be allowed to convert the money any time soon. Such heavy renminbi buying would place an intolerable upward pressure on China's currency, forcing the authorities to buy dollars and borrow renminbi to soak up the local currency liquidity released. That would defeat the object of using foreign exchange to recapitalize the banks. But if the banks cannot convert the new cash, holding it on their capital accounts will free up existing capital for writing off bad loans. It will also give them leeway to raise more capital in the form of subordinated debt, much of which will also be com-mitted to write-offs ... At the end of September 2003 China Construction Bank, regarded as the healthiest of the Big Four, had an official NPL ratio of nearly 12 per cent, down from about 15 per cent at the end of 2002. At first that appears encouraging. But the fall in the proportion of NPLs must be seen in the light of a rapidly growing loan book ... Most international observers estimate the real levels for all of China's banks to be much higher, with Standard & Poor's saying the true ratio is as high as 45 per cent, or about $850 billion ... Then there are questions about the quality of new loans in China ... [One analyst says that] 'When the cycle turns down, that is when the bad loans will start to appear' ... Not only have banks enthusiastically embraced lending to developers in China's highly speculative property sector, but they have con-tinued to make new loans to many of the state-owned enterprises that were the source of their original problems. While some of the most hopeless companies have gone to the wall, there are plenty of inefficient state-sector companies still receiving new loans as a form of social welfare ... [Experts] say the biggest danger is that the banks will continue their unsound lending and poor risk man-agement ... By injecting foreign reserves into its bank, Beijing makes an upward revaluation of the renminbi far less likely this year.

(*FEER*, 22 January 2004, pp. 26–9)

By boosting the banks' capital the injections increase the banks' abilities to make more loans, decreasing their bad-loans ratio and making them look healthier. It also enables them to write off more of their bad loans and sell them. About a third of China's estimated $500 billion in bad bank loans – many backed by struggling state-owned factories and derelict construction pro-jects – were transferred to the four AMCs at full face value in 1999. Since then the liquidators have been trying to resolve, sell and auction off the loans. But the pace has been slow. To date they have only disposed of about 35 per cent of the total loans on their books, and the rate of cash recovery on those loans is only about 17.3 per cent of their original value. As the loans get older and more difficult to resolve foreign investors are becoming less willing to pay more than 10 cents on the dollar to take on the bad debts.

(pp. 26–9)

In preparation for foreign competition China's four biggest state-owned banks could issue nearly $36 billion in subordinated bonds as early as the first quarter of 2004 ... New rules issued by the banking regulator in December [2003] opened the door for [the four banks] ... to recapitalize by issuing subordinated bonds – debt that only ranks above equity if a company is wound up.

(*FEER*, 12 February 2004, p. 25)

('Switching part of the sale to subordinated debt would help a bank increase its capital. China's banking regulator said in December [2003] that it would let banks sell subordinated debt to domestic investors for the first time. Banks cannot count funds raised from convertible bond sales as part of capital': www.iht.com, 18 February 2004.)

China's ministry of finance is preparing to write off its $41 billion stake in two of the country's biggest banks to help the banks dispose of non-performing loans and prepare them to issue stock, Chinese bankers said Tuesday [13 January 2004] ... The planned write-off by the ministry of finance comes a week after Beijing officials announced that they would invest $45 billion of the country's foreign exchange reserves in the same two banks, the Bank of China and the China Construction Bank ... [The moves are] aimed at preparing both banks for the sale of shares in Hong Kong and overseas later this year or in 2005 ... Until late December [2003] the ministry of finance was the sole owner of both banks, holding $26.6 billion in equity in the Bank of China and $14.5 billion in equity in the China Construction Bank. At the end of December [2003] the state administration of foreign exchange moved $45 billion of the country's foreign exchange reserves into a specially created management concern, Central Huijin Investment, which in turn bought stakes in both banks, thereby increasing the banks' equity ... Central Huijin, controlled by the central bank, continues to play an active role in allocating money into various investments denominated mainly in dollars. Partly as a result, the banks have now worked out a deal in which they will write off non-performing loans against the ministry of finance's stakes in them ... Beijing is in the process of converting the Bank of China and the China Construction Bank from state-owned enterprises into joint stock holding companies. Under Chinese regulations this means they must have at least five owners, instead of just one, the ministry of finance. Having the ministry of finance write off its large equity stake in the banks will make it easier to find room in the two banks' ownership for four investors to join Central Huijin in preparation for the sale of stock, with the ministry of finance itself possibly reacquiring a stake in the banks at some point ... The medium-term deadline for fixing China's banks is 2007, when China is supposed to throw open its banking sector to foreign competition under the terms of its accession to the WTO ... China's big four banks are awash with reserves right now, a byproduct of the central bank's huge purchases of dollars for yuan that were made to prevent the yuan's appreciation. The big four have been using their reserves to lend huge sums, raising fears that they might be creating another wave of non-performing loans.

(*IHT*, 14 January 2004, p. 13)

China plans to impose a stiffer regime of corporate governance on those state banks that recently benefited from a $45 billion capital boost ... The clampdown will include ending life-long employment contracts, scrapping the titles of staff and taking resolute supervisory action if bad loan levels rise again ... Once the Bank of China and China Construction Bank are transformed into shareholding banks, a stiffer supervisory regime will click in. If the capital base of either bank was again eroded by a build-up of non-performing loans, authorities would restrict new lending and curtail the remuneration of employees ... Following the $22.5 billion injection into each bank this month, the capital adequacy ratios of both are thought to be well above the 8 per cent minimum required by international rules. But if the ratio fell considerably below the 8 per cent benchmark, senior managers might be punished for misconduct ... Lending will be based on commercial – rather than political – criteria ... Government titles such as 'section chief' and 'division chief' will be abolished. Life-long employment ... is no longer common practice at the Bank of China and China Construction Bank. Staff are to be employed under contracts and paid by performance. In further attempts to improve efficiency the closure and merging of loss-making branches and businesses will be accelerated, along with redundancies.

(*FT*, 16 January 2004, p. 7)

China Construction Bank completed China's first successful international auction of real estate assets that were pledged as collateral on failed loans ... Only a handful of bad-asset deals involving foreigners have been completed in China. Previous deals were for non-performing loans rather than real estate assets.

(*FEER*, 10 June 2004, p. 27)

China Construction Bank, the nation's third largest, said Thursday [10 June 2004] that it would split into two companies as part of a restructuring plan in preparation for an overseas share sale ... The bank ... will separate [in September] its commercial banking operations and related assets into a unit that will be listed ... The parent company will take over remaining assets and liabilities ... Construction Bank and Bank of China each received $22.5 billion in a government bailout in December [2003] ... Selling stakes in state-owned banks would cap a decade of government asset sales, including China Life Insurance's $3 billion initial public offering in Hong Kong in December [2003] ... Chinese state companies that sell shares overseas, including China Life Insurance and China Telecom, have typically shifted their best assets into a listed unit that is separate from the parent ... The country's regulators require lenders to cut bad-debt ratios to below 15 per cent to conduct domestic share sales and to below 10 per cent to sell stock overseas ... Construction Bank cut its bad-loan ratio to 8.77 per cent in the first quarter [of 2004], the lender said on 27 April ... China's banks are racing to reorganize to meet competition from overseas rivals, including Citigroup and HSBC Holdings, the world's biggest lenders, which will be allowed to operate freely on the mainland from the end of next year [2005] under WTO guidelines.

(www.iht.com, 12 June 2004)

'China has held a ground-breaking auction of non-performing loans with a face value of 280 billion renminbi ($34 billion), pitting four state-owned Asset Management Companies against each other for the first time' (*FT*, 23 June 2004, p. 11).

'Bank of China ... [reports that] for the first nine months of 2004 ... its ratio of non-performing loans fell by more than 11 percentage points to 5.16 cent' (www.iht.com, 28 October 2004).

> Chinese legislators have passed a set of amendments to the central bank law aimed at strengthening financial risk control. The new rules precede a planned deregulation that will allow banks to invest in the country's stock market. The National People's Congress agreed Saturday [27 December 2003] to the creation of a new government agency that would supervise and co-ordinate the country's bank, insurance and stock market regulators ... [It was also said that] amendments were approved to China's commercial bank law, aimed at diversifying investment opportunities for lenders. The new rules will come into effect on 1 February [2004]. China has forbidden lenders from buying stocks or bonds or offering non-banking services that might collapse through poor investment decisions ... The amendment to the commercial banking law may allow the country's twelve commercial banks ... to invest in the stock market, real estate and other non-banking financial businesses at some point in the future ... In a third change legislators passed a banking supervision law to legalize the status of China's Banking Regulatory Commission. The banking regulator ... was split from the central bank in April [2003] with a mandate to oversee all banks in China.
>
> (*IHT*, 29 December 2003, p. 10)

'In June [2004] Cinda [Asset Management] won an auction for renminbi 280 billion worth of non-performing loans from Bank of China and China Construction Bank, marking the introduction of competition between AMCs' (*FT*, 22 November 2004, p. 26).

> Bad loans at the four big state-owned banks ... increased in the third quarter [of 2004] by 15.7 per cent of their total lending, according to the China Banking regulatory Commission. Standard & Poor's has said it would cost $656 billion to resolve bad loans at all of China's banks ... Cinda Asset Management this year [2004] bought ... bad loans from Bank of China and Construction Bank, the first time an asset manager acquired distressed assets at a discount ... Cinda had recovered 33.2 per cent of bad loans ... at the end of September ... That was the highest recovery rate among the four Asset Management Companies set up by the government to dispose of bad loans at the four big banks in 1999.
>
> (www.iht.com, 8 November 2004)

The Asset Management Companies have disposed of less than a third of the $230 billion they have acquired from their affiliated banks since 1999 ... Overseas investors have bought bad loans valued at $6 billion in China, the world's number two market for distressed loans after Japan. China's four biggest commercial lenders and eleven shareholding banks had $205 billion in soured loans at the end of September [2004], according to the China Banking Regulatory Commission.

(www.iht.com, 10 November 2004)

China on Thursday [25 November] started its biggest sale of bad loans, inviting Citigroup, Morgan Stanley and other companies to bid for assets valued at $18.1 billion, more than four times the total sold so far to overseas investors. Great Wall Management, which disposes of non-performing loans for Agricultural Bank of China, is selling all its distressed assets, with a face value of 150 billion yuan ... Overseas investors previously purchased loans in China valued at 33 billion yuan, or $4 billion. Clearing bad loans is essential for Chinese banks as the nation prepares to give overseas investors greater access at the end of 2006. By 30 September China's four state-owned asset managers had disposed of 31 per cent of the 1.9 trillion yuan of loans they collected from the nation's four largest banks since 1999 ... Great Wall had recouped 10.6 per cent of the face value of its loans as of 30 September ... compared with a recovery rate of more than 20 per cent at the three other agencies. The nation's fifteen biggest banks hold about 1.7 trillion yuan of bad loans, according to [China].

(www.iht.com, 25 November 2004)

'By September [2004] China's four state-owned asset managers had recovered about ... $14.5 billion in cash from bad loans since 1999 – a fifth of face value' (*IHT*, 30 November 2004, p. 15).

'The official non-performing loan ratio for Chinese banks is 13.37 per cent, down from 17.76 per cent at the start of the year [[2004]' (*FT*, 2 December 2004, p. 11).

'Independent estimates of bad loans in the Chinese financial system [are] at 35 per cent or more, twice the official level' (*FT*, 3 January 2005, p. 32).

'At the end of September [2004] the non-performing loans ratio ... [of] the Industrial and Commercial Bank ... stood at 19.46 per cent' (*FT*, 1 January 2005, p. 17).

China's biggest four banks reduced their bad-loan ratio by 4.8 percentage points to 15.6 per cent last year [2004] ... The bad-loan ratio at the nation's twelve joint stock banks dropped by 2.7 percentage points to 4.9 per cent ... [The combined] bad-loan ratio ... at the big four and twelve joint stock commercial banks [fell] by 4.6 percentage points to 13.2 per cent at the end of last year [2004], the banking regulator said.

(www.iht.com, 13 January 2005)

At the end of last year [2004] virtually unrecoverable loans accounted for by China's four big state-owned banks ... stood at about 16 per cent. The Bank of China's non-performing loans ratio was 5 per cent; the Construction Bank's was 4 per cent.

(www.iht.com, 7 March 2005)

[On 21 April China announced that it had approved] a $15 billion capital injection for the Industrial and Commercial Bank of China, the country's largest lender ... The capital injection ... will be financed from China's foreign exchange reserves, which stood at about $610 billion at the end of last year ... The ICBC has a higher non-performing loan ratio – about 19 per cent – than ... Bank of China and China Construction Bank ... which now claim their bad debts are less than 10 per cent of total assets ... Independent rating agencies put the overall non-performing loan ratio for the large banks at closer to 30 per cent to 35 per cent.

(*FT*, 22 April 2005, p. 28)

If you believe official figures, their [China's banks'] non-performing loan ratio fell to 13.2 per cent at the end of last year [2004], from nearly 18 per cent in 2004 ... Standard & Poor's, a credit-rating agency, reckons 35 per cent of loans will go sour, down from its previous estimate of 50 per cent.

(*The Economist*, 23 April 2005, p. 87)

Bank of Communications had [according to official figures] a bad-loan ratio of 2.91 per cent per cent at the end of December last year [2004], compared with 15.6 per cent at the four state-owned lenders ... China's commercial banks reduced their bad-loan ratio by 0.5 percentage points, to 12.4 per cent at the end of the first quarter [of 2005].

(www.iht.com, 6 June 2005)

'China's commercial banks had a combined non-performing loan ratio of 8.71 per cent as of 30 June [2005], down 4.14 percentage points from the end of 2004, according to the China Banking Regulatory Commission' (www.iht.com, 22 August 2005).

'At the end of 2004 the China Construction Bank's non-performing loan ratio was 3.92 per cent ... Its bad-loan ratio was 3.47 per cent as of 31 March' (www.iht.com, 9 June 2005).

'The Industrial and Commercial Bank of China's non-performing loan ratio for 2004 was 18.99 per cent ... The ratio was revised from a 19.1 per cent [preliminary] figure' (www.iht.com, 28 June 2005).

The four [asset management] agencies have disposed of 53 per cent of the $169 billion of distressed assets transferred to them at inception ... ... [They] are expected to dispose of the remaining loans transferred to them in 1999 by the end of 2006 ... International investors to date have bought distressed assets worth less than $5 billion in the world's second biggest market for non-performing loans.

(www.iht.com, 30 June 2005)

('China's four asset disposal agencies have sold less than $15 billion of non-performing loans to overseas buyers': www.iht.com, 30 November 2005.)

'The companies set up to dispose of non-performing loans previously owned by the banks are recovering about 20 per cent of their face value and so eventually there will be a need for the government to provide for their refinancing' (OECD 2005: website Chapter 3).

Agricultural Bank [is] the nation's fourth biggest lender ... The bank [on 18 July] did not disclose the bad-loan ratio. At the start of 2004, the last time it reported the figure, the ratio was 29 per cent ... The Industrial and Commercial Bank of China, the country's biggest lender ... said Wednesday [18 July] that its bad-loan ratio had fallen to 4.58 per cent at the end of June, down from 19 per cent at the beginning of the year ... China's overall bad-loan ratio fell to 10.15 per cent as of 30 June, down 3.95 percentage points from 31 December [2004].

(www.iht.com, 18 July 2005)

China will reorganize the State Post Bureau to create the country's fifth biggest lending institution, measured by deposits, the China Banking Regulatory Commission said Thursday [28 July]. The new China Savings Bank will hold deposits of 1.23 trillion yuan, or $152 billion, a tenth of household savings in the nation ... The post bureau will become a purely regulatory body while its businesses, including post services and deposit and savings units, will be split into five parts and transferred to a new group company ... The bank, whose ownership structure has not been defined, will be formed by the end of this year [2005] and will compete on an equal footing with China's 130 commercial banks, offering lending to companies and individuals ... China's banking regulator has ordered the nation's 130 commercial banks to direct more loans to small and private companies, at the same time extending restrictions on lending to some industries including steel and real estate ... Foreign banks will be allowed to attract yuan-denominated deposits at the beginning of 200.

(www.iht.com, 28 July 2005)

China Post has remained an opaque and bureaucratic hybrid combining the roles of regulator, mail deliverer and one of the country's biggest financial institutions ... China Post's savings system boasts ... 9 per cent of total financial sector deposits. China Post started taking deposits in 1986 and was initially credited with easing inflation by reducing liquidity, since all funds were redeposited with the central bank ... [with] favourable interest rates paid by the central bank ... The State Council plans to turn the postal savings system 'quickly' into a real bank – China's fifth largest – while dividing the rest of China Post into a regulatory department and a commercial group ... Beijing has not mentioned privatization.

(*FT*, 12 August 2005, p. 8)

'Royal Bank of Scotland said it had secured "appropriate warranties and protections" when it bought into Bank of China, although the bank did not provide details' (*IHT*, 22 September 2005, p. 13).

Since 1998 the government has spent almost $283 billion to shift a mountain of bad loans off the books of state-owned banks. In a report last week the OECD said $203 billion more was needed to clean up the rest. Taken together this rescue amounts to more than 30 per cent of GDP for 2004.

(*IHT*, 22 September 2005, p. 13)

An IMF working paper published yesterday [30 March 2006] says that the banks' working practices have hardly changed ... The paper reviews the lending of the four big banks in the seven years to the end of 2004 . . . Not only was the profitability of the enterprises that the banks lent to not taken into account, the big banks' share of lending 'was actually lower in the more profitable provinces' . . . [The paper] also raises questions about the reported dramatic fall in the new rate of non-performing loans generated in recent years . . . Only 2 per cent of the loans made since 2000 have gone sour, compared with 45 per cent for the period before 2000.

(*FT*, 31 March 2006, p. 22)

Despite costly efforts to rescue China's major banks, they continue to make high-risk loans to money-losing state-owned enterprises, according to a new IMF working paper. The paper said it was difficult to find evidence in banking date from 1997 to the end of 2004 to show that China's four big state-owned banks had changed their behaviour . . . About 2 per cent of loans made since 2000 were reported as non-performing, whereas that proportion was as high as 60 per cent for older lending . . . Banking analysts have warned that bailouts will be wasted if the banks continue to accumulate bad loans.

(*IHT*, 31 March 2006, p. 15)

GITIC and China Aviation Oil

On 6 October 1998 the central bank ordered the closure of the Guangdong International Trust and Investment Corporation (GITIC) after it was unable to repay loans. Since then other non-bank financial institutions have been closed. The central government has made it clear that it will not act as automatic guarantor for all the debts of such companies, especially those foreign loans unauthorized by the central authorities. (The idea is to help combat moral hazard. For details, see the chronology below.)

China Aviation Oil (Singapore) said Monday [24 January 2005] that it would try to stave off bankruptcy after a trading [derivatives] scandal . . . [in which] the company lost $550 million betting on oil prices . . . by repaying about two-fifths of its debt . . . The Singapore unit's Beijing-based parent [is] China Aviation Oil Holding . . . The parent's decision to lead the bailout may do little to reassure investors in other Chinese government-owned companies . . . For other China-owned companies . . . there is no guarantee the parent will [do likewise].

(*IHT*, 25 January 2005, p. 11)

The jet fuel trader China Aviation Oil will receive $130 million in funds from its parent, the oil group BP and the Singapore state-owned investor Temasek as part of a rescue plan, it said Monday [5 October 2005]. The plan comes a year after it collapsed with half a billion dollars in trading losses. The company, known as CAO, whose shares have been suspended since the scandal broke in November 2004, said BP would inject $44 million into CAO in exchange for a 20 per cent stake, giving BP access to China . . . Temasek Holdings will pay $10.2 million for a 4.7 per cent stake in Singapore-listed CAO, while its parent, the state-owned China Aviation Oil Holding Company, will invest $75.8 million and cut its stake in the firm to 51 per cent ... BP has also signed an agreement with CAO to inject assets into the Singapore-listed company six to nine months after the shares resume trading.

(www.iht.com, 5 December 2005)

A chronology of financial developments 1995–2003

1995. The Central Bank Law was approved by the National People's Congress in March 1995. The law increased the central bank's independence, but some delegates wanted a stronger supervisory role for the NPC. The final draft placed the central bank under the direct supervision of the State Council (cabinet), but also obliged the bank to submit work reports to the Standing Committee of the NPC. Details of the People's Bank of China Law are to be found in *China Briefing* (July 1995, pp. 1–2). The central bank was to implement monetary policy under the leadership of the State Council, without interference from government departments, local government, civil bodies or individuals. Monetary stability was to be the prime policy goal. The use of indirect monetary control measures was endorsed, but their use was not expected to be immediate.

1997. On 25 December 1997 China announced plans to eliminate quotas on lending by four state banks as of 1 January 1998, namely the Bank of China, the Industrial and Commercial Bank of China, the China Construction Bank (formerly the People's Construction Bank of China) and the China Agricultural Bank. Instead of imposing quotas, the People's Bank of China would issue a plan to serve as a guide and reference for commercial banks when deciding lending volumes. Commercial banks would have to balance the inward and outward flow of funds themselves. 'A major change spurred by the Asian financial crisis' (*IHT*, 26 December 1997, p. 13). 'A move intended to promote the development of a modern commercial banking sector and ease the supply of credit' (James Harding, *FT*, 27 December 1997, p. 2). Banks would be allowed to adjust interest rates within a modest band to take risk into account (*IHT*, 2 March 1998, p. 11). Banks would be allowed to set interest rates for corporate loans according to risk, albeit within a prescribed band (*FEER*, 12 March 1998, p. 20).

1998. On 16 January 1998 the governor of the central bank unveiled a three-year plan for the reorganization of the banking system. Tackling the problem of bad debt and political lending would require a different system of supervising banks. The central bank would eliminate the branches it operates in each of the thirty provinces and instead establish regional headquarters in order to prevent local authorities from forcing local banks to finance their favoured projects. Write-offs of bad debts to banks would be accelerated. Local commercial banks would be established in some 300 centres to provide financing for local business, while smaller loss-making branches of state banks would be closed (*IHT*, 17 January 1998, p. 9; *FT*, 17 January 1998, p. 2, and 19 January 1998, p. 4). The scheme (partially) to recapitalize four state banks afflicted by large amounts of non-performing loans was approved by the National People's Congress in March 1998. The plan, unveiled on 28 February 1998, involved reducing the banks' reserve requirements to allow them to buy state bonds. (*FEER*, 12 March 1998, p. 20; *IHT*, 2 March 1998, p. 11, and 6 March 1998, p. 6.) On 17 August 1998 it was announced that the government had approved a special bond issue worth 270 billion yuan ($32.6 billion) to recapitalize the state banks. The finance ministry would issue the thirty-year bonds, which would carry an annual interest rate of 7.2 per cent. On the same day the central bank ordered all commercial banks to divest themselves of their non-bank subsidiaries (e.g. trust, securities and property firms) by the end of 1998, the process having already begun in the big four state banks (*IHT*, 18 August 1998, p. 9; *FT*, 18 August 1998, p. 4).

Non-performing loans are classified by more lenient standards than the international norm (Lardy 1998: 79). But even the official figures show that non-performing loans increased from 20 per cent at the end of 1994 to 25 per cent at the end of 1997 (p. 83). It is planned to inject 270 billion renminbi into the four largest state-owned banks (p. 86). The reforms also include a reorganization of the local branches of the People's Bank along regional lines to reduce political interference in lending decisions (p. 86). The central bank will also allow greater flexibility in setting interest rates. The long-standing practice by which the central bank set uniform lending rates for each type of loan precluded banks from pricing loans according to risk. The banks will henceforth be given increased authority to set lending rates and will be encouraged to take risk into account for individual borrowers. The system of mandatory lending quotas, which has placed a ceiling on total lending and mandated loans to specific projects, is also being phased out. The precise implications of this reform remain to be seen, however, since a system of 'guidance quotas for lending' will remain in place (p. 87).

On 18 November 1998 the People's Bank of China's Shanghai branch became the first regional office of the newly restructured central bank. The central bank is replacing its provincial offices with some nine branches covering large regions of China, along the lines of the US Federal Reserve. 'The reorganization of the central bank is intended to reassert the authority of the head office in Beijing and eliminate some of the political meddling in the provinces that has made it harder for officials to expose financial corruption and incompetence' (*FT*, 17 November 1998, p. 4). The central bank has set up a regional structure along the lines of the US Federal Reserve Board in an effort to limit the influence of local governments, especially their actions which undermine central monetary policy. Instead of having branches in every province and major city, the People's Bank of China will have nine main branches – in Tianjin, Shenyang, Shanghai, Nanjing, Jinan, Wuhan, Guangzhou, Chengdu and Xian (*IHT*, 18 November 1998, p. 19).

On 6 October 1998 the central bank ordered the closure of the Guangdong International Trust and Investment Corporation (GITIC) after it was unable to repay loans. Since then other non-bank financial institutions have been closed. (The central government has made it clear that it will not act as automatic guarantor for all the debts of such companies, especially those foreign loans unauthorized by the central authorities. (The idea is to help combat moral hazard.)

On 27 October GITIC defaulted on an international bond payment, 'the first time such a Chinese company had done so since the communist revolution in 1949' (*IHT*, 28 October 1998, p. 13). Since GITIC was shut down two more international trusts from Guangdong province have failed to meet interest payments (p. 23). Some say that the central government intends to reduce the number of such companies from about 240 to forty.

> China's trust and investment companies, largely creatures of the 1980s, were set up to provide financing in a time before this country had stock and bond markets, which are still small but emerging as more efficient financiers ... A typical Chinese trust and investment company essentially operates as the investment arm of a local government ... [Such a company would] use political connections for easy access to debt and sink much of its borrowing into real estate ventures and derivatives ... Lending from Japanese and South Korean banks dried up this year.
>
> (*IHT*, 26 October 1998, p. 15)

> The ITICs represent a fraction of China's financial system ... at the end of 1996 ... roughly 3 per cent of the banking sector's assets ... Many investment trusts are now struggling with a mismatch of maturities, having taken on short-term borrowings to finance long-term infrastructure and industry projects. And in many cases access to foreign capital has meant ITICs have built up large positions in the derivative projects.
>
> (*FT*, 29 October 1998, p. 19)

On 29 October 1998 the central bank ordered the closure of twelve credit co-operatives in Guangxi province. Earlier in the year about thirty local credit co-operatives on Hainan Island had been taken over by the Hainan Development Bank, which itself was then shut down (*FT*, 30 October 1998, p. 7). (The Hainan Development Bank was closed on 21 June 1998.)

On 4 November 1998 the governor of the central bank said that only a 'tiny few' of the 240 ITICs would be closed down and indicated for the first time that some could be bailed out: 'Troubled ITICs will be merged, reorganized and some may have capital injected ... After the restructuring there will be a need for the ITICs and they must be allowed to develop.' Foreign bankers have lent GITIC more than $2 billion. Beijing has said that creditors should seek repayment from the Guangdong provincial government and indicated that by no means all of the debt is likely to be repaid (*FT*, 5 November 1998, p. 6).

> The governor of the central bank said this week that China intended to make good on the debt obligations of the investment companies ... But he made a distinction between loans that had been properly registered with the central government and other kinds of lending, suggesting that the properly registered loans would be paid first.
>
> (*IHT*, 6 November 1998, p. 21)

Of the 243 TICs (trust and investment corporations), about 100 are ITICs (international trust and investment corporations) (*Transition*, 1998, vol. 9, no. 5, p. 18).

> Foreign banks are angry about China's announcement that Guangdong International Trust and Investment Corp. will file for bankruptcy and that creditors will have to go through the Chinese legal system to claim what they are owed.

More than 100 foreign creditors of ... GITIC were told Sunday [10 January 1999] that the company would file for bankruptcy. The move will put the foreign banks at the end of a long line of creditors seeking repayment of GITIC's debts ... Creditors were particularly shocked that Beijing was unwilling to repay loans that had been registered with the state administration of foreign exchange. Historically the government has guaranteed such loans with state funds.

(*IHT*, 12 January 1999, p. 13)

'GITIC ... was the first bankruptcy of a financial institution in communist China's nearly fifty-year history' (*IHT*, 15 January 1999, p. 17).

In December 1998 the State Development Bank took over the China Investment Bank (*FT*, 17 March 1999, p. 4).

1999.

If China's state-owned commercial banks seem perilously burdened by bad debts, consider the even more precarious position of the country's rural financial sector. In the villages the only formal banking institutions are what are known as rural credit co-operatives. These enjoy the distinction in China of having been officially declared insolvent. The rural credit co-operatives are ill-named. They are often reluctant to provide credit and they are not run as co-operatives, for their customers have no say in their operations and do not share any profits. Until 1996 they were offshoots of the big Agricultural Bank of China. Since then they have been supervised by the central bank, the People's Bank of China, though they are pretty much run by county governments ... [In 2001] they accounted for 12 per cent of deposits and 11 per cent of loans ... [There is] one in almost every township, as the larger villages or small rural towns are known ... [Problems include] unclear ownership rights, government interference, bad management and a lack of competition ... [In 1999] the government decided to close down another class of financial institution in the countryside, the ill-regulated rural credit foundations. These had sprung up across China in the 1990s, attracting deposits by illegally setting higher interest rates than the co-operatives and banks. But reckless lending to rural enterprises ruined them, prompting the government to step in to prevent a wider financial crisis. The co-operatives inherited the bad-loan portfolios of the credit institutions ... Over the past two years the government has experimented with reforms in the coastal province of Jiangsu. With the help of interest-free loans from the central bank, the co-operatives have been turned into commercial banks complete with shareholders.

(*The Economist*, 20 July 2002, pp. 67–8)

12 January 1999.

The debt problem extends beyond companies that are controlled by the various provincial governments, reaching the so-called red chips, Hong Kong incorporated companies with some mainland Chinese backing. A report ... published in November [1998] said that red chip debt could total almost $13 billion. In a statement Tuesday [12 January] to the stock exchange here [Hong Kong] a subsidiary of ... Guangdong Enterprises said its parent was having trouble finding funds to pay back $1.2 billion in debt due by April [1999].

(IHT, 13 January 1999, p. 1)

('Red chip' companies are Hong Kong-based companies controlled by a powerful mainland Chinese firm or ministry: *FEER,* 28 October 1999, p. 64.)

13 January 1999.

Stocks of major Chinese-controlled companies trading here [Hong Kong] plunged Wednesday [13 January] amid fears that their lines of credit were drying up as a second state controlled company stunned investors by announcing that it was effectively insolvent, with debts far larger than expected ... Investors sold stock after a subsidiary of Guangdong Enterprises (Holding) Ltd announced that its parent company had debts of $2.94 billion and could not make principal payments to creditors due by April. More surprisingly, the subsidiary company, Guangnan (Holdings) Ltd ... said it had debts of $391 million, at least 50 per cent more than most analysts had expected.

(IHT, 14 January 1999, p. 1)

A report late last year ... said the parents of many red chip companies had 'borrowed aggressively' over the past two years and put most of the proceeds into the stock and property markets ... On Tuesday [12 January] the Guangdong provincial government said it would pump money into Guangdong enterprises to help the company pay its debts.

(p. 4)

14 January 1999.

A third company backed by a provincial government joined the list of the insolvent ... A third Guangdong company, Nam Yue (Group), joined the list of troubled state-backed companies Thursday [14 January]. Nam Yue, a so-called window company in the Portuguese enclave of Macao, was declared insolvent.

(IHT, 15 January 1999, p. 17)

18 January 1999. Guangdong Overseas Trust and Investment Corp. becomes the latest fundraiser in the province of Guangdong to seek talks with foreign bankers after defaulting on a $50 million syndicated loan, which matured in December 1998. The investment agency has offered to continue making interest payments while seeking to defer principal repayment (*FT,* 19 January 1999, p. 8).

19 January 1999. Guangdong Overseas Chinese Trust and Investment Corp. says it is talking with foreign banks after failing to repay a $50 million syndicated loan, but denied it is in default (*IHT,* 20 January 1999, p. 17).

20 January 1999.

The governor of the central bank outlined measures Wednesday [20 January] to clean up the balance sheets of four debt-ridden state-owned commercial banks by transferring their doubtful loans to separate companies. China plans to establish four asset-management companies ... The plan expands on an original plan to start a pilot debt-management plan with one of the four banks, China Construction Bank. The three other banks involved in the plan are Industrial and Commercial Bank of China, Bank of China and Agriculture Bank of China ... [The governor] has estimated that about 20 per cent of China's bank loans ... are non-performing and that 6 per cent to 7 per cent are unrecoverable. Foreign estimates have put non-performing loans [at a higher level].

(*IHT*, 21 January 1999, p. 16)

[Debt for the four banks] is estimated to amount to 25 per cent to 40 per cent of the banks' outstanding loans ... The Chinese asset management corporations apparently have little of the freedom enjoyed by the [US] Resolution Trust Corp. to sell off the bad loans.

(*IHT*, 16 January 1999, pp. 9, 13)

The asset management companies will take on those problem loans that fall into a specific category of non-performing assets, namely loans overdue by two years or more. Bad debts, for which the banks should have already made provisions, and loans that have just fallen overdue will be handled by the banks themselves.

(*FT*, 28 January 1999, p. 29)

21 January 1999. 'Fujian Enterprises told foreign creditors it would service the interest but be unable to meet the principal repayments on a syndicated loan falling due yesterday [21 January]... Fujian Enterprises ...[is] an investment company owned by the government of Fujian province' (*FT*, 22 January 1999, p. 3).

27 January 1999.

Dai Xianglong [governor of the central bank] threw a lifeline to 239 international trust and investment companies (ITICs) ... The governor said that the ITICs could change renminbi into foreign currency – presumably by tapping the central bank reserves – in order to honour their foreign debts. He hoped foreign creditors would help restructure ailing ITICs and said even the Guangdong ITIC, which was closed last year, could yet be restructured with the help of foreign creditors.

(*FT*, 28 January 1999, p. 30)

'The ITICs would be allowed to exchange Chinese currency to meet their registered foreign debt payments' (p. 29). 'ITICs would be able to change renminbi ... into foreign currency to help them repay those foreign debts in their portfolios which are "registered and legitimate"' (p. 6).

The central bank said it was easing a restriction on foreign banks by allowing them to operate in all major cities of China. The central bank did not say when the change would take place nor to what extent foreign banks would be allowed to do business in yuan.

(*IHT*, 28 January 1999, p. 14)

2 February 1999.

Plans are revealed for overhauling the 240 trust and investment corporations. Five more of the troubled financial institutions are to be closed by the end of February. Last week the central bank governor said the bank had altered its original plans to shrink the 239 remaining trust companies to only thirty or forty. Instead, there will be fewer mergers but tighter supervision of the industry.

(*IHT*, 3 February 1999, p. 17)

20 April 1999.

China yesterday [20 April] announced the injection of 10 billion renminbi ($1.2 billion) into the first asset management company to handle the bad debts of a state bank ... China Construction Bank, one of the big four state commercial banks, yesterday offered details of how it planned to improve its balance sheet by repackaging and selling on bad debts through an asset management company – a move that is likely to be the model for the other four state banks. China Cinda Asset Management will have registered capital of 10 billion renminbi provided by the finance ministry ... The debt will be sold both to foreign and Chinese investors. Cinda will be able to ask the central bank for permission to relend, issue bonds, underwrite shares or bonds and securitise debt. Cinda will be exempt from all business taxes.

(*FT*, 21 April 1999, p. 5)

The finance ministry will inject 10 billion renminbi ($1.2 billion) in registered capital and will also guarantee a bond issue. Cinda will then buy roughly 200 billion renminbi in non-performing loans from the China Construction Bank at face value and try and recover as much as possible by selling on the loans at a discount or as securitized instruments to foreign and Chinese investors. The government will step in to write off the debts that Cinda proves unable to recover.

(*FT*, 5 May 1999, p. 34)

China's first asset management will buy most of the non-performing loans at China Construction Bank ... The company has the power to restructure state-owned enterprises – including forcing layoffs – to make them more efficient and better able to repay their bad debts ... The central government has given Cinda the power not only to force restructuring but to convert unpaid debt into equity ... Cinda will raise the capital needed to purchase the bad loans by issuing five- and ten-year bonds backed either wholly or in part by the ministry of finance. China Construction Bank will purchase all the bonds. Cinda will then increase pressure on debtor companies to repay their loans. It will be able to implement restructuring plans, including debt-equity conversions, among debtors and liquidate those that cannot cough up the money ... The central bank governor, Dai Xianglong, recently raised his estimate on non-performing loans at the big four state banks to 20 per cent of total loans. Most analysts, however, believe the actual figure is significantly higher ... Who will foot the bill [for debt write-offs is unclear].

(*FEER*, 6 May 1999, pp. 44–5)

The People's Bank of China ... says a fifth of loans made by the four major banks – China Construction Bank, Industrial and Commercial Bank of China, Bank of China and Agricultural Bank of China – are non-performing ... Foreign economists say the true figure may be as high as 40 per cent ... a third of China's GDP ... While it is clear that central government officials are serious about halting local government interference in bank decisions, Beijing still wants to bend the banks to its will. Since the economy began slowing last year [1998] it has pressed the banks to step up lending ... The central bank dictates how much banks can charge large companies for loans, no matter what the risk factor ... Banks can charge small and medium-sized companies up to 30 per cent more ... China Construction Bank has off-loaded most of its bad loans to the newly created asset management company [Cinda Asset Management] that will recover or sell them ... Cinda is acquiring the bad loans at face value, using ministry of finance-backed bonds, while it will be considered fortunate to recover as much as a third. It is empowered to restructure debtor companies, bring in outside management and sell them off whole or in part ... On the other hand, much of the residual sum may have to be written off because only loans that had some hope of recovery were allowed to be transferred to Cinda.

(*FEER*, 9 September 1999, pp. 75–6)

(On 12 September 1999 it was announced that Cinda would also take over some non-performing debt from the China Development Bank, the government's agency for financing long-term infrastructure: *FT*, 13 September 1999, p. 6.)

April 1999. 'Last month [April 1999] ... foreign creditors were told that they would recover less than 16 per cent of their loans to the now-bankrupt Guangdong International Trade and Investment Corporation' (*IHT*, 13 May 1999, p. 12). (Some foreign creditors of GITIC can expect a higher return on their claims. GITIC defaulted on $4.7 billion in loans in 1998. Recoverable assets are now estimated at $927 million instead of $785 million: *FEER*, 4 November 1999, p. 79.)

3 June 1999. The central bank says it will stop accepting yuan transfers from banks overseas and will close its yuan accounts of foreign banks starting 10 June 1999 in a move that will now require all conversions of yuan to take place in China. Some foreign banks have been allowed to convert the yuan at overseas branches; this will now cease (*IHT*, 4 June 1999, p. 18).

'The Bank of China announced that it would stop accepting renminbi transfers from banks overseas and that it would cancel all renminbi accounts in Hong Kong and foreign countries in an effort to retain better control over monetary policy' (*FEER*, 17 June 1999, p. 62).

It was announced in July 1999 that 1.2 trillion renminbi (equivalent to some $145 billion) owed to these banks by state-owned enterprises would be converted into equity; such an amount was equivalent to about 14 per cent of GDP. A sizeable proportion of these loans, perhaps around 30 per cent, was deemed recoverable given time and an upturn in consumer spending.

(United Nations, *Economic and Social Survey of Asia and the Pacific 2000*, p. 114)

August 1999.

The Chinese government agreed in August [1999] to allow foreign banks to raise large loans on fixed maturity terms direct from Chinese banks. Their only sources of Chinese money before was very short-term borrowing in the inter-bank market ... The rules on funding lending business were relaxed last summer ... Foreign banks see lucrative opportunities in renminbi lending in China but are not allowed to take deposits from the public and may only lend Chinese currency to corporate ventures financed with foreign investment.

(*FT*, 19 October 1999, p. 1)

Events after 17 October 1999.

Beijing has launched an asset management company to take over bad loans held by the Bank of China ... China Orient Asset Management is the second such company to be set up ... [It] would be allowed to sell stock and creditor rights as part of its efforts to raise funds to buy Bank of China's non-performing loans ... Debt-for-equity swaps are expected to be the main method for disposing of the bad loans ... The city of Shanghai has also launched its first state-owned asset management company.

(*FT*, 18 October 1999, p. 12)

China's central bank governor ... [says] that after the completion of a current endeavour to shift many of the state banking system's bad loans into asset management companies (AMCs) there will be no more handouts ... The state-owned industrial sector uses up two-thirds of the country's credit resources to produce just one-third of its output ... Four asset management companies were set up last year [1999] to assume the bad debts of many state enterprises in return for equity stakes in those companies ... [But] the AMCs have not yet been invested with the power to dismiss poor managers ... [The AMCs can only] recommend that management teams are replaced ... The powers of AMCs to dismiss staff are to be similarly circumscribed ... There may be some chance, however, for the AMCs to get their way not by firing the old socialist-era factory bosses but by outnumbering them – by creating boards of directors in their client corporations and staffing then with AMC appointees.

(*FT*, 20 April 2000, p. 10)

Much is being done to recapitalize the big four [state banks] ... Four asset management companies are due to take about renminbi 1,200 billion in problem loans – believed to be more than half the total – off the big four. However, the programme has run into implementation problems.

(*FT*, 1 June 2000, p. 22)

Beijing set up four asset management companies, or AMCs, last year [1999] to implement debt-equity swaps, by replacing state banks' bad debts with inter-est-yielding AMC bonds on bank balance sheets. The plan is that the AMCs will sell off these assets to recoup their costs. (Note that this process has been painfully slow to date.) Beijing has pledged to make up the losses incurred in the asset sales. Hence the fiscal burden of cleaning up the banks inversely contingent upon the prices of the asset sales. Assuming these bad debts, estimated at $218 billion, would be sold at a 70 per cent discount, Beijing would have to spend $153 billion to help recapitalize the banks.

(*FEER*, 23 March 2000, p. 34)

About 20 per cent of outstanding bank loans are officially considered to be non-performing, most of them owed by large state enterprises. (By Chinese standards a non-performing loan is one that has not been serviced for a year or more, whereas the international standard is six months.) Cinda was set up in April 1999 and the other three asset management corporations (AMCs) were set up in the final quarter of 1999: Great Wall (Agricultural Bank of China); Oriental (Bank of China); and Huarong (Industrial and Commercial Bank of China). Asset management corporations obtain their initial capital from the finance ministry but they are expected to raise additional capital by selling bonds and, in time, by listing on stock exchanges. Their scheduled ten-year lifespan can be extended by the central bank.

The centrepiece of the financial restructuring of state enterprises and the four main commercial banks is the government's plan for a massive debt–equity swap. The debt to be swapped is about half of the outstanding loans of the banking sector. Broadly there will be two linked transactions: the swap of selected enterprise debt for equity and the purchase of the swapped debt from banks. The swap of debt for equity is intended to reduce the leverage (debt-to-equity ratio) of state enterprises ... provide them with additional funds for investment in technological upgrading and pave the way for market listing. The purchase of the debt is equivalent to writing off the banks' non-performing debt and providing them with additional capital ... The swaps are confined to debts contracted before 1996 to prevent banks and enterprises from engaging in reckless lending and borrowing in response to the programme ... The swap will consist of two transactions. The asset management corporations will purchase the designated debt of the commercial banks with which they are paired at face value ... They will also acquire an equivalent equity stake in debtor enterprises, which may be sold to a third party or bought back by the enterprise ... It is accepted that the proceeds from the sale of the equity will fall short of the outlays on the purchase of the debt ... The finance ministry is committed to covering the deficit of asset management corporations.

(*Transition*, 2000, vol. 11, no. 1, pp. 15–16)

At a conference on financial reform in Beijing in mid-May [2000], Chinese officials admitted for the first time that the loan-recovery companies will eschew hard-nosed tactics in order to give state enterprises more time to work out their problem debts ... But taking the soft approach means the recovery rate on loans will be low – perhaps as low as 10 per cent. It also means that there is a greater risk that more bad debts will be created ... The AMCs are officially shooting for recovery rates of 30 per cent ... By the end of last year [1999] the four newly created asset-management companies (AMCs) had bought 350 billion renminbi in bad loans at face value from the four state banks in return for ten-year bonds carrying a minimum coupon rate of 2.25 per cent. Central bank officials say that the total bad debts taken over by the AMCs should reach 1.2 trillion renminbi by the end of this year [2000], representing about half the banks' bad debt. Although Beijing declines to say explicitly that it will back the AMC bonds, thereby hoping to press the asset managers to recover as much as possible, it will have no choice but to do so to ensure the state banks get repaid, analysts say ... The initial plan was to act like tough loan-recovery agencies, forcing repayment through threats of bankruptcy or converting loans into equity stakes that could be used to implement management changes at state enterprises.

(Bruce Gilley, *FEER*, 15 June 2000, pp. 58–60)

Debt-for-equity swaps by the four loan-recovery agencies that Beijing set up last year [2000] have so far been limited to about 500 companies nationwide. Beijing hopes those equity stakes can be kept in state hands, either through future buy-backs or by sales to other state firms. But a more likely outcome is massive downsizing of stricken firms and disposal of the most valuable bits to private investors ... The Zhengzhou Coal Industry Group, a state-owned energy and manufacturing concern, is at the cutting edge of efforts to resolve China's bad debt problems. About 970 million renminbi ($117 million) of the troubled firm's non-performing loans from three state banks have been handed over to ... [Cinda Asset Management] ... making this one of China's biggest debt workouts. Under a plan that awaits approval from Beijing ... Cinda Asset Management will swap the bad debts for a majority [51 per cent] stake in a new company [Zhengxin Energy] to be mined out of the best bits of Zhengzhou Coal ... Under the plan ... Zhengxin Energy will be given a new executive team and board of directors ... All the retired workers, schools, hospitals and other parts of the 'little society' that drag down so many state enterprises will be taken over by the provincial government ... An official 'red letter document' ... from the provincial government contains a promise to relieve the new company of its welfare burden ... What is left of the group will have eight years to turn its fortunes around and buy the stake back. If it does not the shareholding will be sold to private investors, including foreigners ... Left behind will be a loss-making, bloated collection of run-down assets ... That makes it unlikely that the company will recover the Cinda stake in Zhengxin after the eight years elapse. Indeed, company officials say a more likely outcome is that Zhengzhou Coal will be forced to sell down its own stake in Zhengxin as it struggles to pay wages and close down money-losing subsidiaries ... While the overall plan has Beijing's blessing, final approval is being held up by a tussle between Zhengzhou's creditor banks and the central government main overseer of state assets, the state economic and trade commission ... The creditor banks' resistance stems from the fact that they have been given a fixed quota for the amount of bad loans that they can hand over to the salvage companies. They would naturally prefer to part with only their most hopeless cases. Since loans to Zhengzhou Coal still pay some interest and represent claims on an asset-rich company, the banks want to hold on to as many of them as possible. On average, Zhengzhou's long-term loans carry an interest rate of 8 per cent ... That contrasts with the niggardly rate of 2.25 per cent that banks earn from ten-year state-backed bonds they are given by Cinda.

(Bruce Gilley, *FEER*, 13 July 2000, pp. 62–3)

The original idea behind the debt–equity swaps was to assert the banks' claims over the recalcitrant borrowers. But it has not quite worked out that way, as the bankers have recently discovered. 'These swaps are only meaningful if there is real pressure for returns on the equity,' says ... [the] executive associate director at Xinda [Cinda] Asset Management Co., the vehicle for China Construction Bank. 'Otherwise it is just debt forgiveness in disguise' ... Since most of the companies on the list got there by virtue of their political clout in the first place, it is unlikely the banks can put enough pressure on many of them to improve their performance sufficiently to generate dividends. 'The purpose of the swaps is to save the state enterprises,' adds a senior banker at China Construction Bank. 'It was never to save the banks. After all, if these companies cannot pay interest on the loans, how can anyone expect them to pay dividends on their equity?' ... When the scheme was first announced many thought that the banks and the more progressive managers at the chosen state-owned enterprises would form a powerful alliance against the local authorities that are usually in charge of SOEs and would introduce reforms that would revitalize the troubled debtors. But bankers say there have been few such cases, even when they have become majority shareholders – especially if reforms involve such politically sensitive matters as lay-offs. It isn't even the banks themselves that decide which of their borrowers qualify for such swaps; instead, the state economic and trade commission presented banks with a list of 600 target companies ... Outside China, when asset management companies, or AMCs, have been created to take bad loans off overburdened banks, they have taken them at less than face value. But in China, where the chance of recovery is no better than 30 per cent, according to ... [one estimate], 1.3 trillion renminbi in bad loans has been transferred at official book value rather than real-world market value. 'The banks' capital would have been wiped out completely if the bad loans were purchased at market value,' said a paper that a China Construction Bank official presented at a recent conference in Korea ... The banks get ten-year bonds from the AMCs in exchange for what is effectively toxic waste in their loan portfolios. These bonds are supposed to be guaranteed by the ministry of finance and, of course, the banks are supposed to receive interest on them. But so far neither the AMCs nor the ministry have paid any money to the banks ... There have been a few signs of more dramatic change in cases where the banks have been able to go to court to press their claims ... Politics continues to undermine change; the independence of banks is still subject to political contingencies. Healthy banks are only a secondary priority – counters to be sacrificed whenever growth falters – and once more they are being asked to lend to policy projects at Beijing's behest.

(Henny Sender, *FEER*, 28 September 2000, pp. 62–6)

China is set to launch an unprecedented scheme to sell off billions of US dollars' worth of the bad loans of state-owned enterprises later this year ...

[via asset management companies] . . . Foreign investors would be able in most cases to take a controlling stake in enterprises by converting debt into equity.

(*FT*, 10 May 2001, p. 13)

The Bank of China, the nation's most prestigious state bank, announces a level of bad debt that is much higher than previously acknowledged . . . The bank's non-performing loans amount to 28 per cent, compared with previous estimates that have ranged between 11 per cent and 15 per cent . . . Some put the total amount of non-performing loans [in the big four state banks as a whole] at 40 per cent, compared with the official estimate of 25 per cent . . . Last year [2000] the banks transferred 400 billion renminbi in bad loans to asset management companies . . . The selling of assets through the asset management companies is expected to be an uphill struggle, meaning the finance ministry will eventually have to foot most of the bill . . . The People's Bank of China has dropped a previous three-year timetable for the liberalization of interest rates.

(*FT*, 14 May 2001, p. 10)

('[The central bank governor, Dai Xianglong, said on 17 January 2001 that] the percentage of the big four banks' loans that had to be written off was only 3 per cent, which foreign analysts say seriously underestimates China's bad debt problem': *FT*, 18 January 2001, p. 10.)

[It was announced] this week that nearly 30 per cent of the Bank of China's loan book is non-performing . . . AMCs [asset management companies] have all but given up on . . . forced liquidation . . . It would require a firesale of much of the state sector . . . By default the AMCs have therefore been swapping debt for equity in the SOEs. As owners, overstretched and undertrained, they are no better than the incumbent managers at improving corporate governance and profitability. The AMCs now talk about auctioning bad loans to foreign investors . . . The AMCs 'bought' the bad loans by issuing bonds to the banks; interest now has to be paid on these. The cash for this, less what can be raised at auction, can only, eventually, come from the taxpayer . . . As a sop to the big four banks, plans to liberalize interest rates within three years have been delayed.

(*The Economist*, Saturday 19 May 2001, pp. 97–8)

Central bank chief Dai Xianglong said [in November 2001] banks must do more to reduce bad loans, and estimated that non-performing loans at state banks accounted for 26.6 per cent of their total lending at the end of September. Some foreign analysts put non-performing loans at about half the lending of the 'Big Four' state banks – China Construction Bank, Bank of China, Industrial and Commercial Bank of China and Agricultural Bank of China.

(*FEER*, 15 November 2001, pp. 30–1)

'China's central bank governor said non-performing loans at the four major commercial state-owned banks amounted to more than a quarter of total lending. The bad loans totalled 1.8 trillion yuan ($217 billion)' (*IHT*, 2 November 2001, p. 15).

'China launched its first international tender for $1.8 billion in the distressed assets of state-owned enterprises yesterday [19 November] ... [a] mix of bad loans, property, equipment and collateral being sold by Huarong Asset Management Company' (*FT*, 20 November 2001, p. 14).

'China will sell about $3 billion in overdue loans and assets, including property, used as collateral for foreign credit to the Industrial and Commercial Bank of China' (*IHT*, 20 November 2001, p. 21).

'China Huarong Asset Management Company held the first public auction of non-performing bank debt ... Foreign and domestic investors made three separate bids for a pool of $1.9 billion in distressed assets' (*FEER*, 29 November 2001, p. 34).

'China Huarong Asset Management Company sold non-performing loans to a consortium of investment banks for 10.8 billion yuan ($1.3 billion). The price was 79 per cent below the value of the outstanding principal on the loans' (*IHT*, 30 November 2001, p. 13).

A consortium led by Morgan Stanley of the United States will try to recover what it can from a parcel of non-performing loans, or NPLs, to 254 debt-ridden enterprises with a face value of $1.3 billion ... The consortium claims it will, if necessary, seize assets or collateral and run the businesses ... The Morgan Stanley consortium on 30 November agreed to pay China Huarong Asset Management about $17 million in cash for the package of NPLs owed by enterprises around the country ... In addition to the cash payment, which amounts to about 9 per cent of the face value of the loans, Huarong will take a minority stake in a joint venture with Morgan Stanley and its consortium partners ... to split the proceeds of recovery ... Huarong's bad loans came from the Industrial and Commercial Bank of China ... Only $1.3 billion of the $1.8 billion Huarong put up for auction was taken up ... Even official figures show that NPLs continue to accumulate. This threatens to undo efforts to restore the balance sheets of the big four [banks] before they begin.

(*FEER*, 20 December 2001, pp. 30–2)

A consortium led by Morgan Stanley has bought the first batch of distressed assets in Chinese state-owned enterprise ever auctioned to foreign investors, paying 'about 9 per cent' of the book value of the $1.31 billion sold, officials said ... Four of the five blocks were sold but the fifth, which has a book value of $590 million, remains on the books. About 60 per cent of the assets underlying the non-performing loans are in state-owned factories, with the remainder in commercial property, industrial parks, hotels, residential precincts and a free trade zone ... There is a total of 1,400 billion renminbi in non-performing loans slated for sale by four Chinese Asset Management Companies.

(*FT*, 30 November 2001, p. 31)

'China's four Asset Management Companies ... sold about $15 billion of bad loans in 2001, about 9 per cent of their holdings' (*IHT*, 15 January 2001, p. 13).

China announced plans yesterday [16 January] to allow its big four state banks ... which together control more than 70 per cent of Chinese banking assets ...

to issue long-term bonds and seek stock market listings ... In 2000 the banks transferred renminbi 1,400 billion in bad loans to four Asset Management Companies.

(FT, 17 January 2002, p. 10)

The Asset Management Companies [AMCs] buy the non-performing loans at face value from the banks and swap them for equity shares in the enterprises concerned. They also sell off the loans for whatever they can get for them – on average around 20 per cent of their face value. But this ratio will plunge in future, because the best assets in the AMCs' portfolios have been sold first. The AMCs are having to borrow money to pay interest on the bonds they issued to the banks in return for the non-performing loans. When the bonds mature the government will have to bail out the AMCs. There is little evidence that the AMCs have helped to improve the governance of enterprises in which they have acquired a stake. Nor have they encouraged the banks to become any more responsible in their lending. The banks know that if their non-performing loans build up again the government will probably transfer them to the AMCs.

(The Economist, Survey, 15 June 2002, pp. 9–10)

For the first time China's central bank chief, Dai Xianglong, admitted in public that bad loans at [the four] big state banks were higher than official estimates. He said they could be up to 30 per cent of the banks' total lending if international accounting standards were used. Some Western estimates put the level of bad loans at 50 per cent. Dai said in January [2002] the combined level of the 'big four' state banks stood at 25.37 per cent in 2001, down 3.81 percentage points from 2000.

(FEER, 11 April 2002, p. 25)

International ratings agency Standard and Poor's ... estimated the Chinese banking sector's average non-performing loan ratio at least 50 per cent ... China is unlikely to cut banks' non-performing loans to 15 per cent within five years as the [Chinese] central bank wants ... China has transferred $169 billion in non-performing loans to four state-run Asset Management Companies.

(FEER, 23 May 2002, p. 26)

The central bank said that China's four Asset Management Companies reached a below-target accumulative cash recovery ratio of 21.6 per cent by the end of June [2002]. Debt-clearing firms had recovered 45.45 billion renminbi ($5.49 billion) in cash by the end of June after disposing of 210.36 billion renminbi in bad assets, the central bank said. The ministry of finance has set a minimum threshold of 30 per cent. Ernst & Young estimates that of China's non-performing loans – worth some $480 billion – about $170 billion has been transferred from the balance sheets of the big banks to AMCs.

(FEER, 15 August 2002, p. 25)

The four Asset Management Companies (AMCs) set up in 1999 to help China's biggest banks get rid of bad debt are themselves turning into a substantial financial risk, according to a report by the Bank of International Settlements (BIS) ... The AMCs are making only slow progress on recouping the non-performing loans that they took over from the Big Four state-run banks ... When the AMCs – Huarong, Orient, Cinda and Great Wall – were established they issued bonds and exchanged them for non-performing assets. The idea was to wash clean the books of the Big Four banks and allow the AMCs to sell the bad debts or try collecting the debts themselves. But the report ... warned that the four are not collecting fast enough and now pose a risk to the banking system. It noted that they had collected only 45.5 billion renminbi ($5.5 billion) in cash by the end of June [2002] and that they faced combined annual interest obligations of 30 billion renminbi on more than 1.1 trillion renminbi in bonds held by the Big Four and the central bank.

(*FEER*, 19 September 2002, p. 25)

Four government Asset Management Companies [were] set up in 1999 to help dispose of non-performing loans, which by some estimates amount to more than $450 billion, or just under half of China's annual economic output. The companies took over almost $170 billion in bad loans from four state banks in the past three years.

(*FEER*, 31 October 2002, p. 30)

In 1998 $33 billion was injected into [the big four state banks] to improve capital adequacy. A year later ... $169 billion in non-performing loans was stripped from their books and shifted to four government-owned Asset Management Companies, or AMCs. In return the AMCs issued bonds worth $141 billion to the banks, topped up with $28 billion in cash.

(*FEER*, 14 November 2002, p. 32)

The asset management corporations have sold just 9 per cent of their loan portfolios for cash over the past two years. Even though these tended to be the best loans in their portfolios, the corporations collected an average of just 21 cents for each dollar of face value. The result is that the asset management corporations have only raised cash equal to 1.9 per cent of the original values of all of the loans transferred to them by the banks ... While many more deals have been done for stock, it is not clear what value, if any, can be assigned to stock in companies that have not paid interest on their bank debts since at least the mid-1990s ... Banks were so sloppy in issuing many of the loans that collateral was not properly registered and titles of ownership were not checked. This misstep makes it almost impossible for buyers to take the borrowers to court to force settlements ... An even bigger problem is that ... state-owned factories ... have work forces and well-connected managers whom local officials are reluctant to antagonize [by closing the factories down].

(*IHT*, 28 October 2002, p. 14)

New estimates [have been made] by outside analysts of China's bad-debt problem. According to probably imprecise official figures, 25.4 per cent of all loans by Chinese banks are unlikely to be repaid in full. The true figure is more like half, maybe $500 billion to $600 billion, say independent experts.

Goldman Sachs thinks it would cost between 44 per cent and 68 per cent of China's GDP to clean up the mess.

(*The Economist*, 18 January 2003, p. 69)

China's debt-recovery firms retrieved 22.4 per cent of the face value of bad debts disposed of by the end of 2002 ... well below a government target of 30 per cent ... The four Asset Management Companies (Huarong, Cinda, Orient and Great Wall) ... had recovered 67.5 billion renminbi ($8.16 billion) in cash by year end and had disposed of 301.4 billion renminbi in bad assets.

(*FEER*, 6 February 2003, p. 23)

Unofficial estimates put bad loans at 40 per cent or more of the total ... Nicholas Lardy now puts bad loans in the system at around $500 billion or over 50 per cent of the total ... In 1999 four Asset Management Companies [were set up] ... Over the following couple of years the government transferred, at face value, roughly $170 billion of bad loans from the four big banks to their respective AMCs, equivalent to more than one-fifth of the banks' loan books ... Since then another $40 billion of bad loans appear to have been transferred to the AMCs ... Even after the relief provided by the first batch the banks' bad loan ration still stands at 22 per cent, according to ... the Bank for International Settlements ... In order to buy the $170 billion of banks' bad loans the AMCs needed to be capitalized. At the outset the finance ministry injected capital of $1.2 billion into each new AMC ... accounting for just 3 per cent of assets acquired. The People's Bank of China put in. .. up to $50 billion. But in return for that cash a big chunk of state banks' liabilities to the central bank appears to have been transferred to the AMCs: that is, state banks' debts were forgiven, while new ones owed by the AMCs were created. Lastly, the AMCs themselves issued $140 billion worth of ten-year interest-bearing bonds. These were given to the banks, along with $40 billion-odd in cash, in return for the bad loans ... So far only 25 per cent of loans, by face value, have been sold ... The central bank's claim on the AMCs is larger than its own capital base.

(*The Economist*, Survey, 8 February 2003, p. 12)

'[According to official figures] the "big four" state banks ... had cut non-performing loans to 24.1 per cent at the end of March [2003], down from 26.1 per cent at the end of 2002' (*FT*, 30 May 2003, p. 9).

'No interest is being paid [on non-performing loans]' (*IHT*, 19 June 2003, p. 17).

In another development the China Banking Regulatory Commission cleared the way for local banks to issue debt as a way to boost sagging capital adequacy and enhance their overall financial strength. The CBRC's guidelines formalized the process for allowing commercial banks to offer debt in terms of five years or more, with the subordinated issues expected to carry a higher interest rate than bonds, which are currently sold on the interbank market by China's major state-run banks.

(*FEER*, 18 December 2003, p. 28)

(More recent financial developments have already been discussed in the preceding section.)

The reform of state industrial enterprises

It was during the First Five Year Plan (1953–7) that the operation of the typical Chinese state industrial enterprise came nearest to its Soviet counterpart (including soft budget constraints). But even then the Chinese enterprise differed from the latter in significant ways. Thus manpower was allocated to the Chinese enterprise, virtually all profits were transferred to the state budget and management bonuses were much less important. The *danwei* (workplace) provided housing, health and social welfare services and the party took an increasingly important role in running the enterprise. Chaotic conditions prevailed during the Cultural Revolution.

Experimental reforms began in 1978 but general reforms in the industrial sector did not begin to be implemented until October 1984. Ma (1998: 380) divides the period 1978 to 1997 into five successive programmes: (1) delegation of greater autonomy to enterprises (1978–80); (2) delivery of contract profit to the state (1981–2); (3) substitution of profit with taxes (1983–6); (4) negotiation of responsibility contracts with enterprises (1987–93); (5) corporatization of SOEs (1994–7).

> The Chinese government first allowed the SOEs to share part of the performance improvement by a profit-retention programme, which initially gave 12 per cent of the increased profits or reduced losses to the enterprises ... for paying bonuses to workers, supporting welfare programmes, and investing in capacity expansions. The managerial autonomy was gradually deepened through the replacement of the profit-retention system by a contract responsibility system in which the SOEs agreed to deliver predetermined amounts of revenue to the state and retained the residual, and later the replacement of the contract responsibility system by the modern corporate system in which the state was entitled to the dividend on its shares in the SOE assets.
>
> (Lin *et al.* 1998: 424)

In the 'contract responsibility system' contracts typically ran for three to five years and stipulated the minimum amount of output, profit and tax to go to the state. There is considerable debate about the effects of these reforms on productivity.

With the aim of giving state enterprises a greater incentive to improve efficiency, the gradual, partial industrial reforms have taken such forms as the following:

1   allowing an increasing part of the capacity of an enterprise to respond to market forces (market prices being paid for inputs bought and output sold on the market; thus there is a 'dual' pricing system);
2   allowing an increasing part of profit to be retained by the enterprise for such purposes as decentralized investment;
3   permitting the manager more control at the expense of the party;
4   the state relaxing its controls on the allocation of manpower.

There was no labour market in the old system in the sense that state industrial enterprises were allocated labour. Workers typically had a job for life in the same enterprise (which, as stated, typically provided housing, health and social security benefits) and a guaranteed (and relatively equal) wage. This was the so-called 'iron rice bowl' (literally, everybody eats from the same pot).

The adverse effects on work incentives have led to reforms. A major reform in the area of manpower involves new entrants to the labour force being subject to *contracts* lasting only a number of years (after which workers can be dismissed). These contracts (a supply-side measure) have resulted in greater labour flexibility in the state sector, despite evidence that some contracts have been more or less automatically renewed.

The proportion of the labour force covered by contracts in all state enterprises was as follows (with the figures for industrial enterprises only in brackets): 1986, 5.6 per cent (7.8 per cent); 1987, 7.6 per cent (10.7 per cent); 1988, 10.1 per cent (14.1 per cent); 1989, 11.8 per cent (16.4 per cent); 1990, 13.3 per cent (18.4 per cent); 1991, 14.9 per cent (20.4 per cent); 1992, 18.9 per cent (20.4 per cent); 1993, 21.9 per cent (31.6 per cent); 1994, 26.2 per cent (38.0 per cent) (Wu 1997: 1244).

> Workers in Chinese state industries ... will find pay increasingly linked to performance under new wage and salary guidelines, the official *China Daily* reported Thursday [21 December 2000]. The ministry of labour and social security guidelines encourage state enterprises to offer incentives for better work ... Among the approved measures state employees can vary pay given to workers holding the same jobs and may offer commissions or stock in the company. To spur product development scientists and technical experts will also be able to trade research for company shares.
>
> (*IHT*, 22 December 2000, p. 19)

The state is reluctant to see unemployment and enterprise bankruptcies on too large a scale for fear of serious worker unrest. ('Unity and stability' is a slogan frequently emphasized.) Loss-making state enterprises are a continual source of worry (i.e. soft budget constraints still widely apply, especially in the case of larger enterprises). Policies like mergers with healthier state enterprises are preferred to bankruptcy, but many smaller enterprises have been closed down. Some estimates of the number of state enterprises making losses are as follows:

1   According to official figures, 9.6 per cent of state enterprises made a loss in 1985, 27.6 per cent in 1990, 60 per cent in 1993, 40 per cent in 1994, 44 per cent in 1995 and 50 per cent in 1996 (70 per cent in the case of large enterprises).

2   At the end of 1997, according to official figures, China had 16,874 large and medium-sized state enterprises, of which 6,599, i.e. 39.1 per cent, lost money. By the end of 1998 the number of money-losing state enterprises had been reduced to 5,121, through either bankruptcy or improved management. It was claimed that the plans announced in 1998 to eliminate the debt of large and medium-sized state enterprises by the end of 2000 were being kept to (*IHT*, 4 August 1999, p. 16). (There are 304,000–370,000 state enterprises, estimates

varying, of which 118,000 are industrial enterprises. Ma says that in 1996 there were 113,800 industrial SOEs: Ma 1998: 379.)

3   In the first half of 1999 about one-third of large and medium-sized state enterprises were making losses (*Transition*, 2000, vol. 11. no. 1, p. 15).

4   'The number of state firms has tumbled from over 300,000 to 150,000 in the past decade ... The OECD has analysed a new financial database covering around 160,000 firms ... [including] private sector industrial firms ... [Around] 35 per cent [of state firms] still make a loss' (*The Economist*, 17 September 2005, p. 91). 'Over 35 per cent of all state-owned companies are not earning a positive rate of return' (OECD 2005: website Chapter 2).

(See the section on unemployment in economic performance.)

The discarding of social functions

In the original system the enterprise was not just a production unit. It was also, as we have already seen, a social unit. The shift to a more Western-type system of social security, health and housing is a difficult, costly and painful one. Such reforms are needed for state enterprises to compete more effectively with private enterprises in a market economy.

Experiments to provide unemployment compensation.

> In 1987 retirement pensions and unemployment insurance for employees in state enterprises began to be established in some cities ... The regulation on unemployment insurance for state enterprise employees was enacted in early 1993, extending unemployment insurance across the country. But its coverage is still very limited.
>
> (Wu 1997: 1244–5)

> In China being a 'laid off' worker (one who is not working but is still attached to a factory) does not mean being 'unemployed'. This helps explain why the official unemployment rate is only 3.0 per cent to 3.6 per cent, while one estimate puts real unemployment at 15 per cent to 20 per cent. Once a person is registered officially as unemployed he becomes the responsibility of the local government, while the welfare of a 'laid off' worker is the responsibility of his enterprise. Unemployment insurance funds are insufficient to cover all workers. Since cities started these funds in 1986 about 9 million people have received benefits. While the schemes vary from city to city, generally employers contribute 1 per cent of each worker's annual salary. Workers in some cities make a personal contribution of 1 renminbi a month. Once registered as unemployed a worker can receive payments from a public fund for a certain period of time (e.g. up to 2 years or from 6 to 24 months), the amount depending on area and length of employment. Some areas stop payments after a worker has rejected three job offers. 'Laid off' workers are cared for by their enterprises although there are sometimes delays in the monthly payments and not all cities have funds to help loss-making enterprises.
>
> (Pamela Yatsko, *FEER*, 30 October 1997, pp. 53, 56)

An unemployment insurance scheme, set up in the mid-1980s, was strengthened in 1998 when the central government raised the contributions to the unemployment fund from 1 per cent to 3 per cent of the enterprise total payroll, requiring employees to contribute 1 per cent of their earnings. Some 15.8 million people were covered under this scheme as of 1999.

(United Nations, *Economic and Social Survey of Asia and the Pacific*, 2001, p. 113)

Those who are laid off are supposed to receive a small living allowance from their factories for two or three years; then local governments are supposed to provide benefits. In north-east China's Heilongjiang province ... the best local governments can offer is 28 renminbi a month. Some laid-off workers have not received anything for more than a year.

(*FEER*, 25 February 1999, p. 47)

In March 1998 the minister of labour mentioned an experiment that required enterprises to contribute 0.621 of wages to an unemployment insurance fund. There was a proposal to increase the percentage to 2 per cent, with employees providing a further 1 per cent of their wages (*IHT*, 9 March 1998, p. 6.)

Last year [1998] the government mandated the creation of thousands of 'reemployment centres' in every city and required local governments to share the costs of living stipends with laid-off workers' former companies. Workers enrolled at the centres are supposed to get training and job referrals, and in the meantime are supposed to receive monthly subsistence payments ... [which vary] depending on the location. But the coverage is spotty and many failing companies still pay little or nothing to their former employees ... Under current policy the reemployment centres are supposed to be phased out at the end of 2001.

(*IHT*, 19 November 1999, p. 13)

Experiments to shift the social security, housing and health burden away from enterprises and towards various levels of government and/or individuals

These reforms have generally been plagued with problems. They are costly. In July 2001 the central government forced 10 per cent of the proceeds of initial public offerings (IPOs) to be paid into a national social security fund (*FT*, 8 August 2001, p. 23.)

Pensions

In 1987 retirement pensions and unemployment insurance for employees in state enterprises began to be established in some cities. But by 1991 only 10 per cent to 25 per cent of contractual labour and 15 per cent to 25 per cent of permanent employees in state enterprises were covered by retirement pensions.

(Wu 1997: 1244–5)

Perhaps one-third of state enterprises renege on their pension obligations. Since 1997 most urban workers have had to pay part of their wages into a social security fund. But those contributions have mostly been spent on current retirees or, worse, the money has gone into cadres' pockets. The system is heading for bankruptcy.

(*The Economist*, 9 September 2000, p. 126)

'China's pension system – still mainly confined to large urban areas and only established in 1995 – is on the brink of collapse ... There is no pension provision for China's ... farmers' (*FEER*, 11 April 2002, p. 48).

In the late 1990s China began to switch from paying for pensions from current contributions to a funded system, in which the contributions made by workers today are set aside in funds to pay their own pensions when they retire tomorrow. The trouble is that converting from the old method to the new leaves a big hole in the accounts ... Under the 1997 pension reform plan state-owned enterprises would continue to pay existing pensioners, while also paying funds into the individual accounts of active workers. As a result, in some areas of China state companies now face having to pay out up to a quarter of their entire wage bill to meet pension obligations. That is unsustainable and many companies have opted to skim off money destined for current workers' pensions to meet their obligations to today's pensioners. Aware of the problem, the central government has stepped in to top up payments out of tax revenues ... But even with central government help the situation continues to deteriorate ... [In 2001] China took its first steps toward tackling the shortfall, introducing a new pilot scheme in the northern province of Liaoning. Among the key elements of the plan was a move to isolate individual pension accounts from other funds to prevent skimming, and to manage them at the provincial rather than the local level ... Now China is preparing to roll out the Liaoning model to the country as a whole ... Under the new plan pension funds will have to invest at least half their money in low-risk bank deposits and Treasury bonds. A further 10 per cent can be invested in corporate bonds and no more than 40 per cent in securities funds and stocks.

(*FEER*, 3 May 2002, pp. 42–3)

A belated pilot project in Liaoning province foundered after local government did not pay their share of contributions. The other problem with the fledgling pension system ... [is that] most of the money that did arrive appears to have been pilfered by managers and local officials.

(*FT*, 27 May 2002, p. 11)

Retirees used to receive [pension] payments from their work units ... The funds came from work units' coffers ... Workers who retired before the mid-1990s continue to be paid under this system ... China has tried to switch to a fully funded system, whereby employers and employees contribute to the funds that the same employees will draw on when they retire. In 1997 the State Council introduced ... [a] framework.

(Hirschler 2002: 9)

Since the nationwide reform of 1997 the public pension system, which only covers 14 per cent of the active population, has been a two-part system. The first part provides a basic flat rate pension while the second part provides a pension proportional to contributions.

(OECD 2005: website Chapter 4)

'About 173 million people, or less than a quarter of China's workers, are covered by basic pensions. The government said it aimed to increase the insured population to 220 million by 2010' (www.iht.com, 22 December 2005).

Health

'Health care reform, which Zhu Rongyi promised in March 1998, has scarcely been mentioned since' (*The Economist*, 18 July 1998, p. 76).

Since 1979 state subsidies to hospitals have shrunk to 15 per cent of their total revenues ... As increasing numbers of state enterprises go bankrupt their workers are losing access to medical benefits. A complicated government plan for medical insurance policies is only slowly being implemented. A World Bank report estimates that 90 per cent of the rural population and 50 per cent of the urban population have no medical coverage ... In recent years the government has quietly sanctioned alternative health care providers – not only small private clinics ... but private wards spun off by state hospitals and larger joint venture facilities between state hospitals and foreign health care firms.

(*FEER*, 24 February 2000, p. 42)

Five years ago the government started pilot health care programmes in fifty-nine cities to experiment with locally administered health insurance schemes funded by contributions from employers and deductions from employees' wages. The intent was to relieve state-owned enterprises of the burden of running their own hospitals and give a break to individuals, whose out-of-pocket medical payments had risen from 20 per cent of national medical spending to around 50 per cent. Local insurance schemes cover 50 million people and insurance provided through the work place covers another 50 million. Some 600 million workers, or 85 per cent of the labour force, have no insurance at all.

(Hirschler 2002: 8)

In the countryside 90 per cent of the population now has no health insurance. In the cities nearly 60 per cent are uncovered ... Cities currently enjoy 80 per cent of health resources despite having only 35 per cent of the population ... In the countryside they [the authorities] have designated more than 300 counties (about 10 per cent of the total) where a new 'co-operative medical system' is being tried, with a plan to make it countrywide by 2010. Funding is shared between voluntary participants, the local authorities and the central government. In addition, a new a new insurance scheme, paid for by central and local governments, has been introduced for the poorest of urban and rural families to cover the cost of serious illnesses. The scheme is due to be implemented next year [2005]. But both projects have serious drawbacks. Local governments are often unwilling to make the necessary contributions, especially in poorer areas. And individuals are often unwilling to pay for a service they feel they may not immediately need. For the past two decades local governments have gouged farmers for contributions to an almost non-existent health care system, with the money being used mostly to pay staff (many surplus to requirements or simply non-existent, with the money being used to line officials' pockets) rather than to pay for services. Consequently, there is reluctance to join any new scheme . . . By 2005 state enterprises are supposed to cease their support for all hospital facilities . . . Private businesses are supposed to pay for medical insurance, but most do not bother.

(*The Economist*, 21 August 2004, pp. 22–4)

'Between 1993 and 2003 the number of people with no medical insurance rose from 900 million to 1 billion – about 80 per cent of the population – according to official figures' (*IHT*, 12 October 2005, p. 11).

The state began cutting hospital subsidies in the early 1980s and by the mid-1990s it covered just 20 per cent of urban state hospitals' costs . . . About 130 million people in China have health insurance, leaving almost 90 per cent of the population without coverage . . . The majority of the uninsured – most of them rural residents – avoid going to hospitals for treatment because they cannot afford it.

(*IHT*, 30 March 2006, p. 17)

Housing

In the early 1990s state enterprises provided housing for 93 per cent of their employees and 51 per cent of all urban residents. In 1991 housing reform was introduced to encourage commercialization of the housing stock, but the response by residents has been slow.

(Wu 1997: 1244–5)

Whereas urban workers have typically been allocated housing by enterprises or municipalities at highly subsidized rents, farmers have typically provided their own housing on land owned and allocated by the community. There have been many local experiments since 1982 involving the sale of public housing, but the first serious proposals for urban housing reform were published by the central government in February 1988. The proposed rent increases, coupled with wage compensation, and house purchases were supposed to begin in 1990. But there has, in fact, been no serious attempt to introduce the reforms on a large scale; substantial reforms have been confined to very few cities, e.g. Shanghai.

(Pudney and Wang 1994: 4–5)

Soon after being appointed prime minister in March 1998, Zhu Rongyi declared that the state would cut its links to mass housing. In April 1998 the government said that the programme was about to begin, e.g. state employees would have to pay about 30 per cent of their income into a housing provident fund that would then help people to buy their own homes. Rents would rise to reflect true costs for those who do not buy. Cities such as Guangzhou, Shanghai and Tianjin have already moved to scrap free state housing. In Shanghai workers and employees contribute a monthly sum and the provident fund lends the money as mortgages. Shanghai has also been selling flats; work units now control only 30 per cent of cheap housing, while 40 per cent of homes are privately owned and the remaining 30 per cent are rented.

(*The Economist*, 18 April 1998, pp. 68–9)

'Zhu Rongyi announced in March [1998] that the subsidized housing traditionally made available by state sector employers to Chinese workers would be phased out' (*FT*, Survey, 16 November 1998, p. v). Under the new housing policy most urban residents will have to either buy their homes or pay much higher rents. Housing currently accounts for just 3 to 4 per cent of household expenditure. The government is to raise rentals over the next three years, until they account for 10 to 15 per cent of household spending (*Transition*, August 1998, vol. 9, no. 4. p. 21). Rents would slowly rise to about 15 per cent of tenants' incomes and work units would phase out housing assignments, forcing people to buy. However, the government would continue to grant subsidies and encourage mortgage lending (*FEER*, 16 April 1998, p. 63.)

Housing reform was meant to begin on 1 July 1998. Work units were to have ceased to allocate housing at nominal cost to employees, who were to have faced rent increases or become homeowners (*FEER*, 9 July 1998, p. 76). The allocation of new state-subsidized housing was to have ended on 1 July, but the deadline has been postponed until the end of 1998 (*FEER*, 30 July 1998, p. 45).

Housing reform was meant to start from 1 July 1998, but rent increases will not now begin before the end of the year (*The Economist*, 18 July 1998, p. 76).

State housing was to have been sold to occupants at significant discounts to market prices. Extra deductions were to have been made to reward long and distinguished service in a state organization (*FT*, 30 April 1998, p. 6).

'Starting this year [2000] work units are not meant to buy flats. Instead, they must give employees money for housing ... The employee can buy the work-unit flat he is already in at a heavy discount' (*The Economist*, 30 September 2000, p. 95).

In late 1999 [the government lifted] ... a ban on the resale of privatized public housing – the kind of housing occupied by most city dwellers ... The government ... relaxed the rules to permit resales, as long as the work unit agreed.

(*The Economist*, 16 June 2001, p. 93)

'Only three years ago the People's Bank of China allowed banks to issue mortgage loans' (*FEER*, 21 February 2002, p. 32).

Housing reform regulations passed in mid-1998 halted the provision of free housing by state institutions. But ... instead of giving out homes many state entities heavily subsidize housing for employees ... Beijing is mandating public auctions for the transfer of most types of commercial land

and introducing other reforms ... Beijing is making the business of buying land-use rights more straightforward in a bid to increase government revenues and bring order to a murky side of its evolving market economy ... All land is owned by the state but land-use rights can be purchased for up to seventy years for the construction of residential property and up to fifty years for industrial and forty years for commercial use ... Regulations due to take effect nation-wide on 1 July [2002] say that land intended for commercial use must be sold by auction or open tender to the highest bidder.

(*FEER*, 27 June 2002, pp. 28–9)

State enterprises have been selling off houses to workers at low insider prices. By 1995, seven years after state units began selling houses to its occupants, 29 per cent of urbanites lived in apartments they had purchased by means of this mechanism and 11 per cent owned housing they had built for themselves or had inherited. However, homeowners who bought housing from their work units do not own their apartments outright, as they are not entirely free to sell them. Work places must still approve any sale and often have the right to buy the apartment back. If the unit is sold to a third party the work place claims the lion's share of the profit on the sale ... Newly hired workers still line up for assigned housing ... The private rental market for ordinary housing is virtually non-existent ... In the late 1990s state-owned enterprises still owned about two-thirds of all urban housing.

(Hirschler 2002: 8–9)

A new policy announced last week bans employers from blocking owners of state-assigned housing from selling properties ... It was only in 2001 that China took tentative steps to scrap the requirement that *danwei* [the government-controlled work unit] approval – or if a citizen has no state-owned *danwei*, police permission – be given for the issuing of passports. Last year [2002] Shanghai joined the handful of cities to try this out. Officials say that this group, which Beijing has now joined, will grow to 100 cities by the end of this year [2003]. By 2005 every city in China, officially 658 of them, is sup-posed to be included ... More recently a *danwei* might have vetoed a marriage because of concerns about providing housing (a practice that the *danwei* aban-doned only four years ago). Bribery was often the only way of getting permis-sion. From 1 October the *danwei* will no longer be involved and couples will not have to undergo health examinations before getting married ... Housing reforms in the 1990s did not entirely release the *danwei*'s grip. Although employees were no longer given free housing, and instead had to buy or rent it, they often could not resell without their *danwei*'s permission. According to last week's directive, the *danwei* can no longer stop them except for legal or con-tractual reasons (such as the property being under joint ownership of the *danwei* and the occupier). Beijing has announced that from 1 October 800,000 homes that were once owned by central government organizations may be put on the market, a move that could double the amount of second-hand housing available in the capital.

(*The Economist*, 6 September 2003, p. 66)

Following extensive privatization during the past decade a residential housing market has emerged, with the owner occupation rate approaching 70 per cent in urban areas. Nonetheless, the short length of commercial and residential leases (fifty and seventy years, respectively) may constitute a barrier to effective improvement of land, as property on the land reverts to the state at the end of a lease.

(OECD 2005: website Chapter 1)

Later reform periods

There have been various stages of reform:

1994 to 1997

Ma describes 1994–7 as the period of the corporatization of state-owned enterprises (SOEs) (Ma 1998: 380). Only the corporatization programme has had implications for ownership in SOEs. In November 1994, 100 large and medium-sized SOEs were selected to be corporatized within two years as limited liability companies (LLCs) or shareholding enterprises (SHEs) (p. 381).

> If a SOE is corporatized into a SHE ... the SOE must be incorporated by means of share offer. As sponsor the state is required to subscribe not less than 35 per cent of the total shares issue, and the remainder is to be offered to the general public ... However, according to the corporatization blueprint most of the SOEs would be incorporated as LLCs and only a few would be converted into SHEs. In other words, the corporatization programme was not intended to be a major breakthrough in terms of state ownership. As such its results have not been significantly different from previous reforms. The LLCs, still solely state-owned, have remained subject to arbitrary government intervention in their operation. More importantly, the corporatization programme, like the earlier reform schemes, failed to improve SOEs' financial performance.
>
> (p. 382)

In July 1996 a senior Chinese official admitted publicly that the corporatization programme had stalled. A year later the State Council confirmed that the corporatization experiment would be finished by the end of 1997 (p. 383).

In November 1993 it was announced that a start was to be made on a 'step by step' conversion of some state enterprises into corporations (including those jointly owned, in varying proportions, by the state and by other shareholders, including private ones), which would shed their social welfare activities (paying a payroll tax instead), be responsible for their own profits and losses (i.e. no automatic subsidies) and be free to make wage and manpower decisions. A pilot scheme involving 100 large state enterprises was supposed to start in 1994. But the reform did not get very far because of fear of the social consequences such as unemployment.

> Two years ago Beijing allowed 100 large state-owned enterprises to become 'corporate entities'. The experiment failed. The reason: firms that sought non-state buyers would have barred themselves from buying wholly state-owned

assets. So quite naturally, seventy-nine of the 100 entities turned their backs on shareholders and chose to remain entirely state-owned. Beijing has yet to change its incentive scheme.

(Matt Forney, *FEER*, 28 August 1997, p. 36)

Shareholding and privatization (sales and leasing)

SHAREHOLDING

The essence of the shareholding system reform, according to Ma, is to convert SOEs into shareholding enterprises (SHEs), with shares issued to the state, enterprises and individuals (Ma 1998: 379).

> It may be argued that if corporate shares are also taken into account, the state still holds controlling stakes of most of the SHEs. Since the holders of corporate shares are state agents or institutions, such shares are indirectly owned by the state. In 1993 and 1994 corporate shares accounted for about 45 per cent of the total capital stock of SHEs.
>
> (p. 388)

> Unlike the rapid privatization in many East European countries, it took thirteen years – from the establishment of the first Chinese shareholding company in 1984 to the recent endorsement of the shareholding system – for this option to be recognized as the mainstream reform scheme. This process is yet another manifestation of the gradual and incremental characteristic of China's economic reform.
>
> (p. 380)

In December 1986 an expansion of the shareholding system experiment was ordered (p. 383). In March 1988 there were some 6,000 enterprises with shareholding characteristics. They fell under four major categories of enterprises issuing shares to employees, other legal-persons (enterprises or institutions), the public, or enterprises owned by workers on the basis of the capital they contribute to the enterprises (p. 384).

> The early development of the shareholding system, which was basically a spontaneous process, took place in the absence of a legal framework. The experiment was attempted mainly by small-sized collective enterprises. Shares were issued primarily as a means to raise capital rather than to establish a new form of corporate governance. Most of the shares received guaranteed interest plus high dividends. They could be redeemed when mature and investors bore little risk. As such the shares were more like bonds in nature. Only a small amount were traded over the counter.
>
> (p. 385)

There was a setback to the shareholding system in 1989 (p. 385). The Shanghai stock exchange opened in December 1990 and the one in Shenzhen opened in July 1991. The shareholding system regained momentum after Deng Xiaoping's call for further reform in January 1992 (p. 386). A variety of share types have emerged under the shareholding system, including state, corporate or legal-person, individual and foreign shares (p. 388). There has been a reduction of state ownership in previously wholly state-owned enterprises (p. 391). But by the start of 1993 the proportion of state shares in each listed SHE ranged from 51 per cent to over 80 per cent (p. 388).

By the end of 1992 only 120 state enterprises had been authorized to sell their shares to the public, although a much larger number were making less formal arrangements for shared ownership between state enterprises (Perkins 1994: 40).

In October 1992 China Brilliance Automotive Holdings became the first state enterprise to sell shares abroad (in the United States to be precise) (Jeffries 1993: 497).

A mere handful of SOEs have been transformed into shareholding companies, in which shares are owned by the state, by legal entities (or corporations) and by employees. The government holds a majority of shares, with employees entitled to a maximum of 20 per cent (Wu 1997: 1256–7).

China has 4,000 shareholding state-owned enterprises, only a small percentage of which have been listed on stock exchanges (*China Briefing*, January 1998, no. 59, p. 1).

Of the 530 listed enterprises, 373 are controlled by the state. The second largest stockholders own no more than 5 per cent of the shares on average (*Transition*, February 1998, vol. 9, no. 1. p. 5). According to the International Finance Corporation, of the nearly 1,000 companies listed on the Shenzhen and Shanghai markets for domestically traded A shares only eleven are private (compared with three at the end of 1998) (*FEER*, 29 June 2000, p. 61).

> The government holds a majority stake in almost all companies listed on China's two stock exchanges, in Shanghai and Shenzhen ... Speculation in the country's volatile markets provides seed capital for many entrepreneurs who have few alternatives. Capital market are otherwise beyond the reach of most entrepreneurs ... [Private businessmen are also] barred from operating a securities company or owning a seat on the exchange ... The most pressing problem is getting a bank loan. The bank requires a guarantor, almost impossible for a private businessman to find in China. Even if a private company has a guarantor, most loans are for only three or four months – eighteen months in exceptional cases ... Entrepreneurs ... are systematically shunned by Chinese banks, often discriminated against by government regulators and barred from entering many industries ... Because relationships with officials are still so crucial, many private business owners are really just opportunists exploiting their party connections. The resulting corruption has not helped improve the private sector's image. One of the most celebrated entrepreneurs, Mou Qizhong, was recently sentenced to life in prison for fraud.
>
> (Craig Smith, *IHT*, 13 July 2000, p. 16)

'Of the more than 1,000 companies listed on the Shanghai and Shenzhen exchanges, at least 900 are majority-owned by the state' (*IHT*, 5 August 2000, p. 1).

'Only a tiny fraction of ownership rights of large firms in China was in the hands of individuals ... The ownership of each of China's large SOEs has spread gradually among a variety of public institutions' (Nolan and Xiaoqiang: 1999: 190–1).

'Since 1993 more than 6,000 state companies of all sizes have been reorganized as shareholding companies. Although the state usually remains the major share-holder, mergers and acquisitions are quietly increasing the private stake in many' (Kathy Wilhelm, *FEER*, 18 February 1999, p. 12).

Six firms – three American, two Chinese and one European – [have been] invited to bid for the right to manage the initial public offering [IPO] of China Telecom, the country's flagship telephone company ... China Telecom is the latest of a string of initial offerings that began in 1997 with the cellular giant China Mobile. So far China's megaofferings have been in telecommunications and petroleum ... [including] the $4.2 billion China Mobile offering ... a $3 billion offering of PetroChina, the number one oil company ... $5.6 billion for China Unicom, the number two cellular provider, and $3.5 billion from an offering of Sinopec Corp., the number two oil company ... [There was] a $7.6 billion secondary offering of China Mobile that was the largest Chinese stock deal ever.

(*IHT*, 18 December 2000, p. 15)

Vodaphone Group PLC paid $2.5 billion this year [2000] for a 2 per cent stake in China's biggest mobile phone telephone company, China Mobile Communications Corp. ... Hutchison Whampoa Ltd holds a 2 per cent stake in China Unicom Ltd, China's second-largest mobile telephone operator.

(*IHT*, 20 December 2000, p. 23)

'At the end of 1999 the state owned about 68 per cent of the 285 billion shares outstanding of China's 1,007 listed companies, according to the official *China Daily*'s business weekly' (*IHT*, 18 April 2000, p. 19).

China said Monday [19 February 2001] it would allow local investors to buy stocks that had been reserved for foreigners. Chinese investors will now be able to buy so-called B shares, or domestically listed stocks denominated in foreign currencies. The new rule ... will not take effect until approved by China's cabinet ... [The] market was created nine years ago ... China's private entrepreneurs ... are free to raise capital on the B-share market if they meet the government's listing requirements ... The B-share market never gained wide acceptance because it remained too illiquid to attract many foreign investors, and domestic companies looking for hard currency opted instead to list their shares on the Hong Kong stock exchange or on markets abroad. As part of the restructuring of its markets the government has stopped issuing quotas that restrict the number of companies allowed to list Class A shares. When the quota that has already been issued is used up this year domestic companies, including private ones, will be free to sell stock based largely on market demand, not government regulation. Private companies were almost never granted quotas under the old system ... Other changes in the markets expected this year [2001] or next [2002] include the merging of the stock exchanges in Shenzhen and Shanghai and the creation of a Nasdaq-style second board that will give younger companies a chance to raise cash ... Already B-share trading is dominated by domestic investors, who use a variety of schemes to open trading accounts.

(IHT, 20 February 2001, pp 1, 17)

The regulators also decided to abolish the quota system for issuing A shares, which are reserved for residents. The quotas had prevented most private companies from listing their shares ... The B shares are a small and hitherto illiquid market ... Most of the scant turnover in these issues has long been conducted by local investors with dollar accounts. Foreigners have been little interested because of the small size and generally poor quality of the B companies.

(IHT, 27 February 2001, p. 15)

The government has promised to phase out its practice of setting aside quotas for favoured enterprises on the A shares market. By next year [2002] all Chinese companies meeting standard listing criteria will be free to issue shares according to market demand.

(IHT, 1 March 2001, p. 13)

'Chinese individuals hold about $75 billion in foreign exchange savings accounts and domestic companies hold another $55 billion in bank deposits' *(IHT,* 8 March 2001, p. 13).

The change in policy is expected to be a precursor to merging the larger local exchange for A shares, with B shares previously reserved only for foreigner investors ... although local Chinese are already responsible for about 80 per cent of B share transactions, using regulatory loopholes ... There are five different categories – A shares, B shares, H shares in Hong Kong, N, or New York-listed, shares and red chips.

(FT, 20 February 2001, p. 9)

The B share market, with just 1 per cent of A shares' capitalization, is trivial. Most foreigners invest only in mainland companies that have issued H shares listed in Hong Kong ... or in state-controlled companies that are incorporated and listed in Hong Kong (so-called 'red chips') ... Regulators say they will delist companies that make losses for three years running ... They also intend to ditch a quota system that determines the order in which companies may list and that favours politically connected SOEs at the expense of private firms.

(The Economist, 3 March 2001, p. 100)

('Red chips' are: 'Hong Kong-incorporated mainland companies': *IHT,* 2 January 2001, p. 15; 'Chinese companies incorporated in Hong Kong': *FEER,* 24 May 2001, p. 54. '"Red chips" are mainland companies listed in Hong Kong': *IHT,* 18 August 2002, p. 11.)

Foreign investors showed so little interest in China's B shares, denominated in US and Hong Kong dollars, that the CSRC [China Securities Regulatory

Commission] is officially opening B shares to domestic investors starting on 28 February. Analysts estimate that Chinese investors have already acquired more than 70 per cent of the outstanding B shares through various stratagems.

(*FEER*, 8 March 2001, p. 47)

The delisting [on 24 April 2001] ... [of] a money-losing washing machine manufacturer off of Shanghai stock exchange ... was the first since China's stock exchange was established in 1990 ... [The] appliance maker has posted losses for four consecutive years ... Under new rules companies that post losses for more than three consecutive years would be given a six-month grace period to post gains.

(*IHT*, 25 April 2001, p. 11)

All state-owned shares of listed companies remained non-tradable until recently ... The State Council announced in June [2001] that when state-owned enterprises issue new shares to the public (either domestically or abroad) the government will sell some of its shares equivalent to 10 per cent of the IPO [initial share offering] proceeds to finance the national social security fund.

(Deutsche Bank, *Global Markets Research: Emerging Markets*, July 2001, p. 11)

China is drafting laws to allow foreign companies to sell local shares ... The new rules would let companies sell stock either in local or foreign companies ... They must seek ministry approval [from the ministry of foreign trade and co-operation] ... Foreign listings on China's two domestic stock exchanges would polish the country's image as it prepares to enter the WTO ... Until now China's stock markets have been limited to local companies, though they are divided into so-called A shares, those denominated in yuan, and B shares, denominated in dollars ... So far, just one foreign firm – a local unit of Taiwan-based Tsann Kuen Enterprise Co. – has sold shares for a Chinese listing. Foreign investors have access to only one-tenth of Chinese shares, Class B shares denominated in US and Hong Kong dollars ... Under the new rules, foreign companies must retain at least 25 per cent of their capital as non-tradable shares, and must keep them from flowing onto the stock market for at least a year after the sale.

(*IHT*, 12 July 2001, p. 17)

The Beijing government has issued long-awaited guidelines for foreign-funded groups doing business on the mainland to list their shares in China ... Over-seas-backed companies could list on both the A and B share markets. A shares are available only to Chinese investors, while B shares were reserved for for-eigners until February [2001] ... Foreigners must keep at least 25 per cent of the listed company's shares in a non-tradable form. The circular ... follows the initial announcement in September 1999, allowing foreign companies to issue shares in China ... China's stock markets do have foreign-invested groups, but, with few exceptions, these are minority stakes.

(*FT*, 12 July 2001, p. 22)

Until late last year [2000] the state ... rarely granted the privilege ... [to] list stock on the country's two exchanges ... to private companies ... But that has changed, first in the so-called B-share market where stocks are denominated in foreign currency and now in the much larger A-share market, where ... two weeks ago ... UFSoft [a private software company] was the first to be listed under the new rules.

(*IHT*, 4 June 2001, p. 11)

Only about 30 to 40 per cent of listed [state] companies' shares in China are tradable with the remainder held by the government or related entities ... Non-tradable shares generally changed hands in legal off-market auctions or were used as collateral for bank loans at prices set by a company's net asset value.

(*FT*, 8 August 2001, p. 23)

'According to some estimates, the state continues to own around 60 per cent of companies listed on the domestic markets' (*FT*, 14 June 2001, p. 11).

On average companies listed on the domestic stock market ... have a public float of only about 30 per cent. The balance is held in two other categories – those owned by the government and so-called 'legal person' shares which are held by approved state institutions.

(*FT*, 14 May 2002, p. 34)

'Of China's 1,250-odd listed companies, only about fifty are private' (*FT*, 4 February 2002, p. 22).

'The government has offered only about 30 per cent of individual company shares to the public' (*FEER*, 9 May 2002, p. 27).

('About 60 million Chinese citizens, or about 13 per cent of households, have opened trading accounts': *IHT*, 3 September 2001, p. 1. Open ended funds 'allow investors to buy and sell their holdings at any time': *IHT*, 13 October 2000, p. 24.)

China has suspended the sale of shares in state-owned companies used to fund a national social security fund in a policy reversal which it hopes will steady its weakening stock market. The China securities regulatory commission announced the suspension last night [22 October 2001] ... The government announced in July that money raised by the sale of 10 per cent of the shares of companies sold in initial public offerings would be put into a welfare fund ... Although a crackdown on share price manipulation by the ... commission ... has contributed to ... depressing the value of shares ... most commentators have blamed the state sell-off ... The government still holds about 65 per cent of the shares in listed companies ... [The commission's] statement last night backed the continuing sale of state shares but said it was a 'long-term task which needed constant improvement' ... China has about 60 million retail trading accounts, but with many of them held in false names only about half are genuine investors.

(*FT*, 23 October 2001, p. 17)

[The government] said in June that the equivalent of 10 per cent of the proceeds of initial public offerings, or any new share issues, would be set aside to provide money for a national welfare fund ... Most of China's 1,100 listed companies are majority-owned by the government with the free float of tradable shares equivalent to about 35 per cent. The remaining shares are held by the government or government entities.

(*FT*, 25 October 2001, p. 44)

China unexpectedly suspended the sale of state-owned shares in listed companies ... The China securities regulatory commission said the government would maintain its long-term policy of reducing the state's holdings in listed companies, but it would implement the plan step-by-step, rather than through dramatic sell-offs.

(*IHT*, 24 October 2001, p. 13)

The China securities regulatory commission ... [aims to] clean up Asia's second largest market in terms of capitalization ... But some analysts say it will take more deep-seated changes to clean up the eleven-year-old Shanghai and Shenzhen stock exchanges ... [There are] 1,150 listed companies.

(*FEER*, 18 October 2001, p. 42)

Majority foreign-owned companies in China will be allowed to list on the country's domestic stock exchanges under regulations that were published on 8 November [2001]. The rules allow companies with at least a 25 per cent stake to list on the markets, including the highly liquid local currency markets. The foreign stake must remain above 25 per cent after the listing for the country to enjoy foreign investor privileges and may never fall below 10 per cent even after secondary issues ... Until now only a few companies with minority foreign stakes have been allowed to list on China's markets. The new regulations open the door to majority-owned companies as well, something that Beijing had promised in July.

(*FEER*, 22 November 2001, p. 36)

A city government enterprise has been tasked with selling off stakes in state assets and shares in order to fund Shanghai's plans to build a hi-tech base. What is new is that for the first time financial institutions that are relatively strong players within China's financial sector are on offer ... The Shanghai State-owned Assets Operation, or SSAO ... founded in 1999 ... holds the sole right to trade state assets in Shanghai ... Beijing municipality and Jiangsu province have also established their own version of the SSAO ... The assets on offer may not be distressed, but neither are they blue chip ... [The SSAO] is also tasked with finding buyers for state equity in publicly listed companies, much of it not currently tradable on the stock market ... The sale of A shares is generally restricted to mainland Chinese citizens and entities, but there are exceptions to this. In certain industries Sino-foreign joint venture companies can purchase A shares indirectly, something SSAO can broker using a method whereby a Chinese entity buys A shares and transfers them to an investment company set up to receive the shares. The investment company can then sell the shares to the foreign-invested joint venture.

(David Murphy, *FEER*, 9 August 2001, pp. 40–1)

An estimated fifty private firms have listed on stock markets in China and abroad ... For years China's government refused to allow private firms to list on domestic exchanges ... That injunction was lifted in 1997, but only a trickle of private firms have made it onto domestic exchanges since local governments, with a quota of firms to list, continue to give precedence to state firms. Of the 1,154 companies listed on the Shanghai and Shenzhen exchanges only two dozen are privately held. Most of the private firms which have reached the market, like Minsheng Bank, software retailer UFSoft, appliance-maker Meidi and medicines concern Taitai Pharmaceuticals, are owned by politically well-connected entrepreneurs. Fifty more have been approved for listing in China and more than 200 are believed to have applied ... [In 2000] leading private entrepreneurs [were invited] to join the ruling Communist Party. Swinging into line banks, securities regulators and bureaucrats have changed policies to help private companies. One result: a flood of private companies seeking stock market listings.

(Bruce Gilley, *FEER*, 17 January 2002, pp. 52–3)

(By July 2002 there were 1,284 listed firms: *FEER*, 1 August 2002, p. 22.)

The government on 23 June [2002] officially abandoned its attempts to raise money for its national security fund by selling state-owned shares on domestic stock markets ... Last June [2001] the China securities regulatory commission announced plans to start selling state shares – untraded equities that make up around 60 per cent of the Shanghai market's capitalization – and to devote the proceeds to the national social security fund. But in October [2001], with Shanghai's domestic A-shares index, which tracks renminbi-denominated shares, down 24 per cent since the sales began, the CSRC suspended the plan. On 23 June authorities buried it ... The State Council had approved the decision to stop sales.

(*FEER*, 4 July 2002, p. 23)

[The town] of Shenzhen is set to pilot a scheme to sell off stakes to foreign investors in important state-owned enterprises, launching an experiment into whether such sales can provide an effective way to fund China's vast pensions shortfall and improve corporate governance ... [The] mayor of Shenzhen said minority stakes of 25 per cent in Shenzhen Energy Group, 45 per cent of Shenzhen Water, 24 per cent of Shenzhen Gas Group and 45 per cent of Shenzhen Public Transportation would be offered to foreign investors, Two overseas companies have already expressed interest in taking stakes in Shenzhen Food General, he added ... The sales would be conducted on a trial basis and would be repeated in Shenzhen and other parts of China only if they were deemed to be a success, official sources said ... The proposed sales of stakes in the Shenzhen companies differs from previous offers of state assets to foreigners in that the Shenzhen companies are viable and even profitable, analysts said ... An attempt in 1998 by the then mayor of Shenyang to sell off several moribund enterprises at knock-down prices by going on roadshows overseas was a failure, mainly because the assets on offer were deemed to be virtually worthless.

(*FT*, 29 August 2002, p. 7)

[The] mayor of Shezhen points to a recent pilot scheme by the city to sell stakes in state-owned utilities to foreign investors through a global bidding process. If successful it will be emulated by other Chinese cities as a way of raising money to fund pension schemes and improve corporate governance.

(*FT*, 11 December 2002, p. 15)

The Chinese government is likely to allow sales of some of its stakes in pub-licly traded, state-controlled companies ... likely to allow sales of such stakes to Chinese subsidiaries and to joint ventures of international companies ... to allow foreign-financed companies here to acquire non-tradable state-owned shares ... China would be expected to sell only minority stakes in the publicly traded state-controlled enterprises to foreigners ... China will also allow multi-national corporations to sell shares in their Chinese operations to Chinese cit-izens ... While some of China's largest state-controlled enterprises are traded on stock exchanges in New York and Hong Kong, where foreigners can buy shares, more than 1,000 are traded only on the A-share stock markets in Shang-hai and Shenzhen, in which foreigners are not allowed to invest ... A third of the shares ... are held by Chinese citizens and can be traded. The government holds the remaining two-thirds ... currently designated 'non-tradable' ... China already allows foreign companies to buy stakes that are not publicly traded or that are traded on the very small B-share market, which are open to foreign investors.

(*IHT*, 31 August 2002, p. 11)

The initial public offering ... in the Bank of China's Hong Kong unit ... [which took place in Hong Kong on 20 July 2002] ... represented a milestone as the first international stock listing by a mainland Chinese bank. The state-owned Bank of China sold a 22 per cent stake in its Hong Kong unit, which is the territory's largest lender and second-largest [after HSBC] taker of deposits ... China Telecom, the near-monopoly provider of fixed-line phone service in southern China, is preparing an even larger public offering for this year [2002] ... Retail investors living in Hong Kong were allowed to buy 35 per cent of the shares in the offering at a 5 per cent discount that foreign and institutional investors had to pay for the rest of the shares.

(*IHT*, 26 July 2002, p. 15)

George Soros, Pilkington PLC and twelve other overseas investors will now be allowed to sell or trade their shares in Chinese companies for the first time ... American Aviation Ltd., a Soros unit that owns a 15 per cent stake in Hainan Airlines Co., will be allowed to either sell its shares to another investor or trade them on China's stock exchanges ... Other overseas investors, including Pilk-ington, a maker of car windshields, will also be permitted to trade their so-called Class B foreign-currency shares.

(*IHT*, 22 August 2002, p. 10)

China will allow foreign institutional investors to buy yuan-denominated stocks and domestic bonds for the first time, the government said Thursday [7 November 2002]. Foreign banks and funds with at least $10 billion in assets

and approval from the Chinese government will be allowed to enter ...
markets in Shanghai and Shenzhen beginning on 1 December [2002] ... Overseas investors must leave their money in the [Class A shares] market for at
least three years.

(IHT, 8 November 2002, p.15)

The 'qualified foreign institutional invest' [QFII] scheme will be launched on 1
December ... China's A-share market has about 1,200 companies, with only
about one-third of shares being tradable. The rest are held by the state or state-
approved bodies. The government announced last week that foreigners would
be allowed to buy into the non-tradable shares of these state-owned companies
... The second initiative, announced yesterday [7 November] will allow
foreign institutions to buy and sell the companies' tradable shares ...
Approved investors will also be able to put money into domestic treasury and
corporate bonds. Investors that qualify under the scheme are foreign fund management companies with five years of operations, insurance companies and
brokerages ... Securities and insurance companies need at least thirty years of
experience and paid-in capital of at least $1 billion.

(FT, Friday 8 November 2002, p. 30)

('The vast majority ... of about 1,200 listed companies ... are state-owned corporations in which only a minority stake, often about 25 per cent, is floated': *FT*,
9 October 2002, p. 25.)

To become a qualified investor a fund management firm, insurance company or
bank must have had a minimum of $10 billion in assets under management in
their last financial year. In addition, fund management companies must have
had at least five years of operational experience while insurance companies and
brokerages must have had thirty years of experience and paid-in capital of at
least $1 billion. Banks meanwhile must be one of the world's 'top 100' institu-
tions ... The capital invested in closed-end funds (the preferred form of investment) set up under QFII can only be repatriated after a minimum of three years
and even then only at a rate of 20 per cent of the principal per month.

(FT, 11 November 2002, p. 11)

China has said it would lift a ban on foreign ownership of stakes in listed companies held by the government. So-called state shares and institutional shares
cannot be listed and comprise two-thirds of ... stockmarket capitalization.
Listed companies would be able to sell previously non-tradable stakes held by
the government and other institutions to foreign parties by tender.

(FEER, 14 November 2002, p. 28)

'Overseas investors will not be allowed to buy more than 20 per cent of a
company's stock, and no one investor will be allowed to buy more than 10 per cent
of a company' (www.cnn.com).

The new scheme – known as QFII, because it is aimed at the qualified foreign
investor – is an import from Taiwan ... [which] was cautious about encouraging volatility ... China's market ... consists of 1,212 companies. But only

'Some 60 per cent of the average listed company remains in state hands' (*FEER*, 28 October 2004, p. 32).

Privatization Chinese-style consists of putting the best assets into a new company and listing just a fraction of its shares, while the (typically) huge, unlisted, state-owned rump retains the inefficient bits ... [For example] Baosteel [is] China's biggest steelmaker ... Baoshan Iron and Steel, the Shanghai-listed subsidiary of Baosteel ... employing some 15,000 people, accounts for less than half of the group's total ... [and] is highly profitable ... The unquoted rump consists of another seven smaller steel businesses, a trading arm and a motley collection of construction, IT and financial services operations. This part of the group, in typical SOE fashion, takes care of social obligations, such as the housing, schooling, pension and medical needs of the group's 100,000-plus workers. It is also the holding vehicle for four loss-making steelmakers which the government forced Baosteel to take over in 1997 – with the additional proviso that it could fire no more than 10,000 every year of the 180,000 redundant workers it was saddled with. And Baosteel is lucky. As a comparatively new company, founded in 1978, it has fewer over-manned factories with rusting equipment than many of the SOEs that originated in the Mao era ... [Baosteel] still needs official approval for large capital investments, though ... [Baosteel] says that today it would at least not be forced to buy another bunch of loss-making rivals ... Baosteel ... is an attractive partner for foreign firms such as Arcelor, Nippon Steel and ThyssenKrupp that each has a joint venture with it.

(*The Economist*, 22 November 2003, p. 85)

China National Offshore Oil Company (CNOOC), the mainland's third largest oil producer ... controls offshore oil exploration and production in China ... CNOOC is planning to list more than 1.6 billion shares, representing a 27.5 per cent stake in the company, in New York and Hong Kong. The shares will begin trading in New York next Tuesday [27 February]. The success of the issue is critical to China's programme of reforming its lumbering state-owned enterprises through partial privatizations on international markets ... CNOOC ... [was] forced to pull an earlier attempted IPO [initial public offering] in October 1999 because of a lack of demand.

(*FT*, 22 February 2001, p. 29)

Shares ... will begin trading in New York on Tuesday [27 February] and in Hong Kong on Wednesday [28 February] ... China National Offshore Oil ... was created from scratch by the Chinese government in 1982 to drill for oil in Chinese waters, as well as be the local partner for companies like Chevron ... and Texaco.

(*IHT*, 22 February 2001, p. 11)

'The company ... raised $1.26 billion in its stock offering' (*IHT*, 28 February 2001, p. 16).

The Bank of China, Agricultural Bank of China, China Construction Bank and

Industrial and Commercial Bank of China have won permission from the central bank to sell shares to foreign investors. The state-controlled banks will also be allowed to form alliances and restructure.

(IHT, 20 September 2001, p. 12)

The government plans to merge dozens of state-owned electronics research institutes and firms into a conglomerate with global reach. The China Electronics Technology Corp. is being organized by the ministry of information industry and will be launched later this year [2001].

(FEER, 18 October 2001, p. 34)

China Telecom ... was formally broken up yesterday [16 May 2002] ... China Telecom will continue as a much-reduced company operating in twenty-one provinces in China's south and west. Ten of its former provincial operations in the north are now part of a competitor, the new China Netcom Group, which also includes an existing data communications operator, the China Netcom Corp. ... [The two] will rank as China's second- and third-largest telecoms operators respectively, after China Mobile Telecommunications Corp.

(FT, 17 May 2002, p. 31)

'The introduction of China Netcom Group is part of a huge government-planned overhaul to increase competition in China's telecoms market. A third operator, China Netcom Corp., was set up three years ago and will provide high-speed services to corporate clients' *(FEER*, 23 May 2002, p. 26).

China Telecom on Thursday [7 November] sold shares worth ... 60 per cent less than originally targeted ... The biggest fixed-line phone company in China sold stock ... at the bottom end of the price range, giving investors a 10 per cent stake in the company ... The initial public offering [IPO] was saddled with glitches even before it was delayed and scaled back.

(IHT, 8 November 2002, p. 15)

'China Telecom was forced to drastically down-size and relaunch this week after receiving lacklustre interest from investors' *(FT*, 8 November 2002, p. 30).

China on Sunday [29 December 2002] broke up its massive state power company into eleven smaller businesses in a move to encourage greater competition ... The dismantled State Power Corp. will spin off its power generating assets to five smaller companies, each controlling less than 20 per cent of the country's electricity capacity ... Two other companies will operate power grids and four companies will handle peripheral business operations ... The five electricity generators will be forced to compete for contracts with the grid operators, State Power Grid and Southern Power Grid.

(IHT, 30 December 2002, p. 10)

China Life Insurance sold $3 billion worth of shares in the year's biggest initial public offering [IPO] ... [offering] 25 per cent of its stock ... China Life controlled 45 per cent of China's life insurance market last year [2002] ... [China] started selling shares in state-owned enterprises to foreign investors [in 1992] to help end subsidized industrial production. The government has sold $60 billion worth of such shares and plans to almost double that amount in the next decade, including sales by Bank of China and other state-owned lenders ... Prime minister Wen Jiabao ... pledged to improve corporate governance as China raises the amount that foreign investors can buy of domestic companies.

(*IHT*, 13 December 2003, p. 15)

[The issue was over-subscribed] ... [There was] strong demand in Hong Kong and New York ... The company ... is understood to have decided to sell an additional 970 million shares to meet investor demand, bringing the total to $3.47 billion ... Analysts have warned about the return of a speculative bubble to Hong Kong as investors bought shares in IPOs of China-based companies, including insurer PICC and carmaker Great Wall Auto.

(*FT*, Money and Business, 13 December 2003, p. 6)

IPOs typically offer 25 per cent to 30 per cent of an SOE's shares. Subsequent issues often dilute state holdings, but the government almost always remains the biggest shareholder. One 2002 study estimated that only 11 per cent of China's listed companies by market capitalization are privately held. State enterprises control the rest ... IPOs by state-owned enterprises primarily offer new shares, not existing government-held stakes. Whether or not the firm has good investment opportunities, funds raised go to the SOE, not the government.

(*FEER*, 15 July 2004, p. 59)

'Bank of China, the second biggest lender, said Thursday [26 August] that it has begun operating as a shareholding company as it reorganizes in preparation for an initial public offer to overseas investors in the second half of 2005' (www.iht.com, 26 August 2004).

China Construction Bank, the nations' third biggest lender, sold stakes to three state-owned companies, the buyers said Wednesday [15 September]. The price of the deal indicates that Construction Bank may raise $5.9 billion from an initial public offer. China Yangtze Power, Shanghai Baosteel and State Grid said they would pay $966 million for a combined stake of 4 per cent.

(www.iht.com, 15 September 2004)

'China NetComGroup (Hong Kong), China's second-biggest fixed-line phone company ... [has conducted] an initial public offering [in Hong Kong]' (www.iht.com, 17 November 2004).

'Air China, the nation's biggest international carrier, has raised $1.08 billion in an initial public offering [in Hong Kong]' (www.iht.com, 9 December 2004).

China announced on Monday [21 February 2005] that selected commercial banks could set up fund management companies in an effort to buoy capital markets and prepare lenders for competition. Shanghai stocks rose on optimism that money would flow into equities ... China last week issued rules allowing insurers to invest directly in stocks. Previously they could invest only through funds ... The State Council, or cabinet, gave approval in principle in September [2004] for banks to set up fund units.

(*IHT*, 22 February 2005, p. 18)

The government launched Shanghai's [stock] exchange in 1990 (and Shenzhen's a year later) ... The mainland's stock market is in dismal slump. On 1 February [2005] the domestic A-share indices in Shanghai and on the junior exchange in Shenzhen hit their lowest level for more than five years. Even after recovering a little since then, they are still down by more than 40 per cent and 50 per cent, respectively, from the record highs of June 2001 ... At that point the government got greedy and tried to sell its remaining holdings, a plan that started the current decline. Even though it was hastily withdrawn the threat of another mass sell-off of state shares continues to spook the market. Four years after the first sell-off a full two-thirds of the market's $460 billion capitalization remains tied up in non-tradable or 'legal person' shares held by state-controlled entities ... And the market's inexorable decline has pole-axed the Chinese broking industry, which not only guaranteed investors double-digit returns but also often speculated corruptly with their funds. Most of the 130-odd securities firms are, in effect, insolvent ... China has private savings of at least 12 trillion yuan ($1.4 trillion) sitting unproductively in banks. The country also has thousands of entrepreneurial firms crying out for funds. If the stock market were allowed to bring the two together, it could, through better allocation of capital, both raise the efficiency of the economy and help maintain its growth rate. Instead, much of that fallow cash has found its way into property, inflating a bubble. Better still, developing China's capital markets would reduce the primacy of the banks ... On 21 February ... [China] announced a fund worth up to $6 billion to compensate investors for the bankruptcy or incompetence of local broking firms. Last weekend regulators launched a test allowing commercial banks to set up mutual funds arms and the week before selected insurers received the green light to invest up to $7 billion in shares ... In December [2004] Goldman Sachs [was allowed] to buy 33 per cent of Gao Hua Securities with management control and the right to raise its stake.

(*The Economist*, 26 February 2005, pp. 81–2)

[On 1 May 2005 China gave] the official go-ahead for the sales of the state's huge holdings in quoted companies, which account for about two-thirds of the equity in businesses with a stock value of $400 billion. The China Securities Regulatory Commission [CSRC] said ... that rules taking effect immediately would allow a small number of companies to take part in a trial programme of state share sales ... The regulator and two-thirds of shareholders have to approve sales of state shares, giving the commission and existing shareholders a veto over disposals. Buyers of state shares will not be able to sell their stake in the first year, and after that will be restricted to sales of a maximum of 5 per cent of a company's equity in each twelve-month period ... The trial programme is intended to allay fears of the potential impact on share prices of a sudden disposal of state holdings ... State shareholdings included stock held by the central and provincial governments, cities and other state-owned companies. Regulators experimented with ways of selling state shares in 1999 and 2001, but had to abandon the attempt, in part because of a sharp drop in market values ... The Shanghai and Shenzhen exchanges have performed badly this year [2005], with the Shanghai composite index down about 8 per cent and Shenzhen market 10 per cent lower.

(*FT*, 2 May 2005, p. 29)

State-owned shares, also known as non-tradable or 'legal person' shares and held by provinces, cities or the central government, account for two-thirds of the $400 billion market value of the companies on the Shanghai and Shenzhen exchanges. The threat that they will one day flood the market has helped send mainland share prices to near six-year lows, although the economy has been booming and other Asian markets have risen in the past two years. The equity market paralysis is in turn holding back the development of other financial markets, for instance in derivatives and corporate bonds. It has also stopped the authorities raising cash to shore up China's underfunded national pension scheme ... In order to avoid depressing prices further, the CSRC and two-thirds of the public, minority shareholders will in each instance have to approve the conversion of non-tradable into normal shares ... Overseas fund managers, who have recently started to invest more in Chinese domestic shares under the government's Qualified Foreign Institutional Investor scheme have long argued for ... existing shareholders [to be] ... granted preemption rights to buy what the state is selling, perhaps even at a discount ... in order to minimize the dilution they will otherwise suffer.

(*The Economist*, 7 May 2005, p. 82)

'The Shenzhen index [was at] its historical peak in 2000' (*IHT*, 30 April 2005, p. 16).

Market regulators on Monday [9 May] announced a trial programme to fully privatize listed companies in an effort to revive China's depressed stock exchanges. Share prices hit a six-year low, although some analysts said the reform measures might ultimately help revive the markets. State companies that hold shares in four companies listed on the Shanghai stock exchange ... will relinquish control and offer their currently non-traded equity for trading on the exchange ... The four companies selected for trial have a combined market value of ... 1 per cent of China's total market capitalization ... The trial may eventually be extended to all of China's listed companies, the commission said ... Last year [2004] Shanghai's stock market was the fourth worst performing of eighty markets tracked by Bloomberg, while Shenzhen's was the second worst. But with Chinese banks straining under bad loans, the government has turned to the sales of state-held equity in companies to fund the country's swelling social welfare and pension payments. A previous effort to unload state holdings onto the share markets in 2001 was abandoned after shareholders revolted.

(www.iht.com, 9 May 2005; *IHT*, 10 May 2005, p. 13)

Shares held by government bodies and state-owned enterprises in more than 1,370 companies listed in China account for about two-thirds of the market's capitalization ... Critics have said that the government's shareholdings was not the only serious problem depressing Chinese markets. They argue that a big proportion of the companies floated in the early 1990s were badly managed and dogged by corruption.

(*IHT*, 18 May 2005, p. 11)

'[China has] 1,377 listed companies' (*FT*, 23 May 2005, p. 7).

Bank of Communications, China's fifth largest lender, plans to raise as much as 14.9 billion Hong Kong dollars in the first of three overseas share sales by the nation's banks this year [2005]. Bank of Communications will offer ... 13 per cent of itself.

(www.iht.com, 6 June 2005)

('Bank of Communications raised $14 billion in its IPO in June': www.iht.com, 5 October 2005.)

China stepped up efforts to revive its struggling equity market yesterday [13 June] when the government said it would offer loans to at least two local brokerages and cut taxes for retail investors ...Local media have suggested the move could be the start of a $7.2 billion bail-out package for the industry ... Although the financial problems of the brokerage sector were much smaller than those at the main banks, they could still cause significant instability in the financial system ... The local brokerages have been one of the main problems facing the market because of the heavy losses many have built up by offering guaranteed high returns to investors. These proved impossible to honour once share prices started to fall ... In another move to shore up the markets the finance ministry said it was temporarily halving income tax on dividends earned by individual investors. The ministry also said it was suspending temporarily income and corporate tax on the sale of state-owned shares.

(*FT*, 14 June 2005, p. 10)

Chinese investors will have to pay tax on only half their stock dividends as part of an attempt to bolster the nation's share markets. Investors previously had to pay income tax on all stock dividends received ... Chinese investors pay a 20 per cent dividend tax. The new rule went into effect on Monday [13 June] ... Another rule went into effect Monday will suspend levies, including transaction tax, corporate tax and personal tax, on shares and cash transferred between investors as part of a share-sale programme to put about $250 billion of state-owned stock holdings, now non-tradable, into the markets. Government and founding shareholders offer minority shares and cash in exchange for the right to trade the rest of their stakes publicly.

(www.iht.com, 13 June 2005)

Bank of America said Friday [17 June] that it had agreed to acquire a 9 per cent stake in China Construction Bank for $3 billion ... Foreigners can buy as much as 20 per cent of a Chinese bank [under current restrictions].

(*IHT*, 18 June 2005, pp. 1, 4)

On Friday [17 June] the state assets supervision and administration commission ... issued a notice reaffirming that the government would continue to maintain control of many listed companies, especially those in 'importance industries and key sectors' ... The government has plans for a $15 billion fund to revive the stock markets.

(www.iht.com, 20 June 2005)

China's stock market regulator said yesterday [19 June] that forty-two companies, including some of the country's biggest and best know corporate names [such as Baosteel, Sinochem, Shanghai Port and Container and Yangtze Power, which owns the Three Gorges Dam project] ... would take part in the second stage of its planned reform of the shareholder structure of listed companies... Of the four [companies in the pilot scheme], all relatively small, the shareholders in one have rejected the company's offer of compensation in return for having their stakes diluted.

(*IHT*, 20 June 2005, p. 5)

'None of the companies nominated are traded on the sectors of the Shanghai and Shenzhen markets that allow foreign investors to buy and sell stock and none are traded on stock exchanges abroad' (*IHT*, 21 June 2005, p. 14).

'China COSCO Holdings, the nation's biggest container shipper, raised 9.52 billion Hong Kong dollars, or $1.22 billion, in a Hong Kong initial public offer' (www.iht.com, 27 June 2005).

Baoshan Iron and Steel, China's largest steel maker, said Thursday [28 June] that it was increasing its offer of free shares to minority stockholders ... to compensate them for any losses resulting from sales of government-owned stakes ... Shareholders would also receive warrants giving them an option to buy one share for every ten held.

(www.iht.com, 28 June 2005)

The government plans to more than double the maximum amount of domestic shares that can be owned by overseas funds to $10 billion as part of a round of measures to prop up the nation's stock markets ... The China securities regulatory commission will also extend a moratorium on share sales and encourage buying by domestic institutional investors, such as the social security fund and insurers ... Foreign access to China's domestic stock markets is now capped at about $4 billion and limited to twenty-seven institutions [each with individual quotas], known as Qualified Foreign Institutional Investors, or QFIIs ... Money entering China through the QFII programme is locked up for a year ... [It was announced that] the securities regulator would suspend new share sales until the forty-six companies picked by the government for the first and second phases of its disposal plan had completed the conversion of their non-tradable shares ... The securities regulator also said it would work on detailed rules governing the non-tradable share disposal after the forty-six companies complete the conversion of their non-tradable stock ... The programme would be applied to all publicly traded Chinese companies after the rules were approved by the State Council, or cabinet ... There are 1,381 publicly traded companies in China ... The Shanghai index has dropped 28 per cent in the past twelve months, while the Shenzhen index is down 32 per cent, putting the indexes at the bottom of a list of eighty stock benchmarks worldwide tracked by Bloomberg over that period.

(www.iht.com, 11 July 2005)

Foreign investors previously had a quota of $4 billion to invest in mainland stocks and corporate bonds ... This will be lifted to $10 billion ... The China securities regulatory commission, the stock market regulator said it would suspend initial public offerings for the time being to allay fears about a flood of new issues on the market ... But this did not prevent the Shanghai composite index falling 0.6 yesterday [11 July] to a new eight-year low, leaving the market down 20 per cent so far this year [2005] ... Stock and bond issues accounted for [only] 1 per cent of the funds raised by companies in the first quarter of the year, with the rest coming from the banking sector ... In other measures announced yesterday the government indicated that it would give state-owned companies greater freedom to buy equities on the stock market.

(*FT*, 12 July 2005, p. 9)

Chinese companies with at least 300 million tradable shares will be allowed to issue warrants that can be traded on the share market to meet demand as the government moves to sell its stock holdings, the Shanghai and Shenzhen exchanges said Monday [18 July]. The companies must have a market capitalization of tradable shares of not less than ... $362 million in the preceding twenty days when the warrants are listed ... A warrant is a company-issued certificate that represents an option to buy a certain number of shares at a specified price before a predetermined date. A warrant has its own value and can be traded on the open market. About thirty of the 1,381 companies listed on China's two stock exchanges are qualified to sell warrants ... Among the forty-six companies selected by the government to participate in the share disposal programme only Baoshan Iron and Steel plans to issue warrants as compensation for losses caused by the increase in the stock supply ... The plan to allow warrants comes as the government is proceeding with a project to sell about $230 billion of stockholdings in listed companies and convert them into common stock that can be bought and sold on the market. In the past similar plans have been scrapped after stock market plunges.

(www.iht.com, 18 July 2005)

China may soon decide to allow its publicly traded companies to use as much as 10 per cent of their stock as incentives for employees in a bid to improve corporate governance, according to a draft of the proposed regulations. China's securities regulator will let the 1,381 publicly traded companies give shares, stock options and warrants to directors, senior managers and other employees ... Stock options and warrants are rights to buy a certain number of shares at a specified price during a set time period ... The draft rules say that companies that have not converted all their equity to tradable stock cannot take part in the incentive programme. The government wants publicly traded companies to convert about $230 billion of mostly state-held non-tradable shares to ordinary stock that can be bought and sold on China's two exchanges ... Companies will be allowed to grant at most 1 per cent of shares outstanding to an individual, the draft rules state. Independent directors and supervisors will not be allowed to take part in any incentive plans.

(www.iht.com, 21 July 2005)

Shareholders of China Yangtze Power ... have approved a plan to dispose of part of the stake in the electricity generator. Yangtze Power is the second biggest of forty-six companies the government has chosen in a trial that aims to sell about $250 billion of state-owned stock now held as tradable shares. Results of the vote were released on Friday [5 August] ... Citic Securities, China's biggest publicly traded brokerage firm, said Saturday [6 August] that shareholders had approved a plan to dispose of the government's holdings in the company.

(www.iht.com, 7 August 2005)

Shareholders of Baoshan Iron and Steel, China's largest steel maker, have approved plans to compensate small investors for losses tied to the sale of the government's holdings in the company ... Baoshan Steel is among forty-six companies in a programme aimed at selling about $250 billion of state-owned stock held in the form of non-tradable shares. The government wants to cut its stake to cover a pension shortfall and improve corporate governance. Minority shareholders have to be compensated because converting non-tradable stock into equity that can be bought and sold on the market may drive down prices.

(www.iht.com, 15 August 2005)

China's fund management companies will be allowed [subject to restrictions] to invest in warrants, a type of derivative ... This has clarified from the regulatory side that mutual funds can invest in derivative products ... Previously there were no rules regarding whether fund management companies could do these kinds of investments.

(www.iht.com, 17 August 2005)

A group of investors led by the Royal Bank of Scotland and Merrill Lynch, two of the world's biggest financial institutions, has agreed to pay $3.1 billion to acquire a 10 per cent stake in the Bank of China ... The British Bank said that it would pay $1.6 billion and that Merrill Lynch and the Li Ka-shing Foundation, which is run by the Hong Kong businessman of the same name, would pay another $1.5 billion to get a share of Bank of China ... Bank of America said in June that it would pay $3 billion to acquire a 9 per cent stake in the China Construction Bank, which plans to go public later this year [2005] ... The Royal Bank of Scotland ... [is] to acquire a 5 per cent stake ... The investors led by the Royal Bank of Scotland said they would retain their investment in Bank of China for at least three years.

(*IHT*, 19 August 2005, p. 13)

The consortium ... won unprecedented warranties and protections from Beijing to shield its investment from a sudden deterioration in the state lender's finances and other risks. The concessions won by the Royal Bank of Scotland are believed to be the first such guarantees granted to a foreign investor in a Chinese state company. Investment bankers said the move could have profound implications for future Chinese privatizations and prompt other foreign companies to seek similar safety nets ... [Bank of China controls] 12 per cent of the Chinese market for loans and 14 per cent of the country's deposits.

(*FT*, 19 August 2005, p. 1)

The financial authorities have widened a programme to make $270 billion of mostly state-held stock publicly traded ... More than 1,300 companies, including Asia's biggest refiner, China Petroleum and Chemical, can gradually convert their non-tradable shares, the regulator said in a statement on Wednesday [24 August] ... Non-tradable stock accounts for about two-thirds of the market value of publicly trade companies, and 74 per cent of the shares are owned by the state. By making all of China's shares tradable the government aims to raise funds to plug a pension shortfall, increase private ownership of companies and make management more accountable to shareholders. The changes will also broaden the choices for the twenty-six overseas investors that are now allowed to buy as much as $4 billion of China's yuan-denominated A shares ... The government said it planned to increase the combined quotas of overseas investors to $10 billion. That may happen by the end of this year [says an analyst] ... To bolster demand for stocks the government in April permitted banks to set up fund management companies. Bank of Communications and China Construction Bank are among those to have done so. Insurance companies have been allowed to directly invest as much as 5 per cent of their assets in stocks and a maximum of 15 per cent in mutual funds. Like the forty-six that took part in the trial programme companies will need to win approval from holders of two-thirds of tradable A shares ... From being the world's worst performing stock benchmarks over a one-year period, in the past month China's key indexes are among the top ten of seventy-nine tracked by Bloomberg. The Shanghai composite index has advanced 12 per cent; the Shenzhen index has added 13 per cent.

(www.iht.com, 24 August 2005; *IHT*, 25 August 2005, p. 12)

China is to free up trading in all listed companies on mainland stock exchanges ... The government said yesterday [24 August] that all 1,400 listed companies on mainland stock exchanges would be encouraged to change the status of their large holdings of non-tradable shares so that they can be bought and sold, in a move intended to open the way to flotations and secondary share offerings ... The government said companies that had completed the reform of their shareholder structure would be given priority in raising new funds ... The reform gives the government scope to reduce its stakes in many of the companies it controls and could facilitate future privatizations.

(*FT*, 25 August 2005, p. 8)

Temasek Holdings, Singapore's state-owned investment company, has agreed to pay $3.1 billion to buy 10 per cent of Bank of China ... which holds 9 per cent of the $1.65 trillion of savings in China ... The investment company also agreed to buy $500 million of shares in China's second biggest lender when the bank sells shares for the first time ... Royal Bank of Scotland, Merrill Lynch and a foundation set up by the Hong Kong businessman Li Ka-shing agreed to invest $3.1 billion for 10 per cent of Bank of China on 18 August.

(www.iht.com, 1 September 2005)

Temasek Holdings ... [has announced] a proposed investment of up to $6 billion in two large Chinese state-owned banks ... buying a stake in Bank of China and pledging to buy a minority holdings in China Construction Bank, the second and third biggest banks ... Temasek announced this week it would spend $3.1 billion for 10 per cent of Bank of China before the bank's IPO [initial public offering] next year [2006], with plans to spend an extra $500 million on shares once listed. The 10 per cent stake in China Construction bank will cost it $2.4 billion ... Recent Chinese deals have included 5 per cent of Minsheng Bank, a privately owned bank.

(*FT*, 2 September 2005, p. 23)

'It was reported that the Industrial and Commercial Bank of China ... had agreed to sell a 10 per cent stake to a consortium led by Goldman Sachs for $3.1 billion' (*The Economist*, 3 September 2005, p. 9).

On 30 August it emerged that China's biggest lender, Industrial and Commercial Bank of China, had secured $3 billion in investment from two American financial institutions, Goldman Sachs and American Express, and Allianz, a big German insurer. The three will take a combined 10 per cent stake in the state-owned bank ... In June Bank of America invested $3.1 billion in China Construction Bank; in July Temasek, Singapore's state investor, put in $1 billion. Last month [August] Royal Bank of Scotland, Merrill Lynch and Li Ka-shing, a Hong Kong tycoon, bought 10 per cent of Bank of China, which on 31 August said it would offload another 10 per cent to Temasek for $3.1 billion. Temasek also promised to spend another $500 million on Bank of China shares at floatation. All three [Chinese] banks are now on course for listings on foreign stock exchanges ... Royal Bank of Scotland ... will get some of its cash back if Bank of China discovers big problems. It seems that investors in Industrial and Commercial Bank of China, at least, have agreed something similar.

(p. 76)

('The Asian Development Bank, a government-funded institution that promotes regional development, said Monday [10 October] that it would invest $75 million in Bank of China. The ADB stake would represent less than 1 per cent of Bank of China's total share capital': www.iht.com, 10 October 2005.)

'PetroChina, the largest Chinese oil company, plans to sell as much as 19 billion Hong Kong dollars of stock as it increases spending globally to meet soaring demand in the fastest growing major economy' (www.iht.com, 1 September 2005).

Petro-China ... has heightened speculation about further cross-border acquisitions by raising up to 21 billion Hong Kong dollars through an international share placement ... The Hong Kong and New York-listed company ... is believed to be selling 3.52 billion shares to institutional investors, representing 20 per cent of Petro-China's outstanding Hong Kong-listed shares. More than 90 per cent of the placement comprised of new shares while the rest are being sold by the state-owned parent and majority owner, China National Petroleum Corporation.

(*FT*, 1 September 2005, p. 25)

China has set up a renminbi 6.3 billion fund to protect investors in bankrupt securities companies in the latest attempt to boost confidence in its struggling stock market ... The fund was established at the end of August with an initial injection of public funds. The fund is designed to compensate investors who have accounts in bankrupt brokerage companies, an industry that has been plagued in recent years by scandals, poor controls and mismanagement.

(*FT*, 8 September 2005, p. 14)

'The programme ... to convert non-tradable stock holdings into common shares ... was widened last month after forty-five of the forty-six companies involved in the trial stages had their plans approved by shareholders' (www.iht.com, 12 September 2005).

China has widened the overseas investment scope for insurers, allowing them to buy foreign currency funds and mortgage-backed securities as well as stocks ... Insurers will be able to use a maximum of 10 per cent of their foreign exchange capital to invest in overseas stocks of Chinese companies ... China originally outlined its move in June. Domestic insurers had combined foreign exchange reserves of around $10 billion at the end of 2004 ... Insurers will be able to invest in foreign currency products in nine major currencies, including the US dollar, Euro, yen and pound.

(www.iht.com, 12 September 2005)

China may ease restrictions on ownership of its domestic lenders by foreign banks by the end of next year [2006] ... said the chairman of the China Banking Regulatory Commission [on 12 September] ... China allows foreign banks to own up to 25 per cent of its lenders. No single financial institution can own more than 20 per cent, an increase from 15 per cent in 2003 ... Last Tuesday [6 September] ...Standard Charter ... agreed to pay $123 million for 19.9 per cent of newly set-up Bohai Bank.

(www.iht.com, 13 September 2005)

'Bohai Bank [is] the first national commercial bank set up in China since 1996 ... Standard Charter ... plans to expand Bohai from its base in Tianjin' (www.iht.com, 6 September 2005).

China Construction Bank will become the first of China's four biggest lenders to trade on the Hong Kong stock exchange, after an initial public offering of about $6 billion ... The company aims to sell a 12 per cent stake to investors next month [October] and have its trading debut by 28 October ... The Beijing-based lender would beat Industrial and Commercial Bank and Bank of

China, which are planning offerings in 2006 . . .Bank of America, the second biggest US bank, agreed in June to pay $3 billion for . . . a 9 per cent stake in . . . China Construction Bank, including $500 million of the IPO. Temasek Holdings, the Singapore government's investment arm, agreed in July to invest $1 billion in the sale. Credit Suisse First Boston, an arranger of the sale, committed to invest $500 million in the IPO, people familiar with the plan said in August.

(www.iht.com, 25 September 2005)

UBS . . . the Swiss bank . . . said Tuesday [27 September] . . . it will take a $500 million stake in the Bank of China . . . The $500 million stake represents about 1.6 per cent of the Chinese bank . . . The accord comes just as its rival Credit Suisse Group appears to be having a setback in its plans for China. People familiar with the situation said that Credit Suisse's expected investment of $500 million in China Construction Bank had been scrapped to prevent a delay in the Beijing-based lender's $7.7 initial public share offering, scheduled for next month [October] . . . China Construction Bank did not want to wait for Credit Suisse to obtain a waiver from the Hong Kong stock exchange.

(*IHT*, 28 September 2005, p. 18)

[The decision by UBS, the Swiss bank] to spend $210 million to bail out Beijing Securities, an ailing brokerage, in exchange for management control and a 20 per cent stake . . . [goes] beyond the current regulatory framework . . . The deal announced yesterday [28 September] breaks new ground. UBS will only take a minority stake in the yet-to-be-named venture, with the Beijing city government, three state-owned companies and the World Bank's private sector arm buying the rest. However, its right to manage is understood to be enshrined in written approval from the State Council . . . Also the new company will not shoulder past liabilities, although the $210 million invested by UBS will go to cover Beijing Securities' accumulated losses . . . [It is] the first direct investment by a foreign group into a domestic brokerage . . . Other international banks [have been] limited so far to joint ventures that can only underwrite domestic listings.

(*FT*, 29 September 2005, p. 28)

China has set up a fund to protect investors at brokerage firms, as part of efforts to bolster confidence in the country's stock markets after four years of declines, the securities regulator said Thursday. Investors will be able to claim payments of debts and settlement capital from the fund in case of closure, bankruptcy or regulatory takeover . . . The securities regulator wants to draw money back to the equity market, whose value has been halved from record highs reached in June 2001. Investors have been reluctant to buy shares because of the ailing securities industry, which is under scrutiny for mismanagement and misappropriation . . . The government has stepped up efforts to strengthen an industry that had combined losses of 15 billion yuan, or $1.95 billion, last year [2004], by providing loans to bigger and better-run brokerage firms and encouraging mergers.

(www.iht.com, 29 September 2005)

The Chinese stock market is known for the relatively wide assortment of share classes floating on its bourses: A share, B shares and H shares. To this alphabet soup add another: G shares ... The newly released shares are called G shares, after Gugai, meaning share reform ... And that is the key to understanding the recent rise in the Shanghai and Shenzhen stock markets ... Since 2001 the Shanghai and Shenzhen markets have fallen by about half, with the Shanghai index touching a low ... in mid-July ... The government started a pilot programme in April in which forty-six companies would sell their non-tradable shares into the market. By August most of the first tier of companies had won shareholder approval for the plan ... They [analysts] figured that the plan would spread to the rest of the 1,400 or so listed Chinese companies. By late September an additional 139 companies had prepared plans to divest themselves of non-tradable shares and numbers are growing by the week ... Companies with the G distinction include China Yangtze Power ... and Bao Steel ... Most of the G share companies, however, are small.

(www.iht.com, 19 October 2005; *IHT*, 20 October 2005, p. 14)

China Construction Bank is expected to raise more than $8 billion from the sale of up to 14 per cent of its stock when its shares begin trading in Hong Kong on Thursday [20 October] ... After the China Construction Bank listing, the government will still hold more than 70 per cent of the bank's shares.

(www.iht.com, 20 October 2005; *IHT*, 21 October 2005, p. 12)

Shares of China Construction Bank had a lacklustre start on the Hong Kong stock exchange on Thursday [27 October]. But it was still China's biggest initial public offering ever, and the world's largest since 2001, raising $8 billion for the lender ... China Construction Bank is the first of China's big four state-owned banks to publicly list its shares with overseas investors ... China's Bank of Communication raised more than $2 billion after it was listed on the Hong Kong stock exchange.

(www.iht.com, 27 October 2005; *IHT*, 28 October 2005, p. 13)

'China Construction Bank's listing, which raised $8 billion from foreign investors for 12 per cent of its shares, is the largest global floatation for four years' (*The Economist*, 29 October 2005, p. 93).

Bank of America and other foreign institutions that have invested a combined $13 billion in China's banks will be required to hold their shares for at least three years and will not be allowed to buy stakes in more than two lenders, an official of the banking regulator said on Wednesday [2 November]. The restrictions, in addition to an existing cap of 25 per cent on foreign ownership, are aimed at safeguarding financial stability and preventing overseas dominance of the banking industry ... China's government defines a foreign strategic investor as one that buys a stake of more than 5 per cent ... A total of eighteen foreign institutions have invested in sixteen Chinese lenders.

(www.iht.com, 2 November 2005; *IHT*, 3 November 2005, p. 18)

The banking regulator this week confirmed reports that the investment arm of China's central bank, Central Huijin Investment, which is the biggest shareholder in Bank of China, has voted to block a long-mooted plan by Singapore's Temasek to take a 10 per cent stake in the lender.

(*The Economist*, 5 November 2005, p. 91)

'Temasek Holdings of Singapore has still not yet received approval from Bank of China's state-owned controlling shareholder to buy a $3.1 billion stake in ... Bank of China' (www.iht.com, 15 November 2005).

In Beijing some have claimed that foreign lenders have been able to buy stakes in Chinese banks too cheaply. *Caijing*, a Chinese financial magazine, reported yesterday [26 December] that, because of such concerns, Temasek Holdings ... had received approval to buy only a 5 per cent stake in Bank of China rather than the 10 per cent it had originally sought.

(*FT*, 27 December 2005, p. 15)

The government said Monday [7 November] that it would allow foreign investors to buy strategic stakes in more than 1,300 state-controlled companies for the first time, extending moves to transform the ownership of about $200 billion worth of mostly state-held shares ... Participation in the domestic market [is] now capped at $4 billion of quotas given to thirty qualified foreign institutional investors ... The statement, dated 26 October, was published on Monday ... Under the rules, effective immediately, overseas investors who buy strategic shares will be subject to a lock-up period ... Publicly traded companies with 25 per cent or more of their shares held by overseas investors would become eligible for benefits, like preferential tax rates, allowed to 'foreign-invested enterprises', and would remain entitled to those benefits so long as the stake held by overseas investors remained above 10 per cent. The statement did not say how a strategic investment would be defined, nor did it set limits on the stakes that foreign investors could hold. Under the government's campaign to convert shareholdings to common stock, current holders of non-tradable shares can sell up to 5 per cent of their stakes one year after implementing a conversion plan, and up to 10 per cent within two years.

(www.iht.com, 7 November 2005)

In the third quarter [of 2005] the Shanghai and Shenzhen stock exchange indexes ... surged about 25 per cent from four-year lows ... [after a] mid-year turnabout ... But the markets have since given up about half those gains ... So far some 1,400 mainly state-controlled companies have their A shares, or yuan-denominated stock, listed on either the Shanghai or the Shenzhen market ... But only five have all their shares listed.

(*IHT*, Special Report on China, 14 November 2005, p. II)

China will exempt foreign investors in local currency securities from paying capital gains tax, the latest attempt to revive stock markets that have lost more than half their value in the past four years. The state administration of taxation announced the exemption, which applies to foreign investors licensed to buy yuan shares and bonds, in a statement dated 1 December ... The ruling places foreign investors on an equal footing with domestic institutions, which are exempt from capital gains and business tax.

(IHT, 14 December 2005, p. 17)

Citigroup agreed on Monday [26 December] to quadruple its stake in Shanghai Pudong Development Bank to the maximum permitted in return for the chance to invest in other Chinese lenders. The purchase would increase Citigroup's stake to 19.9 per cent from 4.6 per cent ... Citigroup is leading a bid of about $2.7 billion for 85 per cent of Guangdong Development Bank ... It is bidding for Guangdong against [other] groups ... Any bid by Citigroup for another lender needs approval from Pudong Bank because Citigroup agreed in 2003 that it would not invest in a second bank.

(IHT, 27 December 2005, p. 14)

'State-controlled Guangdong Development Bank [is] the first bank in China to offer a majority stake to foreign groups' *(FT*, 27 December 2005, p. 15).

A consortium led by Citigroup has been named the preferred bidder for Guangdong Development Bank after doubling its offer to about $3 billion, putting it on the brink of becoming the first foreign-led group to own a mainland Chinese bank. The consortium, which has raised its bid to 24.1 billion renminbi for 85 per cent of Guangdong Development Bank, is understood to have won rights to hold exclusive talks with the state-owned bank for one month ... The deal with Citigroup ... [which will have] a stake of less than 50 per cent ... and its Chinese partners [is] expected to close in the first quarter of next year [2006] ... [Citibank's] local partners, including China National Cereals, Oils & Foodstuffs, would own the remainder ... Guangzhou-based Guangdong Development Bank ... is regarded as one of the most troubled Chinese lenders ... [and] is the first mainland bank to sell a majority stake to foreign groups. Foreign banks are allowed to own not more than 20 per cent of a Chinese lender alone or 25 per cent jointly. The Guangdong Development Bank deal will, therefore, require special permission from Beijing.

(FT, 31 December 2005, p. 15)

Citigroup itself could own 40 per cent to 45 per cent of Guangdong Development Bank ... a medium-sized bank ... if the deal proceeds ... Citibank for two years has had to sit and watch while rivals have grabbed strategic positions in the Chinese banking market ... Citigroup is paying a high price ... Guangdong Development Bank's financial state is precarious ... Shanghai Pudong's permission ... has been granted, but only on condition that Citigroup raise its stake to 19.9 per cent at a rumoured cost of $800 million, four times the original price per share. Remarkably, Citibank also had to agree not to set up a joint venture with Guangdong Development Bank in credit cards, China's most promising financial business and the only one the Guangdong Bank appears to be good at ... By last October [2005] twenty-two foreign banks had spent $16.5 billion on stakes in seventeen mainland lenders, but had gained little real influence ... Liu Mingkang, the banking regulator, gave warning last month [December 2005] that should foreigners be granted more than a quarter of a

Chinese bank, that bank should be considered foreign, subject to restrictions that, among other things, allow yuan-denominated business in only a few cities.

(The Economist, 7 January 2006, p. 68)

Public companies in China, among the world's worst stock market performers in 2005, started the year [2006] with a new tool: stock incentives to improve profits and governance. Incentive programmes, involving as much as 10 per cent of a company's stock, have been allowed since the start of the new year ... Both shares and options can be used. Incentive programmes – which can be for directors, supervisors, senior executives or other employees – should be carried out only by companies that have disposed of non-tradable stock ... An individual employee can now get as much as 1 per cent of a company's stock as an incentive ... The Shenzhen and Shanghai indexes dropped 9.5 per cent and 6 per cent respectively last year [2005], the third and fourth worst performers among seventy-eight stock benchmarks tracked annually by Bloomberg.

(IHT, 5 January 2006, p. 15)

Goldman Sachs, Allianz and American Express have clinched a $3.8 billion deal to buy a combined 10 per cent stake in Industrial and Commercial Bank of China, the country's largest, in the biggest foreign investment in China's financial sector. The deal [is] to be announced as early as today [27 January 2006] ... Goldman Sachs was expected to take a 7 per cent stake for about $2.6 billion ... Allianz was likely to pay about $1 billion for a 2.5 per cent holding, with American Express investing some $200 million for the remainder ... The three groups will invest separately rather than as a consortium.

(FT, 27 January 2006, p. 21)

A group of investors that includes Goldman Sachs, Allianz Group of Germany and American Express said Friday [27 January] that they would together pay about $3.8 billion to acquire a minority stake in Industrial and Commercial Bank of China [ICBC], China's largest state-owned bank ... The chairman of Goldman Sachs said that his investment bank had agreed to raise about $2.58 billion to close the deal ... Allianz, the German insurance company, agreed to invest about $1 billion and said it would form a strategic alliance with ICBC in the insurance business. And American Express, which is already involved in a credit card venture with ICBC, agreed to invest about $200 million ... The Goldman Sachs-led group paid a hefty price for a 9 per cent or 10 per cent stake in ICBC.

(FT, 28 January 2006, p. 17)

New rules that make it easier for foreign companies to buy shares in listed Chinese companies, which start today [31 January], could encourage a surge in mergers and acquisitions ... The rules allow 'strategic foreign investors' to purchase stakes of more than 10 per cent of a company's A-shares, the most liquid class of shares on the mainland stock market, if the purchaser holds the equity for longer than three years. The rule change has been a factor behind a recent rebound in China's stock market, which has risen 13 per cent in the past two months after a four-month slump. Until now only a small group of foreign investor institutional investors had been allowed to buy A-shares. Investors wishing to buy stakes in listed companies usually had to purchase so-called non-tradable shares. Beijing has introduced a plan to phase out this category.

(*FT*, 31 January 2006, p. 21)

[On 14 February China said it] may ease requirements for foreign investment in its stock and bond markets as early as April ... Fund managers and insurance companies applying under the new plan should have a minimum of $5 billion in securities assets under management, half the current minimum ... Insurance companies that have been in business for at least five years will also be able to apply ... compared with the current thirty-year minimum. China first allowed foreigners to invest in its financial markets in 2003 under the Qualified Foreign Institutional Investor plan, permitting mutual funds, insurance companies, securities firms and banks to buy domestic stock and bonds. Under that programme China granted investment quotas for twenty-seven companies, according to the state administration of foreign exchange, which determines the size of the quota for each participant. Four others have been given initial approval to join the programme, but are awaiting their quotas. The government has granted the participants combined quotas of $5.645 billion to invest in domestic markets. Inclusion in the programme allows foreign investors to trade in so-called A-shares in more than 1,400 domestically listed companies, as well as government securities and corporate bonds. China said last year [2005] that it would double, to $10 billion, the amount that foreign firms could invest in its primary stocks and debt markets, from $4 billion. The government said it wants to bring in foreign capital and expertise to help develop China's capital markets and prop up stock markets that, before a rally began in December [2005], were mired in multi-year lows. Programme participants so far include UBS, Citigroup, Morgan Stanley, Goldman Sachs, HSBC Holdings, Deutsche Bank, ING, J.P. Morgan Chase and Merrill Lynch.

(www.iht.com, 14 February 2006)

The bear market that made Chinese stocks the world's worst performers during the past five years may be over. The Shanghai composite index has climbed 25 per cent since July [2005] as the government permitted overseas investors to buy more shares ... Shanghai's index has had one of the biggest gains this year [2006] among Asian benchmarks ... The Shanghai index has climbed 9.2 per cent this year. The Shenzhen index, China's other stock market, has gained 11 per cent ... China's performance contrasts with losses of 35 per cent for the Shanghai index and 47 per cent for the Shenzhen index during the past five years. They were the world's worst performers among seventy-eight global benchmarks tracked by Bloomberg ... Stocks tumbled from June 2001 through July [2005], when both indexes reached eight-year lows ... China's government is giving overseas fund managers more opportunity to buy shares under a so-called qualified foreign institutional investor programme. About a third of the $5.75 billion of investment authorized under the three-year-old programme was approved during the past seven months. Investors that have at least

$10 billion in assets are eligible for the programme, allowing them to invest no less than $50 million in yuan-denominated securities. The government is also inviting overseas companies to buy stakes in local counterparts that have yuan-denominated shares. The companies will be required to acquire at least a 10 per cent holding and keep the stock for three years.

(*IHT*, 20 February 2006, p. 12)

PRIVATIZATION (SALES AND LEASING)

Large privatization along Eastern European lines has not been adopted in China. Initially China concentrated on deregulation (i.e. gradually opening up certain sectors to private activity). Later on small enterprises began to be sold off in significant numbers and even some medium-sized and large companies have now been sold. Although the state still dominates ownership in medium-sized and large companies, an increasing number of companies have sold a proportion of their shares to private (including foreign) individuals and companies (see the preceding sections for details).

(The stock markets are very underdeveloped and unstable, although some shares are listed elsewhere, e.g. Hong Kong and New York. 'H' shares are traded on the Hong Kong stock exchange – the first company involved was the Tsingtao Brewery in July 1993 – while 'N' shares are traded in New York's Wall Street. 'B' shares are supposed to be purchased for hard currencies such as the US dollar by foreigners only. In reality they have been bought by Chinese citizens, but the state periodically clamped down on the practice. As we have seen above, on 19 February 2001 it was announced that Chinese citizens would be allowed to buy 'B' shares and in November 2002 there was a relaxation of controls on foreign purchases of A shares in Chinese companies.)

'Public ownership' formally remains the 'mainstay' of the economy, but the term has been interpreted more liberally.

Permission has been given to sell or lease small enterprises, but 'some cities and provinces have spontaneously started to sell their large and medium-sized SOEs [state-owned enterprises] to foreign investors' (Wu 1997: 1256–7). Only about 200 state industrial enterprises have been authorized to sell their shares to the public on the stock market, although a much larger number has less formal arrangements for shared ownership between state enterprises (p. 1251).

No one knows exactly how many companies have been sold so far ... The state economic and trade commission estimates that as of November [1998] Liaoning province in the north-east, formerly a bastion of state industry and conservative thinking, had already shed 60 per cent of its small and medium-sized state companies, while coastal and southern provinces had sold almost all of them.

(Kathy Wilhelm, *FEER*, 18 February 1999, pp. 11–12)

Several years ago the Chinese leadership decided that the central authorities would select 1,000 large, high-priority state-owned enterprises, with the intention of reinvigorating them, and divest most of those remaining. But to date relatively few state-owned enterprises – perhaps 10 to 15 per cent – have been divested to the non-state sector, and almost all of these have been small ... In some provinces nearly 50 per cent of small state-owned enterprises have been divested ... Today China's state-owned industrial enterprises account for one-third of national production, more than one-half of total assets, two-thirds of urban employment, almost three-fourths of investment ... [and] absorb more than three-fourths of domestic bank credit.

(Broadman 1999: 52–3)

According to the International Finance Corporation (the private sector arm of the World Bank), in 1998 the state sector contributed 37 per cent of GDP. Private businesses generated 33 per cent, while the balance came from agricultural companies and businesses (*Transition*, 2000, vol. 11, no. 2, p. 40).

Holley Group, the country's market leader in sales of electricity meters to the power industry ... has been trying to privatize since 1994. So far it has succeeded in transferring just 10 per cent of the company to private hands. Even so, its improvised management buy-out scheme is being closely watched by provincial officials and state-enterprise bosses as a possible model for other Chinese companies ... In all 5 per cent of Holley's assets is now in the managers' hands ... [with] plans to slowly build their stakes up to 30 per cent.

(Susan Lawrence, *FEER*, 17 August 2000, pp. 42–4)

[A] massive sell-off of troubled factories, mines and other businesses began quietly in the early 1990s and accelerated after 1997, when Beijing decided to allow the privatization of all but the largest state enterprises ... At first local government favoured the workers ... But ... these worker-owned businesses seem to have encountered serious difficulties. At some factories workers have been unwilling to make the radical changes needed to improve efficiency, including layoffs. At others they have little real power over managers and are unable to demand better results or stop embezzlement. As a result China appears to be undergoing a second ... round of ownership change. This time managers and outside investors are taking enterprise away from workers, almost always with the support of local officials and often through corrupt or questionable methods.

(Philip Pan, *IHT*, 7 December 2002, p. 12)

'China is selling more than 190,000 state companies to private investors. The State-owned Assets Supervision and Administration Commission announced last year [2003] that it was focussing on restructuring just 190 or so large state-owned companies and selling the rest' (www.iht.com, 26 October 2004).

'The top 190 or so state-owned enterprises are directly controlled by the State Assets Supervision and Administration Commission – set up in 2003 to restructure these often moribund firms' (*The Economist*, 3 September 2005, pp. 63–4).

'The country now has about 150,000 state-owned companies, down from 238,000 in 1998, according to figures released in September [2004]' (*FT*, 1 February 2005, p. 13).

'The number of state firms has tumbled from over 300,000 to 150,000 in the past decade' (*The Economist*, 17 September 2005, p. 91).

Conglomerates

China has encouraged the growth of large manufacturing companies to help them compete internationally:

1 Qingdao Haier, well-known for the quality of its home appliances such as washing machines and fridges, has just become one of a half-dozen 'national-level experimental enterprises', model companies expected to rank among the world's giants in a few years' time. The South Korean *chaebol* has been influential. But the government still pressurizes these companies to take on problem enterprises (*The Economist*, 20 December 1997, pp. 119–20). (The *kieretsu* is the Japanese equivalent.)

2 'Chinese big business has grown rapidly, modernized at speed and substantially changed its operational methods. Despite large remaining problems ... China's large SOEs have played a central and essential part in China's new industrial revolution. China's bureaucrats have played an active role in the institutional reconstruction and modernization of large SOEs' (Nolan and Xiaoqiang: 1999: 194).

3 'During China's reforms a powerful group of large SOEs emerged which are gradually becoming genuinely autonomous competitive firms. The "merger boom" has involved large SOEs "merging" with small ones, or small ones merging among themselves. But, up to the time of writing (early 1997) not one merger of a large SOE with another has occurred ... In the mid-1990s, despite large changes in their behaviour, with powerful growth and modernization, even the largest of China's large SOEs was still small compared to the global giants in all aspects other than employment ... The powerful growth of China's large-scale upstream SOEs has already lasted for sixteen years' (Nolan and Xiaoqiang 1999: 191–2). China has had second thoughts about foreign models after the Asian financial crises began in July 1997, which, for example, exposed the weaknesses of organizations like the *chaebol*. But the National People's Congress held in March 1998 confirmed the move towards conglomerates. The deputy minister of the state economic and trade commission: 'While we are going to learn in real earnest the lessons from the South Korean cases, our overall plan on amalgamating enterprise groups will not be affected. We believe that we will have a smooth process of establishing enterprise groups in China. In some key sectors and fields it is necessary for China to establish very large enterprises or enterprise groups in order to develop economies of scale' (*IHT*, 9 March 1998, p. 6). The deputy director of enterprises at the state commission for restructuring the economy: 'China will not change its strategy of developing large enterprise groups despite the fact that some large enterprises in South Korea have gone bust in the ongoing financial crisis. We are aware of the problems but we will not change our plan' (*IHT*, 10 March 1998, p. 6).

4 State-owned holding companies have spread over the petrochemical, chemical, non-ferrous metals, aviation and defence-related industries (Wu 1997: 1256).

5 'The state economic and trade commission has been charged with creating vast

... conglomerates in the all-important steel, energy, chemicals, motor and textile industries' (*FT*, Survey, 16 November 1998, p. vi).

[A] directive [was] issued by the cabinet in April ... outlawing 'regional blockades in market activities' ... While opening up to global markets in the past two decades, China's domestic economy has become more and more fragmented, riddled with local protectionist measures from crude roadblocks to sophisticated technical standards ... Beijing has a vested interest in breaking down local barriers. In addition to making consumers worse off, they are one of the biggest obstacles to the creation of strong national companies which will be able to survive the competition brought by WTO membership ... [There] are twenty-seven provinces and four vast provincial-level cities ... Overcapacity in many sectors is one obvious result [of local protectionism]. Virtually every province has a maker of washing machines, colour televisions and refrigerators. The country also has 120 automakers, most of them surviving on various forms of local protectionism. Beijing wants to reduce the number to just half a dozen, but twenty-two provinces or cities have declared the sector to be a core industry for the coming decade ... Alwyn Young ... [in the November 2000 edition of the *Quarterly Journal of Economics* argues that] when local governments won control of capital and technology ... they rushed to invest it in sectors like heavy industry and consumer products that the state was still protecting with easy money and high prices. When that led to over-investment in many sectors, local officials protected their companies with trade barriers. The result: fragmented markets and investment decisions that often went against comparative advantage.

(Bruce Gilley, *FEER*, 12 July 2001, pp. 17–19)

('China has more than 100 automakers': *IHT*, 19 November 2004, p. 15.)

'[On 27 June 2001] China unveiled a five-year plan to restructure its auto industry by building two or three domestic giants while forcing dozens of smaller manufacturers out of business' (*IHT*, 28 June 2001, p. 19).

('VW's joint ventures in Shanghai and Changchun account for about half of China's passenger car sales. Other joint ventures make up nearly 45 per cent, leaving the twenty-odd domestic makers with just 3 per cent': *FT*, 28 January 2002, p. 25.)

('A growing band of small, Chinese car makers are posting strong sales with less expensive vehicles ... [especially Geely and Chery] ... In the 1990s Beijing said it wanted to merge or shut down almost all of China's small domestic makers, leaving the market to a handful of large companies, most of which were already in joint ventures with foreigners. But the rise of Geely and Chery is instructive. Both companies ignored Beijing's restrictions on new car ventures and with protection from their provincial governments went into production without an official licence. Once they were employing people and selling cars the central government had no option but to formally approve them, though Chery was forced to let domestic giant Shanghai Industrial Automotive Corporation take a 20 per cent stake in the company ... In June 2000 ... a plan [was unveiled] to fundamentally restructure thirteen industries, including the car industry. In a new version of an old plan the government now wants to push most of China's 120-odd car companies towards mergers with the three big domestic car companies': *FEER*, 4 July 2002, pp. 15–16.)

> Shenzhen Investment Holding Corp. [SIHC] is reinventing itself as an institutional investor committed to enhancing shareholding value ... SIHC was set up in 1987 as China's first holding company for managing state enterprises. The idea was to keep them out of the reach of bureaucrats ... It quickly made use of stock markets, incentive pay and mergers to improve performance ... But the real reforms began in 1997, after a party congress in Beijing endorsed a massive dilution of state ownership in the economy ... [SIHC] could hold the key to state-owned enterprise reform in China ... Shenzhen is home to an innovative experiment in commercializing state-owned enterprises that, if successful, could radically transform the management of state-owned enterprises across the country. The reforms are centred on SIHC, the powerful yet little known company for most of the city's government's vast business empire ... SIHC plans to turn itself into a kind of hard-nosed institutional investor ... to turn itself from a passive holding company into a strategic investor ... SIHC has been relieved of worries that constrain other state holding companies in China. These include preserving jobs, providing cheap public services, keeping more than 50 per cent ownership in companies and monopolizing sensitive sectors like telecoms ... Its aim is to act like a large institutional investor or direct investment fund whose managers use ownership to push for better company performance ... The plan is twofold: selling unwanted enterprises and making those remaining perform better ... SIHC has dumped a total of 645 companies in the past two years ... SIHC [has] 1,000-odd companies ... More than 300 of the ... companies are targeted for disposal ... The aim is to consolidate the remaining 600-odd companies into twenty or thirty groups ... As incentives, managers at SIHC companies will be given shares in the companies ... SIHC will also get tough and fire managers ... Stock market listings are another way to help SIHC bolster company performance ... The hardest transformation may be of SIHC itself. At present SIHC's board is dominated by cadres from the city's State Assets Commission, which implement national policies on state enterprises ... Consideration is being given to electing outside businessmen to the SIHC board.
>
> (Bruce Gilley, *FEER*, 15 February 2001, pp. 44–7)

Anshan Iron and Steel, the second largest steel maker in China by output, said Monday [15 August 2005] that it would merge with a smaller rival, the biggest move so far in the government's effort to make the steel industry competitive. Anshan Iron and Steel is combining with Benxi Iron and Steel Group, the nation's fifth biggest producer, to form Anben Steel Group, which will have an annual output of almost 20 million tonnes. Shanghai Baosteel Group, the biggest, produced 21 million tonnes last year [2004] ... The government plans to shut smaller mills among the 264 steel makers and force mergers to create two companies big enough to compete with [international] rivals ... The government hopes that China's top ten steel makers will account for half the country's output by 2010 and 70 per cent by 2020. The top fifteen steel makers account for 45 per cent now. Wuhan Iron and Steel, China's third biggest steel maker, said in May that it would acquire Liuzhou Iron and Steel, a smaller rival in the southern province of Guangxi.

(www.iht.com, 15 August 2005)

The long delay in finalizing the deal led to suggestions the talks were foundering. The companies, both based in the north-east province of Liaoning, are the listed arms of Anshan Steel and Benxi Steel. The news that the merger is to go ahead comes a month after Beijing launched a sweeping blueprint for the steel sector which included a plan for rapid consolidation and the creation of two or three companies to rank in size with the global top ten.

(*FT*, 16 August 2005, p. 24)

(See the section on direct foreign investment on outward investment by Chinese companies.)

A chronology of developments in ownership policy and state enterprise reform

At the Fourteenth Party Congress held 12–18 October 1992) general secretary Jiang Zemin said that:

[Shareholding will] help promote the separation of the functions of government from those of enterprises ... We must change the way in which state-owned enterprises operate and push them on to the market ... [China should allow] efficient enterprises to prosper ... Inefficient ones will be eliminated ... [The public sector, which includes collective enterprises, will remain dominant, but should compete] in the market on an equal footing ... [The private sector will act as] a supplement [and some small state enterprises should be leased or sold to collectives or individuals].

(Jeffries 1993: 497–8)

At the Eighth National People's Congress, held in March 1993, prime minister Li Peng stated that 'small' state enterprises could be sold or leased 'by public bidding'. He warned that the government would 'resolutely stop subsidizing those enterprises that have no prospect of making a profit'.

The third plenary session of the fourteenth Central Committee took place in November 1993. Public ownership was to remain the 'mainstay' of the economy. But there was a call for a 'modern enterprise system which suits the requirements of a market economy'. There should be a separation of 'government administration from enterprise management' as part of the transformation of state enterprises. The enterprise should be more responsible for its own profits and losses. The Communist Party would be removed from the boardroom, company directors being responsible for appointing management (*IHT*, 6 January 1994, p. 13). A start was to be made on a 'step by step' conversion of some state enterprises into corporations (the first corporation law was due to be considered by the National People's Congress in early 1994). The aim was to turn as many as possible into limited liability companies (and in some cases joint stock companies), which would stand on their own feet (responsible for their own profits and losses, i.e. no automatic subsidies). In a document issued on 16 November it was stated that persistently loss-making state enterprises should apply for bankruptcy (the failing enterprises would be 'eliminated in the market competition'). Small state enterprises could be leased or sold. But these changes 'should be adopted in a gradual manner after experiments. It must not be done for show or rashly on a mass scale.'

Although the dominance of public ownership was affirmed in 1993,

> public ownership is now being interpreted more flexibly and accommodates not only collective ownership but also joint stock companies, or public–private joint ownership, in which the state would hold either majority or minority equity positions depending on the perceived importance of the enterprise or industry.

The reform of state enterprises is currently being attempted through a programme of adopting 'modern company systems', a programme of corporatization aimed at clarifying property rights by converting state enterprises into Western-type corporate forms with clearly defined capital structures and improved corporate governance systems. 'Since 1992 thousands of SOEs [state-owned enterprises] have been converted into limited liability companies, and listed and unlisted joint stock companies. But they constitute only a minor percentage of the total number of SOEs' (Lin 1995: 12). 'The privatization of major SOEs may be desirable in the long run, but it is not currently on the government's agenda and is unlikely to be feasible in the near term' (p. 21).

(On 20 June 1995 an experimental plan was announced whereby profitable state enterprises that merge with unprofitable ones will assume the total debt, which must be repaid over five years. But interest will not be charged for two years on loans used for circulating funds or for three years on fixed asset loans. Eighteen enterprises were already targeted, but all eligible state enterprises would be able to participate: *IHT*, 21 June 1995, p. 17.)

Several sources (*IHT*, 25 November 1993, pp. 1, 21, and 6 January 1994, p. 13; *FEER*, 9 December 1993, p. 75) reported a pilot scheme to operate in 1994 (later postponed to 1995). Around 100 large state enterprises were to become corporations (limited liability companies owned jointly by the state and by shareholders), shedding social welfare activities but assuming responsibility for the failure or success of the business. (A payroll tax would pay for welfare services such as pensions, health care and unemployment benefit, while private insurance schemes could act as a supplement: *The Economist*, 20 November 1993, p. 85.) If successful, the reform would spread to all 11,000 medium-sized and large enterprises within three to five years. Some enterprises could become multinational corporations. According to Carl Goldstein (*FEER*, 23 December 1993, p. 46), the new plan permits major stakes (in some cases even majority stakes) in state enterprises to be sold to private or foreign investors (although the state has to retain control in, for example, arms manufacture and other basic industries). On 7 January 1994 it was announced that the enterprises in the pilot scheme would be granted autonomy in wage determination (provided that wage increases did not exceed 'a rate representing economic efficiency') and the authority to dismiss workers in the name of efficiency (note that on the same day a regionally varying minimum wage scheme for urban areas was announced; it requires provinces and municipalities to pay at least the average wage in the region) (*IHT*, 8 January 1994, p. 13). On 3 November 1994 it was announced that the enterprises had been selected.

(The outcome of the reform has been dealt with above.)

(Reformers call for intensified efforts to restructure the governance of state enterprises by distributing shares among multiple owners – provincial and local governments, other state enterprises, banks, newly established asset management companies and individuals – in the expectation that arm's-length relations between owners and managers will enhance performance: Jefferson and Rawski 1994: 65.)

At the Tenth National People's Congress in March 1995 prime minister Li Peng said that the aim was 'to invigorate the state sector as a whole so as to give fuller scope to its dominant role'.

In September 1997, in his opening speech to the Fifteenth Communist Party Congress, Jiang Zemin gave priority to economic reform. He stressed the need to 'downsize' state enterprises and make them more efficient in general despite the 'temporary' difficulties experienced by workers laid off. China should 'quicken the pace' of state enterprises reform, including 'reorganization, association, merger, leasing, contract operation, joint stock partnership or sell-off'. The state must retain 'a dominant position in major industries and key areas that concern the life-blood of the national economy' but 'diverse forms of ownership' should be encouraged. Jiang Zemin did not use the term 'privatization' but stressed an increasing role for 'public ownership'.

> We should strive to seek various forms of materializing public ownership that can greatly promote the growth of productive resources ... Public ownership can and should take diversified forms ... We must have a comprehensive understanding of what is meant by the public sector of the economy. The public sector includes not only the state- and collectively-owned sectors, but also the state- and collectively-owned elements in the sector of mixed owner-ship ... Even if the state-owned sector accounts for a smaller proportion of the economy, this will not affect the socialist nature of our country ... We cannot say in general terms that the shareholding system is public or private, for the key lies in who holds the controlling share.

Chinese officials say that state control will be maintained over some 3,000 core enterprises (*FT*, 15 September 1997, p. 6).

> President Jiang Zemin indicated that some 10,000 of the 13,000 medium-sized and large enterprises owned by the state will be sold. Sold to whom was not explained. President Jiang indicated that they would not be privatized but would go into 'public ownership', a conception yet to be clarified ... The government appears to want takeovers, fusions and bankruptcy ... so as eventually to produce a small number of industrial-banking-marketing conglomerates on the model of the big Japanese and Korean trading and manufacturing groups. Those are close to their governments, following national industrial and trading strategies.
>
> (William Pfaff, *IHT*, 18 September 1997, p. 8)

The number of wholly state-owned enterprises will be reduced from 130,000 to 512 of the largest ('priority') ones, the 512 enterprises accounting for about half of the state sector's assets and sales (*IHT*, 16 September 1997, p. 18). Of the 118,000 industrial enterprises 512, being among the largest, will remain entirely state-owned. The 512 enterprises account for almost half of state assets and sales (*FEER*, 25 September 1997, pp. 5, 15). (After remaining relatively stable – in the range of 100,000 during the past ten years or so – the number of state industrial enterprises sharply fell during 1997–8, from about 110,000 in 1997 to 64,700 in 1978: *Transition*, 1999, vol. 10, no. 5, p. 32.)

After the Fifteenth Congress of the Chinese Communist Party, held in September 1997, three major policies were announced to develop large and medium-sized enterprises:

1   It is hoped to establish three to five large firms in the world's biggest 500 enterprises by the year 2000. To this end the central government would channel extra funds into a select number of large enterprises. Included among the first six firms selected in November 1997 to receive funds for technical renovation were the Shanghai Baoshan Steel Works and the Haier Electrical Appliances Group.

2   The aim is to develop a modern enterprise system in large SOEs by the year 2100. As part of the Ninth Five Year Plan the central government has selected 1,000 SOEs to form the 'core' of the 'modern enterprise system'. In 1996 the central government announced that a main bank relationship would be developed in these 1,000 enterprises, with a pilot programme involving 300 firms.

3   A number of enterprise groups is being developed in strategic sectors. The central government has chosen 512 enterprises to form the basis of these enterprise groups. At the national level the State Council is backing fifty-seven enterprise groups (while others are being promoted at lower levels). The two largest enterprise groups are in petrochemicals, the third biggest one is the Baosteel Group in Shanghai and there are other ones in aviation, electrical household appliances and foreign trade (Smyth 2000: 722–3).

China's 305,000 state enterprises employ 70 per cent of the urban work force (109 million workers) and generate 30 per cent of total industrial output. 'The government is nurturing 1,000 of the larger enterprises – of which 120 will be turned into big business groups – under the credo "grasp the big, release the small" adopted at the Fifteenth Communist Party Congress in September 1997' (Pamela Yatsko, *FEER*, 21 May 1998, p. 14). Included among 'the 120 state enterprises earmarked for conglomerate status' are Sichuan Changhong Electronics Group (which is diversifying into areas other than television sets), Qingdao Haier (which makes goods such as refrigerators and air-conditioners), Baoshan Steel, Peking University Founder Group, Jiangnan Shipyard Group and North Pharmaceutical Group. The aim is to form two megafirms in the oil industry (pp. 10–13).

'One of the most important decisions made in the . . . Fifteenth Chinese Communist Party Congress [September 1997] was the endorsement of the shareholding system as the "mainstream reform programme" for state-owned enterprises (SOEs)' (Ma 1998: 379). Jiang Zemin reported to the congress:

We cannot say in general terms that the shareholding system is public or private. The key lies in who holds the controlling share. Under the premise that public ownership is dominant, a decline in the relative proportion of state ownership will not affect the socialist nature of China.

According to Jiang, public ownership includes not only state and collective ownership but also the state's and collectives' share in the mixed economy (p. 395).

China's sluggish state-owned enterprises continue to be a fiscal drain on the government and a drag on the economy. One reason for their poor showing is top staffers traditionally have been chosen because of their excellent political connections and not their management acumen ... Most managers at state-run factories are still appointed by local governments, boards of directors and cadres. But since the Fifteenth National Congress of the Communist Party of China in September 1997 ... more and more companies and district governments realize that true management change lies in creating competition to fill top posts ... Since 1997 a handful of state companies have begun to experiment with salary and bonus schemes that link a manager's earnings to a company's performance. Many are called 'stock options', though they bear little relationship to traditional Western incentives in which executives are given options to buy company shares at below market price ... [For example, one general manager] had to agree to purchase 200,000 renminbi worth of stock in the company upfront. To do so she had to spend 100,000 renminbi of her own savings and borrow 100,000 renminbi from family and friends. She is also committed to buying additional stock worth 880,000 renminbi. Each year she is awarded a bonus – depending on how well the company is doing – that is used to pay off her 110,000 renminbi a year stock bill. No money actually changes hands and she cannot touch her stock until she completes her eight-year contract at the company. At the end of her tenure she can sell her stock to her successor or an outside investor ... If times get tough and bonuses drop she will have to use her own savings or borrow funds to pay off her bill ... [In another example the achievement of] net profits equal to or above 3 per cent of its assets, then the manager is rewarded with 2 per cent to 5 per cent of the additional profit in the form of a stock option. The manager can only sell stock when his or her contract ends.

(Trish Saywell, *FEER*, 8 July 1999, pp. 66–8)

At the National People's Congress held in March 1998 the following important issues were discussed:

1   Li Peng tackled the problem of bureaucracy: 'The incompatibilities of government institutions to the development of a socialist market economy have become increasingly apparent. Unwieldy organization and failure to separate the functions of the government from those of enterprises have given rise to bureaucracy, promoting unhealthy practices and created a heavy financial burden.'

The total number of civil servants was to be halved over three years, with those in central government reaching that figure by the end of 1998. The reasons included combating bureaucracy, corruption and idleness. The total number of ministries was to be cut from forty to twenty-nine. Fifteen State Council ministries and commissions were to be disbanded or reduced in size, with four 'super-ministries' created. (The four are the state commission for science, technology and industry for national defence, the information industry ministry, the ministry of labour and social security, and the ministry of land resources.)

('A bold promise to cut the central-government bureaucracy by half appears to have run into the sand': *The Economist*, 18 July 1998, p. 76. 'A pledge to cut the central government's bureaucracy by half this year has almost been achieved': *FT*, Survey, 16 November 1998, p. i. 'The complement of ministries has been cut from forty to twenty-nine and staff numbers slashed by nearly half': p. vi.)

2 Businesses and enterprises were to be hived off from government departments and state subsidies to non-administrative units phased out over three years.

The deputy minister of the state economic and trade commission:

> The most important objective in this round of government reorganization is to separate government administration from enterprise management. The government reform will take ministries that originally managed enterprises, retain their administrative functions and make them bureaus under the state economic and trade commission. In this way enterprises can become legal entities and enter the market. Those state enterprises that meet requirements can gradually be listed [on stock exchanges]. We have been talking about the separation of government administration from enterprise management for more than ten years. Some progress has been made, but basically the question has not been resolved.

The deputy minister said that inspections of enterprises spun off from ministries would be allowed, but operations would fall into the hands of professional managers (*IHT*, 9 March 1998, p. 6). ('The mechanism by which the government will try to separate the regulatory role of ministries from their commercial interests . . . was far from clear': *FT*, 9 March 1998, p. 3. The idea is that ministries with regulatory powers no longer do business in the markets they oversee. Otherwise problems arise, e.g. foreign companies are regulated by their competitors: *FEER*, 19 March 1998, p. 40.)

(In 1994 the government authorized the creation of a second telecoms operator, China Unicom, to compete with China Telecom. In 1998 the government forced the telecoms regulator, the ministry of information industry, to give up operating China Telecom so that the ministry could play a more neutral role: *FEER*, 30 September 1999, p. 70.)

On 10 July 1998 local governments were told to curb 'the prevalence of selling small state-owned enterprises'. According to the state economic and trade commission, 'The practice has exerted a negative impact on local economic development and social stability and relocation of laid-off workers' (*FEER*, 30 July 1998, p. 46). The sale of small state enterprises is to be supervised by the state economic and trade commission. 'Random' sales of small enterprises are to be banned (*FT*, 11 July 1998, p. 5). The sale of small enterprises is claimed to have confused people and 'seriously affected' the social stability of some areas. Merger and restructuring of such enterprises is recommended rather than auctioning them (*FT*, 13 July 1998, p. 20). On 10 July 1998 the government issued a notice critical of 'blind' privatization. The government is concerned that the sale of such enterprises is often accompanied by cronyism and corruption (*The Economist*, 18 July 1998, p. 76). 'Abuses were rampant. To make companies attractive local authorities had written off at least 100 billion renminbi ($12 billion) in debt without consulting the banks, and some managers were forcing workers to buy shares or lend them cash for buy-outs' (*FEER*, 18 February 1999, p. 11). 'Other critics allege that many companies were sold cheaply to the cronies of local officials ... Some managers forced workers to buy shares under threat of losing their jobs' (p. 15).

> China has ordered [on 29 November 1998] its vast bureaucracy to cut ties with all its businesses next year [1999] in a bid to stamp out corruption ... Organs of the Communist Party and the government were told to give up enterprises under their control.
>
> (*IHT*, 30 November 1998, p. 17)

> China has stepped up its drive to divorce government from business with an order that the ruling Communist Party and state organizations sever links with enterprises starting next year ... A first step will be to place China's largest 512 state enterprises, currently controlled by ministries and other government bodies, under supervision by a newly established 'large enterprise work committee', itself a government body ... Financial firms tied to the bureaucracy are to be run temporarily by the finance ministry and central bank ... The reports said the aim was to curb corruption, boost competition and end favouritism in lending, share listing rights, foreign investment and tax collection.
>
> (James Kynge, *FT*, 30 November 1998, p. 6)

Seeking to counter recent reports that China's ambitious economic reform plan is losing steam, Chinese officials strongly restated their intention Monday [1 December 1998] to overhaul the country's debt-ridden system of state-owned industries by the end of 2000, streamlining larger companies and generally allowing smaller ones to be sold to private owners or to go bankrupt. Acknowledging that the task had proved more difficult than anticipated, in part because of the Asian crisis, Sheng Huaren, the head of the state economic and trade commission, nonetheless insisted that the country had made significant progress toward its goal of establishing a more 'modern corporate system'. 'The goal of lifting the great majority of state-owned enterprises out of difficulty in three years is absolutely achievable,' Mr Sheng said, although he also noted that China had encountered 'unprecedented issues and difficulties' since the beginning of the year ... He insisted that by the end of the year the government planned effectively to 'de-link' the Communist Party, government ministries, the army and the police from their multitude of business interests ... Mr Sheng's remarks came just three days after prime minister Zhu Rongyi ... again took centre stage in a very public tour of Liaoning province, the epicentre of large, inefficient state-owned enterprises ... praising those state-owned enterprises in Liaoning that had for the first time turned a profit generally through greater efficiency and reducing the number of employees. Strongly worded statements from both Mr Zhu and Mr Sheng came as something of a surprise, since economists both in and out of China had recently said that the government had slowed the restructuring of state enterprises, instead pumping money into them in a desperate effort to stimulate economic growth.

(Elisabeth Rosenthal, *IHT*, 1 December 1998, pp. 1, 6)

On the reform of state companies, the report said measures would be taken to separate the administration from the management of enterprises, prevent duplication of projects and set up a social security system. Financial reform efforts, especially at state-owned commercial banks will be accelerated, state radio said.

(*IHT*, 10 December 1998, p. 18)

On 18 December 1998 Jiang Zemin, in a speech marking twenty years of economic reforms, stressed that the economy would continue to be dominated by the state-run sector. But he added that private enterprise also played an important role in China's development (*IHT*, 9 December 1998, p. 8).

When the National People's Congress meets next month [March 1999], delegates are expected to declare private businesses 'an important component of the socialist market economy' ... [Currently the constitution] merely permits private businesses to 'exist and develop' ... as a complement to the state-owned economy ... Of all forms of discrimination the one that most rankles with large private companies is a ban on listing on China's two stock exchanges or issuing bonds ... Several companies have found back-door routes to listing [e.g. buying controlling stakes in companies already listed], but all needed special political support. Private businesses also remain barred from controlling companies in certain sectors of the economy, notable finance, railways, power and telecommunications.

(Susan Lawrence, *FEER*, 25 February 1999, pp. 50–1)

The Ninth National People's Congress (held 5–15 March 1999) agreed to alter Article 11 of the constitution. It was amended to state that 'non-public sectors' constitute 'an important component of China's socialist market economy' rather than merely 'a complement to the socialist public economy'.

Chinese officials said Tuesday [3 August 1999] that they would embrace a broad programme of debt-for-equity swaps that will include the possibility of some foreign ownership ... China's leaders also agreed that a larger percentage of government-owned shares can be sold on the nation's stock markets, the officials said ... [although] China's Communist Party leaders still insist that the state will maintain majority ownership even in the companies that sell stock ... Chinese officials said that foreign buyers would be allowed in some cases to buy stock that is converted from debt.

(*IHT*, 4 August 1999, p. 16)

Shares of listed state companies were to be traded more freely on China's stock markets. The government would keep a controlling share in listed state firms, but would not require the state to hold a specific percentage of shares (*FEER*, 12 August 1999, p. 47).

A Communist Party plenum was held on 19–22 September 1999.

> In a gesture of support for premier Zhu Rongyi the communiqué restated the party's commitment to pulling 'most' state enterprises out of the red in 'about' three years from late 1997. For those who want a slower timetable, however, the communiqué also said the party had set goals for state enterprise reform extending to 2010. Again in deference to Zhu, the communiqué explicitly committed the party to developing a 'mixed ownership' economy and loosening control over small and medium-sized state enterprises. But it also put a new emphasis on 'strengthening and improving party leadership' over such enterprises.
>
> (*FEER*, 7 October 1999, p. 14)

'Two years ago the government committed to reforming the state-owned sectors of the economy in three years, but the September [1999] report [of the Central Committee] pushed that deadline back a decade, to 2010' (*IHT*, 29 October 1999, p. 4).

A statement was released on 27 September 1999. While affirming that 'the public-ownership economy, which includes the state-owned economy, is the economic basis of China's socialist system', the statement also warned that enterprises needed to stop relying on government bailouts. About 240,000 state enterprises employ 90 million people. Enterprises were urged to raise money by selling stocks and bonds instead of depending on bank loans. State enterprise would be allowed to transfer land rights, plant and equipment to obtain cash for working capital or debt reduction (*IHT*, 28 September 1999, p. 15).

> [On 4 January 2000] the state development planning commission announced that private enterprises should be put on an 'equal footing with state-owned enterprises' for the first time since the communists took power in 1949. The announcement was made by planning minister Zeng Peiyan ... Mr Zeng said China's economy faced 'problems that need urgent solution'. Nineteen straight months of deflation caused by a lack of consumer spending, slowing investment in both state and non-state sectors and an excessive reliance on state investment have all contributed to a weakening economy. Mr Zeng said the government would 'actively guide and encourage private investment' and would 'eliminate all restrictive and discriminatory regulations that are not friendly toward private investment and private economic development in taxes, land use, business start-ups and import and export' .... The statement dangled the prospect of unprecedented access to two Chinese stock markets, in Shanghai and Shenzhen, for domestic private companies. 'Except for the areas that are related to national security and those that must be monopolized by the state, all the rest of the areas should allow private capital to enter,' the planning commission statement said. Most economists

say that everything will be open to private companies except the military, telecommunications and energy-related areas, along with some parts of the transportation sector. Currently, private companies face numerous obstacles. Lack of access to capital – either through bank loans or public offering of stocks – has long stymied their development. Private business leaders are often forced to pay huge bribes simply to get a business licence ... In China 50 million people join the work force each year. The state-run sector is contracting at a rate of at least 3 million workers a year. Without the private sector, most economists here [Beijing] predict that massive social unrest would rock Chinese cities.

(John Pomfret, *IHT*, 5 January 2000, pp. 1, 4)

His [Zeng Peiyan's] remarks raise the prospect that for the first time since the 1949 communist revolution a virtually level playing field will be created. Private companies will enjoy the same treatment as the state sector, which consumes more than 70 per cent of state bank lending and employs more than 50 per cent of the urban work force ... 'In the area of stock listings private enterprise should enjoy equal opportunity which was enjoyed by the state-owned enterprises,' Mr Zeng said ... Chinese economists said the new emphasis on private enterprise was driven by Beijing's disquiet over the most worrying aspect of the country's economic performance in 1999 – a significant decline in investment. Official figures show that total fixed asset investment was ... down from last year [1998] ... Only a handful of some 950 listed companies were privately held and state banks remain wary of lending to non-state companies.

(James Kynge, *FT*, 5 January 2000, p. 10)

Two years into a three-year programme, the government said Tuesday [25 January] that the coming year marked a 'decisive battle' in turning around ailing state enterprises ... The head of the commission overseeing the programme expressed confidence that the government would meet its target of getting most key state enterprises out of chronic debt and ready for membership in the WTO by early 2001. He listed signs of success over the past year; losses were reduced or eliminated at many enterprises; profits rose 70 per cent ... The rust-belt north-east and the textile industry made profits for the first time in six years ... The government would continue measures to remove years of debt on the companies' books and subsidize technological renovations. He also said that more enterprises would be merged or allowed to fail. Restructuring will be intensified.

(*IHT*, 26 January 2000, p. 16)

'The party has quietly moved this year [2000] from a policy of "permitting and encouraging" the private sector to a policy, included in the communiqué of the party's recently concluded [fifth] plenum, of "supporting and guiding" it' (Susan Lawrence, *FEER*, 26 October 2000, p. 34). 'In October [2000] a key communiqué pledged the party to "support, encourage and guide" the development of the private sector' (*FT*, Survey, 13 November 2000, p. i).

At the National People's Congress held in March 2002

> Mr Zhu [Rongyi] reaffirmed the need to 'deepen' the reform of state-owned enterprises and restructure state companies to form 'as quickly as possible a number of large companies and enterprise groups that are internationally competitive'. Beijing is currently engaged in directing mergers in the airline, telecommunications and power industries.
>
> (*FT*, 6 March 2002, p. 10)

Jiang Zemin (speech made on 8 November 2002 at the Sixteenth Communist Party Congress held on 8–14 November):

> We need to respect and protect all work that is good for the people and society and improve the legal system for protecting private property ... [The] dominant role [is played by the state sector] ... Controlling shares in lifeline enterprises must be held by the state ... [The private sector is] an important component part ... We should admit into the party advanced elements of social strata [including private entrepreneurs, employees of foreign funded firms and the self-employed] who accept the party's programme and constitution in order to increase the influence and rallying force of the party in society at large.

'[It was announced on 11 November 2002 that] private businesses would be granted equal access to bank credit ... [More] areas closed to private businesses in the past ... would be opened to private capital soon' (*IHT*, 12 November 2002, p. 8).

'The Shanghai gold exchange, the first in China's communist era, began formal trading on Wednesday [30 October 2002] ... China is one of the world's top five gold producers' (*IHT*, 31 October 2003, p. 16).

> Until late last year [2002] the central bank fixed the domestic price of gold. It bought all the gold produced by China's 1,000 or so mines and allocated it to jewellers. This ended in October [2002] when a gold exchange opened in Shanghai where producers and wholesalers trade directly with one another. In March [2003] the central bank went further and gave up its power to license producers and retailers. Now anybody can enter the gold business in China. A far bigger change is planned for June [2003] when individuals will be allowed to invest in gold, either by buying ingots or by opening gold accounts at their banks. China has one of the highest savings rates in the world, officially about 40 per cent ... International trade, however, is one aspect that the central bank is not eager to liberalize.
>
> (*The Economist*, 10 May 2003, p. 80)

China's new government spelt out a cautious strategy yesterday [23 May 2003] for the reform of its state-owned enterprises ... The new government also shied away from setting a target for the transformation of the lumbering state sector ... The new approach to state-owned enterprise reform ... relies mainly on reconfiguring the relationship between the government and the enterprises it owns. As a first step, state enterprises will have their ownership transferred to a new State Assets Supervision and Administration Commission (Sasac). This means that, in theory, regulators will no longer own enterprises they are supposed to regulate. So far, ownership and supervision of 196 enterprises ... had been transferred to Sasac, said Li Rongrong, commission director. He did not say how many of 174,000 state enterprises would be transferred to Sasac or when. The overarching aims of Sasac, Mr Li said, would be to build large, successful state-owned groups able to dominate the sector in which they operated. 'The state-owned economy must be the dominant part of the economy' [he said].

(*FT*, 23 May 2003, p. 13)

The National People's Congress will preside over the slimming down of the central government from twenty-nine to twenty-one ministries and oversee efforts to separate ministries from the state enterprises they own. The symbiotic relationships between enterprises and their owner/regulators has been blamed for both high levels of official corruption and unfair competition in certain industries ... The congress is expected to approve the establishment of a new body, the State Asset Management Commission. Over time ... the transfer process may take at least a year ... the commission and its local offshoots will assume ownership from ministries and other regional organs of ... 190,000 state-owned enterprises ... Central and local authorities will decide which level of government owns which enterprise. This will enable local authorities to sell stakes in the corporations they own without seeking permission from Beijing.

(*FT*, 4 March 2003, p. 12)

'[The director] said Sasac had taken control of 196 [state] enterprises ... There are currently around 174,000 state companies' (*FEER*, 5 June 2003, p. 23).

The State-Owned Asset Supervision and Administration Commission (SASAC), created in 2003, consolidated its powers at the centre and took over the restructuring process of the largest SOEs. With the SASAC's release of over 300,000 smaller SOEs to the control of provincial and local governments, many local governments quickly disposed of these firms through privatization schemes and management buy-outs.

(Gallagher 2005: 25)

'The first private insurance firm in China since 1949 ... Minsheng Life Assurance ... [has] opened for business' (*FEER*, 5 June 2003, p. 22).

The 'Third Plenum' meeting of the party's ruling Central Committee [held on 11–14 October 2003]... called for more equal treatment for private business ... The communiqué made clear leaders' commitment to greater legal guarantees for private business ... 'Non-state sector enterprises [should] enjoy equal treatment in such areas as investment, taxation, land use and foreign trade,' it said. It softened the call, however, by offering only a vague promise of protection for property rights rather than explicit guarantees for private ownership, and stressed a continuing commitment to the role of state industry ...

'Increasing employment should be given a more prominent position in economic and social development,' the communiqué said, adding that greater effort should be made to spread wealth more evenly.

(*FT*, 16 October 2003, p. 11)

There was talk of the need to perfect the 'socialist market economy' (*FT*, 22 October 2003, p. 17).

The communiqué committed the government to delivering 'a modern system of property rights' ... At the moment, however, legal protection for business profits, and the right of individuals to get compensation for forcible removal of property are based on administrative discretion rather than any clear or enforceable set of laws ... The final communiqué offered only a vague reference to the need actively to 'promote political system reform and widen socialist democracy'.

(*FT*, 18 October 2003, p. 15)

The new leaders ... have closed a secretive annual planning session [known as a plenum and lasting four days] with a broad pledge to deepen market reforms and to help the poor, but without detailing any new economic or political policies ... A communiqué ... did not reveal details about a plan to amend the constitution that had been widely discussed in state-controlled media ... The statement issued at the close of the party meeting did not depart markedly from past policies. But it emphasized the need to guarantee legal property rights, a key demand of private entrepreneurs. It also promised to allow the use of private capital in traditionally public endeavours, like building hospitals and schools. Officials said they intended to alter the constitution, but they did not say how or when ... The party is committed to pursuing a more balanced vision of economic development by addressing sensitive social issues. It pledged to reduce unemployment in declining industrial cities and the countryside, to narrow gaps in income between rural and urban labourers, to set minimum income levels and to pursue other 'mechanisms for sustainable economic and social development'. No details were provided.

(www.iht.com, 16 October 2003)

At the end of a four-day, low-key meeting, the party's Central Committee plenum backed legal and regulatory changes that it said would 'perfect' the economic system, including fairer treatment for private enterprises and equal 'treatment in investment, financing, taxation, land use and foreign trade'. It said private enterprises should be encouraged to enter previously closed sectors, such as infrastructure and public utilities ... ['Although the establishment of private oil companies has not been expressly permitted by Beijing, the drilling of wells by private entrepreneurs in Shaanxi was authorized with contracts signed by local governments': *FT*, 14 July 2003, p. 6] ... The official Xinhua news agency said the plenum approved a proposal to revise the constitution, but gave no details of what it was ... 'We should protect all kinds of property ownership – and private ownership as well' ... Hu Jintao [said on television] ... Xinhua said the plenum approved a decision on improving the 'socialist market economic system', but gave no specifics. But an overall change of public stress under Hu in tackling the gap between rich and poor is a reaction to a strategy that favoured hard infrastructure projects – roads, bridges and buildings – to keep the economy growing rapidly and producing new jobs. This worked, but at the cost of investment in soft infrastructure such as the health system, social welfare and rural education. Economist Zhang Zhuoyuan ... [says] the blow from the outbreak of SARS earlier in the year contributed to a rethink of Beijing's pursuit of GDP growth while paying less attention to social management, public services and the development of society ... His point chimes with the more caring image of Hu and premier Wen Jiabao projected by the party propaganda machine and also in private meetings with both men. Since taking power they have stressed the need for a more broad-based development and being seen to care more about ordinary people. 'Economic growth is not our only goal. We aim to balance economic growth, political developments and social undertakings,' Hu [said recently] ... Hu said after the plenum that it was important that jobs should be found for people in the northeast. That focus sets Hu and Wen apart from Jiang's high-profile drive to develop the west and plays to their image of being truly concerned for those who lost out in reforms under Jiang and former premier Zhu Rongyi ... The government has stated that it wants to see the establishment of a full market economy in China by 2010.

(*FEER*, 23 October 2003, pp. 34–7)

The Central Committee called for a narrowing of the rural–urban gap, for a better social security system and for private firms to be treated as equals of their state-owned counterparts. It also called for 'greater efforts' to accelerate the growth of cities – essential if the 300 million people in the countryside with little or nothing to do are to get a chance to work.

(*The Economist*, 18 October 2003, p. 69)

China is changing its constitution to protect private property rights for the first time since the 1949 communist revolution ... A constitutional amendment endorsed by the Communist Party was put before legislators on Monday [22 December 2003] ... The proposed amendment on property says 'private property obtained legally shall not be violated', according to the official Xinhua press agency. The press agency said that would put private property 'on an equal footing with public property'. The amendments were submitted to the Standing Committee of the National People's Congress, a smaller, party-controlled body that handles lawmaking when the full legislature – which only meets two weeks a year – is out of session ... The party leaders also sent the National People's Congress a proposed amendment to enshrine in the constitution the theories of Jiang Zemin ... who invited capitalists to join the party ... The amendment on Jiang's theories says they shall be considered guiding principles along with the ideology of Mao Zedong and the late leader Deng Xiaoping, who initiated China's economic reforms ... Xinhua did not say whether Jiang would be mentioned by name.

(www.iht.com, 22 December 2003)

China's Communist Party has called for protection of private property to be written into the constitution, along with references to the political theory of Jiang Zemin ... though it is unclear if Mr Jiang's name will be written into the constitution ... Xinhua said Mr Jiang's political ideas – known as the 'Three Represents' ['advanced forces of production, advanced culture and the interests of the majority of the people'] – would be established as 'guiding principles of the nation', alongside Marxism, Leninism, Mao Zedong Thought and Deng Xiaoping Theory ... The constitutional proposals must still win formal approval from the National People's Congress [meeting in March 2004].

(*FT*, 23 December 2003, p. 5)

'A revised Article 5 will read: "Citizens legal private property is not to be violated ... The state protects citizens' property rights and inheritance rights according to the law'" (*FT*, 14 January 2004, p. 19).

China has set a floor price for the sale of government shares in listed companies ... [namely] that state shares could not be sold below their net asset value ... aimed at preventing a firesale of state assets and their acquisition on the cheap by executives leading management buy-outs. The news contradicts a statement last month [November 2003] by Li Rongrong, chairman of the cabinet's state-owned assets and supervision and administration commission, that the market would set the price for such sales.

(*FT*, 27 December 2003, p. 10)

The government body responsible for overseeing the restructuring of state assets ... the state-owned asset supervision and administration commission ... issued a set of guidelines to standardize reforming state-owned companies. The guidelines reiterated previous rules that non-tradable state-owned shares of listed companies cannot be sold below their net asset value per share. Non-tradable state shares represent two-thirds of China's stock market ... [But the commission] plan lacks key points such as a concrete pricing mechanism, and was not expected to stir up a storm over getting rid of state shares.

(*FEER*, 25 December 2003, p. 25)

'Chinese regulators gave preliminary approval to plans for a private airline to set up in the south-western city of Chengdu' (*FEER*, 19 February 2004, p. 27).

Okay Airways [is] China's first attempt at a privately, low-fare airline ... In January [2005] China's civil aviation regulators introduced new rules that in principle allow any company with three planes to operate an airline. Foreign investors can take a stake of up to 25 per cent in these private airlines.

(www.iht.com, 28 February 2005)

'[Because of allegations of abuses] in December 2004 the central government body responsible for managing state enterprises banned management buy-outs for large companies and set stringent conditions for such transactions for smaller government-owned businesses' (*FT*, 1 February 2005, p. 13).

China issued new rules yesterday [15 April 2005] to prevent large state-owned companies from conducting management buy-outs ... The new regulations confirm a change in policy that was announced in December [2004] by Li Rongrong, head of the State-Owned Assets Supervision and Administration Commission (SASAC), the government body that controls the companies. Under the new rules all the subsidiaries of large public groups as well as the parent companies are to be banned from selling shares to the senior management.

(*FT*, 16 April 2005, p. 8)

[China has banned] management buy-outs of large state-owned companies ... Of China's 3 million registered private companies 550,000 (or nearly 20 per cent) were previously owned by the state, said a government survey in February [2005]. The textile industry, once almost completely under the control of government, is now dominated by privately owned and managed enterprises.

(*FT*, 12 May 2005, p. 8)

('For loss-making enterprises the government has announced a four-year programme that will involve substantial additional restructuring. In some cases asset sales may be possible in which case it is important to follow the regulations, issued in the spring of 2005, that ensure transparency in management buy-outs': OECD 2005: website Chapter 2.)

China has opened up a number of state-owned and once-strategic sectors of its economy to local and foreign private investment ... The sweeping reform – which was announced in a policy document released by the State Council, China's cabinet – will legalize private investment in sectors including power, rail, aviation and oil. Private investment will now also be allowed in the growing local defence industries, including military research companies and weapons manufacturers, the document said ... The document will provide legal cover for a series of existing investments in sectors that are officially off-limits to private capital, but where in fact private capital has already begun to play a role ... The new document ... [includes] a rule giving local entrepreneurs the same rights as foreign investors, while also putting them on level terms for finance, tax and land-use rights with the state. Entrepreneurs will be allowed into any industries unless they are specifically excluded, the new document says ... [but] entrepreneurs will not necessarily be allowed to own majority stakes in all sectors. Chinese corporate law will set the limits of ownership in different sectors ... However, the new policy further extends the recognition and protection of private property and interests which was begun by the ruling Communist Party in 2002.

(*FT*, 26 February 2005, p. 9)

A government document issued in February [2005] allows private investment in any business not banned by law and supposedly guarantees equal access to bank loans. The official media said the document was the first devoted entirely to promoting the interests of private business since the communist takeover in 1949.

(*The Economist*, 19 March 2005, p. 86)

[On 28 March 2005 it was officially reported that]: 'In four years state-owned enterprises will follow market rules and apply for bankruptcy according to the same laws and regulations as foreign and private companies' ... Five provinces or cities – Beijing, Shanghai, Jiangsu, Zhejiang and Fujian – have already stopped bailing out bankrupt companies, the report said.

(*IHT*, 28 March 2005, p. 14)

The government has promised [that by 2008] more than 2,000 sizeable state-owned factories and businesses ... will be shut down, while the rest will be turned into profitable companies under modern management. It is a sign of the ambition and complexity of that transformation that just two years since its founding, the government agency charged with reforming state enterprises, the State Assets Supervision and Administration, or Sasac, has parlayed its control of 178 of China's biggest companies into a powerful influence over many areas of economic policy, an influence that has some economists wondering about the strength of Beijing's commitment to a full-blown market economy. In recent months [for example] Sasac has unilaterally shifted around the senior managements of the four biggest telecom companies ... Even as Sasac has pushed local officials to accept sales of less crucial state assets, it has exerted increasingly tight control over the 196 state-owned companies ... which the government considers crucial to its economic interest ... From 1998 to the end of 2003 the government reduced the number of small and medium state-owned companies from 238,000 to about 150,000, often by shutting them down or selling them off.

(*IHT*, 1 June 2005, p. 11)

China is revising a draft property law after delaying its passage because of fierce ideological debate among officials and academics over its balancing of state and private rights. The dispute over the long-awaited legislation high-lights political sensitivities that continue to surround China's embrace of the market and echoes differences on other issues such as the degree to which the economy should be opened to foreign and private investment ... [There has been] a surge of objections from conservative academics and officials who believe the draft gives too much weight to protection of private property. The most widely cited opposition came from Gong Xiantian, an expert in Marxist jurisprudence at Peking University, who issued an open letter arguing that the draft law would 'undermine the legal foundation of China's socialist economy' ... Professor Gong argued that property protections in the law could shield those who stole state assets or who took bribes ... The law is now scheduled to be voted on at the 2007 NPC plenary session.

(*FT*, 10 March 2006, p. 9)

The government recently shelved plans to submit a new property law to the congress after a chorus of opposition, led by a Peking University academic, Gong Xiantian. He argued that the draft, which protected property rights, was un-Marxist and unconstitutional.

(*The Economist*, 18 March 2006, p. 62)

For the first time in perhaps a decade the National People's Congress, the Communist Party-led legislature, now convened in its annual two-week session [5–14 March 2006], is consumed with an ideological debate over socialism and capitalism that many assumed had been buried by China's long streak of fast economic growth. The controversy has forced the government to shelve a draft law to protect property rights ... Gong Xiantian, a professor at Beijing University Law School, [has] accused the legal experts who wrote the draft of 'copying capitalist civil law like slaves' and offering equal protection to 'a rich man's car and a beggar's stick'. Most of all he protested that the proposed law did not state that 'socialist property is inviolable' ... The proposed property law has taken eight years to prepare and is intended to codify a more expansive notion of property rights added to China's constitution in 2003.

(Joseph Kahn, *IHT*, 13 March 2006, pp. 1, 4)

The economic activities of the People's Liberation Army

'Since he [Deng Xiaoping] allowed government, party and military units to establish their own enterprises, Chinese bureaucrats supported reform more than their Soviet counterparts' (Ezra Fogel, *FEER*, 25 November 1999, p. 43).

'While it is doubtful that the military establishment likes depending on the market to generate extra income, that dependence gives the military a stake in continuing the economic reform (Thomas Bickford, *FEER*, 1994, vol. XXXIV, p. 473).

On 20–21 July 1998 an anti-smuggling conference was held in Beijing. The *People's Daily* had recently accused the army and the People's Armed Police of involvement in smuggling. Army businesses are easily involved in smuggling because military vehicles do not pay tolls or get stopped by the police for inspection. During the conference Jiang Zemin ordered the People's Liberation Army to cease to engage in commercial activities (although it appears that it would still be allowed to produce weapons). Jiang Zemin:

> To focus efforts to fully build the military, the central authorities have decided that the army and armed police forces must earnestly carry out checks on all kinds of commercial companies set up by subsidiary units, and without exception from today must not engage in their operation. The whole army must earnestly implement the anti-smuggling work and deployment and strictly investigate problems with some units and people involved with the army and armed police.

(*IHT*, 23 July 1998, pp. 1, 4)

On 22 July 1998 Jiang Zemin ordered the military to withdraw from management of its business empire, stating that the People's Liberation Army and the People's Armed Police should 'conscientiously put in order all kinds of commercial companies' their units operate and 'from now on categorically engage no more in commercial activities'. Jiang ordered police and judicial organs to do likewise. Jiang's edict does not apply to China's defence industries, such as China North Industries Corporation (Norinco), China Aerospace Corporation and Aviation Industries of China. They all grew out of ministries, rather than the People's

Liberation Army itself. Jiang also said that 'Some units and individuals of the military and the People's Armed Police' have been involved in smuggling (*FEER*, 6 August 1998, pp. 68–9).

> Experts estimate that the armed forces run some 20,000 industrial, production and service companies ... Initially encouraged by the leadership to offset budget shortfalls, these pursuits mushroomed. They eroded military professionalism and fostered a wide range of illegal activities, such as bribery and smuggling ... The [anti-corruption] campaign provides a convenient cover but not the whole explanation. No less important is the stark fact that economic involvement undermines military modernization. It interferes with war preparations, impairs specialization, erodes discipline and fosters factionalism ... A generational shift in the army high command ... has brought to the top ranks officers with professional qualities and aspirations ... The other factor is Mr Jiang. Intent on establishing his credentials in the armed forces, he has strongly supported the professional military – including their desire to curb the army's economic development.
>
> (Ellis Joffe, *IHT*, 10 August 1998, p. 8)

On 3 November 1998 it was announced that the state economic and trade commission would take over the business empire of the PLA by mid-December 1998 (*IHT*, 4 November 1998, p. 19). On 20 November 1998 it was announced that the transfer of military, judiciary and police-owned enterprises would be completed by the end of December 1998 (*IHT*, 21 November 1998, p. 5). By the end of 1998 control of the army's major companies, such as Poly Technologies, Carrie Enterprises and Xin Xing Group, was to be transferred to the state economic and trade commission. Provincial governments would take over smaller companies now run by the seven military regions, while counties and cities would to absorb the rest (*IHT*, 24 November 1998, p. 7).

On 14 December 1998 it was announced that the armed forces had finished handing over their businesses to civilian control. Henceforth enterprises formerly under the People's Liberation Army and the People's Armed Police were to be controlled by the Takeover Office for Military, Armed Police, Government and Judiciary Businesses, a state body (*FT*, 15 December 1998, p. 8).

> In October [1998] a receiving office was established under the new economic super-ministry, the state economic and trade commission. Two months later every major PLA department and military region announced they had formally handed ownership of their companies to the office, which was supposed to find new owners for these businesses ... The PLA has refused to part with some ... The official *China Daily Business Weekly* alluded on 21 March [1999], saying some sectors of a 'special nature' would be exempt from the business ban. Sources say companies at stake include China United Airlines ... The PLA says the planes might be needed in time of war ... Parts of the two biggest PLA conglomerates have been retained under divestiture rules which allow the military to keep firms that primarily service the military.
>
> (*FEER*, 20 April 1999, pp. 22–3)

The order to the military to divest also included the paramilitary People's Armed Police, the judicial system and the police. The government has since announced that all government, party and legislative branches should give up their companies starting this year [1999].

(p. 24)

The People's Liberation Army still remains in the telecommunications field (*IHT*, 2 February 2000, p. 11).

Two years on the effort appears to be a qualified success. The People's Liberation Army and the paramilitary People's Armed Police have either closed down or handed over to civilian control most of the purely commercial enterprises covered by the divestiture order ... But ... in defiance of the civilian authorities the PLA still has not given up control of some businesses it should have. And bureaucratic infighting has broken out over what should happen to some of the businesses the army has surrendered. Even as he declared in late May [2000] that divestiture work was 'basically completed' in March. Vice-president and Central Military Commission vice-chairman Hu Jintao admitted 'shortcomings still exist' ... What is more the divestiture order has allowed the PLA to continue operating many not-so-purely commercial businesses, such as farms and factories employing soldiers' family members ... The civilian leadership declared from the start that the PLA would not be compensated for individual companies. Instead, the army was offered a single lump-sum payment with annual rises thereafter in the military budget ... The lump sum was ... paid in March 1999 ... The initial deadline was December 1998 ... But ... an early 1999 audit found that the military had failed to declare approximately 10 per cent of the businesses covered by the divestiture order. The civilian leadership set a second deadline of August 1999 for the PLA and PAP to hand them all in ... Even now, however, between 100 and 200 cases may still be outstanding ... Disputes have arisen after the military has closed down or handed over enterprises ... The work has been slowed down by contentious bankruptcy proceedings. Banks that lent money to PLA businesses now being shuttered have been demanding their money back, but the central government has been unwilling to bail out the banks. Other disputes have erupted over restructuring plans for transferred enterprises ... Many less lucrative parts of the army's business empire have so far been left with the army. These are the military businesses that existed before the PLA's aggressive push into commerce in the late 1980s and early 1990s ... The PLA is retaining its extensive network of farms. It is keeping some factories set up to provide jobs for soldiers' relatives, particularly in remote areas where the relatives have no other options for employment. It is keeping some enterprises that provide cover for intelligence-gathering. And its hospitals and research institutions will continue to offer fee-paying services to the public, though they are under order to limit the scale of those businesses. A more complicated story is businesses primarily providing logistical support to the military, such as repair shops, munitions plants and factories making uniforms, tents and other supplies. The original divestiture left these businesses with the military, even though many of them also run unrelated commercial operations on the side ... [e.g. renting out] real estate ... The PLA is now starting to close down or to divest some businesses in this category and move toward outsourcing instead ... [e.g. transferring] cafeteria and gardening staff to a civilian company.

(*FEER*, 13 July 2000, pp. 14–16)

The Chinese military's long-delayed move out of commercial telecommunications is on again ... Both the military and China's dominant telecoms operator, China Telecom, are in the process of transferring their shares of assets [mobile phone networks in four cities] of the closely watched Great Wall Telecommunications Co. to China Telecom's competitor, China Unicom.

(*FEER*, 27 July 2000, p. 10)

Although it gathered steam as economic reforms began in 1978, the People's Liberation Army's move into business really took off in 1984, when Deng Xiaoping endorsed a plan under which China's military would drastically increase its commercial activities ... Deng gave two reasons to justify the move: it would provide money for both the army and central government coffers, and it would make the army a better fighting machine. Cadres would learn about administration while soldiers would learn to 'develop their ability to deal with difficult struggles and sacrifice their blood for the revolutionary spirit' ... Yet rather than make the PLA a better fighting machine, going into business brought corruption, an inattention to training, conflicts with civilians and factional infighting ... Problems like those eventually led ... Jiang Zemin to order the military out of business in July 1998. Since then most of the empire has been handed over to civilian control. Notable exceptions remain, including a green light for the PLA to remain in telecoms, on the grounds that it helps develop military communications networks. But by and large the handover has gone ahead ... The PLA won ... financial compensation ... Its budgets rose, debts were taken over by the state and, most important, many PLA executives were allowed to simply walk off with their companies.

(*FEER*, 7 June 2001, pp. 66–7)

The economic activities of party and state officials

On 25 August 1993, on the final day of a six-day session of the party's Commission for Discipline Inspection, a new code of conducted was announced barring party and government officials from engaging in business on their own account or helping relatives and friends to profit from their activities (*IHT*, 26 October 1993, p. 7).

On 29 May 1995 state enterprise officials were banned from setting up private businesses, using their influence to help relatives or diverting enterprise assets for themselves. This move followed one the previous week ordering state and party officials to declare their incomes and a string of earlier edicts banning government workers from accepting meals, gifts and other favours from the public (*IHT*, 30 May 1995, p. 4).

China has ordered [on 29 November 1998] its vast bureaucracy to cut ties with all its businesses next year [1999] in a bid to stamp out corruption . . . Organs of the Communist Party and the government were told to give up enterprises under their control.

(*IHT*, 30 November 1998, p. 17)

Sheng Huaren, the head of the state economic and trade commission . . . insisted that by the end of the year [1988] the government planned effectively to 'de-link' the Communist Party, government ministries, the army and the police from their multitude of business interests.

(*IHT*, 1 December 1998, pp. 1, 6)

'[In 2000] Beijing barred senior cadres' children from taking part in business "within the scope of the powers" of their parents' (*FEER*, 18 October 2001, p. 34).

The non-state, non-agricultural sectors

The non-state sector includes:

1 the private sector, although in China the distinction is made between 'individual' enterprises (employing fewer than eight people) and 'private' enterprises (employing eight or more people);
2 foreign-invested enterprises (dealt with below);
3 collectives, mainly 'township–village enterprises' (TVEs).

The percentage of industrial output contributed by various sectors

In 1978 the state sector accounted for 78 per cent of industrial output (TVEs 21 per cent and the private sector 1 per cent). But the non-state sector has grown much more rapidly than the state sector. The share of the non-state sector in total industrial output increased from 24.5 per cent in 1980 (0.0 per cent for category 1, 0.5 per cent for category 2 and 24 per cent for category 3, respectively) to 47 per cent in 1991 (5.7 per cent, 5.7 per cent and 36 per cent, respectively) and 57 per cent in 1994. TVEs accounted for 10.9 per cent of total exports in 1987, 44.4 per cent in 1993 and 32.6 per cent in 1994 (Sachs and Woo 1996: 3).

During the period 1980 to 1997 the state's share of industrial output fell from 76 per cent to 25.5 per cent, while collectively owned enterprises saw their share increase from 23.6 per cent to 38.1 per cent. 'Other', including private firms and foreign joint ventures, increased from 0.5 per cent to 36.4 per cent (Smyth 2000: 724).

In 1994 state enterprises accounted for 43 per cent of industrial output (compared with 78 per cent in 1978) and employed about 70 per cent of industrial workers (*The Economist*, 10 June 1995, p. 69). In 1995 state enterprises accounted for less than one-third of industrial output, compared with over three-quarters in 1978 (*The Economist*, 14 December 1996, p. 87).

State enterprises generate 30 per cent of total industrial output (*FEER*, 21 May 1998, p. 14).

The share of state enterprises in industrial output fell from 77.6 per cent in 1978 to 28.8 per cent in 1996, although they still employed 57.4 per cent of urban workers in 1996 (Lin *et al.* 1998: 422).

The state sector's share of industrial output has fallen as follows: 1978, 78.0 per cent; 1988, 57.0 per cent; 1995, 34.0 per cent; 2000, 23.5 per cent (Hirschler 2002: 7).

In 1994 collectives accounted for 39 per cent of industrial output (*IHT*, 19 June 1995, p. 2).

In 1996 rural industrial enterprises contributed 26 per cent of GDP, 44 per cent of gross industrial output and 35 per cent of total earnings from exports (Smyth 1998: 784).

'Foreign-owned companies' share in the gross output of industrial enterprises rose from nothing in the early 1980s to 12 per cent in 1995 and 29 per cent in 2002' (*FT*, 9 December 2003, p. 21).

The private sector as a whole as a percentage of GDP

> In 1992 ... a survey by *The Economist* [28 November 1992] put the state sector at no more than 25 per cent of the economy ... Most analysts today guess that the private sector [as a whole] accounts for around 25 per cent of total output ... Fresh work in the latest *China Economic Quarterly* (CEQ), an independent publication, concludes that both guesses are way out ... Since 1978 [in agriculture] ... the transformation has nearly been completed ... Since half of China's 700 million workers are engaged in farm-related work, the privatization of farming is the biggest reason why three-quarters of China's workforce is today in private employment. The private contribution to ... construction, industry and mining is harder to measure, in part because many 'collectives' are private firms in disguise. But CEQ's educated guess is that 51 per cent of industrial GDP is now in private hands (including foreigners) ... Private firms [account for] just 37 per cent of services output. Rolling ... [all] sectors together gives an estimate for the private share of the whole economy of ... 53 per cent ... If agriculture and foreign-invested companies are stripped out the private sector shrinks to less than two-fifths of GDP.
>
> (*The Economist*, 19 June 1999, p. 104)

'State enterprises that account for less than one-third of the country's output command more than two-thirds of all credit' (*The Economist*, 9 September 2000, p. 125).

> Only about a third of China's economy is still directly controlled by the government through state-owned enterprises. But these are concentrated in key areas like defence and utilities. While many of the biggest state firms have publicly quoted subsidiaries on international stock markets, the government retains ultimate ownership ... The top 190 or so state-owned enterprises are directly controlled by the State Assets Supervision and Administration Commission – set up in 2003 to restructure these often moribund firms ... Two-thirds of the economy is in private hands ... ... [but] private companies are

often beholden to state banks for capital and to local officials for favours and contracts.

(*The Economist*, 3 September 2005, pp. 63–4)

The OECD estimates that in 2003 private companies accounted for 63 per cent of China's business sector output (which in turn accounts for 94 per cent of GDP). This compares with 54 per cent in 1998 and virtually nothing in 1970s. If you add in 'collective' enterprises, which are officially controlled by local government but in practice operate more like private firms, the private sector's share was 71 per cent in 2003.

(*The Economist*, 17 September 2005, p. 91)

'The non-state sector now accounts for 75 per cent of GDP if collective and agricultural output is included' (*FEER*, 12 July 2001, p. 49).

The private sector ... now accounts for half of China's GDP and 75 per cent if the essentially privatized activities of agriculture, rural collectives and share-holding companies are included, according to estimates by the World Bank's ... International Finance Corporation. The figure is expected to rise.

(*FEER*, 30 August 2001, p. 19)

The OECD (2005: website Chapter 2) provides information on the percentage of GDP contributed by the various sectors (value-added by firm ownership) in 1998 and 2003. The private sector accounted for 50.4 per cent and 59.2 per cent, respectively, for the two years. The public sector is split into state-controlled and collectively controlled firms (figures in brackets). In 1998 the public sector accounted for 49.6 per cent of GDP (36.9 and 12.7 percentage points, respectively), while the 2003 figure was 40.8 per cent (33.7 and 7.1 percentage points, respectively).

The private, non-agricultural sector as a percentage of GDP

The International Finance Corporation estimates that nearly half of the companies that call themselves collective should in fact be called private (*FT*, 11 May 2000, p. 14).

According to the International Finance Corporation (the private sector arm of the World Bank), in 1998 the state sector contributed 37 per cent of GDP. Private businesses generated 33 per cent, while the balance came from agricultural companies and businesses (*Transition*, 2000, vol. 11, no. 2, p. 40).

By 1998 the domestic private sector had grown to about 27 per cent of GDP, making it second only to the state sector in economic importance. (The other sectors are the foreign, collective and agriculture sectors.) Despite its growing importance, at the end of 1999 the private sector accounted for only 1 per cent of bank lending and only 1 per cent of the companies listed on the Shanghai and Shenzhen stock exchanges were non-state firms ... Chinese firms rely more on internal sources of financing than do firms in transition and developed economies.

(Neil Gregory and Stoyan Tenev, *Finance and Development*, 2001, vol. 38, no. 1, pp. 14–15)

'About 20 per cent of . . . GDP last year [2000] came from its 1.2 million purely private enterprises' (*IHT*, 2 July 2001, p. 4).

The private sector, concentrated on the country's south-eastern coast, remains a small slice of an economy still dominated by government-owned enterprises. Even the 800 million ostensibly independent farmers grow crops on state-owned land and sell grain to state-owned grain companies. Private companies, excluding those controlled by foreigners, accounted last year [1999] for less than 20 per cent of economic output.

(Craig Smith, *IHT*, 13 July 2000, p. 16)

Though many people cite figures that show China's economy is now mostly private, those data include foreign-owned and collectively owned businesses, most of which are still controlled at some level by the government. True private companies, those that are majority-owned by individuals, still account for less than 20 per cent of economic output and for only about 50 million jobs.

(Craig Smith, *IHT*, 4 June 2001, p. 11)

'China's private sector is now responsible for 33 per cent of economic output, state-controlled media reported' (*IHT*, 8 April 2002, p. 11).

Private firms now produce a third of China's GDP – just a few percentage points less than the state sector. In the first quarter of this year [2002] they created almost 30 per cent of new jobs. Many others came from what are known as 'collective enterprises', which in practice are often also privately run.

(*FEER*, 16 May 2002, p. 24)

China's private sector provides 25 per cent of GDP and is set to boom over the next few years . . . the official *China Daily* quoted a National Bureau of Statistics report as saying. Some Western economists, however, estimate that the non-state sector, including foreign firms, accounts for 50 per cent to 70 per cent of China's GDP.

(*FEER*, 17 October 2002, p. 28)

A Beijing think-tank reckons that the private sector contributes just over 60 per cent of GDP, counting TVEs and businesses with foreign investors (worth about 15 per cent). Yet the World Bank's report in January 2003 put the share as low as a third.

(*The Economist*, Survey, 20 March 2004, p. 15)

'While small and mid-sized private enterprises account for nearly 50 per cent of GDP, they only receive 10 per cent to 15 per cent of China's total commercial loans' (*FEER*, 18 September 2003, p. 48). According to the Asian Development Bank, SMEs account for 60 per cent of industrial output . . . Most of these companies are now privately run' (*FEER*, 17 June 2004, p. 34).

The Chinese government estimates that the private sector now accounts for a third of the economy, up from less than 1 per cent in 1978. Analysts say the private sector's share is much higher than official figures suggest. However, assessing that share is complicated by the opaque ownership of many companies and their shareholding structures.

(*FT*, Money and Business, 25 February 2005, p. 6)

'[According to the OECD] the private sector now generates between 57 per cent and 65 per cent of non-farm GDP, depending on how it is measured' (*FT*, 17 September 2005, p. 6).

Precise measurement of the size of the private sector is difficult, but a definition which considers as private all companies that are controlled neither by state nor collective shareholders suggests that the private sector was responsible for as much as 57 per cent of the value-added produced by the non-farm business sector in 2003. Even amongst larger companies in the industrial sector the private sector produced over half of value-added in 2003 and that share appears to have risen even further in the following two years.

(OECD 2005: website Chapter 2)

The OECD (website Chapter 2) provides information on the percentage of value-added by firm ownership for 1998 and 2003. The non-farm business sector (79 per cent of GDP) is divided into the private sector (43.0 per cent and 57.1 per cent, respectively, for the two years) and the public sector (57.0 per cent and 42.9 per cent respectively: this is further split into state-controlled firms and collectively controlled firms – 40.5 percentage points and 16.5 percentage points respectively for 1998, and 34.1 percentage points and 8.8 percentage points respectively for 2003).

(The 2004 upward revision of GDP has, of course, implications for the above estimates of the importance of the non-state sector in GDP. The main reason given for the upward revision was the considerable underestimation of the private service sector.)

The underground economy

'According to recently published official figures ... the underground economy is the equivalent of 20 per cent of GDP (actually twice that, say independent estimates)' (*FEER*, 21 June 2001, p. 60). 'The chief economist at CLSA in Hong Kong ... argues that China's underground economy is worth anywhere between 50 per cent and 100 per cent of official GDP' (*FEER*, 17 June 2004. p. 35).

The D'Long Corporation

Central bankers have moved to bail out a private corporation, a step that many analysts say marks the first time China's government has extended support to a private business. The central bank will put together a loan package of as much as $1.8 billion for D'Long Corporation, a private conglomerate whose collapse threatened to shake China's stock market and banks ... [It was] reported on Monday [23 August] that D'Long, with companies that make products from tomato paste to auto parts, would be placed temporarily under the control of a government asset management company that would reorganize it and its debt.

Details of the bailout remain vague ... The company said it had 30,000 employees and assets worth $12 billion ... D'Long's problems are in part a result of banks' renewed reluctance to lend to private businesses while the economy is trying to cool the economy.

(www.iht.com, 24 August 2004)

D'Long [is] a tangled, private Chinese group with interests in a wide range of agricultural, industrial and financial products ... [It has an] enormously complicated shareholding structure ... [It is] sometimes described as China's largest private company ... In late August [2004] investigators designated Huarong, a state-backed asset management firm, to find buyers for some of the group's assets. It remains unclear how much of the group's assets will be sold or whether a partial bailout is planned ... D'Long started in the 1980s ... [by] four brothers ... Chinese banks have long been loath to lend to China's private sector ... It can be tough for Chinese private firms to raise money through stock or bond issuances ... D'Long was one of the early movers among private Chinese companies investing overseas ... D'Long is like many private Chinese companies: a history of monumental entrepreneurial zeal combined with a penchant for shady ways of gathering funds to finance their ambitions.

(*FEER*, 2 September 2004, pp. 24–7)

Tang Wanxin, whose D'Long Group was once China's biggest stockholder, went on trial Thursday [19 January 2006] and pleaded no contest to manipulating share prices ... The government alleged that D'Long, which is now bankrupt, amassed deposits worth more than 45 billion yuan, or $5.6 billion, by illegally offering guarantees to its clients ... Tang pleaded not guilty to the charge that he had engaged in illegal banking, an offence with a maximum sentence of ten years' imprisonment. However, Tang did not contest the lesser charge of stock price manipulation, which carries a maximum of five years. D'Long was once China's biggest owner of publicly traded shares. It ran into trouble in 2004 as creditors began demanding repayment after reports that it had pledged equity in listed companies as collateral for bank loans. The reports provoked worries that it might have financial difficulties, causing a sell-off by shareholders.

(www.iht.com, 19 January 2006; *IHT*, 20 January 2006, p. 17)

Township–village enterprises (TVEs)

'The larger villages or small rural towns are known ... [as] townships' (*The Economist*, 20 July 2002, pp. 67–8).

TVEs have aroused the greatest interest. They have to survive in a competitive atmosphere and face hard budget constraints. Weitzman (Weitzman and Xu 1993: 550–5) describes the TVE as the driving force of the Chinese model. The TVE is a

vaguely defined co-operative ... a communal organization about as far removed from having a well-defined ownership structure as can be imagined ... Legally, the TVE is collectively owned by all the people in the community where it is located. There is no stipulation of any individual owners nor does anyone have rights to appropriate assets of the firm. There are no shares at all, formally speaking ... Reward structures are extremely vague and informal.

Naughton (1994: 266–70) says that TVEs are controlled by township and village governments. In most cases that have been studied township and village officials in their official capacity possess all the key components of property rights. Bolton (1995: 7) suggests possible advantages of township–village governments in terms of corporate control (they appoint and monitor managers). But critics of TVEs point to weaknesses of township–village governments in terms of short time horizons (they may be moved on) and local corruption and the limited role of workers in decision-making. In the long term the importance of TVEs is likely to decline as a more individually orientated society develops and conventional property rights become more important. Chow (1997: 322) notes the advantages possessed by TVEs stemming from 'the local government's power to enforce contracts and from the credibility of such a "public" enterprise in raising funds as compared with an entirely private enterprise'.

In the mid-1980s the commune structure was dismantled and townships and villages assumed responsibilities for rural enterprises (Smyth 1998: 786). Commune and brigade enterprises were renamed township and village enterprises (TVEs) (p. 285).

Woo is sceptical of some of the reasons put forward to explain the importance of TVEs, such as culture, a lack of entrepreneurs, the raising of capital and reducing the principal-agent problem. He favours explanations such as the early restrictions on private ownership, tax and other benefits endowed upon TVEs and early low labour mobility (Woo 1997: 316–17).

> Many of China's once-booming township enterprises are being privatized in an effort to revive flagging rural industry ... In recent years ... the township enterprise miracle has started to fade ... With so many domestic and foreign companies rushing to get a piece of China's booming market in the first half of the 1990s, China today has a surplus of just about everything, especially the low-value-added, labour-intensive items ... In this intensely competitive environment only the best-managed and most efficient companies will survive. While some township enterprises have made the changes necessary to remain contenders, many have not, underscoring the limitations of the township-owned model. Low-skilled labour, unsophisticated management and capital shortages make it difficult for many of these firms to upgrade quality, move into higher-value types of manufacturing and increase their scale of production ... [Local] government intervention [means] ... that town-appointed managers are not held responsible for failures ... Ideological objections to private ownership have relaxed over the past few years – a trend formally sanctioned at September's Fifteenth Party Congress.
>
> (Pamela Yatsko, *FEER*, 5 February 1998, pp. 52–3)

'The township and village enterprises that fuelled China's economic growth for most of the past fifteen years are flagging as their low-tech, low-wage approaches reach their limits (Steven Mufson, *IHT*, 13 April 1998, p. 13).

'Increasingly sophisticated urban corporations with easy access to capital have driven many TVEs to the brink of financial collapse' (*FT*, 25 July 2000, p. 22).

'Township enterprises that brought wealth and jobs to millions of rural Chinese are faltering in many areas' (*IHT*, 5 September 2000, p. 5).

Since 1988 there has been experiments with 'shareholding co-operatives':

1   The 'shareholding co-operative system' is an experiment which has been running since 1988 'in order to improve some of the TVE's internal draw-backs: to define the property rights of the TVE, to improve the incentive system and democratic management, strengthen the role of entrepreneurs and to attract scarce resources'. By May 1995 the number of 'shareholding co-operatives' had increased to 204,000 or 12.4 per cent of all TVEs. 'The main idea of a co-operative is participation, democracy and the principle of one and equal voice for each member. The main idea behind "shareholding" is the pref-erence of capital (on workers) and allocation according to one's shares' (Amir Helman, *The CEA (UK) Newsletter*, December 1996, vol. 8, no. 4, pp. 24–5).

2   TVEs face problems in terms of interference by local governments, decreased incentives to invest locally when labour mobility increases, the attractions of risk diversification, increasing difficulties of raising outside capital and restric-tions on managerial autonomy (Woo 1997: 317–19). 'In addition to the above five problems, there has been a recent development that has pushed the TVEs to "clarify" their property rights. The capacity expansion of many of the coastal TVEs in southern China has forced them to rely increasingly on migrant labour from the poorer provinces. The original inhabitants want to prevent the new residents from having an automatic share in the dividends of the collective-owned enterprises, and so they have corporatized the TVEs and divided the shares among themselves' (p. 320). 'Many TVEs have transformed themselves into shareholding corporations in the search for a more efficient organizational form, but their shares are legally not transferable (p. 300). 'The fact that there are informal markets for these legally non-transferable shares speaks volumes about popular expectations about the future institutional basis of economic transactions in China' (p. 322).

3   'As rural enterprises have started to get bigger and become more marketized, informal relationships are no longer sufficient. For example, in the start-up phase in southern Jiangsu it was common for the township or village govern-ment (TVG) to provide either financial assistance or a guarantee to the lending organization to help the rural enterprise to raise capital. Toward the end of 1997 the ministry of agriculture issued "proposals for expanding the reform of township enterprises". As a result, China has started to experiment with such alternative forms as joint stock companies and shareholding co-operatives as well as mergers, outright sales and bankruptcies (Smyth 1998: 785). 'The downside of TVEs with strong TVG involvement is that it is difficult to know who is the true owner. This places the TVG in a powerful position to use profits from TVEs to finance municipal government budgets or cross subsidize unprofitable enterprises under its control' (p. 791). 'Many large rural enter-prises have formed enterprise groups and/or converted to joint stock limited

liability companies ... Large firms are being encouraged to form enterprise groups with both other rural enterprises and entities with different ownership forms such as private firms, local SOEs and research institutions like universities ... In addition, a number of larger rural enterprises have been converted into joint stock or limited liability companies in which each shareholder's liability is proportionate to his/her investment' (pp. 792–4). 'The major avenue for reforming small and medium-sized rural enterprises has been to transform them into shareholding co-operatives ... Under the shareholding (or Shandong) model, management and workers are sold shares in the enterprise.' At the end of 1995 there were over 3 million shareholding co-operatives accounting for more than 10 per cent of rural enterprises (p. 795). 'A number of benefits have been claimed for shareholding co-operatives ... It is argued that it clarifies the relationship between TVE and TVG through creating a "government share" in the enterprise ... In most instances it accounts for about 20 per cent to 25 per cent of total shares, but in some cases it is higher ... Issuing shares provides a means to raise capital from management and workers (p. 796). 'Other approaches that have been used in small enterprise reform include auction or sale to private investors and joint ventures with domestic and foreign investors' (p. 797). 'While recent reforms have brought a range of benefits there are still a number of problems ... In some instances workers have been forced to invest their savings in purchasing shares ... One of the objectives of introducing shareholding co-operatives is to make the workers the true owners of the enterprise. It is thought that if ownership is clarified internal management will be improved; however, in practice in many cases shareholding co-operatives have not reduced the power of local government ... In some cases local government continues to exercise tight control over the appointment of managers even after the reforms' (pp. 797–8).

Along the eastern seaboard these ... rural industries ... developed rapidly from the mid-1980s to the mid-1990s (far less in inland areas such as Henan) ... By the end of 1996 they employed 135 million people, contributing nearly half of China's exports, compared with one-sixth at the beginning of the decade. But since then they have gone into decline. Last year [2001 the number of] rural enterprises fell by 620,000 and employment was down 5 million on the 1996 peak ... Many were, in effect, under the control of township and village governments ... resulting in poor management and irrational investment decisions. Many of these have now been privatized, but the private sector is especially starved of capital ... Many small and isolated rural enterprises will be unable to compete as larger-scale private businesses develop in urban areas.

(*The Economist*, Survey, 15 June 2002, p. 11)

'Entry occurred rapidly in China [in the period 1979–84]. Most of the new entrants were not private firms, but rural enterprises run by local governments, called township and village enterprises' (McMillan and Woodruff 2002: 157).

These firms were publicly owned, by communities of a few thousand people. They were managed by village government, and the profits were shared between villagers and local government by explicit rules. Around 60 per cent of profits were reinvested, and the remainder was paid as bonuses to workers or used for local public goods such as education, roads and irrigation. Managerial discipline ... came from the fact that these enterprises had no access to government subsidies to cover any losses and faced intensely competitive product markets ... [They] received some benefits from having village government as a partner. Access to state banks and to rationed inputs was eased [for example] ... After a decade and a half of growth they began to be privatized. By the late 1990s more than a half of them were partially or fully privately owned.

(p. 165, citing Hongbin Li and Scott Rozells, *Agricultural Economics*, 2000, vol. 23, no. 3, pp. 241–52)

The 'open-door' policy

In 1978 the policy was announced of opening up the economy to foreign trade, capital, technology and know-how in order to modernize and speed up the growth of the economy:

Foreign trade

The importance of foreign trade to the Chinese economy has increased substantially, as the following indicators show:

China's place in the world ranking of exporters

China has climbed rapidly in the world ranking of exporters from its position at number thirty-two in 1978

'[China is] the world's ... fifth largest trading power' (*FEER*, 27 September 2001, p. 12).

'China ... [is] the fifth biggest trader' (*FT*, 12 November 2001, p. 10).

'[China is] the seventh largest trading economy in the world' (Nicholas Lardy, *IHT*, 10 November 2001, p. 13). 'By 2000 it was the seventh largest trading nation' (Nicholas Lardy, *Foreign Policy*, March–April, 2002, p. 20).

'China ... [is the] seventh largest exporter' (*FT*, 10 December 2001, p. 22).

'China ... was the world's fifth largest importer last year [2000]' (Mike Moore, director-general of the WTO, *IHT*, 19 September 2001, p. 10).

'Trade had reached a peak in 1928, when it accounted for 2.3 per cent of the world total – a level not surpassed until 1993. In 1977, before the reforms, China's share had fallen to a mere 0.6 per cent' (*The Economist*, 20 November 1999, p. 27). 'Even today, at 3.4 per cent, its share is no bigger than that of the Netherlands' (*The Economist*, Survey, 8 April 2000, p. 16). 'China now accounts for nearly 5 per cent of world exports' (*The Economist*, Survey, 8 February 2003, p. 5). 'China, the world's fifth largest exporter last year [2002], accounted for 5.1 per cent of global exports' (*FEER*, 17 April 2003, p. 24).

'In 2001 China accounted for 4.4 per cent of all world exports ... Since 1978 ...

the country's share of world trade has more or less quadrupled ... Japan's figure for 2001 was 6.6 per cent' (*The Economist*, 15 February 2003, p. 74).

> In a little over two decades China has jumped from being an insignificant trading nation to rank fourth behind the United States, Germany and Japan, according to the WTO's 2001 figures. In that year China accounted for 5.6 per cent of global exports and 4.9 per cent of imports. US exports were 11.9 per cent of the world total and imports 18.3 per cent.
>
> (*FEER*, 18 September 2003, pp. 32–3)

'Between 1980 and 2002 China's share in global exports and imports rose from 1.2 per cent and 1.1 per cent to 5.2 per cent and 4.2 per cent, respectively' (*FT*, 12 November 2003, p. 23).

'China's share of world trade has grown to about 7 per cent, almost triple what it was a decade ago. China is the world's third largest importer' (www.iht.com, 12 July 2004).

'[In 2004, according to the World Trade Organization China, overtook] Japan as the world's third largest exporter ... China is now the biggest merchandise trader in Asia and the third largest in the world for both exports and imports' (*FT*, 15 April 2005, p. 9).

'[China is] the third largest exporter and importer' (*FT*, 31 August 2005, p. 14).

'Total foreign trade topped $1.4 trillion ... in 2005 ... making China the world's third largest foreign trade after the United States and Germany' (*IHT*, 12 January 2006, p. 11).

Foreign trade increase as a percentage of GDP

Foreign trade as a percentage of GDP has increased to a remarkable extent and of late there are signs that China's exports are improving as regards value-added.

It is important to stress that *both* exports and imports have grown rapidly, a sign of increasing overall integration into the world economy that contrasts with the experience of Japan (which stressed exports).

> Through foreign direct investment China runs a huge processing operation for the world on behalf of multinational corporations. This is one reason why its trade/GDP ratio is inordinately high for a continental country – more than 40 per cent compared with about 20 per cent for the United States.
>
> (*FT*, 8 June 2004, p. 19)

> Exports are ... worth around 20 per cent of GDP and the value-added is low, with about half of all exports consisting of processed imports ... The preponderance of low-technology consumer exports like toys and shoes has protected China from the plunge in electronics demand that has hammered Taiwan and [South] Korea.
>
> (*FEER*, 25 October 2001, p. 68)

> While the ratio of exports to GDP for China is relatively high (22 per cent), the impact of slowing external demand on China's overall economic growth is

unlikely to be as large as that for many other Asian economies. One reason is that a substantial proportion of China's exports consists of simple processing of imported materials with low value-added.

(United Nations, *World Economic and Social Survey 2001*, p. 108)

Much export manufacturing, in other words, consists of processing industries that ship in components, bolt them together and ship them out again. The foreign-dominated export sector, especially in China's handful of 'special economic zones', should be thought of as an enclave ... China, says Mr [Nicholas] Lardy, is only shallowly integrated with the world economy.

(*The Economist*, 10 March 2001, p. 26)

'In 2000 exports totalled $249.21 billion, the Chinese government reported, or nearly a quarter of the GDP of $1.07 trillion' (*IHT*, 19 December 2001, p. 15).

Exports grew from $10 billion in 1978 to $278 billion in 2000, making it the sixth largest trading nation in the world (from about the thirtieth in the late 1970s). The trade-to-GDP ratio increased from 10 per cent at the beginning of the reforms to about 40 per cent in the late 1990s.

(*Finance and Development*, 2002, vol. 39, no. 3, p. 22)

'China's ... ratio of trade to GDP at market prices was 44 per cent in 2001' (*FT*, 12 November 2003, p. 23).

'Some 50 per cent of China's imports are materials destined for reexport' (*FT*, 29 October 2002, p. 11).

'[China's] ratio of exports to GDP stands at around 30 per cent' (*The Economist*, 20 November 2004, p. 14).

The sum of exports and imports – a traditional measure of a country's openness to trade – now amounts to more than 50 per cent, compared with 20 per cent of GDP in 1989 and less than 10 per cent of GDP in 1979 ... In the 1980s and early 1990s China's exports were concentrated mainly in clothing, footwear, toys and other light manufacturing products. Since then its shares of world exports have risen in all categories and have grown especially rapidly in office machinery and telecommunications products (including electronics), as well as furniture, travel goods and industrial supplies. More recently China has made substantial gains in more hi-tech export categories, including automated data processing equipment. Electronic goods now account for as much as 25 per cent of exports ... The rapid expansion of exports is only half the story. It has been accompanied by sharp increases in imports, especially imports for processing and reexport, which have led to a significant increase in regional trade within Asia.

(Prasad and Rumbaugh 2003: 46–9)

'Exports amounted for 36 per cent of GDP in 2004' (*IHT*, 27 June 2005, p. 11).
'China's exports have grown from 20 per cent of GDP in 1999 to 35 per cent in 2004' (*FT*, 22 April 2005, p. 19). 'The ratio of trade (exports plus imports) to GDP is 70 per cent' (*FT*, 27 June 2005, p. 17). 'Last year [2004] the ratio of trade to GDP, at market prices, reached 70 per cent, much the same as in South Korea ...

The United States and Japan have ratios of trade to GDP that are below 25 per cent' (*FT*, 5 September 2005, p. 17).

> For its size . . . [China] is unusually open to the rest of the world in terms of trade and foreign direct investment. The sum of its total exports and imports of goods and services amounts to around 75 per cent of China's GDP; in Japan, India and Brazil the figure is 25 per cent to 30 per cent.
>
> (*The Economist*, 30 July 2005, p. 66)

> Up to half of China's exports are made up of intermediate and semi-finished products imported from other countries to be processed and shipped out again. If the double accounting of the import content is stripped out, the ratio of China's exports to its GDP tumbles to about 18 per cent of the 36 per cent seen in the crude data.
>
> (Qu Hongbin, *IHT*, 12 October 2005, p. 8)

China as a net importer of grain and oil

China became a net importer of both grain and oil in 1993.

'Since 1993 China has become a net oil importer' (*IHT*, 12 April 2005, p. 6).

'By 1994 . . . [China became] a net importer of oil . . . China today imports about 30 per cent of the oil it consumes' (*IHT*, 29 October 2001, p. 8).

'China's crude oil imports are expected to exceed half its total usage by 2015–20, up from 30 per cent today' (*FEER*, 7 February 2002, p. 30). 'By last year [2001] 34 per cent of total oil needs were imported. By 2030 that figure . . . will reach 82 per cent' (*FEER*, 24 October 2002, p. 36). 'China became a net importer of oil in 1996' (*FEER*, 13 February 2003, p. 28). '[In 2002 China] derived around 30 per cent of its oil needs from imports': *FT*, 24 February 2003, p. 7. 'As a percentage of China's oil needs, imports are expected to grow from 34 per cent in 2002 to more than 80 per cent by 2030' (*FEER*, 24 July 2003, p. 12). 'China imports a third of its oil supply. About half of China's crude comes from the Middle East' (*FEER*, 3 April 2003, p. 23). 'China overtook Japan last year [2003] to become the world's second largest oil consumer' (*FEER*, 10 June 2004, p. 27). The United States imports 55 per cent of its oil (*IHT*, 19 November 2003, p. 15). 'Last year [2003] China surpassed Japan to become the world's second largest consumer of oil after the United States' (*FEER*, 17 June 2004, p. 31).

'China imports 35 per cent [of its oil], of which 60 per cent is from the Gulf' (*IHT*, 9 February 2006, p. 8). 'Oil imports from Saudi Arabia . . . account for 14 per cent of China's total oil imports' (*IHT*, 24 January 2006, p. 12).

'China this month [January 2006] noted that its ratio of imported oil declined by 2.2 percentage points to 42.9 per cent last year [2005]' (*The Economist*, 11 February 2006, p. 64).

'China's grain imports are expected to rise to 10 per cent of total consumption by 2020, up from 3 per cent today' (*FEER*, 7 February 2002, 31).

'For the first time in twenty years China became a net importer of food last year [2004]' (*FT*, 28 July 2005, p. 10).

(Further statistics on China's impact on world commodity markets are given in the section on economic performance.)

China's foreign trade surplus

China has not typically run large foreign trade surpluses, but the surplus surged in 2005. 'After a sharp rise in China's overall trade surplus during 1993–7 the surplus has remained relatively stable in the range of about $35 billion to $45 billion since 1997' (Prasad and Rumbaugh 2003: 49). 'China ran a trade surplus in 2004 of $31.9 billion, the highest since 1998' (*The Economist*, 15 January 2005, p. 102).

> China said Wednesday [11 January 2006] that its trade surplus with the rest of the world tripled in 2005 to a record $102 billion ... [China's official estimate of its] trade surplus with the United States reached a record $114.7 billion ... Excluding the United States, China actually had a trade deficit with the rest of the world of about $12 billion in 2005, largely with Japan and oil exporting countries.
>
> (*IHT*, 12 January 2006, p. 11)

The United States continually complains about its huge bilateral trade deficit with China (apart from other things such as China's poor record with regard both to human rights and to observance of international patent law). (The United States has exerted pressure on China to revalue its currency against the dollar: see below.) 'China said its trade surplus with the United States was $42.7 billion last year [2002] ... while the United States, which counts exports through Hong Kong, estimates its deficit at about $100 billion' (*FEER*, 27 February 2003, p. 28). The United States puts the trade surplus at $103 billion (*FT*, 24 February 2003, p. 7). In 2002, according to the United States, China's trade surplus was $103 billion. China said it was only $43 billion (*FT*, 30 October 2003, p. 2). The figure of $103 billion 'surpassed the size of Japan's surplus for the first time' (*FT*, 3 September 2003, p. 11). The United States said that in 2003 the surplus was $124 billion compared with China's figure of $58.6 billion (*The Economist*, 17 April 2004, p. 60).

> [The United States claims that] the US deficit with China in 2004 was $162 billion ... China says the deficit is only $80 billion ... The United States counts exports from Hong Kong as Chinese exports, and China does not include exports from the mainland to the United States from China-based American companies.
>
> (*FT*, 22 March 2005, p. 10)

> [China's official estimate of its] trade surplus with the United States reached a record $114.7 billion ... in 2005 ... up from $80 billion a year earlier and $28 billion in 2001 ... [According to the United States] through October 2005 China already had a trade surplus of over $166 billion.
>
> (*IHT*, 12 January 2006, p. 11)

'[China's] current account surplus doubled last year [2005] to $125 billion' (www.iht.com, 27 February 2006).

Despite the big shift to China, US imports from Asia as a whole have hardly changed in the last fifteen years ... Asia's share of imports into the United States has held remarkably steady, at 38 per cent ... While China now has an estimated $200 billion trade surplus with the United States, it also has a $137 billion trade deficit with the rest of Asia.

(*IHT*, 10 February 2006, pp. 1, 6)

'[According to the United States, in 2005 the] US trade deficit with China [increased] to a record $201.6 billion' (*IHT*, 16 February 2006, p. 18). '[The] US trade deficit [as a whole in 2005 reached a] record $725.8 billion' (*IHT*, 15 February 2006, p. 13).

Reduction in tariffs

Tariffs are being reduced, a trend encouraged by WTO commitments (see below).

The average tariff rate fell from 43 per cent in 1992 to 17 per cent on 1 October 1997. On 1 July 1999 China announced that it would reduce the average tariff on imported goods from 17 per cent to 15 per cent in 2000. It also indicated that it would fulfil its promise to cut the average tariff on imported capital goods to 10 per cent by 2005 (*FT*, 2 July 1999, p. 4).

By last year [2001] quotas and licensing requirements restricted only 5 per cent of all imports, compared with about half little more than a decade ago. China has pledged to eliminate the remaining import quota and licence restrictions by 2005, a pace of opening that is actually less rapid than the recent past. Restrictions on trading rights, which at one time gave a single or small number of state companies a monopoly on the right to import all goods, have been slashed and now apply to little more than a dozen products. The government has committed itself to phasing out restrictions on trading rights for about half of these commodities over a three-year period.

(Nicholas Lardy, *FT*, Survey, 15 March 2002, p. ii)

(See the section on the WTO, below, for later developments.)

End to state monopoly of foreign trade

The state monopoly of foreign trade was ended and an increasing number of state enterprises were allowed to conduct foreign trade on their own and to retain a percentage of foreign exchange earnings. Private companies (both domestic and foreign) have been allowed to engage in foreign trade. The sector has become increasingly controlled indirectly, e.g. via the exchange rate system and tariffs (although, for example, licensing still exists).

China's foreign trade ministry was to allow overseas companies for the first time to set up foreign trade joint ventures with Chinese partners (*IHT*, 1 October 1996, p. 17).

In November 1995 it was announced that three or four foreign trading joint ventures would be approved in Shanghai and other locations. In July 1996 four applications were approved by the Shanghai authorities, while the first joint venture was approved by the central authorities in late October 1996. The regulations include high levels of trade turnover, location in Shanghai's Pudong zone or the Shenzhen SEZ, and a minority shareholding for the foreign partner (*China Briefing*, January 1997, p. 3).

The first joint venture foreign trade company has been set up (*IHT*, 12 July 1997, p. 15).

The first three joint venture trading enterprises began operation in Shanghai on 28 August 1997, foreign companies taking stakes of 49 per cent in each case (*FEER*, 11 September 1997, p. 64).

On 14 October 1998 it was announced that China would open its export trade (currently restricted to state enterprises) to private enterprises by 1 January 1999 (*IHT*, 15 October 1998, p. 19).

> China said yesterday [5 January 1999] that it had allowed twenty private companies to engage directly in foreign trade in an effort to boost the country's flagging export performance... Private companies have previously been allowed to import and export only through state-run trading houses ... Exports in 1998 fell slightly against 1997, failing to meet a trade ministry target of 10 per cent growth, and falling far short of 1997's 20.9 per cent year-on-year increase.
>
> (*FT*, 6 January 1999, p. 6)

> State media reported that China had cleared twenty privately owned companies to conduct foreign trade as part of a move to increase exports ... The ministry of foreign trade and economic co-operation issued trade licences to twenty companies, including the [New] Hope Group, China's biggest animal feed producer. 'This is the first time that private firms have been allowed to enter foreign trade,' said an official of the ministry. Until now only state-run trading companies, selected state-owned manufacturers and Chinese companies in which foreigners have a stake have had the right to conduct foreign trade.
>
> (*IHT*, 6 January 1999, p. 15)

The WTO

China did not succeed in gaining founder membership of Gatt's successor, the World Trade Organization (WTO), when it was established on 1 January 1995. China's entry into the WTO has been delayed by such factors as quotas, an extensive licensing system and large subsidies to state industrial enterprises. It has been argued that WTO entry has implications for the overall economic reform process in China. 'The WTO rules are the lever that China's reformist prime minister, Zhu Rongyi, wants to use to overcome his domestic opponents and force more openness on China' (Thomas Friedman, *IHT*, 1 September 1999, p. 6). 'President Jiang apparently needs the weight of international commitments to help overcome domestic opposition to his ambitious plan to drive his economy away from state controls and towards markets' (Michael Weinstein, *IHT*, 10 September 1999, p. 6). 'Prime minister Zhu Rongyi ... wants to use commitments to the WTO to make it hard for domestic opponents to overturn reforms. Violations of China's commitments to the WTO invite retaliation by China's trade partners' (*The New York Times*, editorial: *IHT*, 4 November 1999, p. 8).

Controls on the Chinese economy (such as on capital flows) helped shield China to some extent from the effects of the Asian financial crisis (which started in July 1997). This had a dampening effect on China's desire to join the WTO. But prime minister Zhu Rongyi had talks about WTO entry with President Clinton in the USA in April 1999. (President Clinton rejected the Chinese concessions then because he thought they would not be sufficient to convince the US Congress. He subsequently regretted this and the public disclosure of the details of the talks caused great embarrassment for Zhu Rongyi, who was subjected to considerable criticisms at home in China. Many argue that the concessions made by China in the November 1999 agreement with the USA are, on balance, less than those the USA could have achieved in April 1999!)

China has to negotiate first with individual countries or trading blocs, such as the EU. On 27 April 1998 the EU agreed to remove China from a list of 'non-market' economies. The decision revised the EU's criteria for judging 'dumping'. The EU would henceforth use China's own price information rather than prices from Western producers to determine, on a case-by-case basis, whether China was selling goods below cost. China was not designated as a market economy, but the new policy would enable the EU to take account of cases where market conditions existed (*IHT*, 28 April 1998, p. 13).

On 15 November 1999 the USA and China announced that an agreement had finally been reached – the negotiations had lasted, off and on, for thirteen years! The failure of the USA and China to agree on their bilateral deal had been the main obstacle to China's membership of the WTO.

The deal did not need the approval of the US Congress before China could proceed into the WTO, but Congress would eventually have to grant China what in the USA is called 'permanent normal trading relations' (PNTR) instead of having to take an annual vote (which started in 1974) if US companies were not to be penalized by China. (PNTR is more commonly known as 'most favoured nation' or MFN status, the idea being that the most beneficial concessions apply to all countries. The US House of Representatives voted in favour of PNTR on 24 May 2000 by a surprisingly comfortable margin of 237 to 197, surprising in the sense that a long, passionate and acrimonious debate had seemed to herald a very close run result. Some critics were appeased by a promise to set up a commission to monitor human and labour rights in China. The US Senate voted in favour of PNTR on 19 September 2000. The majority in favour, eighty-three to fifteen, was again surprisingly large.) China had already reached agreement with twelve other countries, including Japan and Australia but also had to reach agreements with the EU, Canada and twenty-two other countries, including Brazil, India and Switzerland. A new round of WTO negotiations were to begin on 30 November 1999.

There was to be a general reduction in China's import tariffs to 17 per cent by 2004 from the current average of 22.1 per cent.

1   Tariffs on major US farm products will fall to between 14.5 per cent and 15 per cent. Deep cuts in tariffs will be made by January 2004, to just 14.5 per

cent for commodities such as wheat and maize (from an average of 31.4 per cent). There will be quotas in China for imports of wheat, corn, rice and cotton and the phasing out of state trading of soy oil. China will also halt export subsidies.

2   A range of industrial tariffs will be reduced from an average of 26.4 per cent in 1997 to 9.4 per cent by 2005. Tariffs on automobile imports, which now range from 80 per cent to 100 per cent, will be reduced to 25 per cent by 2006. Foreign auto companies and banks will be able to offer consumer loans for car purchases.

China will import twenty foreign films a year, double the current number, and allow foreign film and music companies to share in distribution revenues. Foreign companies will be allowed to form joint ventures for the distribution of video and sound recordings.

Protective measures to respond to Chinese 'import surges' into the USA will last for twelve years, while US anti-dumping measures will last for fifteen years. The USA will end import quotas on Chinese textiles by 1 January 2005, but with special 'anti-surge' safeguards for four years after that.

Foreign companies can import and export without government middlemen and distribute and sell products directly to consumers in China. They can also handle after-sales, repair and maintenance services.

Foreign companies will be able to own up to a 49 per cent stake in the Chinese telecommunication services sector, and 50 per cent (with management control) beginning two years after China's entry to the WTO. Foreigners may invest also in internet companies, including content providers, but it was not clear whether the same terms applied. 'New laws will regulate content on the internet and foreign ownership of internet companies will be limited to 50 per cent, minister of information industry Wu Jichuan said in an interview [in December]. He added that companies will need licences' (*FEER*, 23 December 1999, p. 50).

> The landmark trade agreement ... opens the door to foreign ownership of up to 50 per cent of internet content companies by 2002 and up to 49 per cent of internet service providers by 2006 ... The minister of information industries has made it clear that Beijing could tie up foreign investors in cumbersome licensing procedures.
>
> (*IHT*, 18 December 1999, p. 13)

(There remains some doubt about whether existing foreign investment in some internet companies will be permitted under a clause which provides for the continuation of existing joint ventures in all service sectors. On 5 January 2000 the minister of the information industry said that the limit of foreign participation in internet service providers would be 50 per cent. 'The question of foreign participation in internet content providers (ICP) ... remains more complex. Wu Jichuan said ICPs would be subject to "relevant government regulations", which he said would be published in the first three months of this year [2000]. Many foreign companies have combined stakes well in excess of 50 per cent in mainland ICPs and government officials have said that these must be sold down to abide by China's WTO agreement. Some companies have tried to circumvent Beijing's regulations by styling themselves not as ICPs but as Internet Technology Providers or Internet Application Providers': *FT*, 6 January 2000, p. 12.)

Important provisions will open Chinese retail banking to foreign companies over several years and improve market access for insurance companies, legal and accounting firms. Foreign banks can offer services in local currency to Chinese enterprises, two years after China joins the WTO, and to Chinese citizens five years after joining. In the insurance industry geographical limits on foreign companies will be eliminated over five years. China agreed to allow 50 per cent ownership for life insurers on accession. Non-life and reinsurance companies will be allowed 51 per cent ownership on accession and wholly owned subsidiaries after two years. ('China is preparing gradually to relax restrictions on foreign companies offering "group" insurance policies ... The easing would begin three years after China accedes to the WTO, officials said. Foreign insurers are at present limited to dealing with individuals, and are therefore unable to sell policies to companies or other "group" entities ... The deal also states geographical limits on the operations of foreign and foreign-invested insurance companies will be lifted over a period of five years after accession, officials said': *FT*, 22 December 1999, p. 8.)

In the infant financial securities field in China, foreign companies are held to minority stakes in such activities as underwriting stock issues. Foreign firms can have a stake of up to 33 per cent in financial services such as mutual funds and securities fund management, rising to 49 per cent three years after China joins the WTO.

Foreigners will not have to submit to local-content requirements, and deals that insist on transfers of technology will be subject to WTO rules. Chinese state enterprises may not discriminate against foreigners: commercial considerations must apply when purchasing goods or services.

(*IHT*, 16 November 1999, pp. 1, 10, and 17 November 1999, pp. 7, 16–17; *FT*, 16 November 1999, pp. 1, 18–19, 26, 17 November 1999, p. 16, 19 November 1999, p. 14, and Survey, 29 November 1999, p. vi; *Guardian*, 16 November 1999, p. 2; *The Economist*, 20 November 1999, pp. 27–31.)

China is to phase out preferential tax policies for foreign enterprises following its accession to the WTO ... Beijing's top tax official said yesterday [11 January 2000]. But the creation of a 'level playing field' between foreign and local companies will not happen immediately after WTO entry and concessions already promised or enjoyed by foreign companies will be continued ... the director of the state bureau of taxation said yesterday. 'In line with the general WTO principle of national treatment, we will adjust tax rates within China in order to create a level playing field for Chinese and foreign companies,' he said ... All corporations in China are taxed at the flat rate tax of 33 per cent, but after various deductions most foreign companies pay around 15 per cent. In special industrial zones companies typically enjoy two years free of corporate tax followed by three years of taxation at the rate of 7.5 per cent ... He appeared to leave the door open to some degree of flexibility by saying the WTO principle of national treatment would have to be viewed alongside not only 'the domestic situation in China'. 'The tendency for China is to move toward unification. But this is only a trend,' he said.

(*FT*, 12 January 2000, p. 10)

Foreign investors are due to lose preferential tax rates after China enters the WTO, he said. Companies that are at least partly foreign owned now pay as little as 15 per cent in income tax, less than half the 33 per cent that local companies pay. That disparity will be removed over time, he said, though he did not give a timetable for the move toward the WTO principle of 'national treatment', or equal rates for local and foreign companies. 'This is a sensitive question which requires a step-by-step approach,' he said.

(*IHT*, 12 January 2000, p. 16)

(Note that there are concerns about the prospects for China's *implementation* of the agreement. There is also domestic *regional* protectionism within China, so getting the regions to adhere to WTO rules will be difficult. Disregard of its rules and rulings could also have a negative impact on the WTO itself.)

On 26 November 1999 China and Canada signed a bilateral agreement resolving outstanding issues. The agreement would bring Chinese tariffs on priority Canadian goods down from an average 12.5 per cent to 5.2 per cent over two-and-a-half years. The agreement met Canada's demands for improved access for agricultural goods such as wheat and barley, which are Canada's largest exports to China (*FT*, 27 November 1999, p. 6). China and India concluded a deal on 22 February 2000.

The EU and China announced an agreement on 19 May 2000. This was the last major agreement to be reached, but those with Switzerland, Mexico, Costa Rica, Guatemala and Ecuador were still to be concluded.

The main points of the agreement with the EU were as follows:

1   Tariffs on 150 goods not covered by the deal with the USA (EU-priority goods such as cosmetics, spirits, footwear, glass, ceramics, leather goods and items of machinery) would be cut by an average of 40 per cent to an average of 10.9 per cent. Tariffs on cosmetics would be reduced from an average of around 30 per cent to 10 per cent. Tariffs on all spirits would be reduced from 65 per cent to 10 per cent. China rejected the EU demand for car import tariffs lower than in the US agreement.

2   The state monopolies on the import of oil, oil products and high-grade fertilizer would be dismantled. From China's accession into the WTO, foreign oil and oil product exporters would be allowed to sell 20 per cent of imports to non-state Chinese companies at market prices. This proportion would increase by 15 per cent every year. According to some estimates, China would import up to 40 per cent of its oil needs in 2010. Fertilizer exporters would be able to export a quota of 2.7 million tonnes a year from accession at an agreed 4 per cent tariff. Any unused portion of the quota would be carried over into the following year.

3   There would be further liberalization of tariffs and quotas on products including rape oil, pasta, butter, milk powder, mandarins, wine and olives.

4   The export monopoly on silk would be liberalized.

5   The EU failed to raise the percentage of foreign ownership in mobile telecommunications, internet services and life assurance agreed in the US deal. But China agreed to bring forward by two years the dates by which foreign companies would be allowed to form telecoms and insurance joint ventures. (For example, foreign ownership in mobile telecommunications would be allowed to reach 49 per cent within three years of WTO accession instead of five.) At least seven insurance company licences would be granted to European companies in both life and non-life sectors. China also agreed to lift equity share restrictions on foreign retailers, allowing them to establish wholly foreign owned networks throughout the country. Limits on floor space were also abolished. There would be a relaxation of restrictions on foreign joint ventures in car, van and truck production.

6   Foreign companies would be allowed to offer services on Chinese law and to benefit from a relaxation of some recruitment restrictions.

     (*FT*, 20 May 2000, p. 7; *IHT*, 20 May 2000, p. 1; *FEER*, 1 June 2000, p. 20)

On 26 July 2000 China announced that it had concluded a bilateral market access accord with Ecuador. Mexico and Switzerland were still to settle (*FT*, 27 July 2000, p. 12).

Long Yongtu (chief Chinese negotiator for entry to the WTO):

> If there is no competition China's industry will not develop well. The globalization process is irreversible. Nobody can be isolated from it ... We believe that globalization will enhance China's competitiveness ... We decided to open gradually our telecommunications market. If we do not open it we will become isolated in the new economy that is based on advances in communications and information technology ... China is committed to a market economy, not a planned economy, because it wants to be an economic power in the twenty-first century ... We used to believe that the government could create a group of first-class entrepreneurs. We now realize that they have to be created in the marketplace. One of the main problems with the planned economy is that there is too much government interference.

> (*IHT*, 17 November 2000, p. 21)

Further developments

> [A] directive [was] issued by the cabinet in April [2001] ... outlawing 'regional blockades in market activities' ... While opening up to global markets in the past two decades, China's domestic economy has become more and more fragmented, riddled with local protectionist measures from crude roadblocks to sophisticated technical standards ... Beijing has a vested interest in breaking down local barriers. In addition to making consumers worse off, they are one of the biggest obstacles to the creation of strong national companies which will be able to survive the competition brought by WTO membership ... [There] are twenty-seven provinces and four vast provincial-level cities ... Inter-provincial restrictions on the flow of goods are well known. Tobacco and alcohol products from other localities face outright bans in some places ... Provincial fees and taxes [vary] ... Agricultural products like grain,

flour and soybeans remain subject to internal trade barriers, while the circulation of bottled water and medicine is also heavily restricted by local standards. Even newspapers are affected ... Construction ... [companies are also affected by] local protectionism ... Overcapacity in many sectors is one obvious result [of local protectionism]. Virtually every province has a maker of washing machines, colour televisions and refrigerators. The country also has 120 automakers, most of them surviving on various forms of local protectionism. Beijing wants to reduce the number to just half a dozen, but twenty-two provinces or cities have declared the sector to be a core industry for the coming decade ... Alwyn Young ... [in the November 2000 edition of the *Quarterly Journal of Economics* argues that] when local governments won control of capital and technology ... they rushed to invest it in sectors like heavy industry and consumer products that the state was still protecting with easy money and high prices. When that led to over-investment in many sectors, local officials protected their companies with trade barriers. The result: fragmented markets and investment decisions that often went against comparative advantage.

(Bruce Gilley, *FEER*, 12 July 2001, pp. 17–19)

According to a new study, regional barriers within the country are as high as those between countries of the EU, or between Canada and the United States. Worse, inter-provincial trade barriers have risen steadily since the 1980s even as barriers to imports have fallen. The findings by Sandra Poncet ... are the latest evidence that China's reform era has resulted in the creation of an array of separate markets protected by non-tariff barriers - like licensing and 'buy-local' rules ... Even as China joins the WTO and opens its markets to imports, domestically produced goods still face major obstacles in crossing provincial borders.

(Bruce Gilley, *FEER*, 22 November 2001, p. 44)

[The USA and China] announced Saturday [9 June 2001] that they had agreed on several issues that had been blocking Beijing's entry into the WTO, paving the way for China to join the global trade body this year [2001] ... The big sticking point involved farm subsidies ... China must still complete similar deals with the EU and other trading partners.

(*IHT*, 11 June 2001, p. 11)

'Other stumbling blocks have included Chinese attitudes toward opening its insurance and retail markets' (*FT*, 1 June 2002, p. 8).

The USA said ... that China had agreed to restrict agricultural subsidies and open its markets further to foreign insurers and retailers as part of a deal ... China's current domestic [agricultural] subsidies are in the 1–2 per cent range ... China had sought developing-country status that would allow for domestic subsidies of as much as 10 per cent of the value of agricultural output. The USA had insisted on 5 per cent; the two appear to have split the difference. The USA also won agreement on product-specific caps to keep China from heavily subsidizing certain crops such as apples or garlic ... The EU and Mexico must still finalize deals with China.

(*FT*, 13 June 2001, p. 12)

('The two countries [China and the USA] settled on 8.5 per cent': *IHT*, 28 June 2001, p. 19.)

> China agreed to phase out rules curtailing American firms' access to the markets for reinsurance and big-ticket property insurance; a consensus was reached on limits to the spread of American retailers in China; and China agreed to lift restrictions on foreign companies' rights to import and export ... China's agricultural subsidies at present amount to only about 2 per cent of output, and it would be hard pressed to afford more ... Mexico has yet to agree the necessary bilateral obstacles at all. And there are outstanding disagreements with others, such as the EU, which has accused China of backtracking on promises to open its insurance market.
>
> (*The Economist*, 16 June 2001, p. 94)

> China plans to raise tax rates on foreign companies, bringing them in line with taxes paid by local companies, a state-run newspaper reported Monday [11 June 2001]. The move would scrap preferential policies that have helped funds flow into China for two decades. The change has been prompted by China's pending entry into the WTO and the timing of the new unified tax regime will depend on when the country finally becomes a member.
>
> (*IHT*, 12 June 2001, p. 13)

'China and the EU reached an agreement Wednesday [20 June 2001] resolving their outstanding differences on Beijing's membership in the WTO ... Details of the agreement [were not given]' (*IHT*, 21 June 2001, p. 1.

'The EU and China yesterday resolved the remaining differences over access to the Chinese market for European insurance and retail distribution companies ... Progress was also made on broader issues relating to trade in services and goods' (*FT*, 21 June 2001, p. 12).

> China will remove price controls on 128 items from 1 August [2001] in preparation for the country's entry into the WTO, it was announced yesterday [11 July]. But Beijing will keep controls on thirteen broad categories that cover key areas of the economy. The lifting of the controls, which mostly formalizes the prevailing situation, was part of Beijing's intensifying efforts to rid itself of a 'non-market economy' classification that disadvantaged it in dumping disputes ... The items on which price controls are to be lifted include sugar, silk, natural rubber, pure gold jewellery, steaming coal and tea for sales in border areas ... The lifting of such curbs, though, is little more than symbolic. Most of the 128 items were already being traded according to market forces ... More significant are the areas in which guidelines are to be maintained. These include natural gas, electric power except for that portion sold through pooling, train tickets and fees, fees charged by key sea ports and ports along the Yangtze river, basic telecommunication services, some fertiliser, some pharmaceuticals and educational materials for elementary schools, middle schools and universities. In a move towards making pricing more transparent, China would soon unveil rules for holding public hearings on government pricing policy decisions ... The government would supervise local government price

setting procedures and monitor allegations on inter-regional dumping. The reduction in price controls will assist China in its arguments to overturn its classification as a 'non-market economy' in international trade disputes. This means that when Beijing fights a dumping case it is not allowed to cite domestic costs in its defence but has to submit to the application of costs in a 'surrogate' country such as India. Of the 420 cases it has had to fight over the last twenty years, sixty-eight have come from the USA. China, by contrast, has brought only seven dumping suits over the past three years ... [A Chinese official] predicts a surge in anti-dumping cases brought by Beijing after China enters the WTO.

(*FT*, 12 July 2001, p. 7)

. On 19 July 2001 the US House of Representatives voted to back President George W. Bush's request to continue normal trade relations with China.

On 13 September 2001 China and Mexico reached a deal on WTO entry. This was the final bilateral agreement.

A WTO panel ... the working party on China's accession ... was expected to approve on Monday [17 September 2001] the terms for China's entry ... Taiwan ... is expected to win approval the next day ... The last stumbling blocks ... were resolved on Saturday [15 September] ... The standoff over access to China's insurance market pitted Washington against Europe over the treatment of a US company, American International Inc., that has operated in China for years and wholly owns its operations there ... The working party's ... formal recommendation ... [will set] the stage for their approval at the [WTO] ministerial conference in Doha [Qatar] this November.

(*IHT*, 17 September 2001, p. 13)

Negotiators in Geneva gave formal agreement Monday [17 September] for China's membership in the WTO ... China will formally begin its membership after a vote by the 142 trade ministers of the international body in Qatar in November and after China ratifies the agreement. The process should be finished by early next year [2002]. Taiwan ... is expected to sign a similar agreement Tuesday [18 September].

(*IHT*, 18 September 2001, p. 13)

WTO ministers ... meet in Qatar in mid-November ... China will become a member after notifying completion of ratification procedures, probably early next year ... Today [18 September] a separate WTO working party will approve membership terms for Taiwan, which has been waiting for China to complete its negotiations. Under a 1992 understanding Taiwan will join the WTO after China as a 'separate customs territory' by the name of Chinese Taipei.

(*FT*, 18 September 2001, p. 12)

Nationalist China was one of the founding members of Gatt in April 1948. In March 1950 Taiwan pulled China out of Gatt after the communist takeover in 1949. China applied to rejoin Gatt in July 1986 (p. 12). 'It has been estimated that some

30 million Chinese workers may face unemployment in the next five years or so. ... State sector jobs have been cut by 35 million in the last four years' (*FT*, 19 September 2001, p. 18).

'[On 18 September 2001] Taiwan ... won formal clearance to join the WTO ... Hong Kong and Macau ... became members under the separate category of a "customs territory" not as countries' (*IHT*, 19 September 2001, p. 17).

'China ... insisted that Taiwan ... join as "the separate customs territory of Taiwan Kinmen and Matsu" or Chinese Taipei' (*FEER*, 22 November 2001, p. 34).

China's membership of the WTO was formally approved on 10 November 2001. (Taiwan was accepted the following day.)

> Immediately after the formal signing ceremony yesterday [11 November] China notified the WTO that it had ratified the membership terms, paving the way for ... the fifth biggest trader to become the WTO's 143rd member on 11 December [a month being required for actually joining the WTO after notification of ratification is given] ... instead of following immediately after ministers approved China's entry terms on Saturday [10 November], Beijing's signing ceremony was postponed a day to just after WTO endorsement of Taiwan's membership yesterday evening [11 November]. The staggered procedure was introduced to allay Taiwan's concern that China could in some way block accession. Taiwan, which will join as a 'separate customs territory' under the name Chinese Taipei, was only permitted to negotiate WTO entry on the basis of a 1992 understanding that China would enter first ... George W. Bush, US president, last week committed the USA to granting China permanent normal trade relations from the date of entry by certifying to Congress that its WTO membership agreement met all the US requirements.
>
> (*FT*, 12 November 2001, p. 10)

> According to the constitution, the decision to ratify entry into an international treaty should be made by the standing committee of the National People's Congress. But this has not happened in the case of China's admission into the WTO. Instead, the NPC standing committee took a 'decision' in August 2000 ... The NPC's standing committee had [thus] approved WTO accession even while negotiations on the terms of entry remained unfinished. China is supposed to become a full member on 11 December but will not start to implement the tariff cuts and market opening agreements until 1 January [2002].
>
> (*FT*, 20 November 2001, p. 14)

'Under the agreement with the United States, Washington will cease the annual review procedure in which Congress considers whether to end "normal trade relations" with China because of its record on human rights' (*IHT*, 12 November 2001, p. 11).

> At US insistence, other countries have the right to deploy against China special protective measures that would normally violate WTO rules. They may, with limited risk of retaliation, curb its textiles and clothing exports for eight years and any products for twelve. They also remain free to impose anti-dumping measures, of which China is already the world's biggest target.
>
> (*FT*, 10 December 2001, p. 22)

'China agreed to allow foreign securities firms to set up joint venture funds in a bid to bolster competition ahead of ... entry into the WTO' (*IHT*, 29 November 2001, p. 15).

(While China formally became a member of the WTO on 11 December 2001, Taiwan did not until 1 January 2002. 'Taiwan became the 144th member of the trade organization under the name of the "separate customs territory" of Taiwan and its islands of Penghu, Matsu and Jinmen, which is also known as Kinmen or Quemoy ... In a largely symbolic move Taiwan on Tuesday [1 January 2002] opened its doors to Chinese tour groups for the first time in more than five decades, but there were no sightings of such groups on the island. Travel agents said the response from eligible applicants, mainland Chinese living or studying overseas, has been lukewarm. Those in China are not allowed to travel to Taiwan as tourists': *IHT*, 2 January 2002, p. 11.)

('South-East Asian leaders yesterday [6 November 2001] endorsed a proposal to create a free-trade area with China over the next ten years ... Beijing advanced the proposal at last year's Asean summit': *FT*, 7 November 2001, p. 12. '[It was announced] that China and the ten-member Association of South-East Asian Nations will establish a free-trade zone – encompassing nearly 2 billion people – in the next ten years. The agreement to begin negotiations [was] struck at the early November Asean-plus-three summit in Brunei': *FEER*, 15 November 2001, p. 15).

China has secured a compromise in a thorny dispute between the EU and the USA over the treatment that AIG, the US insurance company, will receive following Beijing's accession to the WTO ... Official sources said yesterday [6 December 2001] that the compromise balanced the US desire for AIG to be allowed to continue opening wholly-owned insurance branches in China and the EU's insistence that the company should have to abide by China's WTO terms that limit foreign insurers to 50 per cent ownership in joint ventures. The deal, which appears to have won preliminary acceptance, is that AIG ... [which] currently has four wholly-owned operations in China ... will be given permission to open two more 100 per cent owned branches, but will thereafter have to abide by the same 50 per cent rule as all other foreign insurers in China's market ... The deal is seen as consistent with WTO rules because the two extra licences are to be awarded to AIG before China enters the WTO on 11 December, even though they will be exercised at a later date ... Some nineteen foreign insurers are [currently] offering services to China but they are subject to strict city limits.

(*FT*, 7 December 2001, p. 12)

[China] lowered the general tariff level by one percentage point to 11 per cent from 1 January 2003, a move that would affect more than 3,000 products ... The average tariff level on agricultural products would fall to 16.8 per cent from 18.1 per cent, while that on industrial products would be cut to 10.3 per cent from 11.4 per cent.

(*FEER*, 9 January 2002, p. 23)

China will allow companies that are not state-controlled to import 20 per cent of the country's oil products this year [2002] ... Currently 90 per cent of

China's oil product imports are controlled by four state-owned companies. That will fall to 79 per cent ... by the end of this year ... China is the second largest importer of oil in Asia, after Japan ... Beijing will stop setting quotas for oil products as of 1 January 2004.

(*IHT*, 23 January 2002, p. 12)

China will further reduce tariffs on imports as part of efforts to meet it made to join the WTO ... China has cut overall import tariffs to 11 per cent, down from 15.3 per cent before WTO membership two year ago ... The average tariff on imported industrial products has fallen to 10.3 per cent from 14.7 per cent over the same period and is expected to be cut to 9.3 per cent by 2005. Most duties on imported mechanical products will be cut to 5 per cent to 10 per cent by 2005 and some will be reduced to zero.

(*FEER*, 4 December 2003, p. 25)

In a bid to undercut United States critics of its trading success and save billions of dollars annually, Beijing decided to cut from 1 January [2004] a tax rebate given to exporters. The ministry of finance said China would cut the rebate by an average of three percentage points from the current 17 per cent. China introduced the rebate in the aftermath of the Asian financial crisis to boost the competitiveness of its exports without resorting to a devaluation of the renminbi. But the surge in exports and the renminbi's peg to the US dollar has come under a barrage of fire in recent months from US officials and manufacturers, who accuse Beijing of manipulating its currency to give an unfair advantage and steal American jobs ... [China] has refused to revalue the renminbi.

(*FEER*, 23 October 2003, p. 32)

The United States filed the first case by any country against China at the World Trade Organization on Thursday [18 March 2004], charging that Beijing imposes unfair taxes on imported semiconductors ... [The United States alleges that] China's tax is as much as 14 per cent higher on imported computer chips than those on those designed or manufactured in China, whether by domestic or foreign companies.

(*IHT*, 19 March 2004, p. 13)

The Bush administration filed the first complaint against China with the WTO over a tax on imported semiconductors. At issue is a 17 per cent value-added tax that China imposes on all semiconductor sales in China. To encourage domestic production, China gives an immediate rebate of all but 13 per cent to producers of chips designed and made in China.

(*FEER*, 1 April 2004, p. 26)

'[China says that] any company that makes chips in China can claim the tax break' (www.iht.com, 1 April 2004).

('The EU on Wednesday [31 March 2004] joined a US complaint against China in the WTO': www.iht.co, 31 March 2004. 'Japan on Thursday [1 April 2004] backed a US complaint to the WTO over tax breaks for chip makers in China, the world's fastest growing semiconductor market': www.iht.com, 1 April 2004.)

'The Chinese government ... reduced export-related rebates to an average 13 per cent of tax bills effective 1 January [2004] from as much as 17 per cent previously' (www.iht.com, 26 February 2004).

[China said it] would crack down on rampant piracy of American intellectual property such as films, computer software and music ... [and] pledged to delay implementing a new standard for wireless telephones that would have locked out foreign competitors and cost them market share by forcing all imported cellphones to use a Chinese-designed encryption standard. In addition, the Chinese agreed to speed up legislation that would allow foreign companies to import goods into China without needing costly Chinese middlemen.

(*FEER*, 6 May 2004, p. 25)

US officials said Thursday [24 June 2004] that they had agreed to twice-yearly talks with China aimed at granting the country official status as a market economy, a designation that would give Beijing more leverage in trade disputes ... As a non-market economy China is assessed in US anti-dumping cases on production costs in India ... Last week the United States imposed duties totalling $1.2 billion on exports of wooden furniture ... 'Non-market' status makes it difficult ... to prove low prices are a result of market competition, not government manipulation ... When China joined the WTO in 2001 it agreed that the United States did not have to reconsider its non-market status until 2015. Other countries, including New Zealand and Thailand, recently granted China market status ... But as a market economy China would be exposed to anti-dumping charges brought because of unlawful financial subsidies rather than distorted prices ... You cannot bring an anti-subsidy case against a non-market economy.

(www.iht.com, 24 June 2004)

The EU will refuse to recognize China as a market economy after an in-depth probe by Brussels found the Chinese economy suffering from too much state interference, weak rule of law and poor corporate governance ... China is the target of most US and European anti-dumping measures ... Beijing has already won over New Zealand, Singapore and Malaysia ... [The United States says] that China's leaders need to make substantial progress in reducing the state's role in the economy before it could expect US recognition ... If classified as a market economy the EU could no longer find Chinese producers guilty of dumping on the basis of comparing their prices with those of other emerging economies. Instead, Brussels would have to accept Chinese prices and costs as the benchmark – a much tougher burden of proof.

(*FT*, 28 June 2004, p. 7)

China is not yet a 'market economy' the European Commission concluded in a report Monday [28 June 2004]. State interference in industry, combined with a lack of adequate accounting, property and bankruptcy laws mean China must continue to be classified as a 'transitional economy' for the purposes of settling trade disputes with the EU ... The EU changed its rules four years ago to allow it to grant market economy status to individual companies from transitional economies, if they could provide reliable enough information. Since then 111 Chinese companies have requested the change in status but only twenty-eight have been granted it. The EU has thirty-two anti-dumping disputes with Chinese exporters, including cases involving the makers of bicycles and bike parts, and a further twenty-two cases are under investigation. The United States is imposing anti-dumping duties on fifty-two Chinese exporters, including exporters of steel concrete reinforcing bars.

(*IHT*, 29 June 2004, p. 15)

The United States said Thursday [8 July 2004] that it was dropping its case against China at the WTO after Beijing agreed to eliminate a tax break that US semiconductor makers said harmed their exports ... China would gradually eliminate a tax advantage that effectively raised the price of American imports of semiconductors by 14 per cent ... China will phase out the tax advantage over the next nine months, ending it in April 2005. The accord came after Washington threatened to bring the case before a WTO panel ... It would have been the first case ever filed against China by any of the WTO's 147 members ... Among other 'successes' the [US] administration has achieved in gaining market access to China is an agreement struck last April, under which China gave up a plan to impose its own software encryption standard for wireless computers.

(*IHT*, 9 July 2004, p. 11)

'The United States slapped punitive duties on shrimp imports from China and Vietnam of up to 113 per cent because of alleged dumping' (*FEER*, 15 July 2004, p. 29).

'A complex system of quotas has limited international trade in textiles and apparel for decades, but this will expire on 1 January [2005] under an agreement worked out in 1993 as part of the creation then of the WTO' (www.iht.com, 13 December 2004).

The commerce ministry in China plans to impose tariffs on some exports, a step that could avert a trade war with the United States and the EU over a new influx of low-cost Chinese garments that had appeared likely to flood Western markets starting on 1 January [2005] ... The commerce ministry said that the goal of the tariffs would be to encourage Chinese producers to manufacture higher-end textiles and apparel instead of selling a full range. A minimum tax will be set for each garment regardless of what each one costs.

(*IHT*, 14 December 2004, p. 6)

On 31 December 2004 the Multifibre Agreement, a tortuous quota system that has ruled (and distorted) trade in textiles for thirty years, is due to expire ... One widely cited study estimates that China's share of world textile trade will rise from 17 per cent in 2003 to over 50 per cent by 2007.

(*The Economist*, 18 December 2004, p. 138)

[China wants] to win formal US recognition as a 'market economy' ... as soon as possible ... Formal status as a 'market economy' would make it easier for

Chinese businesses to fight anti-dumping complaints brought to US trade offices by US manufacturers, because it would mean China's pricing system is assumed to reflect competitive market conditions.

(www.iht.com, 13 January 2005)

[On 10 January 2005 the United States said] that the new tariffs were so low that they would have a 'negligible' effect on Chinese exports of clothing to the United States ... An unexpected [US] court ruling at the end of December has limited the ability of [the United States] ... to restrict Chinese apparel exports ... [The US court] unexpectedly agreed on 30 December to a request by American retailers for a preliminary injunction barring the safeguard quotas.

(www.iht.com, 10 January 2005)

Hoping to ease growing trade frictions with the United States and Europe, China said Friday [20 May 2005] that it would raise tariffs sharply on many of its textile and apparel exports. The move comes as Beijing is under increasing international pressure to revalue its currency and to dampen the surge of textile and apparel products to the United States and Europe that occurred in the first quarter of this year [2005] ...... [China] said that as of 1 June China would impose substantially higher tariffs on seventy-four textile and apparel products, with tariffs quintupling on average ... The tariffs are generally to rise to the equivalent of 12 cents apiece from about 2.5 cents ... The United States said this month that it would impose quotas on certain Chinese textile and apparel imports to limit growth to 7.5 per cent a year. The EU is also weighing new restrictions on Chinese textile and apparel goods.

(*IHT*, 21 May 2005, pp. 1, 4)

China has sharply raised taxes on its own textile exports in the hope of heading off import curbs by the United States and the EU amid a deepening global trade dispute ... Tariffs on most items will rise to 1 renminbi and sometimes reach 4 renminbi ... This compares with the 0.2 renminbi to 0.3 renminbi tax imposed on 148 categories in January [2005] ... The United States has twice imposed quotas on Chinese textiles in the past week.

(*FT*, 21 May 2005, p. 10)

'[On 27 May the EU announced that it] would limit imports of Chinese T-shirts and flax yarn at a maximum of 7.5 per cent above imports from March 2004 to February 2005' (www.iht.com, 29 May 2005).

The government said Monday [30 May] that it was revoking [on 1 June] duties that it had placed on textile exports ... [specifically] the duties it had placed this year [2005] on garment exports that are being restricted by the EU and the United States.

(www.iht.com, 30 May 2005)

[China] said that all eighty-one product lines for which the duties are being revoked were threatened by US and EU quotas ... On Friday [27 May] the EU formally asked Beijing to resolve the dispute through the WTO ... The commission's decision to open a formal dispute proceeding gives China fifteen days to take action itself or face the reimposition of quotas.

(*IHT*, 31 May 2005, p. 10)

'Textiles account for just 6 per cent of China's trade' (www.iht.com, 6 June 2005).

The EU and China stepped back yesterday [10 June] from a potentially bitter trade dispute by negotiating a three-year 'transitional arrangement' for the import of Chinese textiles to Europe. The sides agreed to limit the increase in Chinese textile imports in each of the next three years to about 10 per cent a year before trade is fully liberalized in 2008 ... The EU will suspend planned sanctions against two categories of exports – flax yarn and T-shirts.

(*FT*, 11 June 2005, p. 9)

'The deal will cap the growth in imports of ten categories of Chinese textiles to between 8 per cent and 12.5 per cent a year between 2005 and 2008' (*FT*, 13 June 2005, p. 8).

The growth of certain textile and apparel exports to Europe [will be limited] to about 10 per cent a year through the end of 2008 ... The two sides agreed that Chinese textile exports would be managed to allow for 'reasonable growth' between 2005 and 2007.

(*IHT*, 11 June 205, p. 1)

'The [EU] deal limits Chinese export growth to 8 per cent to 12.5 per cent a year until 2007' (*IHT*, 18 June 2005, p. 14).

'The European trade commissioner ... said Monday [29 August] that he had begun procedures to release 80 million garments' (*IHT*, 30 August 2005, p. 8). 'The European trade commissioner ... has begun consultations with EU countries on a plan to release the backlog of sweaters, trousers and bras' (www.iht.com, 30 August 2005).

The breakthrough came as talks between China and the EU to revise a two-month-old textiles pact stretched into a fifth day. EU customs officials have impounded millions of Chinese sweaters, trousers, bras and other goods because most of the ceiling set by a deal reached in June that capped growth in ten lines of textile exports at 8 per cent to 12 per cent a year has been reached ... The EU's twenty-five member states have been split over the unanticipated pile-up of hundreds of millions of Euros' worth of garments from China ... [There are] demands for protection of EU textile producers against complaints from retailers.

(www.iht.com, 29 August 2005)

The new [10 June] quotas were quickly filled, prompting EU customs officers to block additional goods valued at hundreds of millions of Euros. The issue has exposed a rift between countries with big retail interests but little textile manufacturing, which want to ease the import restrictions, and the mainly southern European nations that remain significant textile producers.

(www.iht.com, 30 August 2005)

The European trade commissioner ... is facing resistance from France, Italy, Spain, Greece and Portugal, which want to protect their textile companies, including those with plants in places like north Africa and eastern Europe ... His proposals are backed by Germany, Sweden and the Netherlands, which have big retailing sectors ... European ports have been flooded by clothing ordered before the [new quota] system came into place or right after.

(*IHT*, 1 September 2005, p. 13)

A lobby group for retailers, wholesalers and trading firms has called on ... the European trade commissioner ... to let in all goods that were ordered before the [new] quotas came into effect on 12 July ... When China became a member of the WTO in 2001 it did so under special terms that allowed importing countries to impose short-term 'safeguards' on Chinese goods until 2013 if they could show those goods to be causing 'material injury' to domestic producers. And separate measures for textiles allow safeguards to be imposed whenever imports threaten 'market disruption'.

(www.economist.com, 1 September 2005)

'[There was a] month between the agreement's signing (11 June) and the announcement of regulations (12 July)' (*The Economist*, 3 September 2005, p. 41).

The United States imposed quotas on imports of bras and certain expensive fabrics from China on Thursday [1 September] after American and Chinese trade negotiators failed to reach a deal in a brief meeting in Beijing on Thursday morning. But the commerce department in Washington softened the blow by postponing until 1 October any decision on whether to impose special limits on imports of Chinese sweaters, robes, wool trousers and knit fabrics. The department had set a Wednesday deadline for imposing quotas on these categories and the bras and fabrics.

(*IHT*, 2 September 2005, p. 17)

'On 1 September America decided to restrict imports of Chinese-made bras and some synthetic fabrics' (*The Economist*, 3 September 2005, p. 26).

'Two rounds of talks [between the United States and China] – the second of which ended Thursday [1 September] in Beijing – failed to produce a settlement' (www.iht.com, 4 September 2005). '[The United States] said that it would limit imports of fabrics made with synthetic filament threads and also bras and other body-supporting undergarments' (www.iht.com, 5 September 2005).

China and the EU and China reached an agreement on Monday [5 September] to unblock millions of Chinese garments that had piled up at EU ports because they exceeded import quotas ... The EU's twenty-five member states will need to approve the deal before the clothing can go on sale in European stores. The agreement effectively raises import limits to allow in excess clothing amid growing concern that a flood of cheap Chinese goods undercuts European producers. European governments still have to agree the details of how the extra imports should be unblocked. Talks broke off in Brussels on Friday [2 September] and are due to continue Monday ... [The European trade commissioner] said Friday that European governments had reached 'broad agreement' behind his proposal to allow in goods ordered and shipped during the month following a 10 June textile deal with China and subtract goods ordered from next year's quota ... The EU negotiated new and higher limits with China in June but the month-long delay before the restrictions came into effect meant many importers placed huge orders in an attempt to get quota-free goods into Europe before the deadline. Imports of sweaters, men's trousers, bras, blouses, T-shirts and linen cloth overshot the new limits barely weeks after the deal was signed. Actual sweater imports are close to double the 2005 quota of 69 million garments.

(www.iht.com, 5 September 2005)

The negotiations [were] about how to handle some Euro 400 million, or $500 million, of Chinese garments that had been blocked from entry into Europe under the quota agreement made in June. The EU agreed to let in all the unlicensed goods, comprising around 80 million items, that had been blocked at European borders. In a burden-sharing arrangement the EU said it would accept 50 per cent of the goods unconditionally. China agreed that the remaining 50 per cent would be included in its quota for 2006 or from unfilled quotas of other products in 2005.

(*IHT*, 6 September 2005, p. 1)

'[The EU and China] agreed to release Chinese garments impounded at Europe's ports "as soon as possible"' (*FT*, 6 September 2005, p. 1).

Europe yesterday [7 September] finally agreed to end its dispute over Chinese textile imports, clearing the way for about 77 million impounded pullovers, trousers and bras to be released into shops next week. Only Lithuania, which has a big textiles sector, refused to back the deal struck between the EU and China under which half the blocked goods would be waved through by the Europeans while the other half would count against textile quotas for 2006 or against other unfilled quotas.

(*FT*, 8 September 2005, p. 10)

The United States signed an agreement with China on Tuesday [8 November] placing quotas on items including cheap shirts and trousers over the next three years. The deal raised the volumes of clothing that the United States would accept from China when compared with previous arrangements, but it placed limits on those volumes and included a wider range of products than those already subject to restrictions ... Under Tuesday's agreement clothing imports would be allowed to grow 10 per cent in 2006, 12.5 per cent in 2007 and 15 per cent to 16 per cent in 2008. The new terms would apply to more than thirty products. The United States would also move to release clothing piled up at American ports, although stocks could remain impounded for longer ... To avoid stockpiles at ports in future disputes, China could borrow quotas in following years, or, if such borrowing was not possible, because those quotas were also exhausted, then the customs authorities could still decide to lift restrictions.

(www.iht.com, 8 November 2005; *IHT*, 9 November 2005, p. 13)

'So far this year Washington has imposed an annual growth limit of 7.5 per cent on $3.4 billion worth of Chinese textile imports, which represents more than one-fifth of US imports of textiles and clothing from China' (*IHT*, 7 November 2005, p. 12).

> The deal ... will set quotas covering nearly half of Chinese textile imports into the United States ... It covers thirty-four different categories that account for 46 per cent of Chinese textile imports into the United States. The quotas will be introduced in two months to give manufacturers and retailers time to adjust to the changes.
>
> (*FT*, 9 November 2005, p. 11)

> After a nine month investigation ... [the EU] is set to introduce anti-dumping duties of almost 20 per cent on shoes from China and Vietnam ... The duties will affect exports that already represent 8 per cent of shoes sold in the EU ... Peter Mandelson, the EU trade commissioner ... is confident his proposal will be backed by a majority of the twenty-five EU member states as early as this week, with a view to introducing the duties on 7 April. But he is demanding that the duties be raised progressively over six months ... As with textiles, the issue has split the EU ... Vietnam has invested heavily to boost its shoe production in recent years and is now exporting 120 million pairs of shoes a year to the EU. Mr Mandelson hopes the temporary sanctions will persuade China and Vietnam to negotiate and offer a solution ... Failing a settlement by October, the EU could decide to keep the duties in place for another five years. China is already subject to about fifty EU anti-dumping measures.
>
> (*FT*, 20 February 2006, p. 4)

'Peter Mandelson is recommending that advanced sports shoes and children's shoes be exempt' (*FT*, 8 March 2006, p. 13).

> Countries like Italy want greater protection ... [while] countries in Scandinavia look askance at tariff plans ... Imports of leather shoes to the EU from China amounted to 95 million pairs in the eleven months ended March 2005. Over the same period imports to the EU from Vietnam totalled 120 million pairs ... Imports from China rose 300 per cent from January to October 2005, compared with the like period in 2004 ... Under the EU suggestions, if a majority of member state governments agree, tariffs could start as low as about 4 per cent by early April. That temporary level could rise to just below 20 per cent by early October. But Peter Mandelson would aim to ratchet any duties lower if China and Vietnam later show signs of making changes ... To meet a 7 April deadline Mandelson must send proposals to EU member states this week or next.
>
> (*IHT*, 21 February 2006, p. 15)

> Even tougher measures are demanded by European shoe manufacturers, but opposed by retailers and importers who warn that they will push up prices in stores ... The EU said this week that its imports of leather shoes from China soared 320 per cent in the twelve months up to March 2005, to 950 million pairs. Vietnamese imports grew 700 per cent to 120 million over the same

period, the EU said. A nine-month EU investigation into the market found evidence of state support to the footwear industry in China and Vietnam, including cheap finance, non-market land rents, tax breaks and improper asset evaluation. Brussels says that this allows it to introduce anti-dumping measures under international trade rules ... If approved, provisional measures could come into force on 7 April for six months while the EU continues its investigations. They could be extended for five years if the situation does not change.

(www.iht.com, 23 February 2006)

Peter Mandelson announced on Thursday [23 February] tariffs to slow the flow of leather shoes into Europe from China and Vietnam, while calling on European retailers to absorb the extra charges so consumers can continue paying for brands like Puma and Adidas ... [It is estimated that] 40 per cent of Puma shoes would be hit by tariffs ... Mandelson is preparing to phase in import duties of 19.4 per cent on some Chinese-made footwear and duties of nearly 16.8 per cent on some Vietnamese-made shoes beginning in early April ... starting at 4 per cent ... although EU governments must still approve the measures ... Mandelson said the measures would affect only nine of every 100 pairs of shoes in Europe, and just 2 per cent of total trade between the EU and China. They would also exclude shoes under size thirty-seven-and-a-half, or children's sizes.

(*IHT*, 24 February 2006, p. 15)

The EU, which imported shoes worth $5.9 billion from China and Vietnam in the past year, will impose tariffs starting at 4 per cent on some imports from the two countries on 7 April ... The EU duties will rise to a maximum 19.4 per cent on Chinese shoes after five months and 16.8 per cent on Vietnamese imports. The phase-in is designed to ensure that European retailers with goods in transit are not faced with sudden changes in tariffs. The duties will cover 9 per cent of shoes sold on the EU market and exclude children's shoes and some sports footwear ... China's clothing and textile exports increased 21 per cent to $115 billion in 2004 ... The country exported 95 million pairs of shoes to the EU in the past year.

(www.iht.com, 24 February 2006)

The EU imported $6 billion worth of shoes from China and Vietnam in the past year. On Wednesday [22 March] it agreed to impose tariffs starting at 4 per cent, rising to a maximum 19.4 per cent after five months, on some imports from the two nations starting on 7 April. The duties, which will cover 9 per cent of the shoes sold in the EU, exclude children's shoes and some sportswear.

(*IHT*, 23 March 2006, p. 12)

'The EU will start by imposing duties on leather shoes from China and 4.2 per cent on shoes from Vietnam. The tariff is set to rise to 16.8 per cent for shoes from Vietnam, and 19.4 per cent for shoes from China' (*IHT*, 24 March 2006, p. 13).

The EU and the United States turned to the WTO on Thursday [30 March] to try to force China to lower restrictions on imports of car parts, a long-standing complaint of Western automakers. The complaint accuses China of imposing high taxes on auto parts imported from the United States and other countries in violation of pledges it made when Beijing joined the WTO in late 2001 ... Beijing has ten days to respond and thirty days to start talks. If the issue cannot be solved within sixty days, all three parties can ask a WTO panel to hear and rule on the dispute. If such a panel were to rule against Beijing, penalty tariffs could be levied against its exports. The EU said China could be breaking trade rules by applying the same tariff for finished cars to the imported spare parts that make up 60 per cent of more of the value of the vehicle ... The EU said China had promised not to treat parts as whole cars when it joined the WTO ... China says that the car tariffs are intended to prevent the importing of what are essentially whole cars in large chunks, to avoid the higher tariff rates for importing finished cars ... Before the case over auto parts the United Sates was the only country ever to file a trade case against China before the WTO. The earlier case, involving a Chinese tax rebate for semi-conductor chips, was resolved during the consultation phase ... The United States is also looking at filing another trade case with the WTO against China over what the trade representative's office says is rampant piracy of intellectual property rights to products including movies, music and computer programmes.

(www.iht.com, 30 March 2006)

'The EU and the United States joined forces Thursday [30 March] against China in the WTO ... Both the United States and the EU have alleged that China is flouting trade rules by applying the same tariff for finished cars – about 28 per cent – to imports of automobile parts if those parts make up 60 per cent of the value of the finished car. They said the tariff on spare parts should be about 10 per cent' (*IHT*, 31 March 2006, pp. 1, 8).

'The United States and the EU claim China is imposing unfair "local content" rules through a complex tariff system that raises the import tariffs from 10 per cent to 25 per cent if parts make up more than a certain percentage of a car' (*FT*, 31 March 2006, p. 5).

Implications of WTO accession for China's economy

China's WTO entry follows a long period of opening of its trade and investment going back to the 1980s. This opening has brought the average tariff rate down from 43 per cent in the early 1990s to just above 15 per cent now ... China's accession will further reduce tariffs, from 31.5 per cent to 17 per cent for agricultural products and from 24.6 per cent to 9.4 per cent for industrial products. It will also expand the opportunities for FDI [foreign direct investment] in China by opening sectors previously closed to foreigners, such as telecommunications and financial services, and by improving the overall business climate for foreign firms. However, because China is already substantially exposed to international competition, its economy is not expected to experience the severe shock suffered by Russia and other Eastern European countries following their opening up in the late 1980s. Labour-intensive industries, which are China's comparative advantage, are the clearest winners from WTO entry. Some studies suggest that China's textile output could double after the multi-fibre agreement regulating world textile trade is eliminated in 2005. Some capital- and technology-intensive industries, such as automobiles, telecommunications and segments of the chemical and metallurgical industries, are expected to lose ground, at least initially. In agriculture markets for land- and water-intensive crops, notably wheat, corn, soybeans and other crops produced mainly in the north of China, will be opened up to lower cost competing products from abroad. Labour-intensive crops such as vegetables and flowers will enjoy expanded opportunities in foreign markets. The impact on the grain market will be limited as long as China's grain procurement system, which sets minimum producer prices and which is not covered under its WTO agreement, is maintained. However, the higher cost to the government once import controls are lifted will create strong incentives for the system's modification or elimination. Some estimates suggest that accession could boost annual FDI inflows by more than two-fold in the medium term. Worry that domestic banks will suffer severely from China's commitment to allow foreign banks to compete on comparable terms by 2005 has been one of the chief concerns within the country about the effects of WTO entry. However, foreign banks are likely to be selective in their activities and to avoid most lending to domestic businesses until the performance of those businesses improves. The direct impact of WTO entry on China's macroeconomic performance should be positive in the medium term ... China's import controls will begin falling immediately after accession and the effect on imports should start to become apparent by 2003. The main impact on exports is only likely to occur after the multi-fibre agreement lapses in 2005. Finally, the overall effect of WTO entry, and the extent to which China realises its potential benefits, will depend on the ability of the economy to reallocate its resources and to restructure the business sector to correct the widespread inefficiencies that now exist. These adjustments are being impeded by government interference in enterprise management, weaknesses in the financial system, local protectionism, and other problems. Success in addressing these problems will help some sectors that initially lose, such as automobiles, to restructure so as to be able to better exploit China's low cost of labour and large market.

(OECD, *Economic Outlook*, December 2001, p. 128)

[It was announced on 19 June that] under a new rule, which is to take effect on 20 July, companies exporting textile products on which other countries have set import limits will need to apply for a temporary export permit ... Permits will apply to categories specified in the EU agreement.

(www.iht.com, 20 June 2005)

Yuan convertibility and exchange rate policy

The yuan (renminbi or 'people's currency') has gradually been made more and more convertible. The first local foreign exchange markets ('swap centres') were set up in 1985 (a valuable boost to direct foreign investment since profits earned by 'foreign-invested enterprises' could be repatriated without having to export).

On 1 January 1994 the official and swap rates were unified, with the yuan subjected to a managed float.

> Unification of the yuan's official and market exchange rates appeared to imply a 50 per cent devaluation in the official rate; but at the time more than four-fifths of China's trade was already conducted at the market rate, so the devaluation was in effect less than 10 per cent.
>
> (*The Economist*, Survey, 7 March 1998, p. 7)

'In late 1994 Beijing first pegged the yuan to the dollar' (www.iht.com, 22 July 2005).

> China has fixed the value of the yuan at 8.277 to the dollar since 1995 ... The yuan can be freely exchanged only for trade purposes. Restrictions on the capital account, covering investment, prevent foreign investors from moving short-term capital into China and local investors from shifting funds overseas.
>
> (www.iht.com, 2 July 2004; *IHT*, 3 July 2004, p. 11)

> Officially the renminbi is already floating. It is, in theory, allowed to fluctuate 0.3 per cent either side of a reference rate determined each day by the central bank as a weighted average of the previous day's trades. But in practice the renminbi is pegged to the dollar. Normally the central bank is the biggest player on the Shanghai market, buying and selling currency to keep the exchange rate in a stable range between 8.2770 renminbi and 8.2800 renminbi to the dollar.
>
> (*FEER*, 4 May 2000, p. 58)

'The renminbi ... is now pegged near 8.28 to the dollar within a band of 8.276 to 8.280' (*FEER*, 5 February 2004, p. 23).

In the Asian financial crisis (see below) there was relief that China did not devalue the yuan. More recently there has been the opposite pressure to revalue the yuan. The United States (with its large bilateral trade deficit with China) is particularly keen that China's currency strengthens against the US dollar in order to make Chinese exports less competitive. (While it is generally thought that the yuan is undervalued, there is considerable disagreement as to the extent to which this is so. See, for example, *The Economist*, 25 June 2005, p. 100.)

'China's central bank bought about $180 billion of US Treasuries last year [2004] to maintain the value of the yuan as foreign currency flowed into the economy' (www.iht.com, 13 January 2005).

> China and other Asian countries have – because of massive dollar purchases to prevent their currencies appreciating – emerged as the financiers of the US's [large] current account and fiscal deficits, providing cheap capital that has kept the dollar's decline orderly and helped bring economic growth and low interest rates ... Foreign central banks, mainly from Asia, buy US Treasury paper ... [Asian countries] face capital losses on their reserves as the dollar declines ... Economists estimate that three-quarters of China's foreign reserves of more than $600 billion are held in US dollar assets ... A shift in exchange rate

policy would allow the government to use monetary policy for domestic goals, rather than subordinating interest rate decisions to the management of the renminbi [the government having to buy dollars with renminbi in order to maintain the exchange rate, thus increasing the money supply] ... The government has been able to offset the impact of the accumulation of reserves on the domestic economy by selling Chinese government securities – a process called sterilization. Reserves increased last year [2004] but the central bank drained about two-thirds of this out of the system through sterilization, ensuring that the impact on the money supply was minimal.

(*FT*, 14 April 2005, p. 17)

Money is pouring into China, both because of its rapidly rising trade surplus and because of foreign investment. Normally this inflow would be self-correcting: both China's trade surplus and the foreign investment pouring in would push up the value of the yuan ... making China's exports less competitive and shrinking its trade surplus. But the Chinese government, unwilling to let that happen, has kept the yuan down by shipping incoming funds right back out again, buying huge quantities of dollar assets – about $200 billion worth in 2004, and possibly as much as $300 billion worth this year ... This money flowing in from abroad has kept US interest rates low despite the enormous [US] government borrowing required to cover the [US] budget deficit.

(Paul Krugman, *IHT*, 21 May 2005, p. 6)

'Reports in the official Chinese media say that Beijing has invested about two-thirds of its $750 billion of foreign currency reserves in US government and corporate debt' (*IHT*, 7 November 2005, p. 14).

China's foreign currency reserves of $660 billion are rising by $17 billion or so a month. To mop up the liquidity created from buying these reserves, China's central bank has to issue ever more domestic currency bonds. With more than 1 trillion yuan of these bonds now outstanding, the country's commercial banks are becoming more reluctant to buy them.

(*The Economist*, 21 May 2005, pp. 85–6)

The combination of a rising current account surplus and foreign direct investment inflows has led to a need to purchase dollar assets to stabilize the exchange rate. The authorities have been able to sterilise much of this inflow through changes in reserve ratios, open market operations and window guidance to restrain the growth of bank lending without raising interest rates ... Reliance on window guidance to limit bank lending goes against the government's policy of increasing the use of market-based instruments to control monetary developments.

(OECD 2005: website Chapter 1)

Massive, sustained one-way intervention in the foreign exchange market (averaging 12 per cent of GDP in 2003 and 2004 and rising in 2005) has kept the renminbi from appreciating against the dollar in nominal terms and has induced moderate depreciation in China's real effective exchange rate.

(Morris Goldstein and Michael Mussa, *FT*, 3 October 2005, p. 19)

On 21 July 2005 there was a small revaluation of the yuan against the dollar, with the peg against the dollar scrapped in favour of the yuan moving within a daily trading band of 0.3 per cent either way against a basket of currencies (including the dollar). (For details, see the section below.)

Developments in yuan convertibility and exchange rate policy

In the spring of 1996 foreign-invested enterprises were allowed to conduct their foreign exchange transactions at designated banks.

On 1 December 1996 China formally accepted Article 8 of the IMF's articles of association on current account convertibility (restrictions remaining on capital account transactions).

At the National People's Congress held in March 1998 it was announced that the date of full convertibility of the yuan was to be put back because of the Asian financial crisis that started in July 1997 in Thailand. The deputy governor of the central bank said that it could take ten years instead of the unofficial target date of 2000 (*IHT*, 6 March 1998, p. 6).

> Dai Xianglong, the central bank governor, said in a recent closed-door meeting that Beijing should strive to create the conditions for full convertibility during the next five years ... Zhu Rongyi, the prime minister, said in March [2000] that China could not outline a timetable for capital account convertibility until its ability to supervise foreign exchange transactions was much improved.
>
> (*FT*, 10 July 2000, p. 11)

> Pressure for a devaluation of the yuan is much less than during the Asian financial crisis as the real effective exchange rate has depreciated over the past two years owing to domestic deflation and the rebound of many Asian currencies. Moreover, China continues to have large foreign reserves [$165 billion].
>
> (United Nations, *World Economic and Social Survey 2001*, pp. 108–9)

'The central bank chief, Dai Xianglong, said Wednesday [17 January 2001] ... the People's Bank of China planned to move ahead with the liberalization of its rigid interest rate regime and make its exchange rate more flexible after WTO entry' (*IHT*, 18 January 2001, p. 15).

> Dai Xianglong, China's central bank governor ... maintained his line on gradual liberalization for China's own currency, saying it would be allowed to trade in a slightly broader range this year. The increased flexibility of the renminbi, which trades in a tight band of a fraction of 1 per cent, will be to handle the rise in trade which is expected to come with China's entry into the WTO. The Chinese currency is backed by huge foreign exchange reserves, which the central bank said yesterday stood at $165.6 billion at the end of last year [2000].
>
> (*FT*, 18 January 2001, p. 10)

'Last year [2000] ... Dai Xianglong ... governor of the People's Bank of China ... said the renminbi would be ready for convertibility in five years. Now it is slated for "some time in the twenty-first century"' (*FEER*, 24 May 2001, p. 51).

China will need another decade before the country is ready to open its capital account and entirely remove controls on its currency, state media said Thursday [3 January 2002] ... The local currency, the yuan, is effectively pegged to the US currency at about 8.28 yuan to the dollar, although local officials refer to the system as a 'managed float' ... 'In the coming ten years China should not rashly open up its capital account ...' 'The yuan should maintain its long-term stability under the managed float system in order to prevent excessive international capital flows and the spread of financial crises, and in order to cope with a Japanese devaluation ... Over the next decade China should concentrate its efforts on the economic restructuring necessitated by WTO entry,' Xinhua said. China had said it would open up its capital account by 2000, but it abandoned the deadline as policymakers witnessed the turmoil of the 1997–8 Asian financial crisis.

(*IHT*, 4 January 2002, p. 15)

China's foreign exchange market will start trading Euros, its fourth currency, in April [2002] ... The Euro will join the US and Hong Kong dollars, which have been traded in China since ... 1994, and the yen, which was added in 1995. The change means Chinese companies engaged in international trade will be able to change yuan directly for the European currency without having to change to US dollars first.

(*IHT*, 26 March 2003, p. 12)

In a new move to relax capital market restrictions and aid investments overseas, the State Council agreed to broaden an experiment easing foreign exchange controls on Chinese companies ... The cabinet approved the expansion of a trial that began in Zhejiang province in October [2002]. Under that programme many Chinese that want to invest overseas no longer have to obtain central government approval or meet strict requirements from Beijing. They can apply to provincial authorities for approval. The programme will be expanded to include Shanghai and Guangdong, Jiangsu, Shandong and Fujian provinces ... It is also likely to be extended to the cities of Beijing and Tianjin this year [2003]. The policy still limits provincial and city government to approving deals worth up to $200 million a year.

(*FEER*, 30 January 2003, p. 23)

The continuing weakness of the Chinese banking system hinders the move to capital account convertibility. The savings ratio in China is very high and ordinary citizens place a high proportion of their savings in banks. Portfolio choice is still relatively restricted.

China said Friday [31 October 2003] it would allow businesses in some regions to invest more money abroad, the country's latest move to deflect US pressure for a revaluation of its currency ... Fourteen provinces or regions would be allowed on a trial basis, to approve overseas investment of up to $3 million, increased from a previous ceiling of $1 million.

(www.iht.com, 31 October 2003)

('[As regards] Chinese citizens travelling abroad ... officially there is a limit of 6,000 renminbi each': *FEER*, 29 May 2003, p. 26.)

China's government indicated Friday [2 July 2004] it would let insurers invest overseas, easing controls on the movement of capital and allowing companies that now hold $8 billion in foreign currency assets to seek higher returns. Regulators are drawing up rules after getting the go-ahead from the State Council, or cabinet ... Insurers' foreign capital was mostly in domestic banks, where dollar deposits offer annual interest of less than 1 per cent ... Easing controls on capital flows also marks a step toward making the yuan freely convertible ... Insurers will be permitted to invest abroad under a so-called qualified domestic institutional investor programme that has been installed in the State Council since March 2002 because of concern that it could trigger an outflow of foreign currency deposits ... China has fixed the value of the yuan at 8.277 to the dollar since 1995 ... The yuan can be freely exchanged only for trade purposes. Restrictions on the capital account, covering investment, prevent foreign investors from moving short-term capital into China and local investors from shifting funds overseas. The government has started to ease controls on capital inflows through a QFII programme under which twelve companies were allowed to invest a combined $1.8 billion as of the end of last month [June 2004] ... [China is] preparing regulations that will allow insurance companies to invest directly in domestic stocks.

(www.iht.com, 2 July 2004; *IHT*, 3 July 2004, p. 11)

China has granted preliminary approval for local insurers to invest in overseas capital markets ... No timetable for the scheme [was given] nor indication of the guidelines ... Insurers have about $8 billion in foreign currency ... Chinese insurers have to keep their foreign funds in local banks, which offer a meagre yield through interest rates of less than 1 per cent ... About 30 per cent of the sector's foreign currency assets are in demand deposits and the rest in fixed-term deposits. Insurers are prohibited from investing directly in stocks.

(*FT*, 3 July 2004, p. 8)

China will expand a programme that allows multinational companies to buy and sell yuan for non-trade purposes, easing capital controls as it moves toward making the currency freely exchangeable, the government said Tuesday [13 July 2004]. The pilot programme, started last year [2003] in Beijing, Shanghai and Shenzhen, will go nationwide on 1 August and be extended to include some domestic companies ... Tuesday's statement did not give figures for how much yuan companies can exchange under the programme ... Chinese and overseas multinationals will be allowed to use yuan to buy and remit foreign currencies to pay wages, buy commercial insurance and fund travel, research and other expenses ... Firms that qualify included multinationals with affiliated units in China, Chinese holding firms with overseas affiliates and foreign-owned holding firms based in China ... Individual foreign-invested companies in which the overseas partner owns at least 25 per cent are also eligible, provided their businesses have a 'significant impact' on the local economy and they have a clean record for three years.

(www.iht.com, 13 July 2004)

Ping An Insurance (Group), China's second largest life insurer, on Monday [10 January 2005] received approval to invest as much as $1.75 billion in overseas capital markets, the first such licence granted by the government ... The investment limit granted Monday was not part of plans to allow local investors to invest abroad under a so-called qualified domestic institutional investor plan ... [China] said in August [2004] that insurers would be allowed to invest as much as four-fifths of their combined $10 billion in foreign currency assets overseas.

(www.iht.com, 10 January 2005; *IHT*, 11 January 2005, p. 12)

China will allow global agencies, including the World Bank, to sell yuan-denominated bonds for the first time, promoting the use of the local currency by overseas investors and broadening the nation's debt market. Foreign development institutions that have provided loans of more than $1 billion for projects or companies in China will be eligible for approval, according to rules posted Tuesday [1 March 2005] ... China is preparing to make the yuan fully convertible and is trying to develop its bond market to reduce companies' reliance on bank lending. The World Bank, Asian Development Bank and Japan Bank plan to sell a combined 4 billion yuan, or $483 million, of bonds in China ... [it was] reported on 30 December [2004]. China's bond market is currently small and hasn't any foreign players yet ... Plans to let foreign institutions sell yuan-denominated bonds were announced in a statement Monday [28 February] ... The government also plans to ease curbs on overseas investment by local companies, including insurers, as part of its relaxation of capital controls ... China's government will choose one or two institutions to conduct trial sales before deciding whether to expand the programme ... Foreign institutions cannot transfer proceeds of yuan bond sales overseas ... They can remit returns from their yuan-funded investment or lending ... Under current rules approved overseas investors with at least $10 billion in assets and $50 million to spend may buy Class A shares, bonds and mutual funds. Investors can withdraw a maximum of 20 per cent of their capital at any one time.

(www.iht.com, 1 March 2005)

China's currency traded briefly outside its tightly controlled band yesterday [29 April 2005] ... Traders said the renminbi, pegged to the dollar for a decade, was briefly in the market at a rate of 8.2700 renminbi to the dollar, outside the usual band of 8.2760 to 8.200.

(*FT*, 30 April 2005, p. 6)

'The dollar unexpectedly fell to 8.2700 and stayed there for twenty minutes ... before returning to its usual level of 8.2760' (*IHT*, 30 April 2005, p. 4). ('On 18 May 2005 Hong Kong widened the band within which its currency may move against the dollar, in order to make it less attractive to speculators betting on a revaluation of the yuan': *The Economist*, 21 May 2005, p. 86.)

China moved yesterday [10 May 2005] to limit upward pressure that growing capital inflows have put on the renminbi by announcing new limits on offshore borrowings by local and foreign banks ... Restrictions were introduced [in the middle of 2004] ... Overseas lenders have been using foreign currency to fund their books in China because it is much cheaper to borrow offshore. But many banks have been positioning themselves for a revaluation of the renminbi.

(*FT*, 11 May 2005, p. 10)

The central bank of China on Wednesday [18 May] allowed the country's smaller lenders to have greater access to the foreign currency market, preparing them for a flexible yuan exchange rate. Citigroup, HSBC Holdings and five other foreign banks began dealing in the US dollar against seven other currencies [the Euro, yen, Australian dollar, British pound, Canadian dollar and the Hong Kong dollar] and the Euro against the yen ... through the China Foreign Exchange Trade System in Shanghai ... [The banks] will act as market makers for the new trading system. Market makers provide continuous buy and sell quotes, ensuring liquidity ... Three domestic lenders will also act as market makers: Bank of China, CITIC Industrial Bank and Industrial and Commercial Bank of China. The expansion of the country's foreign exchange market helps prepare the conditions for China to widen the yuan's trading band ... Under the new system participants will be anonymous and the exchange will assume the credit risks for all trades ... This system will help smaller Chinese banks, often deemed too risky to deal with international lenders, to enter the market ... The exchange provides trading in the yuan against four of the currencies – the US dollar, Euro, yen and Hong Kong dollar – through a separate platform.

(www.iht.com, 19 May 2005)

'China seems to be preparing the way for a slightly freer currency. This week it allowed some currencies to be traded against each other for the first time' (www.economist.com, 19 May 2005). 'In a long-scheduled move a new foreign exchange trading system began, allowing Chinese banks to deal in eight currency pairs (seven involving the dollar, plus Euro-yen trades)' (*The Economist*, 21 May 2005, p. 85).

China has increased the amount of foreign currency that companies can buy for investment abroad by 52 per cent, encouraging enterprises to expand globally and seeking to ease pressure for a revaluation of the yuan. Companies can invest a combined $5 billion this year [2005], up from $3.3 billion previously ... The new rules took effect on 19 May [2005].

(www.iht.com, 23 May 2005)

Premier Wen Jiabao on Sunday [26 June] ... reiterated that China's long-term goal remains what he called a 'market-based, well managed and floating exchange rate system'. He also said the goal of that system is to keep the exchange rate of the yuan 'stable at a reasonable and balanced level' ... [He] rejected foreign pressure for an immediate shift in China's currency regime, saying China would set its own timing for reform and warning against what he called undue haste.

(www.iht.com, 26 June 2005)

In a surprise announcement ... China on Thursday [21 July 2005] revalued the yuan to 8.110 for every dollar, scrapping a decade-long peg to the US currency in favour of a more flexible band using a 'basket of [unspecified] currencies' ... Until the announcement the yuan sold for 8.277 for every dollar ... The adjustment of the exchange rate is only slight, but China's central bank seemed to indicate that the adjustment is only the first step in a gradual move towards a looser exchange rate system ... A statement by the People's Bank of China: 'Our country has begun to implement a managed floating based on market supply and demand, and adjusted by referring to a basket of currencies. The renminbi's exchange rate will no longer be pegged to the dollar, and it will form a more flexible exchange rate mechanism' ... The bank explained ... [that] 'for the present stage' ... the yuan will be allowed to move 0.3 per cent up or down in value against the dollar, while the value of other currencies will also be allowed to move up and down within a range announced by the bank ... 'The People's Bank of China will adjust the band of the exchange rate when appropriate, based on the maturation of the market and financial circumstances,' the bank said ... The new system puts tight daily limits on changes in the yuan's value but could allow it to change substantially over time. Beginning Friday [22 July] the yuan will be limited to moving within a 0.3 per cent band a day against a collection of foreign currencies, the government said. But the officially announced price at the end of each day will become the mid-point of trading for the next day, which could let the yuan edge up incrementally.

(www.iht.com, 21 July 2005)

China said Thursday that it had revalued the yuan and would no longer peg it strictly to the dollar ... The central bank said that it had slightly increased the value of the currency and that the yuan would now be managed against a basket of currencies, which were not identified ... Nicholas Lardy: 'I think ... the currency is 15 per cent to 20 per cent undervalued.'

(*IHT*, 22 July 2005, pp. 1, 14)

The People's Bank of China ... said that each evening it would set a new trading range for the yuan to move within on the next trading day. To add to the uncertainty each day's new range may not necessarily be expressed in terms of dollars, the bank warned ... To determine the new peg the central bank will look at how a basket of foreign currencies moved the day before. But the central bank did not reveal which currencies it will track or their relative weightings within the basket ... The only limit that the central bank put on its moves was a promise on Thursday [21 July] that the centre of each day's trading range would not move more than 0.3 per cent in either direction from the centre of the previous day's range. But with twenty or so trading days in a month that means China could in theory push its currency up by 6 per cent a month, or push it down by the same amount ... In late 1994 Beijing first pegged the yuan to the dollar and then allowed it to crawl upward by a small fraction of 1 per cent each trading day. This resulted in a total increase of 3 per cent in 1994 and smaller increases thereafter ... A day after China moved to revalue its currency the country is bracing itself for a huge influx of speculative capital ... or 'hot money' ... as investors bet that the yuan will continue to appreciate against the dollar ... Some of the speculative money entering China is being used to acquire property and other assets; other foreign money has been invested in the stock market or simply sits in bank accounts awaiting a currency move, experts say.

(www.iht.com, 22 July 2005)

'Beijing announced that the yuan will now be pegged to a basket of currencies – without saying which currencies were in the basket or how those currencies would be weighted' (*IHT*, 8 August 2005, p. 7).

'From now on the yuan will be linked to a basket of currencies, the central parities of which will be set at the end of each day' (*The Economist*, 23 July 2005, p. 71).

> Most estimates suggest the renminbi is at least 15 per cent to 30 per cent undervalued ... The daily trading band is of 0.3 per cent is very narrow. But China could allow the currency to appreciate by this amount daily. Over time that could add up to a significant revaluation: 15 per cent in less than two-and-a-half months.
>
> (*FT*, 22 July 2005, p. 18)

> The People's Bank of China ... [talks of the new system being a] 'managed floating exchange rate regime based on market supply and demand with reference to a basket of currencies' ... Although the new mechanism allows the renminbi to rise or fall up to 0.3 per cent against the dollar each trading day, China's domestic currency market is dominated by the People's Bank of China ... with other traders playing a relatively minor role ... Within China expectations of future currency moves were seen as likely to fuel a renewed inflow of speculative funds by companies and individuals who can find ways around the country's capital controls.
>
> (*FT*, 23 July 2005, p. 8)

> China ... has strict capital controls which can help limit the impact of speculative investment ... [One view is that] although the currency was only likely to move in one direction, the potential gains to speculation might be negligible ... [because] the government has shown that any changes are going to be small and gradual ... Zhou Xiaochuan, governor of the central bank ... said the modest revaluation of the renminbi was only an 'initial' step ... Zhou Xiaochuan: 'We have made an initial adjustment of 2 per cent ... China's exchange rate reform will not have too much influence on US deficits ... The Asian financial crisis has taught us many lessons. Exchange rate reform needs a healthy financial market and healthy financial institutions.'
>
> (*FT*, 25 July 2005, p. 8)

For more than a month John Snow, the US Treasury secretary, carried with him a closely guarded secret: that China would soon scrap the renminbi's decade-old peg to the dollar ... A week before Thursday's announcement the Treasury received a firm signal from China that revaluation was imminent ...

China mainly assembles imported parts and components manufactured elsewhere. The local value-added in its exports is as low as 15 per cent. Any loss of competitiveness from a stronger exchange rate would be largely offset by cheaper imports. Even a 25 per cent revaluation would raise prices of many Chinese exports by only about 4 per cent ... Between 1994 and 1997 the Chinese currency rose from 8.7 renminbi to the dollar to 8.28.

(p. 15)

China will not move to full convertibility of the yuan for at least five years because it worries that hedge funds may attack the currency, much as happened to the won and the baht during the 1997 Asian financial crisis, Li Deshui, a member of the central bank's monetary committee, said ... Friday [22 July] ... Li Deshui: 'There is more than $800 billion to $1 trillion of hedge funds in the world and the Chinese financial system is relatively weak ... [If the yuan became fully convertible] it would be attacked by these hedge funds ... Over the next five years I do not foresee the renminbi becoming fully convertible. Our banks are not good enough and the monetary system is not quite up to international standards ... [The restriction of full convertibility of the yuan is] China's last economic and financial defence ... [The government would] not easily allow [a change in the policy]' ... Economists and institutions including the IMF have urged China to gradually make the yuan convertible on the capital account, which would allow money to flow freely in and out of the country for investment purposes. The currency is already convertible on the current account for trade in goods and services.

(www.iht.com, 25 July 2005; *IHT*, 26 July 2005, p. 12)

The central bank said on Tuesday [26 July] that last week's 2 per cent revaluation of the yuan did not mean that additional adjustments would follow. Foreign news reports describing the revaluation as an 'initial adjustment' to the exchange rate were incorrect, the People's Bank of China said in a statement. The revaluation of the yuan ... was simply the first step in changing China's currency system, the bank said. 'It does not mean that the renminbi was adjusted by 2 per cent as an initial step, with further adjustments to come later,' the central bank said ... The central bank said the new yuan–dollar level of 8.11 ... reflected the equilibrium level, or the rate that balances supply and demand, based on the fundamentals of the economy. The People's Bank of China said the size of the revaluation was based mainly on what was needed to adjust the trade surplus.

(www.iht.com 26 July 2005)

The central bank issued a statement Tuesday [26 July] denying that there were any plans for further revaluation of the currency. The People's Bank of China appeared to be trying to quell widespread speculation that over the next year China would allow the yuan to further appreciate against the dollar. In its statement the central bank said that the revaluation against the dollar last Thursday by about 2 per cent 'does not imply an initial move which warrants further actions in the future' ... Some economists estimate that the yuan is between

15 per cent to 30 per cent undervalued ... China has beefed up its capital controls over the past year, trying to prevent speculative capital from flowing into the country. And in what may have been an effort to dampen the spirit of speculators, the People's Bank of China issued what it called a 'solemn statement' insisting that there were no plans for further revaluation. The government said that the recent changes were made to restore balances in the country's foreign trade but also took into account the risks such a move would pose to Chinese companies ... The central bank also said that: [The] 'reform of the renminbi exchange rate regime must be proceeded with in a gradual way. The reform is focussed not on the quantitative adjustment of the renminbi exchange rate but on the improvement of the renminbi exchange regime.'

(*IHT*, 27 July 2005, p. 11)

'China on 26 July tried to damp speculation that the 2.1 per cent gain would be the first in a series of changes. The government said it would not revalue the yuan again in the 'foreseeable future' (www.iht.com, 1 August 2005).

China's central bank has moved to cool expectations of a further revaluation of the renminbi, insisting that last week's 2.1 per cent increase against the dollar had been calculated to leave the currency at a 'reasonable and balanced' level. In a solemn declaration that appeared to reflect worries about possible speculative capital inflows, the People's Bank of China said the revaluation and simultaneous scrapping of the dollar peg were initial moves in reforming its currency regime. 'This certainly does not mean that the 2 per cent adjustment of the renminbi is a first step that will be followed by further adjustment,' it added ... Zhou Xiaochuan, People's Bank governor, reinforced such expectations ... [of] more substantial but gradual revaluation ... on Saturday [23 July] ... [when he said]: 'We have made an initial adjustment to the exchange rate level of 2 per cent' ... Mr Zhou is widely believed to have pushed for a greater revaluation. The central bank insisted that Mr Zhou had meant Thursday's revaluation was only an initial step in reform of the exchange rate regime.

(*FT*, 27 July 2005, p. 6)

China's central bank yesterday [29 July] insisted there would be no more government-led revaluation of the renminbi, saying that the currency's exchange rate was already reflecting market forces ... The central bank statement: 'Some foreign people ... to suit their own purposes ... have tried to create misunderstanding by saying this adjustment is an initial move and there will be more to come ... [In fact the renminbi is being set] according to objective rules ... These movements will be created by the floating mechanism and there will be no more official adjustments of the renminbi level' ... The new regime – a 'managed float' based on 'market supply and demand with references to a basket of currencies' [is opaque] ... Many analysts say the lack of such clarity is intentional, aimed at giving Beijing more flexibility in setting its new renminbi policy.

(*FT*, 30 July 2005, p. 6)

Nearly three weeks after China revalued its currency and dropped its longstanding peg to the dollar, the head of the central bank disclosed on

Wednesday [10 August] that the currency was now largely being managed against a basket of leading currencies dominated by the dollar, the Euro, the yen and the won ... But he did not reveal details of the percentage that each currency holds in the basket. He said the yuan's rate was also being influenced by several smaller currencies, including those of Singapore [the Singapore dollar], Britain [the pound sterling], Malaysia [the ringgit], Russia [the rouble], Australia [the Australian dollar] and Canada [the Canadian dollar] ... Zhou Xiaochuan: 'China's major trading partners are the United States, the Euro land, Japan, [South] Korea, etc., and naturally the US dollar, Euro, Japanese yen and Korean won become major currencies of the basket' ... [The announcement] suggests that while the dollar remains influential in determining the value of the yuan, the Euro and the yen have gained significant influence ... This week the central bank also announced measures to liberalize its currency trading system, a move intended to help banks and companies deal with uncertainty surrounding a stronger yuan. ... The central bank said it would also introduce foreign exchange forwards on the domestic inter-bank market, which would allow banks to buy or sell foreign currencies at the current price with future delivery as a hedge against fluctuations.

(*IHT*, 11 August 2005, p. 11)

('Futures are agreements to buy or sell assets at a set date and price': www.iht.com, 11 August 2005.) 'Non-banking businesses will be allowed to trade in China's onshore foreign exchange market' (www.iht.com, 10 August 2005). 'Presumably for political reasons, the Taiwan dollar is omitted, despite Taiwan being in the same league as Japan and [South] Korea] as a source of components for export industries' (*IHT*, 12 August 2005, p. 7).

Other currencies included in the basket, but with smaller weightings include ... the Thai baht ... Analysts differed about the weight allocated to the dollar, with estimates ranging from 30 per cent to 70 per cent ... The People's Bank of China, in a series of announcements this week, has said it will expand the onshore currency swap and renminbi futures markets with the issue of new trading licences to local banks ... Since China abandoned the peg ... the renminbi ... has fluctuated only marginally in daily trading.

(*FT*, 11 August 2005, p. 8)

Based on bilateral trade patterns, the assumption is roughly 20 per cent for the US dollar and 20 per cent each for the Euro and yen. But naming the [South] Korean won and not the Taiwan dollar (which should command a similar weighting of about 10 per cent) shows how academic all this is. The won itself is not fully convertible. Thus the dollar will remain the anchor currency ... [China has also enlarged] the pool of banks permitted to trade renminbi forward.

(p.20)

The basket also contains the currencies of Singapore, Britain, Malaysia, Russia, Australia, Thailand and Canada. The Hong Kong and Taiwanese dollars are conspicuously absent ... All transactions between China and

Taiwan are in [US] dollars ... The choice of currencies ... said Zhou Xiaochuan ... depended not only on the pattern of China's trade, but also on the sources of its foreign direct investment and the currency composition of its debts ... China also announced this week a further liberalization of foreign exchange trading, allowing non-banks to trade in the spot market and more banks to conduct forward trading. Currency swaps will also be introduced into the onshore market.

(The Economist, 13 August 2005, p. 60)

The China Banking Regulatory Commission ... said Thursday [11 August] that it would allow domestic and overseas companies to act as money brokers for the first time ... Brokers with a minimum capital of 20 million yuan, or $2.5 million, will be allowed to trade financial products on behalf of customers in foreign exchange, money market and bonds at home and abroad ... The central bank said Wednesday [10 August] that companies that import and export at least $2 billion a year would be able to trade directly in the domestic foreign exchange market.

(www.iht.com, 12 August 2005)

[On 23 September] the People's Bank of China announced after the close of trading that it would allow the yuan to fluctuate more widely in value against currencies other than the dollar. But the central bank made no change to the tight trading range between the yuan and the dollar ... [There has been an] extremely gradual appreciation in the yuan's value against the dollar since a 2.1 per cent revaluation on 21 July ... [China] has allowed the currency only to strengthen by 0.03 per cent per week against the dollar since then, which worked out to an annual rate of appreciation of just 1.6 per cent ... China announced with the revaluation that the yuan's value in terms of other major currencies, like the Euro or yen, would not be permitted to vary more than 1.5 per cent from the yuan's value relative to the dollar ... [But on 23 September China] widened the daily trading band for other major currencies to 3 per cent from 1.5 per cent ... China's central bank said Friday [23 September] that it would allow the yuan to strengthen by as much as 3 per cent from a daily fixed rate against the Euro [for example], from 1.5 previously ... China's [currency] is traded almost exclusively within its borders ... The dollar closed Friday at 8.091 yuan.

(IHT, 24 September 2005, p. 15)

On Friday [23 September] China said it would let the yuan fluctuate as much as 3 per cent from a daily fixed rate against the Euro, yen and other currencies except the dollar ... [The yuan] has only gained 0.2 per cent against the dollar in two months.

(www.iht.com, 26 September 2005)

China widened the renminbi's trading band against non-dollar currencies yesterday [23 September] ... China said it would double the renminbi's trading range against currencies such as the Euro and the yen to plus or minus 3 per cent ... China dumped a decade-old peg to the US dollar in July, revaluing the renminbi by 2.1 per cent against the dollar ... The People's Bank of China added a 1.5 per cent trading range for the renminbi against non-dollar currencies but has since come under pressure from local banks to change this because of difficulties in managing two trading bands.

(*FT*, 24 September 2005, p. 7)

On 23 September the People's Bank of China said the yuan would be allowed to fluctuate by 3 per cent a day against the Euro, yen and other non-dollar currencies, compared with 1.5 per cent previously. Daily movements against the dollar, meanwhile, remain limited to only 0.3 per cent ... Allowing non-dollar currencies to fluctuate by 3 per cent gives the Chinese authorities a little more leeway, lessening the need for expensive intervention ... [to] nudge the dollar back up against the Euro ... [Some] 80 per cent of China's foreign trade is settled [in dollars].

(*The Economist*, 1 October 2005, p. 83)

[China allowed the yuan] to inch up on Friday [28 October] through a psychologically important benchmark against the dollar ... The yuan rose to 8.084 to the dollar on Friday, for a total increase of 32-hundredths of a per cent in the fourteen weeks since China revalued its currency on 21 July. At the time of the revaluation the Chinese authorities said they would not allow the yuan to rise or fall more than three-tenths of a per cent against the dollar in a single day ... The decision to let the yuan finally breach the mark of three-tenths of a per cent on Friday proved that the Chinese were not using the daily trading limit as a brake on the yuan's value.

(www.iht.com, 28 October 2005)

'Chinese officials argue that manufacturers have paper-thin margins in a competitive export environment. Officials fear that anything other than incremental currency moves could threaten stability': www.iht.com, 20 October 2005.)

China took a big step yesterday [25 November] towards allowing a stronger, more flexible renminbi ... by launching a domestic currency swaps market with a $6 billion deal. The transaction came after the country's foreign regulators announced late on Thursday [24 November] that they were going ahead with a long-awaited system of market makers to trade the renminbi against foreign currencies. The dollars lent out by the central bank will help grease the wheels of this new market, reducing its dominant role. Dealers said the central bank sold dollars at the current exchange rate of 8.0810 renminbi per dollar with an agreement to buy them back in a year's time at 7.85 renminbi. The implied renminbi rise of about 2.9 per cent reflects the difference between US and Chinese interest rates.

(*FT*, 26 November 2005, p. 8)

[The US Treasury Department has decided] to refrain from accusing China of currency manipulation in its periodic report on currency policies of US trading partners ... In its previous report the Bush administration warned that it would accuse China of currency manipulation if it failed to make substantial changes to its fixed peg between the yuan and the dollar ... This time ... the Treasury Department simply expressed disappointment that trading in the yuan was 'highly constricted' and said it would 'intensely scrutinize' its practices in future reports, which are issued every six months. In Congress two leading critics of China ... Charles Schumer and Lindsey Graham ... quietly renewed threats to seek legislation that would impose steep tariffs ... of 27.5 per cent ... on Chinese imports if the yuan was not allowed to float more freely ... Branding China a 'currency manipulator' would be largely symbolic, but it would be the first time in eleven years that the United States has made such a charge and would represent a much more confrontational approach.

(*IHT*, 30 November 2005, p. 16)

The government allowed thirteen banks, including HSBC and Citigroup, to begin trading yuan directly with each other on Wednesday [4 January 2006] using a tightly regulated over-the-counter market in China, instead of requiring all currency trades to be made with a government agency ... The yuan has climbed just half of 1 per cent against the dollar since ... 21 July [2005] ... although it has appreciated more sharply, along with the dollar, against other currencies.

(*IHT*, 5 January 2006, p. 4)

On 5 January [2006] Beijing announced that it would abolish limits on the amount that domestic companies could invest offshore ... Foreign exchange reserves ... [at the end of 2005 reached] a record $819.9 billion ... Only Japan, with $847 billion at the end of October [2005], has bigger foreign exchange holdings ... An estimated 70 per cent of its reserves [are] in US dollar-denominated assets ... [including] about $247 billion in US Treasury bonds ... relatively low-yielding investments ... There have been suggestions that China will diversify its foreign exchange holdings away from dollars.

(*IHT*, 17 January 2006, p. 13)

'Last year's rise of the dollar meant that on a trade-weighted basis the renminbi appreciated by one-tenth in 2005' (*FT*, Survey [*The World: 2006*], 25 January 2006, p. 3).

The yuan has appreciated 0.8 per cent since China revalued the currency by 2.1 per cent and began managing it against a basket of currencies, including the Euro and the yen. The biggest daily fluctuations have been less than 0.1 per cent. China's currency closed Wednesday [15 February] at 8.0479 per dollar.

(*IHT*, 16 February 2006, p. 18)

'The remninbi has only risen by another 0.8 per cent since July [2005] and never approached the daily up-or-down trading limit of 0.3 per cent against the US dollar' (*FT*, 22 February 2006, p. 9).

China will soon release statistics showing that it has passed Japan as the biggest holder of foreign currency the world has ever seen. Its reserves already exceed $800 billion and are on track to reach $1 trillion by the end of the year [2006], up from just under $4 billion in 1989.

(*IHT*, 27 February 2006, p. 16)

'China will soon release statistics . . .' (*IHT*, 27 February 2006, p. 16).

[On 14 March] prime minister Wen Jiabao . . . announced that China would not revalue its currency in the coming year . . . Wen said there would be no 'surprise' revaluations of the yuan this year [2006]. A year earlier . . . Wen had suggested that any changes in currency policy might come as a 'surprise'. Later last summer China unlinked its currency from the US dollar for a new, more complicated currency regime. Since then the value of the yuan has risen by roughly 3 per cent against the dollar . . . Wen noted, however, that China's currency would probably continue to move within the parameters of the country's new currency formula . . . Wen Jiabao: 'There is room for the yuan to fluctuate either up or down on its own in line with changes in the market. It is no longer necessary for us to take one-time administrative measures.'

(*IHT*, 15 March 2006, p. 13)

Prime minister Wen Jiabao . . . ruled out any further sharp adjustments in the value of the renminbi . . . Mr Wen said it was 'no longer necessary' to take one-off administrative measures to raise or lower the renminbi's value after July's 2.1 per cent revaluation against the US dollar . . . His remarks forestall any sharp changes in the currency, which has appreciated by less than 1 per cent under the tightly managed float introduced with the July [2005] revaluation.

(*FT*, 15 March 2006, p. 11)

A week-long trip to China by two US senators sponsoring a trade bill targeting China's currency has revealed differences between them . . . Senator Charles Schumer, Democrat of New York, and Senator Lindsey Graham, Republican of South Carolina, have introduced legislation that would impose a 27.5 per cent tariff in two years on all imports to the United States from China unless Beijing's officials allow 'substantial' appreciation in their country's currency . . . The senators said [in an interview on 25 March] that Schumer had been more impressed than Graham by promises from Chinese officials to liberalize their currency policies, although those promises included no timetable . . . China has allowed its currency to creep up slightly faster in the past three weeks . . . China allowed the yuan to appreciate by 2.1 per cent on 21 July and the currency has very gradually appreciated by another 1 per cent since then (*IHT*, 27 March 2006, p. 6). Charles Schumer: 'The jury is out . . . [but] we are more optimistic that this can be worked out than we were in the past.'

(www.iht.com, 27 March 2006).

A week after they travelled to China . . . Charles Schumer and Lindsey Graham . . . said Tuesday [28 March] that they would delay until 29 September a bill that would have imposed a 27.5 per cent tariff on goods from China . . . to give Chinese officials more time to act . . . This is not the first time the senators have agreed to put off a vote on the measure until March after Treasury Secretary John Snow assured them that China would change its policies and the Bush administration would press harder on the issue . . . China has overtaken Japan as the world's largest holder of foreign exchange reserves with $853.7 billion in holdings at the end of February ... Japan's reserves at the end of February stood at $850.06 billion.

(*IHT*, 29 March 2006, p. 13).

American manufacturers claim that China is unfairly undervaluing the yuan, by as much as 40 per cent (*IHT*, 31 March 2006, p. 1). 'The yuan did rise this past week ... and it finished the week at its highest level since July [2005] ... The dollar eased to 8.017 yuan on Friday [31 March] from 8.027 on Thursday, adding to a gain for the yuan of about 0.5 per cent since early February.

(www.iht.com, 31 March 2006).

The 27.5 per cent tariff proposed in the Schumer–Graham bill is the middle of a range, from 15 per cent to 40 per cent, of estimates of the yuan's under-valuation against the dollar that the two senators knew about. However ... the IMF finds little strong evidence that the yuan is that much undervalued. Esti-mates by several investment banks suggest that 10 per cent to 15 per cent is nearer the mark ... Since it was revalued by 2.1 per cent in July [2005] the yuan has crept up by a [further] mere 1 per cent against the dollar ... [But] on a broader basis than simply against the dollar, the Chinese currency has risen by more than is commonly claimed. And even against the greenback the pace of appreciation has picked up in recent weeks ... On this trend there could be less than eight yuan to the dollar (compared with the old peg of 8.28) by late April ... Last year [2005] the yuan gained 18 per cent against the Euro as the dollar itself rose briskly ... [The yuan's] trade-weighted value rose by 10 per cent in 2005, before slipping a bit this year [2006] ... On 28 March a milder rival to the Schumer–Graham bill was proposed by Charles Grassley and Max Bancus, the senior men on the Senate finance committee. This would have the Treasury determine whether a currency if 'fundamentally misaligned against the dollar', implying a lower standard of proof than 'manipulation'. If a cur-rency were found to be misaligned the government would be required to impose sanctions.

(*The Economist*, 1 April 2006, pp, 73–4)

The Asian financial crisis and subsequent developments

A summary

China did not nominally devalue the renminbi (effectively pegged to the US dollar) during the Asian financial crisis, although there was some real devaluation because of factors such as deflation and export subsidies. China was highly praised for not starting off another round of competitive devaluations.

The government has a policy of gradual interest rate liberalization. Much remains to be done, however, despite some liberalization of interest rates on foreign currency loans and large deposits on 21 September 2000 and even more significant developments in December 2003 (see below).

Foreign exchange controls have been tightened.

Capital flight has been a problem. 'China's illegal capital flight was about

$20 billion last year [2000] though in earlier years it was estimated at more than double this amount' (*FEER*, 21 June 2001, p. 58). '[The] economist Dong Fureng estimates [that] $50 billion left China illegally last year [2002]' (*FEER*, 27 March 2003, p. 29).

> Between 1996 and the end of 2001 about $80 billion was registered under the 'errors and omissions' column in China's balance of payments ... This capital flight despite strict currency control includes money from smuggling and frauds. Most of it, however, seems to be controlled by state companies that shared the widely held lack of confidence in the renminbi ... Chinese official data show illicit capital inflows in 2002 instead of the usual drain, indicating new confidence in the Chinese currency.
> (*FEER*, 29 May 2003, p. 27)

> For the first time China recorded a positive figure under the category of 'errors and omissions' in the central bank's annual statement of balance of payments. That meant that the movement of illicit capital in China had reversed course and was now flowing back in. The $7.79 billion errors and omissions figure represents the part of 2002's capital flows the government cannot trace.
> (*FEER*, 22 May 2003, p. 23)

Foreign exchange reserves are very high. (See Table 1, p. 000.) 'China's ... foreign exchange reserves [are] the world's second largest after Japan' (*FT*, 7 January 2001, p. 9). 'China's reserves, second only to Japan's, were $212.2 billion at the end of 2001' (*FEER*, 16 January 2003, p. 29).

More recently there has been pressure, especially from the United States (because of China's large trade surplus with the United States: see above) for China to allow the renminbi to strengthen in order to reduce the competitiveness of Chinese goods.

To counter the adverse effects of deflation on growth on spending (7 per cent growth is the minimum deemed necessary to avoid unemployment getting out of hand) the government increased its spending and decreased taxation. The government also used other measures to boost spending, such as taxing interest earned on bank deposits, larger salaries for civil servants and longer holidays.

The government made clear in words and deeds that it would not act as an automatic guarantor of loans made by foreigners to Chinese financial institutions. In January 2003 new rules meant that high-level government approval was needed before Chinese entities could borrow funds from abroad.

An analysis and a chronology of developments to January 2003

> The Asian financial contagion has so far left China largely unaffected ... Nonetheless, Chinese policymakers are genuinely concerned that they may contract the Asian financial contagion and have taken a number of bold steps to bolster their resistance. Unfortunately, China has many of the same structural problems that South Korea, Thailand and Indonesia had, most notably bank-dominated financial systems, weak central bank regulation and supervision of

commercial banks, excessive lending, and a large buildup of non-performing loans.

(Lardy 1998: 78–9)

Bank-dominated financial systems, where markets for equity and debt are small, tend to create a high potential for the systematic underpricing of loans. That, in turn, encourages excessive borrowing by firms with preferred access to credit (state enterprises in China). 'Capital markets do not provide enough competition for banks.' Politicians can more easily influence the pattern of bank lending (p. 79). China has an excessive buildup of domestic credit, shown by the following: an extraordinary deterioration in the balance sheets of state enterprises (the chief recipients of bank credit); excess capacity in many industries; 'asset bubbles', especially in the real estate market; an enormous buildup of non-performing bank loans (pp. 80–3).

> Despite these vulnerabilities, China is unlikely to catch the Asian flu. The Chinese currency is not convertible for capital account transactions. Chinese savers concerned about the viability of the country's financial institutions cannot legally convert their renminbi deposits and purchase foreign currency-denominated financial assets. Moreover, because their ability to convert currency back into dollars is severely limited, foreigners own only small amounts of renminbi-denominated financial assets such as bank deposits or company stock.
>
> (p. 83)

Non-residents are only allowed to buy foreign-currency-denominated 'B' shares and have to find foreign buyers willing to pay dollars.

> The absence of capital account convertibility also means that speculators, both foreign and Chinese, have no way to act on a suspicion that the renminbi is over-valued and likely to depreciate. Only buyers with a demonstrated need related to trade, tourism, repayment of an approved foreign currency loan, or repatriation of profits derived from a direct investment can purchase foreign exchange.
>
> (p. 83)

China's capital inflows are also predominantly direct investments, while China runs foreign trade surpluses (p. 84). Foreign exchange reserves reached $139.9 billion by the end of 1997, second only to Japan's (p. 78).

> Many ask whether ... China will also collapse ... China has had a property market boom that is ripe for a crash ... China's banks are broke ... They are government banks ... forced to make huge loans to the large, money-losing industries that are being propped up by the central government in order to stop unemployment from rising ... The bad debt problem is a government problem ... In the end the government is probably willing to pump in any amount of liquidity and simply live with the resulting inflation. A property bust will make China's banking problems quantitatively worse in China, but it won't change the nature of its basic problems ... China has a big trade surplus. It does not need to borrow money to finance its imports.
>
> (Thurow 1998: 24)

As far as is known, neither the government nor Chinese companies have many loans denominated in foreign currencies. China has $100 billion in foreign exchange reserves.

> Since China does not have a convertible currency, it is under no obligation to convert Chinese currency into foreign currencies if investors decide that they wish to liquidate their holdings; but this does not mean that it cannot have a foreign currency crisis. If Chinese exporters stop bringing their funds back to China and Chinese importers, fearing a future devaluation, start paying for their imports early, large outflows of funds can rapidly emerge despite currency controls. While a collapse of China's economy seems unlikely, an economic slowdown is almost a certainty.
>
> (p. 24)

(On 6 October 1998 the central bank ordered the closure of the Guangdong International Trust and Investment Corporation – GITIC – after it was unable to repay loans. This and other earlier developments are dealt with in the section on monetary policy, discussed above.)

A chronology of later developments is as follows:

12 September 1998. China is tightening control over outflows of foreign currency ... Authorities have banned four banks in the southern city of Shenzhen from selling foreign exchange because of irregularities ... The retail price index fell 3.3 per cent in August against the same month a year ago. In July the RPI fell 3.2 per cent' (*FT*, 14 September 1998, p. 3).

27 September 1998. Stringent new foreign exchange regulations are announced, aimed at checking China's exposure to overseas debt and stemming the outflow of foreign currency. There are demands for stricter supervision by banks of the sale of foreign exchange and calls for restrictions on the issue of foreign debt. Local governments are told to stop issuing overseas debt and offering financial guarantees to foreign-funded projects without central government approval. There have also been several as yet unpublished restrictions in recent weeks on foreign currency transactions. These include curtailing renminbi lending by Chinese banks to foreign companies wanting to hedge their currency risk by prepaying foreign currency loans (*FT*, 28 September 1998, p. 4).

> Eager to stop hard currency leaving China, the state administration of foreign exchange ruled that companies should no longer be lent renminbi to pre-pay foreign currency loans, a move that prevents many foreign companies hedging against future renminbi devaluation ... Another official ruling states that approval should be gained for each repatriation of earnings above $10,000. Foreign diplomats said the ruling, which it seems is only sporadically enforced, has incensed some foreign companies.
>
> (*FT*, 29 September 1998, p. 8)

28 September 1998.

> In the latest move to protect China's foreign exchange reserves, the central bank has given domestic companies until Thursday [1 October 1998] to

repatriate foreign currency held overseas and has blocked new loan guarantees by foreign banks ... Foreign bankers estimate that more than $30 billion may have been taken out of China in the first half of the year, as investors and businesses prepared for a possible devaluation of the yuan ... The repatriation order is part of a series of measures to stem the outflow of funds. Over the weekend the foreign exchange administration also ordered measures to prevent unauthorized foreign currency loans.

(*IHT*, 29 September 1998, p. 19)

Chinese officials estimate that billions of dollars leak abroad each year ... Last year [1998] leakages reached $17 billion ... Some companies inflate the value of the goods that they import, depositing excess payments into foreign bank accounts. Sometimes fake invoices are used for products that were never imported. And in some cases exporters underreport their sales and keep the unreported income offshore. Concerns about capital flight prompted China to tighten its foreign exchange controls. Under new rules issued in September [1998] all Chinese companies holding foreign exchange illegally abroad had until 1 October [1998] to repatriate or face stiff penalties. New rules were also decreed that required all mainland bank branches in China to conduct foreign exchange trading through their headquarters in Beijing. In addition ... Chinese companies will be allowed to buy foreign currency needed for trade only in the cities where they are domiciled. Companies are also prevented from prepaying for imports; if a company wants to make an early repayment of foreign exchange loans it must get approval from the state administration of foreign exchange ... China's currency trades in a small government-controlled inter-bank market that keeps the exchange rate pegged at roughly 8.28 renminbi to the US dollar, but the rate has slipped ... on an active black market.

(*FEER: Asia 1999 Yearbook*, 1999, pp. 24–5)

('China's illegal capital flight was about $20 billion last year [2000] though in earlier years it was estimated at more than double this amount': *FEER*, 21 June 2001, p. 58.)

29 September 1998. 'China yesterday [29 September] ordered local enterprises to repatriate by tomorrow [1 October] billions of US dollars they are believed to hold illegally overseas' (*FT*, 30 September 1998, p. 1).

A consequence of yesterday's measures could be felt by foreign banks and companies that export to China. Many exporters sell their goods to Chinese import agents, which buy the products with hard currency loans from foreign banks. But these import agents are now the subject of SAFE [state administration of foreign exchange] investigations into whether they used fake documents to shift foreign currency offshore. If they are found to have generated more than $1 million in illegal dealings, their trade licences will be revoked.

(p. 8)

On Tuesday [29 September] China's central bank announced new restrictions on foreign exchange transactions to try to control the flow of hard currency out of China ... Officials in Beijing say Chinese companies are improperly moving dollars overseas, presumably in fear of a possible devaluation of the nation's currency. Although China's foreign exchange reserves are still strong, at $140 billion, they have remained largely unchanged this year while China has run up a trade surplus of more than $30 billion and absorbed $27 billion in new foreign investment ... Chinese companies [are required] to bring back any illegal foreign currency deposits being held overseas by Thursday [1 October] or risk severe punishment ... Under the new currency restrictions, banks must demonstrate that all actions involving more than $100,000 are fully backed by documentation before they can be cleared by customs. The state administration of foreign exchange will closely scrutinize any transactions of more than $200,000.

(*IHT*, 30 September 1998, p. 13)

Since mid-September [1998] China's foreign exchange authorities have issued more than twenty different notices and regulations, tightening the supervision of forex transactions and raising the requirements for official documentation, conversion and remittance on hard currency transactions.

(*FT*, Survey, 16 November 1998, p. iii)

9 December 1998.

As most of its neighbours suffer through their worst financial crisis of modern times, China stands almost alone. It has held its currency steady, kept its economy primed and continued its economic reforms. Now it is collecting its reward, raising $1 billion from foreign investors. On Wednesday [9 December] China became the first Asian country to issue an international bond since Russia devalued its currency and defaulted on its debt in August. The issue, originally set for $500 million, was doubled in response to overwhelming demand. More-over, investors appear to be crowning China as Asia's best borrower outside Japan: it will pay a lower interest rate on its new debt than South Korea, Thailand or other neighbours would if they tried to raise money today ... With a $140 billion hoard of foreign exchange China does not need the fresh hard currency that this dollar-denominated bond ... will bring. The offering, in fact, is a bit of muscle-flexing by a country that wants everyone to heed Asia's new economic order. Some bankers and investors say China is raising capital precisely because many of its neighbours cannot – at least without paying far more for the privilege ... China will join Argentina as the only developing country to raise big money from foreign creditors since the Russia crisis began.

(Joseph Kahn, *IHT*, 10 December 1998, p. 13)

The bonds were China's first in dollars since October 1997, when a $400 million five-year issue coincided with a sharp deterioration in sentiment towards emerging market paper. Bankers say that the bonds are designed to differentiate China from other Asian borrowers (*FT*, 10 December 1998, p. 38).

5 January 1999.

China said yesterday [5 January 1999] that it had allowed twenty private companies to engage directly in foreign trade in an effort to boost the country's flagging export performance... Private companies have previously been allowed to import and export only through state-run trading houses ... Exports in 1998 fell slightly against 1997, failing to meet a trade ministry target of 10 per cent growth, and falling far short of 1997's 20.9 per cent year-on-year increase.

(*FT*, 6 January 1999, p. 6)

State media reported that China had cleared twenty privately owned companies to conduct foreign trade as part of a move to increase exports ... The ministry of foreign trade and economic co-operation issued trade licences to twenty companies, including the [New] Hope Group, China's biggest animal feed producer. 'This is the first time that private firms have been allowed to enter foreign trade,' said an official of the ministry. Until now only state-run trading companies, selected state-owned manufacturers and Chinese companies in which foreigners have a stake have had the right to conduct foreign trade.

(*IHT*, 6 January 1999, p. 15)

In 1998 the trade surplus grew 7.9 per cent to a record $43.59 billion, rising exports to Europe and North America offsetting the effects of the recession in Asia. Exports increased by 0.5 per cent, while imports fell by 1.5 per cent. (In 1997 exports increased by 20.9 per cent and imports increased by 2.5 per cent.) Trade volume in 1998 fell by 0.4 per cent, the first fall in total exports and imports since 1983. In the first nine months of 1998 exports to the rest of Asia fell by 6.3 per cent compared with the same period of 1997 (*IHT*, 12 January 1999, p. 13).

13 January 1999. Brazil devalues its currency and triggers another bout (albeit relatively modest) financial turbulence around the world.

25 January 1999.

China's central bank insisted Monday [25 January] that it would defend the value of the yuan after an article in an official Chinese newspaper reawakened fears of a devaluation and sent share prices and currencies plummeting across Asia. A spokesman for the People's Bank of China dismissed the article in Sunday's [24 January] English-language *China Daily* as 'a private opinion' that did not 'reflect the point of view' of the bank. While the article noted that Chinese officials opposed a devaluation, it quoted 'some analysts' as saying that a devaluation of the yuan 'would not definitely be a bad thing and may not trigger a fresh round of currency devaluation'.

(*IHT*, 26 January 1999, p. 1)

'Some analysts say that even without an official devaluation, China is paving the way by achieving the same effect through internal policy: giving bigger tax and duty rebates to exporters and ... cracking down on smuggling' (p. 6).

27 January 1999. Dai Xianglong (governor of the central bank):

We have a solid foundation for a stable exchange rate ... As a person in charge I can say the renminbi will not be devalued ... During the Asian crisis the renminbi was not devalued and at the moment it is not necessary for the renminbi to be devalued ... The renminbi would only devalue when there is a great imbalance in the balance of payments of China and there is a great increase in the cost of exports. But I do not think these conditions exist this year.

(FT, 28 January 1999, pp. 28–9)

Dai Xianglong: 'There are no benefits to devaluation. It would hurt foreign investors and increase the foreign debt burden of China, and it is not conducive to the stability of the financial sector' (*IHT*, 28 January 1999, p. 14).

> Exports rose 0.5 per cent last year [1998], compared with a 20.9 per cent climb in 1997 ... Mr Dai said economic growth this year [1999] would be about 7 per cent ... A key barometer of the pressures for devaluation this year will be foreign exchange reserves, which grew only $5.1 billion last year to $145 billion. Zhu Rongyi, China's premier, has ordered that these reserves must not be allowed to fall below current levels, officials said. The reserves have been under pressure partly because of widespread currency fraud, capital flight and smuggled imports.

(FT, 28 January 1999, p. 30)

'Fears of devaluation have led to capital flight. More than $20 billion was spirited abroad last year, illegally circumventing the currency laws' (p. 29).

From 1990 to 1997 exports growth averaged 17 per cent a year. But in 1998 exports increased by only 0.5 per cent, while imports fell by 1.5 per cent. The trade surplus increased by 7.9 per cent to $43.6 billion (*FEER*, 25 February 1999, p. 61).

> China ... may find itself actually more competitive than before the crisis. One reason is that China will increasingly be able to compete on quality rather than just lower cost ... Several mechanisms effectively devalue the Chinese currency ... China is suffering from an oversupply of commodities ... Trade-finance arrangements did not break down in China as they did elsewhere in the region ... Current deflation ... already amounts to an effective devaluation ... China can subsidize exporters in other ways, such as through tax rebates, which currently represents a de facto 3 per cent cut in the exchange rate [e.g. rebates on value-added tax: p. 61] ... Other tricks are surfacing. Exporters are beginning to offer an exchange rate of well over 9 renminbi to the US dollar ... [compared with] the official rate of about 8.3 ... China imports little from [the rest of Asia].

(Henny Sender, FEER, 25 February 1999, pp. 17–18)

12 March 1999. It is reported that in the first two months of 1999 exports fell by 10.5 per cent compared with the same period of 1998. Imports rose by 2.2 per cent (*IHT*, 13 March 1999, p. 21).

3 June 1999. The central bank says it will stop accepting yuan transfers from banks overseas and will close its yuan accounts of foreign banks starting 10 June 1999 in a move that will now require all conversions of yuan to take place in China. Some foreign banks have been allowed to convert the yuan at overseas branches; this will now cease (*IHT*, 4 June 1999, p. 18).

The Bank of China announced that it would stop accepting renminbi transfers from banks overseas and that it would cancel all renminbi accounts in Hong Kong and foreign countries in an effort to retain better control over monetary policy (*FEER*, 17 June 1999, p. 62).

4 August 1999.

China has promised to offer financial support to Chinese companies establishing processing operations overseas in order to help flagging exports ... Companies in the textile, garment and home electric appliances sectors would be encouraged to set up processing facilities overseas to import raw materials and components from China ... Banks [have been urged] to finance the companies' purchasing of equipment and raw materials ... The extension of credit on favourable terms to Chinese companies setting up abroad is the latest in a series of policy initiatives to help revive exports. These have included tax rebates, rewards for foreign currency earnings and reduced levies on exporters.

(*FT*, 5 August 1999, p. 4)

China repeatedly announced its firm commitment to the exchange rate parity of the yuan and at the same time took several supportive measures to boost exports and relieve pressure on the exchange front. Such responses included higher rebates of export taxes, allowing private companies to export directly rather than through foreign trade enterprises and ensuring access to export credits by joint venture enterprises. As a result of these measures and aided by the economic recovery in the region and elsewhere, merchandise exports expanded significantly in the latter part of 1999 and pressure on exchange rate of the yuan has subsequently abated.

(United Nations, *Economic and Social Survey of Asia and the Pacific 2000*, p. 112)

Chinese customs authorities have suspended imports of all wines from France ... They cited reports that vineyards in a few provinces in southern France were ignoring a ban on a byproduct of bovine blood because of concern over the possibility ... of a connection with 'mad cow' disease ... In the past few months, as domestic stockpiles of various foods and manufactured products have grown, China has banned a variety of imports, including pigs from Madagascar, horses from Zimbabwe and meat and dairy products from the Netherlands, France and Germany. China also banned Dutch poultry after a single chick was found to have chicken plague.

(*IHT*, 11 August 1999, p. 17)

(The ban on French wine imports was lifted on 17 August 1999: *IHT*, 18 August 1999, p. 17.)

30 August 1999.

China approved an expected fiscal stimulus package yesterday [30 August] ... Parliament approved a renminbi 60 billion bond issue for infrastructure spending and amended a law to pave the way for China's first tax on bank deposits ... Payments to millions of laid-off workers are to be increased by 30 per cent from 1 July ... Civil servants have already received a 30 per cent pay rise ...

An infrastructure spending programme began last year [1998] with a renminbi 100 billion bond issue . . . The finance minister said that the renminbi 60 billion issue approved yesterday would stimulate some renminbi 300 billion in spending, mainly because banks would have to complement state infrastructure expenditure with loans. Total fixed asset spending last year [1998] was up 14.1 per cent on a year earlier.

(*FT*, 31 August 1999, p. 4)

China's legislature approved a tax on savings account interest, trying to help the slowing economy by encouraging consumers to save less and spend more . . . The government's top policy-making body has proposed raising the national debt by 60 billion yuan to fund state spending to stimulate economic growth . . . The State Council said the money should be raised by selling Treasury bonds to banks. Half the money should go to the central government and half would be lent to local governments. The money would be spent on infrastructure construction, technological innovation and environmental protection projects . . . State spending was a central factor in China's strong economic growth late last year [1998] after the government issued a special 100 billion yuan infrastructure bond and pushed state banks to increase their lending by the same amount.

(*IHT*, 31 August 1999, pp. 14–15)

The 20 per cent flat rate tax may come into effect on 1 October 1999. China has a high savings rate, of the order of 40 per cent of GDP (*IHT*, 1 September 1999, p. 19). (The 20 per cent tax on interest earned on personal bank savings actually went into force on 1 November 1999: *FT*, 15 October 1999, p. 14.)

1 September 1999. A bar comes into force on all plans for new production of a broad range of ordinary consumer items, from refrigerators and air conditioners to candy, apple juice and liquor in a move to combat deflation. The ban on new projects also covers the construction of luxury hotels, apartment and office buildings and department stores (*IHT*, 19 August 1999, p. 1). 'Yesterday [23 August] the official *China Daily*, declaring that overproduction of electrical goods damaged the economy, said new projects to manufacture video compact disc players, refrigerators, air conditioners and other household appliances, would be banned from 1 September' (*FT*, 24 August 1999, p. 6).

5 September 1999.

China yesterday [5 September] announced extra spending this year [1999] on increased social security benefits or civil service salaries for 84 million people . . . State benefits for the unemployed, as well as for low- and middle-income families, would be raised by 30 per cent, backdated to 1 July . . . Pensions would be increased by an unspecified amount . . . 42.8 per cent of total central budget revenues last year [1998] was spent on servicing existing debts.

(*FT*, 6 September 1999, p. 4)

The pay increases, which are generally in the range of 15 per cent to 30 per cent and are retroactive to 1 July, will go to workers and retirees in government offices, schools and other state-funded facilities. In addition, monthly subsidies paid to millions of unemployed workers and urban poor will increase by an average of 30 per cent.

(IHT, 7 September 1999, p. 16)

Basic salaries for civil servants and the allowance for the unemployed will go up by 30 per cent. Pensioners will receive an extra 15 per cent and workers in state-owned enterprises will get rises depending on their employers' circumstances ... Central and local authorities are to pay arrears owed to millions of workers and pensioners.

(The Times, 7 September 1999, p. 14)

The People's Bank of China ... says a fifth of loans made by the four major banks – China Construction Bank, Industrial and Commercial Bank of China, Bank of China and Agricultural Bank of China – are non-performing ... Foreign economists say the true figure may be as high as 40 per cent ... a third of China's GDP ... While it is clear that central government officials are serious about halting local government interference in bank decisions, Beijing still wants to bend the banks to its will. Since the economy began slowing last year [1998] it has pressed the banks to step up lending ... The central bank dictates how much banks can charge large companies for loans, no matter the risk factor ... Banks can charge small and medium-sized companies up to 30 per cent more ... China Construction Bank has off-loaded most of its bad loans to the newly created asset management company [Cinda Asset Management] that will recover or sell them ... Cinda is acquiring the bad loans at face value, using ministry of finance-backed bonds, while it will be considered fortunate to recover as much as a third. It is empowered to restructure debtor companies, bring in outside management and sell them off whole or in part ... On the other hand, much of the residual sum may have to be written off because only loans that had some hope of recovery were allowed to be transferred to Cinda.

(FEER, 9 September 1999, pp. 75–6)

29 December 1999. Official figures are released showing that in 1999 exports increased by 6 per cent and imports grew by 18 per cent. The trade surplus narrowed to $30 billion, down from $43.6 billion in 1998.

Imports rose 18 per cent to $165 billion. Exports grew 6 per cent to $195 billion, accelerating in the second half of the year as demand for Chinese goods picked up in Japan and other Asian markets that had been slowed by the economic crisis.

(IHT, 30 December 1999, p. 9)

'After declining in 1998 and the first half of 1999, China's exports have been rising strongly since the second half of 1999, helped by strong global, and particularly regional, demand growth' (OECD, *Economic Outlook*, June 2000, p. 144).

Recent developments suggest a decline in the external vulnerability of China during 1999. The real effective exchange rate has continued to depreciate from its peak reached in early 1998 as a result of domestic price deflation and recoveries in other regional currencies, reducing pressures for a nominal depreciation and supporting export growth. And net capital inflows have resumed (mainly reflecting a reduction in outflows), offsetting a decline in the current account surplus and contributing to a further increase in official reserves to almost $160 billion.

(IMF, *World Economic Outlook*, May 2000, p. 29)

1 January 2000. China's foreign exchange reserves rose by $9.72 billion in 1999 to stand at $154.67 billion at the end of December 1999 'in a further sign that pressures on Beijing to devalue its currency have eased'.

The improved performance compared with 1998, when reserves climbed by just $5.1 billion, was due in part to measures taken by the authorities to curb capital flight, economists said. The level of China's foreign currency reserves is regarded as the leading barometer of confidence among Beijing policymakers over the exchange rate of the renminbi.

(*FT*, 3 January 2000, p. 6)

China said that a crackdown on smuggling and illegal currency trading had helped raise its foreign reserves by $9.7 billion in 1999, to $154.7 billion, despite a sharp decline in its trade surplus. The increase was nearly double that of 1998, when the drain from illegal currency outflows was so great that reserves grew just $5.1 billion despite a $45 billion trade surplus.

(*IHT*, 3 January 2000, p. 15)

Official figures show that China had a trade surplus of $29.1 billion in 1999 compared with $43.6 billion the year before. China's foreign exchange reserves stood at $154.7 billion at the end of 1999 (*FEER*, 13 January 2000, p. 73, and 9 March 2000, p. 54).

6 March 2000.

A key component of the 2000 budget derives from a 100 billion renminbi issue of state bonds for spending on infrastructure projects. This follows a 60 billion renminbi bond issue last year [1999] and a 100 billion renminbi issue in 1998 ... [There is] pressure on state banks to support state infrastructure spending with the required lending. Such pressures conflict with years of official exhortation that the 'big four' state banks should increasingly apply commercial criteria to the granting of loans.

(*FT*, 7 March 2000, p. 12)

12 April 2000.

China announced a series of new regulations on the issuance of foreign debt yesterday [12 April] ... The regulations ... make all medium and long-term debt issues subject to approval by the state council (cabinet). The current system, under which certain types of institutions have permission to borrow abroad, is to be abolished. This means that China's troubled ITICs (international trust and investment corporations) will not be allowed to borrow abroad unless they have cabinet approval. China has signalled that it wants to conduct a thorough clean-up of the country's 240 ITICs, merging many and closing several to leave only the most creditworthy in operation.

(*FT*, 13 April 2000, p. 12)

26 June 2000. Hainan International Trust and Investment Corporation (HITIC), an investment company (owned by Hainan province and set up as a conduit between the government and the world's financial markets), misses an interest payment on a yen-denominated bond. But it has a fourteen-day grace period in which to pay before being declared in default (*IHT*, 29 June 2000, p. 12).

27 June 2000.

China's central government sold 30 billion yen of five-year bonds to Japanese investors, the country's first foray into international debt markets in eighteen months. It also marked China's first sale of samurai bonds – debt denominated in yen and issued in Japan by foreign governments and companies – in five years.

(*IHT*, 29 June 2000, p. 22)

10 July 2000. The Hainan International Trust and Investment Corporation, which is owned by the government of Hainan province, fails to make an interest payment to holders of its Samurai bonds which came due on 26 June 2000. Samurai bonds are yen-denominated bonds sold by foreign governments or companies to Japanese investors. Failure to pay within fourteen days after that date (i.e. by 10 July) means default, although the payment agent was prepared to wait until midnight to receive payment before formally declaring a default (*IHT*, 11 July 2000, p. 16).

At midnight Monday [10 July] the fourteen-day grace period ... expired, sending the company into official default. A Hainan province official said Tuesday [11 July] the provincial government was considering how to pay bondholders but could not say when obligations would be met ... [There was a] default last week of a Zhuhai expressway bond that could be a harbinger of trouble for China's many infrastructure bonds.

(*IHT*, 12 July 2000, p. 16)

26 July 2000.

HITIC ... has said it will make an overdue interest payment to bondholders that bought into its 1994 ... Samurai bond issue ... No official default announcement was made ... An official at HITIC ... said yesterday [26 July] that it would 'pay in a few days'.

(*FT*, 27 July 2000, p. 36)

HITIC paid the overdue interest payment the following day (*IHT*, 28 July 2000, p. 19).

4 August 2000.

Dalian International Trust and Investment Corp [DITIC] has become the first Chinese trust to resolve debt problems with international creditors by offering a 60 per cent cash principal settlement ... In a sign that other trusts might be following in its footsteps ... GZITIC [Guangzhou International Trust and Investment Corp] creditors have been asked to choose between a one-off 40 per cent cash settlement in the second quarter of next year [2001] or a restructuring scheme that theoretically repays debt in full over ten years.

(*FT*, 5 August 2000, p. 16)

The Guangzhou International Trust and Investment Corp has proposed two plans to its creditors for repayment of $1 billion owed to them. They can either get half their money in six months or wait up to a decade for a full repayment.

(*IHT*, 26 August 2000, p. 14)

5 September 2000.

The central bank announced Tuesday [5 September] that it would ease controls on foreign-currency lending and deposit rates, a first step toward allowing eventual free trading of the Chinese yuan. A directive issued by the People's Bank of China gives greater play to international market conditions in setting lending rates and allows banks greater say in determining deposit rates. Although the changes, which are to take effect on 21 September, would not make it easier to borrow foreign currency, they would prevent hard currency from leaking into offshore bank accounts, where interest rates are higher. The People's Bank governor, Dai Xianglong, recently signalled the changes as part of a three-year programme to liberalize China's tightly controlled interest rate system. After that, Mr Dai said, China could begin studying when to make the yuan freely convertible. Currently interest rates are set by the central bank, although banks are given a small margin to vary lending rates based on credit risk. Borrowing foreign currency remains difficult, with the yuan virtually pegged to the US dollar within a narrow band of around 8.26 to one dollar. The move would also create more competition for foreign banks seeking to attract the country's growing volume of foreign currency deposits ... Foreign banks ... generally offer higher interest rates on foreign currency deposits than do Chinese banks ... In April [2000] the yuan briefly traded outside its normal range, prompting speculation that officials were experimenting with allowing the currency to float more freely.

(*IHT*, 6 September 2000, p. 20)

China will free interest rates on foreign currency loans and some deposits ... From 21 September financial institutions will be allowed to set their foreign currency rates in line with the international market ... Rates on deposits of more than $3 million would also be liberalized but the central bank would maintain control over deposit rates for lesser sums. The initiative was also partly aimed at stemming the outflow of foreign currency that has picked up since US rates began to climb ... The liberalization of foreign currency rates has been seen as the first step in a gradual process towards full interest rate liberalization ... In July [2000] Dai Xianglong ... said the interest rate regime would be relaxed over the next three years by allowing the market to set most lending and deposit rates. Loans to most Chinese companies are permitted to fluctuate within a band 10 per cent above or below levels set by the People's Bank of China.

(*FT*, 6 September 2000, p. 11)

For the first time the People's Bank of China has laid out a timetable for liberalization [of interest rates on deposits and loans]: within three years ... On 5 September the People's Bank of China announced the first stage: interest rates on foreign currency loans and large deposits are to be freed from 21 September ... Thereafter lending and deposit rates for the domestic yuan will be set by the market, first in rural areas. City banks will later be allowed more latitude to set their lending rates, and after that rates for certificates of deposit and then for other deposits. Freeing interest rates is necessary before China can make its currency fully convertible.

(*The Economist*, 9 September 2000, p. 125)

September–October 2000.

Hainan International Trust and Investment Corp. ... is being forced to sell stakes in three companies as a deadline on a foreign debt payment expired Monday [9 October] ... HITIC ... [has] still not made an interest payment on 14 billion yen ($129 million) of yen bonds that was originally due on 25 September ... The bonds mature in 2004 ... A two-week grace period in which to make the payment ended Monday ... The sales [of the stakes in three companies] were ordered by a Guangzhou court ... In June HITIC twice missed an interest payment on 14.5 billion yen of so-called Samurai bonds. Samurai bonds are yen-denominated bonds sold to Japanese investors by non-Japanese borrowers. The payment was made on 27 July, a month past its due date, after China's central bank governor threatened to shut the trust firm.

(*IHT*, 10 October 2000, p. 16)

'HITIC failed to meet a payment deadline on 24 September and 10 October ... the first Chinese company to fail in the Samurai bond market ... HITIC's 14 billion yen seven-year bonds were taken up mainly by Japanese investors' (*FT*, 14 October 2000, p. 7).

17 January 2001.

The central bank chief, Dai Xianglong, said Wednesday [17 January 2001] ... the People's Bank of China planned to move ahead with the liberalization of its rigid interest rate regime and make its exchange rate more flexible after WTO entry ... Mr Dai said China would close a 'small number' of its 239 trusts this year [2001] ... Beijing also planned to introduce new rules on trust companies this year, he said. Mr Dai was more positive on the banking sector, saying the worst of its loan problems was past.

(*IHT*, 18 January 2001, p. 15)

Dai Xianglong, Chian's central bank governor ... maintained his line on gradual liberalization for China's own currency, saying it would be allowed to trade in a slightly broader range this year. The increased flexibility of the renminbi, which trades in a tight band of a fraction of 1 per cent, will be to handle the rise in trade which is expected to come with China's entry into the WTO. The Chinese currency is backed by huge foreign exchange reserves, which the central bank said yesterday stood at $165.6 billion at the end of last year [2000] ... Mr Dai also stuck by the bank's position that interest rate liberalization would be allowed only gradually. Mr Dai said the percentage of the big four state banks' loans that had to be written off was only 3 per cent, which foreign analysts say seriously underestimates China's bad debt problem.

(*FT*, 18 January 2001, p. 10)

9 May 2001.

The chief of China's central bank, Dai Xianglong, said Wednesday [9 May] that the government would recapitalize three of its four biggest commercial banks this year to help them meet minimum international standards. Only one of the four ... [thought to be the Bank of China] now meets the Bank for International Settlements' standard of holding capital equal to 8 per cent of assets ... China shifted 1.4 trillion yuan ($169.1 billion), or 16 per cent of the big four's bad loans, into asset management companies in 1999, the central bank said ... China's securities regulator stepped up its campaign for discipline in the stock markets by restricting trading of four unprofitable companies ... The China securities regulatory commission is delisting chronically unprofitable companies to try to improve management before the country joins the WTO.

(*IHT*, 10 May 2001, p. 17)

15 June 2001.

China said Friday [15 June] that it would take action against illegal foreign exchange dealings, a move analysts said was partly aimed at stemming the flow of 'hot money' into Hong Kong's stock market ... This latest effort follows huge foreign exchange outflows to Hong Kong as mainland investors skirt rules for investing in China-linked stocks, which trade at sharp discounts to locally traded hard currency B shares and domestic currency A shares.

(*IHT*, 16 June 2001, p. 13)

28 November 2001.

The low-key opening [takes place] of a new exchange in Shanghai to trade ... gold ... which has been controlled by a rigid state monopoly for more than five decades ... The initial trading will only be 'simulated' to test the exchange's systems. The exchange is expected officially to begin trading next month or early next year ... The establishment of the exchange, ... will end the monopoly on all old transactions by the People's Bank of China. China was the fourth largest gold producer in 2000 ... after South Africa, the USA and Australia.

(*FT*, 28 November 2001, p. 19)

1 July 2002.

The more than 200 foreign and domestic creditors of Guangdong International Trust and Investment Corp., or GITIC, will be paid 820 million renminbi

($99 million), or about 4 per cent of their claims. It will be only the second payment since the debt-laden trust was shut down by the central bank nearly four years ago ... In October 2000 creditors were paid 690 million renminbi in cash, or 3.4 per cent of their claims. Creditors have claimed more than 20 billion renminbi from what was once the top overseas borrowing vehicle for the Guangdong provincial government.

(*FEER*, 11 July 2002, p. 28)

24 July 2002.

China will allow state companies that owe more than $100 million or more overseas to sell corporate bonds denominated in dollars and other foreign currencies to domestic funds and banks. The provision is aimed at helping companies repay $170 billion of foreign debt.

(*IHT*, 26 July 2002, p. 15)

Rules governing development of an onshore dollar bond market [were announced on 24 July] ... Approved companies will be encouraged to borrow foreign currencies by issuing domestic bonds, allowing them to tap into some of the $144 billion in hard currency held on deposit at Chinese banks. By issuing bonds China's more creditworthy companies should be able to reduce their cost of dollar funding below the 3.75 per cent fixed rate charged by Bank of China for a one-year loan. Initially the only approved buyers will be commercial banks, but rules will open up the possibility that companies will be allowed to sell bonds directly to domestic savers at returns higher than the 1.25 per cent they can currently earn on onshore dollar deposits.

(*FEER*, 8 August 2002, p. 23)

15 January 2003.

New rules published on 15 January require high-level approval before Chinese entities can borrow money overseas. Chinese companies need the state development planning commission in Beijing to sign off on each foreign borrowing arrangement, and international borrowing by state banks and government entities needs cabinet approval.

(*FEER*, 23 January 2003, p. 23)

Trade pacts

[On 29 November 2004 China] signed a trade accord [with the ten-member Association of South-east Asian Nations] that calls for zero tariffs on a wide range of agricultural and manufactured goods by 2010 ... China, along with Japan and South Korea, is one of three partners invited to attend the annual [Asean] meeting. The trade agreement with China marked the first concrete steps toward a China–Asean free-trade area by 2010.

(*IHT*, 30 November 2004, p. 13)

'The [Asean] pact with China ... aims to create the world's biggest free-trade area, with a population of almost 2 billion ... within the next six years' (*The Economist*, 4 December 2004, p. 64).

Direct foreign investment (DFI)

The crucial distinction between portfolio investment and direct foreign investment (DFI) is that the latter involves control. 'Foreign-invested' enterprises refer to both joint ventures and wholly foreign-owned companies. The law on joint equity ventures was promulgated on 14 July 1979. Foreign ownership was then limited to a maximum 49 per cent and certain sectors were excluded. Over time there has been a considerable relaxation of such restrictions, e.g. 100 per cent foreign ownership in some cases.

Wholly foreign-owned enterprises have increased in importance, accounting for 45.2 per cent of the number of newly approved foreign-invested enterprises in the first half of 1997, compared with 36.9 per cent in 1996 and 16.5 per cent in the period 1979–92. The figures in terms of contractual value were 36.6 per cent in 1996 and 22.9 per cent in the period 1979–92. Wholly foreign-owned enterprises are prohibited in sectors seen to be of strategic importance to the nation or the economy (such as telecommunications and transport; note that in September 1998 the authorities closed the loophole that allowed foreigners to invest in telecommunications: see below), a few basic industries (such as automobiles and mining) and many service industries. In some of these areas there are also requirements for the Chinese partner to hold majority shares in joint ventures (*China Briefing*, January 1998, no. 59, pp. 6–7).

(See above for the implications for direct foreign investment of China's membership of the WTO.)

The volume of DFI and other indicators of its importance

China has become a magnet for direct foreign investment (DFI) owing to such factors as its abundant and cheap labour. The deputy governor of the People's Bank of China: 'The cost of labour in China is only 3 per cent of that of US labour' (*FT*, 23 November 2004, p. 1). Other factors include a rapidly growing economy and government policy (such as the opening up, at least partially, of an increasing number of sectors and legislation to give greater protection to property rights).

Figures for DFI distinguish between contracted (committed or pledged) and utilized (disbursed or actual) totals. There are large numbers of ethnic Chinese in other Asian countries and some 70 per cent of DFI came from Hong Kong, Macao and Taiwan before the Asian financial crisis. (Note problems such as 'round tripping', i.e. domestic capital sent to places like Hong Kong and back again. *The Economist* talks of a 'good quarter' of total DFI and 'between a quarter and a third': 26 August 1995, p. 60, and 8 March 1997, Survey, p. 12, respectively. 'Maybe more than half of what is counted as "foreign investment" is actually domestic, recycled through Hong Kong': *The Economist*, 19 June 1999, p. 103. 'A large amount of China's FDI is money that has been earned in mainland China but then booked to accounts in Hong Kong for tax reasons': *The Economist*, 15 February 2003, p. 75. 'At least 25 per cent of China's "foreign" cash inflows likely represent investment by domestic companies. Firms routinely funnel money out of the country to tax havens such as Hong Kong and the Caribbean and then move the cash back to China, where it is counted as "foreign" investment': *FEER*, 15 May 2003, p. 39.)

'By 1991 there were roughly 20,000 foreign ventures, with a cumulative investment of $22 billion. Some $3.5 billion was invested in 1991 alone' (*The Economist*, Survey, 28 November 1992, p. 18).

In 1991 the figure for direct foreign investment was $4.2 billion' (*FEER*, 24 December 1992, p. 72).

In 1995 the world total of utilized DFI was $315 billion. China, with $38 billion, came second only to the USA's $60 billion. The contrast with Russia is remarkable, where cumulative utilized DFI in the period 1992–5 came to a mere $4 billion (*The Economist*, 13 April 1996, p. 72). (The Asian financial crisis, which began in July 1997 in Thailand, was disastrous for Russia. In August 1998 came the so-called Russian financial crisis.)

In 1996 utilized DFI was $42.3 billion and in 1997 it was $45.2 billion. In 1997 China received $64 billion in foreign capital, of which $45.3 billion was direct foreign investment. By the end of 1997 the cumulative total of direct foreign investment stood at $225 billion (Lardy 1998: 84). Figures for utilized DFI for subsequent years are as follows: 1998, $45.6 billion; 1999, $40.4 billion; 2000, $40.7 billion; 2001, $46.8 billion; 2002, $52.74 billion; 2003, $53.5 billion (out of a world total of nearly $560 billion); 2004, $60.6 billion; 2005, $60.3 billion.

UNCTAD [United Nations Conference on Trade and Development] reported that foreign direct investment more than halved last year [2001], falling to $735 billion worldwide. The largest reduction was in industrial countries, with only modest declines in FDI flows to the developing world. In 2001 China attracted just under $50 billion FDI compared with $125 billion going to the United States. But while foreign investment levels in China were growing, the level of FDI in the United States fell from $301 billion in 2000.

(*FT*, 23 September 2002, p. 11)

[UNCTAD] said world investment flows would stabilize this year [2002] after falling by a half from a record $1,393 billion in 2000. Total inward FDI slipped by 21 per cent to $651 billion in 2002 from $824 billion in 2001 after a 41 per cent drop the previous year ... The United States has suffered the most savage drop in inward FDI, from $314 billion in 2000 and $144 billion in 2001 to just $30 billion last year [2002] ... FDI flows into China have increased steadily to a record $53 billion last year [2002], making it the top FDI host for the first time ... [But] UNCTAD said that, excluding 'round tripping' ... as Chinese companies have channelled their funds into Hong Kong and then reinvested them in China ... last year's inward FDI might have been closer to $40 billion.

(*FT*, 5 September 2003, p. 11)

[According to UNCTAD] ... global FDI fell by a fifth in 2002 to $651 billion, its lowest level since 1998 ... [But FDI] in China surged by 12.5 per cent to $52.7 billion ... China's emergence as the top location followed a two-year slump in investment flows in the United States and the UK.

(*The Times*, 5 September 2003, p. 27)

[In 2002] China surpassed America as the world's largest recipient of FDI, with $53 billion-worth. But that had more to do with the collapse of investment in America than with the rise in China. Inflows into America in 1999 and 2000 were $283 billion and $301 billion respectively. The figures for China in the same years were $40 billion and $41 billion respectively.

(*The Economist*, 15 February 2003, p. 75)

'China overtook the United States as the world's largest recipient of FDI, taking in $52.7 billion, the World Bank said' (*IHT*, 4 April 2003, p. 12).

China overtook the United States as a recipient of foreign direct investment in 2003 ... according to the OECD ... Investment into the United States declined to $40 billion last year [2003] from $72 billion in 2002 and $167 billion in 2001, while foreign direct investment in China dipped only slightly to $53 billion from $55 billion [in 2002] – leaving China as the world's biggest recipient of investment, excluding Luxembourg, a tax haven.

(*IHT*, 29 June 2004, p. 15)

'[In 2004] America ... regained its status as the largest recipient [of FDI], a position it has held for most of the past two decades' (www.economist.com, 27 June 2005).

[In 2004] global foreign direct investment [amounted to] ... $648 billion ... The UK attracted more foreign direct investment [$78 billion] than China last year [2004], becoming the world's second largest FDI recipient after the United States ... according to the United Nations Conference on Trade and Development (UNCTAD) ... FDI inflows to the United States rose from $7 billion in 2003 to $96 billion in 2004, while flows to China increased from $54 billion to $61 billion. The big upward revision in US inflows for 2003, originally estimated at just $30 billion, also shows that, contrary to earlier reports, the United States has never ceded its lead to China as an investment destination.

(*FT*, 30 September 2005, p. 13)

'After falling for three consecutive years since their 2001 peak, inflows of foreign direct investment finally turned up last year [2004] ... World FDI inflows amounted to $648 billion, 2 per cent higher than a year ago' (*The Economist*, 1 October 2005, p. 114).

'In 1991 foreign-invested enterprises accounted for 16.8 per cent of total exports and 45.8 per cent of the exports of the SEZs' (Kueh 1992: 668).

In 1995 foreign-funded enterprises (including both joint ventures and wholly foreign-owned companies) accounted for 31.5 per cent of exports and 47.6 per cent of imports (*IHT*, Survey, 28 October 1996, p. v). In 1996 foreign-invested enterprises accounted for 40 per cent of exports (*IHT*, 5 March 1997, p. 6).

Firms with foreign investors are responsible for more than two-fifths of China's exports ... [and] employ about 10 per cent of the urban work force ... But ... [they] accounted for only about one-seventh of all China's fixed investment between 1994 and 1998.

(*The Economist*, 19 June 1999, p. 103)

'Half of all China's exports (and three-quarters of its manufactured ones) are made by companies in which foreign investors have a stake' (*The Economist*, 20 November 1999, p. 31).

'Foreign-invested firms accounted for almost half of China's exports in 2000 ... [and] over half its imports' (Nicholas Lardy, *Foreign Policy*, March–April 2002, p. 20). 'About half of its exports [in 2001] ... consisted of products made by foreign companies or joint ventures of Chinese or foreign companies' (*IHT*, 18 December 2002, p. 14).

'[Foreign-invested enterprises increased] their share of total exports from 1 per cent in 1985 to 50.1 per cent in 2001' (*FT*, 29 October 2002, p. 11).

'[In 2004] 63.3 per cent of China's export growth ... was produced by foreign-invested enterprises, up from 56.8 per cent in 2000' (*The Economist*, 29 October 2005, p. 77).

> By 2003 the ratio of China's stock of inward investment to GDP was 35 per cent – against 8 per cent in [South] Korea, 5 per cent in India and just 2 per cent in Japan – while 57 per cent of China's exports came from foreign-invested enterprises in 2004.
>
> (*FT*, 15 September 2005, p. 7)

> About 60 per cent of China's exports are controlled by foreign-financed companies, according to the latest Chinese customs data. In categories like computer parts and consumer electronics, foreign companies command an even greater share of control over the exports, analysts say.
>
> (*IHT*, 10 February 2006, p. 6)

'Foreign-funded enterprises accounted for 12 per cent of industrial output in 1997, double the share for 1993. By last year [1999] that figure had risen to 17.8 per cent' (*FEER*, 5 October 2000, p. 48).

'According to the World Bank, foreign-funded enterprises now account for more than a third of China's total industrial growth' (*FEER*, 25 October 2001, p. 68).

> Already China's stock of FDI, at $350 billion, and growing by over $40 billion a year, is massive. It is the world's third largest, behind America ($1.1 trillion) and Britain ($394 million) ... Foreign-invested firms have grown to account for half of all exports from China ... Firms wholly or partly owned by foreigners account for about one-half of China's imports as well as its exports. Much export manufacturing, in other words, consists of processing industries that ship in components, bolt them together and ship them out again. The foreign-dominated export sector, especially in China's handful of 'special economic zones', should be thought of as an enclave ... China, says Mr [Nicholas] Lardy, is only shallowly integrated with the world economy ... Some estimates put foreign involvement at about one-tenth of the whole economy.
>
> (*The Economist*, 10 March 2001, p. 26)

'Sales by American companies in China are now almost as large as American exports to China' (p. 28).

'[China said on 14 December 2004] that there were 504,568 foreign-invested companies in China and that China had attracted $559 billion in investment since the government opened the country to overseas investors in 1978' (www.iht.com, 14 December 2004).

'The cumulative total ... of FDI ... by the end of last year [2004] reached $562 billion' (*The Economist*, 29 October 2005, p. 77).

(For foreign-invested companies' contribution to industrial output, see the section on the importance of the private sector above.)

Investment overseas by Chinese companies (outward direct foreign investment)

By the end of 1998 Chinese enterprises had invested a total of $6.3 billion overseas (*FEER*, 15 April 1999, p. 82).

'Chinese companies had invested only $6.7 billion overseas by the end of 1998, puny compared with the $276 billion worth of foreign investment that flooded the mainland, according to the ministry of foreign trade and economic co-operation' (*FT*, 6 May 1999, p. 7).

'Several industries were chosen ... such as those industries in which China lacked its own resources or those already possessing mature technology which could use overseas investment to implement technology transfer to other developing countries, thereby stimulating export growth' (Wu and Chen 2001: 1235).

China has invested heavily in foreign oilfields in a bid to guarantee supply ... The country currently produces only 70 per cent of its oil needs ... [and] still relies on coal for 70 per cent of its energy needs ... Natural gas accounted for 23 per cent of world energy use in 1999 but only 3 per cent of China's consumption.

(*FEER*, 20 June 2002, pp. 15–16)

[In 2002] the amount that Chinese companies invest outside their own borders ... [was] $2.9 billion, or 0.4 per cent of global DFI ... led by natural resource companies still controlled by the state ... to secure the country's booming demand for fuel and raw materials ... [There is also a] hunt for foreign know-how.

(*The Economist*, 6 September 2003, p. 71)

'[China is seeking] the kind of management and technologies needed in China ... technology and know-how that would take years to build up organically' (*FT*, 18 December 2003, p. 32). '[The main aims of outward investment are] to secure raw materials ... and to bring local management skills up to international standards' (*FT*, 8 March 2005, p. 12).

Overseas investment by Chinese companies totalled $2.7 billion last year [2002], the ministry of commerce said ... Total overseas investment by Chinese companies stood at $29.9 billion at the end of 1992. It was the first time that the nation's overseas investment had been officially reported.

(www.iht.com, 17 December 2003)

Chinese companies invested $2.7 billion abroad in 2002, according to the ministry of commerce ... Outward investment still requires official approval. Projects that exceed $30 million must go to the State Council ... Beijing in 2003 gave more leeway to Chinese companies to invest overseas ... [It] raised to ten the number of regions from which companies may invest outside China... The ceiling on outward investments for each approved region is just £200 million ... The bulk of China's investments overseas remain resource-based. But now Chinese manufacturers are scouting the region for production platforms to penetrate new markets ... The United Nations Conference on Trade and Development [UNCTAD] said in a December [2003] report that 'average annual outward FDI flows have grown from $0.4 billion in the 1980s to $2.3 billion in the 1990s'.

(*FEER*, 5 February 2003, pp. 25–7)

'China announced rules to make it easier for its companies to invest overseas' (*FEER*, 21 October 2004, p. 28).

China's accumulated direct investment overseas reached $33.4 billion by the end of 2003, according to the commerce ministry in its first report on overseas investment excluding the financial sector. The ministry said that such investment was $2.85 billion in 2003, which was 5.5 per cent greater than in 2002.

(*FEER*, 16 September 2004, p. 32)

'[China's] outward foreign investment was just $2.9 billion in 2003 ... China's stock of outward FDI amounts to $33 billion, less than half a per cent of accumulated world FDI' (*The Economist*, 7 January 2005, p. 58).

'China's government reported $2.85 billion [outward] DFI for 2003, a 5.5 per cent increase from 2002' (www.iht.com, 22 December 2004).

In 2004 'overseas investment by Chinese companies' was $3.6 billion (*FT*, 9 February 2005, p. 6).

'Worldwide direct investment from China more than tripled in 2005 to about $6 billion, according to *The Economist* Intelligence Unit' (*IHT*, 3 April 2006, p. 17)

The sale [has taken place] of IBM's personal computer business to Lenovo, China's largest maker of PCs ... Under Lenovo's ownership the IBM personal computer business will continue to be based in the United States and run by its current management team. IBM will take a stake of 18.9 per cent in Lenovo, which is based in Beijing but now plans to have its headquarters in New York ... Lenovo ... partly owned by the Chinese government ... is paying ... the relatively modest amount ... of $1.75 billion in cash, stock and debt.

(*IHT*, 9 December 2004, p. 11)

Lenovo ... is owned mainly by public shareholders. But a government institution, the Chinese Academy of Sciences, owns 37 per cent. If the acquisition is completed the government's holding will fall below 30 per cent and IBM will have an 18.9 per cent stake.

(www.iht.com, 7 January 2005)

'[The Lenovo takeover is the] biggest overseas acquisition by a Chinese company' (*FT*, 27 January 2005, p. 1). 'Executives at Lenovo ... have made it clear that [their planned purchase] ... is aimed at learning the skills to protect their diminishing market dominance at home' (*FT*, 8 March 2005, p. 12).

> Lenovo ... is majority-owned by the Chinese Academy of Sciences ... [Another Chinese company called TCL is] the most profitable television producer ... Buying the television business of France's Thomson in early 2004 turned it into the world's biggest volume television maker.
>
> (*The Economist*, 8 January 2005, p. 58)

'Lenovo acquired the right to use the IBM name on its computers for five years' (www.economist.com, 23 June 2005).

> China intends to create world-class companies ... The central government decided some years ago that thirty to fifty of its best state firms should be built into 'national champions' or 'globally competitive' by 2010 ... Over the past decade China has created some quite large companies. More than a dozen [e.g. Baosteel] are in the *Fortune 500* list, though almost all of those are domestic monopolies or near monopolies, such as telecom operators or big commodity producers. A handful of others are starting to compete internationally, though mostly in niche markets and on price rather than with technology or brands. But the global footprint of Chinese companies is still rather faint [see figures above] ... China has so far failed to build world-class companies. Even the natural monopolies and resources companies are mostly just big rather than particularly efficient. In manufacturing, technology and consumer areas a few companies are groping towards international competitiveness, but none are there yet ... Unless China institutes far-reaching political and structural reforms that give Chinese managers the confidence to invest in long-term technological development, it cannot readily build a globally competitive corporate sector ... The most impressive [Chinese companies] are the resources groups. Three big oil companies, PetroChina, Sinopec and CNOOC, are aggressively buying overseas and building pipelines across central Asia to satisfy China's fuel demands. They are in more than a dozen countries: CNOOC, for example, is Indonesia's largest offshore oil producer. Baosteel [is] China's top steel producer ... Chalco [is] China's leading aluminium group ... Yanzhou Coal [is] the largest listed coal producer ... Lenovo [is] in personal computers ... TCL [is] in televisions ... Huawei [telecoms equipment] ... insists it is a private company owned by its employees ... [but there is] speculation that it is really controlled by the military.
>
> (*The Economist*, 8 January 2005, pp. 57–9)

(See the section on conglomerates for earlier material.)

> On 20 June [2005] Haier, China's leading white-goods maker, launched a $1.3 billion cash offer for Maytag, an ailing American rival ... Haier teamed up with two American buy-out firms to bid $1.3 billion for Maytag ... On 23 June China National Offshore Oil Corporation (CNOOC) ... made an offer of $18.5

billion (excluding debt) for Unocal, a California-based oil and gas company ...
The Chinese offer is in cash – the shares even of a well-run Chinese firm are
not yet acceptable as takeover currency ... [The offer is a] contested one. On 4
April Unocal agreed to be acquired by Chevron, the second biggest American
oil firm, in a deal worth $17 billion (excluding debt).

(*The Economist*, 25 June 2005, p. 86; www.economist.com, 23 June 2005)

'In 2004 TCL, its [China's] leading television producer, bought most of the television manufacturing business of France's Thomson plus a mobile handset making
business from Alcatel' (*The Economist*, 2 July 2005, p. 70).

'Unocal [is] a California oil and gas company with extensive fields in Asia'
(*IHT*, 25 June 2005, p. 16). '[Unocal has] natural gas reserves, most of which are in
Asia' (*IHT*, 27 June 2005, p. 8).

CNOOC [is] China's third largest company ... [and] Haier Group its largest
appliance maker ... [China desires] Western brand names ... By acquiring
household names China wants to bolster global sales and distribution capabilities ... China has a dearth of internationally known companies that
operate on a global scale and market their products abroad.

(www.iht.com, 27 June 2005)

[Maytag would be a way] to acquire a brand name and a distribution network
to serve Haier's growing manufacturing capability ... CNOOC, a company
that is 70 per cent owned by the Chinese government, is seeking to acquire
control of Unocal, an energy company with global reach ... Unocal has a
history ... of doing business with problematic regimes in difficult places,
including the Burmese junta and the Taleban.

(*IHT*, 28 June 2005, p. 9)

China's ministry of commerce issued a report this month [June] that said that
even though China's exports were dominated by consumer products, there
were few famous Chinese brands involved in the export trade. Most goods
were shipped abroad with foreign brand labels ... The ministry called on
Chinese companies to start exporting their own 'famous brands'. Every region
was ordered to produce its own famous brands ... By acquiring well-known
brand names, experts say, Chinese companies are hoping to get access to
global distribution networks, sophisticated research and development and rec-
ognizable brand names ... TCL became the world's biggest maker of television sets last year [2004] after it acquired the television set business of
Thomson, the French technology company that also owned the old RCA brand
... Earlier this month [there] was $1.4 billion bid [unsuccessful] by China
Mobile, a huge state-owned telecommunications company, for control of
Pakistan Telecommunication.

(*IHT*, 29 June 2005, p. 8)

('China Mobile was outbid by a competitor from the United Arab Emirates. China
Minmetals failed in its $7 billion offer for Canada's Noranda': *The Economist*, 6
August 2005, p. 53.) 'The takeover bid by CNOOC for the US oil and gas company

Unocal is under review by a US government national security panel' (www.iht.com, 11 July 2005). 'CNOOC is 70 per cent owned by the government-controlled China National Offshore Oil Corporation ... The shareholders of Unocal will vote [on 10 August] ' (www.iht.com, 21 July 2005).

> CNOOC's $19.6 billion bid for Unocal, Haier's $1.28 billion approach to Maytag and Lenovo's $1.75 billion acquisition last month of IBM's personal computer business are proof that Chinese corporations intend to buy companies that help produce the world's oil, assemble its PCs and manufacture its washing machines. Cars and microchips may follow.
>
> (*FT*, 25 June 2005, p. 12)

'Something like half of Unocal's reserves are in Asia' (*FT*, 27 June 2005, p. 19).

'[On 19 July] Haier Group ... abandoned its $1.28 billion bid for the appliance maker Maytag ... saying the group was not prepared for a takeover battle with Whirlpool, a rival bidder' (www.iht.com, 20 July 2005). 'Haier ... was backed in its bid by Blackstone Group and Bain Capital' (*IHT*, 21 July 2005, p. 5). 'Whirlpool ... [is] America's biggest white goods maker' (*The Economist*, 23 July 2005, p. 64).

> CNOOC said Tuesday [2 August that it had] to end its $18.5 billion takeover bid for ... Unocal because of fierce political opposition in Washington. The decision ended a hotly contested battle between CNOOC and Chevron, the second largest US oil company ... The move by CNOOC clears the way for Chevron to finalize its acquisition of Unocal for about $17 billion in cash and stock. Unocal shareholders are expected to vote whether to accept Chevron's bid on 10 August. CNOOC's all-cash bid for Unocal was the largest takeover attempt ever made in the United States by a Chinese company. It came just two months after Chevron had already agreed to a merger, sparking a takeover battle eventually forced Chevron to sweeten its bid to $17.6 billion in cash and stock from $16.8 billion.
>
> (*IHT*, 3 August 2005, p. 1)

> CNOOC ... said that it had 'given active consideration to further improving the terms of its offer and would have done so but for the political environment in the United States' ... The political resistance to CNOOC's bid culminated in the insertion into an energy bill of a clause requiring a four-month study of China's energy policy before the bid could continue ... China is intent on creating up to fifty state-controlled 'global Champions'.
>
> (www.economist.com, 4 August 2005)

> A few weeks ago the government folded the assets of China National Petroleum Corporation (CNPC) and its listed affiliate, PetroChina, into a new, as yet unnamed firm. This new entity's express purpose is to be a 'platform for international business development' and to 'establish significant overseas operations'.
>
> (*The Economist*, 6 August 2005, p. 53)

The fate of Unocal was finally settled on Wednesday [10 August] when a majority of the company's shareholders approved a takeover offer of about

$18 billion by Chevron ... [On] the same day as the vote crude oil prices touched a new high of $65 a barrel in New York.

(www.iht.com, 11 August 2005)

State-owned companies in China and India are trying to buy a Canadian company with oil fields in Kazakhstan ... A joint venture of China National Petroleum, China's biggest oil company, and PetroChina, its publicly traded subsidiary, offered roughly $3.2 billion late Monday [15 August] for PetroKazakhstan ... ... whose shares are traded in Toronto ... [and which has] headquarters in Calgary ... Oil and Natural Gas, India's main government oil company, has already submitted a bid of $3.6 billion in co-operation with the steel maker Mittal Group ... China National Petroleum already has substantial oil investments of its own in Kazakhstan and has been trying to build a pipeline to carry the oil to China.

(*IHT*, 17 August 2005, p. 14)

China National Petroleum Corporation ... would be able to pump its production through its 1,000 kilometre pipeline linking Atasu in Kazakhstan to the Alataw Pass in the north-western Chinese region of Xinjiang. The pipeline is currently working below its 20 million tonnes capacity.

(*FT*, 16 August 2005, p. 24)

China National Petroleum Corporation ... agreed on Monday [22 August] to pay $4.18 billion for ... PetroKazakhstan ... [outbidding] the Indian state-owned company Oil and Natural Gas ... PetroKazakhstan has had a series of legal skirmishes with the Russian company Lukoil, its main partner in the oil fields. Lukoil's main pipeline from Kazakhstan into Russia is already full, but CNPC is expected to finish a pipeline from Kazakhstan into western China at the end of this year [2005] ... PetroKazakhstan previously operated as Hurricane Hydrocarbons ... [which] bought Yuzhneftegaz, a Kazakh state-owned oil company ... for $120 million in 1996.

(www.iht.com, 22 August 2005; *IHT*, 23 August 2005, pp. 1, 4)

'CNPC bid $4.18 billion for PetroKazakhstan ... The deal, which is expected to be approved by PetroKazakhstan shareholders on 18 October, would mark the largest cross-border acquisition by a Chinese company' (*FT*, 5 October 2005, p. 29).

Vladimir Shkolnik, the Kazakh energy minister, said yesterday [4 October]: 'The question of the sale of PetroKazakhstan to CNPC is very serious – we are talking about a strategic project. What shape the deal will take has not been decided, but the government of Kazakhstan will do everything to ensure that strategic control remains with the company. Our national oil company KazMunaiGaz, will have a stake in this company' ... It had been reported earlier that Beijing-based CNPC was in talks to sell part of PetroKazakhstan to KazMunaiGaz, the national oil and gas company in Kazakhstan.

(*FT*, 5 October 2005, p. 29)

On Saturday [15 October] President Nursultan Nazarbayev of Kazakhstan signed changes to a law, changes that would let the government block sales in oil and gas companies ... The bill was approved by parliament on 12 October ... CNPC said Monday [17 October] that it had agreed to sell a 33 per cent stake in PetroKazakhstan to the state-owned KazMunaiGaz in an attempt to ease the Kazakh government's opposition to the purchase ... Another potential obstacle may come from legal actions by Lukoil, Russia's largest oil company. Lukoil is asking an Alberta court to postpone the takeover until its case in a Stockholm arbitration court is resolved. Lukoil said it had filed with the Stockholm chamber of commerce, claiming that a shareholders' agreement gave it the right to buy out PetroKazakhstan's half-ownership of a joint venture that produces oil in Kazakhstan.

(www.iht.com, 19 October 2005)

Under Kazakh law the state oil company, KazMunaiGaz, has a pre-emptive right to buy oil fields. That right was asserted during the sale this fall of PetroKazakhstan, a Canadian-owned company, to China National Petroleum, the biggest oil deal in Kazakhstan this year [2005]. The deal was only approved after the Chinese company agreed to sell assets, including a refinery, to KazMunaiGaz.

(www.iht.com, 23 December 2005)

The leading oil companies of China and India have agreed to jointly acquire Petro-Canada's petroleum interests in Syria ... [it was] reported on Wednesday [22 December 2005] ... China National Petroleum and Oil & Natural Gas have agreed to pay $576 million for the assets ... The companies, both state-owned, are buying Petro-Canada's interests in Al Furat Petroleum. The transaction requires the approval of Syria's government.

(*IHT*, 22 December 2005, p. 13)

A Chinese government drive to secure reliable supplies of foreign energy has been dealt a setback by shareholders in one of China's top oil companies. The oil company, the Hong Kong-listed CNOOC, said Tuesday [3 January 2006] that independent shareholders had blocked a proposal that would have allowed the company's parent, which is owned by the Chinese government, to invest in overseas oil and gas reserves. Energy industry analysts said the proposal suggested that the Chinese government was worried about the country's long-term energy security and wanted CNOOC's parent to have the freedom to make politically sensitive investments in countries like Sudan or Iran, or offer higher than market prices for reserves ... At present the parent, China National Offshore Oil Corp., is barred from investing in foreign petroleum reserves as part of a non-competition agreement offered as a sweetener when CNOOC went public in 2001 ... Under the 2001 non-competition agreement CNOOC was to specialize in offshore domestic oil and gas production and downstream processing. However, in December [2005] the listed company's management asked for shareholder approval to overturn the agreement so that the parent could make investments in oil and gas reserves without fear of a backlash from investors over price or political risk. If these investments were successful the listed company could buy them from the parent, the management explained ... CNOOC said it regretted that 59 per cent of independent shareholders had opposed the proposal in the Saturday [31 December 2005] vote.

(www.iht.com, 3 January 2006)

'Currently only 12 per cent of China's energy requirements are imported compared to 40 per cent in the United States and over 80 per cent in Japan' (*Newsbriefs 2006*, vol. 26, no. 3, p. 35).

CNOOC, China's biggest offshore oil producer, said Monday [9 January 2006] that it would pay $2.3 billion in cash for a stake in a Nigerian oil field ... CNOOC [China National Offshore Oil Corp.] will buy a 45 per cent stake in Nigeria's OML 130 oil area, also known as the Akpo field, from the privately owned Nigerian company South Atlantic Petroleum ... China is competing with India, whose government blocked the state-run Oil & Natural Gas from buying the Akpo stake in December [2005] because of concern over ownership at South Atlantic ... The Indian cabinet rejected the proposal because of a lack of clarity in ownership at South Atlantic Petroleum ... Nigeria is among the world's eight most corrupt nations, according to Transparency International, based in Berlin .... The Akpo field ... will pump 225,000 barrels a day after 2008, or 9 per cent of Nigeria's current production ... Total, based in Paris, holds 24 per cent of the field and Brazil's Petroleo Braasileiro owns 16 per cent. The rest is held by South Atlantic and the state-owned Nigeria National Petroleum.

(www.iht.com, 9 January 2006)

CNOOC said it had agreed to pay nearly $2.3 billion ... $2.28 billion ... to acquire a large stake in a Nigerian oil and gas field ... The oil field is located in the Niger Delta, one of the world's largest oil and gas basins. The field ... is now operated by the French oil company Total, which also has a large stake in the field. CNOOC has also committed to spend $2.25 billion over the next few years to help develop the Nigerian project ... An Indian company, Oil & Natural Gas, last month [December 2005] won the contest for the Nigerian assets with a bid of about $2 billion, but it was blocked from making the deal by India's cabinet. The deal was blocked over concerns about the transparency of the Nigerian ownership, according to Bloomberg News ... Pending the approval from the Nigerian authorities, the deal Monday would be the biggest ever for CNOOC and one of the largest overseas acquisitions ever made by a Chinese company ... CNOOC, one of China's most aggressive energy companies, has spent nearly $2 billion over the past few years acquiring overseas oil and gas exploration assets in such countries as Australia, Indonesia, Vietnam, Thailand, Bangladesh and Azerbaijan.

(*IHT*, 10 January 2006, p. 11)

'CNOOC ... bought a block that a rival energy consumer, India, had shunned after an initial bid. The stake was sold by a former Nigerian defence minister, who was awarded it when Nigeria was under military rule' (*The Economist*, 21 January 2006, p. 58).

China and India ... yesterday [12 January] ... agreed to co-operate in securing crude oil resources overseas ... Under their agreement Chinese and Indian oil companies will establish a formal procedure to exchange information about a possible bid target, before agreeing to co-operate formally. Their memorandum of understanding also covers possible co-operation across the energy industry, from exploration to marketing. But India and China's national oil companies could still compete in third countries.

(*FT*, 13 January 2006, p. 1)

India's minister for petroleum and natural gas ... said the two countries would exchange information in bids for overseas assets ... Some analysts said they believed that India's bargaining power with the Chinese would be limited ... [Other critics said they believed] that India and China would succeed jointly only in going after assets that were not attractive to Western companies.

(*IHT*, 21 January 2006, p. 13)

'Before the ink was even dry on the Beijing agreement, Indian oil ministry officials found out that Myanmar had agreed to sell natural gas from a field partly owned by an Indian company exclusively to China' (*IHT*, 24 January 2006, p. 7).

China and Saudi Arabia signed an agreement Monday [23 January] on energy co-operation ... on 'co-operation in oil, natural gas and minerals' ... during a milestone visit by King Abdulla of Saudi Arabia ... The visit is the first by a Saudi king since the two nations established diplomatic relations in 1990 ... [China] reported that the two sides were hoping to reach agreement to build an oil reserve facility on the southern island of Hainan to store 100 million tonnes of oil ... China's oil imports from Saudi Arabia have already risen from 8.8 million tonnes in 2001 to about 20 million tonnes last year [2005] ... Oil imports from Saudi Arabia ... account for 14 per cent of China's total oil imports ... Among the bilateral deals already in the works Sinopec of China is drilling for gas in the Saudi desert and building a refinery with the Saudi oil firm Saudi Aramco in China's Fujian province. Aramco is also beginning engineering work with Sinopec in the Chinese city of Qingdao.

(www.iht.com, 23 January 2006; *IHT*, 24 January 2006, p. 12)

In 2004 Iran in 2004 agreed in principle to sell China 250 million tonnes of liquefied natural gas over thirty years, a deal valued at $70 billion. China already imports 14 per cent of its oil from Iran. Sinopec ... hopes to develop Iran's enormous Yadavaran oil field.

(*IHT*, 25 January 2006, p. 6)

Japan, South Korea and Taiwan import all their oil, of which 75 per cent is from the Gulf. India imports 75 per cent, of which 80 per cent is from the Gulf. China imports 35 per cent, of which 60 per cent is from the Gulf.

(*IHT*, 9 February 2006, p. 8)

China and Taiwan

> Under the ... policy imposed in 1996 ... businesses in Taiwan are not allowed to undertake any mainland-bound investment project worth more than $50 million and infrastructure sectors are also banned ... Many companies skirt this ban by channelling investments through third countries ... Taiwan entrepreneurs are estimated to have invested more than $40 billion in China since the commencement of civil contacts in late 1987.
>
> (*IHT*, 6 September 2000, p. 20)

'The government on Friday [29 March 2002] eased a ban on computer-chip investments in China ... Companies would be allowed to produce less advanced computer chips in China as long as they are making more sophisticated ones in Taiwan' (*IHT*, 30 March 2002, p. 12).

> Taiwan's parliament approved measures to allow mainland Chinese to invest in the island's property, the latest in a string of steps to encourage mainland companies to put money into Taiwan. Lawmakers also approved the final reading of regulations exempting profits and dividends earned by local companies in China from domestic taxes when repatriated. The property move comes after Taiwan lifted a ban on local [micro] chip makers building plants on the mainland but set tough rules for what is considered a strategic industry by limiting construction to three plants by 2005.
>
> (*FEER*, 11 April 2002, p. 25)

'Taiwan's accumulated investment in China [amounted] to $29.32 billion by the end of 2001' (*FEER*, 21 February 2002, p. 29).

> Taiwan relaxed restrictions on direct trading with mainland China and lifted a ban on importing 2,000 Chinese farm and industrial products. In addition, Taiwanese and Chinese banks will be allowed to make direct remittances, but they will be restricted to currencies other than the new Taiwan dollar and Chinese renminbi.
>
> (*FEER*, 28 February 2002, p. 26)

> Taiwan's state-owned Chinese petroleum and its Chinese counterpart, China Offshore Oil, signed a landmark pact $25 million yesterday [16 May 2002] to explore jointly for oil and natural gas in the Taiwan Strait, which separates the island from China. This is the first big joint venture between state-run companies since ... 1949.
>
> (*FT*, 17 May 2002, p. 11)

> [In May 2002] state-owned oil companies from both sides signed a landmark joint exploration deal. Chinese Petroleum Corporation of Taiwan and China National Offshore Oil Corporation, China's biggest offshore-energy company, will set up a 50–50 joint venture to look for oil and gas in the Tainan Basin between Taiwan and China.
>
> (*FEER*, 30 May 2002, p. 24)

'With or without government approval, Taiwan businessmen have poured an estimated $70 billion of investment into the mainland since Taipei relaxed restrictions in 1987' (*IHT*, 26 August 2002, p. 9).

'China last year [2001] replaced the United States as Taiwan's biggest export market' (*FEER*, 20 June 2002, p. 21).

> Taiwan's cabinet ... yesterday [13 April 2005] passed draft technology protection legislation ... If the legislature adopts the bill the transfer or export of advanced technology by individuals or companies to China will require approval by [the government] ... At present investments from $50 million upwards are subject to approval.
>
> (*FT*, 14 April 2005, p. 11)

Conditions for DFI in China

The trend over time has been to improve the conditions for DFI, although foreigners still complain about the following:

1   Foreign investors have typically taken the long-run view of prospects, but there have been many complaints about the generally low level of profitability. Things, however, are changing. 'Nicholas Lardy ... [has] tackled the increasingly common myth that foreign investors aren't turning a profit ... You find profitability in the second half of the 1990s at about 14 per cent – that same profit margin investors are finding in Brazil and Turkey' (*IMF Survey*, 2002, vol. 31, no. 10, p. 175). 'Plenty of foreign investors still lose money. But they are increasingly outnumbered by multinationals making profit that – if not quite justifying the exaggeration of the 1990s – at least makes China an indispensable part of their global operations' (*IHT*, 6 January 2003, p. 1). 'In a late-2001 survey ... 61.9 per cent of Japanese companies in Vietnam said they were profitable, approaching the 70 per cent recorded in China' (*FEER*, 30 January 2003, p. 14). 'As recently as 1997 the best evidence was that US companies in China were returning an aggregate profit of zero. In 1999 equity-based earnings (those derived from shareholdings in local affiliates) rose to $755 million. By 2003 they had more than tripled to $2.4 billion ... Total China earnings, which includes the affiliates' profits booked through Hong Kong and Singapore, shows income rising from $1.9 billion in 1999 to $4.4 billion in 2003 ... When all other sources of profit are added ... [e.g.] royalty and licensing fees ... [the total for 2003] amounts to $8.2 ... But in 2003 US companies made $7.1 billion in Australia, a market of only 19 million. They earned $8.9 billion in Taiwan and South Korea ... [with] a combined population of 70 million ... In Mexico ... US companies earned $14.3 billion' (Joe Studwell, *FT*, 6 December 2004, p. 21).
2   There is uncertainty over property rights (e.g. difficulties in enforcing contracts; note that land can only be leased). But again things have tended to improve over time in this regard.
3   There is widespread counterfeiting. This is still a major problem although the government has tried to do something about a problem which increasing afflicts domestic Chinese companies as well.
4   There is an initially inadequate infrastructure (such as energy, transport and communications). But there have been major improvements over time (e.g.

power supply problems are now confined to certain inland areas). Since late 2003 there have been increasing reports of power and transport problems as a result of China's rapid economic development.

5   There is still the problem of *guanxi* (the tendency of Chinese to conduct business through personal connections).

On 21 June 1992 it was announced that for the first time a foreign (actually a Hong Kong) company had taken a majority (51 per cent) share in a state-owned enterprise (a textile company) (*IHT*, 13 July 1992, p. 13).

On 13 May 1993 an agreement was signed between the Singapore authorities and China to develop an industrial township in Suzhou, near Shanghai. The Singapore Labour Foundation (a quasi-state body) and the Suzhou municipal government were to put together a consortium of companies to develop the new town (Kieron Cooke, *FT*, 14 May 1993, p. 4). (The scheme subsequently ran into considerable difficulties and Singapore reduced its stake in the venture. One problem was the setting up of a rival scheme by the local authority.)

On 29 June 1993 the Tsingtao Brewery became the first Chinese company to sell shares in Hong Kong.

On 22 November 1995 a new tax on imported capital goods, payable from 1 April 1996, was announced. Companies whose business agreements were completed before the end of 1995 would enjoy a grace period of up to two years before having to pay, but those set up after 1 April would have to pay the new import duties immediately (*IHT*, 23 November 1995, p. 21). For projects up to $30 million, exceptions on duty extend to the end of 1996 and for larger projects to the end of 1997 (*FT*, 10 May 1996, p. 21). (As of 1 January 1998 tax exemptions were introduced for equipment imported by foreign-invested enterprises and domestic enterprises for their own use. Taxes remained on certain listed items to discourage low-technology projects: *IHT*, 31 December 1997, p. 11. Foreign companies in eighteen industries, mostly high-tech ones, were to be exempted from tariffs and (value-added) taxes: *FT*, 5 January 1998, p. 3. 'The presence of certain open-ended formulas on the list suggest that few foreign investment projects will not qualify': *IHT*, 5 January 1998, p. 11.)

More recent state policy has been to try to shift the weight (about 90 per cent) of DFI away from the east coast (especially the south-east coast) areas and towards the relatively neglected interior provinces.

As of 1 January 2000 foreign-invested businesses in western and central provinces would enjoy a preferential 15 per cent rate of income tax for three years. Foreign companies making high-density fertilizers, stainless steel and microelectronics products would also benefit. Most domestic companies pay a 33 per cent income tax, while many local authorities in more affluent coastal areas have already offered foreign businesses preferential rates ranging from 15 per cent to 24 per cent (*FT*, 30 September 1999, p. 4).

The 'Great Western Development' ... campaign, launched in January [2000], is Beijing's latest attempt to prevent the quarter of the country's population that lives in the far west from falling even farther behind people in the prosperous eastern coastal region ... The landlocked west comprises more than half of

China's land area ... The west, which includes Tibet and Xinjiang, is home to 80 per cent of China's official minorities ... Only 3 per cent of the $300 billion foreign investment in China since 1978 has gone to the west. In January [2000] Beijing gave the region the power to approve foreign investment projects of any size and to grant an additional eight years of tax breaks to foreign-invested firms that move some production inland. The problem is that governments in the west have been giving such breaks without Beijing's approval for years just to compete with similar preferential policies that have long applied to coastal areas.

(*FEER*, 4 May 2000, pp. 22–3)

('About 90 per cent of the cumulative foreign investments have gone into the coastal provinces, 40 per cent in Guangdong alone': *FEER*, 24 December 1992, pp. 72–3.)

(For further information, see the section on China's entry into the WTO.)

The opening up of an increasing number of sectors to DFI

An increasing number of sectors have been made eligible for at least joint ventures. Some of the earlier examples are as follows:

TELECOMMUNICATIONS

On 10 May 1993 it was announced that foreign companies were to be prohibited from participating in the management of or from holding shares in telecommunications services (as opposed to manufacturing plants) (*IHT*, 11 May 1993, p. 11).

On 20 July 1994 it was announced that China Unicom would be allowed to compete with the Ministry of Post and Telecommunications in the provision of telephones. But direct foreign investment was still ruled out.

On 12 October 1994 preliminary agreement was reached on a deal to involve foreign companies in telecommunications. But two days later it was made clear that foreigners could not take part in the equity or the management of phone services, being eligible only to build networks, to advise on their operation and to reap returns on the investment (*IHT*, 15 October 1994, p. 15).

'In the past fortnight China has ... decided to close the means through which foreign companies can invest in the local telecoms services market' (James Kynge, *FT*, 29 September 1998, p. 8). 'A week ago China announced new restrictions on foreign investment in the telecommunications industry' (Seth Faison, *IHT*, 30 September 1998, p. 13). China Telecom has a competitor in China Unicom, which was formed in 1994.

The sector has been dominated by China Telecom and its Hong Kong subsidiary China Telecom (HK) ... Lacking government support China Unicom turned to foreign investment partners for its expansion plans, but in September [1998] the ministry for the information industry called off all telecomservice projects involving foreigner companies. Previously China Unicom had circumvented the ban on direct foreign investment by using the formula

'China-China-foreign companies' ... Under them China Unicom formed joint venture companies that were minority owned by foreign firms. The foreign funds flowed indirectly through the second venture which was technically a Chinese company. Now the government appears keen to help China Unicom expand.

(Charles Bickers, *FEER*, 18 February 1999, p. 53)

In September 1999 doubts were cast on the legality of the foreign investment which had taken place in the provision of internet services in China.

In September 1999 the top communications official ... Wu Jichuan, minister of information industries ... suddenly reaffirmed a long-standing ban on foreign investment in Chinese internet service providers ... American companies had rushed into partnerships with Chinese internet providers before Beijing's warning ... Mr Wu has said he will issue new rules on foreign investment by the end of the year [1999] ... Internet service providers connect users with state-run gateways to the global internet.

(*IHT*, 13 November 1999, p. 13)

Before the 15 November [WTO] deal [with the USA] the ministry of information industry had thrown the internet sector into an uncomfortable limbo by declaring it closed to foreign investment while taking no action against the growing number of foreign companies ... that had invested in Chinese internet companies ... The ministry's long-awaited regulations on the operation and ownership of internet businesses in China, which were initially expected on 12 December [1999], have been postponed until early next year [2000].

(*FEER*, 2 December 1999, p. 44)

The Chinese government appears to have reversed its ban on foreign investment in China's dotcoms. Lycos Asia, a joint venture between US-based portal Lycos and Singapore Telecommunications, says it has been granted a commercial business licence that enables it to act as an internet-content provider in China. The 'wholly-owned foreign entity licence', according to Lycos Asia, was issued in mid-August [2000] by the Shanghai foreign investment committee, which operates under the ministry of foreign trade and economic co-operation and has the power to issue business licences to foreign companies ... [The] general manager for Lycos Asia says the licence will allow his company to operate a portal in China as well as create content for that portal ... Last September [1999] China's ministry of information industry ruled internet-service providers and internet-content providers could not use overseas capital ... The large Chinese portals that have received permission to list their shares overseas to raise funds were forced to separate their mainland content operations from the rest of their business ... Once China enters the WTO it will be expected to permit companies with foreign ownership to operate in the country.

(*FEER*, 31 August 2000, p. 38)

Signalling the tough times faced by internet companies in China, an auction of Chinese web sites, domain names, technologies, web content and entire dotcom companies is scheduled for 29 September [2000]. And despite strict government restrictions limiting foreign investment in the internet, the auction will be open to overseas bids.

(*FEER*, 21 September 2000, p. 72)

The first auction of internet companies, which took place on 29 September 2000, was not very successful.

[The] ban on bids by foreign investors may have contributed to the auction's failure ... China's internet companies, like other web stocks worldwide, are having a tough time reviving investor interest after a worldwide decline in demand for internet stocks ... [There is an] absence of clear laws governing internet usage ... China will allow foreign companies to own as much as 49 per cent in domestic web sites a year after China joins the WTO and 50 per cent after that ... [the] vice-president of China's state information centre said at a recent internet conference.

(*IHT*, 2 October 2000, p. 15)

New regulations governing the use of the internet were published on 2 October 2000.

The rules require internet content providers to win the approval of the ministry before they can receive foreign capital, co-operate with foreign businesses or list domestic or overseas stock. 'The proportion of foreign investment must conform with relevant laws and administrative regulations,' the rules say.

(*IHT*, 3 October 2000, p. 19)

More than $1 billion in foreign capital is believed to have been invested in Chinese dotcoms by venture capitalists and many of the world's largest media companies over the past two years ... Many Chinese dotcoms, often majority-owned by foreigners, have not received MII [ministry of information technology and telecommunications industries] permission for their infusions of foreign capital ... Beijing has promised to allow 49 per cent foreign ownership in internet content providers on entry into the WTO, rising to 50 per cent two years after that.

(*FT*, 3 October 2000, p. 12)

INSURANCE

In late 1992 China issued its first licence to a foreign insurance company, though it was restricted to Shanghai (*IHT*, 16 February 1995, p. 13). On 12 July 1995 it was announced that foreign companies would also be allowed to sell insurance in Guangzhou (*IHT*, 13 July 1995, p. 17). The city of Guangzhou has been opened to foreign insurance companies (*IHT*, 21 October 1995, p. 13). Plans to establish the first life-insurance joint venture are announced (*IHT*, 4 May 1996, p. 13).

RETAILING

In 1991 a Japanese retailer became the first foreign company to win permission to open a joint venture department store (*FEER*, 24 December 1992, pp. 72–3).

China Briefing (October 1992, no. 42, pp. 1–5) reported the decision in late June 1992 to open up the retail trade sector to joint ventures with foreign companies on an experimental basis. Until then foreign investment had been confined to food services (e.g. MacDonald's) and small supermarkets (mostly attached to foreign hotels). In early September it was announced that foreign companies would be able to establish joint travel agencies, albeit with operations restricted to holiday resorts catering for overseas tourists.

There are six cities where foreign ventures can engage in retailing: Beijing, Tianjin, Shanghai, Guangzhou, Dalian and Qingdao (*IHT*, 11 April 1994, p. 12). In 1995 China plans to allow one or two foreign retailers to operate supermarket chains in joint ventures. The Chinese partner's stake would exceed 50 per cent (*IHT*, 2 January 1995, p. 7). According to the original policy in 1992, only 'one or two' Sino-foreign joint ventures are permitted in the twelve locations (including the five SEZs, Shanghai, Beijing, Tianjin, Guangzhou, Dalian and Qingdao). It was recently announced that only one Sino-foreign joint venture would be permitted to operate a national chain of stores. In August 1994 it was confirmed that a further six cities would be open to joint ventures in retailing (Harbin, Wuhan, Nanjing, Xian, Shenyang and Chongqing) (*China Briefing*, December 1994, p. 49, pp. 7–8). Fourteen joint venture department stores in eleven cities have been approved (*FT*, 5 October 1995, p. 6).

On 21 April 1998 China announced a ban on direct (door-to-door) selling. Domestic and foreign companies (like Avon Products from the USA) were ordered to wind up or apply for licences as conventional retailers by 31 October 1998. The stated reasons for the ban included 'false publicity', the luring of consumers into buying 'excessively high-priced' goods and pyramid schemes. 'The plight of the major US direct sellers highlights a familiar concern of foreigners doing business in China: they have little protection against wild swings in the commercial environment' (*IHT*, 25 April 1998, p. 15).

> China's rationale for the ban is simple: without thorough regulation, direct marketing can easily turn into a pyramid scheme. In such cases people can buy overpriced products that cannot be returned. The only way to make money is to bring more people into the network. When a network stops growing those who joined last are stuck with their unsold wares. Those who started the scam vanish. These schemes are now rampant, started mostly by domestic companies. There is no evidence that foreign companies are running scams.
>
> (Matt Forney, *FEER*, 30 April 1998, p. 69)

In July 1998 the US company Amway Corporation (a distributor of soap and hair-care products) was given permission to resume direct sales provided that its agents act as conventional salespeople rather than purchasing products for resale (*IHT*, 22 July 1998, p. 15).

> The state economic and trade commission has announced an amendment of the rules to encourage further foreign participation in retailing joint ventures in a

number of cities previously off-limits and to start joint ventures in wholesaling. The new regulations allow foreign companies to operate retailing and whole-saling business in most large cities, including the capitals of provinces and autonomous regions. Foreign retailers had previously been restricted – in theory if not always in practice – to eleven cities including Beijing and Shang-hai. Beijing's plans should help clarify the status of many foreign-invested stores, which have fallen foul of a sweeping review of the retailing sector last year [1998]. This threw into doubt the scores of Sino-foreign retailing joint ventures, mostly in the provinces, which were approved by local administrations but not Beijing.

(*FT*, 12 July 1999, p. 6)

'Foreign retailers in China can hold up to 65 per cent of a retail joint venture' (*FEER*, 24 October 2002, p. 31).

TRANSPORT AND COMMUNICATIONS

On 6 August 1993 it was announced that joint ventures would be allowed in road and dock management.

On 25 January 1993 China announced that foreigners would be allowed to invest solely or jointly in the construction of motorways, bridges and tunnels and to invest solely in the construction of private docks and waterways for cargo shipping (*FT*, 26 January 1993, p. 4).

POWER

China recently announced that it would allow 100 per cent foreign ownership of power utilities (Tony Walker, *FT*, 30 March 1993, p. 32).

On 11 November 1996 it was announced that the contract for the first wholly foreign-owned build–operate–transfer (BOT) power station had been awarded. The station would be transferred to the government after fifteen years of operation (*FT*, 12 November 1996, p. 6). The formal signing of the agreement took place on 3 September 1997 (*FT*, 4 September 1997, p. 6).

CAR PRODUCTION

In April 1994 it was announced that no more joint ventures for cars would be approved for up to three years. After that new car-assembly plants would be approved only if they bought at least 40 per cent of their components inside China and raised the proportion to 60 per cent within three years (*The Economist*, 16 April 1994, p. 103). China's vehicle sector policy was issued in February 1994 and published in full in July. No new manufacturing joint ventures were to be approved until 1996. Preference would be given to foreign-invested companies operating in China whose operations included an element of component manufacture (*China Briefing*, October 1994, p. 5). On 19 October 1995 two Japanese companies won clearance to buy a 25 per cent stake in a Chinese car maker, the first such deal since

China revived stock markets in 1990. Foreigners have been confined to 'B' shares and have not been allowed to buy corporate or 'legal person' shares in listed Chinese companies (*IHT*, 20 October 1995, p. 19). China has announced that it 'has just lifted' its ban on new car plants and that import tariffs will be lowered by 30 per cent as of 1 April 1996 (*IHT*, 8 January 1996, p. 12).

AIRLINES

On 5 December 1993 it was announced that joint-venture airlines would be allowed in 1994. Foreigners would also be permitted to invest in commercial airports and run all operations except air traffic control. Similar investment would be allowed in other parts of the transport system and infrastructure (*IHT*, 6 December 1993, p. 5). The details were announced on 27 May 1994 (*IHT*, 28 May 1994, p. 15; *FT*, 28 May 1994, p. 4): (1) there would be a small number of initial experiments; (2) foreign investors would be restricted to a maximum stake of 35 per cent in airlines and of 49 per cent in airports; (3) foreigners would be allowed a maximum 25 per cent of voting rights; (4) the positions of chairman and general manager would go to (mainland) Chinese.

SHIPPING

On 26 June 1994 it was announced that foreign ownership would be allowed in the shipping industry, but generally only on a minority basis (Tony Walker, *FT*, 27 June 1994, p. 4).

GOLD MINING

China has opened up ten gold mines to foreign investment. Investors must sell all output to the state at 10 per cent below market prices (*FEER*, 1 December 1994, p. 81). (On 4 September 1994 China published its first official figure for gold production, namely 90 tonnes in 1993.)

TOBACCO

New joint ventures in tobacco processing and the production of cigarettes and filters have been banned through the year 2000 in order to help domestic enterprises hurt by a government anti-smoking campaign (*FEER*, 8 August 1996, p. 65).

AGRICULTURE

The forty-six-year-old ban on the leasing of crop land to foreigners has been lifted (*FEER*, 17 October 1996, p. 111).

STEEL

China has permitted foreign control in its strategic steel industry. But even more striking ... China has tentatively begun allowing foreigners an additional liberty ... the right to hire and fire workers on the basis of merit alone ... Officially, as of last week, what used to be the Nanjing No. 2 Steelworks has become Sharp Base Steel Co., a joint venture controlled by Glencore Asia Ltd, part of the giant Swiss commodity-trading group Glencore International ... China has preferred to attract foreign know-how by having overseas companies build factories from scratch. Now that approach may be giving way to a practice of handing over unprofitable state companies that might otherwise have closed ... Critical to sealing the Glencore deal – which involves no technology transfer – was acquiring the right not only to shed excess workers from the state-owned plant but, more important, the right to hire and fire for the life of the deal ... Glencore ... [paid] for the twenty-year right to run the twenty-year-old mill ... [Glencore] committed itself to a profit-sharing agreement with the Chinese government, as well as a fixed amount of revenue it must hand over for every tonne of iron sold. It has committed itself to exporting 70 per cent of its product.

(*IHT*, 21 May 1999, pp. 1, 4)

BANKS

In March 1999 the central bank governor announced that foreign banks would be allowed to set up branches in all major cities. Previously they had been restricted to twenty-three cities and Hainan Island (*FEER*, 25 March 1999, p. 22).

China has relaxed restrictions on foreign banks ... Foreign banks have been permitted for the first time to take interbank loans with maturities of longer than four months, geographical limits on twenty-five foreign banks' activities have been relaxed, and prohibitions on forming lending consortia, charging related fees and on inter-branch transfers within the same twenty-five banks have been lifted ... Only some nineteen foreign banks in Shanghai and six in Shenzhen, a city near Hong Kong, are permitted to conduct renminbi business in China and, even then, they are allowed to take deposits and make loans only to foreign-invested companies.

(*FT*, 27 August 1999, p. 4)

HSBC, the London-based international bank, will today [29 December 2001] sign a deal to take an 8 per cent stake in Bank of Shanghai ... The Shanghai municipal government is Bank of Shanghai's majority shareholder ... The deal marks the first equity investment by an overseas bank in a Chinese counterpart since the communist government came to power in 1949 ... In 1984 HSBC became the first overseas bank granted a Chinese banking licence since 1949 and was among the first permitted to conduct business in renminbi.

(*FT*, 29 December 2001, p. 15)

(HSBC was founded in 1865 in Hong Kong and Shanghai.)

'Becoming the first foreign banks to buy into a mainland Chinese lender, HSBC Holdings and Hong Kong's Shanghai Commercial Bank agree to take minority stakes [of 8 per cent and 3 per cent, respectively] in the Bank of Shanghai' (*FEER*, 10 January 2002, p. 29).

'Foreign banks have less than 2 per cent of all deposits and loans' (*IHT*, 11 May 2002, p. 4).

> Foreign banks ... [account for] about 2 per cent ... of China's total banking assets ... Even the biggest overseas lenders are limited in the services they can provide, because China restricts them to offering foreign-currency accounts to local customers and doing local-currency business with foreign clients in nine cities.
>
> (www.iht.com, 10 May 2002)

> Citibank, the US financial giant, has won Chinese government approval to buy its first minority stake in a mainland bank ... Under the planned deal Citibank is set to buy 8.26 per cent of the Shanghai Pudong Development Bank ... The German savings-and-loans group Bausparkasse Schwabisch Hall has won approval to establish a joint venture in northern China with China Construction Bank.
>
> (*FT*, 2 January 2003, p. 18)

> BNP Paribas has created China's first wholly foreign-owned bank ... BNP Paribas formed the institution, which so far consists of a single office, by taking over the share of its Chinese partner in a Shanghai bank set up as a joint venture in 1992 ... China has promised as part of its commitments to the WTO that by 2006 it will give foreign banks the same treatment as local institutions.
>
> (*IHT*, 28 November 2003, p. 12)

> China on Monday [1 December 2003] made it easier for foreign banks to enter its markets, lowering capital requirements and allowing foreign bankers to enter four more cities and to take bigger stakes in Chinese banks ... A single investor [will be allowed] to hold up to 20 per cent of a Chinese bank, up from 15 per cent.
>
> (*IHT*, 2 December 2003, p. 15)

> Capital requirements imposed on foreign banks' business in China would be reduced ... for banks offering renminbi services to foreign customers ... [and for] foreign banks incorporated in China ... The maximum stake a single foreign investor may take in a Chinese bank has been raised from 15 per cent to 20 per cent, but the maximum stake by all foreign interests remains at 25 per cent ... Foreign banks would be allowed to do renminbi business in [four more cities] ... bringing the total number of cities to thirteen. [Foreign bankers'] market share is a tiny 1.4 per cent.
>
> (*FT*, 2 December 2003, p. 15)

> Just one week after it raised the ceiling for foreign investments in Chinese banks to 20 per cent, regulators in Beijing said on Monday [8 December] that they would ease requirements and procedures for prospective buyers. The changes, aimed at reducing time-consuming procedures to obtain the Chinese government's approval for any purchase of a domestic financial institution, will take effect on 31 December 'The rules change the previous ad hoc approvals for foreign bank purchases of local banks, reduce divergence and

uncertainty of such deals and improve transparency and efficiency of the regulations,' the banking commission said. China is also giving foreign banks more access to its population. Last week it allowed eighty-four overseas banks, including Citigroup and HSBC, to provide local currency services to Chinese companies for the first time. Overseas banks can also operate in four new cities, bringing the total to thirteen. The regulator is also lowering capital requirements for foreign banks operating in China.

(www.iht.com, 8 December 2003)

Gradually opening up the banking market in line with China's WTO commitments, regulators cleared four foreign banking giants to conduct renminbi-denominated business with domestic firms. Citigroup's Citibank, HSBC. Hong Kong-based Bank of East Asia and Japan's Mizuho Financial Group would be allowed to undertake such business in thirteen cities ... including Shanghai, Shenzhen, Tianjin, Dalian, Guangzhou, Fuzhou and Chongqing.

(*FEER*, 19 February 2004, p. 27)

RAIL FREIGHT

'China will allow foreign companies to take minority holdings in rail freight joint ventures next year [2002] and to hold majority stakes from 2004' (*IHT*, 24 October 2001, p. 14).

FUND MANAGEMENT

International fund managers got the right in early December [2001] to operate joint ventures in China ... Foreign fund managers ... under China's WTO agreements can take a one-third stake in local fund-management firms, with the limit rising to 49 per cent after three years ... The joint venture companies will be able to manage funds on behalf of Chinese clients, but not foreign ones.

(*FEER*, 10 January 2002, p. 29)

(See the following section on more recent chronological developments regarding conditions affecting DFI in specific sectors.)

More recent chronological developments regarding conditions affecting FDI

Two pivotal transactions may herald the beginning of a new era of mergers and acquisitions in China. Emerson ... announced on 21 October [2001] it was acquiring Avansys, a specialized power systems maker for telephone networks, owned by Huawei Technologies, the private Chinese telecoms company, for $750 million. Just days later Alcatel, the French telecoms-equipment maker, announced it was paying $312 million to gain control of its joint venture Shanghai Bell Company.

(*FT*, Survey, 15 March 2002, p. iii)

Two recent deals appear to signal the beginning of a proper market for mergers and acquisitions. Emerson, an American electronics company, bought 100 per cent of a division of Huawei, a privately run telecoms-equipment maker that is considered one of China's best companies ... Alcatel of France increased its stake in a state-owned enterprise in Shanghai, thereby gaining control. Both deals were modest – less than $1 billion – but they are the first two foreign takeovers of Chinese companies.

(*The Economist*, 16 March 2002, p. 78)

China gave the first licence to a foreign bank to do business with domestic clients, a landmark in opening its financial sector to overseas institutions. Xiamen International Bank, a Sino-foreign joint venture bank based in Xiamen in the south-east province of Fujian, received approval to provide domestic clients with foreign currency services.

(*FEER*, 21 March 2002, p. 29)

Citibank became the first wholly-owned foreign bank to win approval from China's central bank to provide hard currency services to Chinese individuals at its Shanghai branch ... Before Citibank's success foreign banks were restricted to providing foreign currency services to non-Chinese citizens and foreign companies. They also remain barred from offering renminbi services to Chinese individuals.

(*FEER*, 28 March 2002, p. 28)

The Chinese securities regulatory commission issued long-awaited regulations to give foreign fund managers and brokerages limited access from 1 July to domestic A-shares markets. The new rules ... gave the go-ahead to foreign firms to take up to 33 per cent stakes in brokerage and fund-management joint ventures. From July joint venture asset-management firms can trade A shares and sell their products to domestic investors. Sino-foreign brokerages will be allowed to under-write but not trade A shares. A shares are currently closed to foreign investors ... Foreign firms can take stakes of up to 33 per cent in fund-management firms, rising to 49 per cent three years from China's entry into the WTO last December [2001]. They can either set up a new joint venture or invest in an existing domestic-fund firm. Sino-foreign securities houses can underwrite all Chinese share offerings, but they are restricted to brokering B shares and bonds.

(*FEER*, 13 June 2002, p. 28)

China has allowed its most successful Special Economic Zone, Shenzhen, to accelerate market access for foreign investors ... Shenzhen has recently been given approval by the central government to open up twenty key service sectors ahead of the WTO timetable ... The areas to be opened in Shenzhen ahead of the WTO timetable include financial services, securities, ports, hospitals, procurement centres, tourism and logistics. Details are being formulated, but in several cases foreign companies would be allowed to assume full or majority ownership of business operations one or two years earlier than stipulated under the WTO agreement.

(*FT*, 17 June 2002, p. 8)

China plans to raise the foreign ownership limit for domestic airlines to 49 per cent from 35 per cent ... The new rules, which are to take effect from 1 August [2002], will also allow foreigners for the first time to hold the posts of president or chief executive of a domestic airline. But each foreign investor is limited to a maximum 25 per cent stake and the Chinese partner must always hold a majority.

(IHT, 3 July 2002, p. 13)

Caps on foreign investments in domestic airlines and airports will be lifted from 1 August ... The Civil Aviation Administration ... said it would only require that Chinese partners retain a controlling interest in domestic airlines, doing away with the current 35 per cent ceiling on foreign stakes. A single foreign firm, including its affiliates, would not be allowed to own more than 25 per cent of a Chinese airline ... For airports the new rules are less clear. The current 49 per cent cap on foreign ownership will be capped and Chinese shareholders will have to keep a 'relative controlling interest', according to the statement. A separate report in the state-run China News Service said foreign investors may be able to take control of companies offering airfreight warehousing, ground handling and catering.

(FEER, 11 July 2002, p. 28)

The railways have been one of the most tightly controlled areas of the planned economy but foreigners will be permitted to take a minority stake in cargo joint ventures from this year [2002]. Under WTO rules foreigners can hold majority stakes in railway freight joint ventures from 2004, with all restrictions lifted after 2006. Passenger services will be closed to offshore investment. However, senior rail officials say China will welcome foreign investment in railway construction on long-term build–operate–transfer contracts ... Despite steady growth rail's share of the overall transport market fell sharply until the late 1990s. In 1990 rail carried more than 70 per cent of total freight and over 53 per cent of passengers. By 2000 just 51 per cent of freight and 36 per cent of passengers moved by rail ... With a massive $42 billion in spending the government plans to add 7,000 kilometres of new track to the sprawling 68,000-kilometre rail network by 2005 ... Railway reform is a key plank of a huge infrastructure spending programme ... China is now betting that new east–west rail lines will be catalysts for an internal economic boom ... The growth of the road network ... has been little short of astonishing ... An explosion in trucking and other transport services has complemented rail services on existing routes between major cities.

(FEER, 18 July 2002, pp. 27–9)

With only three exceptions, foreign logistics firms cannot operate outside the country's free-trade zones unless they form joint ventures ... Maersk, APL and O&O Nedlloyd ... are the only firms that can operate nationwide as fully foreign-owned logistics companies ... Until 2004 other foreign firms have to operate as joint venture partners or only in free-trade zones that handle imports and exports. Dozens of companies, though, have joint ventures with passive local partners who simply take a share of revenues ... China's WTO agreements allow full foreign ownership of nationwide logistics companies from November 2004.

(*FEER*, 25 July 2002, pp. 29–30)

'Foreign logistics firms are to be allowed to set up joint ventures in five cities and three provinces' (*FEER*, 8 August 2002, p. 23).

Becoming the first foreign firm to run a Chinese bank, United States-based Newbridge Capital took over management control of Shenzhen Development Bank to give it experience with international management. The medium-sized bank said its board had appointed an eight-member 'interim management committee'. The San Francisco buy-out and investment firm is reportedly in talks with the bank to take a stake of about 20 per cent.

(*FEER*, 24 October 2002, p. 31)

Newbridge Capital, a US investment firm, has won central government approval to acquire a controlling stake in the Shenzhen Development Bank ... the first time that a foreign financial institution has won government approval to acquire the controlling stake in a mainland bank ... Newbridge is negotiating to take a stake of about 20 per cent ... making it by far the biggest stakeholder in the bank because about 72 per cent of the share capital is already listed ... Newbridge is [being] permitted to buy the unlisted 'legal person' shares of a state entity that is listed on China's renminbi-denominated A-share market – a class of shares hitherto off-limits to foreigners.

(*FT*, 9 October 2002, p. 25)

Shenzhen Development Bank, the first Chinese bank to be listed on the stock exchange, announced yesterday [12 May 2003] that the transfer of a controlling stake of about 20 per cent of its shares to Newbridge would not proceed ... Newbridge demanded the Shenzhen city government stick [to the agreement].

(*FT*, 13 May 2003, p. 25)

'In December [2002] China for the first time allowed foreign equity investment in a part of the print media – retail newspaper, magazine, and book distribution' (*FEER*, 10 July 2003, p. 30).

By 2007 foreign banks will be allowed to offer full services in both foreign and domestic firms and individuals in China ... ... Between them the big four [state-owned banks] – the Agricultural Bank of China, the Industrial and Commercial Bank of China, the China Construction Bank and the Bank of China – control three-quarters of the country's deposits and commercial loans.

(*FEER*, 16 January 2003, p. 31)

Citibank, a unit of US financial giant Citigroup, said it had secured the right to raise its stake in China's Pudong Development Bank to a quarter by the end of April 2008. If exercised the option would give Citibank an unprecedented foothold in a largely untapped market of $1.2 trillion in personal savings ... No foreign player now owns more then 10 per cent of a domestic lender.

(*FEER*, 8 May 2003, p. 25)

To help an industry hurt by SARS China will allow foreign investors to set up wholly owned travel agencies, more than two years ahead of schedule, the state press said Monday [16 June 2003]. The new rules take effect on 14 July. Travel agencies will be allowed in Beijing and Shanghai, as well as Guangzhou and Shenzhen ... and Xian in northern Shaanxi Province. They will be restricted to offering tours to citizens of China, for travel in China. Tours will exclude the special administrative regions of Hong Kong and Macau or Taiwan.

(IHT, 17 June 2003, p. 2)

'China said that from 14 July it would allow travel agencies and hold majority stakes in travel agencies ... Certain resorts [in China will also be eligible]' *(FEER,* 26 June 2003, p. 25).

In another development ... [China] said it was opening up the insurance markets in two south-western cities, Chongqing and Chengdu, to foreign companies. In March [2003] the [insurance regulatory] agency opened the insurance market in Beijing, Tianjin and Suzhou. Shanghai, Guangzhou, Shenzhen, Dalian, Foshan, Dongguan, Jingmen and Haikou have been open to foreign insurance companies for some time. By the end of 2004 all geographical restrictions on the insurance business will be lifted.

(FEER, 26 June 2003, p. 25)

China's government needs to do much more to improve its business environment to attract high quality FDI from industrialized countries, according to the OECD ... The OECD said China needs to keep making laws and regulations conform to internationally recognized standards if it wants to attract more high quality foreign investors. 'Much FDI in China still takes the form of short-term, labour-intensive manufacturing, while investment in hi-tech activities, particularly in service sectors, lags behind,' the report said.

(FEER, 17 July 2003, p. 27)

Ending a domestic bank monopoly on car-loan services ... China's bank regulator issued [on 3 October 2003] long-delayed rules permitting [subject to specified conditions] foreign car makers to set up vehicle-finance operations ... The regulations allow both non-financial enterprises such as car manufacturers and non-bank financial institutions to form 'auto-financing companies', or AFCs, to provide loans to both car dealers and individual buyers.

(FEER, 16 October 2003, p. 34)

BP said Monday [12 January 2004] that it would sell its holding in PetroChina, ending a four-year investment in China's biggest oil producer. BP, Europe's largest oil company ... said it was selling the stake, which it bought for about $578 million at PetroChina's initial public offering in 2000, as part of a strategy to divest minority investments ... [BP said] it is not part of BP's strategy to hold minority stakes for a long period of time ... The stake could fetch as much as $1.7 billion ... Though BP's stake is equivalent to 20 per cent of PetroChina's equity, the holding represents a fifth of the state-controlled company's tradable shares ... PetroChina is 90 per cent owned by the state ... PetroChina said the share sale did not signal that BP was pessimistic about prospects for continued growth in China's oil industry.

(www.iht.com, 12 January 2004)

BP has unloaded its 2 per cent stake in PetroChina in a sale that will bring Europe's largest listed company a profit of ... just over $1 billion ... BP, which earned $200 in pretax dividends, sold its share ... for an aggregate of more than $1.7 billion ... [BP said] it remained committed to its business with PetroChina and its other partners in China, where ... [it said it] would be investing $3 billion during the next five years ... Relations between BP and PetroChina have been through strained periods – the most painful in 2002 when BP decided to pull out of talks on taking a stake in an $18 billion gas pipeline ... Another testing period came after pro-Tibet activists campaigned to persuade BP to divest its stake in PetroChina because of the Chinese company's alleged lack of environmental sensitivity in building a pipeline that crossed ancestral Tibetan lands.

(*FT*, 13 January 2004, p. 21)

The divestment by BP, which had been PetroChina's largest foreign investor, has raised concern among investors that ... [BP] might also sell its holding in China Petroleum Chemical, Asia's largest oil refiner ... also known as Sinopec ... BP, Exxon Mobil and Royal Dutch/Shell Group ... bought stakes in PetroChina and Sinopec in 2000 ... [The latter two] are Sinopec's largest foreign investors. Exxon Mobil owned 18.9 per cent of its publicly traded shares as of September [2003] and Shell held 11.7 per cent.

(www.iht.com, 13 January 2004)

'BP sold its 2.1 per cent stake in China's Sinopec in a share placement worth some $744 million after ditching its 2 per cent position in China's biggest oil firm, PetroChina, for $1.66 billion in January.

(*FEER*, 19 February 2004, p. 26)

Regulations that effectively came into force on 1 April [2004] ... foreign construction firms charge ... bar them from taking on new work amid China's furious construction boom – and violate WTO rules. Their cause received reinforcement from visiting EU Commission President Romano Prodi, who, in a speech in Shanghai on 11 April, condemned 'new rules in the construction sector which in practice make market access in this sector almost impossible for our companies' ... [But] it is not all bad news ... Construction companies can now be wholly foreign owned. Previously they had to partner up with a local firm.

(*FEER*, 13 May 2004, pp. 30–4)

'Foreign companies will be allowed to take a 50 per cent stake in joint venture life insurance companies ... The new rule will take effect on 15 June [2004]' (*FEER*, 3 June 2004, p. 477).

Newbridge Capital, a San Francisco-based buy-out company, said Monday [31 May 2004] it will buy an 18 per cent stake in Shenzhen Development Bank ...

The economy 607

after a year-long legal battle with the lender's shareholders ... [In April 2004 Newbridge] withdrew a lawsuit against the shareholders for reneging on a September 2002 sale agreement ... China's government gave Newbridge permission in September 2002 to buy as much as 15 per cent of Shenzhen Bank, a purchase that would have made the US company the first overseas investor to own a Chinese bank. In May 2003 Shenzhen Bank said it ended talks ... Newbridge sued the four shareholders – Shenzhen Investment Management, Shenzhen International Trust Investment, Shenzhen Social Security and Shenzhen Chengjian Development Group – at the Paris-based International Chamber of Commerce, claiming unspecified compensation.

(www.iht.com, 31 May 2004)

Newbridge Capital, a US private equity firm ... whose first attempt to buy control of the bank collapsed in 2003 ... is set to become the first foreign investor to win control of a Chinese lender ... As the largest shareholder in the bank, Newbridge will be entitled under Chinese law to appoint a majority of the board, including the chairman.

(*IHT*, 1 June 2004, p. 13)

Newbridge Capital ... has beaten the world's biggest financial institutions to become the first foreigner to gain control of a Chinese bank ... Because individual foreign holdings in Chinese banks are limited to 20 per cent, Newbridge will buy only 18 per cent of Shenzhen Development Bank ... But the deal, sealed on 31 May [2004] permits the Americans to appoint a majority of the fifteen-strong board. They will thus be able to run SDB, the main bank in the city ... SDB is small enough to let go of, with assets of only $25 million, 300 branches and around 4,000 employees. The ownership of the bank is highly dispersed, with 72 per cent in public hands, allowing Newbridge to gain a lot of power with a smallish stake ... Newbridge was also helped by the fact that its main rival for SDB's affections, Chinatrust of Taiwan, was politically unsuitable.

(*The Economist*, 5 June 2004, pp. 72, 74)

'Under new rules issued by bank regulators in Beijing earlier this year [2004] foreign holdings can go as high as 20 per cent' (*FT*, 1 June 2004, p. 27).

A new law that took effect on 1 June [2004] will throw China's retail and distribution sectors open to foreign competition. From December [2004] foreign retailers will be allowed to set up wholly owned companies and stores anywhere in the country. Currently foreign retailers can only hold up to a 65 per cent stake in a joint venture with a local partner.

(*FEER*, 10 June 2004, 478)

'Honda's new factory is the only car plant in China with majority foreign ownership and the only one manufacturing solely for export ... Honda Automobile (China) Company is 65 per cent owned by Honda of Japan' (*FEER*, 27 May 2004, p. 28). 'A requirement to use China-made parts for at least 40 per cent of a locally produced vehicle was scrapped, but the 50 per cent foreign ownership limit in joint ventures remains' (*FEER*, 10 June 2004, p. 26).

British American Tobacco won approval from the Chinese government on 15 July to become the first foreign manufacturer of cigarettes in China in at least half a century . . . a joint venture between BAT and China Eastern Investments Corp., a BAT importer.

(www.feer.com, 29 July 2004)

(The state tobacco monopoly raised objections.)

China's railway system . . . will begin allowing limited foreign investment. . . [It has been reported that] outside investment would be allowed in branch lines but not, as yet, the most heavily travelled trunk routes. In recent years Beijing has spent heavily to improve the nation's airports and roads but relatively little on rail.

(*FEER*, 5 August 2004, p. 26)

('[In 2004] the government announced that it would allow domestic private invest-ment in local railroads and other infrastructure sectors that were once state monop-olies . . . Today 82 per cent [of railroads] remains under central control, with the rest run by local governments . . . [In June 2005] Shandong province in northern China invited foreigners to bid to build and operate six local rail lines . . . For the first time since 1949 foreign investors could become the sole owners of Chinese rail . . . Shandong's initiative seems to test national investment rules. Those issued last year [2004] do not allow for full foreign ownership of any rail lines, only joint ven-tures': *IHT*, 7 July 2005, pp. 13–14.)

HSBC Holdings . . . said Friday [6 August 2004] that it would acquire a 19.9 per cent stake [worth $1.75 billion] in Bank of Communications in China [BoCom], its third acquisition in the country and the biggest by an overseas lender . . . The deal is subject to regulatory approval . . . The previous biggest financial investment in China [was] also by HSBC. The bank paid about $766 million for 9.9 per cent of Ping An Insurance, China's second largest life insurer.

(*IHT*, 7 August 2004, p. 13)

[The] 19.9 per cent stake [in BoCom is] just below the 20 per cent ceiling on foreign investment in Chinese banks . . . BoCom said that in the wake of its financial shake-up, which ended on 30 June, it had an NPL [non-performing loan] ratio of 3.43 per cent. Shanghai-based BoCom [is] China's fifth largest lender.

(*FT*, Money and Business, 7 August 2004, p. 1)

The investment . . . in Shanghai-based Bank of Communications . . . [is] eight times bigger than any other previous foreign investment in a Chinese bank . . . In recent years it [HSBC] has made other, smaller investments: $63 million for an 8 per cent stake in Bank of Shanghai . . . and $766 million for a 10 per cent stake in Ping An Insurance, China's second largest insurer . . . Chinese regula-tions place a 20 per cent limit on a single foreign investor's stake in a Chinese bank, and a 25 per cent limit on total foreign shareholding of a bank.

(*FEER*, 19 August 2004, pp. 42–4)

'General Motors [GM] has received approval ... to begin lending to car buyers through a joint venture with Shanghai Automotive Industry Corp. The joint venture is the first car loan company to receive official approval to begin operations' (*FEER*, 19 August 2004, p. 30).

General Motors, the world's largest automaker, on Wednesday [18 August] started offering loans through its finance venture in China, betting that access to credit will help bolster sales in the world's third largest vehicle market ... GMAC-SAIC Automotive Finance, 60 per cent owned by the US company, is the first overseas car loan venture ... The four biggest state banks account for more than four-fifths of China's outstanding auto loans.

(www.iht.com, 18 August 2004)

China will let overseas retailers own 100 per cent of their local units on 11 December [2004] ... Currently they are limited to ownership of 65 per cent in their Chinese ventures – a share that has risen from 49 per cent since China joined the WTO in December 2001. To become a member China agreed to let foreign retailers buy domestic competitors without local partners three years after joining. Overseas retailers, currently restricted to provincial capitals and big cities such as Beijing, Shanghai and Shenzhen, will also be cleared to expand to smaller towns nationwide.

(www.iht.com, 31 August 2004)

'The government in December [2004] allowed overseas retailers to open as many wholly owned stores as they like across the nation' (www.iht.com, 27 February 2005).

[It was announced on 8 September 2004] China will let foreign banks conduct local currency business in three more cities, including Beijing by the end of this year [2004]... The addition of Beijing, Kunming and Xiamen brings to sixteen the number of cities where overseas lenders can offer yuan services ... The regulator this month allowed overseas banks to open more branches and eased capital requirements for yuan business ... The chairman of the China banking regulatory commission: 'We have so far kept our commitment on joining the WTO. By the end of 2006 foreign and domestic banks can compete on a level playing field with no differences at all' ... The regulator will open four more cities to yuan services next year [2005] – Xian, Shenyang, Ningbo and Shantou – before fully removing restrictions the following year [2006].

(www.iht.com, 8 September 2004)

[On 1 December 2004] five new cities [were opened] to foreign banks offering local currency services ... Xian and Shenyang [were added to Beijing, Kunming and Xiamen] ... bringing the number of cities ... to eighteen ... Foreign banks still account for just 1.8 per cent of total banking assets.

(*FT*, 2 December 2004, p. 11)

Philip Morris International ... has won approval for the first time to have its Marlboro brand cigarettes made in China, the state-run Longyan Cigarette Factory said Monday [13 September 2004] ... 'The State Monopoly

Administration appointed us to make cigarettes for Philip Morris' [the factory said] ... The monopoly controls production, marketing and trade in China ... Philip Morris, British American Tobacco and other foreign companies, which have a 5 per cent share of the Chinese market, are seeking manufacturing bases in China ... No foreign manufacturer has been allowed to set up its own production facility. Japan Tobacco's ... brands are made in China by Shanghai Gaoyang International Tobacco.

(www.iht.com, 13 September 2004)

'In January [2005] China's civil aviation regulators introduced new rules that in principle allow any company with three planes to operate an airline. Foreign investors can take a stake of up to 25 per cent in these private airlines' (www.iht.com, 28 February 2005).

China has opened up a number of state-owned and once-strategic sectors of its economy to local and foreign private investment ... The sweeping reform – which was announced in a policy document released by the State Council, China's cabinet – will legalize private investment in sectors including power, rail, aviation and oil. Private investment will now also be allowed in the growing local defence industries, including military research companies and weapons manufacturers, the document said ... The document will provide legal cover for a series of existing investments in sectors that are officially off-limits to private capital, but where in fact private capital has already begun to play a role ... The new document ... [includes] a rule giving local entrepreneurs the same rights as foreign investors, while also putting them on level terms for finance, tax and land-use rights with the state. Entrepreneurs will be allowed into any industries unless they are specifically excluded, the new document says ... [but] entrepreneurs will not necessarily be allowed to own majority stakes in all sectors. Chinese corporate law will set the limits of ownership in different sectors ... However, the new policy further extends the recognition and protection of private property and interests which was begun by the ruling Communist Party in 2002.

(*FT*, 26 February 2005, p. 9)

A government document issued in February [2005] allows private investment in any business not banned by law and supposedly guarantees equal access to bank loans. The official media said the document was the first devoted entirely to promoting the interests of private business since the communist takeover in 1949.

(*The Economist*, 19 March 2005, p. 86)

Honda began loading cars aboard a ship Friday [24 June] for export to Europe, marking China's debut as a volume exporter of cars to the industrialized world ... The cars being exported were assembled at a brand new Honda factory that was erected just to supply the European market. By agreeing to export all the cars Honda won the right to own 65 per cent of the factory while its local partners own the rest. China has a 50 per cent cap on foreign investment in car factories supplying the domestic market ... Other multinational automakers in

China already export, but on an extrèmely small scale ... Purely domestic Chinese automakers are starting to export.

(*IHT*, 25 June 2005, pp. 1, 8)

China, the world's biggest producer and consumer of steel, will bar overseas investors from taking controlling stakes in Chinese mills ... It is the first time China has put this in formal regulations, although no foreign producers have ever taken a big stake in mills directly controlled by central government... Overseas steel makers, who own patent technologies, will be allowed to set up joint ventures with Chinese partners rather than build independent new mills.

(www.iht.com, 13 July 2005)

FedEx, the world's largest express freight carrier, said on Wednesday [13 July] that it would shift its hub for Asia-Pacific to the southern Chinese city of Guangzhou ... FedEx's Guanzhou hub will be the company's biggest logistics centre outside the United States ... FedEx will close its current Asia-Pacific hub at Subic Bay in the Philippines ... The agreement signed last year [2004] allowed US cargo carriers to establish logistics hubs in China.

(www.iht.com, 13 July 2005; *IHT*, 14 July 2005, p. 12)

China tightened controls on its television and radio stations, announcing a ban on forming partnerships with foreign broadcasters to operate channels. Chinese broadcasters are also barred from leasing channels to foreign companies ... The rule took effect Thursday [14 July].

(*IHT*, 14 July 2005, p. 14)

In early July China issued a ban on Chinese broadcasters and foreign investors jointly operating television channels, and earlier in the year the government froze Chinese–foreign co-productions of television shows ... China disclosed on Wednesday [3 August] that it had frozen approvals for foreign satellite broadcasters entering its market and would strengthen restrictions on foreign television programmes, books, newspapers and performances in an effort to exercise tighter control over the country's cultural life.

(*IHT*, 4 August 2005, p. 11)

China ... moved to defend 'national cultural security' by ordering tighter controls on foreign involvement in the media market ... The rules forbid 'in principle' the granting of permission for any more foreign television channels or the issuing of new licences for companies to handle cultural imports, areas in which foreign companies are already allowed only minimal access ... This year [2005] Beijing has tightened its limits on production joint ventures and officials are widely seen as moving more slowly to approve investments.

(*FT*, 4 August 2005, p. 7)

General Electric is buying a 7 per cent stake in Shenzhen Development Bank for $100 million ... GE and Newbridge Capital will together own almost 25 per cent of Shenzhen Development, the maximum foreign ownership permitted in a Chinese bank. Newbridge, which bought 17.89 per cent of the bank for $149 million in December [2004], controls the bank's management ...

Shenzhen Development, created in 1987 by municipal government companies, is the smallest of the five Chinese banks traded on domestic stock exchanges. Its $20 billion in customer deposits represented 0.65 per cent of the market at the end of 2004.

(www.iht.com, 23 October 2005)

Carlyle Group, a huge US private equity firm, said Tuesday [25 October] that it had agreed to pay $375 million in cash to acquire majority control of Xugong Construction Machinery Group, the largest maker of building equipment. The deal is one of the biggest private equity deals ever in China and is the first in which a foreign company has engaged in a direct buy-out of a large, state-controlled Chinese company ... Carlyle said that it had agreed to acquire 85 per cent of Xugong from its parent company, which is owned by the city government of Xuzhou, in the south-eastern province of Jiangsu ... Carlyle joined with Prudential Financial this month to take a 24.9 per cent stake in China Pacific Life Insurance, one of the top five Chinese insurance companies.

(*IHT*, 26 October 2005, p. 14)

'The acquisition [by Carlyle Group] ... is the biggest private equity investment yet in China' (*FT*, 27 October 2005, p. 18).

Willis, the New York-listed London-based insurance broker, will announce today [15 November] that it has been granted permission by the Chinese regulator to lift its ownership of Willis Pudong Insurance Brokers, a Chinese insurance broker, to 51 per cent. Willis said it was the first international broker to gain the permission of the China Insurance Regulatory Commission to hold a majority share in a fully licensed Chinese insurance broker. It added that the approval from CIRC gave it control over Willis Pudong, which would become a subsidiary and have its results consolidated into the Wills Group ... Willis gained permission last year [2004] from CIRC to acquire a 50 per cent stake in Pudong Insurance Brokers, a 100 per cent Chinese-owned broker.

(*FT*, 15 November 2005, p. 24)

China has opened seven more cities to foreign banks, raising the number that they can do domestic business in by more than a third and accelerating efforts to attract investment to poorer regions ... The move raised to twenty-five from eighteen the number of cities opened to foreign banks for domestic currency business ... The government is opening five of the cities a year before a 1 December 2006 deadline set by the WTO ... As of 31 October [2005] 138 foreign banks had received approval to do yuan business ... China allows its banks to be 25 per cent owned by foreign banks, with a single institution owning no more than 20 per cent. The 20 per cent cap was raised from 15 per cent in 2003 and Lui Mingkang ... chairman of the China banking regulatory commission ... said it would not be raised again soon. Banks that are more than 25 per cent foreign-owned are classed as joint ventures, and are subject to different operating rules.

(www.iht.com, 5 December 2005; *IHT*, 6 December 2005, p. 19)

Carlyle Group, the global private equity firm, said Monday [19 December] that it had agreed to invest $410 million for a minority stake in China Pacific Life Insurance in one of the largest private equity deals ever done in China. Carlyle said it would acquire a 25 per cent in China Pacific Life, which is the country's third largest insurance company after China Life Insurance and Ping An Insurance, both of which are now publicly listed companies in Hong Kong and the United States ... China Life Insurance and Ping An Insurance went public in 2003 and 2004, together raising over $5 billion ... Together the three life insurers command about 80 per cent of the market ... This is the second major deal in recent months for Carlyle, which last October acquired an 85 per cent stake in the Xugong Group Construction Machinery for 3 billion yuan, or $375 million. That deal marked one of the first times a foreign company had ever engaged in a direct buyout of a Chinese state-owned company.

(*IHT*, 20 December 2005, p. 14)

[In February 2006] Avon Products, the world's largest door-to-door cosmetics distributor, was awarded China's first licence for direct selling after the government lifted a seven-year ban on the practice. The company's permit was issued in February ... The ban on direct selling was imposed in 1998 to wipe out pyramid schemes that caused individuals millions of yuan in losses ... Avon was the first company cleared to test direct selling in China in April [2005] ... in Beijing, the port city of Tianjin and the southern province of Guangdong. Door-to-door sellers have been restricted to selling their products through retail stores since the ban.

(*IHT*, 28 February 2006, p. 21)

Since 1998 a few foreign-invested direct sales companies have been allowed to continue their business in China, but have mainly relied on stores for sales. Last December [2005] Beijing put into effect a detailed set of direct sales regulations that outlined capital minimum requirements, business experience and penalties for violators.

(*FT*, 28 February 2006, p. 7)

China yesterday [2 March] further opened the doors to its natural gas industry when PetroChina, the country's biggest oil company by production, signed an exploration deal with Total, the French energy group. The deal to tap the Sulige field in north-west China is the second such agreement after last year's pact [2005] by PetroChina and Anglo/Dutch Royal Duth Shell to explore for gas in the Changbei natural gas field, which is in the same basin as Sulige ... The [Sulige] field in three to five years' time could produce 5 per cent of China's total gas production ... [PetroChina and Total] have also agreed on the sales side of the deal ... The two companies are also exploring the development of a gas field in Iran.

(*FT*, 3 March 2006, p. 30)

Special Economic Zones (SEZs)

Four Special Economic Zones (SEZs) were set up in 1980, the State Council having given approval in July 1979. They were 'special' in the sense that concessions such as lower taxes and tariffs and more flexible employment policies were granted in order to attract foreign capital, technology and know-how. ('[There] are tax breaks for foreign companies in five SEZs, fourteen "open coastal cities" and some fifty development zones. Foreign investors pay corporate tax at a maximum 15 per cent in SEZs and 24 per cent in open coastal cities and development zones. Chinese companies in the same locations pay a maximum of 33 per cent': *FT*, 18 September 2002, p. 20.)

The SEZs were essentially built from scratch, a means of experimenting with new ideas in a gradual and partial manner. New ideas and Western influences would only be spread to the remainder of the economy if and when they had proved their worth. It is no coincidence that three of the SEZs (Shenzhen, Zhuhai and Shantou) are in Guangdong province adjacent to Hong Kong and Macao, while the fourth is Xiamen in Fujian province opposite Taiwan. Hainan Island became the fifth SEZ in 1988.

> The industrial sector was placed at the centre stage of SEZ economies ... Domestic enterprises, state- and nonstate-owned alike, were purposely allowed to operate alongside foreign-invested firms. Firms in the zone were encouraged to establish connections of various sorts with their counterparts in the rest of the domestic economy in order to foster technology transfers and to promote growth through the expanded economic links ... [But] as a precaution taken to minimize possible negative impacts on the rest of the economy, should the SEZ efforts later fail, all four zones were set up in backward areas.
>
> (Ge 1999: 1269)

> As the testing ground for developing a market-oriented, open economy numerous reform measures have first been experimented in the SEZs and those useful ones are later introduced into the rest of the economy ... One example of these reforms has been the SEZ effort in revitalizing state-owned enterprises ... [e.g.] employment is now based on labour contracts ... Ownership structure is changing from a pure state ownership to a mixed one; private and foreign investors may have a piece of pie by owning enterprise stocks ... Foreign direct investment in the tertiary sector, such as retailing, insurance, banking and other financial and information services are expanding. Stock, bond and futures markets are developing. Experimentation with utilizing foreign portfolio investment is already underway.
>
> (pp. 1281–2)

No new SEZs have been approved since 1988, but there has been a proliferation of economic development zones with various names. In 1984 fourteen major east coast cities (including Shanghai) were opened to foreign investment. Governed by regulations similar to those in the SEZs, several hundred economic and technological development zones were set up in these open areas. Shortly afterwards open areas were extended to the Pearl, Yangtzi and South Fujian deltas, as well as the

Liaoning and Jiaodong peninsulas. In 1988 the 'coastal area economic development strategy' was approved, almost the entire coastal area being opened to the outside world. In April 1990 the Pudong New Area was established in Shanghai. Since the early 1990s the entire border area of China and many inland regions have been opened up (Ge 1999: 1282).

The SEZs have not had a smooth ride. For example, in 1985 Deng Xiaoping described Shenzhen as 'an experiment that remains to be proved' (e.g. the volume of exports and the level of technology attracted were disappointing). Deng visited Shenzhen and Zhuhai in early 1992 and gave his approval. But in early 1993 the central government clamped down on the spread of other zones, often set up without central government approval, in order to dampen the construction boom. Although their immediate future is secure, the concessions granted to all development zones are to be gradually phased out over the longer term. (This is a requirement of WTO membership. The section on the WTO, above, includes material on the conditions relating to DFI.)

> Authorities have already begun dismantling some of the useless projects that officials built in pursuit of GDP growth and promotions. These include thousands of 'development zones', which local governments carved out of requisitioned farmland to build villas, golf courses and resorts, leaving farmers landless and jobless. A report in November [2004] by the ministry of land resources said local governments had cut the number of development zones from 5,658 to 3,612 and frozen approval of new zones.
>
> (*FEER*, 1 April 2004, p. 31)

'China has 6,749 registered industrial and investment zones ... The central government has tried to control their growth but has largely failed because provinces, cities, towns and villages are all competing with each other for business to create local employment' (*FT*, Survey, 7 December 2004, p. 3).

'Official incentives for FDI are shrinking: the preferential 15 per cent corporation tax rate enjoyed by foreign companies, half the level for their Chinese counterparts, will be phased out by 2006' (*FT*, Survey, 7 December 2004, p. 2).

> [On 11 January 2005 China said that it] will maintain preferential tax rates for foreign companies until at least 2007 ... Foreign companies are subject to an average 15 per cent tax rate, less than half of the 33 per cent paid by Chinese companies ... The government [had] planned to unify the corporate tax code as early as 2006 ... [Apart from foreign companies investing in China] Chinese companies that are eligible for tax exemptions are also lobbying for the corporate tax law to be delayed.
>
> (www.iht.com, 11 January 2005; *IHT*, 12 January 2005, p. 13)

'The government said on Tuesday [12 July] that it would keep tax breaks for some foreign investors because rising labour costs and raw material shortages had made the need for technology transfers and management expertise more urgent' (www.iht.com. 13 July 2005).

Economic performance

Although China still has a relatively low *per capita* GDP, since 1978 economic performance has generally been very impressive. (See Table 1: the table presents the earlier official Chinese figures for rates of growth of GDP, whereas the section below entitled 'The upward revision of 2004 GDP' gives the revised figures.) Indeed, China's rapid expansion of late has been of global significance, e.g. world market prices of commodities such as oil, coal, iron ore, steel and cement have been affected, and China has become one of the world's foremost destinations for direct foreign investment.

'[China's is] one of the largest and most sustained expansions in history' (Larry Rohter, www.iht.com, 19 November 2004).

> The pace of economic change in China has been extremely rapid since the start of economic reforms just over twenty-five years ago. Economic growth has averaged 9.5 per cent over the past two decades and seems likely to continue at that pace for some time. Such an increase in output represents one of the most sustained and rapid economic transformations seen in the world economy in the past fifty years. It has delivered higher incomes and a substantial reduction of those living in absolute poverty ... A marked evolution of economic policies over the past two decades has led to a long period of sustained economic expansion. National income has been doubling every eight years and this has been reflected in the reduction of the poverty rate to much lower levels. Indeed, by some accounts, over half of the reduction in absolute poverty in the world between 1980 and 2000 occurred in China.
>
> (OECD 2005: website Chapter 1)

> During their industrial revolutions America and Britain took fifty years to double their real incomes per head; today China is achieving that in a single decade ... Until the late nineteenth century China and India were the world's two biggest economies.
>
> (*The Economist*, 21 January 2006, pp. 12–13)

China's global significance can be gauged from the following:

'China ... consumed 40 per cent of the world's cement, 27 per cent of its steel and 31 per cent of its coal' (*FEER*, 1 April 2004, p. 28).

'The National Bureau of Statistics ... calculated that China consumed 30 per cent of the world's coal production last year [2003], 36 per cent of the world's steel and 55 per cent of the world's cement' (*IHT*, 21 January 2004, p. 11). 'Last year [2003] China accounted for one-half of global cement production and about one-third of all steel and coal consumption' (www.iht.com, 1 October 2004).

'[In 2003] China consumed 40 per cent of all the coal and 30 per cent of all the steel in the world' (*The Economist*, Survey, 2 October 2004, p. 8).

'China overtook Japan last year [2003] to become the world's second largest oil consumer' (*FEER*, 10 June 2004, p. 27).

'Last year [2003] China overtook Japan and the EU to become the world's largest importer of iron ore' (www.iht.com. 5 March 2004).

Table 1 China: selected economic indicators.

Economic indicator	1990	1991	1992	1993	1994	1995	1996	1997	1998	1999	2000	2001	2002	2003	2004
Rate of growth of GDP (%)	3.8	9.2	14.2	13.5	12.6	10.5	9.6	8.8	7.8	7.1	8.0	7.3	8.0	9.5	9.5
Rate of growth of industrial output (%)	7.8	12.9	20.8	23.6	18.0	13.9	12.1	10.8	8.8		9.9		12.6	18.1	
Rate of growth of agricultural output (%)	7.6	3.0	3.7	4.0	3.5	5.0	5.1	3.5	3.5						
Grain output (million tonnes)	435.0	435.3	442.6	456.4	444.5				512.0	508.0		450.0		430.6	469.5
Retail or consumer inflation rate (%)	2.1	2.7	5.4	13.0	21.7	14.8	6.1	1.5	−2.6	−2.9	−1.5		−0.8	1.2	3.9
Population (billion)		1.158	1.170							1.259	1.265	1.272			1.300
Balance of trade ($billion)														25.50	31.90
Foreign exchange reserves ($billion)				21.2				139.9		154.67	165.6	212.2	286.4	403.25	609.9

Source: Various issues of IMF, *World Economic Outlook*; United Nations, *World Economic and Social Survey*; United Nations Economic and Social Commission for Asia and the Pacific, *Economic and Social Survey of Asia and the Pacific*; FEER; OECD, *Economic Outlook*; FT; and *IHT*; Jeffries (1996a: 696).

The State of the World 2006, released by the Worldwatch Institute, says that
last year [2005] China became the second largest importer of oil after the
United States, while consuming 26 per cent of the world's steel, 32 per cent of
rice production, 37 per cent of cotton and 47 per cent of cement ... China now
obtains about 28 per cent of its oil imports from Africa – mainly Angola,
Sudan and Congo.

(*The Times*, 12 January 2006, pp. 42–3)

In PPP [purchasing-power parity] terms the country contributed 1.1 per cent
[percentage points] of the world's 3.2 per cent growth last year [2003], against
0.7 per cent [percentage points] from the United States and 0.2 per cent [per-
centage points] from Japan and Europe.

(*FT*, 21 January 2004, p. 18)

Using GDP converted at market rates China has accounted for only 17 per cent
of the total increase in global GDP over the past three years; but measured on a
purchasing-power parity (PPP) basis it has contributed almost one-third of
global GDP growth, much more than America's 13 per cent.

(*The Economist*, Survey, 2 October 2004, p. 8)

'China accounted for 13 per cent of global growth in 2004, according to the
IMF' (*IHT*, 16 January 2006, p. 13).

Perhaps it would be more accurate to speak of the country's reemergence. In
1820 China accounted for about 30 per cent of the global economy ... The
United States then weighed in with less than 2 per cent. But by the 1950s
American was dominant and China ... accounted for only about 4 per cent of
world economic activity.

(Roger Cohen, *IHT*, 13 April 2005, p. 2)

GDP growth

There are various estimates of GDP growth. It was once generally thought that official figures exaggerated performance. The *Financial Times* itself usually stresses
the need to knock a couple of percentage points off the official figure for GDP
growth. 'Junior officials [at lower levels of the hierarchy are induced] to massage
reality to impress bosses' (*FT*, 15 February 2003, p. 9). 'Many independent economists believe that this [the official figure of 8 per cent GDP growth in 2002] is
exaggerated by several percentage points' (*The Economist*, 15 February 2003,
p. 74). Others are even more sceptical.

[In 2001] Thomas Rawski, the American economist ... [asserted] that – official claims of economic growth rates of more than 7 per cent notwithstanding –
China's economy since 1998 might not have been growing at all ... This year
[2002] the Central Intelligence Agency stated that China was indeed growing,
but at about half the rate that Chinese officials claimed.

(*FT*, 4 July 2002, p. 17)

[There is a] widespread tendency among officials to lie in order to boost their
political fortunes ... Some economists believe the official growth rate could be

even more at odds with reality, because of such factors as a tendency to over-
value the stocks of unsold goods produced by state-owned factories or to
underestimate inflation. Thomas Rawski ... estimates that growth in 2001 may
have been between 3 per cent and 4 per cent, or about half the official figure.

(*The Economist*, 16 March 2002, p. 69)

Other factors, however, might push the real growth rate closer to the official
one ... [in some provinces in order, for example] to conceal the rapid development of private enterprise ... [or] to avoid having to pay more tax to the
central government.

(*The Economist*, 16 March 2003, p. 70)

Since October 2003 there have been increasing reports that the official estimated
growth rate for the year might actually have been underestimated. 'Most economists believe official figures are underestimated. Power consumption, transport
statistics and other indicators suggest an actual growth rate of more than 11 per
cent' (*FT*, 21 January 2004, p. 18).

Economists [have] warned that China's apparent success in cooling the
economy should be viewed with some scepticism. Many economists have long
complained that China's economic data are unreliable and that after inflating
data in the past, officials could just as easily be underestimating growth now.

(www.iht.com, 17 July 2004)

'The Asian Development Bank ... said [in April 2004 that] China's official
numbers might understate growth because statisticians cannot keep pace with the
rise of the private sector' (www.iht.com, 27 July 2004).

'By official estimates *per capita* income quadrupled from 1978 to 1995' (David
Shambaugh, *IHT*, 1 October 1999, p. 10). 'Deng Xiaoping ... [aimed] to quadruple
the 1980 GNP in two decades. Though it appeared extremely ambitious at the time,
that target was actually met in 1995, five years early' (*FEER*, 9 December 1999, p.
33). 'China's *per capita* GDP has increased more than fivefold in the last twenty
years' (*FT*, 30 September 1999, p. 23). In September 1997 a new aim was set,
namely to double GNP in the first decade of the millennium (*FT*, Survey, 8 December 1997, p. 1). 'Economic output has risen eightfold in the past twenty-five years'
(*The Economist*, 9 November 2002, p. 15). 'China has quadrupled the size of its
economy in the past quarter of a century' (*FEER*, 1 April 2004, p. 28).

'Chinese output is about one-quarter of Japan's and one-ninth that of the United
States' (*IHT*, 18 December 2002, p. 14).

'China is now the fourth-largest industrial producer behind the United States,
Japan and Germany' (*FEER*, 17 October 2002, p. 32).

In 1999 GDP per head (excluding Hong Kong and Macao) was $735 at 1998
prices (*The Economist*, Survey, 8 April 2000, p. 5).

'For the first time China ranks itself with Russia, Brazil and Thailand this year
as a lower-middle income country with a *per capita* of more than $1,000' (*FEER*, 1
April 2004, p. 28). 'The average disposable income in China's towns and cities,
home to a third of the nation's 1.3 billion population, last year [2003] topped
$1,000 for the first time' (www.iht.com, 14 June 2004). 'Last year [2003] the

annual income of urban dwellers passed the $1,000 mark' (*Guardian*, 29 November 2004, p. 16). '*Per capita* disposable income in urban areas, where a third of Chinese citizens live, exceeded $1,000 a year for the first time in 2003' (www.iht.com, 6 January 2005).

> The World Bank ... [ceased to provide] soft loan finance for the country from June 1999 ... China graduated from lending under the World Bank's International Development Association, the bank's soft loan window, because the country's *per capita* income rose above $800 a year, the cut-off point for IDA financing ... China, the bank's largest borrower, has absorbed about $35 billion since 1981.
>
> (*FT*, 18 March 2000, p. 7)

In March 1998 the official target for GDP growth in 1998 was set at 8 per cent, aided by a large-scale, three-year infrastructure investment programme in order to counter the ill effects of the Asian financial crises (which started in July 1997) and of private consumption depressed by rising unemployment, deflation and reduced social service provision. These fiscal boosts continued. (In July 2003 the Three Gorges Dam started to generate electricity: *FEER*, 28 August 2003, p. 25. On 27 December 2003 work began on a project to divert water from south to north: *Guardian*, 28 December 2003, p. 18.) Other policies intended to boost private consumption include extended holidays, starting in 1999.

> Growth of 7 per cent is considered the minimum required to generate the 10 million new jobs needed each year over the next five years to cover the increase in the work force and absorb surplus farm labour as well as workers idled as a result of state factory closures.
>
> (*IHT*, 8 November 2001, p. 10)

'[In 2004] the economy must create at least 9 million new jobs for fresh graduates, retired soldiers and others entering the work force, and another 5 million jobs for workers laid off from state companies' (www.iht.com, 15 June 2004). 'Beijing's primary concern remains the same: to keep economic growth high enough and volatility low enough to create the necessary 20 million to 25 million jobs a year needed to maintain social stability' (*FT*, 3 January 2005, p. 32). '"We need to create about 20 million new jobs each year," says ... a deputy director of the Development Research Center, a think-tank under the State Council' (*FT*, Survey 8 November 2005, p. 1).

'[In October 2004] the deputy governor of the central bank ... said that a growth rate of 7 per cent to 8 per cent would allow for a healthy economy for the next two decades' (www.iht.com, 10 November 2004). 'The deputy governor of the People's Bank of China [said that] ... a GDP growth of "around 8 per cent" would be more sustainable than China's current rate of expansion ... of 9.5 per cent in the first three-quarters of [2004]' (*FT*, 24 November 2004, p. 10).

> [In December 2004 China] raised its target [for GDP growth in 2005] to 8 per cent annual growth ['about 8 per cent' was mentioned in March 2005] from 7 per cent ... The government in 2001 adopted a target of 7 per cent average

annual growth in order to achieve its goal of quadrupling the size of China's economy by 2020.

(<u>www.iht.com</u>, 16 December 2004)

In 2004 there was growing concern about the increasing shortages of goods and services such as energy, raw materials (such as coal and iron ore) and transport.

'Power shortages have hit nineteen provinces, affecting cities like Shanghai and Guangzhou' (*FEER*, 18 December 2003, pp. 42–4). 'Power demand nationwide is exceeding generating capacity for a third year, causing shortages in at least twenty-four of thirty-one provinces' (<u>www.iht.com</u>, 30 June 2004)

> China's transportation system has begun breaking down, especially in the past six weeks, causing delays in deliveries of raw materials ... Railways are so overstretched that power plants in southern China are having trouble getting coal delivered from the north. Together with shortages of generating capacity, this has contributed to brownouts that have forced factories to operate on limited schedules or in the middle of the night. Heavy-duty trucks are in short supply as Beijing, alarmed at road damage caused by overloaded trucks, has suddenly clamped down on weight limits ... The problem appears to be most acute in China's ports ... Another problem is that China's heavy spending recently on transportation links has gone mostly to highways instead of rail routes.
>
> (<u>www.iht.com</u>. 5 March 2004)

In 2004 the state set out to try to moderate GDP growth, its target being at least ('more than', as it was officially stated) 7 per cent. The state encouraged investment in those sectors having difficulty meeting demand, but used various measures (including political commands and credit restrictions) to try to reduce demand for their products by reining in investment in sectors such as steel, cement, property, aluminium and cars. (Local governments, with their concern for local rather than national issues, were often to blame for heavy investment in such sectors.) The state had the delicate task of trying to achieve a 'soft landing' for the economy (as opposed to a precipitous 'hard landing'). In fact, GDP growth in 2004 turned out to be 9.5 per cent.

The upward revision of 2004 GDP

> China said Tuesday [20 December 2005] that its economy was far bigger than previously estimated and that new figures suggested that it had probably passed France, Italy and Britain to become the world's fourth largest economy ... China revised its economic data after a year-long nationwide economic census uncovered about $280 billion in hidden economic output in China for 2004. The amount is roughly equivalent to an economy the size of Turkey or Indonesia, or 40 per cent of India's economy. That means that China's GDP in 2004 was nearly $2 trillion, not the $1.65 trillion previously reported. With its GDP up 17 per cent China was the sixth largest economy in the world last year [2004]. And with China expected to report another year of sizzling economic

growth in 2005 its economy may already be ranked fourth, trailing only that of the United States, Japan and Germany ... While still far behind the United States, whose economy was valued at about $11.7 trillion last year, and the EU, if it is considered as a whole, China continues to be home to the world's fastest growing major economy ... Economists say the data suggest that the country's economy is healthier, more diversified and more capable of sustaining growth than previously believed. The revised figures show, for instance, that a much stronger services sector has emerged, taking some weight off the manufacturing sector. They also show that there are more small and midsize companies in the country ... Experts have long cited its high investment to GDP ratio as a troubling and unsustainable factor that could eventually overheat its economy. That ratio now appears slightly more reasonable and sustainable today ... Experts are advancing their forecasts when China might overtake the United States as the world's largest economy. Some have advanced their estimation to about 2035, from 2040.

(*IHT*, 21 December 2005, p. 17)

China could displace Britain as the world's fourth largest economy this year [2005] after Beijing unveiled a 16.8 per cent upward revision to official GDP that pushed it into sixth place in 2004. The revision, based on a nationwide census that recorded previously ignored activity in the fast growing service sector, put China's GDP last year at 15,988 billion renminbi ($1,983 billion). This put it close behind France and the UK, the world's fifth and fourth biggest economies and ahead of Italy, relegated to seventh place. But economists yesterday [20 December] reckoned that China's strong economic growth, coupled with a strong dollar, could propel it into fourth position by the end of this year. The revision implies that China's growth in recent years has been faster than GDP data showed and offers comfort to those concerned about the economy's relative reliance on investment and manufacturing. The census put the output of China's services sector at 6,502 billion renminbi, raising its share of GDP from 32 per cent to 41 per cent, said ... the national bureau of statistics. About 70 per cent of the 2,130 billion renminbi in new services came from transport and communications, the wholesale, retail and catering trades and from property ... Economists say the scale of the upward revision of GDP will not be matched by an increase in the level of investment recorded, leading to a fall in the official investment rate from the worryingly high 44 per cent previously recorded for 2004. Other troubling data, such as the proportion on bad bank loans to GDP and the amount of energy required to fuel economic activity will also now look better ... However ... [the bureau stressed] that China's newly revised 2004 *per capita* GDP still ranked lower than 100th in the world, and that more than 100 million Chinese still lived in poverty ... Some economic measures will now look worse ... Spending on research and development, an area stressed by the government in recent years, looked even lower. Beijing was also likely to find it even harder to reach its target of doubling spending on education to 6.6 per cent of GDP by 2010 following the revision ... Some economists say the official data still underestimate economic activity. Dong

Tao of Credit Suisse Boston estimated that China's service sector accounted for more than 50 per cent of the economy rather than the revised 41 per cent.

(*FT*, 21 December 2005, p. 10)

A national economic census showed that its thriving and mainly private service sector has been underestimated ... The increase is mainly due to the underestimation of the service sector ... A big economic census this year [2005] ... involved 10 million data collectors dispatched across the country to register large hubs of business not picked up in conventional reporting. The data collectors have recorded for the first time many street-level private businesses once not picked up in GDP surveys – small factories, shops, restaurants, hair salons, bars and karaoke lounges ... The share of investment in GDP will fall slightly and the share of consumption will rise. China's savings rate is also expected to be lower.

(*FT*, 14 December 2005, pp. 1, 11)

A nationwide census confirmed that there had been vast under-accounting for activity both in its service sector and in Chinese private enterprise ...China's GDP is now reckoned to have been worth just under 16 trillion yuan, or $1.93 trillion, last year [2004], 16.8 per cent more than it had thought ... Service industries – such as telecommunications, retailing and real estate – accounted for 93 per cent of yesterday's revisions and boosted the service sector's share of GDP last year to 40.7 per cent from 31.9 per cent.

(*The Times*, 21 December 2005, pp. 32–3)

Economists have long believed that China's GDP has been considerably understated thanks mainly to poor measuring of privately run services. The country's first economic census, launched in January [2005], showed that in 2004 it was some 16.8 per cent bigger than the previously announced figure of 13.7 trillion yuan ($1.7 billion). In dollar terms at official exchange rates, this means that China replaced Italy as the world's sixth biggest economy last year [2004]. In 2005 it almost certainly surpassed France, and probably squeaked past Britain too. It adds some $284 billion to China's GDP for last year, a figure almost the size of Taiwan's total ... The survey confirms ... that consumption is higher and that investment and savings as a proportion of GDP are lower. This lot of figures look more sustainable than the old lot. But they are still only a best guess at the truth. And, at a sixth the size of America's, China's economy still has a bit of catching up to do.

(*The Economist*, 24 December 2005, p. 79)

Last month's official revision of GDP revealed an economy worth 16 trillion yuan ($1.9 trillion) in 2004, 17 per cent more than previously thought. Some $265 billion of the increase – 93 per cent of it – was ascribed to the services sector. As a result, services' share of the economy has jumped by 9 percentage points, to 41 per cent, compared with 46 per cent for manufacturing and 13 per cent for primary industries (mainly agriculture and mining) ... In many of these businesses turnover and profits have not previously been captured by a statistical system geared to measuring factory production. The small, often private, companies that dominate these areas have also been at pains to escape notice – and therefore taxes ... [The] national bureau of statistics confirms that most of the newly unearthed GDP comes from three categories. The first is wholesale, retail and catering; the second, transport, storage, post and telecommunications. While postal and telecoms services are still state controlled (and thus readily measured) more than 1 million small trucking and removal companies are not. The third activity is real estate, booming particularly in the coastal cities and increasingly inland too, leading to an influx of private money – not least from overseas speculators. Property development has, in turn, boosted demand for architects, decorators, do-it-yourself stores and other building services ... Recent years have seen a surge in media and technology services, including the internet; in financial services such as leasing; and in education and leisure. In a small way, for example, China is starting to rival India as an outsourcing hub ... China's rapid economic growth is fuelling demand for accountants, lawyers, bankers and all manner of consultants ... Specialists in marketing, advertising and public relations advise on the relatively new area of marketing products and developing brands ... China now has nearly 1 million security guards ... A huge new market is opening up for private education ... [There is] a tourist boom, which is still chiefly domestic ... In reality ... China's services sector, on this basis, is well developed and roughly as large as those of Japan, South Korea and Taiwan were at a similar stage of development, notes the HSBC bank. In reality it is bigger still, since the GDP revision cannot capture activities such as kerbside lending and tax-dodging cash transactions in property or entertainment – all of which Dong Tao, chief Asia economist at CSFB, another bank, reckons add another £220 million to the economy. Even so the 41 per cent of GDP claimed by services in China remains below the 60 per cent to 75 per cent typical in developed countries. It is smaller than India's 52 per cent. One reason for this is a communist bias towards manufacturing.

(*The Economist*, 14 January 2006, pp. 63–4)

The economic census covered the secondary (manufacturing) and tertiary (services) sectors, with the tertiary sector accounting for the bulk of the revisions, 2.13 trillion yuan of the newly found 2.33 trillion yuan. This implies a 49 per cent upward revision of tertiary sector value-added, one-half again as large as the 1993 32 per cent upward revision following the tertiary sector census of 1993 ... In the 2004 economic census 'transport and communications', 'trade and catering' and real estate – which together make up almost half of tertiary sector output – accounted for three-quarters of the revisions to tertiary sector value-added. On average across these three industries ... 2004 value-added was underestimated by 75 per cent ... The new GDP value for 2004 of 16 trillion yuan puts China's economy in sixth position worldwide ... Sometime between 2005 and 2006 China will have surpassed the UK (and France) in GDP ranking, and be in fourth position, catching up with Germany, Japan and the United States. NBS [national bureau of statistics] officials, however, are also quick to stress that on a *per capita* basis China ranks no higher than 107.

(Carsten Holz, *FEER*, January–February 2006, pp. 54–7)

[On 9 January 2006] China revised upwards more than a decade of economic growth ... GDP in 2004 was 10.1 per cent larger than a year earlier, rather than the previously reported 9.5 per cent, the national bureau of statistics said. Growth for every year to 1993 was also revised upward, except for 1998 ... The bureau said China's 2004 GDP had been 16 trillion yuan, or $1.98 trillion, 16.8 per cent more than the previous estimate, giving a precise figure for the new estimates it issued last month [December 2005]. In 2004 the services sector had been 10 per cent larger than in the previous year, which compared with 8.1 per cent previously estimated ... The average growth rate between 1979 and 2004 rose by 0.2 percentage point to 9.6 per cent.

(www.iht.com, 9 January 2006)

China has revised upwards its official annual estimates for economic growth for every year but one in the decade to 2004 in line with the results of a nation-wide economic census announced last December [2005]. The national bureau of statistics lifted the growth of GDP by an average of 0.5 per cent a year between 1993 and 2004 to reflect the economic results, which found that the economy in 2004 was 17 per cent larger than previously reported ... The only year for which the national bureau of statistics did not revise GDP upwards was for 1998, which the bureau left at 7.8 per cent ... Both Chinese and foreign economists have long said China's economy and its growth rates have been substantially larger than the official figures ... But in 1998 many contended the opposite, saying the official figure overstated growth in an economy hard hit by the Asian financial crisis.

(*FT*, 10 January 2006, p. 7)

The official revised figures are as follows (previous figures being in brackets): 1993, 14 per cent (13.5 per cent); 1994, 13.1 per cent (12.6 per cent); 1995, 10.9 per cent (10.5 per cent); 1996, 10.0 per cent (9.6 per cent); 1997, 9.3 per cent (8.8 per cent); 1998, 7.8 per cent (7.8 per cent); 1999, 7.6 per cent (7.1 per cent); 2000, 8.4 per cent (8.0 per cent); 2001, 8.3 per cent (7.3 per cent); 2002, 9.1 per cent (8.0 per cent); 2003, 10.0 per cent (9.5 per cent); 2004, 10.1 per cent (9.5 per cent) (p. 7).

The recently announced revisions to the national accounts may make the levels of key macroeconomic ratios in China look more reasonable, but the basic story remains much the same: gross national saving in China amounts to more than 40 per cent of GDP.

(*IHT*, 12 January 2006)

The economy grew 9.9 per cent last year [2005] ... government statisticians announced on Wednesday [25 January] ... The Chinese statistics, showing economic output of $2.26 trillion, sent China soaring past France, Britain and Italy to become the world's fourth largest economy, after the United States, Japan and Germany. Some economists adjust China's figures for the low value of its currency and low domestic prices to suggest that at comparable prices the actual value of China's output has surpassed Germany's as well.

(www.iht.com, 25 January 2006; *IHT*, 26 January 2006, p. 13)

GDP reached \$2,262 billion in 2005 – bringing *per capita* GDP to \$1,700 . . . Fixed asset investment grew 25.7 per cent in 2005, less than one percentage point slower than the year before . . . [There was] a fall in consumer price inflation from 3.9 per cent in 2004 to 1.8 per cent last year [2005].

(*FT*, 26 January 2006, p7)

'The United States in 2004 had the world's biggest economy at \$11.7 trillion, followed by Japan at \$4.9 trillion and Germany at \$2.7 trillion, according to figures from the IMF' (*The Times*, 26 January 2006, p. 45).

'Industrial production rose by 16.5 per cent in the twelve months to December [2005]' (*The Economist*, 28 January 2006, p. 114).

(Grain output in 2005 was 484 million tonnes. China's balance of trade surplus in 2005 was \$102 billion: *IHT*, 12 January 2006, p. 11. Foreign exchange reserves at the end of 2005 stood at \$819.9 billion: *IHT*, 17 January 2006, p. 13. A slightly different figure has been given of \$818.9 billion: *The Economist*, 21 January 2006, p. 106.)

Purchasing-power parity (PPP)

China's world ranking in terms of GDP and GDP per head in purchasing-power parity (PPP) terms is higher:

Between 1980 and 1995, using market exchange rates, GDP per head rose from \$203 to \$540. On a PPP basis the rise was from \$733 to \$2,068 (*FT*, editorial, 22 February 1997, p. 6).

GDP for the year [2001] reached 9.58 trillion renminbi based on early estimates for the year, according to the state statistics bureau. At the official exchange rate of 8.27 renminbi to the US dollar, that translates into \$1.16 trillion. But using the much stronger 'purchasing power' exchange rate of 1.9 renminbi to the dollar used by the World Bank, the figure represents \$5.04 trillion, making China's economy the second largest in the world after the United States.

(*FEER*, 10 January 2002, p. 29)

'[According to the World Bank] the average Chinese income in 2000 was \$840 at the official yuan–dollar exchange rate, but more than \$3,900 if measured on a purchasing-power equivalent basis' (*The New York Review of Books*, 2002, vol. XLIX, no. 13, p. 52).

In dollar terms its GDP is the sixth largest in the world, just smaller than France's. In terms of purchasing-power parity (after adjusting for price differences between economies) it is second only to the United States with an 11.8 per cent share of world GDP.

(*The Economist*, 15 February 2003, p. 74)

At market prices Japan [is] the world's second largest economy . . . [In 2002 it had a] GDP of \$4,266 billion, while China's was only \$1,210 billion . . . [However] at PPP . . . China was the world's second largest economy . . . At

PPP Japan's GDP was only $3,315 billion, while China's jumps to $5,625 billion ... Japan's GDP per head at market prices is thirty-six times bigger than China's. At PPP, however, it is only six times bigger ... In 2002 China's GDP per head, at PPP, was $4,400 ... For comparisons of standards of living, but not of an economy's international significance, PPP are the right ones ... Poor countries with exceptionally low domestic prices, such as China, have far higher GDPs at PPP than at market prices ... [But] at PPP China has vast expenditures on non-tradable services and a far lower propensity to trade than at market prices. Consequently, China's huge GDP at PPP gives a grossly exaggerated picture of its current significance for the rest of the world.

(*FT*, 22 September 2003, p. 21)

'In 2002 in PPP terms China's GDP accounted for 12 per cent of global GDP. In terms of exchange rates, however, this falls to 4 per cent' (*FT*, 8 June 2004, p. 19).

Measured at market exchange rates, China's GDP accounts for only 4 per cent of global output, making its economy the world's seventh largest. But using PPP to revalue its output at American prices, China moves into second place behind America, with 13 per cent of world output.

(*The Economist*, Survey, 2 October 2004, p. 8)

'The World Bank ranked China's economy seventh in the world last year [2004], in dollar terms, making it about one-seventh the size of the American economy' (www.iht.com, 7 October 2005).
'The Central Intelligence Agency, using the PPP method, ranks the Chinese GDP as the second largest in the world, about 62 per cent of the American and 1.92 times that of Japan's, the third largest' (*IHT*, 21 July 2005, p. 6).

The sources of growth

In the central planning era of 1952–78 capital formation contributed 65.2 per cent and labour input 16.9 per cent of aggregate output growth, while productivity contributed only 18 per cent. In the reform period 1979–94 the respective figures were 45.6 per cent, 12.8 per cent and 41.6 per cent (Hu and Khan 1997: 105).

A variety of market-orientated reforms and increased integration into the global economy are the most likely explanations for the rapid productivity growth observed in China in recent years ... First, there has been a significant reallocation of labour from agriculture to the industry and services sectors ... Second ... output of the non-state sector – broadly defined to include the urban collective sector, rural industry, agriculture, and private and foreign businesses – has risen dramatically over the past one-and-a-half decades ... Third, China's open-door policy and 'special economic zones' helped attract massive foreign direct investment ... Finally, China emerged as an export powerhouse over the last decade.

(pp. 117–19)

'Three-quarters of China's growth comes from capital accumulation, according to ... the IMF' (*The Economist*, Survey, 20 March 2004, 0. 4).

Poverty

There has been a dramatic reduction in poverty.

> Over the past twenty years the GDP of China has more than quadrupled. Real *per capita* disposable income has more than tripled in the cities and has almost quadrupled in the countryside [between 1978 and 1997: p. 472]. According to official statistics, the number of people in poverty was reduced by over 200 million between 1978 and 1995. By 1995 about 70 million people had a *per capita* annual income of less than 318 yuan in 1990 prices, the official poverty line [according to the World Bank: p. 472].
>
> (Yao 2000: 447)

'A quarter of a billion people out of a population of 1.3 billion live in poverty, according to the World Bank' (*FEER*, 30 August 2001, p. 19).

> In the two decades since it opened up ... the economy has grown more than fivefold ... and 270 million have been lifted out of poverty ... [But] average [annual] income is a mere $950 a head and the disparities in wealth are huge. China is still a poor country, in places abjectly so.
>
> (*The Economist*, 10 March 2001, p. 25)

> The UN World Food Programme announced [on 20 December 2003] that China no longer required the international food aid it has been receiving for twenty-five years. Instead it will be asked to become a donor and to share its experience of lifting 400 million people out of poverty ... The World Food Programme's executive director ... announced a new partnership with the government that will see China start to provide rather than receive support from the international community: 'China has lifted as many as 400 million of its own people out of poverty in less than a generation,' he said. 'That is an extraordinary achievement.'
>
> (*Guardian*, 23 December 2003, p. 12)

'The poverty rate has plummeted from one-third of the population in 1979 to less than a tenth today' (*IHT*, 26 March 2004, p. 7).

'China has quadrupled the size of its economy in the past quarter of a century and pulled more than 220 million people out of poverty – nearly three-quarters of the poverty alleviation by the developing world' (*FEER*, 1 April 2004, p. 28).

> The number of people in China in absolute poverty – lacking sufficient food or clothing – has shrunk from 200 million just over twenty years ago to around 29 million today, according to the World Bank ... [but the World Bank says] there are still 400 million people living on less than $2 per day.
>
> (*FEER*, 10 June 2004, p. 30)

> According to the World Bank, China has reduced the number of its people living in poverty from 490 million in 1981 to 88 million today ... Homi Kharas, chief economist of the World Bank's poverty reduction unit, says one of the secrets of China's success in alleviating poverty in the two decades since

it began dismantling the command economy stemmed from liberalizing the agriculture sector. 'Cheap food prices are the single most important driver of poverty reduction,' says Mr Kharas. This is counter-intuitive for many, because China's farmers are the poorest group in a poor country, a status that in many developing countries prompts government to shelter them behind protective barriers. But China's unwillingness to provide much protection for its farmers has resulted in millions of them leaving the land to supplement their families' through employment in the cities.

(*FT*, 28 May 2004, p. 12)

'From 1981 to 2001 422 million Chinese have moved out of (absolute) poverty' (Joseph Stiglitz, *FT*, 27 July 2005, p. 17).

The number of Chinese living in poverty rose for the first time since the beginning of economic reforms in 1979. Based on the number of people earning less than 637 renminbi ($77) per year, which is the threshold under Beijing's poverty definition, the number increased by 800,000 in 2003 ... Based on the new figures [China said that] 29 million people now live in [absolute] poverty ... [and that] the increase should be blamed on natural disasters in 2003. China's definition of poverty is considerably lower than the accepted international definition, which is $1 a day. The World Bank estimates that China has about 200 million people below that threshold. Two months ago, at an international conference, China won praise for lifting 400 million people out of poverty since 1979.

(www.feer.com, 29 July 2004)

This year [2004] the number of destitute poor, which China classifies as those earning less than $75 a year, increased for the first time in twenty-five years. The government estimates that the number of people in this lowest stratum grew by 800,000 to 85 million people.

(*IHT*, 2 August 2004, p. 5)

'[According to China] the rise means that more than 85 million ... subsist on less than 637 yuan a year' (*Guardian*, 20 July 2004, p. 11).

The pace of economic change in China has been extremely rapid since the start of economic reforms just over twenty-five years ago. Economic growth has averaged 9.5 per cent over the past two decades ... It has delivered higher incomes and a substantial reduction of those living in absolute poverty ... National income has been doubling every eight years and this has been reflected in the reduction of the poverty rate to much lower levels. Indeed, by some accounts, over half of the reduction in absolute poverty in the world between 1980 and 2000 occurred in China.

(OECD 2005: website Chapter 1)

('China's focus on economic development has come at the cost of neglecting basic healthcare. Basic services, such as immunization, are no longer free, which has quickened the spread of infectious diseases': Jiang Xueqin, *FEER*, 21 December 2000, p. 87.)

Inflation

Retail price inflation reached a peak in the 1990s of 21.7 per cent in 1994, but this was low relative to many transitional economies in Eastern Europe and the former Soviet Union in the early years of transition. (See Table 1, p. 617.) (This is explained by such factors as control over money supply growth, the high rate of growth of output, a high propensity to save, and the relatively small size of the state sector of industry compared with transitional countries in Eastern Europe and the former Soviet Union, which helps keep subsidies down.)

'The CPI (consumer price index) ... excludes housing costs and [so] understates inflation' (*FT*, 26 January 2005, p. 18). 'The prices of ... [things] such as health care, education and housing are not reflected in the CPI' (www.iht.com, 24 March 2005).

'The retail price index ... measures a narrower basket of commodities than the consumer price index (*FT*, 14 March 2000, p. 14). 'The retail price index (RPI) ... includes readings from sought-after services such as education' (*FT*, 23 May 2001, p. 12). '

There was deflation in China for some time after October 1997, i.e. prices actually fell.

During 2003 modest inflation started to be recorded.

Unemployment

Unemployment is an increasing problem.

'State companies have shed more than 20 million from their work force over the past three years, of whom some 11.3 million have been reemployed, mostly outside the state system' (*FT*, 24 January 2000, p. 10).

'Of the 11 million state workers laid off in 1999, 6.1 million did not find new jobs. They brought the total of unemployed urban workers up to 11.8 million' (*IHT*, 26 January 2000, p. 16).

[On 10 November 2002 it was officially revealed that] in the past few years state-owned enterprises have laid off 24 million to 25 million workers. Each year 10 million more people enter the work force ... State companies have dismissed more than 26 million workers since 1998.

(*IHT*, 12 November 2002, pp. 8, 11)

Over the past ten years bloated state-owned enterprises and 'collectives' (most of them in effect also state-owned) have shed much of their excess labour. Many have been simply closed. Between 1998 and 2002 such closures resulted in job losses for a staggering 24 million workers, or about 10 per cent of the urban labour force, by government reckoning.

(*The Economist*, 11 September 2004, p. 65)

China announced yesterday [7 January 2003] that it would phase out a job-for-life system for the country's 30 million civil servants ... Over the next five years the government will put into place a system under which civil servants work according to contracts and can be dismissed if they fail to perform in line with a set of transparent goals ... In reality a previous cast-iron guarantee of life-long employment for government officials evaporated some years ago, with about 17,000 civil servants being dismissed over the past six years and 22,000 resigning ... In places such as Shenzhen ... such reforms have already begun, along with a rudimentary feedback system that allows the local administration to consider public opinion on the performance of government departments ... A more common reform, also practised at some central government bureaux in Beijing, has been to recruit through an examination and interview system, rather than purely through appointment by superiors.

(*FT*, 8 January 2003, p. 12)

The announcement formalises changes already under way ... It is part of civil service reforms which also include open recruitment examinations and an attempt to encourage educated Chinese to return from considerably more lucrative jobs abroad ... The idea of an 'iron rice bowl' to give security to those favoured by China's rulers predates the communist era.

(*Telegraph*, 8 January 2003, p. 14)

The official Xinhua news agency reported yesterday ... [that] China [is] to end lifelong tenure for public employees ... Within five years judges, policemen, soldiers, teachers and nurses will be forced to sign contracts and ... could be dismissed ... [An] administrator at the foreign trade ministry ... [said that] 'Already my ministry signs contracts with young students, who join the ministry when they graduate from university. Contracts are for five to ten years.' He explained that the aim was to make public sector employment more attractive.

(*The Times*, 8 January 2003, p. 14)

Civil servants should be recruited 'through a system of open examinations in order to build quality and competence'. State employees include everyone working for a government-funded institution, from artists at fine arts academies to junior clerks in tax offices ... Educational institutions and research centres, while still technically under state management, are increasingly obliged to pay staff with money they have raised themselves.

(*Guardian*, 8 January 2003, p. 10)

China created 2.6 million jobs in the first half of 2003, only one-third of its full-year target of 8 million ... The ministry of labour and social security estimated 10 million people would enter the labour force this year [2003], in addition to an urban jobless population of 14 million.

(*FEER*, 28 August 2003, p. 25)

('China recently returned to the council of the International Labour Organization, the ILO, after it was ejected twelve years ago in the wake of the [1989] Tiananmen crackdown': *IHT*, 8 February 2003, p. 4.)

The official urban unemployment rate was only 3.6 per cent at the end of 1996, although other estimates put the actual figure much higher. 'The real unemployment rate in urban areas will be about 12 per cent to 15 per cent if the disguised unemployment turns into open unemployment'(Wu 1997: 1254).

In China being a 'laid off' worker (one who is not working but is still attached to a factory) does not mean being 'unemployed'. This helps explain why the official unemployment rate is only 3.0 per cent to 3.6 per cent, while one estimate puts real unemployment at 15 per cent to 20 per cent.

(*FEER*, 30 October 1997, pp. 53, 56)

'Perhaps 20 million workers, out of some 110 million once employed by state firms, have been sacked or indefinitely sent home ... Unemployment [is] perhaps ten times higher than the official 3 per cent' (*The Economist*, 14 February 1998, p. 67).

The official figure for urban unemployment was 3.1 per cent at the end of 2000 and 3.6 per cent at the end of 2001 (*IHT*, 1 March 2002, p. 15).

The official jobless rate ... of 3.8 per cent, or 6.8 million people, is routinely derided by overseas economists as virtually meaningless. It excludes anyone living in the countryside ... as well as anyone laid off from state-run companies within the last several years. The latter are considered still part of their companies' work forces, even if – as is the case for the most – they receive no pensions or other benefits from their former employers.

(*IHT*, 8 February 2002, p. 13)

[On 7 February 2002] joblessness figures far higher than the statistics usually cited [were given by the] state-run *China Daily* newspaper ... [Quoting the ministry of labour and social security it said] that in urban areas alone about 12 million people had no work. In the countryside the problem was far greater, with an estimated 20 per cent of the ... rural population idle.

(*IHT*, 8 February 2002, p. 13)

'The state-run *China Daily* said about 132 million people are unemployed – many millions more than officially stated ... The paper put urban unemployed at about 12 million and said 120 million rural dwellers were without work' (*FEER*, 21 February 2002, p. 29).

The problem of unemployment was discussed at the National People's Congress on 5–19 March 1998. There would be an estimated 3.5 million job losses in the state sector in 1998.

There were 11.51 million officially counted unemployed at the end of 1997, including 7.87 from the state sector. A deputy minister at the state economic and trade commission:

Within these [state] enterprises, if a third of the workforce were cut, these enterprises could still operate normally. If half of the workers were to be cut some enterprises could operate even better. We cannot lay off all the excess workers at once. We have to do it step by step.

(*FT*, 9 March 1998, p. 3; *IHT*, 9 March 1998, p. 1)

[On 11 November 2002] the labour and social security minister ... said the published [urban] jobless rate of 3.9 per cent rose to 7 per cent, or about 14 million, when workers laid off from state-run companies were included ... State-run companies are assumed to be paying benefits to former workers [who have been laid off] even though this is often not the case . . . China sorts jobless workers into two categories. Those severed from the books are counted as unemployed; those who continue [supposedly] to receive meagre assistance payments from their former employers are considered 'laid off' . . . [But even the 7 per cent] figure does not count the jobless among the 100 million people who have migrated to cities from the countryside, he said . . . State companies have dismissed more than 26 million workers since 1998.

(*IHT*, 12 November 2002, p. 11)

[Workers] laid off . . .[are] still nominally on their company's payroll . . . [The 7 per cent figure does] not cover unemployment among 80 million to 100 million people who have moved to the cities for jobs, or joblessness among another 130 million rural residents who work in the town and village enterprise sector.

(*FT*, 12 November 2002, p. 10)

Last year [2003] the government put the urban unemployment rate at 4.3 per cent . . . What is the real unemployment rate? The government's number only includes those who are officially registered as unemployed. It does not include those who have been laid off from state-owned enterprises but still get a basic stipend for three years after losing their jobs. Taking them into account, and adjusting for other distortions, many Chinese analysts put the figure at around 8 per cent to 10 per cent in urban areas. A survey of five large cities conducted by the University of Michigan and the Chinese Academy of Sciences found unemployment rose overall from 7.2 per cent to 12.9 per cent between 1996 and 2001. Regional variations are considerable. By the government's conservative calculations, Beijing's unemployment rate was 1.4 per cent last year . . . But in some areas at least unemployment estimates may imply that the problem is more serious than it really is. For one thing the official figures cover only those who are registered urban residents. But in some big cities 20 per cent to 30 per cent of the population is made up of migrant workers from the countryside, most of whom are not classified as city dwellers. Migrant workers have very low unemployment rates, because if they cannot find work they return to the countryside. A report published in 2002 said that some unofficial estimates putting unemployment at around 7 per cent that year would have to be revised to 5 per cent if the labour force were taken to include both registered residents and migrants. The migrants' numbers are also certainly higher than official figures show, although in recent weeks unusual labour shortages have been reported in some southern industrial areas, apparently because some migrants feel they are better off staying in the countryside where incomes are showing signs of recovery. Another distortion is the high level of hidden employment. Some analysts believe that as much as 60 per cent of laid off workers (those not yet formally labelled as unemployed by the government but who supposedly have no work) are in fact employed informally . . . The national census of the economy due to be held at the end of the year [2004] . . . the country's first . . . is sure to find that private sector employment is much higher than currently reported . . . China ignores rural areas when calculating unemployment figures in the belief that since villagers enjoy land-use rights they can make a living. Even so 150 million or so rural dwellers have little or nothing to do and in the coming years may move to urban areas.

(*The Economist*, 11 September 2004, pp. 65–6)

'Last year [2004] was the first time the rate [of urban unemployment] had fallen [from 4.3 per cent in 2003 to 4.2 per cent in 2004]' (*FT*, 3 February 2005, p. 10).

Since 1998 a policy of letting small enterprises go and restructuring large companies has been successfully pursued, with the number of state-controlled industrial enterprises falling by over one half in the following five years. Employment contracts were made more flexible, leading to job reductions in the industrial sector of over 14 million in the five years to 2003.

(OECD 2005: website Chapter 1)

Pollution

China has severe pollution problems. e.g. poor-quality air in urban areas.

Only 2.2 per cent of China's energy needs are currently met by gas ... Coal makes up 71 per cent ... But decades of pollution in China's cities, including severe acid rain over 40 per cent of the country, have forced the government to act. In February 1998 Beijing changed its strategy towards gas ... and started aggressively promoting the cleaner fuel for domestic heating, vehicles and energy production.

(*FEER*, 14 September 2000, p. 16)

Floods regularly occur. This flooding is partly man-made owing to such factors as deforestation; cultivation of flood plains exacerbated the ill effects of the floods.

'Five of the ten most polluted cities in the world are in China' (OECD 2005: website Chapter 1).

'More than 100 million people live in cities, such as Beijing, where the air is considered "very dangerous"' (*Guardian*, 31 October 2005, p. 22).

'Roughly 70 per cent of China's rivers and lakes are polluted ... Roughly a third of China is exposed to acid rain ... China is the world's second biggest producer of greenhouse gas emissions' (*IHT*, 31 October 2005, p. 4).

The first Chinese province to calculate 'green GDP' – economic production less environmental costs – has concluded it barely grew ... over the past two decades. Shanxi province, a coal-mining heartland south west of Beijing, found that in 2002 its green GDP was a mere 66 per cent of the officially announced [figure] ... if costs incurred through environmental and resource exploitation were counted. According to a study by the province's academy of social sciences ... subtractions from the headline GDP figure should include ... [an allowance] for coal resources depleted ... for land resources exploited ... for water used and ... for environmental pollution.

(*Guardian*, 19 August 2004, p. 9)

An elaborate points system that determines the careers of officials is often blamed for many of China's problems. In their drive to meet targets for economic growth local mandarins squander money, ride roughshod over citizens and ravish the environment. So now China is trying to devise and embed into its assessment of officials a way of calculating a 'green GDP' – which allows for environmental costs in national accounts – to help mitigate some of these excesses ... Green GDP would be calculated by subtracting the cost of the natural resources used and the pollution caused from regular GDP ... President Hu Jintao first endorsed the idea in March 2004 ... Last February the government said that ten regions, including Beijing, were carrying out a pilot project in green GDP assessment ... A 'framework' for a green GDP accounting system could be unfolded [it is said] within three to five years. This would make China the pioneer of a statistical approach that no other country has adopted – and which many economists around the world eschew as an attempt to quantify the unquantifiable ... The exercise is riddled with complexity ... China's top leaders themselves may be getting cold feet. A draft of the national economic development plan for the next five years ... stresses the need for 'a resources-saving and environment-friendly society'. But it makes no mention of a green GDP.

(*The Economist*, 22 October 2005, pp. 69–70)

'"Green GDP" ... [which] takes account of the impact of economic activity of the environment ... is being piloted in ten provinces' (*FT*, 27 January 2006, p. 17).

Environmental damage from pollution is costing China the equivalent of 7.7 per cent of GDP annually, according to an estimate in a study on Asia's infrastructure needs published last year [2005] by the World Bank, the Asian Development Bank and the Japan Bank for International Co-operation.

(*IHT*, 7 January 2006, p. 15)

In China 36 per cent of the population smokes, according to some studies. Chinese cigarettes are also among the cheapest in the world ... and smoking kills 1.2 million people a year in China, according to the World Health Organization.

(*IHT*, 9 February 2006, p. 12)

China announced a plan Wednesday [15 February 2006] to combat widespread pollution ... The plan, approved by the State Council, or cabinet, focusses on pollution controls and calls for the country to clean up heavily polluted regions and reverse degradation of water, air and land by 2010 ... The plan calls for environmental quality to be considered in assessing the performance of local officials, who until recently were judged mainly on their success in promoting economic development. Regional governments will be asked to set environmental targets and conduct regular evaluations, the announcement said. 'Leading officials and other relevant government officials will be punished for making wrong decisions that cause serious environmental accidents and for gravely obstructing environmental law enforcement,' it said.

(www.iht.com, 15 February 2006; *IHT*, 16 February 2006, p. 6)

Energy sources

In mid-1996 coal accounted for 75 per cent of energy consumption. Gas accounted for only 2 per cent (*FT*, 8 July 1996, p. 30).

'China still relies on coal for 80 per cent of its energy needs' (*FT*, 12 August 2003, p. 7).

> China, the world's largest coal producer and user, plans to spend $10 billion over the next decade on plants that turn coal into motor fuel, as the government struggles to contain a ballooning oil import bill ... China's crude oil imports have risen over the past decade from zero to 40 per cent of local consumption ... China sits on 12 per cent of the world's coal reserves ... Two-thirds of China's energy last year [2003] came from its coal mines.
>
> (www.iht.com, 23 November 2004)

'China is the world's biggest producer and consumer of coal ... Burning coals accounts for more than 65 per cent of total energy production ... Coal-fired power stations account for 80 per cent of China's electricity output' (*IHT*, 18 August 2005, p. 11). 'Coal provides 67 per cent of the country's energy' (www.iht.com, 21 September 2005).

> China, which provides about one-third of the world's coal, accounted for more than 80 per cent of the global coal mine deaths in 2004. The death rate at its mines is 100 times that for pits in the United States. Despite repeated official promises to improve safety, more than 5,000 workers are reported killed every year.
>
> (www.iht.com, 2 February 2006)

Natural gas accounts for 2.7 per cent of energy needs (*IHT*, 20 August 2003, p. 11).

Oil exports first became significant in the mid-1970s. They increased dramatically during the 1980s. China began to import a small quantity of oil in the mid-1980s (*China Briefing*, August 1994, pp. 6–8).

China became a net oil importer in 1993. In mid-1995 it was estimated that China had only 2.4 per cent of proven global oil reserves and 1 per cent of gas reserves (*IHT*, 3 June 1995, p. 9).

('China relies on imports for 6 per cent of its energy, according to official government estimates': *FT*, 27 September 2005, p. 13. 'China imported almost 42 per cent of its oil in 2004, mostly from the Middle East': www.iht.com, 3 January 2006.)

By early 1998 nuclear energy contributed only 1 per cent of total energy output. The plan was to increase this to 5 per cent by 2020 (*FEER*, 26 February 1998, p. 7).

'Nuclear plants make up 2 per cent of the country's power ... [China] wants hydropower to meet 30 per cent of the country's electricity demand, up from a fifth now' (www.iht.com, 5 November 2002).

'China has set a provisional goal of relying on nuclear energy to meet 4 per cent of its electricity demand by 2020, up from the current 2.3 per cent' (www.iht.com, 1 September 2004).

Health and environmental concerns have prompted Beijing to scale back its dependence on coal, which now accounts for more than 70 per cent of its total energy needs ... Imported oil accounted for one of every five barrels it consumed last year [1999].

(*IHT*, 12 October 2000, p. 13)

'China wants to build more gas-fired plants and dams to replace coal-fired plants that generate four-fifths of its power and are some of its biggest air polluters' (www.iht.com, 5 November 2002).

'China's largest oil producer, PetroChina Company Ltd, has discovered a natural gas field that could be the largest in the country ... in the gas-rich Ordos Basin of China's northern region of Inner Mongolia' (*IHT*, 22 January 2001, p. 13).

'PetroChina, China's largest oil producer, has made the nation's biggest oil discovery in a decade [in the north-western province of Gansu], bolstering its reserves by at least a third' (www.iht.com, 27 May 2004).

PetroChina has discovered an oilfield that promises to boost its petroleum reserves by at least a third ... The discovery ... is equivalent to five months of China's oil consumption ... China overtook Japan last year [2003] to become the world's second largest oil consumer.

(*FEER*, 10 June 2004, p. 27)

'By 2020, starting from a miniscule base that it has established only recently, China expects to supply 10 per cent of its needs from so-called renewable energy sources, including wind, solar power and small hydroelectric dams' (www.iht.com, 26 July 2005). 'China plans to raise renewable energy to about 15 per cent of total supply by 2020, from 7 per cent' (www.iht.com, 29 September 2005). 'A law taking effect next year [2006] will require that China produces 10 per cent of its energy from renewable resources by 2020' (www.iht.com, 30 October 2005).

China, the world's second biggest emitter of greenhouse gases, announced plans yesterday [7 November 2005] to more than double its reliance on renewable energy by 2020, which could make it a leading player in the wind, solar and hydropower industries ... [China] said it would aim to provide 15 per cent of its energy needs from non-fossil fuels within fifteen years – up from 7 per cent today, and 50 per cent more than its previously stated goal of reaching 10 per cent by 2020 ... Earlier this year the National People's Congress enacted the country's first renewable energy law, which will promote the use of alternatives to coal and oil.

(*Guardian*, 8 November 2005, p. 25)

'[China] wants gas to supply 8 per cent of the country's energy by 2010, up from 3 per cent today' (*FT*, 3 March 2006, p. 30).

Labour unrest

On 1 June 2001 a report entitled *China Investigation Report 2000–2001: Studies of Contradictions among the People under New Conditions* was published. It was written by a research group in the Communist Party's department of organization, which runs key party affairs such as promotions, training and discipline. The department is headed by Zeng Qinghong, an adviser to Jiang Zemin.

A startling new report ... describes a spreading pattern of 'collective protests and group incidents' arising from economic, ethnic and religious conflicts and the masses are 'tense, with conflicts on the rise' ... [The report says there is] mounting public anger over inequality, corruption and official aloofness ... The reports warns that the coming years of rapid change ... are likely to mean even greater social conflict ... The report ... cites growing inequality and corruption as overarching sources of discontent. The income gap is approaching the 'alarm level' it says.

(*IHT*, 2 June 2001, p. 1)

The report admits that protests by up to 10,000 people are becoming increasingly common, especially in rural areas, and predicts that 'massive grievances are likely to increase' in the next few months. Popular resentment at heavy taxes, levied by often corrupt bureaucrats, has boiled over into attacks, it says ... The unrest is likely to worsen with China's imminent entry into the WTO, it says.

(*Guardian*, 5 June 2001, p. 11)

Fushun is a city of 1.4 million in the heart of China's rustbelt in the north-east. Its main industries are large and state-owned: coal mining, steel and aluminium ... In March [2002] protests erupted simultaneously in Fushun and two other north-eastern cities, Liaoyang and Daqing. Fushun's involved only a few hundred people, but the other two drew tens of thousands and went on for several days. In Liaoyang smaller protests periodically erupted well into May. It was one of the biggest outbreaks of labour unrest reported in China in well over a decade. The government quelled it in the usual manner, rounding up the ringleaders and promising the others more money ... The latest bout of unrest in Fushun and other north-eastern cities was sparked by official attempts to pay off redundant workers and leave them to fend for themselves. In Fushun coal miners complained that their severance packages ... [were] paltry ... The city of Beijing has faced only occasional small protests over labour issues.

(*The Economist*, Survey, 15 June 2002, pp. 13–14)

Protests involving tens of thousands have simmered down over the past few days ... Although China has been no stranger to labour unrest in recent years ... the demonstrations in the industrial city of Liaoyang during the past month [March 2002] marked a notable change ... Liaoyang's protests coincided with large protests in Daqing, an oil production centre also in the north-east. Thousands of Daqing oil workers surrounded a management office to protest against the terms offered to those laid off. Unlike the unrest in Liaoyang, the Daqing protests involved only one group of workers ... Although these protests were by far the biggest reported in China recently, smaller ones also occurred last month [March] among miners in the Liaoning town of Fashun, in the south-western province of Sichuan (involving several hundred unpaid workers at a textile factory), in south-eastern Jiangxi province (involving several thousand coalminers angered by wage cuts) and even in Beijing itself, where about 200 retired workers from a car factory were demanding their unpaid pensions.

(The Economist, 6 April 2002, p. 63)

Since 1 March [2002] tens of thousands have poured ... on to the streets of Daqing ... to protest, angry that promises of pensions and medical care made during their working years have now been watered down by management. Similar protest rocked the city of Liaoyang in adjacent Liaoning province and there have been reports of scattered industrial unrest around the country this month. Since 1998 25 million workers have been laid off from state companies ... the country's economy minister said in Beijing on 8 March. Those sackings have provoked tens of thousands of similar, but smaller disputes since 1998.

(FEER, 4 April 2002, p. 32)

'Unrest resumed in ... Liaoyang with hundreds of laid-off workers peacefully demanding the release of four leaders detained two months ago' (*FEER*, 23 May 2002, p. 24).

Protests of all kinds have become more common ... Workers laid off from failing state enterprises have protested the misuse of company assets by managers and the frequent failure to pay worker pensions and stipends. Farmers angered by unbearable taxes and haughty officials have had numerous deadly encounters with the police ... Security agencies ... have prevented disaffected workers or farmers in different regions linking up.

(IHT, 2 June 2001, pp. 1, 4)

Workers in China's rust belt city of Liaoyang held off on protest for a third day Sunday [24 March 2002], watching to see if the government would release detained leaders of their movement ... Large-scale protests in the north-east industrial city started early this month [March] as workers from a bankrupt ferroalloy plant demanded back pay.

(IHT, 25 March 2002, p. 2)

Hundreds of unemployed workers in the north-western city of Lanzhou staged street demonstrations and blockaded roads Wednesday [24 April 2002] in the latest of a series of scattered protests across China against massive job losses in the country's oil industry ... It was the third day of labour unrest in the capital of Gansu province ... Witnesses ... described seeing 300 to 400 workers ... picketing outside government offices ... Tens of thousands of similar demonstrations have erupted in China over the past few years ... [as] millions of workers [have been laid off] ... But the protests in Lanzhou, involving oil workers, are unusual because they were apparently inspired by large-scale demonstrations ... in Daqing, home to the country's largest and best known oil fields ... Daqing ... [is the place] Mao Zedong once held up as a model for all of China's industries to emulate ... The government has been very successful at preventing labour protests from spreading or gaining broader political support, primarily through ... tough police action against worker activists and payoffs to other protesters ... [e.g. paying back pay] ... the protest in Lanzhou is at least the third in the oil industry since the Daqing demonstrations began. Smaller protests broke out at oil concerns in eastern Hebei and Shandong provinces last month [March], but they quickly collapsed ... All four of the oil industry protests have been directed against what workers describe as meagre severance benefits. And in each case the employer has been a subsidiary of PetroChina, China's largest producer of crude oil and natural gas and one of the biggest Chinese companies listed on the New York and Hong Kong stock exchanges ... Oil industry workers ... have personal and family ties across the country.

(*IHT*, 25 April 2002, p. 3)

The plight of millions of migrant workers toiling for meagre wages in southern China has been thrown under the spotlight by a three-day textile worker riot ... in the town of Shuikou, Guangdong province ... It started after security guards beat up an employee for jumping a meal queue ... The violence involved thousands of people, but was quelled on Thursday [27 June 2002] ... The scale of the riot made it one of the worst incidents of industrial unrest reported in China since one that erupted in Yangjiazhangzi, a north-eastern mining town in early 2000, when some 20,000 people rioted after their redundancy payments were siphoned off by corrupt officials.

(*FT*, 29 June 2002, p. 9)

'As many as 2,000 former workers from a closed brick and tile factory in ... Inner Mongolia have clashed with police and hundreds are occupying the factory, demanding pension benefits' (*IHT*, 19 July 2002, p. 5).

Some 1,400 workers demonstrated over corruption and unpaid benefits in north-eastern China on Monday [4 November] ... More than 1,000 workers who have been dismissed or face layoffs from metal and textile factories protested in Liaoning province, while 400 brewery workers demonstrated in the Jilin provincial capital, Changchun.

(*IHT*, 5 November 2002, p. 5)

(More recent developments are dealt with in the chronology of political developments.)

Postscript

Political developments

Chinese civilization

One of the basic questions asked by historians of Asia is why Japan responded quickly and effectively to the threat presented by the demonstrable superiority of the West, even as China responded slowly, reluctantly, unwillingly. The conventional answer has to do with Japan's tradition of cultural borrowing – mostly from China. It was a tradition of a country that always assumed it had something to learn, and learn it did, so that by 1905, in the Russo-Japanese War, Japan became the first Asian country to defeat a European power, decisively ... China, as is well known, possessed so deep and abiding a sense of cultural superiority, so strong a tradition of needing to learn nothing from the outside, that it was unable to adjust. It was so slow to see that it needed more than to learn a few material techniques to survive in the new globalized world that, in the end, its traditional system collapsed entirely.

(Richard Bernstein, *IHT*, 21 April 2006, p. 2)

China and Taiwan

'Prime minister Wen Jiabao announced [in Fiji] a new package of aid to [eight Pacific island] countries Wednesday [5 April] ... Wen offered new [preferential] loans and aid ... [This was] the first visit by a Chinese prime minister to the Pacific Islands ... [The] six countries that recognize Taipei did not attend the meetings' (www.iht.com, 5 April 2006).

'Last year [2005] a group of towel manufacturers from one of the poorest counties on the island planned to take action under WTO rules to stem a flood of cheap imports from China ... The embattled towel makers ... have worked to curb imports from the mainland, forcing trade authorities from China to negotiate directly with Taiwan. This is the first action of this type under WTO provisions that the island has mounted against the mainland' (*IHT*, 5 April 2006, p. 13).

'Taiwan will raise tariffs on Chinese towel imports for three years to protect local producers, the government said' (*IHT*, 15 April 2006, p. 13).

Taiwanese government-approved direct investment on the mainland stands at a cumulative $48 billion, ranking Taiwan alongside Japan and the United States as an investor in China. However, the island's central bank estimates that the total is in fact as high as $70 billion and private estimates put the amount at more than $100 billion – in either case placing it second only to Hong Kong in the scale of its exposure. But under measures announced last month [March] the island's government will approve mainland investments larger than $100 million, or those of any size that relate to sensitive technology, only if the company allows on-the-ground checks in China by Taiwanese state-appointed auditors, negotiates the remittance of profits and undertakes also to invest within Taiwan ... [The Taiwanese government says that] '70 per cent of our foreign direct investment went to the mainland last year [2005]' ... Taipei has opened up many sectors but bans remain in banking and parts of the technology, infrastructure and petrochemical industries. The most widely used loophole – one that the latest regulations seek to block – is for Taiwanese businesspeople to invest in China in a personal capacity.

(*FT*, 12 April 2006, p. 15)

'Total Taiwanese investment in China has been estimated at more than $100 billion and the island has a $58 billion trade surplus with the mainland' (www.iht.com, 14 April 2006).

President Chen Shui-bian said Friday [14 April] that China was holding talks with a former Taiwanese opposition leader in a bid to conceal the threat it posed to [Taiwan] ... The dialogue between the Communists and the Kuomintang, or Nationalists Party, 'is a cover for China's evil intentions', Chen said... Lien Chan joined top Chinese government figures at a high profile, cross-strait business forum in calling for close economic ties between Taiwan and the mainland ... Lien is visiting the mainland at the head of a 170-strong delegation that includes top Taiwanese business leaders ... While Beijing continues to expand its forces deployed opposite the island, including more than 700 missiles, it is also reaching out to the KMT and other opposition parties with offers of increased co-operation.

(www.iht.com, 14 April 2006)

'Beijing on Saturday [15 April] announced tariff cuts on imports of fruit and fish from Taiwan ... [On 16 April Hu Jintao had a] one-hour meeting with Lien Chan ... and nearly 200 Taiwanese politicians and academics and businesspeople ... During his stay in Beijing Lien also attended two-day government forum on cross-strait business' (www.iht.com, 16 April 2006).

'President Hu Jintao (16 April): 'Only by opposing and checking Taiwan's independence forces can we eliminate the biggest threat harming the peaceful and stable development of ties across the strait ... We must start political talks on an equal basis as soon as possible ... [The two sides] resume talks on an equal footing as soon as possible ... Adhering to the 1992 consensus is the important basis for realising peaceful development between the two sides' (www.iht.com, 16 April 2006; www.bbc.co, 16 April 2006).

'President Hu Jintao said Taiwan should return to a 1992 consensus that the two sides were part of "One China" ... Top level talks have been suspended since 1999 when former Taiwanese President Lee Teng-hui said relations should be "special state to state"' (www.bbc.co, 16 April 2006).

As a precondition to any direct contact with Taiwan, China wants the Chen administration to abide by a 1992 agreement reached with the former Nationalist, or Kuomintang, government that the two sides were part of 'One China'. Under the agreement both sides could have their own interpretation of what 'One China' means, which made possible semi-official talks the following year. But Beijing suspended the exchanges when former President Lee Tenghui suggested in 1999 that the two sides should deal with each other on a state-to-state basis.

(IHT, 17 April 2006, p. 6)

The leader of the opposition [is] Ma Ying-jeou of the Kuomintang ... Ma insists that, according to the [1992] consensus, China, while maintaining there is only 'One China', agreed to a formula under which 'each side can have its own interpretation' ... After ... a recent meeting in Beijing between Hu Jintao and senior Kuomintang politicians ... Hu said that China supports the 1992 consensus, although he did not add the crucial words 'each side can have its own interpretation'. He did add, however, that 'we must resume talks on an equal footing', which some analysts are suggesting amounts to the same thing.

(IHT, 19 April 2006, p. 8)

Hong Kong

The Hong Kong government said Wednesday [26 April] that it would create an audit team to monitor Hong Kong's public broadcaster, which has come under increasing criticism for its critical reporting on government policies, especially the government's stance on broader democracy ... [The government] said that a new audit on the operations of the public broadcaster, Radio Television Hong Kong, found that it had management problems and did not comply with government rules and procedures. The report criticized what was described as the improper granting of overtime and a failure to comply with government procurement regulations ... [The government] said the establishment of the audit team was not an attempt to infringe on the freedom of the press ... The broadcaster ... [is] funded by the government.

(www.iht.com, 26 April 2006)

Tibet

'The Dalai Lama abandoned his call for independence in 1988' *(Independent,* 4 April 2006, p. 24).

[On 13 April 2006 there took place] China's first international religious meeting since the Communist Revolution in 1949 ... The proceedings ... of the First World Buddhist Forum ... were dominated by the presence of Tibet's eleventh Panchen Lama, a controversial figure anointed by the Communists while still a child, and the absence of the ... Dalai Lama ... Gyaltsen Norbu

... now sixteen ... was named as Panchen Lama, the Himalayan region's second most important religious figure, in 1995. The Dalai Lama's nominee was whisked away and is thought to be held under house arrest ... Gyaltsen Norbu shared the stage with Buddhist leaders from South Korea, Taiwan and Sri Lanka ... About 1,000 Buddhist monks and theologians from thirty countries gathered in the eastern city of Hangzhou for the congress ... Delegates emphasized the theme of the forum – 'a harmonious world begins in the mind' – which mirrors President Hu Jintao's campaign to build a harmonious society ... [There are] 27 million Tibetans ... China has about 100 million Buddhists.

(*Independent*, 14 April 2006, p. 25)

'The Dalai Lama's nominee – Gedhun Choekyi Nyima – is believed to have been under arrest since 1995, when he was six' (*The Times*, 14 April 2006, p. 47).

Human rights

'The Paris-based Reporters Without Borders has ranked China 159th on a list of 167 countries in its global press freedom index' (www.iht.com, 13 April 2006).

'Human rights groups say at least fifty people are still in prison because of their involvement in the peaceful Tiananmen demonstrations of seventeen years ago' (*The Economist*, 22 April 2006, p. 12).

Religion

30 April 2006. 'Despite objections from the Vatican, the state-controlled Catholic Church installed as a bishop a senior official ... of the patriotic association and the secretary-general of its Council of Chinese bishops' (www.iht.com, 30 April 2006).

'[The] consecration marked the first time since January 2000 that a Chinese bishop had been appointed without the tacit approval of the Vatican' (*FT*, 1 May 2006, p. 6).

3 May 2006. 'The state-controlled Catholic Church in China installed on Wednesday [3 May] a second bishop over the objections of the Vatican' (www.iht.com, 3 May 2006).

The use of the internet and mobile phones

'China is the world's largest mobile phone market with about 370 million users but mobile penetration is still very low, approximately 30 per cent compared with some 90 per cent in many Western countries' (*FT*, 15 April 2006, p. 17).

In February, while [the US] Congress was drafting its Global Online Freedom Act, the Chinese government was issuing highly restrictive email regulations ... They require ... internet service ... providers to hold and, if requested, turn over personal information about users to the authorities... The regulations require email providers to report to Chinese authorities when an email 'upsets social stability' or 'harms the national interest'. The Congressional bill would require all US-owned search engines and content providers to leave China or risk fines and the threat of prison for employees. The bill would also empower the Department of Justice to block US companies from providing information about internet users to any foreign official.

(www.iht.com, 19 April 2006)

'Yahoo turned over a draft email from one of its users to the Chinese authorities, who used the information to jail the man on subversion charges, according to ... Reporters Without Borders ... Yahoo's Hong Kong unit gave the authorities a draft email that had been saved on Jiang's account ... It was the third time Yahoo had been accused of helping put a Chinese user in prison. Jiang Lijun was sentenced to four years in prison in November 2003 for subversive activities aimed at over-throwing the Communist Party' (*IHT*, 20 April 2006, p. 18).

The numbers of internet-connected computers have more than doubled since the end of 2002, to 45.6 million, and internet users have risen by 75 per cent to 111 million. China now has more internet users than any country but America ... Blogs – online personal diaries, scarcely heard of three years ago – now number more than 30 million. And search engines receive over 360 million requests a day... At the end of last year [2005] China had 393 million mobile phone accounts, nearly 200 million more than at the end of 2002 and more than any other country ... [Internet users] now face a police force of some 30,000 online monitors, say foreign human rights groups. They also say that China has jailed over fifty people for expressing views online or in text messages ... Surveys suggest that [internet] users are ... mainly young, better educated and male ... During the outbreak in the early years of SARS ... many people stayed at home and made extensive use of the internet to gather information and keep in touch. The government's efforts to block news of the outbreak collapsed as word spread by email, computer and text messages.

(*The Economist*, 29 April 2006, pp. 28, 30)

Bird flu

'Humans infected with bird flu [number] 186 in all since 1997 ... Of the world's confirmed human cases ninety-three are from Vietnam' (*IHT*, 28 March 2006, p. 4).

'Two young girls have been infected with bird flu, raising to eight the number of human cases of the virus in Egypt, the health minister said Sunday [2 April]' (*IHT*, 3 April 2006, p. 10).

'The bird flu found in domestic fowl in the eastern German state of Saxony was the deadly H5N1 strain [it was announced on 5 April] ... The confirmation of bird flu at a large poultry farm was the second instance of H5N1 in domestic fowl in the EU after an outbreak in France in late February' (*IHT*, 6 April 2006, p. 4).

'Germany's first case of the deadly H5N1 bird flu strain has been confirmed on a poultry farm east of Leipzig. The cull of the farm's flock of 10,000 geese, turkeys and chickens had begun after about twenty birds were found dead earlier this week ... The H5N1 strain has killed at least 107 people worldwide' (*Independent*, 6 April 2006, p. 23).

'An Egyptian girl died from bird flu on Thursday [6 April], taking to three the country's human death toll from the [H5N1 strain of the] virus ... The government put the number of people who have caught the virus at eleven' (www.iht.com, 6 April 2006).

'The Scottish swan is the first confirmed wild case in Britain of infection with the H5N1 virus that has killed an estimated 200 million birds in forty-five countries, either directly or through preventative culling ... The mute swan was found on 29 March ... Bird flu has killed 109 people' (*FT*, 7 April 2006, p. 2).

'A swan found dead in eastern Scotland [Fife] has tested positive for the deadly strain of bird flu, making it the first recorded case of the disease in a wild bird in Britain. The bird [is] believed to be a native mute swan ... Bird flu has been gradually making its way across Europe, striking countries like Germany, France, Denmark, Italy, Poland, Switzerland and Greece' (*IHT*, 7 April 2006, p. 3).

'DNA tests confirmed a swan found dead of H5N1 in Scotland had been a migrating species ... [It] probably came from Germany' (*FT*, 12 April 2006, p. 9).

'This week Vietnamese health officials said chickens smuggled over the border from China had reintroduced bird flu into their nation, which had reported no cases for four months' (*IHT*, 14 April 2006, p. 1).

'A twenty-one-year-old migrant worker in Hubei province has died of bird flu ... It is China's twelfth known human death from bird flu' (*IHT*, 21 April 2006, p. 8).

'The [H5N1] virus has infected 196 people ... and killed 110 of them, according to the WHO. At least thirty-three countries have reported initial outbreaks in animals since February' (*IHT*, 24 April 2006, p. 15).

'A dozen human H5N1 cases, four of them fatal, have been confirmed in Egypt, according to the WHO. Since late 2003 204 cases have been reported worldwide, the WHO said. Outbreaks of bird flu in poultry and fowl in Africa have been found in Burkina Faso, Cameroon, Egypt, Niger, Nigeria and Sudan, according to the World Organization for Animal Health' (*IHT*, 26 April 2006, p. 13).

A chronology of political developments

A panel of officials and scholars convened to advise senior Chinese leaders on policy matters disagreed on how to advance economic and legal reforms and expressed anxiety about what one official called 'unprecedented controversy and dissent' among China's elite ... Many participants stressed that they were alarmed by the resurgence of socialist thinkers critical of the country's lurch toward capitalism. Some said that the ruling party would face growing social and political instability unless it established genuine rule of law. The leaked minutes show that even as some foreign governments and scholars have touted China's development model, called the 'Beijing Consensus', as a path to prosperity for poor countries, the elite fears the consensus behind two decades of rapid economic growth is eroding ... Shi Xiaomin, a policy adviser to the State Council or cabinet, said at the session: 'The past two years the media has been talking a lot about the Beijing Consensus, the reality is that there isn't one. There is a consensus about where we have been these past twenty years, but not where we are going' ... The Communist Party shows few signs of rolling back market-orientated policies put in place in recent years. But there is considerable uncertainty about the next stages of reform, such as how to manage the widening gap between rich and poor, curtail the explosion of unrest in the countryside and tackle corruption. The party-controlled legislature postponed consideration of a broad property rights measure that had been expected to become law this spring. And officials have sent mixed signals about efforts to overhaul the state-run financial system and permit foreigners to play an ever-larger role in the once tightly controlled banks and securities firms. Debate over those issues was the backdrop for the forum, which was convened on 4 March by the China Society of Economic Reform, a policy group run by the State Council. About a dozen officials, senior economists and legal experts participated in the day-long session, which was intended to provide a sampling of candid views to inform government leaders ... Some participants in the forum argued that the difficulties China faces today are political and legal rather than economic. The solution to rising social tensions, they suggested, is to put the government and ruling party on firmer legal footing, while allowing ordinary people a greater say in public affairs.

(*IHT*, 7 April 2006, p. 5)

China's advice to the world's poor resembles its strategy at home: 'development first, politics later'. This stress on the overwhelming importance of stability – no matter how undemocratic, corrupt or environmentally irresponsible the regime – has led to the coining of a phrase, the Beijing Consensus. This highlights the contrast with the so-called Washington Consensus that emphasizes elections, free trade and accepting the guidance of the US-dominated World Bank and IMF. Beijing has carefully avoided endorsement or even explicit mention of any Beijing Consensus.

(Howard French, *IHT*, 20 April 2006, p. 2)

17 April 2006

The authorities, who last month [March] unexpectedly dropped a state-secrets case against a jailed researcher for *The New York Times*, have started an investigation period that could lead to reinstating the charges against him by early May, his lawyer said Monday [17 April]. The possibility of resuming the case undercuts speculation that the withdrawal was a prelude to releasing the researcher, Zhao Yan ... The prosecutor said in late March, days after the case's withdrawal, the authorities had initiated a new six-week investigation.

(*IHT*, 18 April 2006, p. 7)

18–22 April 2006. President Hu Jintao visits the United States

The Chinese are calling it a state visit. The Americans say it is not ... The Americans ... know what the Chinese know: that Hu Jintao is getting less than his predecessor, President Jiang Zemin, who was accorded a full state visit by President Bill Clinton in 1997 ... At first Jiang tasted American rejection. He spurned a 1995 offer by Clinton for a 'working visit' to Washington. Jiang, still emerging from the shadow of President Deng Xiaoping, insisted on the same state visit hoopla that President Jimmy Carter had accorded Deng. He got his wish two years later.

(www.iht.com, 9 April 2006)

'The Bush administration ... decided to call it a "working visit". Bush and Hu will have lunch at the White House, but no state dinner. Beijing still insists it is a state visit, an honour all of Hu's predecessor's received on their first trips to the White House' (www.iht.com, 16 April 2006).

'The highlight of Hu Jintao's four-day trip will be a meeting Thursday [20 April] with President George W. Bush. But Hu will first touch down in Seattle, where he will tour a production plant of Boeing, whose business has boomed on Chinese orders. Hu will also dine at the $100 million home of Bill Gates, the Microsoft chairman and the world's richest man' (www.iht.com, 18 April 2006).

In a burst of checkbook diplomacy this month, Hu dispatched China's largest-ever buying delegation to the United States, which committed to purchasing $16.2 billion in US aircraft, agricultural products, auto parts, telecommunications gear and computer software. A negotiating team led by deputy prime minister Wu Yi also agreed to undertake a broader crackdown on piracy of US copyrights and trademarks, reopen the Chinese market to US beef, and allow more foreign companies to compete for government contracts ... Hu will tour Boeing's aircraft factory in Washington state ... On the sidelines in Seattle Hu has invited a small group of US statesmen and scholars to discuss bilateral relations with him privately ... The session was organized by Zheng Bijan, a former head of the Communist Party's main training academy for party cadres, who coined the term 'peaceful rise'. The concept of peaceful rise [of China] ... [is one] informally endorsed by Hu ... Deputy [US] Secretary of State Robert Zoellick, who last autumn [2005] called China a 'stakeholder' in the international system, has promoted a high level strategic dialogue, which Beijing has eagerly embraced.

(www.iht.com, 16 April 2006; *IHT*, 17 April 2006, pp. 1, 4)

'In Seattle Hu will meet US and Chinese academics, including Zheng Bijan, a long-time Communist Party adviser who has promoted the idea that China's "peaceful rise" need not provoke severe conflict with Washington ... After Washington Hu will go to Yale University in Connecticut to give a speech on China's "peaceful development"' (www.iht.com, 18 April 2006).

'Robert Zoellick ... deputy [US] Secretary of State ... [has appealed to] China's better instincts to become a "responsible stakeholder" in the international system' (*FT*, 18 April 2006, p. 14).

'[This is] a concept [he] introduced last September [2005]' (*FT*, 17 April 2006, p. 11).

'[On 16 April] Mr Hu said that Beijing was not pursuing fast growth for its own sake. He said: "We are paying more attention to the transformation of the mode of growth, resource conservation, environmental protection and, more importantly, the improvement of the lives of the people'" (*The Times*, 17 April 2006, p. 30).

President Hu Jintao (16 April): '[The government does] not seek high-speed economic growth. We are concerned about the pace of development and the quality and the effect of our growth. We are also concerned about saving our resources, environmental protection and the improvement of our people's livelihood' (www.bbc.co.uk, 16 April 2006).

'[For the meeting with President George W. Bush at the White House] the Chinese ... secured a twenty-one-gun salute, reflecting Hu Jintao's status as head of state and a review of the guard of honour. In China they called it a "state visit" ... In the United States officials called it merely "a visit" ... However, the carefully planned ceremony marking the first visit by a Chinese president in a decade was marred by a protester from the Falun Gong meditation group' (*FT*, 21 April 2006, p. 5).

> The ceremony on the White House lawn was interrupted when an Asian woman standing among news cameramen began screaming ... first in Chinese, then in English ... a protest for religious freedom in China ... A spokesman for a Falun Gong-affiliated newspaper *The Epoch Times* later identified the protester as ... [a] pathologist and Falun Gong practitioner based in New York ... In another gaffe the Chinese national anthem was announced as being that of the "Republic of China", the name often used for Taiwan, and not the 'People's Republic of China'.
>
> (*IHT*, 21 April 2006, pp. 1, 8)

'A Chinese woman shouted at him [Hu Jintao] to stop the persecution of ... Falun Gong ... The woman ... [is] a naturalized US citizen who is working as a journalist for *The Epoch Times* and who had a one-day press pass that gave her access to the platform' (www.cnn.com, 21 April 2006).

> President Hu Jintao concluded his first trip to the United States with a speech Friday [21 April] at Yale University aimed at reassuring Americans about his country's rise ... Hu: 'We must not only become stakeholders. We must become partners in constructive co-operation ... Although China has become, comparatively speaking, stronger, it has a population of 1.3 billion. Any figure divided by 1.3 billion will necessarily become a smaller one' ... He noted that on a *per capita* basis China still does not rank among the 100 richest nations and said that its official development plan called for it to become 'moderately prosperous by 2020' ... Hu promised Bush that he would try to stimulate more consumer demand at home ... Bush referred to China as a 'stakeholder', a word intended as a message that China must use its power for more than commercial ... economic ... gain ... Hu's visit to Yale marks only the second time a Chinese president has addressed an American university. The first time was in 1997 when Jiang Zemin spoke at Harvard University. Hu was speaking at Bush's alma mater and when Bush travelled to China earlier this year he spoke at Hu's alma mater, Tsinghua University... It was the fifth time that the

two men have met in the past year ... During his 2000 campaign Bush described Beijing as a 'strategic competitor' whose ambitions for global influence must be contained. Now he prefers to say that the US relationship with China is 'complicated', reflecting a conversion that he took a step further Thursday [20 April] to declare that 'China and the United States share extensive common strategic interest'.

(IHT, 22 April 2006, p. 4)

22 April 2006. Hu Jintao begins a three-day visit to Saudi Arabia

'Saudi Arabia was China's top oil supplier in 2005, providing 17.5 per cent of its imports ... China's growing thirst for oil has helped push crude prices above $75 a barrel in New York for the first time' (www.bbc.co.uk, 22 April 2006).

In 2004 the two countries agreed to hold more regular political consultations, while Sinopec, China's state-owned oil company, signed a deal to explore for gas in the forbidding deserts of the Empty Quarter of Saudi Arabia. Last year [2005] Saudi Aramco signed a $3.6 billion deal with Exxon Mobil and Sinopec for a joint oil refining and chemicals venture in Fujian province, in southern China. Talks are continuing with Sinopec regarding investing in a plant in Qingdao, a northern Chinese port ... The Saudi now account for almost 17 per cent of China's oil imports.

(IHT, 24 April 2006, p. 5)

24 April 2006. 'President Hu Jintao has begun a week-long visit to Africa ... The trip has started in Morocco ... President Hu will also visit Kenya and make a return trip to Nigeria, which he visited in 2004 – a tour that also included Gabon and Algeria... Trade and oil will top Mr Hu's agenda' (www.bbc.co.uk, 24 April 2006).

Nigeria is finalizing a deal to give China preferential rights in bidding for four drilling licences, in exchange for $4 billion of infrastructure investment in the world's eighth largest oil exporting country. The deal was high on the agenda as President Hun Jintao began a two-day visit to Nigeria yesterday [26 April] ... As part of the agreement China will buy a controlling stake in a Nigerian state-owned refinery and invest in a railway line and power plants. In return Nigeria will offer first refusal rights on four oil exploration blocks to the China National Petroleum Corporation (CNPC) in a bidding round scheduled for next month [May].

(FT, 27 April 2006, p. 10)

'President Hu Jintao ... ended his five-country tour [of Africa] in Kenya, where he signed an agreement Saturday [29 April] for licences that would allow the state-owned China National Offshore Oil Corporation, or CNOOC, to explore for oil off the coast of Kenya' (www.iht.com, 1 May 2006).

30 April 2006. '[The] authorities have compensated the mother of a youth [then fifteen years of age] who died after being beaten [on 6 June] in police custody during the 1989 [Tiananmen] crackdown on pro-democracy protesters, in the first known payment of its kind. A human rights activist said yesterday [30 April] that police in Chengdu had reportedly paid 70,000 yuan (£4,800) as "hardship assistance"' (*The Guardian*, 1 May 2006, p. 16).

Economic developments

Labour

'Labour shortages are very localized and job-specific ... Shortages [of skilled labour] are everywhere' (*IHT*, 8 April 2006, p. 7).

'The country has a surplus labour pool of as many as 300 million people, many living in inland areas with very low wage costs ... The biggest constraint to exploiting that vast labour pool is skill shortages' (*FT*, 20 April 2006, p. 16).

'The urban jobless rate is estimated at more than 8 per cent (far higher in some cities) and at least 150 million people in the countryside have little or nothing to do' (*The Economist*, 29 April 2006, p. 65).

Monetary policy

'A recent paper by economists at the IMF found little evidence that Chinese banks' lending decisions had become more commercial' (*The Economist*, 29 April 2006, p. 82).

> The government will require domestic banks with a 'relatively large number of overseas branches' to adopt the stricter rules of the so-called new Basel Accord starting in 2010–12, according to Liu Mingkang, who heads the China Banking Regulatory Commission ... The rules of the new Basel Accord, also known as Basel II, are scheduled to be phased in from 2008 to 2011. They lay out how banks should set aside capital to protect themselves against sudden shocks like the collapse of major corporate borrowers ... The Basel II rules were drawn up by a committee of international regulators and central bankers and are due to be phased in between 2008 and 2011 ... A total of fifty-three [Chinese] banks, accounting for 75 per cent of banking assets, had met the standard of 8 per cent capital adequacy by the end of 2005, up from eight banks in 2003, Liu said. Most Chinese banks must reach the standard by 2006. Bank of China, China Construction Bank, Industrial and Commercial Bank of China and Bank of Communications, accounting for half of China's total bank assets, had 'basically' resolved their bad loans problems, Liu added.
> (www.iht.com, 10 April 2006; *IHT*, 11 April 2006, p. 14)

A mountain of bad [bank] debts is only the most visible sign of the persistent misallocation of capital. Many more loans do not go bad but yield only negligible returns. In a study to be published on 4 May ... *Putting China's Capital to Work: the Value of Financial System Reform* ... the McKinsey Global Institute, the consultancy's economics think-tank, calculates that China's GDP would be a staggering $320 billion, or 16 per cent, higher if its lenders knew how to lend. Around $60 billion, the think-tank reckons, could be gained from raising the banks' operating efficiency by cutting costs, putting in proper

electronic payment systems, and developing bond and equity training. The rest
– some $260 billion – would come from redirecting loans to more productive
parts of the economy. The banks should switch funds from poorly run state
firms to private enterprises [including foreign enterprises], which contribute 52
per cent of GDP but account for only 27 per cent of outstanding loans. This
would both increase the efficiency of investment and raise returns for China's
army of small savers.

(*The Economist*, 29 April 2006, p. 82)

'The McKinsey study provides 2003 figures, respectively, for GDP percentage contribution and corporate bank loans outstanding by type of enterprise: private and
foreign enterprises, 52 per cent and 27 per cent; wholly state-owned enterprises, 23
per cent and 35 per cent; shareholding (partly state-owned enterprises), 19 per cent
and 27 per cent; collective enterprises, 6 per cent and 11 per cent' (p. 82).

The savings arm of China's monopoly postal service has begun making loans
for the first time, a move intended to help it prepare for its transformation into
the country's fifth largest bank. After years of delay officials say Beijing is
close to launching reform of the Postal Savings and Remittance Bureau ... The
postal savings bureau [has been granted] permission to offer small loans to
rural customers on a trial basis ... The bureau is only permitted to lend money
to existing rural customers in the three provinces of Fujian, Shaanxi and Hubei.

(*FT*, 12 April 2006, p. 8)

China's central bank raised official borrowing costs Thursday [27 April] for the
first time for a year and a half, trying to slow a spectacular surge in lending and
investment that has produced a frenzy of often ill-considered construction and
could trigger another wave of bad debts at Chinese banks. From steel mills and
auto factories to luxury apartment buildings and plush office complexes, China
has been engaged in a nationwide building boom fuelled by easy loans from
banks ... The People's Bank of China announced Thursday evening, effective,
Friday morning, that it was raising the benchmark lending rates that banks may
charge customers by 27-hundredths of a percentage point for loans of all maturities. The increase was the same size it was the last time China raised rates, on
28 October 2004, which in turn was the country's first interest rate increase in
nine years ... The central bank left unchanged its caps on the rates that banks
can offer on deposits. By raising lending rates while leaving deposit rates
untouched, the government allows banks to fatten their profit margins to cover
loan defaults ... Prime minister Wen Jiabao had warned on 14 April that China
would move to tighten controls over lending and real estate. But most economists had expected China to require banks to hold greater reserves at the
central bank, which would have left them with less money to lend.

(www.iht.com, 27 April 2006)

The People's Bank of China ... announced that it was raising the benchmark
lending rates that financial institutions may charge customers by 27-hundredths
of a percentage point for loans of one year ... The one-year rate rose to 5.85
per cent from 5.58 per cent ... The mostly state-owned banks still make many

loans to state-owned companies and politically connected private companies and charge them the lowest rate allowed, which is nine-tenths of the benchmark rate. The yuan strengthened by less that three-hundredths of a per cent in Thursday's [27 April] trading, with the dollar slipping to 8.0161 yuan.

(*IHT*, 28 April 2006, pp. 1, 8)

'The People's Bank of China raised its benchmark one-year lending rate by a quarter point to 5.85 per cent, from 5.58 per cent ... The central bank also moved to reinforce the rise in interest rates by issuing new guidelines to commercial banks to quell lending to a dozen sectors where excess capacity and investment is at its greatest' (*The Times*, 28 April 2006, p. 51).

'Beijing has again caught the markets by surprise, lifting interest rates for the first time in eighteen months in response to a first quarter surge in banking lending and investment. Many economists had predicted the central bank would respond by raising the amount that banks must set aside in reserves and strengthening administrative controls on lending to rein in credit growth' (*FT*, 28 April 2006, p. 9).

'The one-year benchmark rate will increase by 27 basis points to 5.85 per cent from today [28 April] ... The rate rise is a symbolic opening shot in what is likely to be a sustained official campaign to restrain excessive credit and over-investment in steel, cement, property and other sectors ... The central bank left deposit rates unchanged' (p. 14).

'China is expected to raise the banks' reserve requirements next month, after China's spring holidays' (*The Economist*, 28 April 2006, p. 82).

Shareholding

'Stock market regulators said yesterday [17 April] new share offerings would begin again "soon", after a year-long freeze. It also said foreign funds might be allowed to invest more on mainland markets ... A rally in the mainland market [has taken place] this year [2006]. The Shanghai composite exchange, which has risen 17 per cent so far this year after a four-year slump, closed 1.4 per cent higher' (FT, 18 April 2006, p. 6).

China plans to allow investors to take out loans to buy shares and to sell borrowed stock for the first time aimed at tapping the country's $4 trillion of bank deposits and bolstering trading ... [China] is considering plans to select five brokerage firms to start margin-lending and short-selling services this year [2006] ... The pilot programme may be expanded to more firms later ... [It has been argued that the plan] will alleviate concern that the market will be weighed down by listings of big companies ... The plan arrives as the government prepares to end a year-long ban [since May 2005] on public share sales ... An investor buying on margin pays only a percentage of the cost of the stock, with the brokerage house financing the rest through a loan. In short sales investors sell stock they have borrowed in anticipation that they can buy it back later at a lower price and profit from the difference ... The Shanghai composite index has risen 36 per cent from its July [2005] low and the Shenzhen composite index has jumped 46 per cent since 18 July [2005]. On

Monday [17 April] the Shanghai index rose 19.08 points, or 1.4 per cent, to close at 1,378.61 points, the highest level since November 2004. The government will initially allow companies to sell shares through placements, then by public sales of additional shares and finally through initial offerings ... [The plan is] to set up a company, called China Securities Finance, this year to provide loans for brokerage firms to finance margin trading ... It is also proposed to let brokerage firms borrow directly from banks to finance client subscriptions to initial public offerings.

(*IHT*, 18 April 2006, p. 17)

Foreign trade

'China has agreed to hold talks over tariffs on car parts, the commerce ministry said Sunday [9 April] ... China's ambassador to the WTO ... sent letters to his US and EU counterparts informing them that Beijing had accepted their requests for a meeting' (www.iht.com, 9 April 2006).

'The US ... balance of payments ... deficit with mainland China accounts for only a quarter of its overall deficit ... [China] ran a current account surplus of about $150 billion last year [2005]' (*FT*, 19 April 2006, p. 15).

Yuan convertibility and exchange rate policy

'The Chinese currency remains at least 25 per cent below its fair market value' (*FT*, 7 April 2006, p. 14).

'Analysts say that China has been gradually diversifying away from dollar assets in its foreign exchange reserves, but fears of a collapse in the currency will prevent Beijing from making any dramatic shift ... China held $262.6 billion of US Treasury securities as of January [2006], which is dwarfed by Japan's holding of $668.3 billion' (www.iht.com, 4 April 2006).

The European Commission is proposing ... to a meeting of EU finance ministers [15–16 April] ... that Europe back China's policy of switching to a more flexible exchange rate system at its own pace – rebuffing the US call for faster steps to raise the value of the currency ... The commission warned that sudden moves to strengthen the yuan, as demanded by US officials, could further weaken the dollar against the Euro ... The European Commission: 'China should introduce greater exchange rate flexibility in a gradual manner ... [A gradual move would lessen the risk of the dollar., Euro and yen] overshooting [on the markets] ... [An abrupt move to stop pegging the yuan and possibly other Asian currencies to the dollar] could give rise to a sudden reversal of Asian capital flows into the United States, which might risk an excessive additional downward of the dollar against the Euro' ... The twelve countries using the Euro posted a trade deficit with China of $90 billion in 2005. The US deficit with China was $201.6 billion.

(*IHT*, 4 April 2006, p. 13)

'The EU [as a whole] posted a ... $128 billion trade deficit with China last year [2006]' (*IHT*, 10 April 2006, p. 10).

European finance ministers steered clear of public confrontation with China over the value of its currency as a two-day meeting between EU and Asian finance ministers drew to a close [in Vienna on 9 April] ... Nevertheless, a main concern at the talks was the divisive issue of the yuan's valuation. The United States has called strongly for China to allow its currency to appreciate. But European leaders were more guarded Sunday [9 April], noting that Beijing had allowed the yuan to rise, albeit gradually, with some adding that a sudden revaluation could lead to turmoil in currency markets.

(www.iht.com, 9 April 2006)

EU finance ministers called Sunday [9 April] for China to allow its currency to appreciate, but they couched their demands in a gentle tone that contrasted sharply with the tough-talking approach taken by American officials and the US Congress. During a meeting of EU finance ministers with their Asian counterparts in Vienna, EU officials highlighted the need for China to allow the yuan ... to float more freely. But they pointedly avoided giving the Chinese formal advice in a high-profile diplomatic setting ... The final communiqué from the meeting included no mention of the exchange rate issue, though it cited global imbalances as a risk to economic growth ... European diplomacy appears to have embraced the concept that the outside world can do little but try to convince the Chinese that letting the yuan strengthen is in their own interest.

(*IHT*, 10 April 2006, p. 10)

Beijing announced a broad package of currency changes Friday [14 April] that will allow Chinese individuals and institutions unprecedented access to foreign currencies ... The new rules may relieve upward on the yuan to strengthen and may open up foreign stock markets to Chinese individuals for the first time by allowing qualified Chinese brokerage firms and fund managers to purchase foreign securities, including stocks, on behalf of individual clients. Domestic banks and insurance companies will be able to buy US Treasury securities and other overseas fixed-income securities with foreign currency purchased in China ... The real level of capital outflows from China could be constrained by quotas and other barriers contained in implementing guidelines Beijing has yet to issue ... [It is not known] whether the quotas are going to be small or a few billion dollars ... Beijing will increase the amount of foreign currency Chinese individuals can buy when they leave the country. From 1 May Chinese travellers abroad will be permitted to take up to $20,000 a year out of the country, up from $8,000 now ... Until recently China made its companies sell to the government all of the foreign money they earned overseas and it maintained strict limits on the amount of foreign cash Chinese citizens could buy when they left the country.

(*IHT*, 15 April 2006, p. 11)

China is to relax restrictions on companies and individuals making financial investments overseas in the latest stage of the government's gradual efforts to loosen capital controls ... The package of changes, which comes into effect in May, allows individuals to buy up to $20,000 of foreign exchange every year – up from $8,000 – and simplifies the procedures. Certain banks will be allowed to convert clients' deposits into foreign currency to be invested in overseas bond markets, while insurance companies will be allowed to buy overseas fixed income instruments. Some fund managers will be permitted to use funds raised in foreign currencies to buy overseas equities ... Beijing announced yesterday [14 April] that foreign exchange reserves increased by $56.2 billion in the first quarter to $875.1 billion.

(FT, 15 April 2006, p. 7)

The yuan rose a tenth of a per cent on Wednesday [19 April] in Shanghai trading to 8.0163 ... China revalued the yuan by 2.1 per cent on 21 July [2005] and has let it creep up by another 1.2 per cent since then ... Chinese businesses across a range of industries [such as clothing, shoes, ceramics and automobiles] say that their main response to a strengthening currency and rising wages has been to accelerate their move toward higher-end products, from shoes to cars ... Chinese exporters are nervous that their country's currency will keep appreciating and are responding with a race to sell higher-value goods.

(www.iht.com, 19 April 2006)

'On Wednesday [19 April] the yuan had its biggest gain against the dollar since its July 2005 revaluation, rising as much as 0.14 per cent. The dollar eased to 8.0128 yuan' (www.iht.com, 19 April 2006).

National productivity improvements have broadly matched nominal wages growth for more than a decade. Of course, rising costs squeeze manufacturers of highly labour-intensive products, such as T-shirts ... Industrialization is all about shifting continuously from basic products to more advanced ones. The changing composition of China's surging exports shows how successfully it has done so. Textiles and clothing, which generated 28 per cent of the total in 1993, accounted for 9 per cent last year [2005], while the share of machinery and electrical goods trebled to 56 per cent.

(FT, 20 April 2006, p. 16)

Direct foreign investment

[It is said that] UBS, a Swiss bank, has won final approval for a landmark $212 million agreement to take control of troubled brokerage Beijing Securities – the first high-profile deal involving a foreign group to be cleared in months ... The China securities regulatory commission [CSRC] ... [has] approved UBS's purchase of a 20 per cent stake in Beijing Securities ... However, its right to control the management of the venture is believed to have been sanctioned in writing by the State Council, China's powerful cabinet ... An official announcement could come over the next few weeks ... The deal ... would enable the Swiss bank to become the first foreign investment firm to buy directly into one of China's ailing brokerage firms. The regulatory approval follows months during which the authorities hardened their attitude to foreign takeovers of domestic companies in important sectors such as finance and manufacturing ... The CSRC has taken on a sterner, less welcoming attitude to foreign investment in recent months in line with the national mood of increasing antagonism towards overseas buy-outs.

(FT, 5 April 2006, p. 25)

Bibliography

Periodicals and reports

CDSP	*Current Digest of the Soviet Press* (since 5 February 1992 *Post-Soviet*)
EIU	Economist Intelligence Unit
FEER	*Far Eastern Economic Review*
FT	*Financial Times*
IHT	*International Herald Tribune*

Books and journals

Aubert, C. (1990) 'The Chinese model and the future of rural–urban development', in K.-E. Wädekin (ed.) *Communist Agriculture: Farming in the Far East and Cuba*, London: Routledge.

Bai, C., Li, D. and Wang, Y. (1997) 'Enterprise productivity and efficiency: when is up really down?', *Journal of Comparative Economics*, vol. 24, no. 3.

Bergson, A. (1985) 'A visit to China's economic reform', *Comparative Economic Studies*, vol. XXVII, no. 2.

Bideleux, R. and Jeffries, I. (1998) *A History of Eastern Europe: Crisis and Change*, London: Routledge.

Bleaney, M. (1988) *Do Socialist Economies Work? The Soviet and East European Experience*, Oxford: Basil Blackwell.

Bolton, P. (1995) 'Privatization and the separation of ownership and control: lessons from Chinese enterprise reform', *Economics of Transition*, vol. 3, no. 1.

Bowles, P. and White, G. (1989) 'Contradictions in China's financial reforms: the relationship between banks and enterprises', *Cambridge Journal of Economics*, vol. 13, no. 4.

Bramall, C. (1993) 'The role of decollectivization in China's agricultural miracle, 1978–90', *Journal of Peasant Studies*, vol. 20, no. 2.

Broadman, H. (1999) 'The Chinese state as corporate shareholder', *Finance and Development*, September.

Brooks, K., Guash, L., Braverman, A. and Csaki, C. (1991) 'Agriculture and the transition to the market', *Journal of Economic Perspectives*, vol. 5, no. 4.

Cao, Y., Fan, G. and Woo, W. (1997) 'Chinese economic reforms: past successes and future challenges', in W. Woo, S. Parker and J. Sachs (eds) *Economies in Transition: Comparing Asia and Eastern Europe*, London: MIT Press.

Chai, J. (1992) 'Consumption and living standards in China', *China Quarterly*, no. 131.

Chamberlain, H. (1987) 'Party–management relations in Chinese industry: some political dimensions of economic reform', *China Quarterly*, no. 112 (December).

Chan, T. (1986) 'China's price reform in the 1980s', discussion paper no. 78, Department of Economics, University of Hong Kong.

Chang, C. and Wang, Y. (1994) 'The nature of the township–village enterprise', *Journal of Comparative Economics*, vol. 19, no. 3.

Chang, G. and Wen, G. (1997) 'Communal dining and the Chinese famine of 1958–1961', *Economic Development and Cultural Change*, vol. 46, no. 1.

Chen, C., Chang, L. and Zhang, Y. (1995) 'The role of foreign direct investment in China's post-1978 economic development', *World Development*, vol. 23, no. 4.

Chen, K., Hongchang, W., Yuxin, Z., Jefferson, G. and Rawski, T. (1988) 'Productivity changes in Chinese industry', *Journal of Comparative Economics*, vol. XII.

Chen, K., Jefferson, G. and Singh, I. (1992) 'Lessons from China's economic reform', *Journal of Comparative Economics*, vol. 16, no. 2.

Cheung, S. (1986) *Will China Go Capitalist?*, London: Institute of Economic Affairs (Hobart Papers).

Chow, G. (1997) 'Challenges of China's economic system for economic theory', *American Economic Review*, Papers and Proceedings, vol. 87, no. 2.

Dillon, M. (2002) 'China and the US bases in Central Asia', *The World Today*, vol. 58, no. 7.

Dipchand, C. (1994) 'The interbank market in China', *Development Policy Review*, vol. 12, no. 1.

Dittmer, L. (1989) 'The Tiananmen massacre', *Problems of Communism*, September–October.

Dollar, D. (1990) 'Economic reform and allocative efficiency in China's state-owned industry', *Economic Development and Cultural Change*, vol. 39, no. 1.

Donnithorne, A. (1967) *China's Economic System*, London: Allen & Unwin.

Economist, The (various surveys on China):
—— (1992) 'China', 28 November.
—— (1993) 'Asia', 30 October.
—— (1995) 'China', 18 March.
—— (1997) 'China', 8 March.
—— (1998) 'Central Asia', 7 February.
—— (1998) 'China', 24 October.
—— (2000) 'China', 8 April.
—— (2001) 'China's economic power', 10 March.
—— (2002) 'China', 15 June.
—— (2003) 'Central Asia', 26 July.
—— (2004) 'A survey of the world economy: the dragon and the eagle', 2 October.
—— (2006) 'China', 25 March.

Ellman, M. (1979) *Socialist Planning*, London: Cambridge University Press.
—— (1986) 'Economic reform in China', *International Affairs*, vol. 62, no. 3.

Feder, G., Lau, L., Lin, J. and Luo, X. (1992) 'The determinants of farm investment and residential construction in post-reform China', *Economic Development and Cultural Change*, vol. 41, no. 1.

Field, R. (1984) 'Changes in Chinese industry since 1978', *China Quarterly*, December.

Financial Times (various surveys on China): 9 December 1985; 20 August 1986; 5 September 1986; 22 September 1986; 29 September 1986; 30 September 1986; 18 December 1986; 18 December 1987; 12 December 1989; 24 April 1991; 16 June 1992; 2 June 1993; 18 November 1993; 7 November 1994; 20 November 1995; 27 June 1996; 8 December 1997; 19 May 1998 (Shanghai); 16 November 1998; 1 October 1999; 13 November 2000; 15 March 2002 (China and the WTO); 12 December 2002; 8 February 2003 (Asian finance); 29 April 2003 (Yangtze delta); 16 December 2003; 20 March 2004; 7 December 2004; 5 March 2005 (India and China); 8 November 2005.

Fischer, S. and Sahay, R. (2000) 'Taking stock', *Finance and Development*, vol. 37, no. 3.

Gallagher, M. (2005) 'China in 2004', *Asian Survey*, vol. XLV, no. 1.

Gaynor, M. and Putterman, L. (1993) 'Productivity consequences of alternative land division methods in China's decollectivization', *Journal of Development Economics*, vol. 42, no. 2.

Ge, W. (1999) 'Special Economic Zones and the opening of the Chinese economy: some lessons for economic liberalization', *World Development*, vol. 27, no. 7.

Gelb, A., Jefferson, G. and Singh, I. (1993) 'Can communist economies transform incrementally? The experience of China', *Economics of Transition*, vol. 1, no. 4.

Gold, T. (1989) 'Urban private business in China', *Studies in Comparative Communism*, vol. XXII, nos 2 and 3.

Goldman, M. and Goldman, M. (1988) 'Soviet and Chinese economic reforms', *Foreign Affairs*, vol. 66, no. 3

Gordon, R. and Li, W. (1991) 'Chinese economic reforms, 1979–89: lessons for the future', *American Economic Review*, Papers and Proceedings, May.

Granick, D. (1990) *Chinese State Enterprises: A Regional Property Rights Analysis*, Chicago: University of Chicago Press.

Gregory, P. and Stuart, R. (1990) *Soviet Economic Structure and Performance*, 4th edn, New York: Harper & Row (2nd edn 1981 and 3rd edn 1986).

—— (1994) *Soviet and Post-Soviet Economic Structure and Performance*, 5th edn, New York: HarperCollins.

Groves, T., Hong, Y., McMillan, J. and Naughton, B. (1994) 'Autonomy and incentives in Chinese state enterprises', *Quarterly Journal of Economics*, vol. CIX, no. 1.

—— (1995) 'China's evolving managerial labour market', *Journal of Political Economy*, vol. 103, p. 4.

Guardian (various surveys on China):

—— (1986) 'China', 13 October.

—— (1987) 'Regional China – Jiangsu and Guangdong', 16 October.

—— (1987) 'Shanghai', 19 November.

Gungwu, W. (1993) 'Greater China and the Chinese overseas', *China Quarterly*, no. 136.

Halpern, N. (1985) 'China's industrial economic reform: the question of strategy', *Asian Survey*, vol. XXV, no. 10.

Hartford, K. (1987) 'Socialist countries in the world food system: the Soviet Union, Hungary and China', *Food Research Institute Studies*, vol. XX, no. 3.

Hirschler, R. (2002) 'China's experience with transition: what is behind its stunning economic success?', *Transition*, vol. 13, no. 3.

Holzman, F. (1976) *International Trade under Communism*, New York: Basic Books.

Hsu, R. (1989) 'Changing conceptions of the socialist enterprise in China, 1979–88', *Modern China*, vol. 14, no. 4.

—— (1992) 'Industrial reform in China', in I. Jeffries (ed.) *Industrial Reform in Socialist Countries: From Restructuring to Revolution*, Aldershot: Edward Elgar.

Hu, Teh-wei, Li, Ming and Shi, Shuzhong (1988) 'Analysis of wages and bonus payments among Tianjin urban workers', *China Quarterly*, no. 113.

Hu, Z. and Khan, M. (1997) 'Why is China growing so fast?', *IMF Staff Papers*, vol. 44, no. 1.

Huang Yasheng (1990) 'Webs of interest and patterns of behaviour of Chinese local economic bureaucracies and enterprises during reforms', *China Quarterly*, no. 123 (September).

Huang, Y. and Duncan, R. (1997) 'How successful were China's state sector reforms?', *Journal of Comparative Economics*, vol. 24, no. 1.

Hussain, A. (1992) *The Chinese Economic Reforms in Retrospect and Prospect*, London: London School of Economics, Discussion Paper CP no. 24.

Hussain, A. and Stern, N. (1991) 'Effective demand, enterprise reforms and public finance in China', *Economic Policy*, no. 12.

—— (1993) 'The role of the state, ownership and taxation in transitional economies', *Economics of Transition*, vol. 1, no. 1.

—— (1994) *Economic Transition on the Other Side of the Wall: China*, London: London School of Economics, Discussion Paper CP no. 29.

Hussain, A. and Zhuang, J. (1996) *Pattern and Causes of Loss-making in Chinese State Enterprises*, London: London School of Economics, Discussion Paper CP no. 31.

Imai, H. (1994) 'Inflationary pressure in China's consumption goods market: estimation and analysis', *The Developing Economies*, vol. XXXII, no. 2.

International Herald Tribune (various surveys on China): 15 September 1986; 9 July 1986; 11 April 1994; 30 May 1994; 13 March 1995; 24 April 1995; 28 October 1996; 25 November 1996; 12 August 1997; 1 October 1999; 27 June 2002.

Ishihara, K. (1987) 'Planning and the market in China', *The Developing Economies*, vol. XXV, no. 4.

—— (1990) 'Inflation and economic reform in China', *The Developing Economies*, vol. XXVIII, no. 2.

Jackson, S. (1986) 'Reform of state enterprise management in China', *China Quarterly*, no. 107.

Jefferson, G. and Rawski, T. (1994) 'Enterprise reform in Chinese industry', *Journal of Economic Perspectives*, vol. 8, no. 2.

Jefferson, G. and Xu, W. (1991) 'The impact of reform on socialist enterprises in transition: structure, conduct, and performance in Chinese industry', *Journal of Comparative Economics*, vol. 15, no. 1.

—— (1994) 'Assessing gains in efficient production among China's industrial enterprises', *Economic Development and Cultural Change*, vol. 42, no. 3.

Jefferson, G., Rawski, T. and Zheng, Y. (1996) 'Chinese industrial productivity: trends, measurement issues and recent developments', *Journal of Comparative Economics*, vol. 23, no. 2.

Jeffries, I. (ed.) (1981) *The Industrial Enterprise in Eastern Europe*, New York: Praeger.

—— (1990) *A Guide to the Socialist Economies*, London: Routledge.

—— (1992a) 'The impact of reunification on the East German economy', in J. Osmond (ed.) *German Reunification: a Reference Guide and Commentary*, London: Longman.

—— (ed.) (1992b) *Industrial Reform in Socialist Countries: from Restructuring to Revolution*, Aldershot: Edward Elgar.

—— (1993) *Socialist Economies and the Transition to the Market: A Guide*, London: Routledge.

—— (1996) *A Guide to the Economies in Transition*, London: Routledge.

—— (ed.) (1996) *Problems of Economic and Political Transformation in the Balkans*, London: Pinter.

—— (2001a) *Economies in Transition: A Guide to China, Cuba, Mongolia, North Korea and Vietnam at the Turn of the Twenty-first Century*, London: Routledge.

—— (2001b) 'Good governance and the first decade of transition', in H. Hoen (ed.) *Good Governance in Central and Eastern Europe: The Puzzle of Capitalism by Design*, Cheltenham: Edward Elgar.

—— (2002a) *Eastern Europe at the Turn of the Twenty-First Century: A Guide to the Economies in Transition*, London: Routledge.

—— (2002b) *The Former Yugoslavia at the Turn of the Twenty-First Century: A Guide to the Economies in Transition*, London: Routledge.

—— (2002c) *The New Russia: A Handbook of Economic and Political Developments*, London: RoutledgeCurzon.

—— (2003) *The Caucasus and Central Asian Republics at the Turn of the Twenty-First Century: A Guide to the Economies in Transition*, London: Routledge.

—— (2004) *The Countries of the Former Soviet Union: The Baltic and European States in Transition*, London: Routledge.

—— (2006) *North Korea: A Guide to Economic and Political Developments*, London: Routledge.

—— (2006) *Vietnam: A Guide to Economic and Political Developments*, London: Routledge.

Jeffries, I., Melzer, M. (eds) and Breuning, E. (advisory ed.) (1987) *The East German Economy*, London: Croom Helm.

Johnson, D. (1988a) 'Economic reforms in the People's Republic of China', *Economic Development and Cultural Change*, vol. 36, no. 3.

—— (1988b) 'Agriculture', in A. Cracraft (ed.) *The Soviet Union Today*, Chicago: University of Chicago Press.

Jones-Luong, P. and Weinthal, E. (2002) 'New friends, new fears in Central Asia', *Foreign Affairs*, vol. 81, no. 2.

Kamath, S. (1990) 'Foreign direct investment in a centrally planned developing economy: the Chinese case', *Economic Development and Cultural Change*, vol. 39, no. 1.

Kaminski, B., Wang, Z. and Winters, A. (1996) 'Export performance in transition economies', *Economic Policy*, no. 23.

Kane, P. (1988) *Famine in China (1959–61): Demographic and Social Implications*, London: Macmillan.

Kojima, R. (1990) 'Achievements and contradictions in China's economic reform', *The Developing Economies*, vol. XXVIII, no. 4.

Koo, A. (1990) 'The contract responsibility system: transition from a planned to a market system', *Economic Development and Cultural Change*, vol. 35, no. 4.

Korzec, M. (1988) 'Contract labour, the right to work and new labour laws in the People's Republic of China', *Comparative Economic Studies*, vol. XXX, no. 2.

Kosta, J. (1987) 'The Chinese economic reform: approaches, results and prospects', in P. Gey, J. Kosta and W. Quaisser, *Crisis and Reform in Socialist Economies*, London: Westview Press.

Kueh, Y. (1989) 'The Maoist legacy and China's new industrialization strategy', *China Quarterly*, no. 119.

—— (1992) 'Foreign investment and economic change', *China Quarterly*, no. 131.

Kung, J. (2000) 'Common property rights and land reallocations in rural China: evidence from a village survey', *World Development*, vol. 28, no. 4.

Lardy, N. (1998) 'China and the Asian contagion', *Foreign Affairs*, vol. 77, no. 4.

Lee, K. (1990) 'The Chinese model of the socialist enterprise: an assessment of its organization and performance', *Journal of Comparative Economics*, vol. 14, no. 3.

—— (1993) 'Property rights and the agency problem in China's enterprise reform', *Cambridge Journal of Economics*, vol. 17, no. 2.

Lee, P. (1986) 'Enterprise autonomy in post-Mao China: a case study of policy-making, 1978–83', *China Quarterly*, no. 105.

Li, W. (1997) 'The impact of economic reform on the performance of Chinese state enterprises, 1980–1989', *Journal of Political Economy*, vol. 105, no. 5.

Lin, C. (1995) 'The assessment: Chinese economic reform in retrospect and prospect', *Oxford Review of Economic Policy*, vol. 11, no. 4.

Lin, J. (1988) 'The household responsibility system in China's agricultural reform; a theoretical and empirical study', *Economic Development and Cultural Change*, vol. 36, no. 3 (Supplement).

—— (1990) 'Collectivization and China's agricultural crisis in 1959–61', *Journal of Political Economy*, vol. 98, no. 6.

—— (1992) 'Rural reforms and agricultural growth in China', *American Economic Review*, vol. 82, no. 1.

Lin, J., Cae, F. and Li, Z. (1998) 'Competition, policy burdens and state-owned enterprise reform', *American Economic Review*, Papers and Proceedings, May.

Ling, L. (1988) 'Intellectual responses to China's economic reforms', *Asian Survey*, vol. XXVIII, no. 5.

Ling, Z. and Zhongyi, J. (1993) 'From brigade to village community: the land tenure system and rural development in China', *Cambridge Journal of Economics*, vol. 17, no. 4.

Liu, Z. and Liu, G. (1996) 'The efficiency impact of the Chinese industrial reforms in the 1980s', *Journal of Comparative Economics*, vol. 23, no. 3.

Lockett, M. (1987) 'China's development strategy: the Seventh Five Year Plan and after', *Euro-Asia Business Review*, July.

Long, S. (1990) *China Against the Tide*, London: EIU.

Ma, S. (1998) 'The Chinese route to privatization: the evolution of the shareholding system option', *Asian Survey*, vol. XXXVIII, no. 4.

McKinnon, R. (1992a) 'Taxation, money, and credit in a liberalizing socialist economy', *Economics of Planning*, vol. 25, no. 1.

—— (1992b) 'Taxation, money and credit in a liberalizing socialist economy', in C. Clague and G. Rausser (eds) *The Emergence of Market Economies in Eastern Europe*, Oxford: Blackwell.

—— (1994) 'Financial growth and macroeconomic stability in China, 1978–92: implications for Russia and other transitional economies', *Journal of Comparative Economics*, vol. 18, no. 3.

McMillan, J. and Woodruff, C. (2002) 'The central role of entrepreneurs in transition economies', *Journal of Economic Perspectives*, vol. 16, no. 3.

McMillan, J., Whalley, J. and Lijing Zhu (1989) 'The impact of China's economic reforms on agricultural productivity growth', *Journal of Political Economy*, vol. 97, no. 4.

Mancours, K. and Swinnen, J. (2002) 'Patterns of agrarian transition', *Economic Development and Cultural Change*, vol. 50, no. 2.

Mao, Y. and Hare, P. (1989) 'Chinese experience in the introduction of a market mechanism into a planned economy: the role of pricing', *Journal of Economic Surveys*, vol. 3, no. 2.

Meng, X. and Zhang, J. (2001) 'The two-tier labour market in urban China. Occupational segregation and wage differentials between urban residents and rural migrants in Shanghai', *Journal of Comparative Economics*, vol. 29, no. 3.

Murrell, P. (1990) *The Nature of Socialist Economies: Lessons from Eastern European Foreign Trade*, Princeton, NJ: Princeton University Press.

—— (1992a) 'Evolutionary and radical approaches to economic reform', *Economics of Planning*, vol. 25, no. 1.

—— (1992b) 'Evolution in economics and in the economic reform of the centrally planned economies' in C. Clague and G. Rausser (eds) *The Emergence of Market Economies in Eastern Europe*, Oxford: Blackwell.

—— (1993) 'What is shock therapy? What did it do in Poland and Russia?', *Post-Soviet Affairs*, vol. 9, no. 2.

Naughton, B. (1994) 'Chinese institutional innovation and privatization from below', *American Economic Review*, vol. 84, no. 2.

—— (1996) 'China's emergence and prospects as a trading nation', *Brookings Papers on Economic Activity*, no. 2.

Nolan, P. (1992) *Transforming Stalinist Systems: China's Reforms in the Light of Russian and East European Experience*, Cambridge: University of Cambridge Discussion Paper on Economic Transition DPET 9203.

—— (1993) 'China's post-Mao political economy: a puzzle', *Contributions to Political Economy*, no. 12.

—— (1996a) 'Large firms and industrial reform in former planned economies: the case of China', *Cambridge Journal of Economics*, vol. 20, no. 1.

—— (1996b) 'China's rise, Russia's fall', *Journal of Peasant Studies*, vol. 24, nos 1 and 2.

Nolan, P. and Xiaoqiang, W. (1999) 'Beyond privatization: institutional innovation and growth in China's large state-owned enterprises', *World Development*, vol. 27, no. 1.

Nove, A. (1961) *The Soviet Economy*, London: Allen & Unwin.

OECD (2005) *Economic Survey of China 2005*, OECD: www.oecd.org/document-print/0,2744,en. 2649.

Pearson, M. (1991) 'The erosion of controls over foreign capital in China', *Modern China*, vol. 17, no. 1.

Perkins, D. (1988) 'Reforming China's economic system', *Journal of Economic Literature*, vol. XXVI, no. 2.

—— (1994) 'Completing China's move to the market', *Journal of Economic Perspectives*, vol. 8, no. 2.

Phillips, D. (1986) 'Special Economic Zones in China's modernisation: changing policies and changing fortunes', *National Westminster Review*, February.

Platte, E. (1994) 'China's foreign debt', *Pacific Affairs*, vol. 66, no. 4.

Pomfret, R. (1993) 'Mongolia's economic reforms: background, contents and prospects', *Economic Bulletin for Asia and the Pacific*, vol. XLIV, no. 1.

—— (2000a) 'Transition and democracy in Mongolia', *Europe-Asia Studies*, vol. 52, no. 1.

—— (2000b) 'Agrarian reform in Uzbekistan: why has the Chinese model failed to deliver?', *Economic Development and Cultural Change*, vol. 48, no. 2.

—— (2000c) 'The Uzbek model of economic development, 1991–99', *Economics of Transition*, vol. 8, no. 3.

Prasad, E. and Rumbaugh, T. (2003) 'Beyond the Great Wall', *Finance and Development*, vol. 40, no. 4.

Prybyla, J. (1985) 'The Chinese economy: adjustment of the system or systemic reform?', *Asian Survey*, vol. XXV, no. 5.

—— (1986) 'China's economic experiment: from Mao to market', *Problems of Communism*, vol. XXXV, no. 1.

—— (1987) 'On some questions concerning price reform in the People's Republic of China', Pennsylvania: Pennsylvania State University, Working Paper 9–87–16.

—— (1994) Review in *Economic Development and Cultural Change*, vol. 42, no. 3.

Pudney, S. and Wang, L. (1994) *Housing and Housing Reform in Urban China: Efficiency, Distribution and the Implications for Social Security*, London: London School of Economics, Discussion Paper EF no. 8.

Putterman, L. (1988) 'Group farming and work incentives in collective-era China', *Modern China*, vol. 14, no. 4.

Qian, Y. (1994) 'A theory of shortage in socialist economies based on the soft budget constraint', *American Economic Review*, vol. 84, no. 1.

Qian, Y. and Xu, C. (1993) 'Why China's economic reforms differ: the M-form hierarchy and entry/expansion of the non-state sector', *Economics of Transition*, vol. 1, no. 2.

Quaisser, W. (1987) 'The new agricultural reform in China: from the people's communes to peasant agriculture', in P. Gey, J. Kosta and W. Quaisser, *Crisis and Reform in Socialist Economies*, London: Westview Press.

Rawski, T. (1994) 'Chinese industrial reform: accomplishments, prospects and implications', *American Economic Review*, vol. 84, no. 2.

Richman, B. (1969) *Industrial Society in Communist China*, New York: Random House.

Riskin, C. (1987) *The Political Economy of Chinese Development since 1949*, London: Oxford University Press.

Roy, D. (1990) 'Real product and income in China, Cuba, North Korea and Vietnam', *Development Policy Review*, vol. 8, no. 1.

Sachs, J. (1992) 'The economic transformation of Eastern Europe: the case of Poland', *Economics of Planning*, vol. 25, no. 1.

—— (1994) *Poland's Jump to the Market Economy*, Cambridge, Mass.: MIT Press.

—— (1995) 'Consolidating capitalism', *Foreign Policy*, no. 98.

—— (1996a) 'The transition at mid-decade', *American Economic Review*, Papers and Proceedings (May).

—— (1996b) 'Economic transition and the exchange rate regime', *American Economic Review*, Papers and Proceedings (May).

—— (1997) 'An overview of stabilization issues facing economies in transition', in W. Woo, S. Parker and J. Sachs (eds) *Economies in Transition: Comparing Asia and Eastern Europe*, London: MIT Press.

Sachs, J. and Woo, W. (1994) 'Structural factors in the economic reforms of China, Eastern Europe and the former Soviet Union', *Economic Policy*, no. 18.

—— (1996) 'China's transition experience reexamined', *Transition*, vol. 7, nos 3–4.

Schram, S. (1988) 'China after the 13th Congress', *China Quarterly*, no. 114.

Shambaugh, D. (1989) 'The fourth and fifth plenary sessions of the 13th CCP Central Committee', *China Quarterly*, no. 120.

Shen Xiaofang (1990) 'A decade of direct foreign investment in China', *Problems of Communism*, March–April.

Sicular, T. (1988a) 'Plan and market in China's agricultural commerce', *Journal of Political Economy*, vol. 96, no. 2.

—— (1988b) 'Grain pricing: a key link in Chinese economic policy', *Modern China*, vol. 14, no. 4.

—— (1988c) 'Agricultural planning and pricing in the post-Mao period', *China Quarterly*, no. 116.

Skinner, G. (1985) 'Rural marketing in China: repression and revival', *China Quarterly*, no. 103.

Smyth, R. (1998) 'Recent developments in rural enterprise reform in China', *Asian Survey*, vol. XXXVIII, no. 8.

—— (2000) 'Should China be promoting large-scale enterprises and enterprise groups?', *World Development*, vol. 28, no. 4.

Solinger, D. (1989a) 'Urban reform and relational contracting in post-Mao China: an interpretation of the transition from plan to market', *Comparative Communism*, vol. XXII, nos 2 and 3.

—— (1989b) 'Capitalist measures with Chinese characteristics', *Problems of Communism*, vol. XXXVIII, January–February.

Stavis, B. (1989) 'The political economy of inflation in China', *Studies in Comparative Communism*, vol. XXII, nos 2 and 3.

Tam, On-Kit (1988) 'Rural finance in China', *China Quarterly*, no. 113.

Thurow, L. (1998) 'Asia: the collapse and the cure', *The New York Review of Books*, 5 February 1998, vol. XLV, no. 2.

Tsang, S. (1996) 'Against "big bang" in economic transition: normative and positive arguments', *Cambridge Journal of Economics*, vol. 20, no. 2.

Ungar, E. (1987–8) 'The struggle over the Chinese community in Vietnam, 1946–86', *Pacific Affairs*, vol. 60, no. 4.

United Nations (1993) *World Economic Survey 1993*, New York: United Nations.

—— (2001) *World Economic and Social Survey 2001*, New York: United Nations.

Wädekin, K.-E. (1982) *Agrarian Policies in Communist Europe*, Totowa, New Jersey: Rowman & Allanheld.

—— (1988) 'Soviet agriculture: a brighter prospect', in P. Wiles (ed.) *The Soviet Economy on the Brink of Reform*, London: Unwin Hyman.

—— (ed.) (1990a) *Communist Agriculture: Farming in the Far East and Cuba*, London: Routledge.

—— (1990b) *Communist Agriculture: Farming in the Soviet Union and Eastern Europe*, London: Routledge.

—— (1990c) 'Private agriculture in socialist countries: implications for the USSR', in E. Gray (ed.) *Soviet Agriculture: Comparative Perspectives*, Ames, Iowa: Iowa State University Press.

Walder, A. (1989) 'Factory and manager in an era of reform', *China Quarterly*, no. 118.

Wall, D. (1991) 'Special economic zones and industrialisation in China', Discussion Paper no. 01/91, International Economics Research Centre at the University of Sussex.

—— (1993) 'China's economic reform and opening-up process: the Special Economic Zones', *Development Policy Review*, vol. 11, no. 3.

Wang, J. (1999) 'China's rural reform: the "rights" direction', *Transition*, vol. 10, no. 2.

Wang Jun (1989) 'The export-oriented strategy of China's coastal areas: evaluation and prospects', University of Leicester, Department of Economics, Discussion Paper no. 116 (September).

Wang, X. (1997) 'Rural empowerment of state and peasantry: grassroots democracy in rural China', *World Development*, vol. 25, no. 9.

Wang Xiao-qing (1993) *'Groping for Stones to Cross the River': Chinese Price Reform against the 'Big Bang'*, Cambridge: University of Cambridge, Discussion Paper DPET 9305.

Wang Zhonghui (1990) 'Private enterprise in China: an overview', *Journal of Communist Studies*, vol. 6, no. 3.

—— (1993) 'China's policies towards collective rural enterprises', *Small Enterprise Development*, vol. 4, no. 1.

Watson, A. (1988) 'The reform of agricultural marketing in China', *China Quarterly*, no. 113.

Weitzman, M. and Xu, C. (1993) *Chinese Township Village Enterprises as Vaguely Defined Co-operatives*, London: London School of Economics, Discussion Paper CP no. 26.

—— (1994) 'Chinese township–village enterprises as vaguely defined co-operatives', *Journal of Comparative Economics*, vol. 18, no. 2.

Wen, G. (1993) 'Total factor productivity in China's farming sector, 1952–89', *Economic Development and Cultural Change*, vol. 42, no. 1.

White, G. (1987a) 'Cuban planning in the mid-1980s: centralisation, decentralisation and participation', *World Development*, vol. 15, no. 1.

—— (1987b) 'The politics of economic reform in Chinese industry: the introduction of the labour contract system', *China Quarterly*, no. 111.

—— (1988) 'State and market in China's labour reform', *Journal of Development Studies*, vol. 24, no. 4.

White, G., and Bowles, P. (1988) 'China's banking reforms: aims, methods and problems', *National Westminster Bank Quarterly Review*, November.

Wong, C. (1986) 'The economics of shortage and the problems of reform in Chinese indus-try', *Journal of Comparative Economics*, vol. 10, no. 4.

—— (1988) 'Interpreting rural industrial growth in post-Mao China', *Modern China,* vol. 14, no. 1.

—— (1989) 'Between plan and market: the role of the local sector in post-Mao reforms in China', in S. Gomulka, Ha Yong-Chool and Kim Cae-One (eds), *Economic Reforms in the Socialist World*, London: Macmillan.

—— (1991) 'Central–local relations in an era of fiscal decline', *China Quarterly*, no. 128 (December).

Wong, E. (1987) 'Recent developments in China's Special Economic Zones: problems and prognosis', *The Developing Economies*, vol. XXV, no. 1.

Woo, W. (1994) 'The art of reforming centrally planned economies: comparing China, Poland and Russia', *Journal of Comparative Economics*, vol. 18, no. 3.

—— (1997) 'Improving the performance of enterprises in transition' in W. Woo, S. Parker and J. Sachs (eds) *Economies in Transition: Comparing Asia and Eastern Europe*, London: MIT Press.

Woo, W., Hai, W., Jin, Y. and Fan, G. (1994) 'How successful has Chinese enterprise reform been? Pitfalls in opposite biases and focus', *Journal of Comparative Economics*, vol. 18, no. 3.

Woo, W., Parker, S. and Sachs, J. (eds) (1997) *Economies in Transition: Comparing Asia and Eastern Europe*, London: MIT Press.

Wu, H.-L. and Chen, C.-H. (2001) 'An assessment of outward foreign direct investment from China's transitional economy', *Europe-Asia Studies*, vol. 53, no. 8.

Wu, J. and Reynolds, B. (1988) 'Choosing a strategy for China's economic reform', *American Economic Review*, Papers and Proceedings, May.

Wu, Z. (1997) 'How successful has state-owned enterprise reform been in China?', *Europe-Asia Studies*, vol. 49, no. 7.

Yao, S. (2000) 'Economic development and poverty reduction in China over twenty years of reform', *Economic Development and Cultural Change*, vol. 48, no. 3.

Zhu Ling (1990) 'The transformation of the operating mechanism in Chinese agriculture', *Journal of Development Studies*, vol. 26, no. 2.

Zhu, Y. (1995) 'Major changes under way in China's industrial relations', *International Labour Review*, vol. 134, no. 1.

Zhuang, J. and Xu, C. (1996) 'Profit-sharing and financial performance in the Chinese state enterprises: evidence from panel data', *Economics of Planning*, vol. 29, no. 3.

Index